ACCLAIM FOR JASON SOKOL'S

There Goes My Everything

"A subtle, nuanced, and strikingly original study."
—Henry Louis Gates, Jr.

"It's difficult not to approach Sokol's book with sheer astonishment that it has been written by one so young . . . but in truth, just about any scholar in the field would be happy to claim *There Goes My Everything* as his or her own work."
—Jonathan Yardley, *The Washington Post Book World*

"Sokol handles the material so well. . . . *There Goes My Everything* is stark in its portrayal of racism and spirited in its celebration of large and small victories toward freedom for all."   —*Minneapolis Star Tribune*

"To his credit, Sokol . . . never judges his subjects, and instead concentrates on exploring the book's chief theme . . . the divide between conscious, moral choice and human fallibility."   —*San Francisco Chronicle*

"The major premise of this book is extraordinarily important. Sokol recognizes that the full dimensions of the civil rights movement can only be grasped if Southern whites . . . are incorporated into the master narrative. His book, therefore, points the way to a fuller, more satisfying history of one of the most important dramas of 20th-century America."
—*Chicago Tribune*

"Engaging. . . . Sokol provides a kaleidoscopic portrait of Southern whites in the age of Jim Crow's collapse. . . . Mixes long-familiar civil rights stories with new and revealing anecdotes."   —*The Boston Globe*

"Ambitious and insightful."   —*The New Republic*

"Thanks to Jason Sokol, we now have a richer understanding of the hard, soul-searching journey undertaken by southern whites to get on the right side of black freedom."   —*The Weekly Standard*

"Jason Sokol . . . is determined that we not forget how far the South had to go to expel the poison of racism. . . . He means to let no skeptic get away unpersuaded."   —*The Wilson Quarterly*

"For one so young, [Sokol's] book is remarkably prescient. . . . The depth and nuance of what Sokol [captures] in his new book is nothing short of breathtaking."   —*The Tuscaloosa News*

"An apt and even arresting narration of the ways that the white South included hard and soft racism, iron certainty and deep doubt."
                                    —*The Chronicle of Higher Education*

JASON SOKOL

There Goes My Everything

Jason Sokol grew up in Springfield, Massachusetts, and attended Oberlin College and the University of California, Berkeley, where he received his doctorate in American history. He teaches history at Cornell University.

www.jasonsokol.com

There Goes My Everything

There Goes My Everything

WHITE SOUTHERNERS IN
THE AGE OF CIVIL RIGHTS, 1945–1975

JASON SOKOL

Vintage Books
A Division of Random House, Inc.
New York

FIRST VINTAGE BOOKS EDITION, AUGUST 2007

The Library of Congress has cataloged the Knopf edition as follows:
Sokol, Jason.
There goes my everything : white Southerners in the age of civil
rights, 1945–1975 / Jason Sokol.—1st ed.
p. cm.
Includes bibliographical references.
1. Southern states—Race relations—History—20th century.   2. Whites—Southern
States—Attitudes—History—20th century.   3. Whites—Southern States—Social
conditions—20th century.   4. Civil rights movements—Southern States—History—
20th century.   5. African Americans—Civil rights—Southern States—History—
20th century.   6. Southern States—Social conditions—1945–   I. Title.
F220.A1S65 2006
305.8'00975'0904—dc22   2005044488

Vintage ISBN: 978-0-307-27550-9

Author photograph © Betsy Sokol
Book design by Wesley Gott

www.vintagebooks.com

Printed in the United States of America
10   9   8   7   6   5   4   3   2

To my parents, Fred and Betsy Sokol

Contents

There Goes My Everything

Introduction: Change Seeps In

LIFE EMBRACED MYTH in the Jim Crow South, as facade blurred with fact. Hugh Wilson came up in that world, where icy stereotypes were as much a part of everyday life as hot soul food. "Since I was three or four years old I'd go down to my grandmother's, black-eyed peas and turnip greens, hog gravy, Lord have mercy. I mean . . . just good old southern country." In his childhood, Wilson absorbed as many cruel myths as colossal meals. "I was just like everybody else. Too many of us thought that, we knew individual blacks to be awful fine folks but we thought of blacks as a race as being sort of an Amos and Andy situation." Wilson started farming near Chapel Hill, North Carolina, in the 1930s. Jim Crow had defined the minds and lives of southerners, and Wilson bought in to the common image of African-Americans as inferior and content. "These people have felt undisturbed by the Negro race, they were in their place. . . . You had the black fellow as a happy fellow, he sings all day . . . and he don't worry about where his food is coming from tomorrow." Many white southerners, like Wilson, persisted in those views. It was how they were raised, and many believed, how they would die.[1]

When the civil rights movement tore through the southern landscape in the 1950s and 1960s, it challenged the attitudes of millions, undermined their customs, and upended their ways of life. It even penetrated the minds of old farmers like Wilson. "I began to get a lot older before I began to realize." He attributed fundamental changes in his racial beliefs to the civil rights movement. "Honest to God when I was a kid, I believed that junk," Wilson recalled in 1974. "I changed . . . an awful lot of my attitude . . . toward matters of race." Wilson did not count his experience as unique; he glimpsed similar changes in many of his neighbors. "These . . . farmers around here . . . and their wives, not all of them but by and large, they have come a long damn way." As the civil rights movement reshaped the South, it snapped the thin thread that had connected stereotypes to truths. White southerners began to sift through what they had always taken for granted, and made their way in a world divorced from the myths of old.[2]

THE CIVIL RIGHTS MOVEMENT possessed a rare ability to transform all it touched. In its hands, oppressed African-Americans gained legal equality, old white farmers like Hugh Wilson eventually rethought unquestioned beliefs, black power challenged white rule, and in the case of the *Albany Herald,* sarcasm turned into prophecy. "Albany calmly today awaited to be turned upside down by Martin Luther King Jr.," read the Southwest Georgia newspaper's front page on July 17, 1962. While the *Herald* mocked King's claim that the movement would turn Albany "upside down," it gave unwitting expression to a fate that would soon visit thousands of communities across the South. When African-Americans struggled for civil rights, they also struck at the very foundations of southern life. The civil rights movement altered race relations, overturned ingrained practices, subverted traditions, ushered in political change, transformed institutions, undermined a way of life, and even turned cities upside down—from Black Belt towns like Albany, Georgia, and Eutaw, Alabama, to metropolises such as Atlanta and New Orleans, and college communities like Athens, Georgia, and Chapel Hill, North Carolina. Many whites felt these changes just as deeply as, if much differently than, African-Americans. The impact of the civil rights movement differed from person to person, family to family, town to town. In the end, few escaped its long reach. Some white southerners attested to liberating experiences that forever altered their racial attitudes and behavior. Others found new ways to resist racial equality. Many more clung to any sense of normalcy they could salvage, at times willfully ignorant of the tumult around them. Still, change seeped into life—in ways whites had barely conceived and scarcely contemplated.[3]

Most white southerners identified neither with the civil rights movement nor with its violent resisters. They were fearful, silent, and often inert. The age of civil rights looked different through their eyes. The prominent events of the era—the 1955 Montgomery bus boycott, the 1960 student sit-ins, the Birmingham church bombing in 1963, the Selma-to-Montgomery march of 1965, for example—often had less meaning than the changes in the texture of day-to-day life. Few white southerners ever forgot the day they first addressed a black person as "Mr." or "Mrs.";

the time their maid showed up for work, suddenly shorn of her old deference; the day they dined in the same establishments as black people; the process by which their workplaces became integrated; the autumn a black man appeared on the ballot; or the morning white children attended school with black pupils. Taken together, these changes amounted to a revolution in a way of life.

To probe the experiences of white southerners in the age of civil rights is to capture the ambiguous contours of change. It is to explore beyond the pronouncements of politicians and newspaper editors, beneath the rhetoric of leaders and into the lives of their constituents. To seek such voices is often to grapple with antagonisms. As *Newsweek* reporter William Emerson cabled from the magazine's southern bureau in May 1955, "The individual Southerner was left to shift for himself mid the deafening roar of the press, the declarations of politicians and propaganda groups. Just how he felt was a mystery and subject to change." For many, the civil rights movement induced uncomfortable admissions, unwanted realizations, and unwelcome surprises. "It has become gradually apparent that the white man in the South woefully misunderstood the true desire of the Negro. . . . The city man was amazed at the fury of his country cousin. And, the farmer, himself, frequently found that he was at odds with at least one of his half-grown children." As the civil rights movement marched on, many white southerners found themselves swept up in the torrents of a change they were only beginning to fathom. "It's changing down here, that's what's happening," said an Atlanta storekeeper whose business integrated in 1965. "The man in the street, he has to keep up with it, even if he doesn't always go along with it. . . . We're all segregationists, the white people of Georgia; or most of us are. But we've got caught up in something that's bigger than us, and we've got to live with it."[4]

In many cases, white southerners' beliefs could not catch up to events that occurred all around them. Psychologist Robert Coles, who surveyed the Deep South in the 1960s, went a step further: "In Mississippi I have watched certain white people for nearly a decade, and I truly wonder even today what they *do* believe in. In fact, their beliefs are often less important to them than the continuity of their lives. When *that* comes under a shadow, they respond—and so do their beliefs." Through it all, African-Americans drove the motors of change. If they did not force all southerners to rethink their racial attitudes and habitual patterns of discrimination, many whites had to confront, at the very least, the fact that their cherished way of life seemed gone for good. The "Southern way of life" connoted magnolias and gentility, but it also carried specific implications about the region's racial order—one in which whites exercised the power, and blacks ever acquiesced. Some expressed shock that blacks who had been deferential and accommodating for so long finally rose up to challenge their position. Others had seen it coming for years, but were no better prepared for the civil rights movement's power to rupture their lives. "They're leading us around," said an Alabama police officer. "Everything they do, we have to think about. Who says the nigger is on the bottom? He's calling the tune, and we run to hear it; this place, that place, everywhere, it seems."[5] When African-Americans embraced civil rights, a few whites joined them—but many more found themselves bewildered by a struggle they could neither appreciate nor understand.

White southerners often lived under the spell of their own collective history—or a certain interpretation of it. Through family lore or history lessons in school, the white South nurtured its youth on the myth of the happy and faithful slave, told stories of heroic Confederate soldiers in the "War of Northern Aggression," and spun nightmares out of the "tragic era" of Reconstruction. "You would read in your history books about how gallant the South was," recalled Selma, Alabama, mayor Joe Smitherman of his lessons in school, "and the War Between the States and that we were used and misused." Margaret Jones Bolsterli remembered the stories of her childhood on a cotton plantation in Desha County, Arkansas, during the 1930s. "Racism permeated every aspect of our lives, from little black Sambo . . . in the first stories read to us, to the warning that drinking coffee before the age of sixteen would turn us black. It was part of the air everyone breathed." Few could completely divorce themselves from the past, for its vestiges lived on at mid-century—on every cotton field, on every sidewalk, in every interracial interaction. Some whites convinced themselves that blacks deserved their lot in life; others never quite embraced that logic. They were all deeply influenced by the blacks they had grown up with, befriended, employed, or exploited—whether they liked it or not. Reporter Marshall Frady wrote, "In myriad and unwitting ways, the white southerner became, and remains, the creature of the black man he hauled through violence and abasement into his midst." Blacks may not have gained their fair share of economic and political power through the civil rights movement, but they became the primary actors in the region's drama. They pulled the levers of history, and fostered fear in white communities. "We are here . . . frightened in the depths because our past does not sweep us forward or backward," James McBride Dabbs wrote in 1964. "In the person of the Negro, it sweeps us where we are afraid to go." As much as George Wallace or Lester Maddox touted themselves as the faces of Dixie, leaders like King and throngs of marchers molded events in the South, and increasingly, across America. They forced the hands of millions of whites. "During most of the South's history, the Negro stood at the back door, an insistent voice speaking out of the night," Dabbs wrote in 1969. "Now the white man stands at the back door, but this time the back door of history, wondering what is going on inside, wondering how to meet the power of the blacks, in whose hands history increasingly lies."[6]

Observers in the South during the 1960s believed they had witnessed the death of one world and the birth of another. Reporter Jimmy Breslin watched from the lobby of Montgomery's Jefferson Davis Hotel as blacks paraded through town on the 1965 Selma-to-Montgomery march. At first, many whites cursed or even smiled. "Then the people kept coming . . . with their heads high up in the air. . . . And the faces at the windows changed. . . . The owner of the Ready Shoe Repair Shop stood with his lips apart and he watched the life he knew disappear on the street in front of him." While blacks in the Deep South asserted themselves, whites often watched in amazement. As the drama unfolded, some aspects of the Jim Crow South died forever. Breslin wrote:

> You have not lived, in this time when everything is changing, until you see an old black woman with mud on her shoes stand on the street of a Southern city and sing ". . . we are not afraid . . ." and then turn and look at the face of a cop near her and see the puzzlement, and the terrible fear in his eyes. Because he knows, and everybody who has ever seen it knows, that it is over. The South as it stood since 1865 is gone. Shattered by these people in muddy shoes standing in the street and swaying and singing "We Shall Overcome."

To some, change came in sudden flashes and momentary realizations. As Robert Coles recounted after witnessing a sit-in on Mississippi's Gulf

Coast, "I think most people of the South—Negroes and whites alike—have experienced some of that same surprise I did, a jolting flash when one kind of world begins to collapse, another begins to appear, and it all becomes *apparent*." Everyone had a different word for what was taking place. "This thing here is a revolution. And some of us know it," a Montgomery businessman told Breslin. "The world's . . . passed all of us by, unless we start to live with it." Yet some whites could no easier live with the new experiences and the ensuing changes than they could understand or articulate them. When historian William Chafe asked Greensboro lawyer Ed Hudgins about the effects of the civil rights movement, Hudgins responded, "Desegregation was absolutely incomprehensible to the average southerner—absolutely unbelievable." The prospect of integration "would be traumatic to the average southerner and his way of life—a way of life that was fixed without possibility of mutation." While few may have comprehended it, none could deny that if the civil rights movement brought one thing to the South it was change.[7]

Some watched worlds collapse overnight; others saw revolutions occur before their eyes. In the 1960s, it was not yet clear whether the old order was shattered for good, or whether it merely looked and felt like that at certain fleeting moments and in certain specific places. From one perspective, the South had changed forever; from another, parts of southern life looked remarkably similar two and three decades hence. Segregation had mandated two different societies by law, and white southerners continued to drift into their own worlds, defined largely by race. "As I look back, it's unbelievable to me that we lived in two different worlds," Clay Lee, a Philadelphia, Mississippi, minister, said in 1980. "And to a large extent, I think we still do." There were always two stories: one of how southerners experienced those phenomenal moments of the civil rights years; and the other of how, over a period of time, they absorbed the transformation, encouraged it, rejected it, or lived with it. Those two tales, refracted through thousands of lives, held millions of truths.[8]

HISTORIANS HAVE YET TO CAPTURE those narratives of white southerners during the age of civil rights in all their complexity. The civil rights movement has found many authors more than worthy of its import, from biographers of King like Taylor Branch and David Garrow to chroniclers of specific locales like William Chafe on Greensboro, Robert Norrell on Tuskegee, John Dittmer and Charles Payne on Mississippi, Adam Fairclough on Louisiana, Charles Eagles and J. Mills Thornton on Alabama, Stephen Tuck and Melissa Fay Greene on Georgia, David Colburn on St. Augustine, and Diane McWhorter and Glenn Eskew on Birmingham. With good reason, these books collectively emphasize the struggles of black southerners. While many of the authors also study white southerners, the focus frequently remains on the civil rights movement itself. The struggle's lasting meaning often becomes overshadowed, as does its interracial impact on southern life. Many books probe white southerners' experiences through studies of prominent figures. We know the stories of George Wallace, Strom Thurmond, and others who led a political stampede into the Republican Party. We know the writings of leading newspaper editors like Ralph McGill, Hodding Carter, and Harry Ashmore. Two newly published studies—by Kevin Kruse and Matthew Lassiter—offer groundbreaking narratives of the suburban South. But overall, an insistent focus on powerful citizens—such as political leaders and newspaper editors—renders barely visible the populace that buys the papers, and casts the votes. Moreover, the literature on the South during this era privileges the dramatic demonstrations and famous battles of the civil rights movement, often at the expense of analyzing the very realm that those struggles sought to change—southern life, black as well as white. I take these works as my models, and building alongside them, approach the age of civil rights from a perspective many of them have not broached.[9]

Of the many books written during the 1960s, none explores how whites accommodated the upheaval better than Robert Coles's *Children of Crisis.* Coles interviewed students, parents, and teachers who integrated New Orleans and Atlanta schools in 1960 and 1961. As a psychologist, he studied how southerners coped with the tumult of desegregation. Historians now have the benefit of four decades. We can begin to understand in a wider context stories like those that Coles told—and form coherent narratives out of murky experience. We can sift the continuity from the change to understand where, when, and why transformations occurred—and did not. White southerners played decisive roles in determining the depths, and limits, of change. Better understanding of their actions and beliefs can more fully explain why the civil rights movement failed, or triumphed, where it did. And the civil rights movement, in turn, transformed many whites forever. With a critical mass of oral histories, magazine bureau dispatches, newspaper articles and editorials, students' examinations, and other firsthand accounts, we can probe beyond the stories of black versus white, good versus evil, beyond the unforgettable speeches, protests, marches, and boycotts, and into life's protean ambiguities—alternately forgettable and indelible.

Several scholars have urged further exploration in this direction. Charles Eagles pointed out that historians "have tended to emphasize one side of the struggle, the movement side, and to neglect their professional obligation to understand the other side, the segregationist opposition." He urged scholars to take more detached views and seek broader perspectives. When historians analyzed white southerners, in all their diversity, that would "make for a much more complicated story, full of additional conflicts and ambiguities. . . . Told without condescension, the often tragic stories of white southerners' hates, fears, and pride belong in the wider accounts of the civil rights era." Others echoed Eagles's plea. Kevin Mattson asserted that civil rights ought to be made "harder." "Harder to celebrate as a natural progression of American values," Jacquelyn Dowd Hall agreed. "Harder to cast as a satisfying morality tale. Most of all, harder to simplify, appropriate, and contain." In a similar vein, Peter Ling counseled scholars to "delve deeper into the struggles that we believe we already understand. In doing so, we will find new heroes and fresh villains, but most of all we will confront . . . the people who wish it would just all go away." In the South during the days of civil rights, that group proved to compose the majority.[10]

In times of relative quiescence, as well as in moments of drama, white southerners felt the ground shift beneath their feet. Change did not come out of nowhere, but had its roots in a long process that the New Deal and World War II set in motion. A booming national economy blazed into Dixie in the 1940s, while the region welcomed veterans, white and black, back from a war waged in the name of democracy and freedom against tyrannical racism. Against the global backdrop of the Cold War, pressure for civil rights intensified. Some southerners gave in to it; others used anti-communist hysteria to attack any political activity they found unpalatable, particularly support for black advancement. During the first decade after World War II, some white southerners began to open their arms to a more egalitarian ethos as others continued to resist any pushes, however small, toward black civil rights. The Supreme Court's 1954 decision in *Brown v. Board of Education* further polarized these two tendencies. Citizens' Councils rose in massive resistance, and cowed into silence the small segment of white southerners that might have tolerated integration. Even when faced with the 1955 Montgomery boycott, the rising star of Martin Luther King, Jr., and the desegregation of Central High School in Little Rock, Arkansas, in 1957, many whites still refused to believe that southern blacks desired civil rights, or that they possessed the capacity to organize themselves into movements. The 1960 student sit-ins in Greensboro, North Carolina, and Nashville, Tennessee, opened thousands of eyes, if few minds and hearts. Direct action protests provoked gruesome white violence, and some southern communities fractured in the face of such extreme bigotry.

As President Lyndon Johnson ushered the Civil Rights Act and Voting Rights Act through Congress in 1964 and 1965, respectively, some white southerners began to believe that rights for blacks necessarily meant a loss of freedoms for whites. White fears intensified as African-Americans clenched their fists in cries of "Black Power" and urban disorders flared. For thousands of white southerners, the movement only started to take effect in the late 1960s. Communities that had resisted school integration for the better part of two decades began to buckle under the Supreme Court's 1969 integration mandate, *Alexander v. Holmes*. When all the battles ended and the struggles subsided, blacks and whites across the South were left to negotiate the terrain of everyday life—and in the face of unprecedented events after World War II, that terrain had shifted profoundly. White southerners experienced the changes in a multitude of ways.

To illustrate the arc of change in southern life, this book begins in the wake of World War II and continues into the 1970s. After the war's last shots were fired in 1945, southerners began to grapple with larger processes—economic, demographic, industrial, and political—that gripped their land and their lives. It was not a linear path from wartime changes to the black freedom struggles of the 1960s. Industrialization and urbanization changed the outlines of the South as individual blacks began to challenge the substance of its society. In this sense, the decade after the war provides an important context for the later social convulsions. This work focuses most intensely on the 1960s, for the black civil rights movement pulsed with full force during those years. As civil rights confrontations raged and federal laws made their way into various towns, deep changes became apparent in southerners' lives and minds. The book continues into the 1970s because many areas did not begin to feel the effects of integration—whether in schools, at the ballot box, or in the mind—until the late 1960s and early 1970s. After King's 1968 assassination, commentators began to write the civil rights movement's epitaph. If conventional wisdom maintained that King's death killed the movement, the perspective of white southerners—and of everyday southern life in general, black as well as white—demanded a different timeline. While the bulk of the action took place in the 1960s, the 1970s told the story of the civil rights movement's influence on American life, and revealed its lasting legacy.

This book focuses on a handful of episodes in different southern towns. Shifting attention from town to town, and from time to time, allows a comparison of various parts of the South, and also reveals the disparate avenues through which the civil rights movement forced change. Despite the *Albany Herald*'s claims, few whites in Albany, Georgia, lived with any sense of "calm" when local blacks welcomed King and the Southern Christian Leadership Conference (SCLC), an organization of African-American preachers that became active in the civil rights struggle. Whites felt themselves besieged by "outside agitators," and the majority of residents could barely believe their eyes when the "good Negroes" of Albany—"their Negroes"—demonstrated that they were anything but content. In the face of black protest, the white myth of "good race relations" blew away with the wind.

Similar tremors pulsed through New Orleans in 1960 and Athens, Georgia, in 1961, when African-Americans entered white schools. Thousands of whites in New Orleans boycotted the public schools, but a few did continue to send their children to Frantz Elementary and McDonogh No. 19. Children became pawns as white communities alternately unified and fractured under the pressure of civil rights. The New Orleans school crisis brought out hateful prejudices in some and made accidental radicals of others. In that Deep South city, black rights hastened white division. In Athens, some students joined a mob when Charlayne Hunter and Hamilton Holmes integrated the University of Georgia; many more resigned themselves to the inevitability of desegregation and bemoaned its capacity to disrupt their lives. By 1970, school integration began to take hold almost everywhere, even as private "segregation academies" sprouted. School desegregation threw generational differences into sharp relief. Some white students took integration in stride as their parents continued to shout "Never!" Others could not shake off the stigma of their upbringing; black students were to them the agents of a trauma they tried in vain to ignore.

If any pieces of federal legislation touched the lives of white southerners, they were the 1964 Civil Rights Act and 1965 Voting Rights Act. The former made desegregation a reality in private businesses and public facilities everywhere. From Ollie's Barbecue in Birmingham to Pickrick Fried Chicken in Atlanta, and thousands of lunch counters in between, businessmen and their clientele expressed the entire gamut of reactions. Some white employees greeted black customers as though they had been patrons for years; others slammed doors in their faces; still more served them hesitantly and reluctantly. In the wake of black voting rights, locales with large African-American populations traveled the previously unthinkable path from white power to black political control. Greene County, Alabama, was one such area. As in other facets of life, white reaction to black voting gains varied immensely from person to person. One's pragmatic transition to a new political world was another's nightmare. What visited cities sometimes bypassed rural areas or newly developing suburbs, and wrenching realities in one state were foreign to another. For every pattern that seemed to emerge, however, another crumpled under the sheer diversity and complexity of experience.

Roy Blount, Jr.'s, anecdote resonates with anyone who probes the South during the 1960s. As Blount was watching a recent television drama about the civil rights era, a nine-year-old boy asked him, "Which were you in—the Klan or the FBI?" "I was just in Georgia," Blount replied. The vast majority of white southerners were neither Klansmen nor government informants, members of neither the Citizens' Councils nor the Student Nonviolent Coordinating Committee (SNCC). Certainly, bigots and murderers existed. While these intransigents often captured headlines and solidified fears, they do not substantially further one's understanding of the majority's plight. Labels help even less. To identify whites as "extremists," "segregationists," or even "moderates" inadequately explains their beliefs or actions—much less so the tag "racist." Charles Payne analyzed writing about southern whites when he praised Fred Powledge's *Free at Last?*:

> I am particularly thankful that [Powledge] doesn't hold southern racists up to ridicule; he gives them credit for being complex and makes some attempt at understanding the cross-pressures under which they were operating. The opposite tradition, in which racists are pictured as stupid, vulgar, and one-dimensional, is one of

the hoariest conventions of writing about civil rights and one of the most destructive. I take it to be a device by which authors certify their own enlightened status by distancing themselves from the grosser expressions of racism, thus giving racism the face of the ignorant, the pot-bellied, and the tobacco-chewing, an image with which almost no one can identify and which easily supplants more complex and realistic images of racism.

To think of most white southerners simply as "racist" gives them either too little credit or too much. In Adam Fairclough's view, the label is far too generous: "The term 'racist' has become devalued through overuse: it fails to prepare one for the depths of disgust, contempt, and condescension with which whites, to varying degrees . . . regarded their black fellow citizens." These writers attest that a sensitivity for complexities remains paramount in any story of America and its most persistently bedeviling issue—race relations.[11]

Present-day observers can fall victim to simple explanations, and so did those on the front lines of the civil rights struggles. Some civil rights supporters misunderstood the white communities that served as battlegrounds, the very places they sought to transform. Among the civil rights movement's lessons, J. Mills Thornton has argued, "it became clear that white southerners' doubts about segregation were both more extreme and complex than either zealous segregationists or civil rights advocates initially appreciated." White southerners' racial attitudes and behavior frequently revealed a confused and conflicted people, at times divided within and against themselves. Harold Fleming of the Southern Regional Council (SRC) wrote in a 1956 quarterly report, "There . . . needs to be more recognition of the complexity of opinion and attitude on race. Most people hold no simple, single-minded, coherent opinion on the subject; rather they have a number of vague, shifting, often contradictory notions of what their position should be." Fleming unraveled aspects of a mind-set to which white southerners typically clung: they possessed a conviction that segregation was "best for both races" and that blacks desired it; respected "law and order"; believed in blacks' rights to "an equal chance"; supported public education; took pride in the South and hoped that "outsiders" would not think it "benighted"; and feared that, if integration came, blacks would "take advantage" of whites. The list could go on, Fleming maintained. Those lines of thinking that together formed public opinion "at any given time" reflected "the depth, intensity, and balance of the various notions at the moment." The minds and lives of the South were even more complex because they were not fixed, but precarious and mutable. Few forces shook them so thoroughly as the struggles of the civil rights movement.[12]

WHITE SOUTHERNERS WATCHED as African-Americans demanded their freedom and, in Chapel Hill farmer Hugh Wilson's words, ascended "out of their place." Even in those cases where the civil rights movement succeeded in changing whites' attitudes and altering their lives, nothing was simple or straightforward about those transformations. Old beliefs had a powerful ability to endure. "In the back of your head from what came when you were a child, you had this idea," Wilson said. "You still got that thing in there, that black boy, he's trouble." For some, the law forced changes in practices, but it could not touch the recesses of hearts and minds. Others began to question deeply held views even though their lives looked much the same as before. At times, the old stereotypes and everyday practices died hard together. And for still others, change in any form—in law, mind-set, or lifestyle—was something to fear and resist, with denial and bitterness, all the way to the grave. Wilson asserted, "Some rednecks . . . think about themselves as a white person rather than as a person, who happens to be white." Change would eventually visit them, too, but it could take decades. "It'll come one day, but God knows I probably will be dead a long time and rotten too."[13]

When change came, as the story of a self-described "liberal" woman from Fayetteville, North Carolina, further attests, it was a partial and messy process. Few southerners achieved, much less desired, a clean break from the past. The intensity and form of discrimination often changed, not the fact of its existence. The woman—identified only as H.S.—belonged to the generation that came of age during the black freedom struggle. H.S. attributed her own liberal views to her Jewish background, which predisposed her to empathize with other persecuted minorities, as well as to generational differences. "I am a product of my times . . . those glorious 60s. When it was hip to be liberal, I was liberal." Her parents were given to no such liberalism, and they fired their black maid when she became pregnant. "In reaction to my parents, I cried . . . for black political and economic rights." But her experiences in

junior high and high school during the late 1960s and early 1970s began
to push H.S. toward her own type of conservatism on racial issues.
Racially charged fights in school made her wary of blacks, and "I became
a little suspect of the black man's savagery. For the first time, I realized it
was black against white." At the University of North Carolina at Chapel
Hill in the mid-1970s, H.S. felt herself on one side of an unbridgeable
chasm. "Carolina nowadays exhibits a great rift between black and white
society—in living arrangements, student organizations, social affairs,
etc.," she wrote in 1975. "For that reason, I have had little contact with
blacks." The tensions of the late 1960s and 1970s endowed her with a
certain type of racial attitude. It was not the old mind-set that waxed
nostalgic for the lost days of the happy Sambo and "good race relations,"
but a more complex—and perhaps therefore more troubling—kind of
attitude. "Intellectually I am still the equal rights advocate, crying for
political and economic rights for blacks in all areas. But my cry has sub-
dued. And the emotional strains altering my belief in social equality, I
feel will always stand in the way of my desire to give blacks that." Like
the generation before her, H.S. still believed that "social equality" was
something whites could choose to bestow upon blacks. Little else in her
views resonated with the fears and prejudices of the older Jim Crow generation. "As is the case in much of the country, my racism is very subtle
now." A new day dawned in the South; even the racism it spawned was
something novel.[14]

Ben Smith, a professor at North Carolina State University, was one
southerner who admitted to no such prejudices. Smith wished his region
would overcome its past at once, and step into the new world that the
civil rights movement offered. As southern senators filibustered against
the Civil Rights Act in December of 1963, Smith penned North Carolina senator Sam Ervin a futile plea to support civil rights. "It is not
easy for a native white citizen of a southern state to give up the traditions
of his early years," he wrote. "I was born in Prince Edward County, Virginia. I am still proud of my birthplace but not of its politics." Smith
explained how he, like many southerners, cherished his heritage and
took pride in his region's history. He had visited Shiloh and Vicksburg,
Andersonville and Fredericksburg. "I have stood in pride and sorrow
where Jackson fell at Chancellorsville." While many politicians warned
of a "Second Reconstruction," a handful of white southerners, like Smith,
welcomed it. "It is long past time to bury the ghost of the Old South,

that has been dead and gone so long. The ghost has served the purposes of too many murderers and thieves; it has duped countless simple folk who forget that they are free men and Americans. The world is waiting, hoping that we will set our own house in order."[15]

Increasingly, the struggles of southerners during the age of civil rights became contests over competing visions of what made people "free men and Americans." Authors as disparate as Toni Morrison, David Roediger, Nathan Irvin Huggins, and Edmund Morgan have argued that white American visions of freedom historically depended—for their very substance and survival—upon black slavery or oppression. The idea of freedom became more powerful "in a cheek-by-jowl existence with the bound and unfree," Morrison wrote. Huggins argued that slavery and freedom were less polar opposites than interdependent pieces of America's historical fabric: "Slavery and freedom, white and black, are joined at the hip." More concretely, white Americans—aristocrats and workers, in the North and South, from colonial through antebellum times—rooted their economic and political power in African-Americans' lack of it. Whiteness paid wages, psychologically and also economically. Southern whites reinforced their freedom and economic livelihood after the abolition of slavery when they established the sharecropping system, the crop lien, and countless other instruments to keep African-Americans in a "slavery of debt." Legal segregation marked the emergence of the Jim Crow South, an era defined by lynching, intimidation, and disenfranchisement that kept blacks powerless and enslaved by fear. The civil rights movement was death to much of that. While the extent of its legacy may be well debated, the post–World War II era and the civil rights movement won for black Americans undeniable political and legal freedom. And if it is true that white American freedom depended upon black oppression, what happened to that freedom—in its visions and its practices—when the touchstone of bondage disappeared?[16]

In this vein, some white southerners perceived the civil rights movement as a threat to their very notion of freedom. Others saw the civil rights struggles for what they were—attempts to translate American promises of democracy and liberty for all into reality. Where some saw a world turned "upside down," others glimpsed, at long last, the chance for southerners and for all Americans to turn their lives right side up. "You take these country people out here," North Carolina farmer Hugh Wilson offered. "[They're] changing a lot of their attitudes. [They're] learning." The South in the 1970s was a society remarkably similar to that of Jim Crow times in some respects, yet fundamentally transformed in others. Even for those who resisted, change continued to seep into life. At times its arrival was sudden; more often it was halting and gradual, and came in fits and starts. When tranquillity settled over the sites of the civil rights movement, the work of adjusting to life in a new world finally began. White southerners had miles to go. "I don't know how long it's going to take," Wilson said in 1974. "[It] is one hell of a process."*[17]

---

*I have chosen to render quotations exactly as they appeared in historical documents, with punctuation and grammar unchanged. When brackets, apostrophes, plus signs, parentheses, ampersands, misspellings, or the like occur in quotations, it is because they existed in the original documents—in newspapers, letters, and other manuscript sources. Italics are a notable exception: if some people I have quoted chose to underline words, those underlines have been replaced with italics in the text.

ONE

Prelude: In the Wake of the War, 1945–1955

ON BATTLEFIELDS IN EUROPE and the Pacific, World War II blew gusts of change toward Joe Gilmer and Lewis Barton. For these white soldiers who fought alongside blacks, the war left indelible imprints. "Before the war I had the same feeling towards the Negro as the typical Southerner. God didn't intend them to have equal rights with other races, I thought," Petty Officer Barton wrote in a letter to his hometown newspaper, the Lumberton, North Carolina, *Robesonian.* By 1945, his belief became one of the war's millions of casualties. "I am afraid that all race prejudice is gone from the boys who have fought this war," Sergeant Gilmer wrote to the *Fort Worth Star-Telegram.* "White boys who have seen Negroes die to save their 'buddies,' and to help keep America free, are not in favor of the 'Jim Crow' law." In several regiments, by war's end, whites and blacks ate, worked, lived, and fought together. The South's segregation laws seemed petty and absurd by comparison. "Forcing them to ride in the rear of busses and stand for white[s] to sit down, I realize now is narrow-minded childishness practiced by our state," Barton wrote. "I discovered that the Negro is a human being." It was a lesson some white southerners would soon learn. For many others, the humanity of blacks remained a threat of the first order, a fear too immediate to peacefully allow, a reality to indefinitely deny. "It isn't going to be wise for any man . . . to try to abuse the colored people any more," Joe Gilmer warned. "The veterans of this war have learned that freedom means more than just freedom for the white man." Many southern veterans carried this truth back to their communities. The question of the

ensuing decade—between the end of World War II in 1945 and the
beginning of the Montgomery bus boycott in 1955—was whether white
southerners would welcome or challenge it.[1]

Joe Gilmer's and Lewis Barton's transformative experiences placed
them in a minority. Many soldiers who fought alongside blacks felt their
attitudes change, but they constituted only a small fraction of white
southern servicemen. About two-thirds of all white soldiers said blacks
should have the same rights after the war as they had before. Many justified their beliefs with assertions like, "We get along fine with the
Negro, why change?" and, "They're satisfied with the way they are now."
More than 90 percent of white southern soldiers supported separate military facilities and outfits. And white southerners who stayed at home
defended segregation even more vehemently. The sight of blacks in uniform had the peculiar ability to spark violence. "It seems that a Negro in
uniform has stimulated some white civilians and soldiers to protect the
customary caste etiquette of the South," read a 1943 report on the
American soldier. That "protection" often manifested itself in the form
of racial violence. During the war, the South was the site of six civilian
riots, twenty military riots and mutinies, and between forty-five and
seventy-five lynchings. While some soldiers felt that interracial contact
in the army promoted tolerance, "a larger group seemed to have reinforced their pre-Army attitudes while in the service. . . . The job done,
they wanted to get out, get home, and by and large resume where they
had left off." That often meant supporting Jim Crow as staunchly as ever.[2]

Gilmer and Barton both believed their profound wartime experiences
were not unique; they thought many white southern soldiers had similar
changes in attitudes. Although the testimonies of most whites challenge
that generalization, there is some evidence to support it. "All of our servicemen have not reacted in the same way," Guy Johnson said in 1945.
Johnson headed the Southern Regional Council, a progressive group—
made up of mostly white southerners—that came to support integration.
"Some of them have come out with worse attitudes toward the other race
than they had when they went in. I believe, however, that the majority of
our fighting men have had experiences which have taught them a new
appreciation of their fellow Americans of another race." In fact, those
with "a new appreciation" for blacks comprised but a small segment. Yet
their experiences were significant, and augured larger changes in the
years to come.[3]

Before Frank Smith gained notoriety as the rare progressive congress-man from the Mississippi Delta, he fought in the army during World War II. What Smith learned at Artillery Officers Training School in Fort Sill, Oklahoma, in 1942 stayed with him for the rest of his life. "OCS at Fort Sill was a revolutionary experience to those of us from the South, and probably to a good many others from outside the South. Negro offi-cer candidates were scattered among us wherever they happened to fall in the alphabetical list." Smith detected little resistance to this policy among southern soldiers. "The Southerners who expressed themselves to me said they had no objections, and some even voiced approval . . . nobody was bucking the tide." Southerners who would later oppose seg-regation, like Smith, often looked back on the war as a turning point. While Smith grew up as a member of the Mississippi Delta's small mid-dle class, Claude Ramsay was raised in poverty across the state in Ocean Springs. Ramsay carried traditional southern beliefs about race into the war. Yet when he returned to civilian life, he began to believe that blacks should have their rights. He landed a job at International Paper Com-pany shortly after the war, and won the presidency of the state AFL-CIO in 1959. For the rest of his life, Ramsay would consider the war a defin-ing experience.[4]

Georgia native Harold Fleming had similar memories of his service as a commander in the Pacific. "It did more to change my life than any other experience I've ever had," he confessed. "I'm a . . . good old boy at heart." Fleming neither sought nor expected any transformation of racial views, but his war experiences thrust such changes upon him. Stationed in Okinawa, Fleming was placed in charge of African-American troops. "The nearest thing you could be in the army to being black was to be a company officer with black troops," he later told journalist Fred Powledge, "because you lived and operated under the same circum-stances they did, and they got crapped all over." This experience did not instantly convert the "good old boy" to political radicalism, but it opened his eyes and changed his life. " 'Radicalized' would be too strong a word. It wasn't that I came to love Negroes; it was that I came to despise the system that did this." Fleming completed the transition when he went to work for the SRC after graduating from Harvard. He would eventually lead the organization during the 1950s. Fleming kept few friends from his prewar days; he associated mostly with like-minded progressives and friends from the American Veterans Committee. The committee consisted of "usually young veterans, just back from the war, white and black, who thought there was or ought to be a new day on this race stuff. And I exchanged my old friends for a new set of friends and co-workers and collaborators." After the war, nothing in Harold Fleming's life remained the same. "The army experience activated me," he later recalled; it set him along an arc that reshaped his career, his friendships, and the stuff of his everyday life.[5]

Most southern soldiers followed life trajectories unlike those of Frank Smith, Claude Ramsay, or Harold Fleming. Still, the majority of white southern soldiers who fought alongside blacks found that they "got along well together." A platoon sergeant from South Carolina remembered, "When I heard about it, I said I'd be damned if I'd wear the same shoulder patch they did. After that first day when we saw how they fought, I changed my mind. They're just like any of the other boys to us." Many soldiers confirmed that in combat the color line vanished. "We was trapped behind the line, and white was afraid of dying as blacks," African-American veteran Wilson Evans remembered of the Battle of the Bulge. "And there was no color, no nothing. . . . I did see that Americans could become Americans for about eight or nine days." While these soldiers asserted that race was inconsequential in combat, an overwhelming majority of white southern soldiers still resented the army's integrated living quarters. Combat suspended the color line, but the garrison introduced it again.[6]

Seth Lurie, an air force major from New Orleans, was stationed after the war at Craig Field in rural Dallas County, Alabama. He described himself as "a reconstructed southerner," and attributed that conversion to his military career. "The greatest teacher is experience . . . My education on this came solely from the military." Like Frank Smith, Lurie was housed alphabetically at Officer Training School. In that interracial contact, prejudices centuries in the making dissolved during everyday interaction:

> That was my first real contact with Negroes. . . . I learned that a Negro was a human being, with blood in his brain, and perspiration on his brow, with aches the same . . . ambitions the same, thought of home the same. I learned later that he died the same as a white man dies, for the same cause. Also in combat I learned that he has the same courage and daring as a white man. . . . To the

best of my knowledge, there is no resentment on the part of any
white officer.

Lurie's revelations were powerful. They showed that weeks of experience
could undo the received wisdom and ingrained customs of an entire
upbringing.[7]

Seth Lurie was quick to realize that his experiences did not suggest a
region-wide transformation. He could see it firsthand in his interactions
with the residents of nearby Selma. "Old timers in this town are against
progress. . . . Until this segregation-preaching generation dies off and a
new generation takes hold, there will be trouble." Monumental wartime
changes failed to grip all southerners. More than half of the war's veterans predicted "trouble" with blacks, and almost 20 percent foresaw
"trouble" with Jews. A 1946 social psychological survey found "little
reason for doubting the re-absorption of the vast majority of American
soldiers into the normal patterns of American life." White southern soldiers became reabsorbed in the South's traditional way of life. Many
believed they had fought to defend, not overturn, racial customs.[8]

While African-American veterans remembered that some white soldiers lost their prejudices in the war, those memories were far outweighed by accounts of whites who violently defended Jim Crow.
Dempsey Travis was stationed in Camp Shenango, Pennsylvania, where
the only PX excluded blacks. When a black soldier went into the PX
for a beer, whites kicked his eye out. Travis joined an expanding crowd
of African-American soldiers who discussed what action to take. A car-
avan of six trucks arrived, and white soldiers jumped off—wearing battle fatigues and carrying arms. They fired into the crowd, hitting Travis
in several places. He recalled the ambulance ride: "Two guys were sitting in front. The one says to the driver, 'Why we be doin' this to our
own soldiers?' Driver says, 'Who ever told you niggers were our soldiers? Where I come from'—I detected a southern accent—'we shoot
niggers like we shoot rabbits.' " By 1943, Travis had been put in
charge of a troop movement on its way to Camp Lee, in Richmond,
Virginia. It was the first time Travis, a Chicago native, had witnessed
the life of the South. Some sights singed his northern eyes. German
POWs rode in the front of the city's streetcars, blacks in the back.
After Travis received a transfer to Aberdeen, Maryland, in 1945, he
came across the rare white southerner who seemed to have been liber-

ated by the war. A major from Texas made Travis manager of an integrated PX. In the end, Travis "found the most sympathetic white men in the army were actually southerners." White southerners were nothing if not diverse: some welcomed blacks; others brimmed with hostility. In the memories of most black soldiers, however, the hostility far surpassed the acceptance.[9]

Alfred Duckett found few sympathetic whites. A freelance journalist who published articles in many of America's major black newspapers, Duckett was drafted and sent to Camp Claiborne, Louisiana. "The first night we arrived, a white officer told us what the rules were. . . . 'We want you to know we're not takin' any foolishness down here, because we don't shoot 'em down here, we hang 'em.' " When Duckett shipped over to Camp Lucky Strike in France, he found "an almost psychotic terror on the part of white commanders that there would be a great deal of association with the white women." The company's chaplain traveled in advance to each town, and informed the locals that blacks had tails. The commander issued an edict that black troops could not associate with French civilians. When Allen Leftridge disobeyed this order and conversed with a French woman who was serving coffee and doughnuts, a white MP shot him in the back. The white officers were so paranoid about black soldiers that they locked up the regiment's guns. Blacks received arms only in combat. As some white southerners clung to the myth of the "happy Negro," many recoiled in terror at the prospect of black men with guns—or even worse, with white women.[10]

When the last battles were over and soldiers became veterans, whites and blacks alike gazed back toward home. Many black soldiers discovered that if their native Southland had begun to grapple with economic and demographic change, little metamorphosis had occurred in white racial attitudes. Ben Fielder, an African-American from Mississippi, served in both Europe and the Far East, and made his way up the ranks to staff sergeant. After returning to the United States, Fielder and a white veteran embarked on a train ride from California back to their native Mississippi. As the train rumbled across the country, the two dined together and passed the time telling stories. Fielder felt they transcended "this race nonsense" and "became tight." When the train passed into Texas and Louisiana, Fielder realized his mistake. The white soldier assumed a posture of superiority, and informed Fielder that the war was over, that they were back in the South, and that, as Fielder recalled, "I was still just a nigger. Not an American soldier anymore. Just a nigger."

Black veteran German Levy of Brookhaven, Mississippi, concurred that on the level of white racial behavior, little had changed. "The pancake hadn't turned over . . . you come back home right into the same world you left." In many ways, the South at war's end closely resembled the prewar land. Reconstructed or not, white soldiers made their way back to factories, farms, and families, or moved into growing cities. While these soldiers had seen the wide world, some returned to communities that seemed much the same as before they left. Many preferred it that way.[11]

2

MOST WHITES CONTAINED POTENTIAL for both acceptance of and resistance to racial change. It often took powerful events, like a world war, and broad social processes, such as urbanization and industrialization, to bring out those tendencies. As one Alabama man told John Dos Passos, "Looks like the war has speeded up every kind of process, good and bad, in this country." In southern states that had relied upon staple crops for centuries, wartime industry and labor shortages accelerated the processes that diversified and mechanized the economy. "War does a lot of things," Mississippi Delta planter W. T. Wynn reflected in 1946. "Our economics have been disrupted. . . . I believe that in the next five to ten years you will see the greatest revolution that ever happened in this country, happen in this Mississippi Delta." Poor whites and blacks who had known nothing but sharecropping and tenancy moved into newly expanding urban and industrial areas. As a dispatch from *Newsweek*'s southern bureau put it, "The South is in the midst [of] two revolutions, an industrial revolution and explosive urbanization." Numbers help to capture part of that story. In the 1930s, more than 15 million southerners (more than half of the region's people) lived in rural areas. Lured by job opportunities—and more vaguely, by hopes for better lives—both whites and blacks, during and after the war, moved to southern as well as northern cities. Four million of them left the rural South in the 1940s. In 1950, Mississippi was the only southern state where the majority still worked on farms. By 1960, the South's rural population had dropped to 7 million. Many whites felt the transformative effects of these demographic and economic changes. The Lemann family ran a sugar plantation in Palo Alto, Louisiana, for centuries. Arthur Lemann, who represented the fourth generation of that dynasty, deemed the wartime changes revolutionary. "I recall so vividly back in the early '40s that there were no trucks on the farm. . . . I rode a horse like every other overseer, from can to can't." The expanding industrial economy brought with it the mechanical cane-harvester, introduced the tractor, and displaced one hundred of Lemann's workers. "World War II brought about the drastic changes that we're enjoying, or not enjoying, today," Lemann recalled in a 1991 interview. The days of the horse, mule, and human cane-cutter became the stuff of memory.[12]

As farmers left rural areas, their absence often undermined white solidarity and its tendency toward mob rule and lynch law. Small-town sorts began to populate the burgeoning urban areas. Large factories like the Ingalls Shipyard in Pascagoula, Mississippi, attracted thousands of workers, and many more millions of dollars in industry. Corporations moved plants southward, often with implicit promises that southern localities would stamp out the grosser manifestations of racism. Industrialization and urbanization brought economic changes and new hopes for a "New South," and they helped lay the structural groundwork for a loosening in southern race relations after the war.[13]

The war era altered the mind-set of some white soldiers, nudged rural southerners into cities, further industrialized the South, and also injected new streaks of progressivism into the politics of various states. National and international forces thus pierced local fortresses of white supremacy. The Supreme Court destroyed a pillar of Jim Crow when it outlawed the white primary in 1944. Before that time, the Democratic Party's all-white primary had proved the most effective tool for excluding blacks from politics. Yet while an influx of black voters helped change politics in some cities, rural areas remained citadels of disenfranchisement. In rural Mississippi, Alabama, and Louisiana, for instance, whites used violence, intimidation, and legal ploys to keep blacks away from the polls long after the white primary had been banned. In areas where fear was less pervasive, some southerners voted for reformist politicians rather than race-baiters. The states that trod this political path contained smaller percentages of whites who lived among black majorities. Often it was not the presence of blacks per se that fueled white fears, but their potential for power—a potential most evident in heavily black areas. In Texas, Tennessee, Florida, North Carolina, and Virginia, less than 5 percent of whites lived in black-majority counties in 1940. Between 8 and 12 percent of white Arkansans, Louisianans, Alabamians, and Georgians lived in such areas. In South Carolina, the figure was 20 percent; in Mississippi, 37 percent. These figures help to explain which states elected reformist politicians in the 1940s: Estes Kefauver and Albert Gore won victories in Tennessee, Claude Pepper in Florida, Frank Porter Graham in North Carolina (though he was appointed, not elected), Sid McMath in Arkansas, and "Big" Jim Folsom in Alabama. More to the point, the figures help to explain which states did not vote for progressives: notably, Mississippi and South Carolina.[14]

On the level of national politics, both reform and reaction touched Dixie in 1948. Henry Wallace, Franklin D. Roosevelt's former vice president, mounted a presidential campaign under the banner of the Progressive Party. Wallace made substantial—if ephemeral—inroads in Upper South states like North Carolina and Virginia. He was the first national candidate to publicly attack segregation in the South. Wallace was also the first politician to address mixed audiences—and for the deliberate way in which he broke the taboo, he encountered angry crowds and a mob atmosphere. Wallace's efforts failed in the end, although his campaign showed that some southerners might oppose segregation if given a viable forum in which to do so. While 1948 brought Henry Wallace and the Progressive Party to the South, it witnessed the similarly fleeting—yet equally significant—revolt of the Dixiecrats. The States' Rights Party nominated Strom Thurmond of South Carolina for president and Fielding Wright of Mississippi for vice president. Democrats unhappy with President Harry Truman's steps in the direction of black civil rights bolted from the party, and fueled the fledgling Dixiecrats. Both Wallace and the Dixiecrats scored breakthroughs in southern politics, yet neither shattered the one-party Democratic stronghold. That would have to wait until the 1960s.[15]

THE WAR PROVIDED some southerners with novel experiences, brought demographic and economic transformations, and portended wider changes in life, yet it also left mixed legacies. Whereas Guy Johnson teemed with optimism in 1945, he grappled with new realities a year later. "The year 1946 has brought many things. Perhaps we can best characterize it as a year of reaction," he said before the annual meeting of the Southern Regional Council in November 1946. "The Nation has 'let down' after its great war effort, and the inevitable conservative and reactionary trend has made itself felt in unmistakable ways." Johnson did not have a difficult argument to make. He cited the revival of the Ku Klux Klan, the reelection of race-baiting politicians like Theodore Bilbo in Mississippi and Eugene Talmadge in Georgia, and beatings of union organizers, black veterans, and others who threatened to disrupt the status quo. In a 1946 letter to Dwight Eisenhower, Alvin Owsley, chairman of the American Legion National Americanism Endowment Fund, predicted racial violence would mount. Reflecting on the new confidence African-American soldiers had displayed overseas, Owsley wrote, "I do not know . . . where these Negroes come from, but it is certain that if they expect to be returned to the South, they very likely are on the way to be hanged or to be burned alive at public lynchings by the white men of the South." As several grim cases showed, Owsley was not far off the mark. In a four-week stretch during July and August of that year alone, a dozen black men were murdered in the Deep South. A white mob lynched Leon McTatie when he supposedly stole a saddle near Lexington, Mississippi. Maceo Snipes, a veteran, met a similar fate in Butler, Georgia, after he became the first African-American in Taylor County to register to vote.[16]

Incidents in Walton County, Georgia, and Columbia, Tennessee, marked the "year of reaction." The executions of two young black men— Roger Malcolm and George Dorsey (a veteran), who were brothers-in-law—and their wives, Dorothy Malcolm and Mae Murray Dorsey, occurred outside the town of Monroe, Georgia, on July 25, 1946. Roger Malcolm was a laborer on Bob Hester's farm. On July 14, Malcolm allegedly stabbed Hester's son during a dispute. Malcolm spent the next eleven days in jail, until he was bailed out by Loy Harrison—the area's largest cotton grower, and George Dorsey's boss. The Dorseys and Malcolms piled into Harrison's car, and headed for his farm near the Apalachee River. Harrison sped past the Dorseys' house, across a bridge toward a waiting white mob. Rumors of a lynching had swirled about town after Malcolm's arrest, and a visit from Eugene Talmadge roused the rabble to a fever pitch. The gubernatorial candidate told a Monroe crowd, "If I'm your governor, they won't vote in our white primary the next four years." The Dorseys and Malcolms would never get that chance. On July 18, Talmadge carried Walton County by seventy-eight votes in the Democratic primary—and with it the state of Georgia. On July 25, the Malcolms and Dorseys were lynched near Loy Harrison's plantation. The reaction was at its height.[17]

The lynchings and Talmadge's victory made that summer of 1946 a restive one for white Georgians. Talmadge ran his campaign around the race issue, and made many pledges like the one in which he vowed to disenfranchise black Georgians. He targeted rural white voters, in full knowledge that they could carry him to victory. Georgia's infamous county-unit system of elections made that possible. Each county possessed a given number of unit votes, ranging from two for the smallest counties to six for the largest. Of Georgia's 159 counties, 8 of them received six unit votes; 30 possessed four unit votes; and the remaining 121 had two unit votes apiece. The candidate that won a certain county received all of its unit votes. Talmadge captured the Democratic primary with 242 unit votes (twice the number of two-unit counties), to 148 for James Carmichael. More Georgians voted for Carmichael than for Talmadge—a full 16,144 more—but the county-unit system gave voters in rural areas disproportionate power. Urban Georgians expressed outrage. Cliff Owsley of Atlanta felt "completely disfranchised and powerless." Frances Barnes of Marietta was "disillusioned and sick at heart over the inability of the rural sections to understand what is happening in our state." The perspective tilted 180 degrees in the rural areas. Ira Butt, editor of the *North Georgia News,* celebrated the fact that "We've got a WHITE MAN's Governor coming forward now." Rural white Georgians reveled; those in the cities sought cover. Editor J. B. Hardy of the *Thomaston Times* blamed Carmichael's defeat on rural prejudice. "In the country counties where ignorance and prejudice rule . . . Ole Gene got his big votes, but in the city counties where education and enlightenment reign Carmichael piled up a huge vote." Not every rural Georgian breathed segregationist fire, and hundreds of letters to the *Atlanta Constitution* attested to the fact that not every Atlantan took an "enlightened" stance on race relations. Still, Hardy's generalization possessed the ring of truth.[18]

Some white southerners could not reconcile a battle against German racism with the mandates of Jim Crow. One Georgian admitted that while he believed in black inferiority, he could not countenance Eugene Talmadge's racist demagoguery. "We are fighting a Jew-baiter in Germany and I don't see how we can be consistent if we support a Negro-baiter in Georgia." In the wake of the war, Captain James Clark, an air corps veteran, expressed disbelief at Talmadge's victory. "Georgia has elected to follow the leadership of a man, who by his actions, placed himself in the same category as the dictators we so recently condemned. It is difficult to understand how a freedom-loving people failed to grasp the opportunity to banish the influence of Eugene Talmadge from state government." Some white southerners took seriously America's international posture toward freedom—and realized it clashed with Jim Crow.

Clark concluded, "It is my firm conviction that the struggle for the preservation of the rights of men has suffered its greatest defeat in the back yard of its protector."[19]

Thomas Lovett and Henry Steadman, veterans from the college town of Athens, believed that the war's lessons had escaped Georgians. They felt certain that if others understood what had happened in Germany, their racial prejudice would have withered away:

> We would like to put in a word of sympathy for the people of Georgia. Our sympathy comes from the fact that more of the people of the State did not have the opportunity to see Germany after its defeat, as we did. Had they, we feel quite sure that the election of Eugene Talmadge would have been impossible. Those people thrived on racial hatred and intolerance, the very issues that elected Mr. Talmadge. By this election, the State has proven itself to be on the same level with that of Mississippi—in fact, we believe Georgia is worse!

To Lovett and Steadman, World War II left an unquestioned legacy—that all humans would enjoy democracy and freedom, and that white supremacy and totalitarianism would perish in all their forms. But the election of Talmadge showed that many whites (and not only natives of Mississippi) disagreed. "We wonder if the people of this State realize that by this election we are in danger of having a form of government which so many of our native sons died fighting against." Talmadge's victory demonstrated that the war had done little to destroy prejudice in many white southerners; neither could it remove racial politics or corruption from state governments.* The election results spoke for white Georgians in ways that editorials and letters to the editor could not.[20]

Two days after the *Atlanta Constitution* published the letter from Lovett and Steadman, the Malcolms and Dorseys lost their lives. The lynchings in Monroe further shattered any notions that white southerners were moving toward acceptance of democracy and freedom for all. "It

---

*When Eugene Talmadge died of cirrhosis before he could take office, a political fiasco ensued. Powered by a suspect write-in effort and ballot box corruption, Talmadge's son Herman finagled himself onto the list of candidates from which the legislature could select the next governor. The legislature, dominated by old-line Talmadge supporters, voted Herman Talmadge into the governor's office. He had served for sixty-seven days when the Georgia Supreme Court ruled his succession illegal. The previous governor, Ellis Arnall, then installed his lieutenant, Melvin E. Thompson. Thompson kept the statehouse until 1948, when Herman Talmadge won it back.

is very regrettable that mob violence occurs in any section of the country" was all Eugene Talmadge could say, as he equated the Monroe lynchings with wartime racial confrontations that occurred in Detroit and Chicago. Few American politicians were so glib. Senator William Knowland of California called the lynchings "a blot on the whole United States," reflecting the new international atmosphere in which the killings occurred.[21]

Some white Georgians expressed shame at the heinous crime. "Hitler and Germany were indicted at Nuremberg and our fair State was indicted at Monroe," wrote J. L. Thomas of Decatur. "I have reached the point where I do not think it heresy to say I am rapidly losing that boundless pride in my Southern heritage that was instilled in me in my youth." The feelings to which Thomas testified would resonate with many other white southerners in the age of civil rights, through the 1950s and 1960s. Rampant bigotry and violence against African-Americans often upset white southerners much more than black demands and movements appealed to them. Those who began to change their racial views were often repelled by white supremacy, not compelled by civil rights. That spirit animated many Georgians when they attended church on Sunday, July 28, after the lynchings. From Atlanta and Athens to the First Methodist Church of Monroe itself, churches issued resolutions condemning the lynchings. At St. Luke's Episcopal Church in Monroe, Dr. Lester Rumble declared, "The terrible crime of Monroe is a guilt of us all." As Reverend H. C. Holland opened services at Monroe First Methodist, he read a statement that deplored the murders and asked all those who agreed to stand up. "We stand for equal rights and complete justice for all men in all stations of life," Holland said, as the entire congregation rose to its feet.[22]

White southerners might rise for racial justice after the lynchings, but few made that sentiment a genuine part of their lives. Instances of sympathy for the plight of blacks were isolated, and it often took horrific displays of violence like the Monroe lynchings to instill even fleeting compassion. Such sympathy rarely translated into changes in the home, school, church, or workplace, on the bus, in the cotton field, at the ballot box, or in the mind. On July 18, the *Atlanta Constitution* had rung in the election season on a note of hope. "Negroes swarmed orderly and with dignity to the polls yesterday to vote for the first time in a Georgia Democratic primary." Yet in the last weeks of July, Georgia elected a demagogic governor and hosted the execution of four African-

Americans. Nobody yet knew for sure whether the planter Loy Harrison had intentionally driven the Malcolms and the Dorseys to their deaths. It would be 1992 before an eyewitness implicated Harrison in the murders, and named others. The criminals remained at large in 1946. "We have just sent millions of the flower of our young manhood to Europe and to Asia to stamp out Nazism, whose habit has been to take the law into its own hands and murder helpless people," stated the Atlanta Methodist Ministers' Association on July 30. "Now, in Georgia, something closely akin to Nazism in Europe and Asia has arisen, and in every sense it is just as brutal." If white supremacy was at all shaken by the war, those tremors reached Atlanta ministers much more than they touched any whites in rural places like Monroe. Black leaders of the Walton County Civic League pointed out in 1950 that the dissolution of the white primary was meaningless, because the white man "is going to run things anyway."[23]

White residents of Columbia, Tennessee, certainly hoped that they would continue to dominate. The trouble there began in February 1946, when Gladys Stephenson brought her radio to the Caster-Knott store to be repaired. Weeks later, the manager, LaVal LaPointe, told Stephenson's younger son, John, that the radio had been sold. When the store reacquired the radio, LaPointe demanded an exorbitant fee for it. James Stephenson, a nineteen-year-old just back from the navy, accompanied his mother to the store on February 25. Tensions mounted and an argument ensued. A fight broke out between Stephenson and store apprentice Billy Fleming, a white army veteran. Neither man sustained critical injuries. Gladys and James Stephenson were both taken to jail, while Fleming's father secured a warrant for attempted murder. By early afternoon, a crowd of whites had formed on the downtown square. When the Stephensons were released, they returned to the safety of Columbia's black neighborhood, the Bottom. Amid rumors of a lynching, James Stephenson left town for Chicago and blacks in the Bottom armed themselves. The white crowd downtown quickly lost its desire to invade the neighborhood of armed blacks, and African-Americans rebuffed Columbia police. Tennessee highway patrolmen hurtled toward Columbia in time for a predawn raid on the Bottom. State officers ravaged the neighborhood, decimated its businesses, and arrested more than a hundred blacks at random, who were marched to the Maury County Jail. Two were killed in the sheriff's office. An investigator for the SRC asserted, "Any estimate of property damage would not be too high." Columbia blacks were not lynched, but neither were they protected. In the years after World War II, this passed for change in the South.[24]

The events in Columbia offered contradictory lessons. In August, a Lawrenceburg, Tennessee court tried twenty-five of the arrested blacks. The grand jury, composed entirely of poor whites, acquitted all but two of them. If two general stories about the white South unraveled in the years after the war—one of racial reform and the other of reaction—the jury's decision added to the saga of reform. It suggested white southerners were no longer wedded quite as deeply to racial discrimination. Yet seen from another vantage point, white southerners continued to deny the humanity of African-Americans at every turn: LaVal LaPointe attempted to fleece the Stephensons; Billy Fleming's father obtained a trumped-up warrant for attempted murder; a mob formed on the downtown square; the highway patrol destroyed the Bottom, arresting more than a hundred blacks, two of whom died in the sheriff's office. Through it all, Sheriff James Underwood could testify in court, "The relations between the races [in Maury County] has been . . . better than any other classes on earth." It seemed like the same old myths still buttressed the same old oppression. Still, this was different: Underwood initially released the Stephensons from jail; the black community, newly fortified with confidence, armed itself and fought back; whites may have gathered on the square, but they did not lynch anybody; and perhaps most amazingly, the Lawrenceburg jury of poor whites acquitted twenty-three blacks.[25]

Perhaps white southerners had begun to feel the winds of change. In any understanding of the jury's acquittal, southern class dynamics loom large. Many whites who ascended into the middle class after World War II felt threatened by blacks. Will Campbell, a white reverend who became caught up in the movement for racial justice, argued that poorer whites could better empathize with the unfairly accused: they, too, had been dragged into court before, condescended to, exploited, and unjustly indicted. "There continues to be less real racism in redneckism because the redneck participates in our society from a base of considerably less power than the rest of us." This line of thinking contends that the poor whites in Lawrenceburg, having the least to lose, were most apt to acquit the black defendants. Surveys of white World War II soldiers also support this argument. Conventional wisdom long had it that better educated southerners possessed more "enlightened" or "progressive" views on race, but that was not always true. Of white southern soldiers asked for their opinion about integrated work crews, 76 percent of those with a high school or college degree said they would object, while only 57 percent of the less educated did. Status anxiety did not seem to afflict poor whites as it did the middle class; the poor had little status to lose.[26]

Yet there were many southerners, on both sides of the racial divide, who glimpsed in poor whites the most vicious aspects of racism. Sheriff Underwood described members of the white mob as "people who work at the phosphate plants and hosiery mills. . . . This type of white man does not know the Negro as we do and is less friendly to him." Such a reading of southern class dynamics could be buttressed by more than just white myths about "knowing the Negro." One Columbia African-American stated, "The white factory worker, who fears our competition, is the dangerous element in the South." He cited the "Fleming boy who started the trouble here" as a prime example. Fleming was but one of many poor whites who despised blacks—"Because they are, if anything, more insecure than the Negro." Such notions about poor whites made the acquittals in Lawrenceburg that much more surprising.[27]

For all the change the acquittals may have highlighted, an examination of the crowd that gathered on the Columbia square challenges any easy claims to progress. In that crowd, and during the Columbia disturbance in general, white war veterans displayed particularly deep hostility toward blacks. Veterans who changed their racial views after the war—those like Seth Lurie, Joe Gilmer, and Claude Ramsay—stuck out like sore thumbs. Most whites felt immediately threatened by black veterans who exhibited newfound dignity and confidence. For the vast majority, the war's inclusive ideals of democracy, freedom, and antiracism rang hollow. Even those who absorbed such egalitarian wartime ideals often separated the war itself from what came after. Whites thought the legacy of World War II had little to do with the rights of black Americans. Of course, African-Americans disagreed.[28]

As more southerners moved to the cities, as the economy industrialized, and as veterans returned home, the old paternalism started to die out on both sides of the white boss–black worker dynamic. Black veteran Wilson Evans returned to Mississippi with new resolve. But when Evans attempted to lead voter registration drives in 1947, he ran smack into southern whites, as determined as ever to resist black gains. "You came back with Northern ideas of niggers voting," the Gulfport sheriff told Evans. "But us Southern white folks hadn't swallowed it yet." After the war, facades did not coat reality quite so heavily, and interracial interactions assumed rougher edges. "The old expectations and fears no longer applied," John Egerton wrote. "A meaner game . . . was in the offing." Murders that swept the South in the year of reaction were "fueled by white fears that black veterans might become a revolutionary force, and that blacks in general would no longer stay 'in their place.' " Loy Harrison said as much when he spoke of the Monroe lynchings decades later. "Up until George went in the army, he was a good nigger," Harrison told Clinton Adams, a boy in Walton County at the time of the lynching. "But when he came out, they thought they were as good as any white people."[29]

Black veterans brought a double-edged sword with them when they returned to the South. Without deference, they challenged old white stereotypes—and many whites responded in kind. In a stinging irony, the Alabama state legislature uttered a truth in a 1945 resolution arguing that whites and blacks should be "left in peace and harmony to work out their mutual problems." African-Americans returned from the war with the desire to shake the white South out of this unjust peace. Yet "no good can come from changing the normal course of evolution and development of race by arbitrary legal means," the legislature maintained, for "such attempts lead only to violence, misunderstanding, and destruction of the normal and happy relationship now prevailing between the races in this state." If the state legislature was gravely mistaken in its belief that a "normal and happy relationship" prevailed under Jim Crow, it accurately foretold the kind of violence that would erupt when blacks challenged white myths. For all its terror, however, the year of reaction proved to be only that—a year. In light of federal and international pressure, and under the weight of larger demographic and social shifts, the number of southern lynchings drastically decreased. Strange fruit still hung from the South's poplar trees in the 1950s, but these episodes became horrible anomalies instead of standard practice.[30]

While lynching began to disappear from the southern landscape in the late 1940s, racial tension and white prejudice did not. "The tension in the South today makes me sick at heart," wrote A. H. Sterne, vice president of the Atlanta branch of the United Council of Church Women, in 1948. Fellow Atlantan Helene Alford painted a similarly grim portrait of Georgia that year. " 'Civil rights' is dynamite in this state with the political upheaval around us. . . . The picture looks pretty dark." Well before direct action protests hit southern towns, fears of black equality gripped many white southerners. When asked what the most important problem facing the South was in July 1949, 30 percent replied, "civil rights." Eighty percent believed blacks should be required to occupy separate parts of interstate buses or trains. White southern support for segregation remained entrenched after the war. The student sit-ins were eleven years away, and few whites would change their minds in the interim.[31]

Many continued to contest the legacy of World War II. When black protest intensified and the pace of change quickened in the 1950s and 1960s, white southerners referred back to the war as a touchstone. After the *Brown v. Board of Education* decision in 1954, a young Mississippi farmer who had served in the war cast his lot against civil rights. "Fight integration? Why I've just begun to fight," he wrote Congressman Frank Smith. "When I was on a beach in the South Pacific I was fighting and I didn't know why. Now we know what we are fighting for, and nothing is going to hold us back." A certain notion of freedom crystallized among white southerners—and it had little to do with fascism overseas or equal rights. Many began to picture the American government as the fascist, and the white southerner as the victim. When President Eisenhower mobilized federal troops to integrate Little Rock's Central High School in 1957, many whites found the war analogy particularly apt. "My son was in the Marine corps during World war two and spent 14 months in the South Pacific fighting, and for what?" one Broxton, Georgia, woman wrote *Atlanta Constitution* editor Ralph McGill. "I can answer that one, to see Soldiers with rifles and Bayonets pointed to the backs of his children being forced to obey a DICTATOR instead of enjoying a FREE America and choosing their friends and associates." A peculiar conception of individual freedom animated many white southerners—the freedom to segregate oneself by race, regardless of what others desired. For many, World War II became a battle for that specific liberty. The movements for black civil rights that unfolded over the following two decades looked like villainous attempts to challenge whites' freedom.[32]

One Charlotte man believed the 1964 Civil Rights Act and its desegregation of public facilities undermined his war efforts. "Six brothers in my family including myself fought in World War II for our rights and freedom," this veteran wrote to his congressman in 1965. "Then why . . . am I being forced to use the same wash-room and restrooms with negro[e]s. I highly resent this. . . . I'd be willing to fight and die for my rights, but can't say this anymore for this country." When the black freedom struggle chipped away at southern customs, many white veterans began to believe that they had fought in vain. World War II changed the racial attitudes and behavior of some soldiers and some southerners, but it failed to transform the majority. As Seth Lurie remarked about the citizens of Dallas County, Alabama, "I only hope the white people of Dallas learn before they have to learn as I did—through a war." Although the civil rights movement did not bring military war to the South in the 1950s and 1960s, it came with a similar power and depth of feeling. The freedom struggle forced sudden cataclysms and gradual transformations in southern race relations—the kinds of changes that had been felt only one other time in the life of the South: after the Civil War.[33]

3

ALTHOUGH AMERICA HAD WAGED a war against totalitarianism abroad, many continued to condone Jim Crow at home. In rhetoric, if not in action, the federal government displayed an awareness of such hypocrisy. Violent racism in the South handed to America's foes incontrovertible proof that injustice endured in the United States. Russian writer Ilya Ehrenburg took a trip to America in 1946 and described Mississippi as a place where whites "shiver with fright thinking about the mass of unfortunate, angry people who may become tired of singing 'Hallelujah' while waiting their turn to be hanged." In 1955, young Emmett Till was lynched near Money, Mississippi, and his body thrown into the Tallahatchie River. After Till's death, Düsseldorf's *Das Frei Volk* reported, "The life of a Negro in Mississippi is not worth a whistle." Racial violence in the South not only lent grist to the communist propaganda mill, but encouraged other nations to criticize America. White southerners continued to use whatever means they wished to keep blacks in their "place" in the 1940s, but their heinous crimes no longer occurred in a geographic vacuum. As blacks demanded more rights, the federal government and international media became more attuned to their plight. In this atmosphere, white southerners could no longer wield the rope, the gun, or the knife with such impunity.[34]

The coin of internationalism had another side. Even as lynchings decreased, in light of America's Cold War rhetoric and global ambitions, an ascendant ethos of anti-communism lent Jim Crow's defenders explosive fuel. Anti-communist hysteria spawned blacklisting and redbaiting nationwide; its ability to become tangled up in race relations was

especially pervasive in the South. As names like Joe McCarthy, Alger
Hiss, and Ethel and Julius Rosenberg captured headlines across the
country, anti-communism shaped the South with its capacity to derail
any challenge to the status quo—and to Jim Crow, in particular. In
1946, the Congress of Industrial Organizations (CIO) launched its
"Operation Dixie" campaign to unionize southern workers. Instead of
challenging southern traditions, however, the CIO formed segregated
locals and practiced anti-communism. The CIO's fears of integration and
communism resonated with the majority of white workers that it courted.
The Scottsboro trial of the 1930s had first solidified many of these issues
in southern minds. The Communist Party came to the defense of accused
African-Americans, and focused an international spotlight on the horrors
of southern racism. Simultaneously, its prominent role in the Scottsboro
case allowed white southerners to equate black civil rights with communist conspiracies. Many white southerners pictured the National
Association for the Advancement of Colored People (NAACP) and the
Communist Party as one and the same, blacks who struggled for equality
became dupes of a Soviet scheme, and northern advocates of civil rights
looked like communist-inspired "outside agitators." The black and red
menaces shaded into each other. A central tenet of many white southerners' worldview, anti-communism possessed staying power. It colored
white southerners' perceptions of the federal government, the civil rights
movement, and the African-Americans in their towns.

Of all the forces that were unleashed in the 1940s, few proved more
durable than anti-communism. White southerners' fears of the red menace were not confined to the high tide of the Cold War, but endured for
decades. "Before the Supreme Court decision" in *Brown v. Board of Education,* Frank Smith wrote, "Negroes were just one of the hate objects—
Jews, Catholics, labor unions, and communists were indiscriminately
intermingled." The many challengers to white southerners' way of life
soon coalesced, and anti-communism stood as an inseparable part of that
amalgam.[35]

Frank Porter Graham's 1950 bid for reelection to the U.S. Senate from
North Carolina showed anti-communism's southern strength. Graham
was the progressive former president of the University of North Carolina, beloved by many. Governor W. Kerr Scott had appointed Graham
to the Senate in 1949 to finish out the term of the deceased J. Melville
Broughton. Graham ran for reelection, and won a plurality of the vote in
the Democratic primary. He finished ahead of attorney Willis Smith by

a margin of 49 percent to 41 percent, but polled just short of the required outright majority. As a runoff approached, Smith's campaign—spearheaded by Jesse Helms, who later became a leading conservative senator—realized it had to gain ground fast. Smith and Helms played on Graham's past as a member of Harry Truman's Civil Rights Commission and the Southern Conference for Human Welfare (SCHW). The campaign circulated a doctored photograph that pictured Graham's wife dancing with a black man. North Carolinians found handbills in their mailboxes that read, "WHITE PEOPLE WAKE UP!" and asked, "Do you want Negroes working beside you and your wife and daughters?" Helms tagged the University of North Carolina as the "University of Negroes and Communists." Smith and Helms alleged that Graham was "up to his neck" in communists and that he "favors mingling of the races." It begged the question, which did southern whites really fear—communism or integration? In this particular case, the two were so closely entwined in the minds of many that the answer did not seem to matter. Willis Smith defeated Frank Porter Graham in the 1950 election, 52 percent to 48 percent. For supporters of segregation, anti-communism became a juggernaut.[36]

Mississippi senator James Eastland raised the ante when he brought a McCarthy-like spectacle to the Big Easy in 1954. Former members of SCHW, an organization formed in 1938, became Eastland's primary target. SCHW attracted southern liberals like Clark Foreman, Aubrey Williams, and Virginia Durr, as it represented a legitimate movement to reform Dixie's politics. When America plunged headlong into the Cold War, SCHW suffered for its previous refusal to ban Communist Party sympathizers from its ranks. In 1947, the House Un-American Activities Committee (HUAC) alleged that SCHW was a communist front, that it used the issue of race as "explosive and revolutionary tinder in destroying American democracy," and that it advocated "an independent Negro Soviet Republic in the southern Black Belt which in essence is a call to civil war." SCHW disbanded after Henry Wallace's defeat in November 1948. Many of its members had joined an offshoot established in January 1946: the Southern Conference Educational Fund (SCEF). In 1954, Eastland attempted to resuscitate the red ghost of the SCHW in the minds of white southerners. He held a series of hearings in New Orleans, and called to the stand various members of SCEF and former members of SCHW. Eastland accused the defendants of communism, and planted witnesses who would corroborate his allegations. The trials were a sham, and most of the public saw through Eastland's smears. In the short term, Eastland suffered. The *Montgomery Advertiser* called his hearings a "blight on 'Southern honor.' " Yet Eastland accomplished his main objective—he publicly reinforced the connection between civil rights activism and the specter of communism. Virginia Durr asserted that while few of her Montgomery neighbors believed she was a communist, "the fact that we are against segregation was blazoned forth to all the Southern world, and in the minds of most Southerners that is tantamount to being subversive if not actually insane." The curtain for Eastland's southern version of *The Crucible* went up on March 16; the Supreme Court issued its decision in *Brown v. Board of Education* two months later. As that ruling approached, Eastland's hearings suggested to white southerners that supporters of integration were subversive communists at the very least, if not deranged.[37]

Many caught his drift. Whites were poised to shout "communist" at any advance the civil rights movement might make—from the *Brown* decision and the Montgomery bus boycott to school desegregation in Little Rock, the Civil Rights Act, and untold protests in towns across the South. The meteoric rise of Citizens' Councils in 1954 and 1955 saturated the southern air with anti-communist propaganda. Soon after the *Brown* decision, Senator Eastland charged that the Supreme Court was under communist control. The Court has become "indoctrinated and brainwashed by left-wing pressure groups," Eastland contended. The Supreme Court justices must be communists, many white southerners agreed. Jewell Lamm of Middlesex, North Carolina, wrote to her congressman, "Personally I think all nine of the old political hacks ought to be exiled to Russia." When Emmett Till was lynched in Eastland's home state, many white Mississippians glimpsed the hand of communism in the grisly murder. Reporters descended on the courthouse in Sumner, Mississippi, to cover the trial of Roy Bryant and J. W. Milam, who confessed to the crime years after they were acquitted. A well-dressed, bespectacled old woman declared to television cameras, "I'm almost convinced that the very beginning of this was by a communistic front." Everywhere civil rights appeared, white southerners saw red.[38]

The anti-communist furor reached whites across the South—from rural areas to urban centers, Upper South and Deep South alike. Ideas of communist conspiracies seized not only small Mississippi towns or white supremacist strongholds. The constituents of Charles Raper Jonas illustrate this point. Jonas was a U.S. representative from the North Carolina

Piedmont, and a Republican. His district formed the backbone of North Carolina's "progressive mystique," and represented a chink in the armor of an otherwise one-party region. Yet Jonas's constituents were as concerned with communism as any other southerners. When a civil rights bill came up for debate in Congress in 1956, Lamm wrote Jonas, "I beg of you to help defeat President Ike's 'Civil Rights' Bill. . . . We want to resist communism at home as well as abroad. We want the U.S. a proud and sovereign nation like it was before Franklin D. Roosevelt and his 'Marxist' New Deal took over. God and Christ gave us segregation. . . . The commies propose to give us integration." Just the thought of integration dredged up in Lamm fears of a godless and dictatorial society. But to L. G. Blodgett, another of Jonas's constituents, civil rights was not the most pressing issue. When the bill became law, Blodgett argued it was "not too important from the point of negro 'rights,' though many hereabouts would differ from me." Blodgett worried far more about communism than about the toothless, if significant, Civil Rights Act of 1957. "It suddenly dawned on me that the Civil Rights Bill was being used as a 'popular front' for the negroes 'rights,' but Communism was definitely behind the 'race' situation." It was 1957, the heyday of massive resistance, and Blodgett knew his community would not integrate overnight. More threatening than desegregation itself was the red plot behind it. After the integration of Little Rock's Central High School, however, others were not so sure. One University of North Carolina alumnus could barely believe his eyes when he saw the photographs in his hometown *Charlotte News.* "Can this be America? It looks more like a smuggled photo from behind the Iron Curtain!" The Charlotte man did not think communists were behind the desegregation in Little Rock, but was certain the events would aid the Soviets in their deceitful plans. "Those persons behind the integration push have finally succeeded in dividing our nation to an extent that must please Moscow to the 'n'th degree!"[39]

Anti-communism was not the sole province of whites who favored segregation. Liberal nationwide organizations like Americans for Democratic Action (ADA) raised the banner of anti-communism after World War II, and the SRC also dissociated itself from communism. Louis Schulz, minister of the First Congregational Church in Winter Park, Florida, belonged to the state's Interracial Committee. When asked to become a member of the Florida Council on Human Relations, Schulz inquired about the council's stance on communism before considering its offer. "I seldom join an organization like this without using every possible means to be assured that it is not infiltrated by Communism," Schulz wrote in 1956 to the SRC, the parent organization of the state councils. "There is no doubt of my interest in working for justice and fair play and good citizenship rights for all Americans," he noted—so long as they did not bend too far to the left. United in anti-communism, many white southerners—from those who advocated states' rights to those who joined state interracial councils—could appreciate Schulz's prerogative. Through the mid-1960s, southerners as ideologically opposed as head Klansman Sam Bowers and progressive Mississippi newspaper editor Hodding Carter would agree that communists aided the black civil rights movement.[40]

Dixie's leaders, from members of Citizens' Councils to elected officials, painted stark images of communist conspiracies. Most white southerners, in turn, easily accepted and internalized the anti-communist message. Over time, it became an indispensable piece of the puzzle of resistance. The anti-communism of the 1940s and 1950s rode the wave of national paranoia, and became more meaningful to white southerners as the black civil rights movement progressed. The direct action phase of the civil rights movement added a new dimension to southerners' anti-communism in the 1960s, and it later became apparent why anti-communism had such power for them—why many so smoothly incorporated it into their racial attitudes and behavior. White southerners had discovered a force they could mold to their needs, fears, and confusions. Postwar anti-communism may have been the product of specific Cold War circumstances, but once lodged in the minds of southerners, its power did not depend upon that initial context. Later civil rights struggles challenged the southern way of life head-on; white southerners wielded anti-communism to rationalize their customs and combat those threats for as long as they persisted.

4

AS THE YEARS UNFOLDED after World War II, it seemed increasingly likely that southern cities would act as arenas for an impending collision between blacks' desires for freedom and whites' wishes to keep their communities as they had been. Every southerner imagined a different catalyst. Richard Franco, an Atlanta doctor, always considered himself on the liberal side of the race issue. Franco's Jewish identity helped him to empathize with the plight of blacks. When presented with the choice of universal humanism versus provincial individualism, he always chose the former. Franco was right that the postwar era would bring changes in race relations to the South, but he incorrectly predicted their form, and their impetus. "The emancipation of blacks would take place by the enlightened evolution of the white community," Franco had long thought. "Politicians and leaders . . . would by their enlightened attitude make the changes." Mayor William Hartsfield ran a progressive administration in Atlanta, and Franco thought that ethos would evolve, gradually, until it enshrined equality for all. "It didn't really occur to me that the avenue of the change would come from black people themselves, that they would marshal the energy and exert the power and basically make the demand . . . 'that this society isn't going to work unless you let us in the door. We're not going to abide by this.' That was not how I envisioned or anticipated the change." Franco was light-years ahead of many white southerners in that he possessed a vision for racial equality—but it stemmed from a belief that whites would voluntarily grant equality to blacks. Many more white southerners lived in a conflicted limbo; they refused to envision a new racial order even while they braced themselves for it. As blacks' demands for equal rights and white resistance both heated up after the war, many southerners waited for a spark. No one knew precisely what would ignite the flame. By 1954, the Supreme Court reluctantly wielded the matches.[41]

Straight lines did not connect events in the age of civil rights. Groups and individuals responded in ways that were rarely predictable to events that were even less so. White southerners exhibited tendencies toward both acceptance of and resistance to black civil rights in the 1940s and 1950s; upheaval finally forced those proclivities to the surface. The *Brown* decision did not usher in new tendencies among white southerners, but deepened existing trends. At the time, it was often unclear whether the black struggle would advance or fall back—whether the future promised larger jolts, or whether the previous tumult had signified the extent or racial change. Many southerners grappled with both phenomena at once—just as they attempted to adapt to yesterday's news, tomorrow's overwhelmed it and sent individuals on different arcs toward different ends.

The civil rights era began in the relative quiescence of the 1940s, in the push and pull between the old and the new, the change and the reaction. North Carolinians who tuned into Durham's WDNC radio on Saturday night, January 13, 1945, could hear Dr. James Shepard, founder of North Carolina Central University. Shepard entitled his speech "Inter-Racial Progress in North Carolina." "As you well know, the average white Southerner is a fairly decent citizen who wants to do the right things," Shepard quoted a letter he recently received. "He can be persuaded with reasonable arguments; he can even be shamed through a fair appeal to his [conscience], but he cannot be coerced into a course of action however right. He is stubborn, proud, and utterly allergic to threats." Many preferred tranquillity, meaning adherence to segregation, over any kind of turbulence. Examining the civil rights era in its larger postwar context, a report from *Newsweek*'s southern bureau pointed out that race was "an unresolved issue except in the minds of the 'extremist on both sides.' Nice people preferred not to discuss the issue." With every piece of legislation, every court decision, every local struggle, the civil rights years eroded that silence and complacency. "The responses came as events forced them. Bit by bit people began to sound out exactly how they did feel." And bit by bit the civil rights movement drew them toward change.[42]

Between the end of World War II and the Supreme Court's decision in *Brown v. Board of Education,* the past dueled the future in the South. In general, big cities began to look ahead as rural areas clutched old customs. While some examples defied that generalization, the pattern held in Dallas County, Alabama. Harris Wofford, while a law student, took a trip to Dallas County in 1952. Wofford's observations helped to recapture rural white southerners' mind-sets and ways of life before civil rights struggles had become a reality—worldviews and lifestyles too ingrained for a court ruling to upend. "The nigger is well taken care of here," a woman in charge of the Dallas County Chamber of Commerce told Wofford. "I'd say this is a nigger heaven. Segregation there definitely is of course. But no race riots. . . . The niggers know their place and seem to keep in their place. They're the friendly sort around here. If they are hungry, they will come and tell you, and there is not a person who wouldn't feed and clothe a nigger." Paternalism was alive and well in Selma in 1952, replete with stereotypes, myths, epithets, and bedrock assumptions of black inferiority. It rested on a conviction that southern whites knew "their Negroes" intimately, understood their needs and desires, and fulfilled those needs whenever they could. "We in the South are the ones in the whole United States who *love* the colored people," a Selma woman assured Wofford. To prove it, she summoned a black servant and asked him, "Now, Bascum, down here the white people and colored people understand each other, don't they?" "Yes, ma'am," he replied. A series of questions and answers continued along these lines. "Down here we *understand* the colored people," the woman reiterated. Her beliefs suggested that racial attitudes in Selma had not changed much since the first days of Jim Crow.[43]

Wofford pointed out that where this paternalism continued to flourish, life was not all cruelty and tension. "That an underlying affection between Southern blacks and whites exists along with the hostility seems certain. . . . In the tenant and servant systems of the black belt these relationships have been slow to die." The old dynamics did begin to recede, slowly but surely, as larger social processes blazed into Dallas County—the movement of southerners from rural to urban areas, along with gradual economic and political changes. "What the resulting relationship between Negroes and whites will be cannot perhaps be known," Wofford continued, "but one thing is certain: the old relationship between a white cotton planter and 'his niggers' is ending—as the cotton work is mechanized, as the farms switch from cotton to livestock . . . as Negroes become displaced, or tempted to city employment." Race relations were beginning to change well before the *Brown* decision and the Montgomery bus boycott. Despite enduring paternalism, perceptible shifts in consciousness complemented transformations in the rural southern environment.[44]

Wofford saw signs—subtle but substantial—that changes were under way in the attitudes of white southerners. An influential Selma citizen asserted during a public meeting, "We want the Negro to keep in his place, but it must be hard for him to know just where his place is. In buses it's behind; on trains it's up front; in white churches it's up, and generally speaking, it's down." This was a rare acknowledgment that the accepted customs and traditions out of which the fabric of the southern way of life was woven smacked of absurdity. While no admission of black equality, the remark possessed powerful implications. It suggested that even if one believed in black inferiority and the idea of a race's proper "place," that concept made little sense outside of white minds. "Place" was nonsensical in practice, for it required obedience to confected standards. It assumed that blacks could understand a white code, when the code itself was predicated on the belief that African-Americans could comprehend nothing of the sort—and that they thus needed a code imposed upon them.[45]

The expectation that blacks could divine whites' logic also suggested that African-Americans might understand whites quite well. By contrast, the age of civil rights demonstrated over and over that white southerners in fact had no idea who "their Negroes" were. "To state this problem is to assault one of the first assumptions of southern whites," Wofford wrote, "that only they *know* the Negro. 'Come out and *I'll* tell you about the nigger,' . . . 'You can never know them until you come here and live and work with them'—this is the constant refrain." It remained the constant white refrain in a given locale until the civil rights movement tore through that town, and until African-Americans themselves—the very substance of whites' assumptions—exposed such beliefs to be the cruel myths they were. Some whites simultaneously defended white supremacy and sympathized with blacks. The words of one Selma lawyer exposed an underside of the white myth. "This thing is a problem and it has got us worried like the dickens," the lawyer remarked about the prospect of integration, and admitted that if he were African-American, he would move out of Dallas County. This lawyer feared and loathed the possibility of equal rights for African-Americans—but he did not buy into the idea that Dallas County blacks had reason to be content with their station.[46]

Many Selma residents displayed similarly mixed racial feelings. They dreaded federally imposed integration even as they understood its motivation. "We haven't given them a chance. Now the Supreme Court is going to cause us a heck of a lot of trouble, but it is our fault," a white farmer said. If whites could ensure that separate facilities were actually equal, he contended, they might avoid struggles with the federal courts. In 1952, whites in Dallas County already feared that the federal government might intervene against segregation. Schemes for massive resistance and segregation academies predated the *Brown* decision. "We'll just let the public schools fade away; we won't cut them out all at once . . . but gradually we'll drop the sales tax which supports the schools," as one Selma citizen laid out his plan in the eventuality of "forced" integration. "We'll let private schools take over."[47]

Realities in Selma often clashed with those in larger cities like Atlanta, Charlotte, or New Orleans. Many southerners themselves perceived vital differences between rural and urban areas. During the 1940s and 1950s, the South underwent a shift from a majority-rural region to an increasingly urban one. In 1940, only one in five southerners called a metropolitan area home. By 1960, 15 percent lived on farms and 44 percent in the cities. "In the strictly rural areas the feeling is . . . more explosive," *Newsweek's* William Emerson cabled from Birmingham in 1953. "The racial issue has been made a political football for so long . . . that the rural Alabamian has been convinced that it is his duty to prevent the 'pinks' of the cities from de[s]ecrating his state with racial equality. . . . The fear (whether it be real or imaginary) is not so much concern with the end of segregation in colleges. . . . But in grade schools 'Never.' " White southerners could say whatever they wished in the 1940s and 1950s, but no one could predict how they would act when civil rights struggles heightened. During the years of the civil rights movement, opinions would collide with reality. Soon declarations of resistance would not suffice; whites would have to support their words with action.[48]

When the Supreme Court issued its decision on May 17, 1954, southern leaders scurried to position themselves against it. Politicians like Eastland, Herman Talmadge, and Georgia senator Richard Russell quickly condemned the ruling. Russell charged that the Supreme Court had overstepped its constitutional bounds, and demanded a curb on the Court's powers. Across the South, elected officials and state bodies renewed their oaths to uphold segregation. The Louisiana State Education Committee passed a resolution, by a vote of 83–3, in favor of maintaining school segregation. Southern newspapers also beat the drum of Jim Crow. The *Charleston News and Courier* lamented the Supreme Court's decision as "another nail in the coffin of states' rights." As the years before *Brown* showed, this defiance did not come out of nowhere—and it was not predicated solely on the *Brown* decision. Since the end of the war, reformist politicians in the South had battled old-style race-baiters. But the *Brown* decision gave race-baiters a powerful target. The content of southern politicians' exhortations had gestated for years, and their pronouncements revealed multitudes.[49]

Southern leaders who raised the flags of states' rights and segregation betrayed worries that their lives would never be the same. "I hope some means can be found whereby the traditional customs of the past will not be upset in the South," said Robert Arnold, chairman of the Georgia State Board of Regents. The *Birmingham News* made a rare admission that those customs might not have been healthy. "Admittedly segregation has produced emotional reactions that have not always been good. . . . But we are much concerned that the ending of segregation may produce feelings and problems far more difficult to deal with." Indeed, white southerners would at last have to "deal with" the fact that blacks were human, and that they, too, desired and deserved freedom and equality. After a lifetime of being told that blacks were inferior, the end of segregation would most certainly generate "feelings and problems" for many white southerners that could well be called "difficult." Many wished to postpone that trauma. "It really wasn't going to apply to us," Selma school board member Carl Morgan hoped. "A ruling had been made but there were no guidelines as to how it was going to be interpreted, and it seemed like a bad dream. . . . Our initial thought was: 'Well, that's what they decided in Washington, but it may not affect us that much.'" Whites hoped their lives could remain untouched. The superintendent of DeKalb, Georgia, schools, Jim Cherry, hoped the Supreme Court decision could stay "largely an abstraction." For many white southerners, it remained just that.[50]

While the Citizens' Councils proclaimed the day of *Brown v. Board of Education* "Black Monday," few white southerners embraced such Manichaean portraits. Immediate signs of rupture in their lives were not apparent. "Well the Great Decision came on yesterday and has caused far less excitement than anyone thought it would," Virginia Durr wrote from her Montgomery home on May 19. A week later, things still seemed tranquil to Durr. "The reaction here on the decision is calmer than I had thought it would be, but still that might simply be the calm before the storm." Few southerners saw the apocalypse coming anytime soon. The *Brown* decision did not even register on the radar of many whites. "When I picked up a *Courier-Journal* at the student cafeteria," remembered John Egerton, who was a student at Western Kentucky State College, "I took a quick glance at the banner headline—Supreme Court bans school segregation—and then flipped to the sports section." For most white southerners, the *Brown* decision had little immediate impact. It may have energized the careers of politicians and litigators, and nourished the hopes and dreams of African-Americans, but for many whites it meant little—at least until integration actually came to their own town.[51]

While the *Brown* decision loomed as "an abstraction" for the majority, some white teachers and students felt thrust into the fire. Members of the Atlanta area Fulton County Teachers Association bemoaned the decision. "Negroes and whites in the same schools in Georgia just won't work," said Lucien Bell, a science teacher at Roswell High School. Many other educators concurred. "I have been associated with Negroes for more than 40 years and some of them are my good friends, but they are happiest in their own schools," said Mrs. Gaither Cochran, assistant principal of College Park High School. Few whites saw reason to abandon their views about African-Americans. "We are giving the Negroes equal facilities and they have stated they are well satisfied," said Ben Hutchinson, principal at College Park. "Let's maintain that good feeling we've built up." Not all Georgia citizens agreed. While politicians threatened to close public schools and defy the Supreme Court at all costs, many teachers thought that tactic unwise. At least one had the courage to say so in public. "I have taught in the white public schools of Georgia for 16 years," Velma Miller of Thomasville wrote. "Some of the defiant are creating the impression that Georgia can 'go it alone.'. . . Doing away with our public schools would . . . be a catastrophe. . . . Most of us are not ready for Georgia to leave the Union again." When southern communities had to face the reality of school integration, be it years or decades later, this argument—between public education and segregation—would flare up again.[52]

Richard Franco, a student at Atlanta's Grady High School in 1954 and 1955, felt *Brown*'s indirect effects through his teachers. In the classroom, he realized for the first time that racial prejudice was not the sole province of poor white southerners. Bigotry thrived among all social classes. Franco's English teacher, whom he had deeply respected and admired, was the agent of this realization. He "read poetry beautifully . . . and introduced us to Shakespeare and Wordsworth. You could tell he had a real sensitivity about the human condition, about the paradoxes of life, about the fact that life is painful, that there are lessons to be learned, insights about the nature of our existence." While leading discussion on *The Merchant of Venice*, Franco's teacher insisted that Jews and blacks possessed racial characteristics inherently different from those of Anglo-Saxon Protestants—that all races were not equal. "With all of that sense of humanity that I got from him as an individual, it turned out he was as bigoted" as many others. In the wake of the Supreme Court decision, Franco's teacher acted on his beliefs, and resigned from the public school system before racial integration could reach his classroom. Yet in that act, integration had already shaped his life. "He didn't want to even be in a situation where he might have to teach in a public school that would eventually be integrated, even though there was nothing pressing. People were [saying] it would never happen or it would take a decade or twenty years. . . . But he got out of that school system." As his teacher departed, Franco could no longer hold on to his notion that better educated white southerners would gradually bring about integration and racial equality. "My sense that it was going to be done by enlightened people, I don't know how long that would have taken." He realized later that for change to occur, it would have to come through the agenda—and on the timetable—of southern blacks, and of the federal government. Such impositions were necessary, for white southerners "would not have done it otherwise. Now that I look back on it," Franco said in 2003, "who knows when it would have happened. It might have been a hundred years, I don't know."[53]

Along with teachers and students, some southern churchmen felt *Brown*'s immediate effects. The Supreme Court's 1954 ruling forced church bodies to choose between segregation and federal law. While southern politicians rallied to the segregationist cause, most religious organizations backed the law. The Southern Baptist Convention issued an official recommendation at its June 1954 meeting: "That we recognize the fact that this Supreme Court decision is in harmony with the constitutional guarantee of equal freedom to all citizens, and with the Christian principles of equal justice and love for all men." The convention commended the Court, and reiterated its support for public education. The vote on *Brown* garnered 9,000 in favor and only 50 against. While the General Assembly of Presbyterians also supported the desegregation decision, the margin was closer: 239–169. Those who represented the region's Catholic minority followed with statements of agreement. The bishop of Little Rock, Albert Fletcher, urged Catholic churches and schools to admit blacks. "Persons of every race . . . should be made to feel at home in every Catholic church," Fletcher said in September 1954. "All are His, not our, invited guests." But the *Brown* decision posed a momentous dilemma for southern church leaders. Many ministers were forced to negotiate between the stances of their national church bodies and the sentiments of their congregations.[54]

In an article entitled "The Agony of the Southern Minister," Ralph McGill articulated this plight. "Ministers are squeezed between the dictates of conscience and church policy on the one hand, and the prejudices of those who 'run' the church, on the other. Save for the so-called 'Bible floggers' . . . and those who are sure that God himself is chief among segregationists, this is a time of agony of spirit for the ministers of sensitive heart and mind." Ministers either had to flout church policy or enrage their constituents. Reverend Robert Trotman, a minister at Bronwood Baptist Church in Terrell County, Georgia, supported the *Brown* decision during a sermon. In June 1954, the church deacons requested—and quickly received—Trotman's resignation. Events over the following year proved that this type of episode was hardly unusual. Ed Jones, pastor of Fortune Baptist Church near Parkin, Arkansas, preached that segregation was sinful. In February 1955, the church dismissed him. At a meeting of Mississippi's Methodist Conference in June 1955, Roy Delamotte was appointed to one of the state's churches. After Delamotte condemned Jim Crow in a speech, the conference found no church still willing to accept him. In Batesburg, South Carolina, U.S. federal judge (and father of South Carolina's governor) George Timmerman, Sr., led a campaign against his minister at First Baptist Church. In Timmerman's eyes, Reverend G. Jackson Stafford's crime was to vote in support of the Southern Baptist Convention's *Brown* resolution. On October 19, Stafford resigned his pastorate. The torment of ministers knew no state lines.[55]

Across the South, congregants and deacons battled those ministers who spoke out for integration. Presbyterians in central Mississippi targeted Durant's Reverend Marsh Callaway. A native of Texas and sixty years old in 1955, Callaway served in Mississippi churches—first in Drew and Columbia before Durant—for twelve years. In the wake of the *Brown* decision, Holmes County residents alleged that two men—Dave Minter and Eugene Cox, who ran a cooperative farm—were racial "agitators." Citizens of nearby Tchula called Minter and Cox before a mass meeting, and condemned them as advocates of integration. Rev. Callaway stood up and denounced the meeting as "undemocratic and unChristian." The elders of Durant Presbyterian Church then demanded Callaway's resignation. He reported to the Central Mississippi Presbytery that the elders "kicked me out because I spoke against the Citizens' Council." He was referring to the audience at the Tchula mass meeting, where several white supremacist leaders played a prominent role. In November 1955, the Central Presbytery voted to "dissolve" Durant Presbyterian's "pastoral relationship" with Callaway. Callaway asked to stay on through the end of the following March, but the church body terminated his contract as of December 31. Callaway vowed he would appeal the decision to the statewide Presbyterian body, but his pleas proved futile. "I just believe deeply that the future of the church is at stake," Callaway reflected. The Presbytery's decision meant "that every minister will be under the thumb of his elders. . . . The Sunday before the Tchula meeting, we had one of the largest crowds in several months. . . . But because I dared stand up for what I believe, my services were boycotted and I was asked to resign." In the age of civil rights, pastors lost their pulpits for less.[56]

Few congregants detected connections between Christian teachings and black civil rights. One Methodist layperson could not see why so many religious organizations supported the *Brown* decision. "Being a Christian is accepting the Lord Jesus Christ as my personal savior . . . and just because I don't want my granddaughter to go to school with a Negro boy, I don't see what it has got to do with my being a Christian or not." Denominational resolutions could not compel congregants to change their views on race. The real power in the churches continued to rest with those who made financial donations and ran local life. Many ministers were unconvinced, even enraged, by the declarations in favor of *Brown.* The majority of the white southern clergy, like white southerners in general, opposed the rising civil rights movement. At the nation's largest Baptist church, Dallas's First Baptist, Reverend W. A. Criswell lampooned the "bunch of infidels" who "sit up there in their dirty shirts and make all their fine speeches." In the face of ministers who lost their pastorates and congregants who refused to change their racial views, the initial speeches in support of *Brown* seemed almost like flukes. One Southern Baptist tried to explain and excuse why his convention first supported *Brown.* "They were just a little bit exalted. . . . When they got back with the home folks a lot of 'em wondered how they did it." Southern churches were not exalted places; they were indisputably defined and shaped by the customs, traditions, and attitudes around them. At the 1956 Southern Baptist Convention meeting in Kansas City, Missouri, C. C. Warren declared it "unwise for us to reopen any discussion" of the Supreme Court decision. When it came to integration, many southern ministers quickly learned to keep their mouths shut. In the spring of 1956, Reese Griffin, the pastor at Bass Memorial Methodist Church in Macon, Georgia, suggested that black and white children ought to attend church schools together. The usual chain of events occurred, and Griffin resigned in June. "It has come to the place where a minister will lose his pulpit if he says anything in favor of integration," Griffin wrote on June 16, 1956. "It is not a matter of what he says nor how he says it. He must not dare say anything at all."[57]

ONE DID NOT HAVE TO GLANCE at oppressed African-Americans, civil rights supporters, or agonized ministers to see the coming convulsions. They were just as evident in the actions of steadfast civil rights opponents, from high school English teachers to southern politicians and Citizens' Councilmen. At times, those who feared civil rights gains were their most accurate prophets. As the *Albany Herald* mocked King's claim that he would turn the town "upside down" soon before the community was actually thrown into upheaval, so Citizens' Council members and Klansmen who resisted racial equality helped to provoke federal support for it. By 1955, the Citizens' Council movement against integration had established beachheads across the Deep South and the Black Belt. "The feeling on the Supreme Court decision is running high," Virginia Durr wrote in January 1955. "These people down here are so paradoxical—so gracious and kind until you hit the race question and then they are as hard as iron." White southerners, through their everyday mannerisms and interactions, betrayed deep fears that their world would never be the same.[58]

"The most serious challenge to their social order since the Civil War" loomed on the horizon, historian John Hope Franklin wrote in 1972. White southerners responded "characteristically by that remarkable combination of praising things as they were and resisting the change that they abhorred." The most important parts of the coming years would not be the pitched protests, the charged confrontations, the waves of demonstrators, or the impassioned crowds. "It is not the interracial confrontations, important and tragic as they were, that are of prime significance. It is the South's confrontation with change, its response in defending what it regarded as a perfect society, that is instructive." White southerners fought reality with myth, Franklin argued. And that fight—whose battlefields stretched from kitchens and living rooms to minds—revealed more about southern life than armies of attack dogs, fire hoses, and picket lines. The civil rights movement showed defenders of Jim Crow what the Civil War and Reconstruction had taught slaveholders—that just as black slaves were not faithful and happy Sambos, neither were twentieth-century black southerners content with dancing

Jim Crow. And they never had been. As Franklin argued, an illusory ideal rallied many in the white South:

> Its obsession was to maintain a government, an economy, an arrangement of the sexes, a relationship of the races, and a social system that had never existed . . . except in the fertile imagination of those who would not confront either the reality that existed or the change that would bring them closer to reality.

The civil rights movement would attempt to overturn all these interrelated parts of the southern lattice of discrimination. That meant not only confronting many centuries of white myths, but attempting to force changes in hard reality.[59]

The years after World War II painted the backdrop for such changes. Tales of white southerners in the postwar years do not reveal a steady march toward racial progress. Instead, they are full of ambiguities and frustrations, forward sprints and backward stumbles. Moreover, white southerners themselves had differing visions of "racial progress," of what was "forward" and what was "backward." Few denied that World War II was waged for freedom, but "freedom" admitted of different meanings in different minds. Soon the civil rights movement would translate facets of southern life that had always been partially concerned with race—politics, education, everyday interactions with employees—into conflicts that were, on their face, unavoidably about it. The vast majority of "nice people" still preferred not to discuss integration, a choice that became ever more difficult. Those who had always accepted the way the wind blew became caught between rival gusts.

By the time Rosa Parks boarded a Montgomery bus in 1955, no one was yet able to predict the full-blown movement to come. White southerners might have detected subtle changes in "their Negroes," but few felt their everyday lives and beliefs being transformed. More had moved into cities, fewer continued to lynch blacks in the light of day, some had fought beside them in a war, and all had witnessed the Supreme Court of the United States strike down as unconstitutional a pillar of their way of life. On the eve of the 1955 boycott, for those in Montgomery, that way of life was intact. Before the 1960 student sit-ins for whites in Greensboro or the school crisis for those in New Orleans; prior to the 1961 integration of the University of Georgia for Athens citizens, or before the Albany Movement in 1962 for Southwest Georgians; before the massive demonstrations on Birmingham streets in 1963 or the 1964 Civil Rights Act; before the 1965 march on the Edmund Pettus Bridge for those in Selma, or the sanitation workers' strike in 1968 for whites in Memphis, the southern way of life reigned. In that sense, the years between the end of the war and the beginning of direct action protests could be called a prelude. The reckoning awaited.

TWO

"Our Negroes" No More

AN ABYSS SEPARATED white racial attitudes from reality. To traverse it, southerners walked a tightrope. While few were conscious of the mental high-wire act they daily performed, the civil rights movement made plain that prevalent beliefs about blacks had all the substance of thin air. If whites were too diverse to admit of a single "mind of the South," a vast number of them in communities across Dixie subscribed to a similar complex of views about African-Americans.* Before civil rights struggles hit their town, many believed that race relations were good, that blacks were content with segregation, that white southerners understood African-Americans and knew what was best for them, and that their love across the color line was returned. Whites were shocked when African-

---

*In 1941, W. J. Cash argued that there was a discernible "mind of the South." Cash detailed its components in a vivid portrait of white southerners from colonial times to World War II. Joel Williamson's *The Crucible of Race* argued that southerners were of more than one mind. He outlined three specific worldviews: conservative, liberal, and radical. James Cobb offered a welcome clarification to Cash when he wrote: "Crippled by racism, an exaggerated sense of individualism, a tragic proclivity for violence and the 'savage ideal' of hostility to criticism or innovation, what Cash presented as a deeply flawed mind was actually more like a regional temperament, a remarkably consistent behavioral pattern forged in the crucible of Civil War and Reconstruction and still dominant and unyielding more than sixty years later." To this list, one might add that the southern temperament, in Cash's original formulation, marches from present to past. W. J. Cash, *The Mind of the South* (New York, 1941); Joel Williamson, *The Crucible of Race: Black-White Relations in the American South Since Emancipation* (New York, 1984); James Cobb, "World War II and the Mind of the Modern South," in Neil McMillen, ed., *Remaking Dixie: The Impact of World War II on the American South* (Jackson, MS, 1987), p. 3. Also see James Grossman, " 'Amiable Peasantry' or 'Social Burden': Constructing a Place for Black Southerners," in Rick Halpern and Jonathan Morris, eds., *American Exceptionalism?: U.S. Working-Class Formation in an International Context* (New York, 1997), pp. 221–43.

Americans rose up in defiance in the 1960s. Black rebellion clashed so sharply with white perceptions that many disbelieved their own eyes. In turn, white southerners insisted the struggles that hit their towns were the brainchild of distant enemies—of communists, the NAACP, or northern liberals. "Their Negroes" were happy, many reasoned; and in the 1960s, they had become the dupes of "outside agitators." The claims of bewildered whites collided with the reality of organized blacks, who exploded the myth that they were anyone's Negroes, or that they ever had been.

White paternalism found expression—in varying forms and to different degrees—everywhere, from Dallas County, Alabama, to Dougherty County, Georgia; from small parishes in Louisiana to urban centers of the Upper South. Mississippi native David Cohn captured the mind-set that prevailed a generation before the civil rights movement when he described in 1935 what "the white man of the Delta says to the world beyond his gates: I live with my family among an overwhelming mass of Negroes. . . . Nowhere do we receive them on terms of social equality. . . . Most of us have a deep and abiding affection for the Negro. Our paternalism is not designed to enslave him. It is in our blood. The Negroes on our plantations are both our partners and our wards." A white man in rural Mississippi could possess racial beliefs similar to those of a politically liberal woman in a Virginia university town. "I loved Negroes," wrote Charlottesville resident Sarah Patton Boyle, "and, in my segregated way, respected and admired them. . . . I believed that our relationship was complementary and mutually satisfying. . . . When a Negro didn't 'keep his place' I felt outraged." It was a way of thinking that had no definable year of death. Yet almost everywhere black southerners waged struggles for civil rights, whites endured challenges to deeply held beliefs. They responded in diverse ways: some were gripped with shock and fear as they gradually realized "their Negroes" were no more; others denied what their senses told them, unwilling to abandon teachings of a lifetime; still more exhibited ways of thinking that combined fragments of a romanticized past with pieces of a perceptible future.[1]

A predominant white racial temperament stretched in time back before the Civil War, as James McBride Dabbs said in an interview during the late 1960s. "In antebellum days the Negroes were our people and the whites our whitefolk," remembered the native of Rip Raps Plantation in South Carolina. Too often, Dabbs maintained, whites believed affection could take the place of fairness. Some southerners knew that justice was denied African-Americans, yet they evaded the issue of right and wrong. "In our inmost [ears], we knew we were wrong. And so . . . we didn't talk about justice, we talked about love. But love unsupported by justice becomes sentimentality." There was a time and place for such sentimentality, but it had serious limitations. "This isn't bad at twilight. It's like a [quiet] smoke on the piazza. But to be sentimental at high noon and in public is to be in great danger. Unless your eyes are clear, and eyes of the sentimentalist are never clear, you have to get run over or to run over somebody else as we have run over the Negro and then reassured ourselves by saying that we loved him." It was another weight that white southerners had long balanced. Many thought themselves sincere when they said they cared deeply for blacks. But it was a care based upon inequality, rooted in oppression, layered with discrimination, and willfully blind to those very facts.[2]

In the popular attitude, white southerners not only cared for blacks but knew them intimately. Such notions powered the myth of "good race relations." Many white southerners fancied themselves experts on black life, an expertise they grounded in experience. One Charlotte resident claimed to represent "the views of 'the little people.' " "I have employed through the years a lot of negroes," he wrote to Congressman Charles Raper Jonas in 1957. "I understood them and treated them well and, among them, are many respected friends. They know I am their friend and are always glad to see me and would do anything for me, and I for them." Conditions for blacks had gradually improved, the Charlotte man asserted, and he urged his congressman to oppose any federal interference in this process. "Unwise misguided agitation" halted "this progressive improvement and has, in fact, retarded it back toward the condition of a half century ago." Such views put him in the company of many in Charlotte, as well as his rural brethren. Clarence Morrison, a general contractor in Shelby, North Carolina, registered his disapproval of school desegregation. "This letter is coming from a man who has dug ditches along beside Negroes. I have laid brick beside them. . . . I have befriended them in every way possible, and I am still their friend." His legitimacy established, Morrison then asserted, "The relation[s] between the races are the worst in my community than I have known in my lifetime." To many white southerners, the age of civil rights marked the nadir of race relations. They had considered black workers close friends for many years. When civil rights struggles exposed black discontent, whites despaired that the days of "good race relations" were gone.[3]

Natives of the east Tennessee town of Clinton believed that race relations had always been good. According to a *Newsweek* background report, "What the 'good' relations seem to amount to is absence of trouble and submissive acceptance on the part of Negroes of a social system that excludes them from everything except menial job opportunities in the community, occasional friendly exchanges on the streets, access to downtown stores and the annual exchange of church choirs." Whites interpreted black veneers of deference as actual friendship. Furthermore, whites insisted that blacks were content with the racial status quo; thus, attempts at change must have derived "from 'outside influence' . . . the NAACP, the Communists." It was not necessary to travel to bastions of white supremacy on Mississippi cotton fields or Alabama plantations to glimpse the power of these ideas—they resonated powerfully in Tennessee and Kentucky. In Sturgis, Kentucky, Berea College professor Roscoe Griffin found in 1956 that "race relations in the community are described historically both by whites and Negroes as friendly." But the two races invested the concept of friendliness with different meanings; a caste system maintained the peace. "Acquiescence of Negroes to the dominant position of the whites was the condition of the peace. . . . Negroes have 'stayed in their place' and whites in theirs."[4]

When blacks attempted to desegregate the high school in Sturgis, old patterns began to die fast—much faster in black neighborhoods and minds, however, than in white ones. Gone was "the old easiness of their relations within the rigid lines of separation," and in its place existed a tension—a tension that would persist until a new pattern of race relations reigned. Griffin wrote, "Whites in general are not aware that the Negroes are dissatisfied with their status and bent upon change." This lack of awareness ran smack into whites' claims that they knew "their Negroes." White assertions of black happiness stemmed more from whites' "psychological needs" to believe in social harmony than from any evidence that such concord actually existed. This truth defined white communities from the border states and the Tennessee hills to the cities of the North Carolina Piedmont and Georgia's Black Belt.[5]

If white southerners ever wrestled with deeply held beliefs, they did so only after black civil rights struggles hit their town. School desegregation in Clinton and Sturgis forced whites to confront their myths in

1956, while those in Albany, Georgia, could entertain beliefs about "good race relations" into 1961—and well beyond. Howard Zinn eloquently captured white sentiment in Albany in a January 1962 report published by the SRC:

> Again and again—in the office of a political leader, in the anteroom of a businessman, sitting with a newspaper editor, in the living room of a middle-class white family—the statement was made, "Albany has always had good race relations. . . . Our colored folks have been satisfied. . . . We have made considerable progress. . . ." Memories remain poor; for the same statements were made in Montgomery before the bus boycott, in Atlanta before the sit-ins, and all through the South in the days of slavery.

Perhaps these claims had some substance, Zinn speculated. Interracial peace seemed to reign in Albany, and blacks did not voice widespread disapproval prior to the civil rights era. Yet whites mistook black silence for acceptance, and when white claims were transported "out of simple isolation into the texture of life itself," they began to unravel. In Zinn's apt phrasing, "The white South has been notably unequipped with the kind of social seismograph that would detect the first faint tremors of unrest, and too far out of touch with Negroes . . . to hear any but the loudest noises. . . . Thus, southern whites have been hurt and shocked by the eruptions of the past few years." Certain that the era after World War II had brought increasing advancements in black life, Albany whites were seized with confusion when blacks mounted demonstrations for civil rights. "Intelligent and good-hearted white people" failed to understand that token gains did not quell blacks' desires for progress, but whetted their appetite for more. "To the Negro community, all this was like improving the food inside a prison." Few southern whites were able to wrap their minds around this point before black struggles for freedom engulfed them. The paradox, novelist and native southerner William Styron argued, was that few whites had any real contact with blacks. Instead, inequality and pretense saturated all their interactions. Many claimed they felt affection for blacks, but, according to Styron, whites actually harbored a racial animosity rooted in a lack of knowledge. "Whatever knowledge I gained in my youth about Negroes, I gained from a distance, as if I had been watching actors in an all-black puppet show," he wrote in *Harper's* in 1965. The civil rights movement would make it "the moral imperative of every white southerner," Styron hoped, "to break down the old law" and "to come to *know* the Negro," his real desires and fears, in fact rather than in myth.[6]

That white southerners lacked adequate "social seismographs" was little surprise. Many of them were born into families, and reared in communities, that served up traditional southern beliefs about "their Negroes" beside plates of fried chicken and Bible lessons. Beliefs about "excellent race relations" were more than psychological needs; they seemed part of an unshakable landscape. "When you're raised in a custom all your life . . . you just take it for granted," said Chapel Hill drugstore owner John Carswell. "It's like getting up and putting your clothes on every day or brushing your teeth, you do it automatically." Few questioned whether their upbringing was right or wrong; the most important thing was that segregation (and the prejudices it encouraged) spelled reality.[7]

For most white southerners, the system of segregation inspired little reflection. Many accepted it as a fact of life. Birmingham's David Vann pointed out that because segregation was so ingrained, few whites displayed awareness of it. The system was simply a part of one's daily life. Little Rock native Craig Rains remembered that his family's yardman always ate outside. The African-American worker used a separate plate, and a separate Mason jar, that the Rains family reserved only for him. "That was something we all took for granted." Few whites second-guessed such arrangements. "There was very little questioning of the way things were," recalled Ole Miss student Jan Robertson. "It was an all-white world." Like the lakes or the trees, racial separation came to possess the feel of something natural. Journalist Fred Powledge, a native of North Carolina, captured that sentiment with particular effect. Although segregation remained integral to whites' lives, Powledge noted, it was something they barely detected. "If they did notice it, it was in the way they noticed water flowing from a tap or hot weather in the summertime—it was unremarkable." The defining fact of twentieth-century southern life, a system of racial separation codified in the law and buttressed by everyday behavior, infiltrated the collective subconscious and precluded conscious thought.[8]

This reality produced a sort of helplessness. Many whites, like Joe Smitherman, witnessed habitual cruelty to blacks. Smitherman did not particularly enjoy it, and admitted feelings of shame, but, he said, there "wasn't anything you could do." He concentrated more on living with the facts of southern life than on seeing through them. Many resigned themselves; as John Carswell remarked, "I didn't make the custom and I wouldn't be the one to change it." Smitherman worked as an appliance salesman before he became Selma's mayor; Carswell ran a pharmacy. But their feelings of impotence were not limited to whites in the working and middle classes. Such emotions also marked Robert Penn Warren, a Kentucky native and one of the South's most famous writers. In 1930, Warren penned an essay that he described as a "humane defense" of segregation. Even then, Warren "uncomfortably suspected" that segregation carried an inhumane quality. "But it never crossed my mind that anybody could do anything about it." The idea that segregation could cease was a thought that had not occurred to many whites. "The image of the South I carried in my head," Warren wrote in 1965, "was one of massive immobility in all ways . . . it was an image of the unchangeable human condition, beautiful, sad, tragic."[9]

White southerners would not transform life's rhythms. That task fell to African-Americans. When the civil rights movement took the form of civil disobedience, some observers thought such protests would signal the death knell of white racial myths. Faced with undeniable images of rebellious blacks, white southerners would be hard-pressed to claim that African-Americans were happy with segregation. When black North Carolina A&T students sat down at a Woolworth's lunch counter in Greensboro on February 1, 1960, they sent ripples through the South. "The myth" that blacks were content, David Halberstam wrote in 1960, "exploded with the sit-ins." Students in Nashville followed closely on the heels of those in Greensboro, and by April, sit-ins had spread to fifty-four cities in nine states. Halberstam was not the only one who glimpsed in these actions the end of a white mind-set. Ralph McGill wrote, "One of the most persistent falsehoods . . . is the 'stereotype' of the Negro into the 'preacher,' the 'Amos and Andy,' 'Uncle Tom,' 'Boy,' 'Uncle,' 'Mammy.'. . . Most Southerners do not know, or want to know, the facts of Negro development." When the student sit-ins came, they shattered stereotypes and began a revolution in consciousness. "This is one reason why the students in their sit-ins . . . have produced such a revolutionary effect. They have fitted none of the stereotypes." Some southerners asserted that the protesting students had rendered the old stereotypes absurd. The Southern Regional Council's Harold Fleming called the sit-ins "the first step to real change—when the whites realize that the Negroes just aren't having it anymore."[10]

In the aftermath of struggles for freedom, some whites attested to wrenching realizations. When Sarah Patton Boyle discovered that blacks did not cherish their Jim Crow roles, "it was a traumatic heart-twisting experience." Boyle felt that, by 1960, she had stepped into a new world. "The Negroes I now knew bore little resemblance to the Negro I had envisaged since childhood. . . . No greater dislocation of my thought and emotion could have resulted if I had been catapulted to another planet." When blacks exposed the old truths for myth, Boyle could feel the earth shaking. Her entire way of seeing changed. "Nothing I saw in Negroes was familiar. I had landed in a nightmare world, among people who neither liked nor understood me, and whom I could not understand." A white woman from Natchez echoed Boyle's sentiments: "When civil rights came along, a lot of us were shocked. I was shocked to find black people we knew participating in the marches, because we didn't know they were unhappy." Similar feelings penetrated many southerners, whenever and wherever civil rights struggles appeared. The sight of blacks risking their lives for rights and freedom indicated that white images of them were deeply flawed, and could no longer stand the test of reality.[11]

But stereotypes died slowly. They proved rarely susceptible to logic, reason, or even events. Myths thrive on worlds of their own creation, where beliefs can persist in the face of occurrences that seem to dispel them. Many white southerners would explain away acts of black rebellion rather than acknowledge them for what they were. Journalist Dan Wakefield found this mechanism at work in Montgomery in 1960, four years after the bus boycott rocked that city and a few months following the sit-ins elsewhere. Montgomery's black community wielded power through the boycott; it forced changes in municipal laws and disrupted white lives. But the minds of many whites proved beyond reach. "The heart of the problem is not that the white man refuses to sit down at the table," Wakefield wrote in *The Nation,* "but rather that when he does, he refuses to see the real face of the man he is sitting across from." Even when blacks gained white audiences, when they listed their grievances and fearlessly organized their communities, many whites still saw in them the deferential figures of yore. "His whole life has prepared him to believe that the man across the table is good ol' Preacher Brown; and who can blame his blind refusal to see that it is Martin Luther King instead?" In the cradle of the Confederacy, the civil rights movement had yet to change many whites. "The successful boycott did not increase their respect for the Negroes who carried it out, but rather increased the mistrust and hatred of them." While civil rights struggles opened some eyes and changed some minds, they had the reverse effect on others—to further embolden white support for Jim Crow, and more tightly wed some whites to the old stereotypes.[12]

For every white who was at last convinced of black dissatisfaction by direct action protests, there were many others who still failed to hear those pleas. Soon after McGill wrote that student protesters "have produced a revolutionary effect," he received a deluge of mail from white southerners who had experienced no such revolution. "I have never seen a negro in my life that if given an opportunity would not abuse it," a Suffolk, Virginia, man wrote to McGill. "I have employed a great many negroes and I am quite sure that I am respected and liked by each and every one of them . . . but under no circumstances do I consider them my equal." While the direct action phase of the civil rights movement stirred change in some whites, many more joined in the Virginian's endeavor to "hold [blacks] at arms length but practice being polite to them and demand it in return." Black actions only occasionally upended white myths and transformed worldviews. Often, those actions nudged white southerners closer to the comfort of traditional racial visions.[13]

2

THE CHASM BETWEEN the sudden reality of black rebellion and the persistent image of black fealty yawned wide in Albany, Georgia. W. E. B. Du Bois immortalized the city of Albany, and the outlying areas of Dougherty County, in his 1903 classic, *The Souls of Black Folk*. "The corner-stone of the Cotton Kingdom was laid" in Dougherty County, Du Bois wrote, and Albany stood "in the heart of the Black Belt." For the riches that sprung from Albany's soil, nineteenth-century observers called it "the Egypt of the Confederacy." The area admitted at once of "curiously mingled hope and pain," Du Bois mused. "It is a depressing place, —bare, unshaded, with no charm of past association, only a memory of forced human toil." Populated overwhelmingly by black tenants and their masters, Southwest Georgia rooted itself in a history of slavery, followed by sharecropping. White power ruled the Cotton Kingdom, and exposed "the Negro problem in its naked dirt and penury." The pain was obvious. Where, then, was the hope? Du Bois again used the adjective "curious" to describe the Albany area, layered as it was with "untold story . . . tragedy and laughter, and the rich legacy of human life; shadowed with a tragic past, and big with future promise!" Blessed with fertility, the land itself held promise—but so, Du Bois suggested, did its people. Somehow all the toil did not beat hope out of Dougherty County blacks. Albany brimmed with life and spirit when they came to town on Saturdays. It was, in 1903, "a typical Southern county town, the centre of the life of ten thousand souls."[14]

Sixty years later, one could detect the Cotton Kingdom's shell in an expanding commercial city. Albany attracted industry, two military installations, and had grown to 56,000 residents by 1961. Whites clung to a three-to-two majority, though blacks far outnumbered them in the surrounding rural areas. Oglethorpe Avenue cleaved the white section of the city and the downtown from the black neighborhood, known as Harlem. Though poor and disenfranchised, hope still mingled with pain for blacks. Many would say that the mass civil rights meetings held at Albany's Shiloh and Mount Zion churches flowed with fervor rarely attained in other cities. Perhaps the intensity of Albany's blacks during the civil rights years could be matched only by that of its whites. Commerce and growth had remade Albany, but white thinking about race seemed ossified—trapped in a different time. Racial attitudes remained relics of earlier days. "This land was a little Hell," a black man had told Du Bois. "I've seen niggers drop dead in the furrow, but they were kicked aside, and the plough never stopped." Du Bois remarked, "With such foundations a kingdom must in time sway and fall." The kingdom stood tall as the 1960s dawned, but soon it began to wobble.[15]

The civil rights struggle in Albany arose out of local blacks' long-festering grievances. In 1957, African-Americans began to lodge a series of formal complaints, ranging from unpaved roads and sewage problems to segregated polling places and bus stations. The white city commissioners' utter refusal to meet with black leaders magnified the problems. Albany whites still treated blacks with paternalistic condescension, and expected them to embrace their lot in life with smiles of doting subservience. SNCC chose Southwest Georgia as the site of an organizing campaign in 1961, and Albany blacks also formed a local civil rights organization—the Albany Movement. At the movement's request, Martin Luther King, Jr., came to the town on December 15, 1961. Massive civil rights demonstrations soon gripped Albany. Police Chief Laurie Pritchett countered King's nonviolent civil disobedience with restraint of his own. While Albany police imprisoned black protesters by the thousands, and at times held them in wretched conditions, prisoners were rarely brutalized in public. Albany whites showered King with wrath, and Pritchett with praise.

The local newspaper served as a forum for the expression of white racial beliefs. Some citizens signed the letters they wrote to the editor of the *Albany Herald;* many more preferred to identify themselves merely as "Caucasians," "readers," or "Albanians." On July 31, 1962, the *Herald* published one reader's "Open Letter to Dr. King." It contained an exposition of the interlocking opinions that animated many southern whites. "For a century, the white race has lent considerations and provided assistance to the Negroes in overcoming the savage and uncivilized background from which they so recently emerged," the "Advocate" began. Many thought paternalism proved equally beneficial to whites and blacks—and that it established a certain social harmony. "Citizens of Albany (white and black) have heretofore lived happily and in harmony, and offering mutual assistance . . . to one another." The reader informed King of his objection "to total integration (we support equal facilities) until much more progress has been made by multitudes of your race." Whites still believed in the promise of *Plessy v. Ferguson,* the landmark 1896 Supreme Court case that had established the legality of "separate but equal." More than anything else, whites in Albany longed for the days of perceived peace and perfection—of unquestioned white supremacy and habitual black deference. "It is the preference of citizens of Albany to revert back to our normal status—to continue assisting our colored friends in whatever their needs be." Significantly, the writer penned his letter not to the *Herald*'s white readers, but to King and those he represented. "I feel it only fair to use this medium of news to reach our local Negroes with this message." He threatened "our local Negroes" with economic retribution, and promised that African-Americans who joined the fight for civil rights would find themselves without jobs. If white pleas could not coax blacks into the straitjacket of racial stereotypes, then perhaps economic retaliation would do the trick. Many Albany whites mixed nostalgia for an imagined past with fear of an uncertain future. To them, blacks were simultaneously docile and threatening.[16]

A week later, the *Herald* displayed a similar ability to marry two warring thoughts—that the civil rights movement had changed Albany, and that the city could somehow remain the same. In an editorial entitled "King Can't Change Albany," editor and publisher James Gray described Albany "as peaceful as it has ever been in the halcyon period which may come to be known as B.K.—before Martin Luther King's flamboyant intrusion into purely local affairs." Gray saw no apparent contradiction in identifying a fundamentally new era and simultaneously claiming that it was no different from what came before. Southwest Georgians "will find Albany today, as it was yesterday, a friendly community, interested in filling their needs and fully aware of its dependence upon their good will. Martin Luther King can never change that feeling." Whites insisted that harmony had always prevailed—but if blacks wished to disrupt that harmony, they were quite ready to take other measures. Many professed love but threatened hate, a blend of sentiments that only an upbringing and an entire way of life could ingrain—for reason and logic would never abide it. Whites did not know how precarious, tenuous, and conflicted was their worldview until the civil rights movement sent shock waves through the tranquil air of southern cities.[17]

Organizers who arrived in 1961 sought to shake Albany's foundations of white supremacy. Determined to achieve full integration by means of direct action, young SNCC workers found allies in black students at Albany State College. After SNCC wrested control of the NAACP Youth Council, local black organizations formed the Albany Movement—and installed a doctor, W. G. Anderson, as its head. While black students demonstrated, Anderson led community mass meetings. Over a three-week span from the end of November through mid-December, five hundred black protesters were jailed. Demanding the integregation of public facilities and seeking an audience with the city commission, college students sat in at a Trailways bus station lunch counter, high school students waged protests, and two hundred blacks marched on City Hall. Police Chief Laurie Pritchett imprisoned them all. Despite the *Albany Herald*'s claim that demonstrators were "largely ignored," white citizens took in the spectacles. "They herded us into those jails, while the white community stood across Oglethorpe and observed what was happening," an Albany preacher remembered.[18]

At W. G. Anderson's request, Martin Luther King arrived in Albany on December 15. King was arrested the next day, along with 264 other demonstrators. The city agreed to release all the prisoners before Christmas, to desegregate train and bus facilities, and to hear further black complaints—if the Albany Movement would cease its protests. After the protests stopped, the city reneged on its promises. King headed back to Atlanta, and Albany whites applauded as peace displaced black protest in the streets. In January, the Albany Movement attempted to revive its campaign. A successful bus boycott achieved desegregation on city buses, but when the movement (on King's advice) pressed the city for further measures, the bus company shut down. Despite black boycotts of buses, businesses, and the local newspaper, whites yielded little. Try as they might to dismiss black protests, however, few Albany whites were unaffected. "The boycotts are hurting them," reported Marion Page, the Albany Movement's executive secretary. "Not only are we staying out of the stores, but the white people are not going downtown because they are scared." In February, King stood trial in Albany for parading without a permit. He was found guilty, and returned for sentencing in July. That summer, Albany attracted national attention as a center of the civil rights movement.[19]

Through the spring of 1962, whites denied that black demonstrations had led to any changes. The kingdom of segregation stood tall, while paternalistic views of African-Americans flourished. "The South is as staunchly segregationist in its outlook today as it was 50 years ago and even 100 years ago when it fought a war in testimony to its beliefs," the *Albany Herald* editorialized on May 31, 1962. "The South lost that war . . . but a ruinous defeat did not remove the belief." If Albany whites had their way, traditional racial views would reign for another fifty or hundred years. "That thinking will not change," the *Herald* concluded, speaking for many Dougherty County whites. A woman who worked downtown wrote in to affirm that she did not blame Albany blacks for all the turbulence. "We have lots of good Negroes here," the "taxpayer" wrote, "but until the City can throw those agitators out and get Albany back to normal, I guess the other Negroes will be scared half to death." Like many Albany whites, this reader thought of herself as an advocate for the local blacks. Columnist H. T. McIntosh railed, "Albany was deliberately chosen to be the scene of a 'Movement' in which the people of Albany had no part." His perplexity reverberated with many Albany whites, who asked why this "growing, progressive city was chosen as a municipal 'test-tube' for racial conflict." Many wondered, with McIntosh, "Was it because relations between white and Negro citizens had been cordial and friendly for so long?" In this line of thinking, Albany became a target precisely because it was so harmonious. On

July 13, McIntosh argued that Albany "has suffered," the city "has been injured," its people "were bewildered," and Albany "is the victim." Fueled by convictions like these, Albany whites responded to African-American protests with confusion and outrage.[20]

In July 1962, King was sentenced to jail. While many whites thought prison stripes King's proper uniform, Chief Pritchett, Mayor Asa Kelley, and other Albany power brokers realized that a jailed King would attract nationwide publicity and sympathy for civil rights—and potentially ignite a fire in local blacks. Pritchett tossed him out of jail on July 12, after an anonymous person (whom we now know to have been city attorney B. C. Gardner) paid his bond. "[Our] protest will turn Albany upside down," King promised days later. Faced with this prospect, local whites made it known they had no intention of idly watching. "I'm going to stay in my rightful place," D. J. Gillis of nearby Douglas maintained, "and I'm going to place the Negro in his or die trying." Mrs. C. Brown of Blakely, Georgia, agreed, "A Negro is O.K. as long as they stay in their place." As African-Americans mounted protests throughout July and August, whites clung to notions that Albany blacks were satisfied. "I for one believe if the outsiders would tend to their own business and leave Albany colored folks alone they would . . . be as good as they were before this mess all started," wrote Mrs. Roy Logan of Albany. She reported that her black workers seemed "happy and content" and they opposed "all this carrying on King has to offer." Logan continued, "I do hate to see the good colored people of Albany have to suffer when they are innocent." She pictured Albany citizens, black and white, as victims of outside schemes.[21]

Agreement rang out on this score. W. C. Todd ran a lumber mill in Albany and resided in Broxton. Through his interactions with black millworkers since the 1940s, Todd could attest that "they are good Negroes, and would continue to be good if they were left alone by the outsiders." Todd assured his fellow white southerners that federal judges "simply don't know the American Negro as you and I do." Most concurred that local blacks would be happier if civil rights workers departed. "The thinking ones . . . realize they are better off with segregation," wrote Mrs. W. T. Brightwell of Tifton. "The others are easily led by agitators." Even Mrs. David Edwards, a recent transplant to Albany, quickly embraced the local thinking on race. Confident that she was "not biased in my viewpoint," Edwards found, when she moved to Albany, "both white and colored to be friendly and sincere, living together in harmony until 'outsiders' . . . troublemakers, and promoters of hate and strife, came to our city."[22]

White convictions about local blacks, "outside agitators," and civil rights formed a definable worldview and buttressed a way of life. This worldview possessed a certain logic (circular though it may have been) and interpretation of history (inwardly consistent if grossly distorted). If a Jim Crow defender could establish that no past problems existed between whites and blacks, several conclusions followed: civil rights demonstrations were unnecessary, people from outside of Albany devised them, and the local blacks wanted no part. The material and the mental permeated each other at every turn. Whites built prosperity on the lack of black opportunity. Exploitation of blacks both presupposed and encouraged black inferiority. The health of this social order depended upon the white belief that it was tolerable—even pleasant—for everyone. That belief allowed whites to degrade blacks, to justify the degradation, and to then believe that blacks abided it.

The various premises commingled: If one claim stood, the others seemed instantly legitimate. If whites were the best friends of the blacks, surely good race relations prevailed. If Albany blacks were happy with segregation, they were grateful to the whites who powered that system—and they felt victimized by the outsiders in their towns. We "freed them from slavery," Rex Knight of Remerton wrote, and "gave them the right to vote." Instead of responding with grateful thanks, however, blacks demanded further rights. African-Americans gave the lie to these white notions when they demanded freedom and equality. If blacks were in fact unhappy, then whites' entire worldview would be false, and they might have to admit that, for blacks, their city was more purgatory than paradise.[23]

On July 17, *Herald* publisher James Gray appeared on his own television station to praise Albany as a "friendly progressive community." He criticized "the Albany Movement with its get-rich-quick politicians and social quacks." Gray extended to W. G. Anderson the opportunity to answer those claims on the air. Anderson's reasoned defense of black demands moved one Albany white to publicly sift the truths from the tropes and peer through the fog of racial myth. She was the rare white who dissented and possessed the courage to say so. Anderson's candor "came as something of a shock" to this native white southerner— "a shock in that it brought into the open some questions which have troubled me for quite a long time. . . . Dr. Anderson's address . . . will help many Albanians to understand the difficult and heartbreaking road that Negroes must travel in obtaining the simplest of human rights." It was a direct appeal to all those Albany whites who rose in stoic defense of segregation. "Every white citizen of Albany who professes Christianity and democracy," the writer urged, should "take a long, searching look at his prejudices—and . . . his conscience." This "Albanian" stood "convinced that many of us will be able to peep over the wall of our racial prejudice" and "help the Negro rise from the pit we dug for him." The writer acknowledged, "We white southerners were born into an environment of racial discrimination. . . . We were stuck with the horrible practice at birth." But that did not excuse its continuation. As if the challenge to Albany whites' ways of living and thinking was not stark enough, the writer confronted head-on the heart of their traditional racial views. "Stop easing our consciences with nonsensical statements that the Negro community is satisfied with its present lowly status." Perhaps it constituted a lone voice of dissent in a wilderness of conformity— but one public voice surely represented others who preferred to cloak their opinions in silence.[24]

Supporters of segregation sought no such cover. "If what you and Martin Luther King have is religion, I don't want any of it," read a rejoinder. "A.C." praised the city commission, and criticized King and the Albany Movement for their misguided demands. Whites were not responsible for the metaphorical pit in which some blacks found themselves; indeed, it had room to spare. "Why not throw the King boys, the Kennedy boys, Anderson . . . and all the rest of the troublemakers into the pit we dug for them. . . . All your troubles would be over. You can jump in with them if you want to." In times like these, the *Albany Herald*'s "People's Forum" took off on an arc of its own. Letter writers could debate issues for weeks. The *New York Times* characterized the "People's Forum" as a "daily drumbeat" of anti–civil rights rhetoric. And it was a drumbeat inflected with the pulse of white Albany. It served as a sounding board for people gripped by the uncomfortable prospect of change, and exposed a considerable irony. Many insisted that black struggles could not rock Albany whites out of their ways of life, and that the city could withstand any civil rights incursion. At the same time, the panicked nature of those very words revealed the frenzy into which the age of civil rights had plunged so many white southerners.[25]

Beyond the fact that James Gray and his *Albany Herald* slanted reports in defense of segregation, something else was disingenuous about many of its editorial claims. Gray remarked in his television address that, "the Albany Movement . . . cannot possibly undo what has been built with such strength and integrity," and he titled a July 25 front-page editorial "Albany Will Stand." In this portrait, Albany somehow stayed unchanged through the deepest cataclysm to strike its society since Reconstruction. Such an argument quickly became mired in its own naïveté. The *Herald* insisted that King could not turn Albany upside down, that whites felt little change in their daily lives, that the Albany Movement could "undo" nothing, and that the city would stand as ever before. But from time to time it let the word escape that "Albany is caught up in the storm." Gray wrote that, "the dark mutterings of today will pass," and he counseled Albany residents to mind "the old friendships between white and colored which are a bulwark of this community." Albany would "stand its ground against the invader until you-know-what freezes over." Yet few could stand their ground while caught in the throes of a storm. Whatever tranquillity whites experienced in the storm's eye was "an uneasy calm," as the *Herald* reported. Whites knew that the tempest was far from over. They were surrounded by a constant bevy of reporters and national media—who themselves came to embody what many Albany whites disdained. "The white citizens of Albany ache for relief from the national attention focused on the city's racial problems," the *New York Times* reported. To that end, some joined in the claims that little had changed. "Our prosperity is not threatened," attested two Albany youths. "Our streets are not disturbed, and we are not embarrassed before the world." Still more citizens seemed to admit that protests rattled them. "This town's been in the headlines too long already," a barber muttered. "When's this 'nigger business' going to stop?" The persistent civil rights demonstrations, and the resulting media circus, caused in some a physical reaction. "I'll tell you what makes me sick," said an Albany woman. "It's the way those reporters line up and take that man's [King's] picture and ask him questions. They write down everything he says. It makes me sick." Far from an undisrupted way of life, Albany whites showed telltale signs of tumult.[26]

THE STORIES OF ALBANY'S CIVIL RIGHTS struggles in 1961 and 1962 are well documented and well known. Many historians have focused on the Southwest Georgia town as the site of the first major rift between

SCLC and SNCC, whose young organizers mocked King as "De Lawd." Scholars also painted Albany as the place where King suffered his greatest defeat. When Albany appears in the civil rights literature, it is often depicted as an exception. In many of these accounts, Albany whites proved anomalous for their unanimous defense of segregation. Police Chief Laurie Pritchett—who strategically and intelligently combated civil disobedience—looms large in these narratives. "I realize I'm living in a changing world," Pritchett reflected. "You've got to adapt yourself to the situation. We are not in the old school." He tolerated public brutality neither from white supremacist organizations nor from his own police force. Under Pritchett's watch, order, segregation, and peace reigned together. Because whites did not have to choose between peace and segregation, many authors have argued, they stood uniquely united against racial change. These authors assert that Albany whites thereby resisted racial change and defeated the civil rights movement.* James Gray, too, proves an important figure in the argument for Albany as anachronism. A native of the western Massachusetts town of Westfield and a Dartmouth graduate, Gray defended segregation with the zeal of a convert and saturated the media with that defense. It is little surprise that the argument for Albany as anomalous makes its way from the top of the city—from Gray, the most influential man in town, and Pritchett, the most powerful—on down. In this line of thinking, no other city possessed a leadership so capable of encouraging conformity.[27]

A look at everyday beliefs reveals that Albany whites typified a kind of racial behavior that existed throughout the South. A study heavily

---

*In David Chappell's *Inside Agitators,* Albany's white community proves the exception to the book's rule. Albany demonstrated a cohesiveness in its defense of white supremacy "that had never before been witnessed, and was never again to be witnessed, in any southern white community during the years of the civil rights movement." Many cities fractured between segregationists who could stomach violence and whites who preferred law and order—even at the expense of integration. Albany whites did not divide; and for this, Chappell maintains, it was unique. Stephen Tuck argues similarly, in *Beyond Atlanta,* that "Albany proved to be the major exception, with near ubiquitous support for Jim Crow from the white community." To Tuck, Albany was not necessarily the exception to the entire South, but to other sites of urban protest in Georgia. John Ricks, in his essay on King and Albany, described "an amazing cohesiveness in the white community." All these claims remain open to debate, especially Chappell's assertion that such cohesiveness was "never again . . . witnessed . . . in any southern white community." David Chappell, *Inside Agitators: White Southerners in the Civil Rights Movement* (Baltimore, 1994), p. 123; Stephen Tuck, *Beyond Atlanta: The Struggle for Racial Equality in Georgia, 1940–1980* (Athens, GA, 2001), p. 157; John Ricks, " 'De Lawd' Descends and Is Crucified: Martin Luther King, Jr., in Albany, Georgia," *Journal of Southern Georgia History,* Vol. 2 (Fall 1984), p. 12.

reliant upon interviews with Chief Pritchett and biographies of King cannot help but conclude that they invested Albany's air with unique molecules. Indeed, Pritchett proved intelligent in his resistance against civil rights. He read King's books and learned about Mohandas Gandhi's march to the sea in an effort to use King's own peaceful tactics against him. Pritchett helped King to fill the jails. He worked out an agreement with prisons in outlying areas of Dougherty County, and housed every black demonstrator outside the city. Albany City Jail never came close to capacity. The strategy frustrated King and the Albany Movement. This was indeed a striking story. But in time, the civil rights movement would confront white communities just as united in their defense of Jim Crow. And as months and years passed, that movement penetrated even Albany.

In comparison with Mississippi, Alabama, South Carolina, and Louisiana—or even Virginia's Southside or eastern North Carolina— there was nothing extraordinary about white Albany's defense of segregation. There were good reasons SCLC and SNCC did not target places like Philadelphia, Mississippi; Selma, Alabama, and neighboring Lowndes County; or Plaquemines Parish, Louisiana, for massive demonstrations in 1961. Outright rebellion in such areas might possibly have spelled mass suicide. Albany whites were not unique in their racial attitudes; they merely lived in the first Black Belt town to witness direct action protests and demands for widespread desegregation. Deep South protests in Montgomery in 1955 and Little Rock in 1957 did not demand full integration of a municipality—they possessed singular targets, integration of the buses and of the high school. Albany was the first Black Belt area to endure an all-out assault on white supremacy. Sandwiched in the middle of counties with substantial black majorities— Terrell, Baker, and Lee—Albany citizens feared few things more than black power. In this context, Albany whites typified white attitudes in the Black Belt toward civil rights.[28]

This is not the only respect in which the received literature proves shortsighted. It also privileges the drama of the Albany protests, and fails to probe their enduring effects or interracial impact. The movements of 1961 and 1962 fit into a local history of black organizing that preceded the arrival of SNCC and SCLC, and persisted after their departure. Yet even those scholars who extend their inquiries beyond King's tenure in Albany place an almost exclusive emphasis on African-Americans. A focus on whites helps to expose the full dimensions—and promote a fuller understanding of the limits—of the civil rights revolution. The civil rights movement presented the white way of life with an unavoidable challenge. For Albany whites, the civil rights years were shocking and shattering.[29]

The month of July brought a feverish string of events to Albany. On July 11, a crowd outside Shiloh Baptist Church turned to violence. Amid flying bricks and bottles, Pritchett entered the black church in the middle of a mass meeting. It was a rare occurrence for a southern sheriff to communicate with the black community in its own sanctuary. Pritchett counseled Albany blacks to avoid violence, and was surprisingly well received. In a town torn by strife, Pritchett's act was to journalist and South Carolina native Pat Watters "one of the strangest, most deeply significant happenings" of the civil rights era. The next day, Pritchett removed King and fellow SCLC leader Ralph Abernathy from prison. On July 24, a black crowd again became violent, and undercut King's credibility as a prophet of peaceful resistance. As King brought his message of nonviolence to the pool halls and juke joints of Albany's Harlem, the national press narrated his defeat. Advocates of integration and nonviolent resistance, they reported, lost the high ground in Albany. The Albany Movement declared July 25 a "day of penance." On July 28, a black lawyer named C. B. King entered the Dougherty County Courthouse to meet with county sheriff Cull Campbell. Campbell ejected King from his office, followed him to the door, and bloodied King's head with a wooden cane. Like seasoned experts in public relations, both Pritchett and Gray denounced Campbell. At City Hall the next day, only five demonstrators showed up to protest the beating. Throughout, the City Commission refused to sit down with blacks.[30]

Events in Albany piqued the interest of more than one white southerner, including the New York Times's Claude Sitton. Sitton's beat was the civil rights movement, and the newspaper of record his forum. On July 26, Sitton traveled to Mount Olive Baptist Church in the "Terrible Terrell" town of Sasser, Georgia. His article set a standard for civil rights reporting, and it plumbed white attitudes to considerable depths. Sitton recounted the spirit, passion, and song of a mass meeting led by SNCC staffers and interrupted by Zeke Matthews, sheriff of Terrell County. Blacks enjoyed a two-to-one majority in the county of 13,000, but only 51 of them were registered to vote in the summer of 1962. Like many whites, Matthews thought local blacks content with this state of affairs. Sitton opened his article with Matthews's declaration, "We want our colored people to go on living like they have for the last hundred years." For Matthews, these were not idle words but deep beliefs. Matthews was convinced of the happiness of "his Negroes," and doubly certain of his own beneficence. To display this social harmony for the visiting journalists like Sitton, Matthews then questioned African-Americans at the mass meeting. The ensuing dialogue shocked the southern sheriff:

> Sheriff Matthews then turned to the Negroes, saying that none of them was dissatisfied with life in the county. He asked all from Terrell to stand.
>
>   "Are any of you disturbed?"
>   The reply was a muffled, "Yes."
>   "Can you vote if you are qualified?"
>   "No."
>   "Do you need people to come down and tell you what to do?"
>   "Yes."
>   "Haven't you been getting along well for a hundred years?"
>   "No."

With four simple one-word answers, the African-Americans of Sasser, Georgia, debunked decades of white myths. Still, whites like Matthews attempted to ignore the fact of black discontent. Not satisfied with the answers to his questions, Matthews muttered something about his desire to prevent violence and then continued with his boasts. "I've helped more colored people than any man in the South, I reckon."[31]

Although thousands of whites tried to ignore the stirrings of black unrest, they did not as easily dismiss letters that arrived in their mailboxes. The letters bore the stamp of the Georgia Council on Human Relations, and the signature of Frances Pauley, its executive director. In 1960, Pauley gained recognition when she helped lead an Atlanta campaign to keep public schools open amid integration. Two years later, she gazed south toward Albany, where the state's most troubling racial conflict played out. Pauley's letter, dated July 30, reached 10,185 white Albany households. The letter began, "Dear Friend," a feeling few of its recipients reciprocated. "Now in the extremity of misunderstanding and danger in Albany, when racial unrest disturbs the streets . . . and embarrasses Georgia before the country and the world, let us consider what Albany citizens of good will can do to permanently resolve the troubles." Pauley cited other Georgia cities—Savannah, Macon, Columbus—where blacks and whites had come to agreements about desegregation. She encouraged "new understanding between whites and Negroes," and urged Albany citizens to push their leaders toward meeting with blacks. She then mentioned the economic losses that Little Rock suffered in the midst of its desegregation crisis, and warned that a similar fate might befall Albany. Pauley advised Albanians to write their city commissioners, Chamber of Commerce, and meet with their ministers. "Let us open our minds, let us listen to reason and seek the truth. And let us act for a just and happy end to this dangerous, damaging and senseless struggle." Of the roughly four hundred Albany residents who responded, almost all greeted Pauley's suggestions with indignation.[32]

"I am a South Georgia cracker and proud of it," Arthur Johnston replied. Johnston had run a paint and bodywork company in Albany for fifty years. "We have been getting along fine here and were good to the negroes, until . . . King and other trouble makers came down here and started this trouble preaching to our negroes." Many Albany whites shared Johnston's view that African-Americans "already have the best things in the world," and that "outsiders" ought to stay far away from Albany. "You stay in Atlanta, Ga. and tend to your business and I will stay in Albany, Ga. and tend my business." This command echoed through the hundreds of letters that Pauley received. Respondents communicated to Pauley a few principal points: there was no misunderstanding between blacks and whites, blacks enjoyed equal opportunities, and Pauley ought not meddle in Albany's affairs. Pauley had braced herself for resistance, but she was unprepared for the depth of Albany whites' convictions.[33]

Rudolph Greer wanted Pauley to "*understand* that . . . there is no misunderstanding in this city between the races." W. H. Swinney attested, "There is no racial unrest in Albany that I know of." This belief was often complemented by the conviction that "the negro here has better schools . . . than whites," as J. W. Scruggs wrote. "There are thousands that feel the way I do," and under the weight of the mail Pauley received, it was something she started to believe. "I can truthfully state that the colored people have been well taken care of," wrote Milton Merts, the president of an equipment company who moved from Atlanta to Albany in 1950. Most Albany residents believed in that depiction of a harmonious past, and hoped to turn back time. "The Negro and white citizen had lived together in Albany in harmony since its existence, and great progress has been made in . . . the advancement of the Negro," an Albany man wrote to Pauley on August 6. "But thanks to outsiders such as you and your kind this progress has been damaged . . . it will take another 100 years to restore the relationship we enjoyed prior to December 1961." Like the *Albany Herald*, this citizen considered December 1961 to be a sort of watershed moment, the era before to be known as "B.K."—Before King.[34]

If one Albany resident suggested that whites would wage a century-long counterrevolution, many volunteered to serve as foot soldiers in that battle against change. They considered "outside agitators" the prime villains, a species Selma, Alabama, sheriff Jim Clark later consigned to "the lowest form of humanity." Pauley's letter proved that one's physical presence was not needed to achieve "agitator" status—agitation by mail sufficed. Pauley soon rivaled King for the mantle of white Albany's most reviled enemy. "If you outsiders will only keep away, we will clear the trouble in short time," Merts wrote. There was an army behind him, like the citizen who reached Pauley through the *Herald*. "I have talked it over with exactly 18 people and have yet to find one who didn't lose patience with your letter. Whether you know it or not, the real trouble we are having is the meddling of outsiders." Ironically, Chief Pritchett seemed the only one in town who believed that "the bulk of the local Negroes sympathized with King's objectives, even if they did not participate actively in his campaigns." Yet Albany whites were not in complete denial. No matter how hard some Albany whites claimed their lives proceeded as ever before, many more admitted they were in the midst of an upheaval. That upheaval did not have a local root, they insisted—it came from outside, brought by invaders like King, Abernathy, SNCC workers, and Pauley. Many acknowledged that problems existed, but they evaded or dismissed the tumult's real cause.[35]

Bent on denying that blacks were mistreated, Albany whites identified a different source of the problems—"outside agitators." As civil rights supporters flocked to Southwest Georgia, Albany did indeed become a hotbed for outsiders. "Nowhere in the South have we ever had such a concentration of personnel and resources," SCLC's Wyatt Tee Walker said on August 13. Clergymen and church groups from New York, California, New England, and various cities across the Midwest confirmed Walker's claim. Albanians refused to budge. "We have a good crowd of negro's in Albany, Ga. we are very proud of them," one wrote to Pauley. "We are willing to talk to our negro's . . . but we are not willing to do so with all of them trouble makers that are here from all the other places of the U.S.A." Florence Barbee had it on the best authority that "a large percent of the Negroes here wish King and his cohorts would leave. My maid has said this without any solicitation from me." Yet the old way of "good race relations" had blown away with the wind. "Outside agitators" must have turned "their Negroes" into something completely unrecognizable, for blacks breathed with a humanity and dignity whites never admitted they possessed. Chords of affection no longer tied Albany whites to blacks, and the foreign troublemakers were to blame.[36]

Pauley's letter did not push whites toward reconciliation; instead, many claimed that Pauley and the other "outside agitators" generated new resentments. Merts wrote on August 10, "Neither the City Officials or the County officials or Citizens of Albany are willing to let outside trouble makers drive a wedge between the two races who have lived in peace until outside agitators came in." As Pauley tried to bring whites and blacks together, whites insisted she had split them apart. She seemed to have gauged white opinion in Albany about as well as Albany whites understood the desires of local blacks. An Albany woman assured Pauley, "I have never harbored any ill-will toward the Negro race." But the civil rights movement changed that feeling. "Now things are different. We . . . now resent the Negro race, as we would any person or group that tried to force their way into our personal life." Pauley's letter incensed Albany whites of many stripes, even those who previously had considered themselves moderates. "I have attended integrated schools and served with many fine colored soldiers during World War II," wrote W. H. Swinney. When Swinney moved to Albany in 1952, he "was a moderate on integration, but inclined to the 'left' in advocating more integration." While the civil rights movement transformed some moderates into supporters of civil rights, it pushed many in the other direction. The presence of "these 'outsiders' . . . forces us to fight where we would rather concede on some points. You have definitely pushed one moderate into the solid opposition."[37]

Albany whites and blacks were involved in more than a battle for power; they waged war over conflicting visions of American freedom. King pointed out that most Albany whites labored under a "strange illusion . . . not at all uncommon across the South . . . which says that the Negro doesn't really want to be free." Yet Albany blacks often raised their voices in song; they declared, "I'm on my way / To Freedom Land," and marched toward "Freedom's Highway." As protests continued into the dog days of summer, white disbelief seemed unending. "What do the Negroes want?" R. J. Williams of Albany asked. "Their schools are newer and better than the whites." Faye Burnham of Albany asked, "Why do they want integration? They have everything that the white people have." One "Daily Reader" best illustrated the almost callous perplexity. "What I would like to know is what do the colored people call freedom?"[38]

An inability to comprehend black desires often went hand in hand with a certain notion of white freedom. Albany whites perceived in civil rights struggles a threat to their own liberties. A woman who suggested the formation of a committee for "The Removal of the Albany Movement" believed that only with the agitators' departure could her own freedom endure. "I have two children, and I feel that it is my duty to them to do anything and everything I can to preserve the freedoms and lawful way of life we adults knew when we were children." Rex Knight had boasted that whites "freed them from slavery, gave them the right to vote." But "now it looks like this . . . bunch is going to make us wear the yoke." Knight coupled claims about a mythical past with fears of a turbulent future—one that included black rule and white oppression. The historical touchstone of bondage still dwelled in white minds. Alongside worries about black cleanliness, inferiority, and intermarriage lived real political and economic trepidation—that the yoke could be moved from black to white. As J. W. Scruggs wrote to Pauley, "The Negro don't want schooling, he just wants to run over whites." Scruggs's words recalled those of James McBride Dabbs, who said, "You have to get run over or . . . run over somebody else as we have run over the Negro." Whites were so deeply influenced by a racial caste system that few could imagine a world in which blacks and whites would share power. They thought in terms of white supremacy or black supremacy: if blacks gained rights, whites would correspondingly "wear the yoke."[39]

Albany whites would stop at little to preserve "white freedom" and prevent black advancement. Some even sought to imitate the civil rights struggle in their midst. An Albany woman lamented the numerous civil rights organizations active in Albany, but "certainly haven't seen any of them here in the name of White Albany." She urged whites to organize their own movements. Other *Herald* readers were far ahead of her. "You business men of Albany, fire all of your Negro help," an "Interested Reader" implored. "There's plenty of whites needing the jobs." Bainbridge resident Jim Thompson urged whites to fight fire with fire. "Let's come from behind the veil of diplomacy . . . and admit this is a no quarter struggle to the end. . . . When we admit this to ourselves and everyone else then we will organize the white people and show some folks what a boycott really is." The vision of a Manichaean universe prevailed. There were no partial victories or defeats, only black and white, freedom and bondage. H. W. Kinman's detailed proposal for a white boycott appeared in the "People's Forum" on August 27. "As soon as the boycott began to take effect, the Negroes would lose most of their haughtiness, and the entire result would be a great change for the better." The white business community never employed such a full-scale plan, but episodes of economic retaliation occurred. If Albany blacks did not lose their "haughtiness," as Kinman had predicted, many did lose their jobs. An estimated 20 percent of black maids and cooks were fired. "We've been good to her for 20 years," said one white employer who fired the family maid for joining protests. "Now she's done THIS to us." Gone were the "good Negroes" of yore.[40]

Even in what seemed an impregnable fortress of segregation, opposition to Jim Crow peeked through cracks. Those fissures appeared most prominently in Albany's churches. On Sunday, August 19, Albany authorities arrested three blacks who showed up for services at the city's First Baptist Church. When Unita Tumblen, Robert Kenloch, and Johnny Mae Cooper tried to enter the church—in an attempted "kneel-in"—an usher denied them admittance. When they refused to leave the church steps, they were arrested. Reverend Brooks Ramsey was at the pulpit, unaware of the incident as it was occurring. He later made plain his disagreement with the actions of the usher and the police. "This is Christ's church and I can't build any walls around it that Christ did not build, and Christ did not build any racial walls. . . . The church doctrine of love to all men transcends any racial consideration." This was no endorsement of the civil rights movement, Ramsey made clear, but a belief about the freedom to worship where one pleased. "I haven't been a radical in this situation. In fact, I'm not in agreement with all their (the Negroes) methods. I'm not even in agreement with kneel-ins. They hurt the moderates." It was a position that many whites held: while nobody should break the laws of God, neither should blacks push too strongly or swiftly for integration. Ramsey insisted he did not believe the civil rights crusaders "are right in coming at all," but "Christian courtesy demands that anyone—even our worst enemy"—had the right to worship where he wished.[41]

These words were a tough sell to whites in Albany, many of whom treated segregation almost as a religion in itself. Yet Ramsey was not alone. The First Baptist Church Board of Deacons called a meeting the following Sunday, August 26, and unanimously backed their pastor. The Board of Deacons affirmed "the right of individual members of this church and its pastor to arrive at their own Christian convictions on all spiritual matters which may or may not be in agreement with the customs of the church." In this bastion of Jim Crow, the deacons refused to conform. Two days later, Frank Faulk, Jr., a member of the congregation, performed his best Martin Luther impression. Faulk wrote a resolution backing segregation in the church, and nailed it to the door of First Baptist. He demanded that "the minister of this Church make a full and complete public statement . . . that racial segregation as traditionally practiced is consistent with love and morality . . . and that a total . . . continuance of such practice of segregation shall and will prevail at all times on the Church premises." But Faulk did not speak for everyone. In the end, Ramsey retained his position; the board and the congregation upheld his right to interpret the Bible as he saw fit. Elsewhere in Albany, a Catholic church and an Episcopal church both admitted blacks to their services during the summer of 1962. Mrs. John Lapham, a communicant of St. Paul's Episcopal, expressed solidarity with Ramsey and other members of First Baptist. "The Rev. Brooks Ramsey is not alone with his 'moderate' view of Albany's racial problems, although perhaps the moderates are not as vocal as the extremists." Occurrences in Albany's churches cast a rare light on those whites who opposed segregation—a largely silent minority.[42]

The majority opposed civil rights with temerity. Brooks Ramsey was the exception, not Frank Faulk, Milton Merts, Florence Barbee, or Arthur Johnston. While the churches started to bring dissenters further into the spotlight, little changed in the attitudes of many. Danny Hawkes maintained that blacks "infringe on the rights of white people." He wondered, with others in Albany, "Is segregation really discrimination? I don't think so, but if the time comes when the white people can no longer choose their friends, associates, or customers, then that will be true discrimination." Many flinched at such a prospect. "The white children of America will never be seen in a swimming pool with Negroes," Eula Hamilton predicted. A summer of black protests still found racial myths alive and well. These views seemed as deeply embedded in some of the younger generation as they were in the old. As the new school year approached, an Albany High School student, James H. B., wrote to the *Herald,* "If the Negro really wanted to better himself he does have the

chance. . . . It is not a matter of custom being changed, it's a way of life."
Albanians like this student, and like Bill Waiteman, longed for a day in
which blacks "will be happy and peaceful again and so will the white
people, but this can only be accomplished when all the outsiders and
troublemakers have left town." Many others, however, sensed that white
life in Albany could never be the same. "The South must . . . live a different life now," wrote I. Q. Wander. "Peace and harmony can prevail
and we can still be peace-loving people." But Wander thought that violence might be necessary to enforce that peace. "It may take the original
Ku Klux Klan to deal the cards and right about face the entire situation
so that quiet and peace and justice can [again] prevail." While Brooks
Ramsey represented one extreme in Albany, I. Q. Wander embodied the
other. Many whites in Albany recoiled at the idea of a violent vengeance.
They shuddered at Wander's suggestion of the Klan, and espoused
instead the image of happy and good African-Americans.[43]

As autumn approached, many Albany citizens like E. L. Carter continued to tout "their Negroes." "Many of the Negroes in Albany are solid,
respectable citizens," Carter wrote on August 31. Still lacking a reliable
"social seismograph," Carter estimated that 90 percent of Albany blacks
were not "interested in and supporting the movement instituted by the
publicity-mad zealot, M. L. King." The *Herald* titled Carter's letter
"Why Punish Good Negroes?" Although African-American protest
deepened whites' psychological needs for the "good Negro," realities
made that an increasingly difficult belief to retain. The 20 percent who
fired their maids and cooks, for instance, had surely been shaken from
their conception of "our Negroes." Even as some clung to the old images,
many were gripped by shock. The experience of that trauma, a fact that
belied every rhetorical proclamation, constituted the first step in a
process of change.[44]

3

ANTI-COMMUNISM FORMED an integral part of white southerners'
views on civil rights. It helped Albany whites explain the changes in race
relations and in local blacks. The actions of African-Americans were so
novel, so fearful, and so unthinkable that many believed civil rights
protests had to be the work of outside influences—namely the Communist Party. One Albany resident wrote to Frances Pauley, "Get your
communist agitators *out of Albany* and we can settle this without

killing—then the Negroes can settle back in their place + be happy again." After receiving Pauley's appeal, a "true Albanian" concluded that either the NAACP or Communists must have sponsored the mass mailing. "Because this is the way that they operate, by trying to deceive people with an elaborate title like Georgia Council on Human Relations." Like Pauley's mail, the *Albany Herald* brimmed with anti-communist rhetoric. Dallas Powell urged those in his city to "compare the demands now being placed upon the City of Albany and its citizens with those of the communist manifesto. Seeing the similarities therein, let all of us who love this country and hate Communism join hands and fight." The day Powell wrote to the *Herald,* he received Pauley's letter in the mail. It warranted a postscript. "Mrs. Pauley, are you one of those who would like to see the white people fall and the Negro elevated?" Powell asked. "I shall not take the time to answer this letter . . . but instead I shall contact the House Un-American Activities Committee and urge an investigation of this organization for subversive activities." The worldviews of most white southerners had more than two tones: red streaks complicated black and white visions.[45]

WHEN CIVIL RIGHTS GROUPS turned to direct action protests in the 1950s, segregationists intensified their smear campaigns. In 1957, the Georgia Education Commission—led by conservative governor Marvin Griffin—issued a brochure that linked the Highlander Folk School with communism. Highlander, located in the hills of Monteagle, Tennessee, offered workshops on the rudiments of social change—and welcomed progressives of any race. The Georgia Education Commission obtained a photograph of Martin Luther King, Jr., at Highlander during its twenty-fifth-anniversary celebration, and distributed the image across the South. The photo made its way into newspapers and onto billboards. Pictures of King at a "Communist training school" dotted some southern highways. The irony was substantial. Through the early 1960s, King aimed his civil rights appeals at mainstream America. He steeped arguments and oratory in the Constitution and the Bible, and built allies in Washington. Yet even King could not escape the red brush. As King came to personify the black movement, he embodied the sum of white southern fears. Many whites suspected anyone who favored civil rights as being a communist, and vice versa. The allegations against King only reinforced that circle: here was a civil rights leader who had contacts in the nation's capital, ran an influential "outside" organization, and attended communist training schools. Indeed, organizers close to King—Stanley Levison and Jack O'Dell—had been affiliated with leftist organizations. FBI Director J. Edgar Hoover later conducted surveillance on the pretense that King's friends—and King himself—were communists. If even King could be branded a communist so easily, the allegations were sure to stick to many more civil rights activists. More vital than the machinations of segregationist leaders, however, was the way their pronouncements etched themselves in southern minds.[46]

Many whites glimpsed the hand of communism at work in the civil rights movement. "I have kept in touch with certain Negroes in various sections," a Savannah woman wrote to Senator Richard Russell, "and I am of the firm conviction that the very large majority are intelligent enough to know there is something fishy behind these 'spontaneous' Negro demonstrations. They realize that communism is the cause of the trouble, and is promoting a carefully organized campaign." When the civil rights movement hit high tide and waged massive demonstrations throughout the South, it added an extra dimension to white southerners' anti-communism.[47]

From the white side of the southern racial divide, the civil rights movement created a massive conceptual gap. Many thought blacks were incapable of organizing, and were content in "their place." They could hardly divine, or ever acknowledge, a sufficient motivation for black protest. Communism helped to fill that interpretive void. It explained why African-Americans in southern towns—those who had long toiled in whites' yards, tilled their fields, and cooked their meals—would suddenly rise up in mass movements. Southern blacks were not actually unhappy, many whites reasoned; they were puppets on a communist string. If civil rights protests were not legitimate homegrown struggles for freedom long denied, but sinister communist plots, then whites could retain their myths about African-Americans and southern life. Anti-communism enabled whites to deplore civil rights protests without revising their paternalistic views of blacks. This gave southern anti-communism its profound power.

In 1961, the *Jackson Daily News* introduced a column entitled "On Your Guard." Jack Lotto's articles appeared every Saturday to keep readers "posted on the present and future activities of the Communist Party." Lotto's column fed white Mississippians' appetites for anti-communism, encouraged that frenzy, and worked to undermine the black movement for civil rights. The *Daily News* argued that communists had manipulated southern blacks into protesting segregation. "The Communist Party is working to stir the Negro population into nationwide strikes and demonstrations," Lotto wrote in 1962. "The Communists have callously used Negroes for their own purposes while posing as their champions." At times it was unclear which prospect troubled white southerners the most: dignity and confidence for blacks; increased African-American political power and decreased white control; or the triumph of communism itself. All of these fears mingled together. To live in the white South during the age of civil rights was often to view such threats as real and immediate possibilities. "Did these men really believe that the Movement was a communist conspiracy?" asked Diane McWhorter, a Birmingham native whose father was involved in resistance against civil rights. "I think Papa did, and was not simply looking for a noble excuse to get away from his family at night." In the views of many southerners, communists gave blacks their marching orders.[48]

Believing the civil rights movement was a communist conspiracy allowed whites to more easily justify their opposition. Since the enemy was not "their Negroes" but a faceless red monolith, whites could picture themselves the defenders of America—and of freedom itself. Journalist Reese Cleghorn explored how southerners linked happy blacks and victimized whites with a dictatorial federal government and duplicitous communists:

> People who could believe that every day a snickering, South-hating, usurping power-mad, socialistic ilk in Washington was plotting to throttle the South's best interests and set Negroes on their best friends might just as well believe that every day Moscow was chortling as it watched its agents infiltrate and gain control of the government, press, churches and unions of America so that the country was already about three-fourths conquered by Soviet power. The two propositions were, after all, about equally true. And . . . when the Communist scare was nicely linked with the Negro scare, as an explanation of why "our Negroes are upset," the second proposition tended to make still more sense.

White southerners' anti-communism combined reason with paranoia. While anti-communism helped whites to make sense of black rebellion, those fears of a red takeover thrived on nonsensical suspicions. An unreasonable fear helped them reasonably justify their actions. Joining a cam-

paign to abolish HUAC in 1964, the Council of Federated Organizations, a group linked with SNCC, tried to isolate what was so nefarious
about white southerners' anti-communism: "The pervasive feeling
among white Mississippians that the civil rights movement is 'red-
inspired' enables Mississippians to dismiss civil rights protest as illegiti-
mate . . . and to rationalize violence and economic intimidation against
Negroes and civil rights workers as 'patriotic acts.'" Just the charge of
communism could set a community of southern whites against the
accused. "For many, it is a seal that shuts the mind before they ever begin
to think," wrote white civil rights activist Anne Braden in 1964. When
bombs ripped through a Birmingham church in 1963 and killed four
black girls, the *Birmingham News* ran many letters to the editor in which
whites voiced second thoughts about resistance to civil rights. After
George Wallace suggested that "communist agitators" had hands in the
bombing, "the letters stopped," Braden wrote, "as if a magic cleansing
action had occurred." To supporters of segregation, anti-communism
could act as an elixir.[49]

But anti-communism was more than a cleanser. It was an instrument
of state government. As a response to the *Brown* decision, the Mississippi
legislature created the State Sovereignty Commission in 1956. Its official
mission was to "prevent encroachment upon the rights of this and other
states by the federal government." Every southern state formed a similar
anti-subversive organization. Both North Carolina and Georgia had a
Bureau of Investigation, the Louisiana state police possessed a Criminal
Bureau of Identification, and the Georgia Education Commission acted
as a clandestine anti-communist and anti–civil rights organization.
Georgia legislators gave the commission power to issue subpoenas, hire
investigators, and convene hearings. The Mississippi State Sovereignty
Commission served as a model for other states. Agents tapped phones,
bugged rooms, censored newspaper articles, and engaged in many sorts
of espionage. The governor appeared on the commission's letterhead as
ex officio chairman. The commission amassed files on more than 250
organizations, and on 10,000 individuals who supposedly "work for or
represent subversive, militant, or revolutionary groups." In the eyes of
the State Sovereignty Commission, and the many white Mississippians
whose tax dollars powered it, communists worked hand in hand with
civil rights organizations. Albert Jones, director of the commission in
its early years, said as much in 1961: "Regarding the progress that the
Negro is making in our country . . . their efforts are supported by the

Communist. I wish it were some definite way to completely destroy their efforts." Together, communists and civil rights groups constituted a threat of the first order—and their actions begged for organized destruction.[50]

The State Sovereignty Commission worked from the assumption that civil rights supporters had communist ties, and that they aimed generally, in the words of commission investigator Tom Scarbrough, to "overthrow our form of government." The commission counted SNCC—and Bob Moses, its most influential Mississippi organizer—as archenemies. By 1964, blacks constituted 40 percent of Mississippi's population, but still less than 3 percent of registered voters. In the early 1960s, organizers came from outside the state to strike at these conditions. "Spreading from the delta, the [White Citizen] Councils all over Mississippi . . . . girded for the coming attack on Mississippi's way of life," read SNCC's *Mississippi Handbook for Political Programs.* "The attack came . . . in the person of Robert . . . Moses." SNCC's attack on Mississippi's way of life fell well within constitutional bounds—it sought to register black voters, and later to form a political party of its own. To white Mississippians, these goals smacked of subversion and revolution. The State Sovereignty Commission sought to paint the attackers as communists allied with Russia, rather than as democrats inspired by their vision of American freedom. When Scarbrough interviewed Bob Moses in 1962, Moses stated that he was a friend of Carl Braden—a white Kentucky native who supported civil rights, and in Scarbrough's words, "a known Communist." Scarbrough conflated different civil rights groups, and joined them all under the umbrella of a single communist conspiracy. "Martin Luther King, Jr., is the head of the organization for which Moses is working in Mississippi," Scarbrough wrote in his report. "King received his training in this type of work in the Communist School at [Monteagle], Tennessee." Scarbrough was clear in his conclusions. "From my experience by investigating Robert Moses' activities, I must conclude that he is working hand-in-glove with Communist sympathizers if not out-right Communist agitators. It is my opinion that Moses is himself a Communist."[51]

"Communist" became a flexible term for white southerners. The catchall phrase named and discredited anything that reeked of social change. As Clay Lee, a minister in Philadelphia, Mississippi, remembered, white Mississippians failed to distinguish among the various menaces that confronted them—blacks, communists, Jews, and even

Catholics shaded one into the other. "There was no distinction. They were not white, therefore they were not acceptable. Now, when I say white, I'm talking about white, Anglo-Saxon, Protestant." And in the Mississippi Delta, the thought of attempting to register black voters was nothing if not radical. But it also had little to do with communism. SNCC's radicalism was born of the black South; it was infused with the spirit of a people who had endured slavery but had not yet wiped away all of its vestiges. To understand SNCC, and to comprehend Bob Moses's efforts, was to see that many blacks in Mississippi were oppressively poor, not a few were illiterate, and almost none enjoyed the rights of American citizens. SNCC's effort was ostensibly aimed at voting rights, but it was based in loftier goals: education, pride, autonomy, a stake in the democracy that so many had heard about but never actually known, and the chance to make one's life the result of one's own choices. It had nothing to do with communism or the Soviet Union, and everything to do with America. Even if white southerners understood these points, they could never admit it. To do so would be to acknowledge that white supremacy was unjust, and that "their Negroes" were no more.[52]

Yet the charge of communism was not an absolute fabrication, and it did not stem solely from the delusions of white southerners. SNCC accepted legal help in Mississippi from the National Lawyers Guild, formed in 1936 as a pro-labor and pro–New Deal organization. In the postwar years, it quickly earned a reputation for defending communists. That the Guild was interested in civil rights in the 1960s, and not communism, was of little consequence to red-baiters. HUAC's *Guide to Subversive Organizations* described the National Lawyers Guild as "the foremost legal bulwark of the Communist Party, its front organizations, and controlled unions and since its inception has never failed to rally to the legal defense of the Communist Party." To most white southerners, this was incontrovertible proof that SNCC had its roots more in Moscow than McComb. When SNCC workers Mickey Schwerner, Andrew Goodman, and James Chaney vanished in Neshoba County, locals first dismissed it as a communist hoax. The discovery of their corpses beneath an earthen dam destroyed the idea of the hoax, but did little to shake the common perception that communists were running civil rights struggles in the Magnolia State. Theodore White charged in *Life* that "unidentified elements" existed in SNCC, an allegation Bob Moses rebuffed. Rowland Evans and Robert Novak wrote in a *New York Herald Tribune* article, "Liberals view Moses . . . as dangerously oblivious to the

communist menace." The charges scared off even Bob Moses's white liberal ally, the young activist Allard Lowenstein. Lowenstein warned,
"America cannot tolerate a presence as far left as SNCC."[53]

Across the political spectrum, from Klansmen and Citizens' Council
leaders to iconoclastic newspaper editor Hodding Carter, Mississippians
believed communism had sunk into their soil. Carter, as editor of the
Delta Democrat-Times in Greenville, had earned a reputation as one of the
most outspoken "moderates" in Mississippi. His own loyalty had been
questioned in 1959 before a Mississippi committee on un-American
activities. Yet in 1965, he joined in the red-baiting, alleging that "communists have infiltrated the Student Non-Violent Coordinating Committee," and furthermore, that King's SCLC was "slipping out of his
grasp and into the hands of militants under communist influence."
Carter's sentiments jibed with those of the American public. A poll
taken in November 1965 revealed that half of Americans believed communists were involved "a lot" in the civil rights demonstrations, one-
quarter thought communists were involved "some," and only 5 percent
thought "not at all." Among white southerners, the numbers were
doubtless higher. In an irony that highlighted the unifying power of
anti-communism's appeal, on this issue Hodding Carter and Mississippi
senator James Eastland could together speak for the white South.[54]

Such unity propelled legislatures toward greater heights—or, depending on one's perspective, lower depths. White southerners began to arm
their children with ammunition to fight the red menace. In 1963, the
state of Louisiana ordered its universities to teach a course entitled
"Americanism v. Communism." That same year, the Mississippi Department of Education began a campaign to teach about communism in the
public schools. A. P. Bennett, head of the Division of Instruction, sought
to devise a curriculum that would begin in the elementary schools and
work its way up to high schools. "With this approach fully developed we
will have assurance that students are adequately prepared to defend and
perpetuate our way of life." By 1964, the Mississippi legislature adopted
House Bill 459, which added a new requirement for public school students. All schools were to incorporate "new material on the nature and
threat of Communism" by the beginning of the next school year. As
Congressman Frank Smith wrote, "The youth of the state has been
taught that only the Mississippi way is right. . . . Vast numbers believe
that any Mississippian who differs has either sold out for cash or has been
a Communist all the time." By July 1965, communist conspirators had

gained a place in Mississippi history courses—they followed happy slaves, kind masters, fire-breathing abolitionists, the War of Northern Aggression, and the tragedy of Reconstruction.[55]

Many white southerners included the NAACP in that group of villains, despite the fact that by the 1960s it had become a mainstream and comparatively conservative organization. As Frank Smith recalled of the late 1950s and early 1960s, "The favorite question was why didn't those of us in Congress expose the communist control of the NAACP." Constituents directed such questions to their representatives across the South. "The NAACP is definitely communist supported," a Charlotte resident wrote to his congressman in 1962. "The time has come to finally declare war on the NAACP. Negroes are not equal to white people and never will be." Black equality and communism came fatefully together under the auspices of influential bodies that traveled South to "stir up trouble." The irony was that the NAACP went out of its way in the 1940s and 1950s to dissociate itself from communists, and to purge them from its ranks. At its national convention in 1950, the NAACP agreed upon a formal expulsion of any and all communists. The NAACP competed with the Communist Party for members; it advocated reform and not revolt. The NAACP purged Communists to avoid precisely the type of accusations it would repeatedly endure. Yet no action by the NAACP could dispel its reputation among white southerners—and it did not help when W. E. B. Du Bois, a co-founder of the NAACP, became an official member of the Communist Party in 1961. "Dr. Du Bois has just announced to the world how he has been standing all the time," the *Jackson Daily News* gleefully editorialized. "Here is deceit and intellectual subversion in human form." Clearly, the NAACP had nothing to do with communism. But just as clearly, if the NAACP helped achieve the freedom and equality that it sought for blacks in the South, it would have fomented a true revolution.[56]

Allegations of communism were bound up with civil rights challenges, and the one continued to hound the other. By June of 1967, the Sovereignty Commission would claim that communists had quickened their pace. "With the continuing increase of racial unrest and activities relating to the civil rights movement in this country during the past year, there has been a pronounced increase of activities by the Communist Party-U.S.A. concerning the Negro question and the racial movement generally." Civil rights still seemed to many white Mississippians a "Negro question," and many thought of local blacks in the paternalistic modes of the past. "The net result of agitation and propaganda by Communist and other subversive and extremist elements has been to create a climate of conflict between the races in this country and to poison the atmosphere." At every turn, white southerners asserted that increased black radicalism and aggression were not signs of black discontent, but of red conspiracies. As whites linked the idea of a communist plot with beliefs about blacks that had descended from the days before wage labor, they cultivated a paranoid style all their own.[57]

For as long as black civil rights troubled white southerners, anticommunism remained in their arsenal. While the limelight shifted to Black Power, the New Left, the Vietnam War, and the assassinations that felled Martin Luther King, Jr., and Robert Kennedy in 1968, anticommunism retained its power in Dixie. It was pliable in the hands of white southerners. Wherever they felt uncomfortable with racial change and lashed out against it, "commie" was one of the first epithets off their tongues. "Today my heart is heavy, not for Martin Luther King, but for my son and all servicemen fighting communism in Vietnam," Martha Adcock of Durham, North Carolina, wrote in April 1968. Adcock came around to a unique antiwar appeal. "Why is my son and all servicemen fighting communism in Vietnam and our President lowers the flag for a communist leader in this country. Why fight communism in another country and condone it in our own country. Bring these boys home, for they are fighting and dying uselessly." After King's assassination, Governor Lester Maddox attempted to raise the Georgia flag that had been lowered. He proclaimed that King "carried out the policies and programs of communists in this country." Adcock's letter and Maddox's claim underscored the fact that certain strands of thinking proved particularly resilient. Once white southerners, like any other humans, latched on to a belief and internalized it, that belief died only under extraordinary circumstances.[58]

White southerners continued to equate attacks on remnants of segregation with communist conspiracies, because red cries fit snugly into their traditional racial views. Anti-communism occupied the place it did because of its unique ability to explain changes in African-Americans, and to do so in ways that reinforced rather than disrupted stereotypes. Black southerners were happy, docile, and susceptible to manipulation, many whites believed. When they suddenly looked organized, discontented, and autonomous in the 1960s, whites attributed it to a communist plan. Whenever white southerners confronted racial change, they fell back on the crutch of anti-communism. By the time the Mississippi State Sovereignty Commission disbanded in 1973, it had released demons beyond its control.

4

FOR WHITES IN ALBANY, racial confrontation seemed unending. On September 3, 1962, Albany blacks sought to integrate white schools. The nineteen students who showed up at Albany High School ran into a wall of resistance and a sign that pleaded, "No Niggers, Please." Principals told black parents, among them W. G. Anderson, that assignments had already been made for the school year. By the end of 1962, a bitter pall settled over Albany even as SNCC and SCLC scaled back their protests against segregation. After the prominent demonstrations subsided, some observers argued that Albany remained unchanged. Chief Pritchett himself asserted, "Albany is just as segregated as ever." Journalist Reese Cleghorn, in a 1963 article in *The New Republic*, "Epilogue in Albany," termed the city "a monument to white supremacy." But blacks began to expose the monument's clay feet. "Anger and frustration is found among the 37,000 white residents," Claude Sitton wrote in the *New York Times*. "These emotions are laced with fear aroused by the evident animosity among Negroes." Tension mounted, and some Albany whites became caught in the crossfire. In July 1963, when one white businessman drove into the black part of town to drop off his maid, he endured an avalanche of bricks and bottles that fractured his skull. Increasing black aggression jolted white bodies and minds.[59]

Over the ensuing years, the outlines of the city altered. Albany repealed many Jim Crow laws in 1963, even as it sold off public facilities to avoid their integration. In May, the city auctioned three pools and a tennis court rather than desegregate them. James Gray bought one of the pools and the tennis court, and opened them in July on a segregated basis. The City Commission closed the picnic area in a park through the summer of 1963, and padlocked the public library for months. In closing and privatizing facilities, Albany attempted to change the agent of segregation—not the fact of it. Still, some Jim Crow laws had fallen, and whites found it more difficult to deny coming changes. "This movement gave a new sense of dignity and destiny to the Negro citizens of Albany," Martin Luther King said. "Negroes have straightened their backs, and you can never dump your load until you have straightened your back."

To King, such changes in black psychology resonated through the entire town. "For this reason, Albany can never be the same again."[60]

After the 1964 Civil Rights Act passed, African-Americans attempted to swim in James Gray's Tift Park Pool. A local court upheld Gray's right to exclude blacks. Judge Adie Durden sentenced the perpetrators to time on a road gang after he denounced "outside meddlers" and "agitators from New York." Many Albany whites continued to entertain such sentiments. As federal law enshrined black rights in 1964 and 1965, the coming years brought assassinations, riots, and tense episodes on the nation's streets. Albany whites sought refuge from the events all around them. The *Herald*'s "People's Forum" was "about the only place the white man can voice his opinion," Albany's Henry Ledford observed in the summer of 1964. "I'm sick and tired of reading where a Negro's toe is stepped on because he can't buy a piece of bubble gum or he can't mind his own business and stay away from where he ain't wanted." It was a white twist on individual liberties, tinged with a belief about "good Negroes." "No one is going to tell me I have to eat with him, sleep with him or live with him like he's my own brother. . . . I know a few Negroes I respect and admire, for they got what they wanted by working for it." But most blacks were not quite so good, Ledford asserted. "I've lost my respect for them, except the few I told you about because they want to force themselves on us. . . . Why doesn't the Negro leave us alone and mind his own business and quit thinking he's too good for our laws." The laws Ledford referred to were the Civil Rights Act and the Voting Rights Act. Segregated Albany would ultimately bend to the former, and the latter helped blacks on their march toward political rights. In 1964, C. B. King ran for Congress (and lost) and SNCC's voting drive began to bear fruit. By the end of 1965, five thousand blacks in Albany had become registered voters. In 1966, two blacks joined the police force. Mass meetings raged at black churches well into 1968.[61]

In some southern cities, prominent white supremacist victories stalled economic growth. This was not true in Albany. "Few traces remain of the public black eye this southwest Georgia city received," the *New York Times* wrote in 1967. The city's population swelled to 67,000, and in 1968 it won a $53 million Firestone tire and rubber plant. Counting industries as varied as airplanes, golf clubs, and now tires, the old Cotton Kingdom had changed shape. Companies like Firestone, Merck before it, and later Procter & Gamble, helped to moderate racial feeling in Albany.[62]

While few citizens experienced rapid transformation in their racial attitudes, by 1970 paeans to segregation no longer dominated public discourse. A new generation of white southerners began to assert itself—one that was reared on the torrents of the 1950s and 1960s rather than the stale oppression of the 1930s and 1940s. Robert Randall, a 1970 graduate of Albany High School, wrote, "A.H.S. has had its share of racial troubles this year," alluding to an uneasy transition to the widespread integration of public schools. "But what you may not know," Randall advised older Albany whites, "is that the vast majority of our students, both white and black, got along very well together. Integration can work." He rejected the white majority's "view of the entire black race as the white man's enemy. I prefer to view the black as a friend, a living person whom I may know, respect, work with, love, and help, expecting the same from him. We have more in common than not." Randall demonstrated that the youth revolution of the 1960s had reached southern whites. "There's a popular song that goes, 'What the world needs now is love, sweet love.' Y'all try it, huh?"[63]

While Randall preached an interracial love based on equality, others dug into the last ditches. In that same year of 1970, Albany white Jimmy Andrews flaunted a new racism, divorced from the paternalism of old. "I have no love for blacks, race mixers, riot[e]rs . . . I'm a racist." The facade tumbled down. Andrews was no friend of African-Americans, and they were not, in any sense, "his Negroes."[64]

Those who built their lives on the defense of legal segregation had trouble adjusting to a world without it. In 1971, Laurie Pritchett admitted that he was still attempting to live down his reputation as Albany's foremost protector of Jim Crow. "Albany has been an embarrassment to me over the years," Pritchett said from High Point, North Carolina, where he accepted the job of sheriff in 1966. "Albany, Ga., is 500 miles, a bitter 10 years and an embarrassing era away from this quiet Piedmont plateau town," the *New York Times* reported in 1971. Pritchett consciously projected a new image as the old order began to fade away. He "repeatedly referred to himself as a friend of Dr. King and others of the Albany movement." Some in High Point speculated that the town's leaders tapped Pritchett precisely for the reputation he tried to bury. But, as a white official said, "If he was hired to repress blacks, it certainly backfired in the face of whites." Pritchett met with black leaders in 1966, and made two black officers lieutenants. Throughout his tenure in High Point—from 1966 to 1974—Pritchett worked closely and amicably with local blacks. That relationship encouraged interracial peace in High Point on the night of King's assassination. Yet King's movement for civil rights had forever etched Pritchett into the popular consciousness—as a monster to some, and a hero to others; to many in High Point, he was just the local sheriff. Pritchett discovered that life went on after the civil rights movement, but nothing stayed the same. He longed to overcome the events of those years, but found himself inescapably defined by them.[65]

By 1970, the texture of race relations in Albany had changed. The library, tennis courts, and, finally, public schools were opened on an integrated basis. Old prejudices no longer strangled public dialogue, though many white Albanians continued to nurture them. Albany citizens like Helen Johnson could proclaim that "good or bad cannot be determined by the pigmentation of the skin, one must look far beyond the superficial to detect this," and could sign their names without too much fear of reprisal. They had to expect that most whites in Albany disagreed with them, even if all were not so blunt as Jimmy Andrews. The pages of the "People's Forum" still bristled with racially charged rhetoric, with pleas for "freedom of association" and "white rights," with assertions of anti-communism and fears of black political power. Most whites who defended segregation in 1961 and 1962 persisted in their racial attitudes for years. Mrs. B. R. Bannister of Moultrie argued for the abolition of public schools, and Albany's B. Giles called the SCLC, the NAACP, and SNCC "hate clubs."[66]

Portents of change accompanied fragments of stagnation. Ambiguity crept in where harsh oppression and virulent racism once reigned. Whereas white citizens had once hoped to turn back the hands of time, there was little doubt that something new was taking hold. During the height of the 1962 protests, a black porter reflected, "Anybody who thinks this town is going to settle back and be the same as it was, has got to be deaf, blind, and dumb." Many whites kept their eyes closed and their ears covered. But even the most resistant could not escape the civil rights movement's ability to penetrate their lives. In the interactions and negotiations that actual integration forced—often not until the late 1960s and early 1970s—white southerners would at last have to live with a world in which blacks were free and equal. For a time, Albany whites symbolized the white southern racial temperament—a citadel of tradition that shook amid the whirlwind of the civil rights movement. Whites embraced old racial myths and feared the "New Negroes" before them. Yet years after *The New Republic*'s "Epilogue in Albany," the story of white and black southerners in the grip of change was still alive. In many ways, it had just begun.[67]

5

CONFLICT WRACKED MANY WHITE SOUTHERNERS in their racial feelings. "We were taught from early childhood never to speak against segregation and never to question it," Lillian Smith wrote in 1957. "Our honest young eyes might see its cruelty and did. But we must not admit it." Such a state of living at odds, of refusing to freely think and feel, was to Smith a quality that defined the southern way of life. This "mythic mind has its *own mode of thinking* which is of a different nature from that of reason—and because it does think and talk in a different fashion, it can easily trick us. And often does." White southerners viewed the civil rights movement through various prisms of myth, emotion, and logical self-interest. For some people, a racial worldview more in tune with the reality of organized and free blacks replaced the "mythic" one.[68]

For others, the old ways of thinking proved particularly stubborn. Atlanta resident A. Y. Chancellor thought civil rights supporters completely wrongheaded. He asked in 1963, "Are you so foolish as to think that you can undo, overnight, custom and society which has prevailed for these many years?" Even as years passed, ample evidence suggested that they could not. The family of Jimmy Polhill III was involved in urban renewal and community action projects in the town of Louisville, Georgia. His father, Jim Jr., chaired the Jefferson County Community Action Board, and worked on training the poor for new industries. But Jimmy III remained fearful and conformist. He was pained that his family "had been branded Nigger-lovers . . . and had been ostracized. How would you like to be branded a Nigger-lover? . . . You walk into a room full of people and everyone stops talking." Even in a fairly progressive family, traditional feelings persisted. "Polhill says he fears the Negroes. He fears associating with them," the SRC's Susan Bresler reported from Louisville in 1966. It was a fear rooted in his childhood, one he could not rationally combat. "Why do I have this fear? . . . There must be a reason. Before we can communicate, we have to get over this fear." For all the civil rights movement's revelatory power, it could only occasionally undo what had taken centuries to ingrain.[69]

Well into 1966 and beyond, some white southerners continued to think of blacks as "their Negroes." As the town of Edwards, Mississippi, faced an economic boycott, Mayor Clarke Robbins declared, "Our local Negroes have been brainwashed . . . and if we just wait long enough they will learn better." These notions prospered far beyond rural parts of Mississippi. A 1968 poll conducted by the North Carolina Fund proved particularly revealing. More than three-quarters of North Carolina whites agreed with the statement that "whites work harder than Negroes," and 58 percent asserted that "Negroes are happier than whites." Here was the lazy and contented African-American of myth, revived in Upper South minds during the late 1960s. Three-quarters of North Carolina whites maintained that "outside agitators" might cause a riot in the Tar Heel State. Half of the respondents thought that white attitudes toward blacks would improve by 1973; the other half predicted they would worsen.[70]

Martin Luther King's quest for racial justice brought him to Memphis in the spring of 1968. In his last years, King focused on economic inequalities that flourished despite the existence of legal rights. In Memphis, King took up the struggle of poorly paid sanitation workers who had clothed themselves in signs declaring, "I am a Man." He found a city entirely segregated, a metropolis where racial discrimination and black poverty were pillars of the same social order. And while the gains of the civil rights movement had largely bypassed poor Memphis blacks, whites in the "City of Good Abode" had also eluded its reach. "Nowhere is the South's sad talk of 'tradition' more pitiful than in Memphis," journalist Garry Wills wrote in 1968. "The odd thing is that white Memphis really *does* think that—as citizen after citizen tells you—'race relations are good.' Its spokesmen cannot stop saying 'how much we have done for the Negro.' " Albany was not the only southern city whose whites lacked effective "social seismographs." In a time of Black Power and the Black Panthers, King himself angered and bewildered whites in Memphis. Even as many extolled the virtues of "their Negroes," whites began to expect that African-American protest would take the form of violence and "savagery." But they had particular trouble with the threat that King posed. King "infuriated southerners more than all the Stokelys and Raps put together." Whites could dismiss black radical leaders like Stokely Carmichael and H. Rap Brown much more easily than they could dispense with King's challenge. "In him, they saw *their* niggers turning a calm new face of power on them." King spoke of democracy, Christianity, and revolution without bloodshed. He defied every category of white stereotype, from the vicious savage and uppity black to the submissive Sambo.[71]

In many southern towns, integration did not come to schools and other public facilities until the late 1960s and early 1970s. Whites still clung to ideas about "their Negroes" in these newly desegregated worlds. When integration finally penetrated Yazoo City, Mississippi, in 1970 and 1971, local whites shook their heads in dismay. A leader of the Veterans of Foreign Wars wrote to the *Yazoo Herald:*

> To the many fine, colored people I can only say this: you are a part of our community, you have helped to raise our children, worked in our homes, but you have deserted us. . . . May I suggest that you return to the churches you left, and kneel down and ask the good Lord's help. Then ask your trouble makers to go somewhere else, to let you live as you know you must.

The plea was both striking and emblematic. The writer felt abandoned by African-Americans whom he had considered his own, blacks who were a "part" of his "community," and entered it through the back door. He harbored disdain for "outside agitators," and hoped Yazoo's blacks would settle back into stereotypical roles. The position of Charles Stebbins, a Darien, Georgia, attorney, was similarly representative. "I guess I'm just a typical southern person," Stebbins confessed in 1975. "My relationships with black people have hardly changed over the years. . . . From the standpoint of a white person, it was a very orderly . . . existence." Blacks and whites met most often in white homes, and in that circumstance, whites could believe they fully understood blacks. "We always had perfectly happy relationships with them, from my standpoint. Of course, I don't know what they were feeling, but there didn't seem to be any constraint." In parts of the rural South, myths continued to describe race relations into the mid-1970s.[72]

This was true from Yazoo and Darien to Hertford County, North Carolina. A University of North Carolina student identified as "St. Marc" spent most of his childhood in Hertford County. By 1975, the customs of his upbringing still outweighed any change the civil rights movement might have introduced. "How can I destroy the lingering faces of Stepin Fetchit, Amos + Andy, Buckwheat and all the other? They persist in my emotions and in my memory." "St. Marc" admitted that his "world view, is still strongly rooted in Hertford County, a rural, agrarian, black-belt county, which is, in many ways, the same way as it was in 1900." Parts of

society may have changed in those seventy-five years, but everyday practices and attitudes were incredibly undisturbed. "Time is suspended in
Hertford County. . . . It is an insular place, where white men still tip
their hats to white ladies on the street, and think of blacks as Sambos."[73]

This is not quite what the Southern Regional Council's Leslie Dunbar
imagined when he wrote "The Changing Mind of the South" in 1964.
Prior to the civil rights movement, "the endurance—what a Southerner
might call the 'cussedness'—of the old ways was remarkable," Dunbar
wrote. "But now this changes." Civil rights struggles forced change—
whether in the direction of greater tolerance or increased resistance. In a
time of momentous struggle, white southerners' own histories were
"sinking fast beneath them." Dunbar acknowledged that by 1963, many
whites in rural counties could remain "as unengaged as nearly all of us
were but a few years past. But I suspect that no white man living now
in . . . an Albany or a Birmingham can support himself either by mores
or by Faulknerian brooding. For the strong segregationist, the mores
will appear too mild when the protest comes; for nearly all men, the
brooding will seem irrelevant." White southerners could not stand still.
And blacks were on the move: "Negroes are disowning the stereotypes,
the white man's creations, are refusing any longer to acknowledge themselves to *be* what the white man said they were. White southerners are
confronted with a blunt demand from the Negro that he be accepted on
his terms: *and this is the crucial problem of race relations today.*" Blacks
demanded that white minds draw away from their concocted stereotypes
and closer to reality. Dunbar speculated, "I believe we can see the mind
of the white South changing through the action of the black South."
Numerous occurrences lent credence to Dunbar's hope. And mountains
of evidence accumulated in opposition.[74]

SOUTHERN CHURCHES BOTH SHAPED AND REFLECTED the changing—or stagnant—racial attitudes of white southerners. Many whites
had long thought of race relations as harmonious, a belief that was
grounded in more than just their perceptions, desires, and needs. They
imbued the pre–civil rights racial order with elements of timelessness
and righteousness that only religion could impart. Many whites believed
that God had mandated segregation. The Jim Crow social structure
could seem not only pleasant and just, but also divine and blessed.

Few southern whites applied Christian ideals to African-Americans.
"All folks do around here is memorize Bible verses," recalled Mississippi

resident Melany Neilson. "But they never seem to learn anything from 'em." Clara Lee Sharrard, a native of Lexington, Virginia, attended church regularly but never once heard the subject of race addressed. Sharrard's extended family included a minister whose wife "could quote the Bible about anything you wanted. . . . But when it came to talking about blacks and whites it was very obvious that she was not going to apply it to her own thinking and what was going on around her." Many white southerners adhered to a simple axiom, Sharrard remembered: "Love your neighbor, as long as he's white."[75]

Ministers may have helped to establish this perception, but during the civil rights years, many of them tried to avoid the issue. Stories of slavery abound in the Bible, but the "good book" does not lend quite as much ammunition to the cause of racial separation. Some ministers vocally defended segregation in their churches, and others questioned Jim Crow, but they constituted a minority of southern churchmen. Although their forebears a century earlier had breathed fire into the Confederate cause, most southern religious leaders of the mid-twentieth century evaded racial issues. Whereas the churches helped unite Dixie in secession, houses of worship remained deeply divided in the civil rights era. That left their congregations to believe whatever notions they had previously entertained. And many whites thought their system of race relations found sanction in the Bible. As the civil rights movement challenged other racial myths, it also confronted this one head-on.[76]

Almost half of white southerners belonged to Baptist churches. The Southern Baptist Convention (SBC) counted approximately 6 million members in 1945, 10 million in 1961, and 12 million by 1971. Millions of other southerners identified themselves as Episcopalians, Methodists, Presbyterians, Catholics, and Jews. While many Christians thought that segregation had a foundation in the Bible, some ministers advised otherwise. Will Campbell, onetime chaplain at Ole Miss and minister to civil rights workers and Klansmen alike, spoke his mind time and again. In May 1959 Campbell delivered a sermon at Vanderbilt Chapel in which he remembered a childhood experience in his rural southern Mississippi church. In a ceremony, the Klan presented the church with a pulpit Bible. The memory evoked Campbell's great fear—that white supremacy would retain a stranglehold on southern religion, as it had done with much else in society and culture. "The real danger . . . is not racism per se, but that racism becomes a part of faith. The Klan . . . has left its stamp, not only on the pulpit Bible but on the minds and hearts of generations yet unborn." Campbell charged that the Klan—and opponents of racial equality in general—possessed an appeal that was "essentially religious in character." The question of race relations was an almost spiritual one. "No subject has more religious relevance and arouses more religious support than the subject of race in the South today. And the segregationist man in the pew and pulpit who appeals to such support is not simply rationalizing. The stamp of racism has become a part of his religious heritage and it is almost impossible to break through and reach him." Campbell was saying that white southerners' attitudes on race were rooted as much in faith as in reason. And if ministers wanted to help southerners through the trying times of racial change, they would have to appeal to the heart rather than the head. Campbell spoke not of equality, rights, law, and order; those were secular terms. He urged Christians in the South to embrace the language of redemption and reconciliation, to stress the chance for expiation of sin through the civil rights movement. Campbell must have lifted his audience to its feet as he finished his sermon, and ruminated on the image of white mobs who spat on black students: "And I remember who I am and what I am. A white man, a Southerner, a Protestant. And I cry out: Lord, have mercy upon us. Christ, have mercy upon us." To Will Campbell, the civil rights years gave white southerners opportunities to embrace the best of their religious heritage, not the worst. Ministers could play integral roles in transforming white racial attitudes.[77]

Some southern ministers clung to that same hope, while others robed themselves in continued defenses of segregation. Many more remained torn, unsure of what to preach and how to counsel, intent on evading the most pressing issue of the day. The minister at Twin City, Georgia's Methodist church encapsulated the dilemma. "I do not speak bluntly and decisively," he admitted in a 1962 letter to Ralph McGill. "When one does, he immediately cuts his congregation off from him." Some ministers found themselves paralyzed. "Many like myself are not yet sure of the wisest course of action. But time is upon us and we must soon choose. May we do so under the guidance of God." The problem reached its most acute phase when African-Americans challenged ministers and congregations to integrate houses of worship, as they had done in Albany in 1962. This type of episode produced "one of [the] most bizarre spectacles to come out of [the] Negro revolution," according to a *Newsweek* background report. It featured "grim-faced deacons, squinting in Sunday morning sunshine, standing on steps of churches . . . arms akimbe, glaring indignantly at Negroes they are barring from entering sanctuary." Churches confronted the same questions that civil rights protesters posed to schools, businesses, and public facilities: Would they integrate, or close their doors? In the analysis of one *Newsweek* reporter, southern churches had failed woefully in their duties. "The Negro revolution was a massive Christian challenge, and now it must be said there was a massive failure on the part of the Southern church." Most ministers and churches failed to take a stand on integration. The power concentrated in those churches had few parallels in southern society. If meaningful change was to occur, churches would be key—as President Lyndon Johnson understood. In an attempt to garner support for civil rights legislation, Johnson appealed to 150 leading ministers of the Southern Baptist Convention on May 25, 1964. "No group of Christians has a greater responsibility in civil rights than Southern Baptists," Johnson implored the churchmen. "The leaders of states and cities and towns are in *your* congregations, and they sit on *your* boards. Their attitudes are confirmed and changed by the sermons you preach and by the lessons you write and by the examples that you set." Through the civil rights years, few of these churches set the types of examples for which Johnson had hoped.[78]

Some ministers did buck the tide. Up against a wall of conformity and often an opposed board of deacons as well, they attempted to allow integration in their churches and to convince their congregants of its goodness. As a whole, many congregations supported their ministers. But almost everywhere, deacons and members of church boards—who were also, as President Johnson knew, the most powerful members of their communities at large—tended to remain conservative in racial matters. They made the job of pro-integration ministers all but impossible. The *New York Times* carried the story of Reverend Robert McNeill, whose Columbus, Georgia, Presbyterian congregants dismissed him in 1959. In the end, only 50 of the 1,200-member congregation openly opposed him. But those 50 proved both vocal and powerful. Pastors like McNeill "have been men . . . without a country," read a *Newsweek* dispatch, "trying to smuggle some sort of social conviction to their congregations in endless sermons about love and brotherhood, aware all the time that the instant they drop their guise of abstractions they stand to lose their pulpit."[79]

Jackson, Mississippi, provided the backdrop for one such tale. W. J. Cunningham arrived at Galloway Methodist Church on September 1, 1963, two years after the official board had passed a resolution to keep the church segregated. Cunningham's predecessor had resigned over the board's stand on segregation. Galloway, known as the "Cathedral of Mississippi Methodism," stood across from the state capitol. The church board passed a second pro-segregation resolution in January 1963, by a vote of 184–13. In general, that winter had been a restive one for Mississippi Methodists. On January 3, twenty-eight ministers signed and published a statement entitled "Born of Conviction." It urged Methodists to open their doors to all, regardless of skin color. By the following year, more than half of the authors had left Mississippi; by 1969, only seven remained. Not until 1963, at age fifty-seven, did Cunningham "encounter racial antagonism in its full fury." The Citizens' Council cast a strong spell over many of Galloway's 3,500 congregants, as it did over Jackson's white community. "The racial attitude [in Jackson] was like a fog," Cunningham later wrote in a memoir. "You didn't look at it; you just walked through it. You weren't always conscious of it, but it influenced how you walked, just the same." The issue of civil rights consumed Cunningham's years at Galloway. While Cunningham attempted to nudge his congregants toward an acceptance of integration, many of them dreaded that such a thing would come to pass. "They were thinking about, 'Are black people coming into this church?' That dominated everything. It just stifled the atmosphere. . . . There was tension all through the congregation every Sunday over whether black people were coming or not." Cunningham preached sermons about brotherhood at the very moments that ushers—who dubbed themselves "The Color Guard"—barred blacks from the church. The closed-door policy enraged some churchgoers; others made it clear they would leave if the doors were opened. Some referred to Cunningham as "that integrationist," and refused to have him marry their daughters. By the end of 1965, the number of church members had dwindled to 3,100. The board's chairman received numerous calls for Cunningham's dismissal. In December 1965, Cunningham decided to leave, effective the following June. By then, both Jackson and Galloway had begun to take small steps toward change. A devoted segment in the church never stopped trying to overturn the closed-door policy; Cunningham's repeated sermons were not lost on all. In January 1966, the official board voted—by a margin of 65–40—to open its doors. W. J. Cunningham lost the Galloway pastorate in 1966, but African-Americans could finally worship there if they chose.[80]

Few southern religious leaders gained more infamy than the men of Birmingham. Eight leaders, including four bishops and a rabbi, penned the 1963 appeal that provoked Martin Luther King, Jr.'s, "Letter from Birmingham City Jail." King must have been thinking of this group when he reflected, in 1965, on his own "most pervasive" mistake. King initially thought "white ministers of the South, once their Christian consciences were challenged, would rise to our aid." Those in Birmingham, and across the South, exposed the error of King's assumption. "I ended up . . . chastened and disillusioned. As our movement unfolded, and direct appeals were made to white ministers, most folded their hands—and some even took stands *against* us." When King led a direct action campaign in Birmingham during 1963, the city's religious leaders criticized the black protests. In the religious leaders' "Good Friday Statement," they urged "our own negro community to withdraw support from these demonstrations." They deemed the marches "unwise and untimely," and charged they were "directed and led in part by outsiders." Charles C. Carpenter, the nation's senior Episcopal bishop, hand-carried the letter to Birmingham newspapers. Carpenter further claimed that King's protest lacked "Christian respectability." While the Birmingham clerics did not achieve the cessation of protests they desired, their statement gave to history one of the more eloquent writings about social change and civil rights. King scrawled the beginnings of his response on a newspaper in Birmingham's city jail. It contained a scathing indictment of the religious leaders. "The Negro's great stumbling block in the stride toward freedom is not the White Citizen's Counciler or the Ku Klux Klanner, but the white moderate who is more devoted to 'order' than to justice . . . who paternalistically feels that he can set the timetable for another man's freedom." Carpenter seethed, and failed to recognize himself in the paternalistic moderate of King's sketch. "This is what you get when you try to do something. . . . You get it from both sides." Carpenter felt he had made a genuine attempt at racial progress. Rebuffs like King's turned him, as Taylor Branch wrote, "into a more strident Confederate." Two years later, Carpenter termed the Selma march "a foolish business and a sad waste of time" that highlighted a "childish instinct." Indeed, King had in mind religious leaders quite like Carpenter. "Most white churchmen offer pious irrelevancies and sanctimonious trivialities," King alleged in an interview with *Playboy.* "Too much of the white church is timid and ineffectual, and some of it is shrill in its defense of bigotry and prejudice. In most communities, the spirit of status quo is endorsed by the churches."[81]

Few ministers worked to change racial attitudes and ways of life. But as civil rights gains became inevitable, many religious leaders—and their followers—set out along paths toward accommodation, if not quite acceptance. After the Civil Rights Act became law, the Southern Baptist Convention passed a 1965 resolution that supported rights for African-Americans. It adopted a commission report that condemned segregation as "an offense to the gospel" and "a sin against God." Baptists were the most cautious of southern denominations; many others had adopted similar platforms earlier in the 1960s. Change became evident even in W. A. Criswell, the Dallas Baptist who in 1956 had denounced *Brown* supporters as "infidels." In 1968, Criswell declared that biblical segregationists "do not read the Bible right. . . . I don't think that segregation could have been or was at any time intelligently, seriously supported by the Bible." Over time, the civil rights struggle forced substantive changes in white attitudes toward religion and race. Of course, alterations of attitudes did not always translate to physical change in the pews. By 1968, only 127 of SBC churches in the eleven southern states contained black members. In 1980, when W. J. Cunningham wrote that, "integrated churches in the South are a long way off," still no African-Americans worshipped at Jackson's Galloway Methodist Church. As Arkansas native Margaret Jones Bolsterli reflected in 1991, "Eleven o'clock on Sunday morning is . . . the most segregated hour in the South." Whites and blacks continued to worship in separate temples.[82]

6

THE CIVIL RIGHTS MOVEMENT'S assault on the white way of life extended from church pews and southern minds into classrooms, dance halls, and football fields. Change came in a variety of forms. As Chapel Hill businessman Robert Humphreys put it, "I don't remember in a timeline." Simple cause and effect rarely accounted for overhauls in the ways white southerners viewed their worlds. "When Martin Luther King said . . . 'This isn't right.' It was just . . . like a light bulb that went off in a lot of our heads that, 'Well, you know, it really isn't.' It's just the way it had always been and so we accepted it." In the cauldron of dramatic events, momentary revelations challenged deeply held customs. "My parents raised me to be a segregationist or a racist," Humphreys said of his upbringing in the 1950s and 1960s. It was "not because they were hateful people or bad people. It's just the way that everybody raised their kids." But new cultural waves penetrated his mind and life, and they presaged racial changes. Humphreys's band and his high school football team weighed heavier than his parents' lessons. He played "black music" and "emulated a couple of black bands that were here in town. . . . That's what we played and that's what the people we played for wanted to hear." Humphreys played most of his gigs in front of segregated audiences, often at birthday parties of white friends and at community centers. "Black music" pulsed through his instrument. On Friday nights Humphreys trotted onto the gridiron with Eugene Hines—the first black football player at Chapel Hill High School, and in 1966, the first in the conference. As Hines starred, Humphreys sat on the bench. Hines endured taunts from other teams, but the white Chapel Hill players rallied around him. "Guys from . . . these other smaller, rural communities out around North Carolina would say . . . 'We're going to get your nigger,' well, that just fired our team up. 'Cause he wasn't our nigger. He was Eugene Hines. . . . It was a unifying force to us. . . . 'No, you're not! This is our teammate! We're going to kick back!' " As much as politics or protests, music and football could effect changes in racial attitudes.[83]

Sammy Lee Wilson remembered Anne Moody's autobiography, *Coming of Age in Mississippi,* as the book that forced realizations in the minds of white Mississippians. The book itself not only chronicled the past, but shaped the future. Moody wrote of her life as a black woman who came up in the Magnolia State; she detailed poverty, confrontations with violent racism, and participation in the movements that sought to end those ills. "My white history teacher read it and asked was it true," Wilson wrote in 1969, shortly after the book's publication. "A student . . . said that he knew Negroes were being treated bad in Mississippi, but he said the book really surprised him." Most Mississippi blacks saw Moody's hard life as typical—her obstacles and her struggles symbolized those of the multitude. For many Mississippi whites, however, Moody's autobiography seemed to describe another world altogether. "One girl who had read the book met me in the hall one day and rather loudly asked . . . 'Sammy, is this book true?!' " When Wilson affirmed its veracity, the girl replied, "I never knew that this was going on." Wilson urged readers of the *Delta Democrat-Times* to pick up the book. "It will give you a good idea of your black neighbor." Before the civil rights movement, whites exuded confidence that they knew their African-American neighbors and understood their longings. When forced to admit the truth of Moody's world, many reacted in shock.[84]

Transformation extended even into the texture of everyday conversation. "In the Delta no white man will call a Negro mister," David Cohn had written in 1935. "This democratic title is reserved exclusively for white men, as 'Mrs.' and 'Miss' are for white women only. . . . A white man using them in addressing Negroes would fall under the grave suspicion of the community." That taboo held firm when Frank Smith wrote in 1962 that "addressing a Negro as 'Mr.' or 'Mrs.' is still a cardinal sin." Joe Smitherman had several African-American friends, but he "dared not" call them "Mr. or "Mrs." Often these subtle indignities angered blacks just as much as public segregation or the denial of voting rights. "Handshaking, nigger, Mister—these are the little things which, in no simple pattern, are the cutting edges of racial troubles," Harris Wofford had observed in 1953. Imogene Wilson, a black from Memphis, remembered that only in death did southern newspapers occasionally bestow courtesy titles upon blacks. "They wouldn't give you a title until you died." It was little wonder, then, that Hodding Carter attracted the suspicion of Greenville, Mississippi, whites when his *Delta Democrat-Times* extended courtesy titles to blacks in 1952. By that year, more than one hundred southern newspapers were using courtesy titles. For decades many of them had carried two different classified sections—a "Help Wanted" listing as well as a "Colored Employment" section. The *Atlanta Constitution* ceased this practice in the summer of 1964, shortly after the passage of the Civil Rights Act. Ardent segregationist Mary Cain published the *Summit Sun* in the small town of Summit, Mississippi. She devoted an entire news section to the black community, which was originally titled "With Our Colored Friends." In the wake of the civil rights movement, the supplemental section adopted a new title: "The Weekly Mirror."[85]

To both blacks and whites, changes in forms of address symbolized substantial shifts in race relations; they were a large part of blacks' increasing pride, and an affront to many whites. "They used to call you boy," remembered Alice Giles. "Hey boy or girl or hi auntie or uncle." When an African-American slipped up and neglected to address a white as "sir" or "ma'am," "you knew you was in for trouble. You could see them [whites] turning red, getting mad." Whites addressed all blacks with the same generic titles—boy or girl, auntie or uncle—or simply with a casual use of the first name. The civil rights movement was death to the old nicknames. When a reporter from the Mississippi Delta's *Indianola Times* addressed Cora Flemming by her first name at a 1965 rally, she demanded to be called "Mrs. Flemming." "He had it in the paper the next day," Flemming claimed. "People been called Mister and Misses in this town ever since." Many black southerners equated titles with the respect all humans deserved. "Black people became people," said a domestic worker in Clarksdale, Mississippi. "They became 'Mr.' and 'Mrs.' . . . Everybody became somebody." For whites, those admissions of humanity were difficult to grant. A 1964 Supreme Court ruling required lawyers to address black witnesses with courtesy titles. Taylor Branch recounts an incident, shortly after the ruling, in which a Florida lawyer "stumbled so painfully" over the words "Miss Evans." White southerners could endanger their standings in many communities if they showed blacks too much respect. In 1961, a notorious interracial handshake helped determine the next mayor of Birmingham. Bull Connor, Birmingham's police commissioner, and the white supremacist establishment backed Art Hanes against the less extreme Tom King. In May, the Connor faction paid a black man to grasp King's hand in public as a photographer waited. The *Birmingham News* printed a full-page spread, and King soon lost the election. The implication was not only that King dealt with blacks politically, but that he was close enough with them to shake their hands. Edgar Mouton, a Louisiana state senator, "never shook hands with a black person before I ran for office," and "the first time I shook hands it was a total traumatic thing." For whites, trauma was not confined to the days their children attended schools with black pupils or the times black voters dashed to the polls. It was just as harrowing an experience to call a black man "Mister" or to shake hands with him.[86]

Changes in white attitudes manifested themselves in millions of ways. Some loomed on the surface of life, while others remained undetectable. In 1963, Mayor Allen Thompson of Jackson declared that " 'local Negroes' are happy and content." He enjoyed "tremendous underground support from local Negroes," and claimed they were not backing "outside agitators." To Ralph McGill, even this was a change. The supposed "support of Mississippi Negroes for the state government . . . is no longer visible. . . . It has gone underground." Thompson's claim symbolized how much southern whites had changed in their thinking about African-Americans:

> It was but a short time ago that politicians like Mr. Wallace and Mr. Thompson were proclaiming that the Southern Negro was the happiest person on earth. He liked living in a shanty-slum; he was

ecstatic about being deprived of the right to vote. He just loved being kept in his "place" by the benign, kindly cops . . . the really genuine "Southern darky" was happy without [education]. . . . Indeed, so great was his happiness that merchants and planters often would sigh and say to "outsiders," "I wish I was half as happy as my niggers."

But the civil rights movement debunked that myth. "That was such a short time ago, as time moves," McGill wrote. "If it is indeed true, as Jackson's mayor says, that all this happiness has gone underground, then this is important. It would be interesting to know if the mayor really believes it is all there, down in that underground, serene and joyous, just wishing those old agitators would go away so things could be just like they were in the old days." There is much evidence—in the words of Albany citizens, of those in Yazoo, in McIntosh County, Georgia, and in Hertford County, North Carolina—that many white southerners continued to believe such things. But for other whites, attitudes and ways of life were beginning to change.[87]

A planter near Greenwood, Mississippi, lent eloquent voice to a reality riddled with ambiguity. Conflicts occurred between southerners of different stripes as well as within individuals. From a long-term perspective, the civil rights movement forced abrupt change. "Up until thirty years ago there was almost a slave-landowner relationship" in the Mississippi Delta, he said in 1964. "Then all of a sudden—at least it seemed sudden to us—we are told the system we're living under not only is morally wrong but legally wrong and everybody has to change." Such expectations were unfair, he asserted. "To expect a group of people raised and nurtured for 100 years on a system they evidently didn't think was wrong and expect them to agree that the whole thing has been wrong and to reverse themselves and change at once . . . that's asking too much of human nature." The white southerner could no longer stand still; those who could not rapidly transform had few other options. Yet while many in Mississippi preached massive defiance to integration, this planter took a more pragmatic view. "Most of us don't want it to begin with but it's a matter of facing reality . . . a matter of survival." As he understood it, the "big mistake" of white southerners was

to rob the Negro of basic dignity. The system was developed so that it . . . deprived the Negro of human dignity. He was reminded of it every day. The idea of not calling a man and his

> wife Mr. and Mrs. . . . of always saying "back door . . . go round to
> the back door" . . . of having a man 75 years old bend over and
> shine your shoes and you say "here boy."

The planter confessed, "I'm not a very good moralist or a strong religious thinker," but "it seems to me that if there's one sin above others it is to deprive a man of human dignity." He understood, with keen insight, what had happened over the centuries in the Mississippi Delta. At the same time, he prophesied that the "outside agitators" populating Mississippi during the Freedom Summer of 1964 (student volunteers who descended from the North to help blacks gain voting rights) "can so inflame white people against local Negroes that this bitterness will last much longer than just this summer." A deep resentment toward blacks—if no longer a condescension or denial of humanity—lasted well beyond the age of civil rights.[88]

Fear constituted no small part of that resentment. Whites often watched in horror as African-Americans cast aside their old masks of deference. North Carolina native Robert F. Williams induced shock with his 1962 manifesto, "Negroes with Guns." And in Bogalusa, Louisiana, blacks armed themselves to the hilt. Members of the Deacons for Defense—a group formed in Jonesboro, Louisiana, in 1964—fought their greatest battle in 1965, when the Ku Klux Klan became active in Bogalusa. The controversy surrounded the struggle of black union members at the local Crown Zellerbach Corporation, an enormous papermaking complex that dominated the town. When the Congress of Racial Equality (CORE) involved itself, the Klan became increasingly violent. The Deacons attempted to match that capacity for aggression. Their leader, Charles Sims, had been an army sergeant in World War II. He warned, "our weapons are always handy," and boasted of his ability to rally a hundred men in fifteen minutes. When the local police chief informed Sims that a white mob had formed to break up the Deacons' meetings, Sims had a defiant reply: "Tell them to come on—we're gonna stack 'em up like cross ties." Louisiana whites trembled at the prospect of seething blacks—with guns. "They know this," Sims said of whites, "they can't frighten me. They can put me in jail but they have to let me out one day." Overcome by a new willingness to be treated as humans or die, a rebelliousness coursed through black southerners. These changes in consciousness were not lost on southern whites. Such blacks had no resemblance to "their Negroes." African-Americans who rose up during the civil rights movement were "not the first Negroes to face mobs," James Baldwin wrote in 1960. "They are merely the first Negroes to frighten the mob more than the mob frightens them."[89]

Therein lay the civil rights movement's stark challenge to southern white minds and their attendant ways of life. Even while whites clung to old myths in the midst of chaos, that tumult produced inescapable change. To Rev. Will Campbell, a Mississippi native, "harmonious race relations" thrived in white minds only so long as they "had their foot on black people's necks and blacks weren't struggling to get up." Problems ensued when blacks began to struggle. The civil rights movement had staggering effects even on those whites who attempted to evade it. "The white southerner has had a shock," Robert Penn Warren wrote in 1965. "All at once . . . he has been confronted with the fact that what his cook or yard boy or tenant farmer had told him is not true." A whole host of myths went to die, and only with the most intense delusion could whites resuscitate them. "It is not true that the colored folks invariably just love the white folks. It is not true that just a few 'bad niggers' are making all the trouble. It is not true that just some 'Jew Communists' are making trouble. A lot of things are not necessarily true. And maybe . . . never were." For those with eyes to see, segregation no longer possessed the unremarkable feel of water from a tap or oppressive heat in the southern summer. It suddenly seemed mortal, and the "happy Negro" of yore now embodied a distinct threat. In 1964, Warren observed a Mississippi meeting that included civil rights leaders Aaron Henry, Charles Evers, Bob Moses, and others. As Warren strolled out of the auditorium, "my first thought was that I had been witnessing the funeral service for Sambo." The deferential African-American of myth was gone for good.[90]

Some white southerners did not need to attend civil rights meetings or witness the Deacons for Defense to believe that their images of African-Americans were the stuff of myth. For others, those fictions endured no matter what changes might course through the South. "I absorbed the myths . . . into my blood, and they persist," wrote "St. Marc," the North Carolina student from Hertford County. But as James McBride Dabbs saw it, white southerners' problem was their very inability to absorb the lessons before them. He called the white south- erner "the most historic monument of all Americans," for the past— particularly the Civil War—was never dead to him. He had not yet processed the implications of that defeat. "How well we move into the future depends upon how well we take the past," Dabbs commented. If that was so, it did not bode well for the future.[91]

According to Dabbs, southern whites possessed care, affection, and even love for blacks. But these whites gravely missed the point. In a society democratic only in name, shot through with discrimination and layered with inequality, emotional bonds were never enough. "Our love is worth something, but the trouble is we try to make it worth everything." White southerners still laced their paternalism with prejudice. "We like him, perhaps we love him when he is in his place at the bottom." But this alone meant little. "It doesn't do much good to say we love him . . . unless we try to build a just world in which he will have an even break." The civil rights movement asked white southerners not only whether they would change their racial attitudes, but whether they would build a new world, an interracial world, in which no one *was* anyone else's. The paramount issue was not whether white southerners knew or cared for African-Americans. The question was whether whites, under black pressure, could alter their social worlds—or at least adapt to new ones. More than affection was required. Dabbs said, "In an unjust society love is a frail reed." It remained to be seen if and how white southerners would cede those fragile reeds of the past to an interracial future.[92]

THREE

Daughters of Dixie, Sons of the South

FROM CENTERS OF EDUCATION to epicenters of social revolution, southern schools underwent radical transformation during the age of civil rights. In arenas of red brick, leaders, lawyers, and parents waged battles over black civil rights and white ways of life. The children of the South became unwitting pawns and inadvertent warriors. Politicians pledged continued segregation as states appealed the *Brown v. Board of Education* decision, denied its legitimacy, and delayed its implementation. Southern youths waded through the crosscurrents of federal integration mandates and segregationist state interpositions. Some whites took to the streets and to the courts to halt desegregation; many others watched idly, while those of school age found themselves thrust to the fore. As the reach of federal law became increasingly inescapable, whites in the South began to understand the weight that their schools—and their children—would shoulder. A debate between immediate integration and segregation forever was recast in more practical terms: Would public schools survive or perish? From 1954 into the 1970s, southern communities alternately evaded that question, faced its implications, and offered diverse answers. Children, their families, and their teachers bore the everyday burdens of those epic confrontations.

As autumn approached in 1958, "school bells begin to ring children back to their books across the South," *Newsweek*'s Joseph Cumming wrote in a background report. "The most agonizing drama of mid-century America begins another grim act." Students ambled into classrooms and drifted onto history's stage. "Children with their dental certificates and red tin lunch boxes are going scrubbed and bright eyed into what has become the battleground of our time," Cumming's colleague William Emerson wrote. "Wherever the segregation fight swirled, which ever way it turned, it would finally find its center on the school door sill. Somewhere in the background the old, hard effort to educate our children still goes on—but, this will not make the news." In the 1950s, the issue of civil rights most often became a scuffle over school desegregation. The spotlight shined on "massive resisters": parents who boycotted integrated schools, extremists who bombed them, cities that shut down public school systems, and crusaders who opened all-white private schools. Segregationists' violence could "catch the eye of the nation and blind out everything else.... But nowhere would it necessarily represent the attitudes or the actions of the majority of the people," Emerson wrote. "The nation would have to look past violence to see the slow, mighty shifts in the subsoils of custom, tradition, and way of life." School integration came in slow and painful steps. White southerners responded with convoluted combinations of embrace, resistance, adaptation, and apathy.[1]

Border states quickly abided school desegregation, albeit in token form. West Virginia, Delaware, Maryland, Missouri, Oklahoma, and Kentucky implemented desegregation plans in many cities. As one traveled southward, however, resistance to integration hardened. In Arkansas, North Carolina, Tennessee, and Texas, different strategies of delay and tokenism competed. The Deep South states—and with them, at first, Virginia—dug in for a fight to the end. With cries of "Never!" politicians in Alabama, Georgia, Louisiana, Mississippi, and South Carolina rallied their citizens to the unqualified defense of school segregation. While whites in the rural and Deep South denounced a prospect they refused to face, others in cities like Louisville, Nashville, and Greensboro admitted integration could not be stopped—and began to live with it. These instances led the North Carolina Council on Human Relations to proclaim, in March 1956, "The anticipation of desegregation is much worse than actual desegregation ... people are uncertain and fearful of what may happen. Usually nothing much happens." Across Dixie, the next two decades would showcase repeated battles over school desegregation.[2]

Few residents in the eastern Tennessee town of Clinton had invested school integration with much gravity before it occurred in the fall of 1956. "I never thought anything about it before," said a boy who attended school with blacks. "Nobody ever talked to me about it." Hard-core right-winger John Kasper arrived in Clinton to rouse the rabble. Segregationists bombed the high school as well as black homes, but they failed to stop Bobby Cain from becoming the first black to receive his diploma at Clinton High in 1957. Neither could they prevent a gradual process of change that school integration effected in some whites. "The change is evident in individuals," wrote high school teacher Margaret Anderson. "Just as an accumulation of experiences can begin to change an individual, so an accumulation of changed individuals does begin to change a community and ultimately a society." While dramatic acts of violence etched Clinton into the national consciousness, everyday lessons in integrated schools had a deeper impact on local children and their families. In the Tennessee hills, many came to tolerate something they had barely considered years before. But further south, the threat of that very change provoked rage and wrought tumult.[3]

On September 3, 1957, Arkansas National Guardsmen wielded bayonets to block nine black students from integrating Little Rock's Central High School. Governor Orval Faubus affirmed his commitment to Jim Crow education, but three weeks later President Eisenhower ordered the 101st Airborne to integrate the high school. On September 23, more than one thousand white spectators circled Central High. After blacks entered the school, the mob convinced many white students to abandon it. To preempt violence, the Little Rock mayor ordered the black students to withdraw. The next day, Eisenhower dispatched more than a thousand troops to Arkansas, and he federalized the state National Guard. Troopers dispersed the crowd, escorted the black children into school, and patrolled Central High for the next year. Enraged white southerners denounced a scene they thought had died with Reconstruction—that of federal troops protecting blacks' civil rights in the South. Many decried "forced integration," and perceived in it a direct threat. White southerners who backed Ike were few and far between. One was Ralph McGill, who applauded Eisenhower in his front-page *Atlanta Constitution* column entitled "Pulse of the South." But that pulse often appeared to be his alone. On September 29, a Georgian wrote to McGill, "There have been but few times when I would not proudly say 'I am a Georgia cracker.' One of those few times arose the other day when . . . Eisenhower, sent troops into Arkansas and you condoned his unwarranted illegal unthinking action." All but the most liberal of southern whites opposed school integration. A Columbus, Georgia, man wrote, "The sword can force integration on our people without acceptance." Come though it may, many claimed they would never accept integration.[4]

The arrival of African-American students altered that calculus. When white southerners had to face the reality of integration, rather than just stave it off, change coursed through their hearts and minds. The nine black students traveled to Central High classes under armed guard, and they endured manifold taunts and threats. But various white students demonstrated ambivalence and sensitivity absent in the mob that lingered outside. Craig Rains, a student council officer, explained, "If I had my way, [I] would have said, 'Let's don't integrate, because it's the state's right to decide.' " In light of horrific treatment that the black students received, however, Rains was transformed. "I began to change. . . . To someone who felt a real sense of compassion for these students. I also developed a real dislike for the people that were out there . . . causing problems. It was very unsettling to me." When confronted with desegregation, a segment of white southerners would join mobs and jeer at black students. But such displays were repulsive to the vast majority of southerners—those who have become increasingly lost to history. The story of the "moderate white students . . . was never told, to any degree," Rains later reflected. In the uproar over violence and the focus on politicians' machinations, "the little people, the students, got left behind." If few whites possessed any real sympathy for black students, antipathy nevertheless mounted toward violent segregationist defiance. From Little Rock to New Orleans, the polarizing experience of school desegregation created bevies of accidental sympathizers.[5]

Faubus closed four white Little Rock high schools for the 1958–1959 school year. Irked that idle school employees were still receiving pay, the Little Rock school board purged forty-four teachers and administrators. These drastic moves catapulted previously inert whites into action. Upper-middle-class mothers who prized their children's education over any theoretical commitment to Jim Crow formed the Women's Emergency Committee to Open Our Schools. The organization eventually counted 1,600 members. At the end of the aborted school year, the committee organized a recall of three Little Rock school board members. It would emerge victorious on May 25, when Little Rock residents elected three new school board members who favored open schools and compliance with federal law. By 1959, token desegregation reigned in Little Rock. "The new force at work was a shift of issues from segregation vs. integration to public schools vs. no public schools," William Emerson reported. "A region dedicated to the principle of segregation was as firm in its attitude as ever on this point . . . but . . . the survival of public schools was even closer to the hearts of many of the people." The age of civil rights had a way of transforming what seemed a question of racial attitudes into a question of everyday life. The issue was not whether white southerners wanted segregation, much less whether they supported black demands. But when the very survival of public education was at stake, whites in Little Rock chose their public schools over the dogmas of their heritage.[6]

While Little Rock children returned to integrated schools in 1959, segregation trumped public education in parts of Virginia. Given its relatively small black population (20 percent in 1960), its proximity to the Mason-Dixon line, and its varied urban centers, the Old Dominion's soil did not at first glance seem particularly fertile for "massive resistance." Faced with court orders to integrate in September 1958, Norfolk and Charlottesville did not look like prime candidates to shut down their schools. Charlottesville was home to Thomas Jefferson's university, and Norfolk hosted so many industries, transplants from the North, and navy personnel that it scarcely resembled most bastions of southern intransigence. In May 1958, *The New Republic* thought it "inconceivable that the white people of Virginia will give up their public schools to prevent the enrollment of a handful of Negro children in them." Such predictions overlooked the power of Senator Harry Byrd, who had proclaimed his commitment to "massive resistance" immediately after the *Brown* decision.[7]

When September came, Governor Lindsay Almond shut down the Norfolk and Charlottesville schools, along with those in Warren County. Four thousand Charlottesville residents signed a petition for school closure, and a referendum in Norfolk (with wording slanted heavily toward closure) backed school closure by a margin of almost three to two. About 13,000 white students were left without public schools. Soon whites were attending classes at Front Royal's Daughters of the Confederacy Museum, and students populated makeshift private schools in Charlottesville, Newport News, and Norfolk. Discontent animated Virginians beset by school closures. Norfolk parents complained they could not afford tuition fees, one Charlottesville man who hosted classes in his basement carped about the electricity bills, and many teachers objected to the disruption of their lives.[8]

From the rubble of closed schools arose a formidable movement for public education. While more than 12,000 white Virginians joined the segregationist Defenders of State Sovereignty and Individual Liberties, an opposition movement—the Virginia Committee for Public Schools (VCPS)—gathered 25,000 members by the summer of 1959. The state-wide organization grew out of local movements that sprouted in those cities affected by school closure. In Charlottesville, nine mothers formed a committee for public education and challenged the dominance of a private school foundation. In every town plagued by closed schools, rifts divided white southerners. Some lined up in favor of boycotts and fledgling private schools, while others rallied to the cause of public education. In January 1959, the Charlottesville city council and school board both voted unanimously to reopen public schools. But Norfolk politics followed a different path. On January 13, the segregationist city council voted to withhold funds from public schools. Many whites expressed disapproval of the council's action. The Norfolk Committee for Public Schools had already helped file a court case to challenge the school closing law; by May 1959, 7,500 Norfolk whites had joined the VCPS.[9]

A statewide mass movement, together with momentous court rulings, spelled the end of Virginia's "massive resistance" policies. The Virginia Supreme Court of Appeals invalidated the school closing laws on January 19, 1959, and the governor reluctantly yielded to token integration in a January 28 speech. Once Almond adjusted to the court ruling, so did more Virginians. A *Richmond Times-Dispatch* poll found that 60 percent supported the governor. But the ensuing reality of integration was not easy to navigate. "The vast majority of our people are struggling valiantly and honorably for survival of a way of life," said the state's superintendent of public instruction, Davis Paschall, "and . . . for the survival of their schools. . . . They are inwardly confused, hurt, and torn."[10]

The inhabitants of Prince Edward County were not at all torn. Smack in the middle of Virginia's Black Belt, or "Southside," Prince Edward was one of the counties named in the original *Brown v. Board of Education* decision. It was also the first southern community that completely destroyed its schools in order to "save" them. In the summer of 1955, although it did not yet face an imminent order to integrate, the county's Board of Supervisors allocated no funds for public education. The board spoke for its constituents. In a county of about 16,000 (just over half were white), 4,216 whites signed a statement in May 1956 to support closing integrated schools. Where the number of adult whites was about 6,000, that petition contained more than two-thirds of their signatures.

"We prefer to abandon public schools and educate our children in some other way if that be necessary to preserve segregation of the races . . . in the schools of this county." Faced with a final desegregation order in 1959, public education vanished from Prince Edward County. On June 3, the Board of Supervisors voted to levy no taxes for public schools. The board decreased property taxes by more than half, and whites spent the money on private education. Two high schools and eighteen grade schools closed in September 1959. As one official said, they "will just sit on the hillside and rest." Whites founded the private Prince Edward Educational Foundation, which employed almost all of the seventy-two former public school teachers. Most of the county's 1,570 white students enrolled in private schools. "Resistance in Prince Edward has thus far worn the stubborn smile of martyrdom," the SRC reported. The supervisors imbued their actions with the language of sacrifice and goodwill. "Above all, we do not act with hostility toward the Negro people of Prince Edward County." As whites locked the doors of their schools, shuffled teachers around, and shuttled their children to new buildings, the county's black children became invisible to them. "No accommodations have been made for the 1,715 Negro students," the SRC noted. Perhaps Prince Edward County whites did not harbor open hostility toward blacks, only callous indifference.[11]

The civil rights years were hard on white southern moderates. Those who preferred compromise, or supported "gradual integration," found that any middle ground evaporated as quickly as judges could bang their gavels. "There's no middle ground on whether schools are opened or closed," said Ellis Arnall, the prominent former governor of Georgia, on April 9, 1959. Across the region, politicians took solemn stands, mothers formed contrarian movements, businessmen funded private educational organizations, and communities fractured over the issue of public schooling. "There comes a time when a theoretical issue develops into an actuality," Arnall continued. "There's no duty to . . . tilt at windmills." Few people in Little Rock, Prince Edward County, or Clinton managed to escape the issue. Whites either countenanced desegregation, closed schools, or fought to keep them open. Arnall spoke out for open schools in 1959, and he had an undeniable army behind him—a swath of whites in Atlanta who argued that "The City Too Busy to Hate" should take the time to preserve its public schools.[12]

In response to a 1958 court desegregation order, the Georgia legislature—still dominated by segregationists and the county-unit system—

threatened to shut down, and even to sell, public schools. Many Atlantans shuddered at the thought. On November 16, 1958, Mayor William Hartsfield pilloried the "sell the schools" proposal. Two days later, Fulton County representative M. M. "Muggsy" Smith addressed the Spring Street Parent Teacher Association. The former Georgia Tech football star informed a packed school auditorium that he would battle for open schools. "We too long have sat idly by in the hopes that some Moses shall lead us out of the morass of a situation that is not of our own choosing, and for which NO remedy has been found." Caught between court orders and segregationist defiance, many Atlantans found themselves ensnared on the horns of a dilemma. "I have no quarrel with those of our leaders who have striven . . . to preserve the status quo. If any of their efforts could have stopped the cataclysm, I would be the first to congratulate them." But courts ordered school integration—and if Georgians did nothing, the legislature was ready to close their schools. Smith painted a grim portrait of that future. "Where flowers bloomed, the weeds have raised their ugly hydra-like heads. The playgrounds where . . . childish voices had raised a melodic cacophony, stand as silent sentinels of a departed host. . . . Inside . . . closet doors are closed on the thousands of books whose jackets bear the imprint of small, grimy hands." That was only the half of it. Far worse would be the effect of closed schools upon parents, teachers, and children:

> Housework is a problem with the children underfoot, not for a short three months, but ALL THE TIME . . . the baby-sitting problem has become a full-sized nightmare. . . . The older children hang around the corner drug store or record shop, go to movies until sated, then seek various and often ill-advised means of escaping boredom. The teachers—well, God help them, for He alone can—NOW.

Smith's prophecy hit Atlanta whites where it hurt. He detailed how all manner of everyday life would change radically if schools were closed. The proud image of Atlanta as a progressive beacon would vanish when confronted with the reality of a city that could not so much as provide education for its sons and daughters.[13]

The movement to save public schools was rooted in the city's upper-middle-class neighborhoods. In December 1958, mothers from the Northside chartered Help Our Public Education (HOPE). They tried to recapture the middle ground that segregationist crusaders had dissolved,

and sought to save public education without endorsing wholesale integration. In a residentially segregated city, and in affluent white neighborhoods, "integration" meant at most a handful of black students in a
few schools. HOPE trumpeted a vision that looked forward to the pros-
perous urban and suburban Sunbelt South, a place where class trumped
race—where anyone with the money could settle in their neighborhoods
and attend their schools. As they well knew, few black families had the
means to do any such thing. Northside whites pictured an enlightened
"New South," as against the rural Black Belt legislators who wished to
perpetuate a dying old order. HOPE denied that school integration was
a moral issue of black freedom, and argued that school closure smacked
more of an impoverished past than of the bright future. HOPE's message
galvanized many white Atlantans.[14]

On January 14, 1959, Atlanta PTAs voted on whether to close schools
in the event of desegregation. Of fourteen PTAs that released detailed
results, only two voted for school closure. The tally included 3,447 votes
for open schools, and 816 against. But twelve of the nineteen PTAs that
declined to report figures had voted to close their schools. The geograph-
ical breakdown was revealing. As the *Atlanta Journal* reported, "Opposition to keeping open . . . is strongest in the areas where Negro families
live in nearby neighborhoods." The Westside and Southside saw an influx of blacks in the years after World War II; by 1960, many census
tracts in those neighborhoods possessed significant black majorities. In
contrast, the census tracts from which HOPE drew its power base were
more than 90 percent white. Muggsy Smith had spoken at the Spring
Street School—where black children were distant entities, not palpable
threats. At Spring Street, 208 out of 260 voted for open schools. In the
exclusive Northside, whites overwhelmingly supported open schools.
But those in the southern sections of the city, in areas that adjoined black
neighborhoods, voted for school closure. Atlanta itself mirrored, in
microcosm, the dichotomies between Black Belt and urban areas that
defined southern states. Segregation thrived among those whites who
lived near high concentrations of blacks.[15]

Both HOPE and segregationist governor Ernest Vandiver positioned
themselves as protectors of white children. When an NBC station broadcast a neighborhood meeting on January 7, 1959, HOPE conveyed its
message: "To champion children's rights to an education within the State
of Georgia." Through 1959, the legislature remained firm in its commitment to prevent school integration at any cost. As the General Assembly

prepared for its annual meeting, Mayor Hartsfield declared December 6–12 "Save Our Schools Week." HOPE sent each assembly member a telegram that read, "At Christmastime—the greatest gift you can give the children of Georgia is uninterrupted public education." In his State of the State address, Vandiver retorted that he would terminate public funds for education if integration was ordered. Segregation was his salvo for the youth. "Georgia children—their welfare . . . their education— stand uppermost in our minds and in our hearts." In a show of force, HOPE marshaled ten thousand signatures on a petition that it presented to the legislature. Atlanta citizen Jack Walker pointed out that one could not "solve the problems of a great, complicated urban and industrial center by adopting the methods used by . . . small, provincial villages." Georgia's students spoke up on their own behalf. On January 14, 1960, five Northside High School students wrote to the *Atlanta Constitution,* "Even though we prefer not to go to school with Negroes it has come to the point where a decision is necessary. We would much rather integrate our schools than close them, which would mean unhappiness and desolation for all concerned." A freshman at the University of Georgia made that position even clearer. "I am not an integrationist and would be in favor of any plan to keep the schools segregated except closing them." Whites preferred segregated schools to integration. But more than segregation, they cherished the routine and comfort of their everyday lives—and their schools.[16]

Public opinion shifted not with the wind, but under the force of HOPE's organized movement. The mighty subsoils of custom were moving, and even the most intractable politicians realized that many white southerners prioritized the stability of their public schools over the bedrock of their tradition. The General Assembly still delayed, hoping that "tomorrow" might become "never." In February, the assembly endorsed the creation of a commission on school integration. The Sibley Commission, so dubbed because of its head, Atlanta banker John Sibley, became a traveling band that sought out the views of Georgians. It also served as an effective instrument of the legislature's delay. Every congressional district in Georgia hosted a public hearing of the Sibley Commission. Sibley pressed those who testified to support one of two choices—integration or school closure. When Sibley took his show to Atlanta, more than a hundred speakers expressed their preference for open schools. But whenever someone spoke for segregation, the crowd huddled in the Henry Grady High School gymnasium on March 23 cheered. The crowd was split between HOPE sympathizers and those of MASE—the Metropolitan Association for Segregated Education. The hearings showed that while almost all white Georgians preferred public schools to private, 55 percent wanted to abandon them if integrated. "We want segregated schools at any cost," autoworker Ernest Lazarus testified, "the cost of lives if necessary." The commission found that "the beliefs of the witnesses appearing before the Committee vary with the percentage of negro population in their particular locality." And the vehemence of some whites could startle. In Marion County, where 63 percent of the population was black, Alex Bergen testified, "We are in favor of segregated schools at all costs. . . . We may have to give up some of our standard of living. We will be happy to do it. We can ride back in wagons, if necessary, to educate our children in segregated schools." The Marion County audience enthusiastically applauded, perhaps for an imagined rural past rather than HOPE's insistent "New South" vision.[17]

In its April 28 majority report, the Sibley Commission recommended that the state legislature adopt an amendment to keep public schools running. Due to court decisions in other states, and to an apparent diversity of views among whites, it argued that Georgia's "massive resistance" laws were inappropriate. Yet the Sibley Commission also suggested a "freedom-of-choice" option, private school tuition grants, and an amendment that would prevent the integration of opposed whites. In early May, a district court set a date for the desegregation of Atlanta's public schools—the fall of 1961. The days of defiance seemed numbered. In light of an inspired movement that made visible the state's legions of public school supporters, the weight of continued court orders, and an ugly episode of white violence at the University of Georgia, many Georgians caved to open schools in 1961. But before Georgians reached a resolution on public education, events further south made clear the horrors that could afflict southerners if their schools remained battlegrounds. In the instance of New Orleans, the black struggle for freedom fostered deep white division.

2

THREE MONTHS BEFORE the *Brown v. Board of Education* decision, the upheaval on New Orleans's horizon was barely perceptible. In February 1954, *Newsweek*'s William Emerson predicted, "New Orleans should desegregate with ease." By 1960, the furor over integration had enveloped most citizens. New Orleans blacks had set events in motion when parents filed a 1952 lawsuit (*Bush v. Orleans Parish School Board*) to place their children in white schools. In 1956, federal judge Skelly Wright directed the Orleans Parish School Board to draw up a desegregation plan. The board postponed that moment of truth over four years of legal appeals. While New Orleans thought itself a progressive island in the Deep South's river of resistance, it remained to be seen how the city's white population would react to waves of integrated schools. The tides swept everything in Louisiana toward Jim Crow—and they usually originated in Leander Perez's Plaquemines Parish. Perez's brand of white supremacy dominated the state, and his Citizens' Council ally William Rainach rammed segregationist bills through the State Senate. As a New Orleans resident described Louisiana whites in 1959, "They are two billion percent for segregation."[18]

In the Democratic gubernatorial primary of January 1960, Perez and Rainach backed Jimmie Davis, a former country singer famous for "You Are My Sunshine." Davis ran against de Lesseps "Chep" Morrison, who had been mayor of New Orleans since 1946. While Morrison offered himself as a "moderate" alternative, his platform still stated, "Maintenance of segregation is best for all our people." Davis crushed Morrison, ensuring four more years of political control for the Citizens' Council. Journalist Helen Fuller, writing in 1959, believed that Virginia's surrender to integration had ended states' opposition to the Supreme Court. But, she feared, "word of this, as in Andy Jackson's day, may not reach Louisiana until after a second Battle of New Orleans has been needlessly fought." In May 1960, Wright ruled that integration had to begin that fall. After months of legal wrangling among the federal judge, the state legislature, and the Orleans Parish School Board, four black children integrated two New Orleans schools—the first in the Deep South—on November 14, 1960. The ensuing battle over integration featured a white school boycott that left two elementary schools with a grand total of eleven students, mobs of shrieking mothers, two families that fled the city, a white mother who kept her four children in school despite repeated threats, and one African-American girl who braved a violent mob in her sparkling snow-white dress.[19]

As the November day of reckoning approached, the prospect of school integration bedeviled New Orleans whites. In a May school board poll, 82 percent of roughly fifteen thousand white parents preferred closed schools to token integration. Save Our Schools—an organization devoted to continued public education—warned that closed schools could spell economic ruin, bring juvenile delinquency, and cause irreparable harm to the Big Easy's image. Judge Wright tried to make the question moot, issuing his desegregation order on May 16. After the U.S. Fifth District Court of Appeals upheld Wright's ruling, the school board asked the state to interpose. Governor Davis seized control of New Orleans schools on August 17; ten days later, a federal court issued a restraining order against him. Wright then set the first day of integration for November 14. Amid legal uncertainties, many whites in New Orleans remained firmly tethered to segregation. "I do *not* believe that the local Negro citizens are anxious to integrate," a worker at McCrory's department store wrote to Mayor Morrison. "Total forced integration here is not the answer. . . . I am old enough to recall with horror the Tulsa Okla. Race riot . . . and this certainly is not the answer. . . . There must be a way" to "improve the situation. . . . Our way of life . . . in New Orleans depends on it."[20]

The year's flurry of events worked on the minds of New Orleans whites. The federal courts spoke time and again, and Save Our Schools combined forces with the Committee for Public Education, a group composed "mostly of average white [southern] parents of public school children." Some unions, women's organizations, and parents began to support open schools. "I used to be worried about segregation of the schools," a truck driver said. "But after all this monkey business I'm worried about us seceding from the union." Another man asked, "Do you think a city that has survived . . . yellow fever and years [of] Mardi Gras is going to worry about losing its segregation virginity?" In October, the school board adopted a pupil placement plan in preparation for integration. When Orleans Parish School Board member Matthew Sutherland campaigned for reelection, the Citizens' Council ran John Singreen against him. The November 8 election became, in effect, a referendum on open or closed schools. After the *New Orleans Times-Picayune* endorsed Sutherland, Singreen issued a public reply. He wanted voters to understand the stakes: "The sole issue in this campaign is, are the voters willing to accept integration now, or [are] they going to fight now for their rights." Sutherland scored a convincing victory in the four-way race, and garnered 56 percent of the vote. Singreen came in second, with 31 percent. School integration would come after all, it seemed, with sizable white support. Out of an applicant pool of 136, the school board had already selected 5 black students it deemed fit for white schools.[21]

On the morning of Monday, November 14, whites in the city's Ninth Ward awakened from their dreams only to face their nightmares. East of the French Quarter and extending northward from the Mississippi River levee, the Ninth Ward reflected the heterogeneity of New Orleans. Neighborhood whites—German, Irish, and Italian, French and Spanish, Catholic and Protestant—were similar in only a couple of ways: few possessed any wealth, and they all lived within a stone's throw of African-Americans. Narrow one-story homes with small yards sat within sight of public housing projects. A *Newsweek* report called the neighborhood "amazingly integrated," populated by "working class folks." During the years of the Second Great Migration, blacks interspersed themselves through many of the city's poorer neighborhoods. In the 1940s and 1950s, thousands of blacks had migrated from the rural South to New Orleans. While blacks departed Mississippi, Alabama, and Arkansas in droves, Louisiana's black population grew by 22 percent in those decades—and most of them flocked to the "Big Easy." Between 1940 and 1958, the city's black population increased by almost 40 percent; the white population grew by 14 percent. The city's total population swelled by one-quarter million, and by 1960, New Orleans was 40 percent black. The Ninth Ward absorbed many of those African-American transplants. Fully one-quarter of New Orleans blacks lived in the Ninth Ward. "Many white workers feel increasing economic competition from the Negroes on the docks, in the oil plants, on construction jobs," Saul Pett of the Associated Press reported. "And in Ward 9, few people can afford to send their children to private schools. It was, many people think, the worst possible area of the city to begin even token integration."[22]

A closer look at the November 8 election results reveals the political currents at work in the Ninth Ward. On the day that Sutherland won reelection to the school board, John F. Kennedy triumphed over Richard Nixon. Kennedy carried the city of New Orleans by a wide margin, and with it the state of Louisiana. In some Crescent City neighborhoods, Nixon was not even his stiffest competition. Kennedy received half of the Ninth Ward's presidential vote; the States' Rights Party finished second, at 32 percent, while Nixon won just 18 percent. The Ninth Ward also provided John Singreen a heavy base of support. Sutherland garnered 44 percent of the vote, to 36 percent for Singreen. Singreen did not run that close in any other ward except the Eighth, where he won by a single percentage point. More than in other parts of the city, Eighth and

Ninth Ward whites cast ballots against integration. Soon they would vote for the same cause with their feet, their fists, and their voices.[23]

Seven PTAs in New Orleans supported open schools, and two units in wealthier neighborhoods volunteered for token desegregation. But those schools did not fit the school board's "scientific" formula for selecting a testing ground for integration. It chose white schools where students' median achievement scores equaled those of the black students. Many citizens of New Orleans saw this myopia for what it was. "They picked the two worst schools in the city to desegregate," said Rosa Freeman Keller, a well-known local liberal. "It was a very ugly situation." Marion Bourdette, a teacher in a different section of the city, agreed. Ninth Ward whites "just could not accept it. . . . The only thing that separated them from black people was the color of their skin. . . . Economically, they were the same." New Orleans was deeply divided by class. Affluent whites sneered at the Ninth Ward, and acted as though its violent reaction to school desegregation was expected. Many Ninth Ward whites felt picked on by city leaders, threatened by the blacks in their neighborhood, on their docks—and now in their schools. Whites in the Ninth Ward might have little choice of co-workers and neighbors, but no city official could force their children into school with blacks. It was a neighborhood invested with an idiosyncratic history. Fats Domino grew up on a street just behind McDonogh School No. 19. The William T. Frantz School stood on North Galvez Street, four blocks from the junction where the streetcar named "Desire" doubled back through the French Quarter. Mobs of howling mothers and a handful of frightened schoolgirls soon wrote themselves into the Ninth Ward's lore.[24]

In a final effort to halt integration, the Louisiana legislature declared November 14 a statewide school holiday. That morning, officials at McDonogh No. 19 and Frantz each received two notices—one informed them of the state holiday, the other ordered them to proceed as planned with desegregation. New Orleans schools ignored the state's last attempt at interposition, and opened their doors. As parents across the city watched to see whether their children's schools would integrate, three black first-graders walked into McDonogh No. 19; another, named Ruby Bridges, entered Frantz. The fifth girl stayed home. Crowds of several hundred whites formed at each school. They chanted, "Two, four, six, eight—we don't want to integrate." Fifty blacks gathered around McDonogh and cheered. A U.S. marshal escorted Ruby Bridges up the steps at Frantz as she clutched her mother's hand. Cameras flashed while she slipped into the school. Throughout the morning, white mothers streamed into Frantz and McDonogh to withdraw their children. Only 185 of 576 Frantz pupils reported for classes that morning; by the end of the day, 50 remained. Amelia Plunkett ran into McDonogh moments after the black students entered. "I'm getting mine out of there just as quick as I can," she asserted. Friends, neighbors, and other bystanders urged her on as white students from a nearby high school arrived with rebel flags and white sheets. At its peak, the crowd reached 1,000 — but no violence was reported. The relative peace led school board president Lloyd Rittiner to proclaim, "The worst is over . . . the people of New Orleans are going to accept the inevitable." How wrong he was.[25]

The next night at the municipal auditorium, William Rainach urged a crowd of 5,000 to boycott schools rather than "accept the inevitable." Citywide, a total of 10,000 pupils were absent on Tuesday. Frantz counted 65 students that day and McDonogh just 20. One Frantz mother likened the classrooms to tombs. Atlanta representative Muggsy Smith's vision seemed to have become a reality in New Orleans. On Wednesday, white parents organized a march and joined forces with a crowd of 3,000 boycotting high school students. Confederate flags aloft, they marched to City Hall and down Carondelet Street toward the school board building. Police sprayed fire hoses, swung billy clubs, and plowed through the crowd on motorcycles. Some students screamed at Police Superintendent Joseph Giarusso, "I hope all your children are black." During that week, school attendance dropped sharply throughout the city. Many Ninth Ward whites accepted offers from Leander Perez to attend public schools in neighboring St. Bernard Parish. Others began to pay private tuition. By the end of the week, the white boycott of McDonogh and Frantz was almost total.[26]

Many whites berated Mayor Chep Morrison and his police for turning hoses on mothers and barricading them from elementary schools. "I had no idea that you would betray the good white people of your city," wrote a recent Tulane graduate. "I deplore my [tax] money being spent to hire policemen to implement the black Monday decision of the Supreme Court right here in the Crescent City." A high school student was among the minority that applauded the mayor. "While you have seen *all* the young people who are fighting you, you have not seen all of us who are with you all the way." Morrison might take some solace from letters like these, but public opinion flowed strongly in the opposite direction. Another New Orleans resident charged city leaders with "betraying their own race of people . . . but this was taken care of by our forefathers who chased the carpet baggers" like Morrison "into the Mississippi River . . . some have escaped and . . . made their way back to . . . City Hall and to the School Board." Many whites saw a "Second Reconstruction" upon them.[27]

Protest against integration took many forms, from boycotts and mobs to political theater. Because only a small number of Ninth Ward whites gathered in crowds each morning, some observers contended that only a small minority opposed integration. But the abandoned schools told a story difficult to deny. Many whites acquiesced in the boycott out of fear; many others backed it with conviction. "Hundreds of parents peacefully took their children from the affected schools, but because they did not carry clubs and throw stones, it has been said that they 'accepted' integration," Prioleau Ellis, a white mother, wrote to the *Times-Picayune.* "Do not tell me that because I don't use physical violence, I am 'accepting' that which I am doing my best to reject." On November 18, mothers in front of McDonogh adopted creative forms of protest. Two of them dressed up as Native Americans and held signs that read, "American Indians. We can't go to white schools. Why should the Negro go with white?" When New Orleans schools closed for Thanksgiving week, Ninth Ward parents took their show to the statehouse in Baton Rouge. On November 23, mothers walked into the legislative chambers. They were all dressed in black, some had veils, and a little girl carried a black cross. They staged a mock funeral for Judge Skelly Wright, and placed a blackened doll in a coffin. "The judge is dead, we have slaughtered him," one mother yelled.[28]

This protest was restrained when compared with the actions of mothers who clustered daily in front of Frantz. Their display became so notorious that John Steinbeck detoured from his cross-country road trip to observe it. He glimpsed "three hundred years of fear and anger and terror of change in a changing world." Steinbeck described the "group of stout middle-aged women who, by some curious definition of the word 'mother,' gathered every day to scream invectives at children. . . . A small group of them had become so expert that they were known as the Cheerleaders." He marveled at the number of Gulf Coast whites who braved the morning cold to watch the show. Suddenly, the crowd parted as a Cheerleader waded to the front of the police barricade. Minutes before 9:00 a.m., police sirens and two black cars carrying U.S. marshals and

Ruby Bridges signaled the day's beginning. While "a jangle of jeering shrieks went up from behind the barricades," Steinbeck soon learned that this was not the main attraction. "The crowd was waiting for the white man who dared to bring his white child to school." Women hurled epithets at their target. "The yelling was not in chorus. Each took a turn and . . . the crowd broke into howls and roars and whistles of applause. This is what they had come to see and hear." And this was what the Second Battle of New Orleans soon became: not a fight of segregation against black civil rights, but of whites against whites.[29]

Lloyd Andrew Foreman, a minister at St. Mark's Methodist Church, was the white man Steinbeck saw. Foreman's daughter, Pamela, continued to attend Frantz School. So did Yolanda Gabrielle, the daughter of James and Daisy Gabrielle. The ordeals of the Foremans, the Gabrielles, and other white families who brought their children back to school were unique. But they dramatized the ways that the age of civil rights exposed many different white Souths, and cleaved whites as often as it unified them.

As the Foremans and Gabrielles discovered, to walk one's child to school was to endure certain abuse. On November 29, the first day after Thanksgiving break, a fifty-person crowd gathered to block Lloyd Foreman's path to the school. One woman shoved Foreman. He retorted, "Take your hands off me. Talk to me but don't touch me," and tightly clutched his daughter. Foreman dropped Pamela off safely at school, and emerged to speak with reporters. "I simply want the privilege of taking my child to school. If others don't want to send their children that is their privilege." Foreman returned hours later to retrieve Pamela. Fellow minister Jerome Drolet accompanied him, and diverted the crowd's attention while Foreman drove up on the other side of the school. The Foremans soon left, but they would return again the next day.[30]

That morning of November 29, a mob stirred outside the Gabrielles' apartment building as Daisy readied Yolanda for school. The four-bedroom apartment stood five blocks from Frantz, and it housed six children. Daisy Gabrielle waited until the mob had thinned, then brought Yolanda to school at 10:20. "They told me they just wanted us to take the child out of school so that we could have all white schools. If they could change the government's mind I'm all for them, but integration is inevitable." Most white parents who kept their children in school were no lovers of integration, but they believed strongly that their child's

schooling was their own business. Before school integration, Daisy
Gabrielle "had never thought much about the rights and wrongs of segregation." She speculated that many more like herself existed. "A large
majority of the mothers would like to send their children to school but
are afraid of being beaten up." Her child, like Pamela Foreman, wanted
to attend school. "We've had some trouble down here and all the children are mad," Pamela told the *Memphis Commercial Appeal*. "I hope they
won't stay mad long. I hope they can come back so we can play." As the
afternoon's final bell approached, a crowd huddled near the back door of
the school—where Daisy Gabrielle eventually appeared with Yolanda. A
pack of twenty mothers surrounded them. One woman struck Daisy,
who swung back with her purse. "You feel real brave in that crowd," she
yelled. "You cowards." James Gabrielle and a policeman soon broke up
the fracas. "There's no mob rule telling me what to do with my daughter," he said. "It may be my job but my child is going to school where
she's assigned to go." James Gabrielle worked as a meter reader for the
New Orleans Sewage and Water Board, and he acknowledged that his
unwillingness to conform might one day cost him his job.[31]

Days like these took their toll on the Gabrielles, in both tangible and
unseen ways. "I think I lost 10 years of my life the night I made that final
decision," Daisy Gabrielle admitted. Gabrielle kept her daughter out of
school only once. "I was so scared. Who am I to fight the whole state of
Louisiana and the governor, I asked myself. But that night, my conscience tore at me. Are you going to give in to a mob?" Gabrielle awakened the next morning, driven by an almost spiritual urge to defy the
mob. "Whatever it was I heard an inner voice. And when I got up that
morning, I told my husband . . . I'm taking Yolanda back . . . I'm going
to do what I think is the right thing . . . I felt at peace with myself. You
know, I'd rather take a beating from a mob than from my conscience."
Gabrielle maintained, furthermore, that she possessed a certain sympathy for those mothers who attacked her. "They're fear-ridden. . . .
They're scared to death and I feel sorry for them, but I can't let them dic-
tate my life . . . I don't hate or dislike them . . . I really hope someday
they will see my point of view." Integration presented Gabrielle not only
with the choice between public education and a boycott, but between
her beliefs and her friends. "One neighbor told me, '. . . you're foolish to
stand by your principles rather than your friends.' . . . I thought to
myself: 'Neighbors change. Principles don't.' " For Gabrielle to walk

each morning into abusive crowds—to expose her daughter to malice and rage—she had to possess a unique courage. She met the harsh experience with an inner resolve, and invested her own actions with profound meaning. When Gabrielle walked Yolanda to school, she said, "I close myself inwardly and pray, 'though I walk through the valley of the shadow of death, I fear no evil.' When light is walking through darkness, it cannot be touched."[32]

The darkness in New Orleans finally got the best of the Gabrielles. As Daisy Gabrielle experienced abuse each day near the school, her husband, James, was repeatedly threatened on the job. Their eldest daughter, who attended a different school, dropped out. Some local leaders were aware of the situation, and they worried about the amount of suffering that the Gabrielles could endure. Rabbi Leo Bergman of Touro Synagogue warned Mayor Chep Morrison, "If Gabrielle is forced to lose his job and leave town, it will reflect . . . upon you. Isn't there someone in town you can call privately, to give him a job." Morrison made no calls, and segregationists scored a triumph. The verbal abuse James Gabrielle received from his boss and co-workers became so unbearable that he quit his job on December 6. In a typical taunt, one co-worker told Gabrielle he was "contaminating the white race." Unable to find other employment in New Orleans, Gabrielle moved his family to Providence, Rhode Island. By Christmas, boycotting whites had driven the Gabrielle family from their city.[33]

New Orleans citizens debated whether Chep Morrison and his police force did too little to help the Foremans and the Gabrielles, or too much. Some city organizations spearheaded carlifts to transport the children to school. The lifts began on December 1, and on December 6 a car in which Pamela Foreman was riding had its windshield smashed by a brick. A mob also stoned the car that sheltered Yolanda Gabrielle. The situation in front of the families' homes was worse. The Foremans abandoned their own home, its porch splattered with red paint and two arrow-shaped signs affixed to the front lawn that read: "There." The Foremans moved five times in one month, and later left the neighborhood. Foreman was occasionally heckled when he gave sermons, as he preached about times when "life presses in upon us." Foreman's wife called the mayor's office, and word reached Chep Morrison that "they are very worried and feel that the city officials don't care what happens to them inasmuch as they are not important enough." Voices of whites in the Ninth Ward—

especially those who swam against the boycott's current—were easily
lost amid the tumult of the school crisis.* Morrison was concerned primarily with facilitating the image of "law and order," a facade that
existed so long as he confined the upheaval to a few small bands of hecklers in the Ninth Ward. Through the controversy, Morrison attempted to
govern from the center. He claimed he supported open schools, but only
hesitantly sent police to ensure the peace. Had the mayor been more
forceful in dispersing the mobs, many more silent and passive Ninth
Ward families doubtless would have brought their children to school.
While Morrison's equivocations irked both arch-segregationists and liberals and gave the mob license to roam the Ninth Ward, his triangula-
tions sat comfortably with many others in the city who inhabited a sort
of middle ground. Many whites in New Orleans pictured themselves as
suspended between the two extremes of roving white mobs and black
demands for civil rights. Some saw in Morrison what Edwanda and
Charles Macmurdo did: "the quiet voice of sanity." While Morrison's
voice could never have been loud enough to convince Ninth Ward whites
to accept integration, it was too quiet to protect Lloyd Foreman's home
or James Gabrielle's job.[34]

As the Gabrielles made preparations to leave the city, a handful of
other white families brought their children back to Frantz. Marion
McKinley sent two of his children there in the first week of December.
By December 9, the family could count nine times that their windows
had been stoned. "We have moved out of two of our bedrooms and all of
us huddle together at night in one room," Mrs. McKinley noted. A
Mobile native, Marion McKinley moved to study at the New Orleans
Baptist Theological Seminary. Avowedly religious convictions fueled his
family. "We worry about the situation continuously," said McKinley's
Birmingham-born wife. "We are trying to follow God's direction." She
cited other concerns, such as "keeping the family together" and obeying
federal law. "We didn't want this, but . . . we are law-abiding citizens."
Suddenly torn by the school crisis, the McKinleys were driven by their

---

*The anguish of the Foremans and Gabrielles did not go completely unnoticed. The New
Orleans Women's Society of Christian Service pleaded, "Law and Order are not being carried out
in the area of Fran[t]z School. Why are arrests not being made when property is damaged at the
home of the Rev. L. A. Foreman? Or Molestation at the Gabrielle residence?" In addition, a city
sanitation worker named Everett Poling kept two children in Frantz School into December. At
one point, the police did post a twenty-four-hour watch in front of the Poling residence. New
Orleans Women's Society to de Lesseps Morrison (December 7, 1960), de Lesseps Morrison
Papers, City Archives, New Orleans Public Library.

desires to be good Americans and good Christians. Lloyd Foreman found himself encouraged by their actions. A thirty-four-year-old native of Crowley, Louisiana, Foreman did not mention his faith as much as the McKinleys or Daisy Gabrielle—though he based his life and his career on it. Foreman often voiced his belief that the majority of white parents backed the boycott neither in their hearts nor their heads, but were impelled only by fears of violence and ostracism. Gazing at the mob, he reflected, "I can't help but think that the people out there don't represent this city." He hoped that parents and community leaders cowed into silence and submission would soon speak up. "We're not alone in our feelings about the situation . . . but fear has kept so many people away. The voices that need to be heard have been silent—and they need to be heard now."[35]

Margaret and Jim Conner defied the mob, and lost neither home nor job. For this, their tale was remarkable. The Conners were not necessarily stronger than the Gabrielles or the Foremans. Neither were they more clever, more committed, or just plain luckier—but all these things were in some tiny way true. Margaret Conner was born in New Orleans in 1923; her parents and grandparents were also Louisiana natives. Whereas the Gabrielles lived in the Desire Public Housing Project, the Conners owned a house with a front lawn. Frantz was visible from the backyard. Jim Conner worked at Lykes Brothers Shipbuilding, one of the city's first businesses to integrate its workforce. The Conners educated their children in parochial schools until 1958, when it became too expensive and the children transferred back to New Orleans public schools. Out of nine in all, two boys and two girls attended Frantz. Before integration came to New Orleans, Margaret Conner had harbored "mild or unexcited opposition" to school desegregation. "I wasn't brought up to have nigras at school with me or my children." She was shocked when black students entered Frantz. "We never really thought they would do it. . . . I couldn't believe it. First I became angry at the nigras. I figured, why don't they leave well enough alone and tend to their own problems. Lord knows they have enough of them." As Conner maintained, "I wasn't a crusader." But the age of civil rights forced her hand.[36]

Margaret Conner failed to attract the initial attention that Daisy Gabrielle and Lloyd Foreman received—from both the media and the mob—but she brought her four white children to Frantz School just the same. On November 14, Conner received her first phone call from boycotters. Through the rest of the year, she received as many as seventy-five calls on certain days. Conner's decision to send her children to school was less a reasoned choice than a reflexive action. It stemmed not from any views that she possessed about freedom, civil rights, integration, or even education. Or at least it started that way. On Tuesday, November 15, Conner was ready to acquiesce to the boycott. "I was going to stay away, keep my children away, but to tell the truth the idea of having four children home with me, squabbling and making noise and getting into trouble, was too much for me." There were moments when nine children seemed like nine too many—and as if that stress were not enough, she was pregnant at the time. The decision Conner made on that second day of the boycott was one of convenience: it was easier to send four of her children to school than to keep them at home. "I thought . . . maybe things would quiet down, and then we'd all forget one little nigra and our children would go on with school." But when Conner approached Frantz, she saw that the mob had grown overnight. After she witnessed the abuse that Reverend Foreman endured, Conner decided to turn back toward home with her kids. Then she spied the back door to the school, open and welcoming. The mob was "so busy with the minister and shouting at the reporters, they weren't looking at the rear. So I just took the children there and let them go in." At that moment, Conner invested her decision with little meaning. "I thought, 'It's better than their being at home, and better than them listening to those people scream all day from our porch.' It was bad enough *I* had to hear it, and my baby too young for school." Margaret Conner soon came to understand the gravity of her actions. She had unwittingly entered a war.[37]

By the third day of integration, Conner decided to wave the white flag and keep her children home. In the conversation leading to that decision, Jim Conner suggested they move to a different neighborhood so the children might continue to attend public school. But Margaret Conner still believed that the mob might just fade away, that she might bring her children to school without incident. "I said I'd try *one more day*. Maybe the mob would get tired and go away. After all, they had their way— there was only the children of a minister or two left out of five hundred families." She again sneaked her children into school on Wednesday morning. But that afternoon, a few mothers caught a glimpse of Conner when she picked up her children. They "started calling me the worst things I'd ever heard. They followed me home." At that point, Conner came to a realization. "I had the sickening feeling on the way home that I was *in* something, unless I got out real fast." The instant the mob turned its wrath on Conner was the moment she became a crusader. "That night . . . was the turning point." When Conner awakened on November 17, she understood that realities in New Orleans—the existence of school integration, a near-total white boycott, and a vicious mob that now targeted her—presented her with two options, and two options alone. But there was nothing simple about them. "In the morning I couldn't send them, and I couldn't *not*."[38]

Circumstances transformed Margaret Conner into an accidental radical. On Thursday morning, as Conner confronted her impasse, "one woman came here instead of to the school, to swear at me just in case I tried sending the children off." That made Conner's decision for her. "I guess she thought that just her being there would take care of me. Well, it did. I became furious; and I dressed those children as fast as I could and marched them off." The white mob forced Conner to take a stand, and her actions were in large part responsible for the continued integration of New Orleans schools. While Conner's story was dramatic, it was in one sense typical. Of those white southerners who came to accept integration, more were repulsed by segregationist violence than attracted to civil rights demands. Conner detested members of the mobs for their crass tactics, and for their assumption that they could impose their will upon an entire community. Conner despised white coercion far more than she sympathized with black dreams of freedom.[39]

Conner insisted on the accidental nature of the ordeal. "I guess in a sense I did have my way with those mobs. But I didn't plan to, and we were near scared to death most of the time." Conner enjoyed "lucky circumstances," ones that enabled her family to withstand the pressure of the boycott. Most important, Jim Conner enjoyed the backing of his employers. While executives of Lykes Brothers Shipbuilding did not explicitly support the Conners, they took no punitive steps. When Jim Conner's workplace was picketed and threatened, Lykes Brothers officials told him, "We don't understand, but we don't interfere." While James Gabrielle felt pressure to quit his job, Jim Conner dealt with no such dilemma. In time, the Conners learned how to better handle hecklers and abusive mobs. On December 10, two men approached the house. One identified himself as a member of the Citizens' Council, and attempted to persuade Margaret Conner to join the boycott. "I'm not for segregation or for integration," Conner told him. "I'm just for education." Though the Conners were isolated in a neighborhood of resistance, they built their own strength with numbers. Gazing out the window at an ominous crowd, Conner mused, "We are eleven, so we're a mob, too."[40]

There were also times of weakness. Margaret Conner could not always evade the spotlight, and she often pushed through crowds on her way to Frantz. The threatening phone calls also exacted a price. "Yesterday I cried all day long. I'm such a nervous wreck about it." Conner's emotions were conflicted, and they could get the best of her. "My heart is divided, and at the worst of it I thought we'd die, not just from dynamite, but from nervous exhaustion." Conner acknowledged that she eventually helped to break the white boycott of New Orleans public schools, though that was never her intention. "I didn't *mean* to." The viciousness of the mob helped initially to guide her actions. Yet once she took a firm stand, that stand gained a power of its own. Conner's commitment grew as the weeks wore on. Each successive day bore the weight of all those that had come before it, and at a certain point, little could keep the Conner children from Frantz School. "I think I gained my strength each day, so that I was pretty tough in a few months. After a while they didn't scare me one bit. I wouldn't call it brave; it was becoming *determined.* We all of us—my children, my husband, and me—became determined."[41]

Time transformed Conner's initial reflex of convenience into a profound statement about the age of civil rights. While many white southerners believed that "forced integration" endangered their liberties, Conner felt enforced segregation did the same. "I didn't feel any freer than the nigra." Before 1960, she possessed racial views that could only be called traditional for white southerners. Yet those attitudes wilted when she confronted a highly charged situation. The reality of school integration made obsolete Conner's previous opposition. It was a question not of black freedom, but of her own. "I'm just as prejudiced as anyone," she told a reporter. "But all of [a] sudden, after all this, I'm losing some of it." Thinking about the system of Jim Crow, Conner stated, "If I had it to do over, I wouldn't have made this system, but how many people ever have a say about what kind of world they're going to live in." By taking a courageous stand, Margaret Conner did have her say about the world in which she would raise her children. Integration "is bound to come and I'd rather have my children living with it than against it." She looked at a world of milling mobs, vicious epithets, harsh conformity, and abandoned schools—and thought it wrong. In ways both dramatic and subtle, the New Orleans school crisis changed Margaret Conner; in turn, Conner helped to reshape New Orleans. These were the types of changes that the age of civil rights instilled within white southerners. One who mildly opposed desegregation could—with the everyday act of continuing to bring her children to school—become integration's most visible proponent. The change, unforeseeable at first, was in the end undeniable.[42]

The number of white students at Frantz School fluctuated during the 1960–61 school year. After almost all the parents withdrew their children during the first week, enrollment went back up to twenty-three at one point before it fell down to seven. The McDonogh No. 19 boycott was total. John Thompson, an assistant soda fountain manager at Walgreen's, helped to change that. Thompson sent his nine-year-old boy, Gregory, to McDonogh on Friday, January 27. The Ninth Ward stirred that weekend; residents wondered whether Thompson would go through with plans to return his son to the school on Monday. "I didn't send my kid to that school to touch off no integration fuss," Thompson later said. "But I don't want my wife and kids to have to take a lot of guff. And if the cops can't protect 'em, then I will." Thompson not only brought Gregory back to school on Monday, but his other boy—eight-year-old Michael— was also in tow. The next day, segregationist demonstrators picketed Walgreen's—though the manager had already transferred Thompson to a different store location. To make matters worse, Thompson's landlady evicted the family. John Thompson was thirty-three years old at the time; the ex-GI and Native Alabamian made $70 a week to support a family of eight. Facing eviction from his apartment on February 1, Thompson then lost his job. Days later, the Thompsons left New Orleans.[43]

The fate of the Gabrielles and the Thompsons moved and embarrassed some New Orleans citizens. "I am deeply ashamed for our City that two families . . . have been forced to leave us for . . . nothing more than being good Americans and exercising their most obvious rights," Tulane employee James Sweeney wrote to Chep Morrison on February 8. Morrison pointed out that Margaret Conner withstood the pressure of the boycott, and faulted the Gabrielles and the Thompsons for their inability to do the same. "In the case of the Gabrielles, I appealed to the Sewerage and Water Board not to discharge this man, but thereafter he left their employ," Morrison replied. "I received many contributions for the Gabrielles and sent the money on to them. Financially . . . they made out quite well." In Morrison's reading of the situation, the Gabrielles did not look like hapless victims. And "Mr. Thompson was gone from the city before anyone could do anything about him." The mayor then revealed his disdain for the working-class whites of the Ninth Ward. "In this particular section of the city . . . we have found that many of these people are 'floaters.' " They were not genuine New Orleans citizens, Morrison seemed to suggest, perhaps because they did not hail from the Garden District. Their world was more *A Streetcar Named Desire* than *Suddenly, Last Summer.* "They come and they go and they have no real roots in New Orleans, so their parting is of no great moment or importance to them. I am not being critical of the Thompsons or the Gabrielles. . . . However, it is my personal feeling that since they were so prominent in the news—they attracted harassment." This mentality— evinced not only in Mayor Morrison, but among many influential people in New Orleans—allowed the suffering to continue in the Ninth Ward. The chasm between upper- and lower-class whites seemed as wide as the one dividing whites from blacks. New Orleans lawyer Laurence Daspit pleaded, to little avail, "that those who are to blame will see the futility and injustice of the white man punishing the white man in order to hurt others."[44]

At times, it was difficult to know whom to blame. Supporters of the school boycott ruthlessly drove their adversaries from the city. But in a different light, one could see the boycotters themselves as victims—in thrall to the prejudice of their own upbringing, to their poor lot in life, and to the dominant idea of segregation. The school crisis bred many citizen-sociologists. Rabbi Leo Bergman tried to explain the events in his city to the New York–based Union of American Hebrew Congrega- tions. "Try to see the picture, not as you see it on television, but as it is actually taking place here. These people are . . . of not too much educa- tion and not too much understanding of the influences that play upon them. It is an old story in the South that the poor have always been thrown the Negro as bait by the politically ambitious." Bergman revived images of demagogues like Mississippi governor and senator James Var- daman, Eugene Talmadge, and generations of southern politicians who maintained power by setting poor whites against blacks—and against one another. "These people are apt to raise themselves . . . by looking down upon the Negro. . . . It is the only strata that they can consider lower than themselves." Some of this was groundless stereotyping, but some of it was truth. As Margaret Conner contended, class concerns joined with racial ones:

There were all those poor people who were living in the Desire Project. . . . I always felt one of the reasons that they got out in the streets and did what they did was because they didn't have too many people below them. Sometimes you've got to feel like you're top dog, and they didn't have too much. So they wanted to say, "You can't do this to my school. I'll walk out."

Bitterness ran deep. "I can't justify my feelings on any ground, intellectual, moral, or religious," admitted one young parochial school father who opposed integration. "Sooner or later I will have to face the same problems, when our parochial schools are integrated. I'll hate myself for it but I'll yank my kids out of school even if it means excommunication. . . . Why? Why? Why? I keep asking myself, do I oppose integration. . . . Because I know I'm better than they are. I just know it!"[45]

While many whites opposed integration, the tumult it brought could force change. "I am not an integrationist," wrote Neil Lindley, and neither were most whites in New Orleans. "But if the women demonstrators at Frantz school are segregationists I am certainly not that either." Raucous mobs peeled away any layers of respectability from the pro-segregation position. And they threw many whites who thought they inhabited a middle ground into the flames of a revolution. "I am the mother of three children who are caught in the web of the New Orleans integration order," Mrs. Dan Pique wrote days after Thanksgiving. Pique did not "belong to any group for or against integration," but, she acknowledged, "All too soon I found myself involved." Consistent court rulings, extreme actions of mobs on New Orleans streets, and legislators in Baton Rouge spun a sticky web that netted many parents, children, and teachers.[46]

LIKE WHITE FAMILIES, teachers in the Ninth Ward responded to integration in diverse ways. Some of them simply fled. "The inevitable result of forced integration has driven many white qualified teachers to leave the profession," Julie Skoglund wrote to the *Times-Picayune.* Leo Scharfenstein was one teacher who eventually left McDonogh because of desegregation. Scharfenstein saw himself in a trap similar to the ones that ensnared parents and children. "We were in the same position. . . . We were having something forced on us that we really had no choice in." Scharfenstein soon took a job at Arabi Elementary School in St. Bernard—a new school geared specifically toward boycotting Frantz and McDonogh students.

Josie Ritter, a teacher at Frantz, took the opposite tack. Ritter decided to remain at Frantz for the year, but she endured obscene phone calls and drove home from school under police escort each day. "I never dreamed that these people would all pull their children out of school," Ritter admitted. And when they did, teachers confronted difficult choices. In the legislature's efforts to stymie the Orleans Parish School Board, it withheld funds for teachers' salaries. On December 8, 1,300 employees of the New Orleans school system went unpaid; miraculously, an anonymous donor soon volunteered the money. Again on December 22, the legislature adjourned for its Christmas vacation without paying 4,000 New Orleans teachers. "We feel that the teachers have been forced into a squeeze play and they are being made to suffer for merely doing their duty," said Sarah Reed, an official of the New Orleans Classroom Teachers' Federation. Most eventually received their pay, but not before months of depending upon family and friends. "Not very often do professional men and women find themselves unexpectedly . . . in a severe social crisis that challenges the delicate and often undefined relationship between personal beliefs and occupational activity," psychologist Robert Coles wrote. The age of civil rights brought just such a crisis to New Orleans, and desegregation unraveled the tenuous connection between teachers' beliefs and their jobs—or, in Sarah Reed's language, their mere duty.[47]

In the tumult of mobs and legal wars, teachers were as deeply affected as anyone. Many maintained that obligations to their jobs trumped any personal views they held. "The crowds outside wanted *me* to boycott the schools, too," said one teacher. "And I was with them, then, to be truthful . . . I was opposed to desegregation. But I had my job . . . and I just couldn't walk out of the building like that." Instead, teachers took the hands of Pamela Foreman and Ruby Bridges—and persisted despite the upheaval all around them. One Frantz teacher reflected on how the mobs outside upended her nominally segregationist views. "Who can ever forget the looks on those faces?" she recalled three years later. "I always thought I was a segregationist, but I never heard such language, and they became so impossible after a while that they belonged in a zoo, not on the streets. That little nigra child had more dignity than all of them put together." When racial unrest besieged teachers, it could force novel realizations and upend lifelong attitudes.[48]

The white children who left public schools and the black students who entered them were products of the same social forces. Paul Patterson was one white pupil who boycotted Frantz in 1960, and his mother joined the mob that congregated there every morning. The Pattersons had come to New Orleans from a Mississippi farm. Robert Coles described Mrs. Patterson as sad, frightened, obese, bigoted, and typical. "There is no very special reason why this woman joined a mob and said what she did while its member. When I asked her why she joined she replied with conventional hatred for Negroes, not unlike those of other people who never have joined mobs." Life wore Patterson down. "I have enough to do just to keep going and keep us alive." School integration was an added intrusion that taxed an already burdened family. Patterson withdrew her son from Frantz on November 14, and enrolled him in a private school. The Pattersons' story could serve as a model for hundreds of other Frantz and McDonogh families.[49]

While many white families endured great strain, it rarely compared with the pressures that engulfed the Bridges family. Abon Bridges, a Korean War veteran who had earned a Purple Heart, brought his family to New Orleans from the Mississippi Delta in 1958. His daughter Ruby was four years old at the time. The family moved to the Ninth Ward, and rented the front section of a rooming house on France Street. The Bridges could scarcely have predicted the chain reaction that occurred after they agreed to enroll Ruby at an integrated school. They never once guessed that Ruby would be the only black child in that school, let alone that she could so divide their recently adopted city. Abon Bridges soon lost his job at a neighborhood service station. It took the school crisis for Bridges to learn the depths of the hatred that lived in his boss. "I'd give my life to keep the races separate," the service station owner stated. Yet it was not Bridges whom the man most detested. "It's some of those mixing whites who are the cause of this." The fall of 1961 found the Pattersons no longer able to afford private school. That year, Paul Patterson and Ruby Bridges attended Frantz School together. From Mississippi farms to the Ninth Ward of New Orleans, the Patterson and Bridges families trod parallel paths. One migration brought them both to the Big Easy, and one social revolution blew them far apart.[50]

The school crisis overturned everyday life in New Orleans. Chep Morrison claimed that New Orleans residents were impervious to the trouble over integration, but all signs suggested otherwise. As Morrison wrote to a correspondent in December 1960, "It is my sincere wish that you could be here on the scene to witness just how little is going on. Less than 100 people have taken part in the demonstrations and . . . some 627,000 people, are routinely going about their every day business." Yet Morrison could not live his own lie. He admitted in one letter, "This has brought about a drastic social change which has stirred the emotions of most citizens." In another he wrote, "I pray and hope that things will clear up soon and that our wonderful city and people will once again return to its old way of life." In Morrison's assertions, one could almost hear James Gray and the city commissioners of Albany, Georgia, telling the citizenry that the town would not be turned "upside down," even as social upheaval was plain as day. Morrison claimed that everyday life proceeded normally, just as he acknowledged his city to be in the throes of a "drastic social change."[51]

Through the New Orleans school crisis, Morrison displayed the ability to straddle fences. He pleased only those who had no strong views on integration in the first place—and they proved to be a substantial number. Nancy Jones counted herself a member of "the unvocal majority, whose voices [seem] lost in the tumult." Jones claimed a "vast majority of the residents" supported Morrison's position. While Jones bemoaned the loss of her "rights" at the hands of federal judges, she believed the courts were still the proper forums for resistance—not the streets. Reflecting many other constituents' views, Morrison was no friend of integration. He vented to a northern letter-writer who dared pass judgment on his city: "I stand for segregation in the South because we have such a preponderance of Negroes here. When the Negroes have as good facilities, then the Whites have a right to protest. It is not a matter of civil rights; rather, it is a matter of evolution of the cranium and subsequent capacity to learn." Elected mayor in 1946, Chep Morrison presided over the postwar industrial and population booms that transformed New Orleans. The city reached its peak population in 1960. Morrison lost a gubernatorial bid that year, and finally left the mayor's office under the cloud of the school crisis—a crisis that helped to expedite a gradual retreat to the suburbs. In 1961, he accepted the post of U.S. ambassador to the Organization of American States. City councilors voted in Victor Schiro, one of their own, to fill Morrison's unexpired term.[52]

New Orleans welcomed the new mayor in 1961, opened the doors of Preservation Hall, and integrated four more schools. To many families, that last development was the most pressing. The school board was careful not to duplicate its error of the previous year. It integrated schools in wealthier neighborhoods, including the Uptown area. All summer, Schiro fielded letters from anxious parents. To them, images of violence were less fading memories than frightening possibilities. Most parents accepted the fact of desegregation, and requested guarantees of their children's safety. One Robert Lusher School parent wrote Schiro "to request your insistence on maintaining discipline and safety when school opens. . . . All will be well if agitators from other parts of the city are prevented from creating disturbances." Nelda Clements had one daughter at McMain High School, and two younger children at Lusher. She recounted how difficult it was to watch the violence in the Ninth Ward the previous year. "I feel I have no choice morally, or from any other viewpoint, but to send my children to school as usual on September 7th." But those who viewed school integration as a moral issue were in the minority. Many more New Orleans whites shared the opinions of Ann Huey, the parent of two Lusher students. "I do not wish their school to be *integrated,* but if it is to be so, I choose the right to continue sending them there without harassment from segregationist mobs. . . . Preserve for us our rights." Many whites feared desegregation, but they feared violence far more.[53]

The horrors of 1960 weighed heavily on New Orleans whites. Yet not everyone agreed about what constituted the worst of it. To one city resident who wrote Schiro, integration itself was the menace. "Keep our school segregated," he urged. A father in the Members of the Dads and Mothers Club had a similar view. "Do not make the mistake that Morrison made la[s]t year at McDonogh 19 school, by turning the hose on our Mothers. Wives and children. Last year two of our expecting mothers was two of the victims." The Ninth Ward Private School Association, formed during the first days of integration, published a pamphlet in June 1961 featuring caricatures of two confused white children beneath the caption "Dispossessed!" The association wished to construct a school for the one thousand white students "dispossessed" of Frantz and McDonogh. It solicited donations with the plea " 'Buy a Foot of Freedom' Today," and framed the battle in terms of the children's welfare. "The surest way to insure that *your* children will not be embroiled in this integration war is to help defend these children who are on the front line of this terrible mess." It warned white parents throughout the city, "Unless this effort succeeds, your children may be affected next. It's EVERYBODY's fight." With the 1960 New Orleans school crisis barely over, its legacy was already contested. The meaning of freedom for white southerners stood at the center of the controversy. Almost all agreed that liberty was the ability to select a child's school. Disputes revolved around whether that school could exclude blacks, and whether police ought to enforce integration or prevent it. Almost everybody warned Schiro to heed the lessons of the previous year and avoid a repeat of history. But they all perceived different lessons, and remembered different histories.[54]

By 1961, those who accepted token integration began to find their voices. Defending the children did not mean building private schools, they argued, but protecting the right to public education. "You cannot imagine what the parents of Frantz children who wanted their children to go to school had to endure," Anne Dlugos wrote to Schiro. "The stories were not exaggerated. Their jobs, lives, children's lives were threatened, windows were broken, tires slashed and even older brothers in other schools physically and verbally attacked. . . . PLEASE take a strong stand NOW for law and order." On August 16, in the *Times-Picayune,* Schiro detailed his plan to keep the peace. Many citizens argued that the image of New Orleans itself was at stake. Dlugos wrote, "N.O. will not be disgraced again this fall." Lysle Aschaffenburg, president of the Pontchartrain Hotel, expressed his concern about the harm that another disgrace could inflict. "It has always been a great joy for me to tell people everywhere that I am from New Orleans," Aschaffenburg stated. "It has always worked like magic and people always reacted in a very responsive way. . . . All this was true until the school episodes took place. . . . And now I find that everywhere I go I am on the defensive and the great image that New Orleans projected . . . has . . . been badly hurt." Convinced of the potential calamity, Schiro warned again that violence would not be tolerated. On September 1, the A. H. Wilson School Cooperative Club sent a letter to parents. It claimed that a "large majority" of Wilson children would return that year, and offered parents advice on how to maintain order. Still, nobody knew precisely what would happen on September 7. The general outlook seemed optimistic, but the possibility of a Third Battle of New Orleans still lingered.[55]

New Orleans native Marion Bourdette was thirty-six years old in 1961, and her eldest child was enrolled in the second grade at Wilson School. "All summer long there was a lot of tension in the neighborhood." Against her father's pleas, Bourdette decided to keep her child at Wilson—integration or not. On the first day, enrollment dropped from 650 to 200. Along with anxiety about integration and violence, a bomb scare chased away many students. It was a day of trepidation, an experience that words could scarcely render. Books and articles "just couldn't begin to capture what it was like for the parents to know that we're gonna walk through" police barricades and throngs of reporters, unsure of what would happen. "There were policemen and dogs and television cameras and pickets and it was a very scary thing. . . . A lot of people left . . . they were just terrified. And one . . . lady walked down the street with me and said, 'I am shaking all over, I am so afraid.' " Marion Bourdette's walk to school on September 7 was a mixture of high drama and everyday routine. "People acted like the end of the world would happen if the schools integrated. . . . My attitude was if you were gonna live in a city that was 50 percent black, then you should know how to get along with them." Most of the students quickly returned to an integrated Wilson School. While Bourdette continued to send her child to school, friends and family members disapproved. "Oh, you can't send your children to school with Negroes, they'll begin to talk like them," they taunted. "My children don't talk like them. . . . The students for the most part got along well." Bourdette's child took the change in stride.[56]

As students adjusted to integration, parents and teachers fled. Blacks could peacefully attend desegregated schools, but their presence spurred a gradual—and eventually unstoppable—migration of whites to more exclusive neighborhoods, suburbs, and private schools. The contours of education in New Orleans began a radical shift. Teachers at Wilson "saw the handwriting on the wall," Bourdette said, and in the spring of 1962 many asked for transfers to heavily white areas. Claire Chauviere had taught in the public schools for forty-eight years. Then, in the late 1960s, "it became more and more black and more difficult to manage." Chauviere retired, while other teachers and parents gravitated to suburban Jefferson Parish. Margaret and Jim Conner, who in 1962 left the Ninth Ward for the suburbs, were part of that same wave.[57]

By March 1962, 150 children attended Frantz School in peaceful, if partial, integration. Compared with the violence and anxiety that permeated the Ninth Ward during 1960, it seemed a new day had dawned. In September 1962, the city's parochial schools integrated. By the start of the 1964 school year, still only 809 black children attended 31 formerly all-white New Orleans schools. And the city's white population rapidly decreased. In 1968, whites made up 31 percent of the public school population—compared to 43 percent in 1960. So many families had moved or enrolled their children in private schools that, by 1974, New Orleans public schools were only 19 percent white. Although whites no longer boycotted New Orleans schools, they achieved similar ends.[58]

A revolution of sorts had taken place in New Orleans. Those years left an indelible mark on thousands of citizens. The New Orleans school crisis afforded a glimpse into how white southerners responded to the pressures of the age of civil rights—and how diverse those responses were. School integration created white mobs and abandoned schools, but it also produced accidental radicals like Daisy Gabrielle and Margaret Conner. Civil rights struggles forced conflicts within white communities, and within white individuals. When centuries of prejudice collided with new realities, attitudes met everyday life—and the necessities of the latter at times overwhelmed and destroyed the former in untold ways. Episodes of integration did not just push people toward support of civil rights or segregation, but created new spectrums. They asked what one would do when the ground of everyday life shifted, and when one's children were asked to contest that terrain. "I realized . . . we, too, had lived through a revolution," Marion Bourdette said in 1981. "A total social change." She repeated the word, as if it was difficult to believe someone like her had been part of such important changes. "It is truly like we've had a total revolution. The fact that we've come through as unscarred and as able to get along as we can I think is sort of remarkable." It was not a revolution that numbers could measure—either in pupil counts or in years elapsed. The distance from the fall of 1960 to the spring of 1962, or 1972, was best measured not in weeks or months, but in generations. One white girl who returned to a boycotted school in 1961 reflected on how integration changed students, both black and white. "For us white people it will be different, too: when we're parents, we won't talk about the colored the same way our parents did, so naturally our children will grow up with different ideas on the subject of race." The South's sons and daughters held the promises and pitfalls of the future in their hands.[59]

3

IN THE 1960s, universities across America pulsed with the spirit of protest. While students at Berkeley and Columbia captured headlines in the middle and late 1960s, they were not the first to revolt. Earlier in the decade, whites on southern campuses rebelled against the orders of distant courts as well as against the black students they found suddenly in their midst. Through their eyes and stories, school integration became not fundamentally a tale of legal battles, politics, or even parents and families—but of the students themselves, trapped between adolescence and adulthood, between the heritage of their segregationist upbringings and the new racial realities at their schools. Campuses became crucibles in the battle over Jim Crow. Some white children felt thrown into the fires of the time; many others started campus fires of their own.

A year before a riot at Ole Miss attracted federal troops and claimed lives, students at the University of Georgia staged a violent struggle of their own. Few Georgians foresaw that the showdowns over the state's public schools—previously waged between Atlanta parents and supporters of Governor Vandiver—might be settled on the Athens campus, the jewel of Georgia's public education system. In January 1961, Judge William Bootle ruled on the case of two black Atlantans, Charlayne Hunter and Hamilton Holmes, ordering that they attend UGA right away—not in the coming fall, as many had expected. The reaction of white UGA students was immediate. Two hundred of them congregated at the Arch in the center of campus, sang "Dixie," and hanged Holmes in effigy. "We don't like integration being crammed down our throats," said one demonstrator. Public opinion on campus was sharply divided. While Charlie Christian, senior class president, contended, "The majority of the students favor keeping the university open at any cost," fraternity council president Tommy Burnside had a different majority in mind. "I am confident that an overwhelming majority of my classmates will . . . do anything within local reason to maintain segregation of the university." As Vandiver threatened to close the university before Holmes and Hunter could matriculate, many students realized their dilemma. "I'd rather not have it [integration]," said sorority president Carill Morris, "but I'd rather have it than . . . the schools close." Perhaps Tommy Close's mix of feelings best represented the complex emotions and thoughts that swirled within many students. "I'm very distressed that they should try to force something on us," the student council president remarked. "One or two Negro students aren't going to bother me personally but I don't feel that they will ever graduate." In the end, segregation was not the paramount priority. "Of course I don't want the schools to close."[60]

Hamilton Holmes arrived in Athens on Saturday morning, January 7, to begin the registration process. Holmes and Hunter would not be greeted with open arms. As Carill Morris said of Hunter, "I would be friendly to her myself, but there are a lot of girls who are against it. I don't think she'll be very happy here, but if she's coming, she's coming, I guess." The majority preferred a school with Holmes and Hunter to no school at all. On January 8, students held a vigil for open schools in the university's chapel. They collected 2,776 names on a petition—well over a third of a student body of 7,400. Burnside led an opposition movement to keep the university segregated, but things seemed placid in Athens that Sunday night. "Except for the circulation of petitions, life on the sprawling 160-year-old college campus appeared very quiet," the *Atlanta Constitution* reported. "Pretty little coeds and their male companions . . . were concentrating mainly on . . . hamburgers and French fries, and each other." As Monday morning approached, that serenity soon gave way to chaos.[61]

By the end of the day on January 9, Holmes and Hunter were registered. Vandiver ordered UGA closed, but university president O. C. Aderhold claimed he never received official word of the governor's order and kept the school open. Vandiver's action angered some; others were upset by the presence of Holmes and Hunter. That night, more than one thousand students protested. The first day of class was Wednesday, January 11, and white Georgians held their breath. Some despaired that their state's university was falling victim to integration; others prayed that students would resist the temptation of violence. *Atlanta Constitution* columnist Harold Martin penned an open letter to his son, a UGA student. "These last few days have been exciting ones for you and for all your fellows, I know, just as they have been trying and troubled ones for me and for all other parents who have sons and daughters at the university. . . . You are just a freshman . . . and in normal times freshmen don't amount to much." But these were epochal times. Integration forced children to grow up quickly. "In a crisis like this, a man is a man, no matter whether he is a freshman o[r] a senior." Martin hoped his son would carry himself with dignity, and sought to persuade UGA students to accept the ruling. "If the law says that Negro students must be admitted to the University, that's that, and no amount of flag waving and shouting and marching . . . is going to change it." Similarly, many whites around the state urged students to accept integration with grace.[62]

To Ralph McGill, the very image of the white southerner was in Georgia students' hands. "Students at the U. of Georgia have the God-sent opportunity to do a service for the South which we all love. . . . To erase the picture of the 'Ugly Southerner' so starkly and disturbingly shown the nation and the world at Little Rock and New Orleans." McGill deplored those Cheerleaders in the Big Easy, women "slattern" and "vicious." "The ugly Southerner is not the true Southerner," McGill wrote, hoping his belief could help create that fact. Many wondered which face of the white South, the lewd or the dignified, would appear at Athens. Georgia students faced a situation larger than they could have imagined. The question at hand was less how to preserve the open and segregated school they all desired than how to handle imminent integration. "Some things are bigger than all of us," asserted Terry Hazelwood of UGA's *Red and Black,* the student newspaper. Violent demonstrations "won't change a thing; at least in the way we want them changed." All around Athens, many sensed the weight of the moment. "History is being made," a minister had told students on Sunday night. "It is up to us what kind it will be."[63]

That Wednesday, Georgia students came closer to infamy than glory. Although classes started in January, it was the middle of basketball season, and Georgia faced a bitter rival, Georgia Tech, on the night of January 11. The game went to overtime, and Georgia Tech prevailed when the buzzer sounded minutes before 10:00 p.m. An angry group stormed its way to Center-Myers Hall, Charlayne Hunter's dormitory. The outcome of the game led some observers to claim that a mob formed spontaneously, as much in reaction to basketball as to integration. In fact, almost everyone on campus knew that students planned to encircle Center-Myers that night. Some claimed, furthermore, that the Klan and other extremist groups had plotted the siege—but if the Klan had a hand in the protest, it was a small one. In the 1960s, areas around Athens gained a reputation as hotbeds for racist groups. But on that January night, university students led the resistance to integration. Estimates of the mob's number range from 500 to 2,000. At the very least, hundreds of students shouted, toted signs, and flung bricks and rocks through windows of the dorm. At one point, all of the lights went out in the dorm except for those in Hunter's room, so as to provide an easy target—an episode that further suggested the riot was a planned affair. Hunter had already fled her room. William Tate, the dean of men, was the only university official who confronted the mob. He berated groups of students and seized their identification cards. Hours passed before police dispersed the crowd with tear gas and fire hoses. Dean of Students Joseph Williams, acting on Vandiver's orders, suspended Holmes and Hunter "for their own safety." For a night, the mob prevailed.[64]

Afterward, students spoke like victors. "There was some embarrassment but the purpose was accomplished," Joe Collins boasted. "And if they come back it'll happen again." According to P. Wendell Calhoun, Jr., "It was emotionally good for everybody. But it went too far." Incensed by the federal courts, many students echoed a statement made by William Kidd: "That's all we had left. The courts struck down any effort the governor made." Students believed the courts had deprived them of any peaceful options. Kidd, a Thomasville native, told a *Newsweek* reporter, "I know the guys who threw the first bricks, and they aren't any rednecks. They're just guys who feel strongly about this thing . . . they were just real frustrated guys. The rock throwing was bad but the good of the demonstration out weighed the bad. . . . I was there. I think it was justified." Many of the state's best and brightest students agreed.[65]

Other Georgians thought the mob not only wrong, but repulsive. Atlanta resident Peggy Dunbar's letter reflected the humiliated tone of many published in the *Constitution*. "The white students would have been a credit to their race if they had conducted themselves as well as Charlayne Hunter and Hamilton Holmes." On January 13, Judge Bootle ordered Holmes and Hunter reinstated. They returned to school on January 16. A test was scheduled for the following day in Professor Thomas Brahana's calculus class, Math 254. Brahana saw that his students were still visibly shaken by the events of the previous week. Instead of administering the exam, Brahana assigned the class an essay on one question: "What do you think of integration?" Their answers present vital glimpses of the ways white students experienced the last days of Jim Crow.* As a whole, the essays reveal a rare and unadulterated torment and candor. These students did not write for public consumption,

---

*These essays are housed in the Hargrett Library at the University of Georgia. Thus far, only one scholar has focused on this rich resource. See Robert Cohen, "Two, Four, Six, Eight, We Don't Want to Integrate: White Student Attitudes Toward the University of Georgia's Desegregation," *Georgia Historical Quarterly*, Vol. 80, No. 3 (Fall 1996). Cohen points out that the racial attitudes of white southern students have rarely been analyzed. "Even the best accounts of desegregation on Deep South campuses largely neglect the mindset of southern students. . . . To this day we know almost nothing about the racial ideas that prevailed among white students (or their teachers) at southern campuses."

or to be published. For these reasons, their names need not be disclosed—although initials can help to distinguish one author from another. The essays reveal nothing if not the multiplicity of white southern experiences in the age of civil rights—experiences forged on the front lines of the struggle.[66]

Few of the UGA students, no more than thirteen or fourteen years old at the time of *Brown v. Board of Education,* had any inkling how that decision would affect their lives. "Since the Supreme Court ruling of 1954 . . . I have realized that one day [integration] must come to Georgia," TT wrote. "I never thought I would be as personally involved in the matter as I now find myself." What long loomed as an abstract threat began to define campus reality. Contrasting the upheaval of the 1960s to the Civil War a century before, JA wrote, "In the year 1961 another war is also taking place. The center of the action is at the University of Georgia." Students saw the university as the battleground, and themselves as pawns. "I am caught up in this . . . battle due to the fact that I attend the University of Georgia." JA trusted in segregation, as he did most other childhood lessons. "I believe strongly in segregation. This is because I have been reared in a section of the world where there was no form of integration." This student claimed to know blacks well. "I know the Negroes of the South, and when taken as a group, they do not have the higher moral, educational, and ambitional standards of the white race. This belief was inherited by me from my ancestors who gave their lives that the Southern way of life shall live." The ghosts of the Civil War still haunted the Athens campus, as did myths about "our Negroes."[67]

Old racial views animated many UGA students. "I know colored people, most of them servants or workers on the farm," read one anonymous essay. "I . . . have lived among Negroes all my life," another maintained. "Some of my playmates when I was a little boy were Negroes. . . . I know and understand the Negroes." Most students in the class subscribed to TT's belief that "they have their place; we have ours." An unsigned essay read, "The majority are happy and content over the way things used to be. . . . The majority of the Negroes do not want to go to school with us." Sambos inhabited many minds. "A hundred years ago the Negroes were freed from slavery," DW wrote. "They have been given an opportunity to better themselves, but they do not seem to want to. Most of the Negroes are happy living the lives they do." These types of racial views were particularly strong among students who hailed from Georgia's Black Belt:

I was born and raised in Southwest Georgia, where the white man dominates the colored people. . . . I don't want integration . . . and . . . I know the majority of the colored people in Georgia do not want to mix with white people. I have worked with and lived around Negroes all my life. I was . . . looked after by a Negro woman 10 hours out of the day every day for 12 years. I pretty well know what the colored people want and don't want. They're happy where they are.

In effect, the essays were autobiographies. To answer the question "What do you think of integration?" most students went back to what they had absorbed in their youth. Another South Georgia native, HS, began by narrating his childhood lessons. "All my life I have been told that segregation is right, it has been, and always will be in effect, and that if for some reason this . . . was broken down our way of life would be destroyed forever." Most students believed blacks were inferior, and categorically claimed that they "knew Negroes." These same students were just as blunt about their unwillingness to sacrifice their education for those shibboleths. The civil rights movement turned theoretical questions about race relations into practical ones about day-to-day life, and the intangible comforts of traditional beliefs could dissolve in the face of that challenge.[68]

Sentences after insisting "They are happy where they are," an anonymous student completed the transition from theory to practice. "I want my education and I'll get it if I have to go to school with the negro." One could believe racial myths and also tolerate an integrated school. "I'm here to get an education, not to worry about who is sitting next to me." For some, socioeconomic realities made a university education difficult to attain—and the prospect of a closed school frightening. "I come from a family of very modest means," wrote Athens native JB. "I had to work for a year after graduating high school before I had enough money even to enter college . . . the University of Georgia is the only place I can afford to attend." His education could never be sacrificed. "A college education is the most important thing for me. My whole future depends on it." As JG put it, "Not being especially wealthy I cannot afford to throw away 3 years of education." While some poor white families in New Orleans paid private tuition for their children, UGA students decried any such idea. They invested their future in the state's top public university, and no segregationist leader was going to close their school—certainly not because of two black students in a sea of 7,400 whites.[69]

For the majority of Georgia students, token integration was less a question of finances than one of inevitable social changes. As Margaret Conner said in December 1960, integration "is bound to come and I'd rather have my children living with it than against it." Many UGA students adopted that sort of temperament. While such a stance made Conner a radical in New Orleans, it made many UGA students conformists. They resignedly accepted token integration. Out of the thirty-four essayists in Brahana's class, more than half included the phrase "integration is inevitable." Most supported legal resistance to integration—but when it became clear that desegregation could not be stopped, they made an about-face and agreed to adapt. A belief in law and order often buttressed that position. One student wrote, "I do not want to go to school with Negroes but I will not disobey the laws which protect me." Almost all of those who noted integration's inevitability also loathed violence. Integration "is inevitable," JA II stated. "I do not believe in closing down the schools or making a big fuss about it." As JB wrote, "Integration is coming, period, and the sooner it is done and forgotten about the better off everyone will be." JB hoped white southerners would adjust to desegregation as they would any other shift in the course of life. But that might prove difficult. "Integration is inevitable, but I definitely feel that neither the Southern Negroes nor the Southern white people are ready for it," an anonymous essay read.[70]

Few attached any sort of moral judgment to the belief that integration was inevitable. It was simply not an issue that could be fought any longer. "I regret the situation but suggest that all the people of the South can do is to accept it," MHC wrote. "I am all against integration," wrote RC, "but I am all for making the best of it since it is here." Many agreed with the anonymous student who wrote, "We should fight integration every legal way possible, but when it is ordered upon us by the federal courts there is nothing we can do but accept." A measured indifference coursed through the essays, alongside a youthful adaptability to a changing world. HS wrote, "It is inevitable, and whether right or wrong it must be accepted, and will be in the end." While some students refused to attach the words "right" or "wrong" to integration—in the same way that nobody would attach those labels to the lakes or the trees—others hoped acceptance of the inevitable would force deeper acknowledgment.

"As GLC put it, "Negroes are human just as we are." In that same class-room, a handful of students vowed they would never admit any such thing.[71]

Some "lived against" integration, and voiced crass racial stereotypes. "The Negro has an average of one-eighth of an inch more bone thickness on his skull," wrote PC. She considered blacks "shiftless and undepend-able," cited their "jungle instinct," and stated that black students were dupes of the NAACP. Sexual fears drove another student's views. "This is the point I feel most strongly about. . . . In college I feel that the women will be protected better if they don't have to dodge colored boys during the course of the day." In many of these bigoted notions, blacks were depicted as lazy, primitive, and out for white women. AS stated, "I do not personally desire to associate with persons of low moral character," and as proof of blacks' "character" listed "their brand new Cadillac stand-ing in the yard at their one room [tenant] house (neither paid for yet). . . . The frequent number of court cases involving Negro stubborn-ness, wife beating, drunken driving," and "General Sanitation." AS thought white students could still prevent integration, but knew that violence would work against that goal. "Violence only hastens court action and public opinion to integrate." Whether or not students ac-cepted integration, almost all of them deplored the riot that broke out six nights before.[72]

While a small segment of students continued to cling to traditional stereotypes, a similarly small percentage saw through those myths and gave expression to an eloquent dissent. They questioned the wisdom of segregationist politicians, argued the meaning of American freedom, pointed out the paradoxes of separate social systems, and even supported outright integration and civil rights. An anonymous student did not "consider the issue as political, but as moral. I can't understand how some people can consider themselves better than other people." This author admitted that blacks generally lived in worse conditions than whites, "but the reason for this is that the whites have kept them at this low level. I can't see how people who call themselves citizens of a democ-racy can allow these conditions to exist." University of Georgia students disagreed about the contours of American democracy. "A federal judge took away states' rights," GB wrote, "this is wrong and does not make up a democracy." Did true liberty lie in the right of whites to exclude blacks, or of blacks to attend classes with whites? For the students in Math 254, these were open questions. And some could not quite understand why the question existed in the first place. "It seems downright stupid to have segregation," JA II wrote, and noted the waste involved in erecting twin water fountains, schools, and restrooms across the region. If so many whites boasted that they had grown up with blacks and considered them friends, he asked, why were so few willing to attend school with them? "It is still hard to understand why integration is being fought against so violently because 9 out of 10 of the Southern people have been practically integrated with the Negro all their lives. . . . What I can't understand is why we don't mind eating with the Negroes in the kitchen but we wouldn't want to eat with them in the dining room." To this second-generation Georgian, the situation smacked of the absurd.[73]

One essay was blunt in its support for civil rights. "My personal belief is that integration is right," DC wrote. "I, being a south Georgian, have heard the cry, 'Do you want your daughters to marry a nigger?' and 'The Supreme Court is trying to kill the white race in the South' and the other usual statements until it makes me sick." All that was mindless. "There is no possible way to sanely defend segregation." Other backers of integration came to their conclusions in more conflicted, even tortured ways. "When I consider integration, I find myself in mental conflict," read one unsigned essay. "Our Southern doctrine of 'white superiority' . . . has been hammered into my head for the entire time of my life and, yet, I cannot seem to reconcile myself to it." Blacks had been "downtrodden" and "debased," the student asserted, reaching a wrenching conclusion. "I must admit that this is a statement that is quite hard to write, I believe that the only way the Negro will be able to climb up from the hole that we have thrust him in is by his being permitted to secure a[n] education which is exactly that of the white men." Such egalitarianism would not come free of turmoil. "With it will come cries of anguish—the anguish of the great unwashed, no longer 'superior' to anyone."[74]

An invocation of "the great unwashed" highlighted the concern among UGA students with members of their own race. Violent bigotry alternately embarrassed and frightened them. "In the past two weeks, I have seen and heard things that made me very angry and sometimes even ashamed of the race I belong to," one wrote. "I've seen students who were willing to throw away their education, damage their state, and practically destroy their future." Once again, violence transformed previously indifferent whites into advocates of integration. "I welcome integration wholeheartedly when my education is at stake." After Hamilton Holmes and Charlayne Hunter came to the Georgia campus, little remained the same. Students began to reexamine what they cherished—and for most of them, that was a "normal" or "ordinary" college experience. "I do not *hate* these two illustrious members of the Negroid race who are now going to school with me," TT wrote. "I do hate the ugly violence, the unstrung nerves . . . that they have . . . brought about." Only a minority of students loathed Holmes and Hunter themselves; many more hated the controversy that the two new Bulldogs brought to the surface of southern life. Few students had grappled with integration before Holmes and Hunter thrust the issue to the fore, and many attempted to remain apathetic throughout the ordeal. As one essay read, "I can't really say if I've ever sat down and thought about it," but "I *know* my feelings aren't so strong that I would go out and throw a rock at somebody." The vast majority tried to greet integration with this calculated indifference. "Even if I had a strong feeling against integration what is there I could do about it. Play Caveman and throw rocks. NO!!!" In the popular imagination of many Georgia students, those who violently resisted integration tilted at windmills, closed schools with hostile futility, and resorted to the coarse tactics of Neanderthals.[75]

School integration jolted whites from indifference and made passivity difficult. When mobs rampaged, many students wished they could remain above the fray. "I personally don't care whether or not they integrate," JG confided, "just as long as they get it over with and let us go back to our studies." CC hoped that "everybody would leave us alone so things would calm down, and we could do some studying." Above all, most white southerners wanted to protect their daily routines. Integration, "as all can see, if they open their eyes, is bound to happen," wrote an anonymous student. "It is best not to let it hurt our lives too much." While whites in Albany had denied the inevitability of integration when King and SNCC entered town, they—like the UGA students—tried not to let it "hurt" their lives too much. In the midst of the New Orleans school crisis, Chep Morrison claimed his city was similarly immune to ruptures in its day-to-day routine. Yet at its most powerful, the experience of integration upset everyday life and challenged ingrained attitudes. As JB wrote, "My segregationist views and thoughts have given way considerably to the fact that I want a college education more than anything else in the world." To retain his college lifestyle, this student transformed his worldview. In changes like these, many glimpsed a new Dixie. "I dare say that 'the next ten years will bring about more changes in the southern way of life' than any period since the Civil War," DC prophesied. "The South had ample opportunity to make the transition gradually, and without a sudden revolution in our 'Southern way of life.' " But many Georgia students stated explicitly, or sensed intuitively, that the revolution was upon them—and that it would come with sound and fury. "If we are not ready now," wrote GLC, "we will never be."[76]

ONE HUNDRED YEARS AFTER GEORGIA SECEDED from the union, many whites referred back to that historical marker. In a sense, white Georgians had a century to ready themselves for social changes—and still many were unprepared. Some turned the lessons of the Civil War on their head, and expressed disgust at the violence in Athens. A "Disheartened Georgian" was moved to write his first public letter shortly after the University of Georgia riot. "I feel as I imagine my great-grandfathers felt when they . . . stood with [Confederate vice president] Alec [Alexander H.] Stephens," this Georgian wrote to the *Constitution*. He placed the blame for Civil War defeat not on the hated Yankees, but on the Confederacy itself. "The whole South failed because it was committed to a course that was morally wrong. We found that we could not divorce ourselves from the worldwide norms of morality among civilized peoples. Even less can we today." In 1961, some whites waved Confederate flags and protested integration. Indeed, the legislature had voted in a state flag complete with the stars and bars in 1956. But other Georgians read different lessons into the legacy of the Civil War, and the battle currently upon them. W. F. Thomas of Atlanta advised the legislature, "Stop dreaming of a decadent past." He pitted violent, backward-looking rebels of the past against those who would bring a civilized future. W. C. Henson, a UGA alumnus from Cartersville, asserted, "Most Georgians are living in the 19th Century and trying to bring back the days before 1860." One Georgian wrote to UGA president O. C. Aderhold, and gave a final turn of the screw to the Civil War analogies. She praised Aderhold for keeping the campus open, and in that defense of law, order, and peace perceived the historic spirit of the white South. UGA administrators who kept schools open were the "true spiritual descendants of Robert E. Lee, and the soul of the south!" As students on the Athens campus waged battles over the nature of the future, Georgians could not help but reference the distant—yet living—past.[77]

In a story with an endless cast of villains, many UGA alumni championed Dean of Men William Tate as their hero. Tate, a native Georgian, enjoyed a no-nonsense reputation. On the night of the riot, he became the most visible image of order. Tate braved the mob and held students accountable. He lacked sympathy for liberals and integrationists, but had much less tolerance for violence and bedlam. Many white Georgians saw in Tate the very dignity and respectability the mob lacked. In the days after January 11, Tate received hundreds of letters from alumni and other concerned whites: more than five hundred correspondents supported his effort to quell the mob, with fewer than one hundred against. "We are deeply ashamed and upset by the actions of our governor and legislature," wrote Mrs. Edward Downs, "but are proud of both you . . . and the student body as a whole." Many agreed with a retired army colonel from Athens. "Integration of course is bad enough, but as versus . . . order and gentlemanly conduct, it will have to be contested within the law and in the confines of decency, only." For thousands in the middle who would neither speak up for integration nor viciously condemn it, causes still existed in "honor," "decency," and "dignity." Men like William Tate were their icons, and upheaval was not welcome. Atlantan Arthur Murphey, Jr., wrote to Tate, "All of us would probably like to take a ten or twenty year vacation somewhere while it's all being worked out. But it looks like we've used up all of our vacation time." Perhaps they could learn to live with, if not embrace, integration. "Maybe it will be like cold water in the swimming pool. Once you've been in awhile, you get used to it and it just isn't so freezing after all."[78]

As white southerners tested the waters of a desegregated world, Hamilton Holmes and Charlayne Hunter braved that cold every day. Shortly after Holmes and Hunter arrived on campus, Students for Passive Resistance formed: "We hereby pledge ourselves to the use of the ultimate weapon so widely and effectively used by these people—the weapon of 'passive resistance.' We will NOT welcome these intruders. We will NOT associate with them." Not only did black students receive a cold shoulder, but white students who showed them warmth risked ostracism. "We will NOT associate with white students who welcome them. We love our school. We WILL save it." While most white students criticized violence, they practiced a different type of resistance— one in which they could feign indifference while wielding hostility. As a Georgia legislator told the *Atlanta Constitution*'s Celestine Sibley, "Our boys and girls can show them that they aren't welcome—and I don't mean by violence . . . I mean by their attitudes." To that end, women in Hunter's dorm bounced balls in the room above hers into the wee hours of the night. The *Constitution* soon reported, "The hot war has turned into the cold shoulder." It was a parable of what happened on the sites of the civil rights movement, once the drama subsided. Sibley called the "cold and distant civility" practiced by white students "a weapon more cruel to the young than the epithets of the mob." Students in Brahana's class armed themselves with these instruments. One wrote, "I feel that we should try to avoid the negroes, in hopes that . . . they might be psychologically affected and will eventually drop out of school." Another observed, "Even though a negro is allowed to attend classes with white people . . . no one can change his color. Students will not associate with one because they are prejudice[d]."[79]

The full triumph of integration, many admitted, required far more than Holmes's and Hunter's physical attendance. The Students for Passive Resistance could not stop blacks from attending UGA, but they brought misery to those students. Sometimes the fact of interracial contact could alter deeply held white attitudes; at other times, whites changed only in subtle ways, so that their general lifestyles could persist. Celestine Sibley thought that resistance—whether violent or passive— damaged white students more than they knew. Charlayne Hunter "has been taught something I'm afraid we white parents may be realizing belatedly, that those who inflict pain are, ultimately, hurting themselves more than anyone else."[80]

In the end, the university riot changed public opinion in Georgia. "What is the question before us? Segregation?" asked Charles Hartshorne of Atlanta. "That question has been answered" by the thousands who spoke up in favor of open schools after the ugly Athens riot. "Across our state there are reverberations of this one theme," wrote a resident of Suches, Georgia: " 'I believe in segregation, but . . .' " In 1961, beliefs in segregation came under the shadow of what mobs would do to preserve it. "Weather vanes in Georgia are beginning slowly to turn," wrote Julian Longley, "swinging reluctantly on squeaking, squawking pilots, but turning with the new political winds that blow from an aroused and more enlightened public opinion." Many Georgians who did not initially support open schools saw what could happen if integration came without peace. Norman Tolbert of Atlanta phrased the question in a different manner. At stake were the children of Georgia, and their future. "What happens to the pawns, our children," if public schools close? "We cannot sit back and pass on to them what was passed to us and expect them to make the world a better place in which to live." It took the beginnings of change for many people to argue that more change was needed. Tolbert concluded his letter to the *Constitution,* "The proper solution would be to start teaching our children to live without blind hatred." As many students in Brahana's class recounted, their first lessons in life were often about black inferiority. At an early age, whites were endowed with ways of seeing that included cruel blind spots. The civil rights movement may not have imparted light everywhere darkness once reigned, but it forced difficult questions to be asked in southern communities, made many white students see that there were far more important concerns in life than segregation, and gave some older southerners the courage to admit publicly their region's miseducation on race.[81]

While the desegregation of the University of Georgia set many transformations into motion, it offered temporary resolution of one issue: integration would come to many Georgia schools with peace. Politicians and parents saw that if a mob could form in Athens, it could form anywhere. But university integration affected parents and politicians only indirectly. White students were the first to live in the new world that civil rights struggles were creating. To them, integration had much less to do with the attitudes one held than with the experiences and facts one faced. Brahana's students neither boycotted, fomented revolt, nor stood for desegregation. Their experiences were unlike those of either the Cheerleaders in New Orleans, or Daisy Gabrielle or Margaret Conner. Most were just students, not heroes or villains, mob members or martyrs. When Charlayne Hunter and Hamilton Holmes came to Athens, the ensuing mob violence did not begin a debate about open and closed schools; it ended one. But as one fight concluded, many more began. Students grappled with the new experiences of integration, reordered their priorities in its wake, latched on to old beliefs and created new ones, and attempted to resume the routines of their lives. Whites alternately adapted to and fended off a coming social order they could only see slightly but already felt deeply.

On June 1, 1963, Hamilton Holmes and Charlayne Hunter graduated from the University of Georgia. Both quickly stepped into the new future that their pathbreaking actions promised. Holmes was admitted to the medical school at Emory University; Hunter traveled much farther from home. While in Athens, she fell in love with a white student, Walter Stovall of Douglas, Georgia. They moved to New York and married. For an ironic moment, the extremist doomsayers seemed to have it right: token integration led to interracial marriage. Both Holmes and Hunter have had successful careers, he as an orthopedist and she as a journalist. The effect they had on UGA was lasting. In 1960 and 1961, the university administration had waged long legal battles to keep Holmes and Hunter from their campus. Almost thirty years later, in 1988, Hunter delivered the commencement address. Decades after Holmes and Hunter left the university, UGA tethered itself to their legacies. Today, students and alumni, football fans and visiting researchers who stroll down the main quad on campus see the stately Holmes-Hunter Academic Building. This was the building where administrators rejected the black students, where the students were taunted, but also where they finally registered. In 2001, it came to bear their names, and the university formally associated itself with a past it had previously tried to postpone. The Athens campus held the stories of many transformations. Because of the mob violence in 1961, prejudiced white students came to accept—though not to embrace—token integration. The age of civil rights often achieved the unforeseen and made strange bedfellows. Hamilton Holmes, who died in 1995, was buried with a Georgia Bulldog cap atop his coffin.[82]

4

WHEN WHITE SOUTHERNERS LOOKED into the mirror of reality in Athens and New Orleans, they could glimpse a reflection of their own future. With each successive court order, another locale was drawn into the battle over public schools. The fight first came to the Deep South in 1960, and it kept coming. From New Orleans and Atlanta in 1960 to rural Mississippi a decade later, whites throughout the region grappled with the challenge of school integration. By the dawn of the 1970s, towns like Indianola, Mississippi, still possessed segregated public schools, but New Orleans and Atlanta had already experienced desegregation and resegregation. They were well on their way to entire public educational systems that contained heavily black majorities. The process of school integration was alternately torturous and instructive for families, teachers, and children.

While white boycotts in New Orleans were never total, the public schools in Prince Edward County, Virginia, remained empty in 1961. After two years of the Prince Edward Educational Foundation, private schools stood strong—but they brought class tensions to the fore. Those with money could afford private education, a filling station owner observed; "the rest of us got to have public schools." Neither African-

Americans nor white public school advocates gained much ground. In April, seventy-five whites who supported reopening the public schools met to launch an organization devoted to that cause. Many of them endured repeated intimidation, and the group quickly folded. Later that spring, school board members resigned rather than sell off schools and equipment. Despite such acts of dissent, the county's public schools remained abandoned until 1964, when the Supreme Court declared (in *Griffin v. Board of Education of Prince Edward County*) that every child was constitutionally entitled to a public education. Full-scale school integration did not arrive in Prince Edward County until 1968. Still, few whites were eager to return. The public schools were only 5 percent white in 1971.[83]

As Prince Edward whites staved off the inevitable, those in Atlanta began to come to terms with it. In the fall of 1961, Atlantans desegregated schools in peace. "They still say never," Joseph Cumming wrote from *Newsweek*'s Atlanta bureau, "in Alabama cross road towns, on Mississippi cotton farms, at a South Carolina filling station. But the old fight . . . seems to have slipped, dreamwise, one more notch away from the world of reality." Cumming argued that Atlanta's integration "tells a story about the South" and "marks a subtle change that has been going on unawares—an almost sub-conscious shift in the stance of the Deep South that Said Never." In fact, that shift was not subconscious, immediate, or thorough—but it was significant. Atlanta leaders well knew that peace was indispensable to their city's image. And that image propelled their prosperity. Integration of the schools was closely managed, as was the press coverage. Four Atlanta high schools integrated, without incident, in 1961: Murphy, Brown, Northside, and Grady. City leaders congratulated themselves as nine black students entered the schools. More important and more lasting than the fact of tranquillity, however, were the experiences that integration bequeathed to Atlanta's white students and teachers.[84]

The changes that occurred most often happened inside Atlanta schools themselves. Many white pupils avoided black students; some taunted them; others worked and played alongside them. Even those who claimed indifference could not help but react to the black students—and the social revolution—in their midst. "We were as nervous as they were," said a white Atlanta girl. "It's strange, and you feel funny for a while. The rooms were dead silent at first." Over time, daily interactions dissolved theoretical commitments to Jim Crow. "Something happens in the way you think after you get to know people." Many white students who were initially truculent quickly backed down. "I sneered a few times the first few weeks, but I just couldn't keep it up," a high school senior said in 1962. "I felt kind of bad and sorry for them. . . . You have to understand how we've grown up. They were slaves to us. I mean after the Civil War. . . . I was taught to expect them to do anything I wanted." He recounted childhood lessons similar to those of students in Brahana's University of Georgia class. Given such a context, any transformation was cataclysmic. "They've worked in our kitchens and taken care of us, and suddenly you wake up and find them in your schools sitting across from you. . . . It's not the way we've ever lived with them before, and you can't expect us not to find it hard for a while." In the end, new experiences altered him. "I've really changed a lot of my ideas," he admitted, and for that he had to walk a certain social gauntlet: "I argue with my parents . . . I still argue with my friends, they laugh at me, call me a damn 'nigger lover.' "[85]

When Atlanta desegregated in 1961, Clinton, Tennessee, students were five-year veterans of the process. In the early days of integration, teacher Margaret Anderson observed, the vast majority of white pupils neither accepted nor detested their black peers. Most simply tried to avoid the new students. "They seem to feel that if you don't look or don't become involved, it will all go away and everything will be as it always was." The most recognizable changes took place not in vehement segregationists or advocates of tolerance, but in the many students caught in the middle. When mobs set upon blacks, these students at times rose to the victims' defense. They alternately sympathized with black students' travails and retreated when taunted as "nigger lovers." "In these and other situations we saw the inward struggle of the white youngsters," Anderson wrote. Segregationist bombings in Clinton created more white supporters of civil rights than the NAACP ever could have. "The white supremacists in their zeal have . . . done more than they will ever realize to accomplish the very thing they are fighting against." Again, white violence pushed the majority in the middle to the side of token integration. "The 'New South' is on the way: it is ready to be born," Anderson asserted in 1966. When change came, it would cascade along generational lines. Anderson located that "New South" in "the hearts and minds of today's children." A white father in Clinton said, "This [integration] is not really as hard for my children as it would be for me." In his voice was a conspicuous streak of pride.[86]

Racial change in southern schools often followed confrontation. The deeper into the Black Belt school integration ventured, the more violence it attracted—never more so than during an insurrection at Ole Miss in 1962. President John F. Kennedy mobilized troops to counter the uprising as African-American James Meredith registered on the Oxford campus. While that conflagration occupied national headlines and received widespread attention, less well known were the boycotts and pickets—and the subtle changes in attitudes and lives—that school desegregation brought elsewhere in the Deep South. Some Alabama cities faced integration orders in the fall of 1963. Like governors Orval Faubus, Lindsay Almond, and Jimmie Davis before him, George Wallace threatened school closure. He finally caved under a federal restraining order, and on September 10, black students integrated many Alabama public schools. In Birmingham, a total boycott occurred on the first day. In Tuskegee, the rural town of Booker T. Washington's black college, the white community fractured over public and private schools. The epithets "nigger-lover" and "redneck" filled the air. "It's truly brother against brother, father against father," one citizen said. For many white southerners, school integration brought chaos—in the dual forms of black children who disrupted their ways of life, and segregationists who turned their streets and schools into battlegrounds. "We know that something bad's going to happen," a Tuskegee leader said on September 15. "But we are powerless to stop it." By the end of that year, the desegregation of Tuskegee schools had failed. Private white academies began to take over. But when the Tuskegee citizen said, "We know something bad's going to happen," perhaps he had a deeper vision. On Sunday, September 15, a Klan bomb tore through Birmingham's 16th Street Baptist Church and killed four African-American girls. If anyone needed a reminder, the message was clear: in 1963, integration was to some a matter of life and death.[87]

A glance at Little Rock's Central High, almost a decade after *Brown v. Board of Education,* demonstrates the ways civil rights struggles could change—and fail to change—schools, children, and parents. Transformations took years, and they occurred far away from the microscopes of national media, eyes of opportunist politicians, and crowds of protesters. "After the troops turned the mobs away people slowly started forgetting us again," a Little Rock teacher stated in 1962. "You'd think that's all there was to desegregation." The dramatic episodes were only as important as the changes they could effect days and months and years hence.

As the nation saw violence in Birmingham and Mississippi, a gaze toward Little Rock suggested what might visit southern towns after the tension died down. If progress came, it would be slow. By 1963, eight Little Rock junior and senior high schools were desegregated. Of the 2,037 students at Central High, only 20 were black. They almost always sat together in the cafeteria. Two years after University of Georgia students formed an organization for "passive resistance," many whites practiced it at Central High. Yet blacks and whites played together on athletic teams, in school bands, and in other extracurricular activities. What was happening in the schools helped initiate the process of integration in the city at large. The local baseball team—the Arkansas Travelers—gained a black player, Richie Allen. Picketing Citizens' Councilors were overwhelmed by fans who hurried in to see the game. The integrated crowd roared when Allen made his way to the plate. If Birmingham was the South's "laboratory of segregation," Little Rock's citizens often became guinea pigs in Deep South experiments in integration. By 1968, Central High School had become 25 percent black, but West Side High counted only 4 blacks among 1,400 whites. There was reason to highlight both change and continuity. Desegregation was less a way of life than an experiment. It would take years for the results to register.[88]

The unique place of schools in society partially accounted for that ambiguity. Parents often wanted their children to be educated on their own terms. As one mother in Natchez, Mississippi, said, "We wanted the freedom to choose who our child would sit next to in school." White children rarely thought of their own freedom in that light; in general, they were more open to new experiences than were their parents. Samuel Holton was a member of the Chapel Hill School Board when the high school integrated, in 1966. The difficulty, he remembered years later, was not the physical one of educating black and white students in the same building. "You have to remember, you are not just . . . integrating the school, you are also integrating the parental view of the world." Parents formed mobs in New Orleans and Little Rock; parents appeared in front of school boards, time and again, to protest integration. In 1964, for instance, twenty-five parents of Murphy High School students in Atlanta appeared before the Board of Education to argue against an increase in black pupils. The school was "a little too mixed for us," said H. R. Martin, the group's spokesman. Of course, exceptions always confounded the rule. The Foremans, Gabrielles, and Conners were parents, too. And there were also children like the twelve-year-old from Coinjock, North Carolina, who in 1966 wrote to his congressman, "I don't want to go to school with niggers, much less be taught by one."[89]

Crass attitudes like those were prevalent in many towns. When school integration penetrated rural citadels of Jim Crow, boycotts in New Orleans and abandoned schools in Prince Edward County lost their claims to distinctiveness. On August 31, 1966, five black students registered at Woodlawn High School in Louisiana's Plaquemines Parish. At long last, federal courts brought desegregation to the swampy kingdom of Leander Perez. To Perez, school integration was like a natural disaster. He called the "outrage against our people" a "worse catastrophe than Hurricane Betsy." White parents in the parish's East Bank (where black children outnumbered whites three to one) boycotted the school and made plans for private education. Ben Chaupette said, "My kid is never going to an integrated school as long as I've got my health to earn money to send him to private school." But the boycott would not be so difficult for white students, he thought. They had dealt with a comparable hardship. "They were out for a good time last year because of the hurricane but they came back and got good grades." Four days later, he added, "I have faith in these Plaquemines Parish people. They have bounced back from Hurricane Betsy, and they can do it again in this crisis." Surely they could weather another storm.[90]

On Thursday September 1, parents pitched an awning outside Woodlawn to protect their picket line from sun or rain. They carried signs that said, "DON'T," and tried to sway any white parents who might dream of bringing their children to school. Residents settled upon a fitting site for a new private school—one of Perez's former homes, known as the "Promised Land." On September 8, every teacher at Woodlawn resigned. The Promised Land soon employed them. But court orders kept school integration coming. Four more Plaquemines schools integrated on September 12. Desegregation came to those schools peacefully, and without large white boycotts. Bus drivers resigned, citing emotional distress from integration, but many schools possessed working faculties and several black pupils. On September 13, St. Bernard Parish—the buffer between Plaquemines and New Orleans—integrated its schools. Parents waved signs that said "Never," and violence erupted between whites and blacks. Whites streamed out of the high school, and parents clamored to enroll their children at the Promised Land. Nine bullets were fired into the home of one white family that kept its children in school. On September 19, enrollment at the Promised Land was up to four hundred. Battles between public and private education soon raged across the rural South. From Prince Edward to Plaquemines, sprouting private schools, heated boycotts, and torn communities dredged up memories of New Orleans's Ninth Ward.[91]

In 1966, black Mississippians desegregated Grenada High School under protection of the state highway patrol. Constable Grady Carroll assured reporters that after the patrol left town, "we'll have it like we've always had." Many white southerners clung to this idea during the age of civil rights, and many were proved wrong. In white children uprooted from their schools, the lasting changes were evident. Melany Neilson remembered May 1967, when she attended third grade in Holmes County, Mississippi. Neilson's teacher, Lillian Holcutt, informed the class that black students would integrate the school that coming fall. "Things are going to be just the same," Holcutt told her pupils. The following autumn, Neilson's father enrolled her in a nascent private school, Central Holmes Academy. She wondered, "Would things ever be the same?" The short answer was no. Private education changed the texture of life for the entire Neilson family. Tuition "spelled financial strain," Neilson remembered. Her father rented the farm, went to law school at night, and fired the maid. As blacks in Holmes County gained advances, white resistance heightened. Her father received threats when he refused to join the Klan, and soon the family moved to another town. After school integration hit Holmes County, everything changed for the Neilsons. Their story rang true for many more.[92]

Federal law often provided the impetus for those changes. The 1964 Civil Rights Act, and especially the Supreme Court's 1969 decision in *Alexander v. Holmes,* broke the back of school segregation. The 1964 law authorized the Department of Health, Education, and Welfare to withhold funds from any school district that failed to desegregate. HEW drew up desegregation proposals, while southern counties adopted "freedom-of-choice" plans in which black students could choose to attend any nearby school. Yet whites still controlled school boards and city councils, and with them the integration process. In 1967, only 14 percent of 2.5 million black southern students attended integrated schools. By 1968, that number had risen to 20 percent. HEW cut funds off from eighty-one school districts in 1968, and seventy-seven the following year. That same year, the court's *Green v. New Kent County* decision invalidated "freedom-of-choice" plans and directed school boards to abolish dual school systems. In October 1969, the Court handed down its *Alexander* decision; the ruling concerned thirty school districts in rural Mississippi. It mandated immediate and total integration in districts across the South. The Supreme Court ordered "each school district to convert its system from dual to unitary at once." For segregationists, no wiggle room remained. There could be no more delay.[93]

What Skelly Wright had ordered upon New Orleans in 1960 the Supreme Court brought to the rest of the Deep South almost a decade later. Every place could become a Little Rock or a New Orleans. Mississippi Delta whites had been preparing for the "worst" well before *Alexander v. Holmes* ordered immediate integration in October 1969. (In one instance, as early as 1965, a group of planters, businessmen, lawyers, and bankers met in Panola County and planned the formation of a new private school—North Delta.) In May 1969, a district judge ordered that integration in Carroll County begin in 1970. He also ruled that the schools could be separated by sex, and that children could be assigned to schools based upon aptitude test scores. Though hardly an order of total integration, Delta whites panicked. When the private Bayou Academy opened for the 1969 school year, it was immediately overenrolled. "Whites will do all in their power to prevent wholesale integration of county public schools," the *Delta Democrat-Times* had prophesied months before *Alexander*. Beyond that, predictions were useless. "If this fails, anything could happen—from a fairly high level of integration, to all-black public schools and a system of all-white private schools with many whites not in school at all, in complete chaos. Time will tell."[94]

It is difficult to re-create these times of uncertainty. In 1969, African-Americans clenched their fists and chanted "Black Power," National Guardsmen shot students on college campuses, men died by the thousands in Vietnam, and cities smoldered from riots. America was in upheaval, and whites in the rural South did not know exactly how that upheaval would touch them. Would blacks soon try to run their towns? Would white students suddenly find themselves amid seas of black pupils? In Sparta, Georgia, where black students outnumbered whites 2,500 to 300, school superintendent Red Andrews voiced the opinion of many southern whites when he said that total integration would mean "three white children in a classroom with 25 Negroes. Whites just won't put up with it." Many wondered what alternative they had.[95]

Democrat-Times columnist Paul Pittman conveyed their anxiety. "For fearful whites, concerned primarily with the education of their children, the situation is unacceptable." Grassroots concerns about white children's education, and not violent racism or Citizens' Council campaigns, Pittman argued, spurred the growth of private schools across Mississippi. In the summer of 1969, Bayou Academy was renovated to house 500 students, nearly doubling its size—and more than trebling the 160 pupils it had contained in 1968. In October 1969, a week before *Alexander*, Sunflower County's private Indianola Academy counted 600 students in twelve grades, doubling its size from the previous year; Sharkey-Issaquena Academy in Rolling Fork prepared for 300 students, as opposed to 150 the previous year; Deer Creek Day School in the Washington County town of Arcola jumped from an enrollment of 67 to 200. Delta whites not only braced for integration, but they planned to elude it.[96]

Although private schools enjoyed widespread support among Delta whites and desegregation orders earned deep contempt, these white southerners were not necessarily of a single mind. The town of Greenville represented something of a bastion of moderation amid the deeply segregationist Delta, both cause and effect of Hodding Carter and his *Delta Democrat-Times.* In August, *Democrat-Times* staffer Luther Munford questioned the wisdom of white private schools. Segregation academies were ways for wealthy Delta whites to "buy their way out of integration, and make the poorer whites pay the price." Delta children, Munford wrote, "must share the trauma of making our society whole. It will not . . . be easy, yet past integration experiences lead one to believe it will not be as horrible as many fear." At the start of the 1969 school year, the white children of the Delta supplanted those of Little Rock, Prince Edward, New Orleans, Clinton, or Atlanta as the pawns of the hour. The *Democrat-Times* editorialized, "It is ridiculous and it is tragic, it is nonetheless true that the battleground in Mississippi today is the public school system." The state's future was "literally hanging in the balance."[97]

The *Alexander v. Holmes* decision was meant to bring fast and radical change, and it did. Children in thirty Mississippi districts shifted schools at midyear—among them 67,000 blacks and 56,000 whites. Many white parents refused to comply. They sent their children to Bayou Academy or Deer Creek Day School, and many who could not find private schools kept their kids at home or left town. By February 1970, the order had touched forty-six school districts in Mississippi alone. Desegregation of the public schools and formation of private schools, said

Charles Allen Johnson, Jr., executive secretary of the Mississippi Education Association, "hit every kid and parent in the state of Mississippi." That spring, more than 300,000 children were enrolled in almost 400 segregation academies throughout the South. But that was not the most stunning development that occurred in the aftermath of *Alexander.* More remarkable was the fact that some whites stayed in Delta schools—few by choice, almost none because they supported integration, a handful out of indifference and apathy, and many because of financial necessity. Suddenly, some white pupils found themselves surrounded by black students. At Rosedale's West Bolivar County Training School, 21 whites attended alongside 1,133 blacks. In Gunnison, 12 whites and 493 blacks attended formerly all-black Bob Woods Elementary. At the Broad Street School in Shelby, 1,054 blacks attended with only 2 whites. Certainly, the majority of Delta whites did not simply "put up with" immediate integration. But others had little choice. Almost overnight, schools that previously formed the backbone of Jim Crow became extreme tests of integration.[98]

One such story took place in the Wilkinson County town of Woodville. When Wilkinson County School opened after Christmas break on January 5, Annette and Tommy Brown were the only 2 whites among 1,393 students. Dewitt Ginn, the black principal, could hardly understand the Brown children's presence. "I can't figure it out. . . . Their daddy is like most white folks around here. Why should he send his kids to school with black kids!" Annette, an eleven-year-old, explained, "Daddy wanted us to go to a private school. But we didn't have the money." Burnell Brown had built his family's cabin. It lacked running water, was heated by a fireplace, and stood seven miles from the nearest paved road. But Brown admitted that his decision was not simply one of financial necessity. Local businessmen offered to pay his children's way to private schools, but Brown balked. "Education is more important to me than race. Most people around here are prejudiced. They'd rather see their kids grow up ignorant than go to school with the coloreds." As his wife put it, "Mine's not going to be ignorant. They're getting as much education as I can give 'em." Many white southerners across the region could sustain dissent with action—from Lloyd Foreman and Margaret Conner to Burnell Brown. In the end, though, Brown's saga more closely resembled that of James Gabrielle or John Thompson. A week after television and magazine reporters left town and stopped interviewing him,

Brown buckled under the pressure. Tommy and Annette soon attended an all-white private school in Woodville's Protestant church.[99]

The first dip into the icy water of integration was shocking. "I'm still a little numb," admitted Anguilla, Mississippi's, school superintendent Hyram Gerrard. In nearby Holmes County 1,600 whites attended private school by November 3—many at Central Holmes Academy. All 6,000 black students still went to public school, along with 900 whites. Lamenting whites' inability to accept integration, a local lawyer said, "I suppose we've lost the battle." Whites had retreated from the front lines of the school battlegrounds. Yet the lawyer pointed out that perhaps this battle was one they could never "win." "We can't have a unitary school system here any more than they can in Harlem." Of course, Holmes County was not Harlem—but comparisons to the North were becoming more apt. Most southern districts soon contained integrated schools. The controversy became more about busing and residential segregation than about Jim Crow schools. Moreover, by 1973, the South could boast of a higher school desegregation index than any other American region.[100]

One of the many school systems that *Alexander* struck was in Yazoo City. The Fifth Circuit Court of Appeals ruled that integration must arrive by January 7, 1970. Since the *Alexander* decision, wrote *Harper's* editor and Yazoo native Willie Morris, "the white community in Yazoo had been undergoing an agony of survival." Of fourteen thousand Yazoo residents, many whites were like the woman who told Morris, "If I had a child, I'd go out and collect empty bottles if necessary to send [my son] to private school." But the integration order evoked varied responses. On November 23, two hundred whites—many local leaders among them— published an advertisement in the *Yazoo City Herald* that backed public schools. State Senator Herman DeCell vowed he would send his daughter to an integrated school. Many other whites openly agreed. Economics were the motivation cited most often. These citizens believed the town's prosperity depended on luring northern industry; to do so required strong public schools and acceptance of integration. Most were like Owen Cooper, the influential president of Mississippi Chemical Corporation and a devoted Baptist. His support for compliance was "a combination of good religion and good business." Other justifications ranged from defense of children's education to an assault on "pure ole hate." As white students at Yazoo High School braced for the imminent influx of blacks, editors of the school newspaper urged acceptance. Integration might actually benefit students, the *Yazooan* argued, for white students could learn to navigate those racial issues that had long bedeviled their parents.[101]

The day of integration came to Yazoo like most other winter days. Students and parents fought the cold, and fully 80 percent of white children attended public schools. Two teachers resigned, but only two. After another 480 whites left for private schools, the Yazoo public schools had a ratio of three black students for every two whites. The resulting experiences suggested that the new generation of southern youths might stand sentinel over the birth of a New South after all. Students "are groping in pain and innocence toward something new," Morris wrote in 1971, "toward some blurred and previously unheeded awareness of themselves." In March 1970, the sponsors of the student paper refused to publish an editorial by Bruce Darby, a white student. "Mississippians have witnessed the passing of an era. . . . We will not understand the full significance of what has taken place until we try to explain it to our children." Darby suggested that the revolution was upon Yazoo whites there and then, whether they comprehended it or not.[102]

While few Yazoo whites completely embraced integration, almost everyone handled it peacefully. A large majority of Yazoo pupils stayed in school—as opposed to the thousands who left schools in other Delta towns. Many remained confident that the experience of integration might change them, if not their parents. "I don't think the older generation here realizes how much the white people need the colored people," one white student reflected. Another suggested, "If the parents would leave us alone, we'd make it." As time passed, change might surge through the generations.[103]

Harold "Hardwood" Kelley, the former basketball coach and acting school superintendent, observed, "This is a complete social revolution." The whites of Yazoo were living through a certain sort of revolution, one that was embedded in subtleties and at times hidden from view. It was not that attitudes changed overnight, or that Yazoo whites suddenly became arch-supporters of integration. Many still thought of blacks as inferior and bemoaned growing black political power. But white children attended school with African-American pupils, and the impact of that change could be felt all around Yazoo—from the practices of businessmen to the new ability of white dissenters to speak out. Change did not come without pain. Families split over the wisdom of integration. Parents clashed with children, husbands disagreed with wives, and old friends divided over where to educate their sons and daughters. These discussions and debates reshaped life in Yazoo. "An immense facade was beginning to crack," Morris wrote. And beneath it dwelled profound truths:

> it was the little things which were gradually enclosing and symbolizing the promise and the magnitude of what might be taking place here. If a true human revolution implies the basic restructuring of everyday life, the essential patterns of behavior toward other people, then what might be occurring here was a revolution, subtle and intensely complicated.

Blood in the streets and changes in the "power structure" were not necessary accompaniments of revolution. In Yazoo, it originated in the schools, in the experiences of parents and students, and radiated out through society. If new molds of everyday life replaced the old, a revolution would truly have come.[104]

The following decade dashed many claims of revolution, but corroborated others. In its 1971 *Swann v. Charlotte-Mecklenburg* decision, the Supreme Court called for busing as an instrument to achieve desegregation. By 1973, 46 percent of black children attended integrated schools in the South—indeed, the most in America. The statistics suggested a victory for racial equity over the forces of segregation. Yet just when school integration finally penetrated the deepest pockets of southern resistance, some parents and leaders devised policies to beat it back. From Charlotte to Boston, busing came under siege. Vice President Spiro Agnew termed busing an "artificially contrived social acceptance." Congressmen tried to rein in the courts' jurisdiction over local schools and intellectuals fashioned a terminology that deplored "quotas," "reverse discrimination," and "forced busing." To psychologist Kenneth Clark, all this spelled "a sophisticated pattern of retreat from *Brown*." A "new Orwellian semantic" was the "rationale for maintenance of the racial status quo, if not regression in civil rights." Schools had hardly integrated before the backlash against "forced busing" set in. Desegregation was costly to enforce, and it became an easier thing for many politicians and parents to tacitly oppose than to actively support.[105]

The Charlotte story stood out as a significant exception. The lawsuit that found its way to the Supreme Court helped to make Charlotte a national center for the controversy over school busing. In 1969, Judge James McMillan (himself a resident of the southeast Charlotte suburbs) delivered the first ruling in the *Swann* case. McMillan found the Charlotte-Mecklenburg schools "not yet desegregated," and ordered busing to achieve that goal. The Concerned Parents Association, which had sprung up in the Charlotte suburbs, led local resistance to busing. In 1970, the group distributed flyers at shopping malls, community centers, and churches that read, "A Struggle For Freedom Is Coming: Where Will You Stand?" Area residents divided over that question. Some supported McMillan's court order, and their stance gained strength after the Supreme Court affirmed it. The anti-busing movement championed the principle of integration but rejected busing as its means. Yet working-class whites and blacks in the north and west parts of Charlotte united along class lines. They forced the city to pursue a stable system of desegregation that dealt equally with wealthy suburbs and poor urban neighborhoods. This interracial coalition ulimately helped to integrate the school system in the 1970s. Just as blacks boarded buses for leafy suburbs, so whites from outlying areas integrated schools in the city. From the mid-1970s to the mid-1980s, the schools remained 60 percent white and 40 percent black. In Charlotte, for a time, school busing had worked.[106]

Elsewhere, a process of resegregation emerged. In 1970, *Atlanta Constitution* columnist Hal Gulliver called "the cycle of school desegregation . . . a frustrating one . . . 26 schools have gone from all-white to integrated to all-black." The proportion of white students in Atlanta's public schools dwindled over the years, and by 1985 they accounted for only 6 percent of the total enrollment. Yet the process was nothing new. Its outlines were visible in New Orleans as early as 1962. In arenas of school integration, twin legacies often reigned. Resegregation, retreats from *Brown,* private schools, passive resistance, and other stratagems of opposition sprung up in most white southern communities. Places like Yazoo and Atlanta were prototypes. It was not that some cities and towns in the South accepted school desegregation and others resisted, but within every locale existed conflicting realities. There were movements against busing, incidents of hostility toward black students, and booming all-white private schools. There were also private schools that went bankrupt, integrated schools that thrived, and parents and children who felt the power of genuine transformations in lifestyles and attitudes. Often, all of these different facts existed together.[107]

Georgia schools, rural and urban, highlighted integration's ambiguous legacy. In 1970, Atlanta's public schools were less than 30 percent white. In the 1960s, almost 60,000 whites fled the city for the suburbs, and thousands enrolled in private schools; another 100,000 would leave the city in the 1970s. Few schools had integrated faculties, and many of their student bodies remained either heavily white or heavily black. The Fifth Circuit Court of Appeals ruled that schools must possess a racial balance not only of students, but also of faculty. Atlanta's Board of Education presented a faculty desegregation plan that would transfer 1,800 of the city's 5,000 teachers. White students who grudgingly tolerated black classmates feared and loathed taking instructions—and receiving grades—from African-American teachers. On Friday, January 9, more than one thousand white students marched in protest. The heyday of the black civil rights struggles might have passed, but those movements left behind evident lessons—heeded by whites as well as blacks. When white students perceived threats to their own freedoms, they took to the streets—using the same tactics that civil rights demonstrators had wielded with such effect. White imitators followed black liberators.[108]

On Monday, January 12, the throng of protesting students and parents grew to fifteen hundred, and Governor Lester Maddox handed out American flags. Students walked to the capitol chanting "Hell, no, we won't go," and raised banners that read "We Shall Overcome!!!!!!" As Atlanta mother Helen Jaynes explained, "The white child . . . will be forced to attend a school across the city—he will not be taught by members of his own race." This was unacceptable hypocrisy. "No federal funds or state funds will be given to him if he does not comply. This is what the white mothers resent." Through the January ice they trudged toward the capitol, placards held high. Students hoisted their fingers in V-salutes, as police officers offered smiles—not beatings. The *New York Times* called the marchers "the sons and daughters of the Silent Majority," and they represented a segment of Dixie's white children. Traditional narratives of the civil rights movement often end in 1968, but for many white parents and students, the changes just started to take effect in the 1970s. Whites fought back, not always with bombs and court actions, but with marches and protests. Former governor Ernest Vandiver reflected on the desegregation battles that took place at the University of Georgia and in Atlanta a decade before. "Emotions then revolved around the principles. It might have been easier to face the principles than the actuality." Only in the late 1960s and 1970s did principles become actualities. White towns that had experienced upheaval in the 1960s when blacks marched through their streets and sat in at their lunch counters convulsed again when they wrestled with the changes that the civil rights movement had finally achieved.[109]

Some students protested these changes, others accepted them nobly, and many more grappled in varied ways with uncomfortable truths. "Desegregation appears to have been accepted by most white students," the *Atlanta Constitution* could report in 1971, apparently oblivious to the thousands of whites who had left the city and withdrawn from public schools. "They may not personally approve and they may think it's unwise, but they seem to have no illusions that it can be avoided." Yet occasional acceptance of the fact of desegregation did not translate into acceptance of black students, or of the shifts they ushered into southern life. Even at its best, school integration came with great strain. Many students navigated "double lives"—one at home, the other at school. "You don't know what we go through," said a boy in Sumter, South Carolina. "We go home and hear, 'God-damned niggers.' We go to school and the teacher says, 'Now, wait a minute.' " The tension often existed within the school itself, not just in the divide between school and home. Bitter disputes centered on homecoming elections, cheerleading squads, and basketball rosters. At Clarke Central High School in Athens, Georgia, blacks rapidly supplanted white basketball players and cheerleaders. Few whites concealed their disdain. At Valdosta High School, principal Charles Green abolished the selection of a homecoming queen to avoid controversy. Desegregation soon became a matter of school cheers, mascots, homecoming queens, student council officers, point guards, and quarterbacks. This was both the detritus of civil rights controversies and the stuff of social revolution.[110]

On their own terrain, students could forge struggles and carve out realities all but inconceivable to their parents. "The very newness of the experience permits them to bring a freshness to their situations that sets them apart from adults," Paul Gaston wrote for the SRC in 1971. "Youth all over the country are increasingly aware of themselves as a force in their own right." Student protests at northern universities often grabbed headlines. But as the 1970s began, nowhere did youths deal with more profound social changes than in southern schools. The crowds at the Atlanta statehouse showed that many white students did not hope for the days of equal rights and total integration. Others spoke of life-changing experiences. Even if it was overly optimistic to state that the younger generation would overcome all the white South's historic mon-

strosities, there were times and places when that statement came closer
to truth than falsehood.[111]

One such moment existed in Americus, Georgia, during the winter of
1970–1971. Not far from Albany and even closer to Jimmy Carter's
hometown of Plains, Americus sat in Georgia's Black Belt. If one
believed that racial change came to urban centers but bypassed rural
backwaters, Americus showed the error of that generalization. For sure,
many Americus whites fled to private schools after court-ordered desegregation. But those who stayed in public schools adopted the mind-set of
"Good riddance." "They the sorriest damn schools you ever saw," one
civic leader said of the private academies. Nevertheless, they did perform
a service of sorts. "As downright pathetic as they are, they maybe been a
blessing. They've drawn off the reactionaries and allowed us to go on
about our business, so when they fold up . . . these folks will be coming
back into the system on *our* terms." Some white students even invited
blacks to their homes for dinner. Steve Thomas, a sophomore football
player at Americus High School, reflected that desegregation "has made
people understand each other a lot more. . . . Before integration, there
used to be a lot of scare talk from the parents about what was going to
happen. . . . The kids are really a little surprised at how well things have
gone." In this case, the students' "actuality," in Ernest Vandiver's words,
proved far easier to confront than parents' "principles." Student body
president and starting fullback Johnny Sheffield asserted, "The grown
people are just not mature enough to accept it. I don't think they'll ever
really change."[112]

Inside some Americus adults, acceptance of new truths battled against
deference to old reflexes. Mayor Frank Myers was himself a prime example of that inner war. "My children are doing better than they ever did,"
Myers stated in 1970. "I'm still about 40 percent bigoted. There just
ain't no way to grow up like I did without having prejudices." But he
held out hope for his daughter, and for millions of other daughters across
Dixie. Mary Myers was a junior at Americus High. "My daughter . . .
and my other . . . kids, they absolutely rid of *all* of them [preju-
dices]. . . . It's gonna be our children finally who're going to deliver us
out of this thing that's been going on down here ever since slavery." He
believed the white children, with their new range of experiences and
adaptive temperaments, would bring a new South. But another view was
that African-Americans, not whites, would redeem the white southerner

of his sins—or at least move him closer to a better day. To Americus blacks like Thelma Barnum, the wife of a funeral home director, this perspective better jibed with reality. "We gonna give the whites a little soul. We gonna give 'em some *tone.*" In 1970, Fannie Lou Hamer (the sharecropper who helped lead the Mississippi Freedom Democratic Party) said as much to black children who were about to integrate a school just north of Yazoo City. "You not just *frightened,* you scared to death, ain't you? . . . But you . . . remember . . . they ain't gonna be savin' *you.* You gonna be savin' *them.*" Shards of evidence suggested that schools might not only be centers of learning or epicenters of a regional revolution, but could also become hubs of interracial salvation.[113]

Realities in those schools were always messy. Redemption collided with resistance, and old prejudices lingered beside new lessons. Perhaps it was fruitless to debate revolution and salvation, freedom and liberation; perhaps those larger questions would take decades and epochs to parse. The actual occurrences in integrated schools were in a certain context profound, but also entirely mundane. At Decatur High School in the Atlanta area, some of the most volatile race issues revolved around cheers at sporting events. In 1970, Decatur had 1,400 students—broken down evenly between whites and blacks. Out of more than sixty faculty, nine were black. In the fourth year of integration, the varsity cheerleading squad gained its first black members—two girls out of twelve. Many parents ceased hosting team sleepover parties, and controversy arose. "The blacks want more 'soul' in the songs," according to a *Newsweek* background report, "while the whites prefer the stiffly traditional rah-rah-rah." When the team finally incorporated more "soul cheers," the "white girls moan that they just can't shake and shuffle like the blacks." Integrating the school was straightforward enough. But integrating worldviews, lifestyles, and even cheers was something else. "The process of integration here is not completed," said Susan Heard, a white cheerleader and homecoming queen. Chip Lanier, a senior, speculated on what that completion might entail. "I still don't think integration will be all done until blacks and whites live beside each other and are not thinking one is better than the other." Yet Heard and Lanier were not in the majority. The previous year, fifty students had dressed in all white to demonstrate "white power." But they were not in the majority, either. "A minority of blacks and whites are going overboard to mix and learn about each other—an equal minority is heading as quickly in the opposite direction," according to the *Newsweek* dispatch. "In between, is apathy and indecision—kids who don't care much one way or the other . . . kids who don't think that much about race, but kids who eventually will move to one side or the other." In the early 1970s, white children of the South struggled to work out their reaction to integration, to blunt the sharp edges of conflicts, and to make ways for themselves in a new racial order. In this order, the songs that played at dances and the cheers at football games were issues that often formed the terrain of social conflict. When a black Charlotte, North Carolina, principal said that "children are coming up in a brand new world," this was the world he meant. In it, white children shuffled, swayed, and shook.[114]

Black struggle and white resistance turned schools into battlegrounds and children into pawns. But schools were still schools, and children were still students. Schools were the social laboratories of the time, and yet they also contained textbooks, blackboards, dances, and gym classes. Students found themselves wedged between a past that their parents often wished to preserve and a future that they would create with their actions. Through the 1960s and 1970s, southern schools were but one of many civil rights arenas. Fights over school integration were particularly emotional, for they concerned the volatile issue of how to raise Dixie's children. Schools highlighted many showdowns: between federal law and states' rights, between black civil rights and white resistance, between public institutions and private ones, even between alternate meanings of American freedom. Occurrences of school integration could yield dramatic outcomes, but they could also overshadow the fact that similar issues were playing themselves out across the southern landscape—in workplaces and factories, restaurants and ice-cream parlors, rib shacks and juke joints. The civil rights movement affected the whole of southern life. Acceptance, resistance, and even indifference could don millions of different guises.

FOUR

Barbecue, Fried Chicken, and Civil Rights: The 1964 Civil Rights Act

FOR OLLIE MCCLUNG, SR., AND LESTER MADDOX, barbecued pork and skillet-fried chicken flavored the American dream. That the two men came to be mentioned in the same breath seemed in one sense a fitting truth, in another an absurd accident of history. Both McClung and Maddox invested their lives in the restaurant business. Both men came from humble origins, built thriving restaurants, and served inexpensive and traditional southern food. Both avoided profanity and alcohol, and wherever either of them traveled, a Bible was never far behind. Descriptions of both Maddox and McClung often included the word "sincere" or "earnest." But where McClung was modest, Maddox was obnoxious. McClung was unassuming; Maddox could be vulgar. While silent piety characterized McClung, Maddox was given to shrill bluster. Maddox craved the limelight, performed for the cameras, and even ran for (and won) political office; McClung preferred simply to serve his barbecue. In 1964, the Civil Rights Act aligned the two proprietors in the same opposition movement. While they possessed distinct demeanors, McClung and Maddox became similar symbols of resistance against federal law. Both men saw themselves as champions of freedom, and both thought the civil rights movement—specifically its landmark Civil Rights Act—imperiled their vision of the American dream. Millions of other white southerners agreed.

What African-Americans struggled for in the streets, the 1964 Civil Rights Act enshrined as the law of the land. The act increased federal protection of voting rights, linked federal funds for schools to desegregation, and created the Equal Employment Opportunity Commission—

a powerful weapon against job discrimination. Title II covered public accommodations; it prohibited discrimination on government property and in every business that traded in interstate commerce. In effect, nearly every restaurant, cafeteria, movie theater, auditorium, sports arena, soda fountain, and motel had to integrate at once. Everything in the law repelled southern politicians, and they made its passage difficult. Vicious white violence in Birmingham had fueled President John F. Kennedy's initial proposal of the legislation in June 1963. After Kennedy's November assassination, President Lyndon Johnson—a native Texan—vowed the Civil Rights Act would pass. He wielded every power of his office to ensure that outcome. On February 10, 1964, the U.S. House of Representatives passed a version of the act by a vote of 290–130. But Democratic southern senators threw down the gauntlet, and filibustered for a record three months. On June 10, seventy-one senators finally voted to end the debate, and on June 19, the Senate passed the legislation. The House agreed on July 2. That night, Lyndon Johnson signed the act into law.

If Lester Maddox was largely unknown outside Georgia, he quickly made a name for himself. On the afternoon of July 3, three black theology students walked toward the door of Maddox's Atlanta restaurant, the Pickrick. Maddox informed them that the restaurant was closed, and the men replied that they would come back at 5:30. Maddox and his customers were ready when they returned. Pistol in hand, Maddox stood outside the doorway and told the men to leave. A crowd of diners congregated outside, each gripping ax handles that had been purchased in the restaurant. A little boy shouted, "I'm gonna kill me a nigger." The black men retreated to the safety of their car, and as they drove away Maddox swung an ax handle at the Oldsmobile. To those familiar with Maddox, the outburst was no shock. Part showman and part thug, Maddox's flamboyance compelled media attention. Journalist Robert Sherrill described Maddox as "pathetic" and "frustrated," and compared him to the cowardly lion in *The Wizard of Oz*. In a *Saturday Evening Post* article, Marshall Frady described Maddox as "a cracker Don Quixote." But before Maddox was a character played by Bert Lahr or on Miguel de Cervantes's pages, he was a typical working-class man of Atlanta.[1]

Lester Maddox never strayed far from home. Born in 1915, he grew up blocks away from where the Pickrick later stood, on Atlanta's Hemphill Avenue, N.E. Dean Maddox, a steelworker, had seven children; Lester was the second. The Great Depression left Dean Maddox without a job.

Lester dropped out of Tech High in the eleventh grade, and took a job at a drugstore to help provide for the family. He then worked as an apprentice dental technician, and at age seventeen, he landed a job at Atlantic Steel for $10 a week. Maddox built a makeshift candy and soft drink stand in a converted pigeon coop, and manned it in his free time. By age nineteen, he had worked his way up to foreman at Atlantic Steel. That same year, he married Virginia Cox, a seventeen-year-old who rode her bicycle past Maddox's candy business "more often than necessary." In 1940, Atlantic Steel fired Maddox. According to Maddox, he lost his job because he refused to fire two black workers who were seen in the company of union organizers. Maddox left Atlanta for a job at the Bessemer Galvanizing Works across the state line in Alabama, and returned in 1943. The following year, Lester and Virginia Maddox pumped $400 into a ten-by-fourteen-foot building north of downtown Atlanta, where they opened a restaurant called Lester's Grill. Fifteen years after the Depression, the business began to boom. Propelled by his popular fried chicken, Maddox seemed to have found his calling. Maddox ventured in the real estate market, and found himself stuck with a piece of property near Georgia Tech. In 1947, Maddox decided to open a larger restaurant there. He called it the Pickrick.[2]

How Maddox became passionately involved in politics and segregation is not altogether clear. Plainly, the man possessed ambition; it was inscribed in his up-by-the-bootstraps, rags-to-riches tale. Always a religious man, Maddox had aspirations of preaching. He claimed that "the breakdown of the races is ungodly, and . . . verses of the Bible . . . support this." To attract business, Maddox ran column-length ads in the Saturday *Atlanta Constitution* from 1950 through the 1960s. Beneath the caption "Pickrick Says," Maddox advertised much more than his chicken specials. He denounced communism, integration, civil rights, or whatever the moment inspired. Maddox built a following over the years, and the restaurant expanded to hold four hundred patrons. In 1957, Maddox made his first stab at politics. He ran for mayor against the powerful William Hartsfield, in hopes of returning "to honest and clean government, defeat of a dictatorship (Hartsfield) and preservation of segregation." Hartsfield polled 63 percent of the vote to Maddox's 37. Maddox ran again in 1961, this time against the moderate Ivan Allen, Jr. Allen beat Maddox by a similar margin—64 percent to 36 percent—yet Maddox garnered more than half of the white votes. In 1962, Maddox ran for lieutenant governor. While Maddox carried Atlanta, Peter Zack Geer won the office. Where there was an opportunity to champion segregation, Maddox fixed himself on the scene. In the wake of student sit-ins, he founded Georgians Unwilling to Surrender (GUTS). When African-Americans asked Atlanta businesses to diversify their workforces in 1963, Maddox distributed flyers in which he moaned, "WAR HAS BEEN DECLARED UPON WHITE ATLANTA." He formed the People's Association for Selective Shopping (PASS), to boycott businesses that employed blacks. For every civil rights demonstration, Maddox offered an answer.[3]

In the Civil Rights Act of 1964, Lester Maddox met his match. The man who overcame poverty and hardship finally found an obstacle too formidable to surmount—but not for lack of trying. In the aftermath of the July 3 gun-wielding incident, Maddox announced that business was up 40 percent. Customers flocked to the Pickrick to eat plates of fried chicken and support Maddox's defiance. On the Fourth of July, his supporters appeared at a rally in Lakewood Park, an area overwhelmingly populated by the white working class. Featured speaker George Wallace lampooned the Civil Rights Act as a "fraud, a sham, and a hoax." To large applause, Maddox declared, "America will triumph. . . . Freedom will prevail." On July 6, two more blacks approached the Pickrick. Maddox met them at the door and announced, "You're not going to eat in my place tonight, tomorrow night or any other time." Three African-Americans brought a lawsuit against Maddox, and on July 7 he was bound over to Fulton County Criminal Court. The NAACP took up the suit two days later. Maddox's July 11 advertisement publicized the usual specials—drumstick and thigh, 25 cents; breast and wing, 50 cents (he added that these wonderful prices were not available for takeout). But the Pickrick advertised much more than the chicken. "Should I go to jail . . . it won't be Lester Maddox going to jail, nor just the Pickrick closing. . . . It will be freedom and liberty being placed behind bars for LIFE." Many Georgians agreed. Albany citizen John Dorminy argued that the July 4 holiday was "more like a solemn wake," and that "if Patrick Henry and his . . . forces were around today they would be standing with Lester Maddox, fighting just as hard as they fought tyranny two centuries ago." To some white southerners, the federal government had unleashed despotism in its latest law. It was up to lovers of property rights to protect liberty. "I'll use ax handles, I'll use guns, I'll use my fists . . . I'll use anything," Maddox promised. In that spirit, he marched to court.[4]

The Civil Rights Division of the Justice Department took on the lawsuit against Maddox. The Fifth Circuit Court of Appeals tried his case together with that of Moreton Rolleston, owner of the Heart of Atlanta motel. Rolleston also defied the Civil Rights Act—but if Maddox slung a gun, Rolleston wielded an idiosyncratic reading of legal precedent. On the night of July 2, hours after President Johnson had signed the Civil Rights Act, Rolleston traveled to the home of the circuit court clerk and filed an appeal. While the new law banned discrimination from all businesses dealing in interstate commerce, Rolleston argued that the law did not pertain to his business. Yet he operated a motel that advertised with billboards on the nearby interstate highway. People at the Heart of Atlanta, Rolleston maintained, had decided to settle down for the night; as such, they had no designs on interstate travel while at the motel. On August 10, the court ruled that both the Heart of Atlanta and the Pickrick violated the Civil Rights Act. It ordered both to desegregate at once. Rolleston acknowledged that he would obey the law, but appealed his case to the Supreme Court. Maddox took the opposite approach. "Pickrick will never integrate," he insisted. "They won't ever get any of that chicken." While Maddox remained intransigent, he was also ruefully skeptical. "I think the Federal Government will close my establishment. Our government will tell us we no longer can be free Americans. . . . It's involuntary servitude; it's slavery of the first order." In Maddox's view, white southerners were the oppressed ones.[5]

Like public schools that either had to accept blacks or shut their doors, Lester Maddox seemed out of options. On August 11, Maddox again barred blacks who tried to enter his restaurant. "If you live 100 years you'll never get a piece of fried chicken here," he yelled. Pressed by the court the next day to show why he should not be held in contempt, Maddox finally made a decision. On August 13, two young African-Americans headed toward the Pickrick, and Maddox closed it down. He berated the men and began to cry. To Maddox, this was not about the law or even dollars and cents. It concerned his emotions, his beliefs about individual freedom, the restaurant into which he poured his labors—and, in large part, his racial prejudices. Maddox had worked at the Pickrick for seventeen years without a vacation, and established a business valued at $450,000. He believed it was his right to serve whom he pleased, and that did not include blacks. Of course, Maddox still harbored political ambitions. And he must have known, as George Wallace and Barry Goldwater learned, that resistance to the Civil Rights Act earned political capital from white southerners. Goldwater was an Arizona senator who voted against the Civil Rights Act and later won the Republican nomination for president. While Goldwater lost the 1964 election to Johnson in a landslide, he carried the Deep South. So when Virginia Maddox draped her arms around Lester and sobbed, "They've ruined everything we've worked for all our lives," she was only partially correct. The Civil Rights Act dashed Maddox's hopes of maintaining a segregated business, but Maddox's defiant stand launched him on a path that ultimately led toward political victory.[6]

The Pickrick would be no more. Ever astute in public relations, Maddox attempted to portray himself as the victim. "The president and the government and the Communists closed the Pickrick. Not me." Maddox was proud of his fight, and he nurtured a flair for the dramatic until the bitter end. "The only thing I regret is that [Attorney General] Bobby Kennedy . . . could not come down here and get some chicken." Outside the closed restaurant, Maddox pulled up a lectern and recited the Ten Commandments. The affair was staged for the media, and for the crowd—whose hero had truly become a "cracker Don Quixote." Maddox invited his employees—forty-four blacks and twenty-two whites—to sit down in the restaurant and eat their last meal. The crowd roared.[7]

On September 26, a restaurant called Lester Maddox Cafeteria opened in the same building. It was Maddox's short-lived, poorly planned, and last-ditch attempt to keep his restaurant and evade the law. On September 29, Maddox shoved away a group of black would-be diners. Time and again, the courts punished Maddox for his shenanigans and ordered him to admit African-Americans. In February 1965, Maddox finally sold the restaurant to some former employees. It became Gateway Cafeteria, and served blacks as well as whites. Maddox claimed that life without his restaurant was hard to bear. "The torment that has been mine . . . would make death itself seem sweet." Always melodramatic, Maddox never missed a moment to seize the spotlight. And although his resistance to the Civil Rights Act was often calculated, it lacked sophistication and rested on no serious legal argument. While Maddox did not ultimately sell his restaurant until February 1965, he had dropped his constitutional case by the fall of 1964.[8]

Ollie McClung picked up the challenge, and toned down the pageantry. Ollie's was a family business. The restaurant and its barbecue recipe passed through three generations of McClungs. James Ollie McClung and his wife founded Ollie's Barbecue in 1926, on the South

Side of Birmingham. The restaurant specialized in barbecued pork, beef, and homemade pies. In 1927, Ollie's moved to a building on Seventh Avenue South, where it remained for decades. James Ollie's son, Ollie, was eleven years old at the time. He became a junior partner in 1937, and when his father died in 1941, Ollie inherited the business at age twenty-five; at that time, he had a one-year-old son of his own, Ollie Jr. A predominantly black neighborhood grew up around Ollie's Barbecue, and nearly three-quarters of its workforce was African-American. Yet few Birmingham restaurants bucked racial tradition, and Ollie's was no different. While blacks could enjoy Ollie's barbecue from its takeout window in the back, they could not occupy one of the dining room's 220 seats. African-American employees also ate in a separate room.[9]

McClung, like Maddox, was a religious man. Ollie Sr. came to Christianity through a transformative experience. Days before Christmas in 1946, he took Ollie Jr. to Sunday school. Ollie Sr. hung around the church, listened to the sermon, and found himself deeply changed. On New Year's Day, he hauled all the beer in his restaurant to the Birmingham dump. From then on he served only soft drinks, closed the restaurant on Sundays, and equipped each table with cards that banned profanity. They read, "No Profanity, Please. Ladies and children are usually present. We Appreciate Your Cooperation." In 1958, Ollie Jr. became a partner in the business, which grossed about $350,000 a year. A cross section of whites ate lunch at Ollie's, from laborers and the middle class to white-collar executives. Ollie Sr. expressed pleasure at his restaurant's place in Birmingham's social life. "We operate our business as a trust to our customers," he later told a district court. Ollie hoped that his diners had "a place to come in and eat where they will enjoy and where they will leave in a better frame of mind than when they came in. . . . If we fail to do that we feel like we have failed to fulfill our obligation." That Ollie's clientele remained all white formed an aspect of the covenant.[10]

On July 3, 1964, Ollie Sr. left his son in charge for the afternoon. A black man walked into the restaurant and requested the manager. Ollie Jr. informed the man that he could not eat at the counter. He soon returned with three other blacks. They sat down at the counter, as a white customer angrily left. Ollie Jr. asked them to leave, and after the would-be diners scribbled on notecards, they departed. No ax handles were swung at Ollie's, nor pistols waved. Neither were any blacks served. But African-Americans made more headway in other parts of the city. In one stark example of the changes the new law could effect, an old black chauffeur dined at the Town and Country Restaurant in the Dinkler-Tutwiler Hotel. J. L. Meadows ate his meal before dumbfounded whites. He reflected, "I've been driving folks down here for 21 years, and now I'm going to eat where I've been taking these white folks." For the time being, he would not do the same at Ollie's.[11]

After the Civil Rights Act passed, the Birmingham Restaurant Association stirred for a fight. It retained a law firm to explore how restaurants might maintain segregation. The firm concluded that only a restaurant uninvolved in interstate commerce had a chance in opposing the law. A good distance away from interstate highways, train and bus stations, and airports, Ollie's Barbecue seemed like a prime candidate. Unlike the Pickrick or the Heart of Atlanta, it did not advertise. Ollie made his profits by word of mouth. Traumatized by the attempt of four blacks to eat in his restaurant and alarmed by the notion that Ollie's location in a black neighborhood might result in its being overrun by African-Americans, Ollie Sr. was receptive when the restaurant association contacted him about a potential lawsuit. On July 29, the Justice Department filed a suit to end discrimination in Tuscaloosa eateries. To Ollie, this made the threat of integration even more real. He thought a similar suit might be filed against his restaurant, that he might then have to integrate, and that if he did so blacks would flock to his restaurant and his regular customers would leave. Ollie believed his business would be crippled. So on July 31, Ollie McClung filed a suit against the Justice Department. In *McClung v. Kennedy* (*McClung v. Katzenbach* after Robert Kennedy resigned his post), the McClungs sought to prohibit the attorney general from forcing Ollie's to integrate.

Whereas the Justice Department took action against Lester Maddox, the McClungs themselves were the plaintiffs in this case. They maintained that the Constitution's interstate commerce clause did not apply to Ollie's. They contended, furthermore, that Ollie's stood to lose $200,000 annually if it was forced to desegregate. On September 2, a panel of three Alabama judges considered the suit. Ollie Sr. testified that his case was about business and property rights, not race. "I would refuse to serve a Negro as well as a drunken man or a profane man or anyone else who would affect my business." On September 17, the Birmingham-based panel of the Fifth Circuit U.S. Court of Appeals ruled on the case. For that day, Ollie McClung, Sr., and his son prevailed over Congress and its Civil Rights Act. The panel ruled that Ollie's was not engaged in interstate commerce. It argued that Congress had overstepped its authority. The court denounced Congress's attempt to wield "naked power," and declared, "Title II of the Civil Rights Act of 1964, as applied to Ollie's was beyond the competence of Congress to enact." The court feared the day in which "no facet of human behavior" remained beyond legislators' control. Questions of property rights and human rights, judicial authority and congressional power, barbecue and civil rights became closely entwined.[12]

In October, *McClung v. Katzenbach* continued to the Supreme Court. Ollie Sr.'s testimony before the appeals court had already established one potentially damning point. When the McClungs' lawyer asked whether black customers were refused service because of their race, Ollie Sr. affirmed that was the case. "Yes, sir, I would think so. Because we chose not to serve them." Throughout the ordeal, however, Ollie and his son maintained that they harbored no racism. Of course they banned blacks on account of their race, but only because they believed that to do otherwise would injure their business. That decision, Ollie maintained, was legally his to make. Unlike Maddox, the McClungs had no interest in violence or lawlessness. "I felt we were doing right," Ollie Sr. reflected, "but I didn't want anybody thinking that I was violating the law." To obey the law, the McClungs believed, they had to change it.[13]

Because of his victory in court, Ollie McClung, Sr., became something of a hero to segregationists. But Ollie insisted that business and religion were his only concerns. "Ollie takes no delight in the fact that he has become the champion of segregationists everywhere," *Life* reported. In the civil rights era, arguments about property rights—like those about public education—unavoidably became arguments about race. And Ollie was just another part of that experimental revolution. The McClungs stated, "The racial issue just happened to be the issue over which this controversy of federal control of private property and dictation of private business arose." Just as the age of civil rights produced unwitting radicals, it could also turn the unsuspecting into segregationist icons. Some evidence suggested that Ollie respected black people. After his religious conversion, he took time off in 1961 and 1962 to preach in churches across the country. The devotion of African-Americans impressed him. Ollie Sr. insisted, "Many Negroes occupy a higher station in the eyes of God than whites do." But not quite high enough for Ollie to serve.[14]

The Supreme Court soon elevated African-American barbecue-seekers to that plane. On December 14, 1964, the Court ruled against the McClungs. It held that Ollie's did trade in interstate commerce, since a substantial portion of its meat came from outside Alabama. Therefore, Ollie's was subject to the Civil Rights Act and must admit black customers at once. Ollie Sr. was dismayed. "I'm shocked over the decision. . . . The ownership and use of private property is basic to the American way of life. I'm sad that the . . . Court didn't see it our way." The next day, Ollie's agreed to integrate—but not without some choice words. "As law-abiding Americans we feel we must bow to the edict of the Supreme Court." A decade after the *Brown v. Board of Education* decision enraged white southerners, the McClungs declared, "This could well prove to be the most . . . disastrous decision handed down by this court." Then the previously unimaginable occurred. On Wednesday, December 16, five African-Americans entered Ollie's Barbecue. They quietly enjoyed both Ollie's barbecued meats and their own civil rights. Both sides reported "no problems," as Ollie Sr. said. "Everything was all right." One of the black men agreed. "Everything was lovely. Lovely. Not a single incident. We sure enjoyed Ollie's good barbecue." On that table, Ollie's hickory-smoked meat and time-tested recipe must have seemed particularly sweet—if not quite worth a lifelong wait.[15]

2

STRUGGLES TO INTEGRATE BUSINESSES and public accommodations neither originated nor culminated with the controversy over the 1964 Civil Rights Act. In a sense, every previous boycott and sit-in was part of that same effort. The 1955 Montgomery bus boycott may have been the most famous, but it was not the first. Blacks in Baton Rouge waged a bus boycott in 1953; African-Americans throughout the South variously resisted Jim Crow on buses, streetcars, and trains during the 1940s and 1950s. And contests over segregated facilities extended far beyond the realm of public transport. Lunch counters were the scene of many standoffs between segregationists and civil rights advocates well before the 1964 legislation was enacted. The 1960 student sit-ins that occurred in Greensboro, Nashville, and fifty-two other cities might just as well have taken place at Ollie's or the Pickrick. Observers realized how deeply Jim Crow penetrated every nook and cranny of southern life only when African-Americans challenged its authority over those dominions. Shortly after the sit-ins, blacks engaged in direct action of other sorts—

from kneel-ins at churches to oceanside wade-ins. In 1960, blacks swam in the Gulf of Mexico off the coast of Biloxi, Mississippi. The naked eye might have seen human beings cooling off in the water, but many Jim Crow southerners glimpsed deep transgression. Racial custom dictated where a person lived, walked, prayed, shopped, and ate—and into what part of the Atlantic Ocean he or she could dive. When the Civil Rights Act passed in 1964, it attempted to open parts of the world that segregation had closed. Blacks could swim in pools if they wished, and wade in the ocean; they could sit on buses where they liked, shop in stores of their choice, and enjoy barbecue and fried chicken in any restaurant they pleased.

After John F. Kennedy first proposed civil rights legislation in June 1963, many human relations organizations applied pressure on businesses. They advised proprietors to desegregate voluntarily, and thus control the terms of the transition. But nobody wanted to take the lead. "The owners of restaurants, hotels, motels and theaters seem to be saying, 'I will if he does,' " Frances Pauley wrote in July as head of the Georgia Council on Human Relations. "No one wants to be a martyr or a hero. Everyone wants to make his dollar without disturbance." Many seemed to realize that desegregation was ultimately inevitable—it was a matter of when, not if. In 1961, more than three-quarters of southerners polled by Gallup believed the day would come "when whites and Negroes will be . . . eating in the same restaurants, and . . . sharing the same public accommodations." When that moment came, Pauley argued, white southerners would be living in a new world. They had just one choice: to enter it willingly, or be hurled in. "This is revolution, whether people like it or not. They will be caught in the fire whether they choose sides or sit silently." The impact of desegregation was one rare issue on which Frances Pauley and the *Albany Herald* agreed. Days before President Johnson signed the Civil Rights Act, the *Herald* predicted the law would "compel a drastic change in local social customs." Around the South, whites perceived great—and terrible—things in the Civil Rights Act. "Any way you look at it," said an Albany official, "great changes are coming to the Southern way of life." White southern businessmen saw themselves at the center of that change, and they trembled.[16]

Integrating a business was not quite like integrating the Atlantic Ocean. Proprietors were quick to point out that desegregation was not just about black civil rights, but—as Ollie McClung had argued—it affected property rights and jostled the prerogatives of businessmen. In July 1963, the owner of Burlington, North Carolina's, Paramount Theater lashed out at President Kennedy's proposed bill. "It is time that our Congress woke up as to what the Kennedy boys are doing to this country; little by little they are taking away our individual freedoms," Iredell Hutton wrote. "It is getting to be a hell of a note when a person that owns a business cannot sell to or serve whom he chooses." It was not about serving just anybody, but African-Americans in particular. Hutton's justifications of segregation sounded eerily familiar. "When the negro has earned the right, he should be accepted and not until then." Congress deemed that blacks had finally "earned" that most American of rights in 1964, but many southerners disagreed.[17]

As a leading member of the Senate's Judiciary Committee, North Carolina Democrat Sam Ervin found himself in the middle of the fight over the Civil Rights Act. Ervin publicly opposed the legislation, did his best to stall it in committee, and filibustered along with other southern senators. Back home, Ervin's constituents cheered him on. Few were more vehement than Tar Heel business owners who feared integration. Nathan Blanchard ran the Albemarle Bowling Center, a nine-lane alley, in coastal Elizabeth City. Blanchard believed that if any small business integrated, it would lose all its customers and fail. Bowling alleys presented a particularly difficult problem, he maintained, for they possessed a social character other businesses lacked. "Bowling is a social affair and white people in this section will not socialize with negro[e]s." The Civil Rights Act would spell the death of small businesses, he surmised. "I cannot believe that right thinking Americans want to see every small business fail." Segregation in public accommodations was an issue dear to many small businessmen. And the Civil Rights Act was a difficult challenge to stomach. "It is a tough pill," wrote George Colclough, manager of the Burlington (North Carolina) Merchants Association. "I hope that the law-abiding citizens of the South can adjust our thinking enough that we can stay out of jail."[18]

After the Senate voted to end debate on the bill, L. J. Moore sent Ervin a query. He owned Moore's Barbecue in New Bern, and showed that Ollie McClung was not the only barbecue owner who was willing to challenge the law. "I want to operate segregated if possible," Moore wrote to Ervin on June 13, 1964. "We are not a chain restaurant nor connected with any other restaurant and do not ship across state lines and don't believe the federal government has any right to regulate us." Locals came to eat barbecue at Moore's, and its owner believed an all-white clientele was essential to the success of his business. For Ervin's opposition to the bill, "all I can say is thank you from the bottom of my heart." Moore's story was not unlike Ollie McClung's. He was quick to point out that his business avoided interstate commerce, and he believed Moore's Barbecue might be exempt from the law. Moore viewed his opposition to the Civil Rights Act as a statement about the limits of the federal government, not about race. He believed that desegregation would mean a sharp loss of business. When litigation finally forced Moore to integrate the restaurant in 1967, he instead locked the door and bulldozed the establishment. Then he bought a large plot of land down the road, where he erected a new restaurant. This business contained only walk-up windows; it lacked a dining room, and therefore avoided the subject of integration. In 1973, Moore's moved to Highway 17 South in New Bern, and built a dining room. Since then, African-Americans and whites have dined side by side. "Times have changed over the years," said Moore's son Tommy. "People have mellowed out." Moore's Barbecue celebrated its sixtieth anniversary in 2005; for just over half its life, the restaurant has operated on an integrated basis.[19]

Many North Carolina businessmen found themselves torn between two impulses—to obey the law, or maintain their business practices and ways of life. Four years before the passage of the Civil Rights Act, a coin-operated laundromat opened in rural Mount Gilead. The business boasted sixteen washers, five dryers, and no black customers. That was the way the owner preferred it, as did his patrons. In a July 8, 1964, letter to Ervin, the owner's wife stated that only Mount Gilead residents frequented the business, and that no tourists passed through. The proprietors wondered whether they would have to integrate. "We want to do what is right but on the other hand we certainly don't want this unless the law states that every business regardless of what kind must allow the negro." Ervin did not offer legal advice, but sent back a copy of HR 7152 and highlighted Title II. Despite the senator's best efforts, desegregation became the law of the land. Ervin found himself mailing out to constituents the same law that he had opposed with all his might.[20]

Like most whites who preferred segregated schools to integrated ones, a large majority of southern white businessmen preferred to keep their shops all white. But just as court orders suddenly confronted parents with the issue of public education's survival, so the Civil Rights Act changed the nature of the question before business owners. After a 1963

NAACP campaign, the city of Memphis implemented voluntary desegregation in downtown theaters and hotels; conflict among restaurant operators ensued. Many Memphis proprietors were closer in outlook to Ollie McClung than to Lester Maddox. They supported segregation more out of custom than malice, and thought it good for business. Restaurant operators worried that if they served blacks, white diners would flee to a competitor's establishment. At the same time, owners feared black civil rights demonstrations. In the end, members of the Memphis Restaurant Association agreed that civil rights protests would be worse for business than integration. Forty restaurants desegregated by the new year. By April 1964, one hundred previously segregated Memphis restaurants served blacks. Ironically, many integrated out of a sense of solidarity with their fellow restaurant owners. They would go up—or down—together. Harlon Fields owned The Flame and The Pancake Man, and presided over the Memphis Restaurant Association. "Every one" of the members opposed integration in principle, Fields asserted, but they dreaded pickets. It was vital to place all restaurants "in the same boat." When a handful bucked the tide and refused to admit blacks, they attracted the ire of other owners. As the SRC's Benjamin Muse wrote, "The 'hold-outs' in restaurant desegregation seemed to arouse . . . wrath as much as the civil rights movement." Black protesters and the federal government did not attract the most contempt. That was reserved for proprietors who stubbornly clung to white supremacy while others integrated. For some restaurant owners, unity trumped segregation.[21]

Few other areas witnessed widespread desegregation before the Civil Rights Act forced it upon them. Only in retrospect could Mississippi district attorney Jesse Boyce Holleman say, "The Civil Rights Act is probably the best thing that ever happened to the South. . . . It took us over what was inevitably coming, and it was going to come by violence or bloodshed." At the time, many white southerners felt quite the opposite. Even as the Atlanta Chamber of Commerce urged businesses to desegregate with peace and grace, it allowed, "the impact of the law will be difficult for many." In the immediate aftermath of the passage of the Civil Rights Act, responses varied widely. Where peaceful integration of public accommodations reigned in one town, blacks were refused service in the next. On a given city block, African-Americans could have doors slammed in their faces in one restaurant and encounter smiling waitresses next door. The South in the summer of 1964 held different examples of change, resistance to change, and ambiguity.[22]

It was not easy to predict which businesses, or which cities, would prove more hospitable to the new law. On the night of July 2, hotbeds of past racial violence hosted new interracial realities. Ten restaurants and bars in Albany, Georgia, served blacks. "We have no alternative but to comply," admitted the heads of the Georgia Restaurant Association, and many Albany proprietors followed their lead. Two hours after President Johnson signed the law, a racially mixed party walked into the restaurant in Albany's Holiday Inn. As Nathaniel Beech ran toward a table, a white woman murmured, "Oh my soul and body!" A small child pointed in Beech's direction. The waitress served Beech his steak, and rendered him almost paralyzed. "Jus' ain' hungry . . . I was expectin' everything but this. I was expectin' the waitress to say, 'Would y'all min' fallin' back out that door you jus' come in at?' " The white workers and clientele at the Holiday Inn took the new law in remarkable stride. "The waitress was icily gracious all during the meal," Peter de Lissovoy recounted in *The Nation.* "Nobody sat at the tables directly adjacent to ours, but nobody got up and left. Everybody stared or took pains to avoid staring." This counted as progress.[23]

Reactions differed across the region. In Jacksonville, Florida, a site of recent racial skirmishes, a waitress at Morrison's cafeteria greeted two blacks on the night of July 2 with a polite "May I help you?" Other restaurant owners predicted substantial losses in sales. Charlottesville's Buddy Glover closed down his business that night. On July 3, a thirteen-year-old black boy had his hair cut in the same Kansas City barbershop that had denied him service the previous day. Events confounded old notions, created novel realities, and spawned new fears. While many Albany businessmen served blacks, few wanted the world to know about it. One of the rare arrests during integration's first day occurred in an Albany restaurant, where the owner had a television cameraman detained. Blacks in Mississippi did not immediately test the new law, and reports of refused service came from scattered towns and cities, including Selma and Memphis. In places large and small, from Montgomery, Alabama, to Petersburg, Virginia, many became the first-ever black customers in various restaurants and theaters. The legislation itself was historic enough; that compliance greeted it in parts of Dixie proved just as amazing. "The calm with which some hold-out segregationists accepted the change almost matched the historic enactment of the sweeping legislation a century after Lincoln emancipated the slaves," the *Atlanta Journal and Constitution* reported."[24]

In a surprising string of events, some Jackson businessmen abided that change. A mid-sized city and the state capital, Jackson served as a Citizens' Council fortress in the heart of staunchly segregationist Mississippi. The violent rule of Jim Crow in the Magnolia State often obliterated supposed differences between cities and rural backwaters. Jackson trod a path different from that of most other cities in the state. On July 3, the Chamber of Commerce urged compliance with the Civil Rights Act. Mayor Allen Thompson allowed that the law personally repulsed him. "I don't believe in it. I think it is taking away some of the freedoms of our people." But the Civil Rights Act stuck Thompson, along with every other southern politician, between segregation and law and order. He ultimately defended the law. "It's the law and it must be obeyed until it is struck down." On July 5, a total of twelve black guests secured rooms at the King Edward Hotel, Heidelberg Hotel, and Sun-n-Sand Motel. Jackson even provided police escorts for African-Americans from the airport to the Heidelberg. For hotel owners, neither of the available options promised peace: integration would court the wrath of the Citizens' Council; resistance risked black protest and legal injunctions. "Whatever we decided it would have been 'wrong,' " one hotel executive said. "But now that it's done, I can breathe easier." When peaceful desegregation occurred in segregationist citadels like Jackson, it usually followed strong stands by leaders. Businessmen appreciated the guidance of Thompson and the Chamber of Commerce, although some white citizens did not. One mother wrote to the *Jackson Daily News* after her daughter unknowingly attended an integrated theater. "Had we known . . . Negroes were in the theater my daughter would not have . . . been allowed to attend because . . . 'a little integration is just like a little pregnancy; only an abortion or birth can correct it.' " While proprietors of the King Edward, Heidelberg, and Sun-n-Sand helped give birth to new racial realities in Jackson, those at the Robert E. Lee Hotel chose a different approach.[25]

As Jackson's third-largest hotel, the Robert E. Lee had 250 rooms, rose twelve stories high, and stood two blocks from the state capitol. The hotel with its sparkling marble floors served as a popular meeting place for groups that honored the Old South. The Veterans of the Army of the Confederate States celebrated its reunion there as recently as 1952. The brass doorknob to every room, like the door to the elevator, contained a likeness of the famous bearded general. As other hotels in Jackson registered African-American guests, Robert E. Lee proprietor Stewart

Gammill, Jr., put up a sign: "Closed in Despair: Civil Rights Bill Unconstitutional." On July 6, the day that eleven blacks played rounds at the Jackson Municipal Golf Course, the Robert E. Lee turned away guests. Gammill explained he could no longer run the business as he wished. "Unlike its namesake," the UPI's Robert Gordon wrote, "the stately Robert E. Lee Hotel refused to surrender to the forces of the federal government, and had committed suicide instead." Days later, Gammill announced that the hotel would come back to life after all—in a different incarnation. He leased the property to the Robert E. Lee Management Company, which established a private membership. As the state legislature called a special session to aid private schools with taxes, the hotel offered legislators free rooms for the session. While other Jackson hotels integrated, the Robert E. Lee morphed into a private club. There were always some southerners willing to jump into the last ditch.[26]

In a region where the past appeared on doorknobs and elevators, few sites of the civil rights movement provided so dramatic a historical backdrop as St. Augustine, Florida. Black and white protesters waged struggles over the future quite literally on the terrain of the past. St. Augustine's Old Slave Market served as the locus for many downtown demonstrations, and marked the events with an epic quality. Local NAACP leader Robert Hayling pointed out that St. Augustine, the oldest permanent European settlement in the United States, was also the oldest center of black oppression. Founded by the Spanish in 1565, the city prepared to mark its quadricentennial the following year. President Kennedy had appointed a special commission to help with the celebration. Restaurants and motels formed the backbone of the city's economy, one that relied upon tourism for 80 percent of its income. St. Augustine might have been a charming town on the Florida coast, but in race relations it closely resembled Albany or Birmingham. White extremists exerted immense influence over the town of 15,000. Public facilities were entirely segregated; African-American employees suffered frequent discrimination, and the black community of 3,500 endured constant intimidation and brutality. Local black leaders became alarmed that the federal government might pump money into a quadricentennial celebration for a city rife with such injustice. Fannie Fullerwood, head of the St. Augustine area NAACP, alerted Vice President Lyndon Johnson to the racial situation in 1963. The Florida Advisory Committee to the U.S. Commission on Civil Rights then issued a report recommending that the federal government cut off funds for the celebration. Whites seethed and fretted over the potential loss of income. They blamed black activists for such a prospect. Hayling, a new dentist in town and also youth advisor to Fullerwood's NAACP chapter, assured whites that blacks stood ready for any retaliation. "I and others have armed and we will shoot first and ask questions later. . . . We are not going to die like Medgar Evers." Evers, the leader of Mississippi's NAACP, was assassinated earlier in 1963. When white vigilantes shot at Hayling's home, African-Americans returned their fire. Hayling sought SCLC's help, and on May 18, 1964, Martin Luther King, Jr., arrived in the "Ancient City." King came to St. Augustine as the Senate filibuster raged. If King's visit to Birmingham in 1963 had ignited violence that led to Kennedy's initial civil rights legislation, now in St. Augustine, that law met the test of reality.[27]

By the time King set foot in St. Augustine, city residents were well acquainted with civil rights "agitators." The right-wing John Birch Society was powerful. Most whites in town firmly believed that communists drove the civil rights movement. To whites, compromise was impossible when faced with such a malevolent enemy. But the controversy over quadricentennial funds stimulated black demands for a biracial commission; racial tension mounted. Veterinarian Ron Jackson was one white who supported the call for a biracial commission, but he quickly found himself ostracized. One either had to throw in with the John Birch camp, or with the NAACP. "You got pushed to one side or another. If you tried to stay in the middle your friends became your enemies." Although blacks turned to civil rights demonstrations in 1963, they failed to force changes in white attitudes. Most whites in St. Augustine continued to believe they knew what was good for "their Negroes," and it surely was not civil rights. Hayling sent letters to students at New England colleges, hoping that some would travel to St. Augustine and help dramatize the prevailing discrimination. Mrs. Malcolm Peabody, the seventy-two-year-old mother of Massachusetts governor Endicott Peabody, was one who answered Hayling's call. She came to St. Augustine early in 1964, and was promptly arrested. The national spotlight followed Peabody to Florida. A conservative leader called it "an invasion." One man commented, "We're a target city . . . not primarily because of segregation or racial discrimination, but because we are the nation's oldest city." St. Augustine whites railed against the struggle for civil rights and applauded Peabody's arrest.[28]

After King and SCLC arrived, James Brock and his Monson Motor

Lodge moved to the center of controversy. Brock was known as a moderate among St. Augustine businessmen, but like most other white business owners, he banned blacks from his establishment. On June 11, one day after the filibuster ended, King and fellow SCLC leader Ralph Abernathy led a ten-person contingent to the Monson. They requested food at the restaurant. Brock refused service, and King engaged him in an argument that grew long and heated. King explained the types of humiliations blacks endured daily, and Brock replied, "You realize it would be detrimental to my business to serve you." Brock smiled at television cameras and stated, "I would like to invite my many friends throughout the country to come to Monson's. We expect to remain segregated." Police arrived to arrest King and his group. The following week, 300 civil rights supporters marched through the streets and ended up at Brock's motel. On June 18, religious leaders and civil rights activists descended upon the Monson—where 239 demonstrators had already been arrested. Brock blocked the restaurant door and, after the clergymen knelt to pray, shoved them toward the police. Seven protesters then engaged in a swim-in, jumping into the lodge's outdoor pool. Brock poured two gallons of cleaning agents into the water. While the protesters floated in a pool of chemicals, off-duty policemen dove in and arrested them. This was what the fight over public accommodations had become. A "moderate" motel owner poisoned his pool, out of which two soaked cops and seven dripping protesters emerged. Brock then drained his pool, refilled it, and raised a Confederate flag over the Monson.[29]

After the Civil Rights Act passed, St. Augustine's leaders grappled with a new reality. Businessmen met on July 3 to determine their response. Protests against Jim Crow had already devastated the local tourism industry—and now segregation was against the law. The businessmen voted to comply, 75–5, although few of those seventy-five did so happily. As the established public face of St. Augustine proprietors, Brock informed the press of their decision. The Civil Rights Act showed that the law could force what many white southerners, before the 1960s, thought would take generations to occur. King confidant Andrew Young had previously demonstrated at the Monson. But on July 3, Young and others returned to the motel's restaurant. "We went back to that same restaurant . . . and those people were just wonderful. They were apologetic. They said, 'We were just afraid of losing our business. We didn't want to be the only ones to be integrated. But if everybody's got to do it, we've been ready for it a long time.' " The change seemed too swift and complete to be believable. Young recalled that in the same restaurant, before the law passed, a waitress had poured coffee on him. Now she served him with a smile. Perhaps it was the kind of extraordinary change that could be achieved only by people whose racial behavior was conflicted, paradoxical, and full of paternalism and fear. On the other hand, perhaps the transformation was not nearly as thorough as appearances suggested.[30]

Days after the Civil Rights Act was passed, many businesses in St. Augustine desegregated. Black marches died down, as African-Americans tested newly integrated facilities. If a new morning of desegregation had dawned, night fell quickly. In the face of civic leaders' unwillingness to take stands either for integration or a return to segregation, white supremacist organizations stepped into the emerging power vacuum. During some civil rights marches, Ku Klux Klan members had abused police and attacked reporters. On July 4, Klansmen chased blacks from restaurants. The Klan began to picket businesses that integrated, including the Monson Motor Lodge. On July 16, Brock again barred African-Americans from his restaurant. Yet even that act of resegregation could not save him from the punishment of violent segregationists. Although Brock reached a truce with the local white supremacist organization, out-of-town Klansmen firebombed the Monson. Cowed by white supremacist threats, many other St. Augustine businesses resegregated by the third week of July. Lawsuits were filed against a number of proprietors. In a series of hearings at the end of July, defendants confessed that they stopped serving African-Americans after white segregationists threatened violence. The ordeal of St. Augustine businesses exposed the messiness in that sprawling process of social change. Segregation and integration were less permanent states than shifting realities, subject to the powerful winds of the age. The countervailing forces of the federal government, the black freedom struggle, and white resistance pushed southerners this way and that, in thousands of different directions for as many different reasons. When integration finally came, one process ended and another began.[31]

On July 28, a host of restaurateurs appeared before federal judge Bryan Simpson. They all attested to the same basic experience. Leonard Grissom, owner of Grissom's South Seas, recounted a phone call he received on July 5 — two days after he integrated. Asked if he was serving blacks, Grissom responded, "Yeah, everybody is." If he did not stop, the caller threatened, the South Seas would be "closed up." When Grissom arrived at the restaurant the following morning, one window had been shattered by a rock. Whites picketed that day. "I put my hands up and told them, 'you win.'" Segregation returned to the South Seas. After Wallace Colley received a phone threat, Colley's Shrimp House also began to ban blacks. Tom Xynidis, through a thick Greek accent, detailed similar tribulations at his Seafarer restaurant. Xynidis, clearly in torment on the witness stand, constantly wrung his hands. He recalled a beating he witnessed on July 12, when a gang of whites set upon a black man and his white attorney after they emerged from a nearby inn. On July 16, a "peaceable and orderly" group of five blacks approached the Seafarer. Three white men entered at the same time and told the waitresses they would "see whether or not I served the colored people." Xynidis was "afraid if my place exists in the morning. . . . I didn't sleep all night." The Seafarer still stood the next morning, but it resegregated. White supremacists began to focus more energy on business owners who buckled under the Civil Rights Act than on protesting blacks. Sam Russo, owner of the Flamingo Café, recounted that one anonymous caller "told me that I've fed 'em, I'm a bigger sonofabitch than the niggers." Russo, like Grissom, Xynidis, and Colley, soon moved from an integrated business back to a segregated one.[32]

So did James Brock. After Brock took the witness stand, a *Newsweek* reporter dubbed him "the star of the show." Brock embodied the deep strains of the decade's social conflict. In the span of a month, he both doused civil rights protesters with acid and was bombed by the Klan. During an age of intense passions, the middle could be a difficult place. "You're the James Brock who poured muriatic acid in the swimming pool while the Negroes were swimming there?" asked attorney Tobias Simon. Brock admitted he was, and confirmed that weeks after the swimming-pool incident, he served blacks at his motel. Brock then received bomb threats. From July 9 to July 11, whites picketed the Monson. "Delicious food, eat with niggers here" read one of their signs. "Niggers sleep here, would you?" asked another. Cars with Confederate flags watched over the motel, and few white customers crossed the picket line. "I'm scared," Brock said. "I'm scared of elements unknown to me. I'm not scared of what I can see, I'm afraid of what I can't see." Brock was uniquely situated, as one who drew the ire of both Martin Luther King, Jr., and hard-line white supremacists. "I've had the pleasure of being threatened by both sides." One side forced the integration of Brock's motel; the other bombed it after that desegregation occurred.[33]

The Monson became a civil rights battleground, with Brock caught in the crossfire. On July 11, after three days of pickets, Brock requested an audience with Halstead "Hoss" Manucy. Manucy was the powerful leader of the thousand-member Ancient City Hunting Club. In heavily Catholic St. Augustine, the club served as a local complement to the Ku Klux Klan. Several members of the Ancient City Hunting Club doubled as deputy sheriffs. Brock asked Manucy to "get these pickets off my back." Manucy replied, "I don't think they want you to serve niggers." Brock concurred, "Nobody wants to serve them." James Brock was not trapped by his conscience, but pulled in opposing directions by the law on the one hand and Manucy on the other. Another motel owner explained the plight of St. Augustine businessmen. "We have been caught in a dilemma. . . . We are forced to serve Negroes although it hurts our business. If we serve them, the white pickets turn the rest of the business away." As a *Newsweek* dispatch stated, St. Augustine businessmen "have thrust themselves between the grinding forces of the vigilantes and the Civil Rights Act." Put another way, as attorney Tobias Simon said, "These guys have committed suicide." Such was the predicament of many white business owners in the age of civil rights. For a time, firebombs spoke louder than court injunctions. St. Augustine businesses endured segregation, integration, and processes of resegregation and reintegration. Finally, on August 5, Judge Simpson specifically enjoined Manucy and his followers from disrupting desegregation. He also ordered the integration of seventeen segregated or resegregated public businesses. The Old Slave Market still stood at the center of town, but segregation started to fall.[34]

Nothing about that process was smooth. Amid ongoing white attacks, African-Americans continued to fear for their safety through July and August. Few St. Augustine whites accepted the decade's racial changes, and the events of 1964 left the city bitterly divided. While whites embraced traditional racial attitudes, few tried to claim that harmony still existed. A Florida investigative commission issued a report in December that blamed the summer's racial crisis on Martin Luther King. In January 1965, B. C. Roberts, superintendent of the Castillo de San Marcos National Monument, articulated local white sentiment. "If [civil rights leaders] come again, they would be met with the same reaction. The attitudes haven't changed." After 1964, race relations lost all veneers of cordiality. African-Americans could eat in white-owned St. Augustine restaurants, but word would travel back to their bosses—and many of those blacks then feared for their jobs. White-on-black violence persisted into 1965 and 1966, when the John Birch Society attempted to wrest control of the PTA at St. Augustine High School. By 1968, Birch supporters were finally defeated, and school desegregation came to St. Augustine in 1970. Into the 1980s, St. Augustine saw change and stagnation. Hoss Manucy embodied that antagonism. An old NAACP member, James Jackson, reported shock and amazement at the changes he saw in Manucy. When the two almost bumped into each other downtown, Manucy said, "Excuse me, sir." To Jackson, these words marked a previously inconceivable transformation. But while Manucy's racial etiquette may have changed, he continued to believe the Ancient City Hunting Club was in the right during the 1960s. "I thought we was right," Manucy said in 1985. "I still think so."[35]

OBSERVERS ARGUED THAT IF WHITES held out against the Civil Rights Act, and if the new law cultivated violent resistance, it did so in the Black Belt. Claude Sitton wrote, "The change is taking place far more quickly and easily in urban areas than rural ones." David Pearson, a member of President Johnson's new Community Relations Service, a race relations agency created by the 1964 Civil Rights Act, commented, "The pattern so far has been: The larger the city—the greater the compliance. The rural areas will be difficult." In many cities across southern states—Atlanta, Nashville, Charlotte, Mobile, Greenville, and others—blacks successfully tested the Civil Rights Act. Reports of violence most often came from Black Belt areas like Grenada, Mississippi, and Selma, Alabama. "Restaurants, theaters, and courthouse facilities seem as segregated as they were at the turn of the century," journalist Paul Good wrote from Grenada. Conventional wisdom had it that integration came most smoothly to Texas, Virginia, and Florida, and that the fiercest resistance occurred in Alabama and Mississippi. But there were beatings at the Watts Grill outside Chapel Hill, North Carolina; violence and tension permeated St. Augustine, Florida. Blacks were served at Birmingham's Town and Country Restaurant and Jackson, Mississippi's, Sun-n-Sand Motel. In the summer of 1964, realities both defied generalizations and conformed to them.[36]

Georgia exhibited all of these clashing truths, and a study of the state during July 1964 throws these patterns into sharp relief. In the weeks after the passage of the Civil Rights Act, many of Georgia's larger cities boasted compliance. In Atlanta, most hotels and restaurants quickly desegregated. Lester Maddox's Pickrick restaurant and Moreton Rolleston's Heart of Atlanta motel were exceptions, though notable ones. But the Pickrick's location, away from the wealthier "island suburbs," highlighted the point that class lines occasionally revealed more than urban and rural distinctions. In "The City Too Busy to Hate," the desegregation of various facilities—from restaurants and other business to parks, pools, and golf courses—often went smoothly in those areas that poor whites had already fled. Where urban neighborhoods grappled with racial transitions, public places became hotly contested arenas.[37]

Elsewhere in Georgia, cities met desegregation in varying ways. Savannah had experienced racial unrest in 1963. That year, direct action protest came to a place where many still breathed the air, lived in the mansions, and harbored the prejudices of the Old South. But demonstrations succeeded, and on October 1, public and private facilities integrated. By New Year's Day 1964, Martin Luther King could call Savannah "the most desegregated city south of the Mason-Dixon line." In Savannah, no resistance to desegregation followed the Civil Rights Act. Blacks in the state's third and fourth largest cities, Macon and Columbus, integrated facilities shortly after passage of the legislation. Almost every hotel, motel, and restaurant served African-Americans. Macon, like Savannah, experienced black sit-ins prior to 1964. As much as anything else, this fact helped to explain which locales took desegregation in stride. Those that had witnessed black protest before seemed much more willing to abide by the new law. While Columbus hosted protests in the early 1960s, the previous demonstrations were ineffective. But in 1964, most businesses complied with the new law. Two restaurants desegregated despite the threats of a segregationist county commissioner, and a hamburger stand that initially banned blacks was serving them by July 20. In Augusta, the dominion of leading segregationist Roy Harris, reaction to the Civil Rights Act was mixed. Talmadge Memorial Hospital refused service to blacks in its cafeteria, and the city golf course became an all-white private club. But blacks reported no other trouble in desegregating hotels, motels, and restaurants. General compliance with the Civil Rights Act greeted blacks in the southeastern coastal city of Brunswick, but when a handful of teenagers approached a city pool, it was shut down. In Rome, in the northwest corner of the state, lunch counters and motels all agreed to desegregate. A black bellhop who led an African-American to his room at the Hotel General Forrest reflected, "I've waited 33 years for this moment." That moment came to many Georgia cities in the summer of 1964.[38]

As a city wedged firmly in the Black Belt, Albany blurred the line between urban and rural. Because of Albany's previous infamy, national newspapers ran stories about its response to the Civil Rights Act. There were events to fit any argument. Many hotels, motels, and restaurants complied. But at the private pool, ten black would-be swimmers were arrested and convicted for "idling and loitering." The Arctic Bear drive-in refused service to blacks. An African-American reverend who tested the new law had moonshine planted in his car and was arrested. In many national periodicals, shaded maps of the South appeared. Dark splotches colored Mississippi, Alabama, and parts of Louisiana and Georgia to denote resistance to the Civil Rights Act. In Texas, Florida, Virginia, and North Carolina, light shades of gray appeared—apparently to designate a considerable degree of compliance. But realities like those in Albany could not be shaded. They combined dark episodes of resistance with bright instances of smooth compliance. The shade of gray captured nothing and everything about that experience. "Compliance" and "resistance" to the Civil Rights Act were difficult things to track. In many small towns, neither violence nor widespread desegregation occurred. Black fear and white threats could leave towns without tests of the law or with affairs of integration that were so orchestrated they had little meaning. News reports often described towns as either "violent" or "quiet." But those words described few southern locales. One could not say, with any precision, that either "compliance" or "resistance" reigned. The truth was far more muddled.[39]

The march toward integration was more tortuous in rural Georgia than in the cities. Northeast of Macon, motels and restaurants desegregated in the town of Milledgeville. After the hospital forced blacks to the rear entrance for three weeks, the police reversed that policy. In many more small towns, violence propped up segregation. A mob of Winder whites turned blacks away from a theater. Whites in Waynesboro and Washington, two small towns in eastern Georgia, met the law with resistance. Fights broke out at several Waynesboro gas stations when blacks attempted to use the bathrooms. They tested no other facilities there. Businesses in Washington did not integrate because blacks were too fearful of violence to test them.[40]

To many Georgians, a locale did not truly qualify as rural Georgia unless it sat in the southwestern Black Belt—among the twenty-three counties (including Dougherty, Terrell, Baker, and Lee) that formed the second and third congressional districts. There, peaceful integration of public facilities was rare. The situation in Thomasville was exceptional, where motels, restaurants, and theaters complied. Whites in Perry, Tifton, Cochran, Americus, and Valdosta established a volatile norm in Southwest Georgia. Blacks were barred from all three Perry restaurants they approached; the same thing happened in Valdosta. At one restaurant in Perry, state troopers blocked blacks; a white mob stood in their way at another. Many Southwest Georgia whites agreed with the Cochran city official who said about desegregation of movie theaters, "Ain't no niggers going in our show." That mind-set found its most violent expression in Americus. On July 2 and July 3, groups of SNCC workers endured beatings after they ate in newly desegregated restaurants. On July 5, white mobs formed at the movie theater and race riots threatened to break out. "Deceptively sleepy by day," the *New York Times* described Americus, "this small city . . . is tense with terror after dark." To scare African-Americans away from businesses, gangs of whites roamed black neighborhoods at night. Many Americus restaurants and other businesses indeed "complied" with the Civil Rights Act and served blacks. But white mobs often attacked those blacks. In Americus, compliance, resistance, and violence existed side by side. For citizens who, in 1963, "would rather have had their banks and businesses fail than to desegregate their town," according to Frances Pauley, this state of affairs passed for an almost perverse sort of progress.[41]

While whites in Southwest Georgia continued to beat back the Civil Rights Act, their famed senator accommodated. Richard Russell initially served as a lightning rod for opposition to the Civil Rights Act. Before the act was passed, Russell received droves of mail from white Georgians who wished to maintain segregation. The owner of a Macon drive-in restaurant wrote to Russell at the end of May, "I feel that the public accommodations part of this bill will put me out of business if I comply with the act, but I still say I won't feed a nigger in my place." Prior to the law's passage, Russell was receptive to defiance. Indeed, he helped to nurture it and tried to make it respectable. After the Civil Rights Act passed, Russell attempted to respect that law as he would any other. On July 15, following violence in Americus and elsewhere, Russell implored Georgians to abide by the act "for as long as it is there." Russell displayed little hypocrisy in his stand for law and order. "It is the understatement of the year to say that I do not like this statute. . . .

However, it is now on the books." Unlike Russell, some southern politicians (such as George Wallace) urged resistance against the law in *Brown* or the Civil Rights Act, but denounced "anarchic" civil disobedience when it came wrapped in black skins. The Macon storeowner had concluded his May letter to Russell, "The next time you are in Macon stop by with us and I hope we will still be serving just white folks." Among the Civil Rights Act's many achievements, it dashed one proprietor's hopes.[42]

The Civil Rights Act not only crushed white hopes, but caused many jaws to drop. Some greeted the law with sound and fury, others responded in befuddlement, but few were sure what it all signified. Journalist Peter de Lissovoy traveled to Albany during the summer of 1964, and captured with a few illustrations the uncertainty, irony, and very novelty of those months. On Sunday night, July 12, de Lissovoy found his way to the Cabin in the Pines, a bar, dance club, motel, and restaurant just south of Albany's city limits. As the only white in a sea of blacks, de Lissovoy was himself testing the new Civil Rights Act. At about two in the morning, Bo Riggins, the manager, tapped him on the shoulder and nodded toward the door. A police car rolled up, and officers arrested de Lissovoy on charges of trespassing and being drunk and disorderly. His cellmates in the local jail later expressed astonishment "that I could have been so stupid, so lacking in imagination, as to think that I could get away with 'mixin'' in South Georgia." Blacks integrated some of the city's restaurants on July 2, but many of the juke joints and dance halls, poolrooms and swimming pools remained off-limits to would-be mixers. "Troublemakers" were "troublemakers," whether they happened to be black or white.[43]

Albany's African-Americans supported de Lissovoy, and C. B. King served as his lawyer. A Baptist deacon scolded the Cabin in the Pines manager, Bo Riggins. "Now the whites startin' to do right, we can't one of us keep the wrong alive." In jail, de Lissovoy gauged local white views of right and wrong. Stuck in a cell with a mattress thief and an unsuccessful escapee, de Lissovoy found that the convicts had little respect for the Civil Rights Act. It was not that they expected many people to overtly resist it; they simply doubted the law would matter. "It's gonna change some things," the escapee reflected, "but mos' alla life down heah gonna go on jes' the same." The mattress thief took a more defiant position. "It ain' gonna change me. It ain' nothin' but anothuh civil wah gonna change me an' then they hafta shoot me 'fo I sit down t' table with one a them." In his exaggerated declaration, civil war and even death were better than integration. The prisoners believed that local blacks possessed a similar discomfort with the law. According to them, few residents of either race had much interest in mixing in South Georgia. "This heah a Southern white man," the escapee proclaimed, as he pinched the thief's cheek. "But overlook it. S'posin' it works and we all mixed up in the hotels an' restaur'ants. So what? After a while, somebody gonna get tired a the bad feelin'—nigguhs or the white folk . . . an' they'll stop comin'." The crucial question was not whether businessmen would comply with the law, but whether citizens would alter their social choices in light of it. The unsuccessful escapee in a Dougherty County jail was pessimistic. "This law ain't gonna mean shit along the whole run a life."[44]

Some signs pointed in the opposite direction—if not toward grand shifts in social life and racial attitudes, then at least in eye-opening episodes of integration. After C. B. King gained de Lissovoy's release from jail, the reporter witnessed an extraordinary scene in Harlem, the African-American section of town. A microphone and amplifier graced the front yard of an unpainted clapboard house. As a woman serenaded the neighborhood, an audience grew and spilled over the curb. At about 8:00 p.m., a Chevrolet rolled up and three young white men emptied out of it. They joined the crowd. One of them swayed with the music, another engaged some black folks in talk, and the third—the drunkest of them all—proceeded to embarrass the other two. As if the whites did not stick out enough, the drunken man made his way toward the microphone. The singer handed it over. "What y'all starin' at us fo'? We white—sho. But that ain' no reason to stare. The bill a rights done been pass'! We got a right." Here was a different take on the meaning of the Civil Rights Act. Not only could blacks go where they pleased, but presumably so could whites. "We gonna stay, an I'm gonna as' this kin' lady to sing *This lil' light a mine* fo' the white people a Albany, G-A, who need it, God knows." For a city recently wracked by racial confrontation, these words—even if prompted by a strong dose of liquor—had in them the ring of a new Albany.[45]

That new Albany soon arrived at the city's pool halls. On a Friday night in July, five white hustlers visited a Harlem poolroom. An African-American pool shark known as Butterball agreed to their challenge, and the houseman racked the balls. Word of the showdown spread rapidly, and spectators packed the hall. "It looked like the Olympic games," de

Lissovoy wrote, "and, in a sense, it was." The group shot pool until past midnight. They decided to shoot the next night across town, in a white poolroom. The game raged for weeks; at long last, the Civil Rights Act had joined in battle the city's best pool players. "It's the new law," Butterball said. "Integration always starts over sport."* That experiment proved short-lived. After all, pool sharks made their money off unsuspecting amateurs, not each other. "The novelty wore off and the poolrooms, white and black, returned to their normal, and tedious, business." While the Civil Rights Act had changed some aspects of life in Albany, a normalcy—that is, de facto segregation—soon reigned again. But things were never quite the same. Even if the "whole run a life" was not transformed overnight, Albany in 1964 looked nothing like the "Cotton Kingdom" immortalized by W. E. B. Du Bois—or even like Laurie Pritchett's 1962 city. Those old orders were mortal.[46]

As the summer wore on, the Civil Rights Act receded from the spotlight. The bodies of three murdered civil rights workers turned up in an earthen dam outside Philadelphia, Mississippi, and in August, the Mississippi Freedom Democratic Party brought its political and moral challenge to the Democratic National Convention. Leroy Collins, head of the federal government's Community Relations Service, commented in January 1965 that compliance with the law was "remarkable." Many others were given to such superlatives; U.S. Assistant Attorney General Burke Marshall called compliance "massive," and the *New York Times* termed it "overwhelming." Collins estimated that 75 percent of Americans affected by Title II were abiding by it. In a survey of fifty-three southern cities (those with at least fifty thousand people), the Community Relations Service found that more than two-thirds of businesses were com-

---

*White southerners followed professional sports just as other Americans did—and they could not deny the success of Bill Russell, Willie Mays, or the already retired Jackie Robinson. Professional sports did not reach the Old Confederacy until baseball's Braves moved to Atlanta in 1966 (and Hank Aaron broke Babe Ruth's home run record there), but high school and college sports—especially football—were integral parts of southern life. It was also in 1966 when the Texas Western basketball team fielded an all-black starting five, and defeated Adolph Rupp's all-white Kentucky squad in the NCAA championship game. Integration did not penetrate college sports in the Deep South (the Southeastern Conference) until the mid- and late 1960s. Few events jolted southern thinking about race more than the 1970 football game in which USC—and its African-American stars—pounded Bear Bryant's hallowed Alabama team. Soon Alabama possessed black stars of its own. Every booster of the Crimson Tide had to root for black athletes or cease to be a fan. One of the first blacks to play for Bear Bryant was offensive lineman Sylvester Croom. In 2003, Croom became the first African-American head coach of a Southeastern Conference football team when he accepted the position at Mississippi State.

plying in nearly every one. "The national attitude," reported the *St. Petersburg Times,* "is statistically shown to be one of compliance." "Compliance" was the term most often bandied about, and overuse stripped the word of its meaning. Although more than two-thirds of city facilities were complying, many still were not. In such an atmosphere, what exactly did "a national attitude of compliance" mean? Even if a new South had come, it brought along with it myriad confusions and complications.[47]

To illustrate the tangled nature of those realities, the *St. Petersburg Times* ran a seven-part series entitled "Highways to Hope." Samuel Adams, an African-American reporter, and his wife, Elenora, traveled the South for two weeks. The couple drove through twelve states and covered 4,300 miles. "If you're a Negro, and if you're a tourist in the South, things are better these days," Adams wrote in November 1964. "Things aren't good yet. But four months after the passage of the Civil Rights Act there have been some real and meaningful changes. The old ways are dying." Adams and his wife discovered that most restaurants and motels along the region's major highways accepted black dollars. But off those main roads, white businessmen were far less welcoming. Adams found some overt resistance to the Civil Rights Act sprinkled in with a host of subterfuges. Many restaurant tables had permanent "reserved" signs; others had two different menus with different price lists; some closed automatically when blacks arrived, or maintained back rooms and anterooms in which black customers were corraled. A few even possessed newly painted "White Only" signs.[48]

For Samuel and Elenora Adams, it was a journey filled with manifold indignities as well as surprising welcomes. Their first night on the road, after being barred from a Florida state park, the couple secured a room at the Ware Hotel in Waycross, Georgia. "Whites watched curiously, Negro employe[e]s with quiet pride and jubilance as we were shown to our room." There was little curiosity on the faces of whites who worked at the Chuck Wagon Drive-In near Hindsville, Georgia. At 3:30 p.m., a white waitress met the Adamses at the door and said, "We're closing." The couple finally found some food at the Liberty County Truck Center, where a server seated them "in a dingy cubbyhole near the 'colored' rest rooms at the rear of the building." When the Adamses crossed the Savannah River into South Carolina, their bad luck continued. At Lane's Motel in Walterboro, the owner told Adams that he was holding his only vacant rooms for bigger families. A similar story greeted them at the El

Rancho Motel, though they finally found a room at the Travelers Motel. At Green's Restaurant in St. George, Samuel and Elenora Adams were handed two menus with different prices—one intended for black customers, the other for whites. The higher prices appeared on the check. A white couple from Pennsylvania pulled up in Green's parking lot, but quickly left when they spotted the black couple in the window. "Y'all see what integration's doing to us?" Mrs. Green said to Samuel Adams. The Greens might not have preferred integration, but they buckled to it. Businessmen in the Carolinas did not like the law, Adams noted. But most "seemed ready to live with it." The couple traveled a road of hope, as the *St. Petersburg Times* called it, but their path was marked with barriers.[49]

Through the mountain country of Kentucky, Tennessee, Virginia, and West Virginia, Samuel Adams was alternately accepted and rejected at establishments in every state. In Danville, Virginia, a city torn by civil rights struggles, he found that "segregation is still the way of life for many businessmen." The couple did not realize they had entered foreign territory before they set foot in the C&E Grill. On a Friday evening, the jukebox played hillbilly music and the bar was filled with working-class white men. The Adamses ordered coffee. A large man who had been playing air hockey leaned over, and the couple filled with fright. He asked, "Can I rest my beer glass on your table?" Even in the whitest honky-tonk, the Adamses could encounter friendliness and good service. In the South after the Civil Rights Act, appearances continued to deceive. The constant refrains "We don't serve colored here" or "We're closed" could come with sneers or smiles, or anything in between. Samuel Adams heard those lines as frequently as he heard greetings like the one from the owners of Scotty's restaurant in Saint Andrews, Tennessee: "Come back when you all are traveling this way."[50]

It took weeks, months, and even years for some proprietors to obey the law, for lawsuits to unfold, and for district courts to order desegregation in specific places. Selma restaurants first received blacks on January 18, 1965. But owners distributed handbills to white customers, suggesting that desegregation was a passing phenomenon. "We seek your indulgence and understanding of the unpleasant position into which we have been forced. . . . We are confident sanity and good sense will return and that we will be able to revert, in time, to our long-established customs and traditions." They hoped and asserted that the law would leave the pace of everyday life unaltered. The *Selma Times-Journal* urged whites to go about their days as if nothing had changed. "Our community must proceed in its normal routine and our activities must continue in an orderly . . . manner." As 1965 approached, many thought it best for whites to look past their problems with the law, and essentially to forget about it. "Nobody has to like this law," the *Raleigh News and Observer* opined. "But the time of resistance is clearly past. The time for as painless adjustment to it as possible has arrived. . . . It may prove much less disturbing than many . . . white people feared." Some southern whites began to insist that the bill they dreaded, the law they fought, and the change they denounced was not so great a change after all.[51]

The Civil Rights Act, like many other victories of the civil rights movement, changed everything and nothing in southern life. To call the Civil Rights Act ineffectual was absurd; to say it ushered in a social revolution was also a stretch. The fact that blacks possessed the legal ability to enter any establishment was a triumph. That blacks knew they had the law on their side, and the right to go anywhere, helped to erase fear and foster dignity. But some whites felt untouched by the law. "Alabamians, like other southerners, have let down some racial barriers," *Birmingham News* staffer George Biggers wrote in December 1964, "but they have experienced only limited desegregation in the process. Because the extent has been so slight, it would be difficult to draw an unreserved conclusion as to whether rank and file now accepted some desegregation as a part of Life." He echoed the Albany prisoner who doubted it would change "the whole run a life." Southern blacks still lived in segregated neighborhoods, held menial jobs, attended segregated schools, and possessed little political power. Businesses where signs came down were not suddenly bastions of interracial interactions. As the years and decades passed, many of these walls fell gradually, becoming imperceptibly lower until it was no longer controversial for a black man to walk into a white barber shop or for his children to swim in a public pool. But even in 1964, some sensed that ingrained practices, power differentials, and prejudices could take lifetimes to overcome. Biggers wrote, "Whether majority acceptance will ever come is a question only time can answer."[52]

Before Congress passed the Civil Rights Act, even advocates of the bill had worries. They wondered whether the law was strong enough, and its enforcement mechanisms substantial enough, to bring desegregation. "During this time we did not fully appreciate the *positive* effect it would have," Frances Pauley reflected in an October 6, 1965, speech to Atlanta's Hungry Club. In June 1964, the operator of a Holiday Inn in Jessup, Georgia, had told Pauley, "It will never pass." That refrain was uttered often. "Many times we heard, 'It will never happen here. Maybe in Atlanta or even in Savannah—but not here!' " The wonder of the Civil Rights Act was that it brought integration to some of those very places. But not to all of them. "In small towns where there is maybe one dirty village café there still has been little testing and little change. There is no great desire on the part of the local Negro to have his head bashed in for that lousy cup of coffee." That was the ambiguous legacy of the Civil Rights Act. It possessed great power and clear limits. The law could not compel African-Americans to *desire* to integrate many places, much less compel whites to embrace them when they did. The "lousy cup of coffee," as Pauley said, was rarely worth the pain, suffering, and indignity it often took to acquire. "The signs are pretty well down. But . . . the practices haven't changed in all places. . . . All sorts of subterfuges are used . . . to continue to shove the Negro around back." The law enshrined new and all-important rights, but many realms of life remained beyond its reach.[53]

Legal victories set the stage for other phases of the struggle. African-Americans soon fixed their gaze on power, economics, and a set of problems whose resolution had less to do with the law than with subtler forces that lurked beneath it and around its edges. And if whites began to countenance the presence of blacks in restaurants and hotels, some also unleashed racism in nuanced ways. Old prejudices did not necessarily die with the new law, nor did the workings of economic power or the rhythms of social interaction. "Desegregation of public accommodations does not basically alter the pattern of social life anywhere," a Mississippi restaurant owner said in December 1964. "That is why it has been accomplished as easily as it has." This was what Pauley meant when she said, "the law is there, thank God, but it only cracks the door."[54]

3

BEFORE AND AFTER the passage of the Civil Rights Act, white southerners viewed the bill with varying degrees of fear, confusion, outrage, and acceptance. Many railed against the "Civil Wrongs Bill" or raised the banner of "white rights." Others envisioned a newer and better region that the law might help cultivate. In Ethelenida Bland, debate over the law brought out many different racial feelings. The Blands resided in Pineville, North Carolina, a small town near Charlotte on the state's southern border. The couple bred "fine Hampshire sheep" on

Blandhill Farms. Following civil rights protests in Birmingham, Bland wrote her congressman on May 28, 1963. Gazing at the violence that the police unleashed on determined blacks, she wrote, "I cannot see how we can stand the turmoil these infuriated negroes are prepared to make in our cities indefinitely." Desiring peace and order, Bland saw no option but to "give in" to African-American demands. "It is terrible to have to give in to their mob pressure, but there seems to be no other way." Riots would occur, she predicted, unless legislators made headway on civil rights. "We could restrain them . . . but we cannot live constantly in such a state of unrest." Bland advised southern politicians to help draft palatable laws before northerners passed stronger ones. "I hope southern leadership will no longer resist civil rights legislation, but will work to see that some moderate type of legislation is devised which will satisfy some negro demands, without jeopardizing our social customs too seriously." In the universe of Blandhill Farms, white customs and black rights could coexist.[55]

Events moved so fast in the 1960s, and with such force, that new realities could appear in the blink of an eye. During the first week of June 1963, President Kennedy prepared to introduce his civil rights plan. After George Wallace's "stand in the schoolhouse door" at the University of Alabama on June 11, Kennedy went on television and urged Americans to end segregation. Bland had already reassessed the situation. "The negroes are insatiable," she wrote in a June 4 letter. She was no longer sure whites could assuage black demands with "moderate legislation." By June 1963, Bland believed, whites had ceded enough. A few schools had desegregated, a handful of cities integrated businesses, and soon Kennedy would push for strong legislation. "We have . . . lost enough of our freedom. I do not believe we should go any further. The situation is completely out of hand."[56]

Bland's two statements, uttered over the span of a week, revealed that it was possible for seemingly contradictory ways of thinking about civil rights to mingle in the same person. In a third letter, penned on June 8, Bland explained that "integration" admitted of many different meanings—depending upon the circumstance. She could support integration in some contexts and oppose it in others. Bland detailed her support for desegregation in hospitals, labor unions, and employment. She opposed Jim Crow in restaurants and hotels, especially as it applied to "well behaved negroes." Integration did not seem an abstract threat; she imagined how it might affect many aspects of life. Integration at universities was all right, according to Bland, though she stood "unequivoca[l]ly opposed" to it below the college level. While qualified blacks could attend college and graduate school, the average black youngster was so inferior to whites that he would drag down the level of primary education. "It would be the white children who would suffer." In addition, Bland backed Jim Crow housing. "A person should have the freedom to decide whom he wants for neighbors. . . . Neighbors often become good friends, and must meet each other every day or so. Their children will play together." Bland went on to oppose integration of bowling alleys, swimming pools, and other recreational facilities. She drew a distinction between social and business endeavors, deploring integration in the former and supporting it in the latter. "In purely business and impersonal relationships, the two races should be able to work together in peace." Almost seventy years after Booker T. Washington addressed the Atlanta Exposition, the mind's eye could see the former slave holding up his hand and telling the crowd, "In all things that are purely social we can be as separate as the fingers, yet one as the hand in all things essential to mutual progress." White southerners applauded that message in 1895, and over the years generations of them internalized it.[57]

Bland viewed civil rights not as something to which blacks were entitled, but as an intrusion into white life: federal government seized freedoms from whites and redistributed them to blacks. Most whites saw civil rights not in terms of black liberties, but as a loss of white freedom. "I wonder if those who are asking for legislation which intrudes on a person's right of preference, realized that the burden will rest on the poorer white citizen." Along with everything else, the debate over civil rights laws carried with it a controversy about class. As seen in the New Orleans school crisis, for instance, the "burden" of integration did indeed rest with the "poorer white citizen." The working-class white, Bland maintained, "cannot afford to belong to private clubs. He cannot send his children to private schools and summer camps." While wealthier white southerners might be able to evade the dreaded social mixing, it would fall unavoidably on the shoulders of poor whites.[58]

A month before President Johnson signed the Civil Rights Act, one of Senator Russell's constituents alerted him to the plight of Georgia's "poor white people." The Georgia man had dropped out of grade school, and admitted, "i cant spell the words i wont to write." Still, he effectively communicated a position. "In ancer to the Civil Rights Bill . . . we dont wont the bill past thir are other ways of helping the negro

In the face of rising black protest, the southwest Georgia town of Albany became a civil rights battleground. On December 16, 1961, whites looked on as police chief Laurie Pritchett arrested Martin Luther King, Jr., and a throng of demonstrators.

When school integration arrived in New Orleans, whites could not remain
bystanders. Hundreds of white families boycotted Frantz Elementary and McDonogh
No. 19, but a handful of parents kept their children in school. Daisy Gabrielle braved
a mob on December 1, 1960, when she brought her daughter Yolanda to Frantz.

During the height of the 1960 New Orleans school crisis, Yolanda Gabrielle gazed out a window at her family's home. The glass had been smashed by the mob's bricks and rocks.

L. J. Moore opened Moore's Barbecue in 1945. Like many southern restaurants, this New Bern, North Carolina, eatery endured civil rights protests and litigation before the business relocated and finally integrated in 1973.

Ollie McClung, owner of Ollie's Barbecue in Birmingham, Alabama, challenged the 1964 Civil Rights Act. McClung appealed his case all the way to the Supreme Court, where he ultimately lost. Soon thereafter, the restaurant integrated without incident. This photograph shows him outside the Birmingham institution on October 2, 1964.

Joseph Cumming headed *Newsweek*'s Atlanta bureau. Shown here at work in 1972, he later marveled that he had been handed "a ringside seat at the most dramatic social revolution in the USA."

Frances Pauley, depicted here circa 1970, led various Atlanta organizations that supported desegregation. In 1962, as the head of the Georgia Council on Human Relations, she issued a mass mailing to the white citizens of Albany, urging them to keep an open mind about demands for black civil rights. The furious replies she received enlightened Pauley as to the intransigence of racial attitudes in the Deep South.

Cumming (*right*) was one of many white southern journalists whom Representative John Lewis once termed the "sympathetic referees" of the civil rights movement. In April 1969, Cumming traveled to Charleston, South Carolina, where he marched with Reverend Ralph Abernathy (*middle*) during a hospital workers' strike.

In 1973, Cumming (*far right*) covered a remarkable transformation in rural Greene County, Alabama. African-Americans, who had gained political power in the years after the passage of the Voting Rights Act, voted into office William McKinley Branch (*far left*) and Thomas Gilmore (*second from right*). Branch became the county's first black probate judge and Gilmore its first black sheriff.

As the 1970 local elections approached, Ralph Banks worked to defeat African-American candidates. After Greene County blacks swept those elections, Banks accepted the job of county attorney. He would be one of only two whites in county posts.

Thomas Gilmore became Greene County's first black sheriff in
1970. When Gilmore ran for reelection in 1974, Ralph Banks
managed his campaign.

In 2005, Eutaw, Alabama, the Greene County seat, exhibited the mixed legacy of the civil rights movement. Some things remained the same: the Banks & Company building still stood over the center of town. Yet the courthouse had been renamed for Judge William McKinley Branch, testimony to the type of change that the civil rights movement had achieved.

without mistreaten the poor white people." The family led difficult lives. "Prais the good Lord we wont haft to go hungary when we get to heaven." They believed black rights would make life even tougher. Through much of the twentieth century, various reformers held out hope—naive though it seemed at times—that poor whites might over-come racism and join blacks in an alliance to break the planter's eco-nomic rule and his iron grip on southern politics. Yet most politicians both nurtured and responded to racial fears. Poor whites were constantly reminded that even if their hunger was not satiated until the next world, they had one empowering thing in the here and now—white skin. The Civil Rights Act threatened the advantages that their whiteness had con-ferred. "The negro are getting more help now than the poor white. Dont the poor whites have some rits."[59]

White southerners pleaded that the impending legislation was by turns unfair, hypocritical, and oppressive. They wondered why "civil rights" applied solely to blacks. June Melvin managed a clothing store in Southern Pines, North Carolina, west of Fayetteville. She pointed out that the dictionary definition of "civil" pertained to "the private rights of *individuals. . . .* There is no mention . . . that these rights are for Negro citizens alone. However, all civil rights legislation is pointed in that direction." Many whites seemed to believe that rights were mutually exclusive, and finite. Whites would lose freedom for every right that blacks gained. "We should not sacrifice the rights of one group to the detriment of another." Melvin's language may have been misleading, but her meaning was clear. Angered that "civil rights" came in the 1960s to mean black equality, many whites embraced the term "civil wrongs." F. M. Bain lived in Raeford, North Carolina, not far from Melvin's store. Bain wrote to Sam Ervin and thanked his senator "for the stand you are taking in the great Civil Wrongs bill." Its passage would spell "the ruination of our country." Such opinions seeped into the minds of some southern youths. Fourteen-year-old David McDougal, of Athens, Geor-gia, wrote to support Senator Russell's "stand on the Civil Wrongs Bill. . . . It will cost the government money." Though only fourteen, McDougal had some incisive points to make. He wondered why African-Americans were granted access to public facilities when in many places they had not yet integrated the schools. "Don't you think we should at least give them an education first!!!" Doubtless persuaded by Senator Russell's own rhetoric, McDougal called the bill "unlawful" and "un-American." To many whites, everything about the Civil Rights Act seemed wrong. They hoped southern politicians would stand against the president and his liberal allies, while standing up for white southerners and their now imperiled freedom. As a Charlotte man wrote to Representative Charles Jonas, "Make a hit with your constituents by . . . opposing such attempts to coerce the white people and exalt the Negroes." On the precarious seesaw of southern race relations, many believed whites would plummet if blacks ascended.[60]

Those southerners who perceived in the Civil Rights Act a threat to their own freedom also prided themselves on their knowledge of African-Americans. June Melvin noted that her clothing store was open to people of all races. "Some of my best customers are Negroes, and I count them also as my friends." Her friendship was frail, however, and it could "be legislated right out of the picture." F. M. Bain considered himself friends with many blacks; but friendship was one thing, integration another. "I have no hatred in my heart [for] the colored race as I have lived with them all my life. Here . . . more than half of the people are colored and I number amongst them some of my best friends, but I'm not for the social change that so many seem to want." Whites were quick to boast of their friendships with blacks, and just as quick to argue that blacks should not have equal access to facilities. One constituent of Charles Raper Jonas, in Warrenton, North Carolina, held such a view. "The one clause in the Civil Rights bill that is so bitter to me is the Public Accommodation Bill. I . . . have worked hard all my life. Now I feel I have a right to . . . associate with only those I care to, whether at work or at play." She did not see herself as prejudiced; neither did she wish to deny blacks opportunities for advancement. But she did not want to interact with them, and could not see why she should have to. "I am for the negro having every chance of being something but the ones I live near simply do not come up to the standards of living the whites do and never will." Few saw the issue as one of injustice or inequity; from white southerners' vantage point, there was no reason for black and white worlds to mix.[61]

To many of them, segregation and integration had little to do with right or wrong. Blacks and whites were different, and segregation sprang from those differences. As Bland wrote, "We are dealing with an attempt to find a way for two races of decidedly different cultures and backgrounds to live together in harmony." Whites believed they discovered that harmony in segregation. Furthermore, many insisted that while they supported Jim Crow, they had nothing against blacks. "We are all in favor of giving the colored man all the rights we claim for ourselves," wrote a Murphy, North Carolina, doctor. "But we cannot help him by establishing a Dictatorship headed by the Attorney General." He found this "the almost universal opinion of 'the man on the street.' " Indeed, many southern streets teemed with such men. Only a minority thought segregation was unjust. "While I believe the Negroes should have the same rights I do," wrote Florence Wood of Nashville, Georgia, "I do not believe in integration." Remarkably, she saw little contradiction between equal rights and segregation. Equality did not require integration. "I didn't see what we were doing as discrimination," South Carolina hardware store owner Sam Crouch reflected decades later. "I saw it as segregation." Segregation and justice were compatible in some southern white minds.[62]

Other white southerners saw through that paradox. On June 11, 1963, John F. Kennedy proclaimed that the issue of civil rights was "a moral issue. It is as old as the Scriptures and as clear as the American Constitution." The next day, a thirty-two-year-old high school English teacher in Hamlet, North Carolina, wrote her first letter to a politician. "People of my convictions far too often lack the courage of those convictions," Mary Idol Breeze wrote to Charles Raper Jonas. "I wish to declare myself being in favor of the civil rights legislation which the President suggested in his television appearance last night." A North Carolina native, Breeze did not think herself representative of whites in the state—but she believed she was "fairly representative of the age and educational group to which I belong. . . . This group tends to sit in timid, silent disapproval while others do all the talking." Because of the fear that gripped pro–civil rights whites, Breeze reasoned that if she did not speak up, her views would go "unheard and therefore unknown." The issue of black civil rights, while "thorny," was to Breeze essentially a moral problem. Only equality could grant blacks the self-respect all people deserved, and the faster blacks gained those rights, the sooner whites would adjust. "Delay will not lessen the bitterness of some Whites; it is sure to increase the bitterness of Negroes. It will not change the direction of history; it will simply prolong an agony." With their filibuster and rhetoric, southern politicians prolonged that agony.[63]

While Breeze voiced her opinions immediately after Kennedy's speech, it took Augusta, Georgia, resident Nancy Anderson many months to settle her feelings about civil rights. "I've finally reached a personal position of support," she wrote to Richard Russell in November 1963. After Anderson "leaned hard" on her spiritual convictions and beliefs about

American principles, she concluded that all people, regardless of skin color, must be entitled to personal freedom, dignity, and the pursuit of happiness. A Marietta, Georgia, woman agreed that "this bill is simply attempting to provide the means to attain rights undeniably guaranteed all citizens by the Constitution." That perspective made the issue seem almost uncontroversial. Melvin Rockleff of Winston-Salem, North Carolina, "firmly believed" that all "*thinking* people" of his state would throw their support behind any "reasonable" civil rights bill. Rockleff, who identified himself as a veteran of both world wars and Korea, wielded his knowledge of blacks in defense of civil rights—rather than against them. He fought and served with many African-Americans over the years. "My contact with them is not limited to bus boys, household servants," and "bootblacks." Rockleff found the language of white resistance repellent and evasive. "*Individual* rights should not be denied any citizen under the guise of States Rights." Some whites thought blacks unworthy of equality, and politicians alleged the bill would give untold power to the federal government. Rockleff dismissed both claims as overblown and inaccurate.[64]

Rockleff pictured a South tottering between its racial past and future, with the Civil Rights Act as the fulcrum. Many others helped color in the outlines of that portrait. "You are, I know, committed to a certain view of the South and its way of life," Atlanta resident Nancy Collinson wrote to Richard Russell. "But a new age has come . . . a new age and a new way of viewing man, all men. It is my hope that you can live up to it." Some saw in civil rights legislation the potential for that "new age." "I am disappointed that you are not helping to lead us away from the atmosphere that prevailed in 1860," Atlantan James O'Hear Sanders wrote to Russell. "I hope you will turn your back on the racial prejudices of [Mississippi governor Ross] Barnett, [George] Wallace, and Roy Harris facing the new day for the South and the nation." The Civil Rights Act, he argued, presented politicians with the opportunity to step into that new South. But many of them chose an alternate path. They exploited opposition to civil rights, and attempted to extend a white supremacist southern past.[65]

A remarkable document of dissent came not from urban Atlanta, but from Southwest Georgia. On December 8, 1963, Harriet Southwell penned a letter to Richard Russell, and poured into it her heart and soul. Fifty-nine years old and a native of Tifton, Southwell had backed Russell through the years. As debate over the Civil Rights Act mounted, she felt "impelled to write this letter." Any person who took Christianity or democracy seriously, Southwell thought, would also have to take black demands for civil rights seriously. "I truly believe the time is here—(it is late) and that we as Christians—and as true citizens need to acknowledge our wrong and face up to and admit that we have not done to and for the Negro what we, had our faces been black, would have wanted to be done for us." Southwell performed a rare act: she envisioned a hypothetical scenario in which she had been born black, and tried to imagine what she would then call justice. Southwell concluded that blacks must be granted the rights other citizens enjoyed. She asserted that Russell's objections to the Civil Rights Act were the height of hypocrisy. And the age of civil rights plunged her into a tortured process:

> What have we done to the Negro if not exactly what you say you object to in the bill—taken away "freedom of association—and the right to do business with whom one pleases?"
>
> I do not think I am at all by myself in feeling this way—you may hear from many on the other side—but there are *many* who feel as I do. I have seen in these years of soul searching many men and women who with great effort and almost heartbreak have changed their views from those of the days when the Negro was slave and servant. Understand that it took soul-rending change for some of these—some who had been bitter and resentful but who were fair-minded and who examined their souls and *had* to change.*

Southwell was saying that if white southerners explored their innermost feelings (or listened to what writer James McBride Dabbs had called "our inmost ears"), they had to realize that discrimination was immoral, and, ultimately, change their racial attitudes. Claims to the contrary—either from the mouths of southern leaders or others who cried out for "white rights"—were disingenuous or contrived. In the form of Southwell's letter, an idiosyncratic voice for racial equality rang out from the heart of the Black Belt.[66]

---

*When Southwell cited Russell's objections to the Civil Rights Act, she was referring to speeches like the one that Russell delivered on November 27, 1963. Days after John F. Kennedy's assassination, Russell expressed grief for the fallen leader, but made sure to include a plug for the freedoms of white southerners: "The so-called civil rights bill is still the same vicious assault on property rights and the Constitution." Russell thought the bill would destroy more freedoms than it would foster, and would seize "from our society the oldest of our rights—that of freedom of association." *Atlanta Journal and Constitution,* November 28, 1963.

While a portion of white southerners came to support black civil rights in the weeks and months after Kennedy proposed the legislation, others moved in the opposite direction. Audrey Wagner of Charlotte, North Carolina, had long thought herself a progressive, but increasing black demands sparked in her racial antipathy. Wagner had studied at the University of Chicago. She had worked in Nashville with African-American children, and had researched black housing conditions in Greensboro. Throughout her experiences, she asserted, "I have always considered myself a liberal. I have, until recently, felt no personal animosity toward other races. I have always wanted the Negro to improve as rapidly as he was capable, and for him to have his equal rights *under the law.*" Civil rights proposals began to change her thinking. "With the present trend in Civil Rights under President Kennedy, my friends and I are developing an attitude toward the Negro Race that is hostile." As local leaders touted advances in race relations, Wagner suggested that those appearances deceived. "There is not the 'peace and harmony' in Charlotte that the newspapers would have you believe. I have never seen as many educated and refined people 'boiling' under the surface." Wagner claimed she supported black rights in theory, but turned hostile when the time for equality came. Many white southerners concurred. One, a professor of history at the University of North Carolina, Chapel Hill, co-authored the leading textbook on North Carolina history. While the book's first edition minimized the cruelty of slavery and painted Reconstruction as a "tragic era" for whites, it was much more enlightened on racial matters than contemporary histories of other southern states. Upon hearing of the Civil Rights Act, the professor wrote to Sam Ervin and requested a copy of the bill. "It is perhaps the most dangerous proposal *ever* put forth in Congress." Among some self-professed progressives, theoretical support for black rights withered under the prospect of equality. From the Deep South to North Carolina, conservative or moderate, from workers to the upper class, white southerners agonized over civil rights legislation—even those, perhaps especially those, who knew their history.[67]

Calls for "white rights" came from a variety of places. Some originated with leaders like Richard Russell; others emanated from businessmen like Lester Maddox and Ollie McClung; still more found expression in the "man on the street." The apparent doctrine of "white rights" stemmed from—though was not confined to—views about individual liberty, property rights, race, and the law. A worker at the Central Georgia Advertising Co. in Waynesboro informed Russell of the groundswell he perceived. "You will be surprised at the host of people who believe that if the so called 'Civil Rights Bill' becomes law, it not only will strike down basic rights of all Americans, but will alter our . . . system of constitutional government." Ideas about white freedom also contained arguments less tangible, and more powerful. O. W. Hines of McLeansville, North Carolina, captured the growing sentiment. If the Civil Rights Act became law, he had for Sam Ervin a simple prophecy: "We will be slaves."[68]

Some white southerners couched their protests in the vernacular of states' rights. Others warned of a government allegedly in thrall to communists, or claimed that constitutional rights to property and freedom of association were in grave peril. In practice, that amounted to new possibilities in everyday life. It meant that when whites went to the train station, passengers in their coaches—and not just the shoeshine boys and the porters—could be African-Americans. At hotels, not only would the bellhops be black; so might the family in the next room. When whites went out to eat, they would not only have their food prepared by blacks and their tables bused by them, but African-Americans could dine nearby. It seemed only a matter of time before the interracial future overwhelmed past customs. Confronted with these images of tomorrow, white southerners cried that the federal government had trampled upon their rights. They sent telegrams to elected officials, urging opposition to the bill. Many wrote letters to the editor; they counseled businessmen never to allow African-Americans on their premises; they criticized Lyndon Johnson, local blacks, and northern politicians; they charged union members would lose seniority, proprietors would lose control of their stores, and more generally, white Americans would lose their freedom. As one Athens, Georgia, couple explained in their letter to Richard Russell, "We recognize all races and colors of people as human beings. However, we do not feel that there should be legislation to force such people upon us. Our rights are as sacred as theirs."[69]

To some white southerners, the Civil Rights Act challenged much more than their personal freedoms and rights. It threatened their conception of themselves—specifically, their own racial identity. *Albany Herald* editor James Gray broached the subject in an editorial published the day after President Johnson signed the Civil Rights Act. Gray first argued that the law could force only surface changes. "There will be obedience to the letter of the law, but no subservience." The law might admit blacks into public accommodations, but it could never effect transformations in society, economics, attitudes, or even race relations. If those relations were to change in any way, Gray argued, the Civil Rights Act would continue a polarizing trend that Martin Luther King, SNCC, and "outside agitators" had begun years before—further driving a wedge between blacks and whites, and severing them from the harmonious (and mythical) racial past. "This new 'civil rights' law . . . is certain to make a white man more aware that he is white and a black man more aware that he is black." If African-Americans were beginning to celebrate their "blackness" during the 1960s, Gray argued, the Civil Rights Act would help whites realize their "white" identity. Perhaps "whiteness" and "blackness" were more social construction than biological fact, as many scholars later suggested. But the facts of whiteness and blackness had sat so baldly on the surface of southern life for so long that such points seemed irrelevant. Of course, many southerners had mixed racial heritages, dating from the early days of slavery; indeed it was ridiculous to send a man with one black great-grandfather to a certain water fountain and a man with mixed blood further down the line to a different fountain. Though theoretically unstable, that racial system defined social reality. Gray argued that the Civil Rights Act made whites more aware of race. But whites were always cognizant of their "whiteness," and knew that skin color gave them authority and spelled oppression for blacks. They were rarely afraid to wield that power.[70]

The Civil Rights Act did not so much heighten awareness of "whiteness" as spur fears that "whiteness" would stop paying wages. To Selma mayor Joe Smitherman, race and economics were bound together. The civil rights movement "built up . . . fears of losing your white skin or losing your job." Many other whites believed the black freedom struggle posed that sort of threat. In a letter to the *Albany Herald,* J. S. Reynolds of Fitzgerald, Georgia, warned local businessmen that black protesters meant to destroy the "white" race and the privileges that came with it. "Take a stand for your rights. . . . Just be a white man and help keep white white and black black." Overall, whites were much more concerned with the power whiteness gave them than the apparent facts of race and color. After all, these were facts that they had by turns constructed, twisted, overlooked, and suppressed for many years.[71]

The Civil Rights Act served as a rallying point for assertions of white freedom. The new law wrapped together concerns about black protest, the federal government, and states' rights with worries about freedom and "whiteness." Moreton Rolleston, owner of the Heart of Atlanta motel, barely mentioned blacks when he described his resistance to the bill. "The main reason for the suit is the new law's unwarranted invasion of ownership of private property." Rolleston thought it was his right to refuse blacks at his motel, and he seemed to genuinely believe that the Civil Rights Act amounted to "involuntary servitude" for businessmen. After the Supreme Court ruled against both Rolleston and Ollie McClung on December 14, some whites believed that their worst fears had become reality—not in the form of black freedom, but in the sway the federal government held over individuals. Nationally syndicated columnist David Lawrence called December 14 "a fateful day in history," for "what many historians will describe as a federal dictatorship was established in the United States." Few future scholars would reach that conclusion, and neither would they agree with *Birmingham News* columnist Walling Keith, who feared that the Court's ruling against Ollie's might "open a hole in the dike where chaos lives." The ruling had "nothing to do with race or color, but may have all too much to do with civil rights and individual freedom in the years to come." Keith was concerned primarily with the freedom of property owners—that is, white businessmen. Similar racialized understandings of freedom, oppression, and individual rights had been at the very bottom of Ollie McClung's and Lester Maddox's first forays into resistance.[72]

If white southerners felt threatened by civil rights struggles prior to 1964, that threat mostly fostered fear, discomfort, and anxiety. Before the Civil Rights Act, white southerners harbored vague notions that their own freedom was in jeopardy; when the bill passed, those intermingling worries congealed into something concrete. The law applied directly to business owners' everyday lives. Many, like Ollie McClung, believed their businesses would endure a gradual trek from all-white to all-black, and might soon fail. The federal government's primary role in that imagined process bred widespread resentment. If that discontent had hardened into a movement, its banner would have read "white rights" or "civil wrongs." If that movement had a leader, it would have been George Wallace, Barry Goldwater, or Lester Maddox—depending on where the rally occurred and on what face the situation called for. And if the movement had an emblem, it would have been a Pickrick ax handle.

Maddox came to master most all of the arguments against the Civil Rights Act; he was the very champion of "white rights." The hundreds of ads he ran in the *Atlanta Constitution* through the 1960s had reached a fever pitch by the time he stood trial in 1964. One July 18 ad drew together many of Maddox's arguments and tactics. He opened by thanking those who called, wrote, or patronized the restaurant, and thereby supported his family's effort to "remain FREE Americans and protect our 'Civil Rights.' " He seized the language of "civil rights" for whites. Maddox took pride in a call he claimed to have received from an African-American mother.* The woman allegedly supported Maddox's defense of his business. Maddox asked her not to blame black leaders, for the fault belonged "to White citizens who have used her people to make their own gains in the political world possible." This line of thinking held that many politicians favored the Civil Rights Act not because they thought it appropriate legislation, but because with it they could win the fabled black bloc vote. Maddox cited many other blacks who phoned in to support his stand. They were welcome to call, but Maddox never mentioned that if they appeared at the restaurant they would have been run off with a pickax or pistol.[73]

Maddox listed recent episodes of racial violence—from the four little girls killed in a Birmingham church to "three 'civil rights' (agitators)" missing in Mississippi. "The spilled blood, violence, robbery, rape and death, is on the hands of the Communists." The ad moved smoothly among praise for blacks, vitriol for the federal government, blame of communists, and defense of white civil rights. "Many Negro and White Americans, law-abiding citizens are absolutely innocent victims of the grave racial crisis that is upon us." In a plan hatched by "outside agitators," communists, and politicians desirous of black votes, freedom-loving Americans stood as hapless victims. Maddox positioned the government as the aggressor and white southerners as victims. The Civil Rights Act gave that brand of "victimology" more resonance, and brought it even closer to home. A similar appeal carried George Wallace to national political fame, and different forms of it helped Richard Nixon and eventually Ronald Reagan ascend to the presidency. While those powerful politicians did not wield ax handles, they donned various

---

*The ad stated that "Mrs. Pickrick" took the telephone call from the African-American woman. But Maddox proceeded to write, "she told me," and "she assured me." Together with the general fact that few black people supported Maddox's right to wave a gun at them, these inconsistencies only add suspicion to Maddox's claim. Factual or not, the ads themselves remain revealing documents in the fight over "white rights."

cloaks of "white rights." The "forgotten Americans" and the "silent majority" became national forces. The roots of these movements found powerful first expression in white resistance to the Civil Rights Act.[74]

4

THE LINE BETWEEN URBAN AND RURAL areas carved the legacy of the Civil Rights Act. Business owners across the region challenged the new law and worried about its effects. Some politicians denounced the federal government, and various other whites defended certain conceptions of their own rights. But many white southerners, especially those who lived outside large cities and away from centers of civil rights activity, remained all but untouched by the Civil Rights Act. In the wake of the 1954 *Brown* decision, whites had worried more about the sports pages, their sororities, or paying the bills than about actions taken by the Supreme Court. And in 1964, similar mundane concerns occupied more white minds than did the recent additions to federal law. From the Deep South to the Mason-Dixon line, many whites could live just as though the law had never been passed. Clara Lee Sharrard remembered little change in Lexington, Virginia, a small town that was home to Washington and Lee College. After the Civil Rights Act, restaurants "remained segregated. There weren't that many restaurants in town to start with . . . whites and blacks did not come in and sit together, or even in the same restaurant." African-Americans did not attempt to integrate eateries; segregation was an uncontested fact. Journalists and government officials might call places like Lexington "quiet." While in a sense accurate, this was generally misleading. In some rural areas, businesses did not witness integration attempts until the 1970s and beyond. While it was different in most cities, the resulting reality could not without qualification be called a victory for civil rights. In many out-of-the-way places, integration was rarely attempted in the months and years after the Civil Rights Act passed, much less achieved.[75]

It was the spring of 1969 before federal officials appeared at Glenn's Frozen Custard stand in Burlington, North Carolina, where Howard Glenn sold milkshakes, hot dogs, hamburgers, and frozen custard. Glenn's stand was so small that he "never considered my place to be a restaurant by any stretch of the imagination." In a letter to Sam Ervin, Glenn detailed his experience with federal officials. Glenn affixed his signature to whatever papers he was presented, and an FBI agent later visited the premises. In May, Glenn received a court order to integrate his business, and to put up a sign advertising its compliance with the Civil Rights Act. Flummoxed by the ordeal, Glenn quickly put up the sign. "I can't understand why the Federal Government can require me to put up such a sign when most places of business have a sign reading, 'We reserve the right to refuse service to anyone.' " Ollie's Barbecue once possessed the latter sign. But Ollie had learned quickly what took Howard Glenn, and many other business owners, years longer to absorb. "If the Civil Rights Act applies to my little place of business," Glenn wrote, "then it must apply to everything under the sun." If the new law could cover a custard stand at an anonymous intersection in Burlington, it could effect change anywhere.[76]

While some white southerners smoothly internalized such a change, it was to others an agonizingly slow process. Few whites embraced the civil rights movement and the advances it achieved, but one did not have to welcome change to live with it. "I don't like all this," a Louisiana lawyer confided in 1967. "I never did and I won't—ever. The nigra doesn't even want what those civil-rights types keep saying." But he married a stubbornly traditional racial view with an adaptability for the future. "There's nothing to do but go on. We've got to take it and most of the time we just forget about the whole thing and just go about our business. The nigra likes his people and we like ours, and if there's mixing in libraries or restaurants, that's O.K. It won't bust us; we know that, now." Some adjusted to the new law rapidly enough so that the same reality they thought would "bust" them in 1964 had become "O.K." by 1967. The manner in which whites highlighted this type of progress was itself telling. One rarely said that he or she tolerated blacks in public facilities; far more often, whites simply "forgot about the whole thing." They claimed not to notice African-Americans. Sid Smyer, a powerful Birmingham businessman who made a fast transition in 1963 and 1964 from segregationist to moderate, spoke in that vernacular of invisibility. In November 1964, he lauded gains the Civil Rights Act had so swiftly achieved. "My wife and I went to see *Hamlet* the other day. . . . It is at the best theatre in town and I guess there were three to four hundred Negroes there. Nobody paid them any attention." As *Newsweek*'s Joseph Cumming wrote, "All of this is to suggest only that a new calm prevails. I doubt if anyone has much changed their mind about segregation." In

Birmingham, tranquil integration seemed to have replaced racial unrest. Whether it was the "negative peace" that Martin Luther King called the absence of tension, or a positive one that possessed the presence of justice, was still up for debate.[77]

Whites stopped noticing the blacks who invaded their facilities in part because so much else in the country—and the world—demanded their attention. The year 1964 exposed a nation on the brink. Events threatened to shatter the sterile ethos of an increasingly middle-class, suburban post–World War II society, and offered a glimpse of the later 1960s, when youth breathed the spirit of protest and conversed in the language of revolution. Signs appeared of that coming tumult even in the 1950s. It was 1955 when Martin Luther King, Jr., burst on the scene, and 1957 when the showdown in Little Rock occurred. Black students sat in at lunch counters in 1960, Bob Dylan released his first album and the Students for a Democratic Society issued its Port Huron Statement in 1962, and Betty Friedan published *The Feminine Mystique* in 1963. Horrifying deaths stained the fall of 1963, as Kennedy's assassination followed the murder of the four girls in Birmingham. But those episodes captured only a fraction of the upheaval to come. When the reformist feel of the early 1960s exploded with pitched battles later in the decade, still more episodes awaited: riots in cities and on campuses; the rise of the Black Panthers, the women's liberation movement, the sexual revolution, and the movement for gay rights; the assassinations of Malcolm X, King, and Robert Kennedy; the Democratic Party's bloody unraveling in Chicago; thousands of deaths in Vietnam, and thousands more protesters in America.

White southerners greeted integration in this larger context. Against such a backdrop, they measured responses to the admittedly shocking sight of black citizens who strode into whatever establishments they pleased. "After a while, people got used to it," Atlanta doctor Richard Franco recalled. "Initially, people might glower and refuse to sit next to somebody, but that didn't last long." All of those fears that first surrounded the proposed legislation "really became nothing. Changing in the dressing rooms. All these things that before had been considered taboo." To some white southerners, the integration of public facilities was the stuff of drama, shock, and disgust. To others, the fall of Jim Crow signs was but the least of society's changes. "Between the civil rights movement, Vietnam, the women's movement," Franco reflected, "those [episodes of integrating facilities] became relatively minimal." There were times when shifts in everyday life constituted revolutions in themselves, and times when more dramatic events nudged them into the background. "Everything was in tumult, and so segregating a bathroom became kind of irrelevant. Besides, it was against the law." Jim Crow laws had once built walls around southerners, walls that few could see above or beyond. They could make enforced segregation seem natural. When that order died and legal equality struggled to supplant it, some people had difficulty remembering exactly how those walls used to feel. Forty years after the Civil Rights Act, Franco reflected, "When something disappears it's hard to conceive of how ridiculous it was, but when it's occurring, it's hard to see how it's going to change."[78]

In some rural towns, it took decades for Jim Crow to disappear. At Georgia's Terrell County Medical Clinic, blacks sat in the "East" waiting room as late as the 1980s, while whites thumbed through magazines in the "West" waiting room. "That's where we always went," explained a black patron, "so that's where we go." As recently as 1985, the county courthouse boasted two different men's rooms—one in the basement and the other upstairs. In many Terrell County towns, the *New York Times* reported, "there are bars where blacks know they cannot buy drinks, restaurants in which they cannot eat," and "motels in which they cannot get a room. . . . An unwritten code perpetuates what was once enshrined in law and announced by 'Colored entrance' or 'Whites only' signs." Those stories do not stand as freakish anomalies that prove the rule of progress; rather, they question those very claims to progress, and expose the underside of its most glorious triumphs. When African-American Margaret Rogers accepted a teaching job in Walterboro, South Carolina, she was shocked to discover segregation in physicians' waiting rooms. "I never expected to find that, not in 1974." When the other teachers went roller-skating, the rink prevented Rogers from entering. These experiences forced her to rethink the legacy of the civil rights movement. Segregation "hasn't completely died out and . . . you still may run into it in what we call the 'backwood communities,'" she said in the 1990s. "There is still Jim Crow. It's just called something differently now and it's not as out in the open as it was." The Civil Rights Act outlawed segregation, but forms of it would persist for years. It was not until 1985 that officials in Butts County, Georgia, tore down a chain-link fence dividing the black part of the graveyard from the white. Twenty-one years after the Civil Rights Act became law, blacks and whites in Butts County gained the freedom to perish together.[79]

FOR LESTER MADDOX, the legacy of the Civil Rights Act never entirely disappeared. The state capitol in which Maddox later worked was not far from his restaurant. In most stories about Maddox, his antics at the Pickrick serve as a sensational prologue to the tale of how he won the statehouse. But Maddox was first an entrepreneur, and his political story more appropriately serves as the spectacular postscript. Maddox realized his dreams in his restaurant. "My dream came true. I was Mr. Maddox. I was Mr. Pickrick. I was Mr. Somebody." Maddox's defiance of the Civil Rights Act earned him political currency, and the bill that ended his segregated business thrust Maddox squarely into the political arena. His resistance had unforeseen consequences. Maddox's 1966 campaign for governor of Georgia was "borne aloft" at the Pickrick.[80]

After the immediate furor over the Civil Rights Act had died down, Maddox's pick handles still followed him everywhere. Once Maddox finally sold the Pickrick, he continued to hawk autographed ax handles in the guise of "Pickrick drumsticks." He then opened a souvenir shop that featured "mama-sized drumsticks and junior-sized drumsticks"— what journalist Marshall Frady called a "complete family backlash kit." He also sold Lester Maddox sweatshirts and "Wake Up, America" alarm clocks. Maddox even opened a furniture store and named it the Pickrick. On April 21, 1965, an all-white Atlanta jury took just forty-four minutes to acquit Maddox on charges stemming from the gun-waving incident. Given the chance to defend segregation—or at least its local standard-bearer—white Atlantans wasted little time in proclaiming that they stood with Maddox. After the civil rights struggles in Selma, Alabama, Maddox picketed the federal courthouse in Atlanta with a sign: "Down with Johnson, Justice Department, socialism and communism— Up with Wallace, free enterprise, capitalism, liberty, private property rights, America." In August 1965, Maddox brought his case to Washington. He paraded along Pennsylvania Avenue and held before the White House a banner reading "Mr. President: I want my private property rights NOW!" Maddox may no longer have owned a restaurant, but he still had a cause. The Voting Rights Act of 1965 only furthered his sense that the federal government endangered white liberties. Shortly after Maddox returned from Washington, he led a crowd of two thousand whites down Atlanta's Peachtree Street to protest the legislation. So that nobody would misconstrue the meaning of the demonstration, Maddox declared, "This is a march for freedom!"[81]

Maddox threw himself into politics with all the energy and abandon he had formerly used to peddle fried chicken and defy desegregation. His path toward the statehouse wound through almost every Georgia county. While his opponents' billboards cast shadows over highways, Maddox journeyed—ladder and signs in hand—across hundreds of back roads and into town centers. Soon the words "THIS IS MADDOX COUN-TRY" called out from the tops of telephone poles and pine trees across the state. Even as they snickered at the "cracker Don Quixote," other politicians soon discovered that his signs spoke a truth.[82]

The 1966 gubernatorial field included many established names. The Republicans nominated Congressman Howard "Bo" Callaway, the first Republican representative from Georgia since Reconstruction. In the Democratic primary, Ellis Arnall's candidacy generated the most excitement. The reform-minded Arnall occupied the governor's office twenty years before, and he retained formidable support. In a field of many primary candidates, Arnall captured the most votes—but not enough to avoid a runoff against the second-place finisher, Lester Maddox. Any Georgian, regardless of party, could vote in the Democratic runoff. Republicans thought Maddox would lose handily to Bo Callaway in a general election, so some 75,000 of them crossed party lines to vote— and they voted for Maddox. They unwittingly cast ballots for the next governor of Georgia.[83]

Neither Lester Maddox nor Bo Callaway favored integration. Callaway picked up his congressional seat in 1964 on the back of Barry Goldwater's resistance to the Civil Rights Act. Maddox gathered votes not only from sly Republicans, but from admirers of his stand at the Pickrick. Maddox gained the endorsement of Calvin Craig, head of the Georgia Klan. Yet Georgia included a sizable collection of racial liberals and moderates—a substantial number of black voters, and also whites who had earlier supported open schools, feasted on the words of *Atlanta Constitution* editor Ralph McGill, and voted for Arnall in the primary. Callaway figured they would surely support him over Maddox. But the liberals launched a write-in campaign for Arnall. In the general election, although Callaway polled 3,000 more votes than Maddox, the Arnall write-in siphoned away enough (almost 53,000 votes) to deprive Callaway of the required clear majority. By Georgia law, the election was thrown into the state legislature, a body dominated by Democrats. Callaway challenged the law, and a federal appeals court upheld his argument; the Supreme Court overruled by a margin of 5–4. So if Republicans helped Lester Maddox win the Democratic primary, liberal Arnall supporters helped lift him into the governor's office. On January 10, 1967, the legislature voted for Maddox, 182–66. That was how Dean Maddox's second son, a newspaper boy–turned drugstore clerk–turned steelworker–turned restaurateur–turned segregationist icon, became the governor of Georgia.[84]

Once in office, Maddox confused nearly everyone. At his inauguration, the new governor sobbed during the singing of "God Bless America." He asked the choir to sing it again, and urged the crowd to join in. Through four years in office, Maddox consistently offered just one thing—contradiction. A reporter described his inaugural speech as "bogglingly gentle-tempered and conciliatory, brimming with goodwill for everyone." The same man who had brandished a gun in 1964 now talked of "respecting the federal government," maintained there was "no place in Georgia during the next four years for those who advocate extremism," and confirmed there existed "room enough in the great state for every ideal and every shade of opinion . . . for the right of dissent as well as the right to conform." Maddox might have won over former critics, but he never wiped away the stain of his past actions. After the legislature installed Maddox as governor, Martin Luther King confessed he was "ashamed to be a Georgian." Then Maddox became the first governor in the Deep South to appoint blacks to state boards. A blend of stuffiness and irreverence, Maddox banned short skirts among capitol workers. He also coasted through the halls on a bicycle, often pedaling backward. Maddox decreed Sundays as "Little People Days." He opened his doors to any citizen who wished to drop by. One Sunday, a convict visited Maddox, presented a list of complaints about prison conditions, and turned himself in. Maddox quickly began to reform the state penal system.[85]

Something like egalitarianism bubbled up in Maddox even as he continued to disdain black movements for civil rights, asserted that communists were behind them, and adopted an "I told you so" attitude when cities exploded in riots. Following his initial burst of evenhanded moves, Maddox made something of a rightward turn. After King's assassination in 1968, flags outside the capitol were lowered in mourning. Photographers captured the embarrassing scene of Maddox running out to hoist the flags back up. King was a communist, Maddox maintained, and the state of Georgia would honor communists neither in life nor in death. "I didn't think we oughta use our flag to honor an enemy of our country." As the network news cameras fixed upon him, Maddox decided to leave the flags alone. Atlanta mayor Ivan Allen, Jr., looked on from nearby City Hall. "I will never forget how utterly perplexed he was when he realized the eyes of television were watching him." Maddox, who had once waved pistols to stave off the law, was now the very embodiment of state law. He didn't quite know how to act, torn as he was between his personal past and his current position as governor—but also between the stale days of Jim Crow and a more stormy present. Perhaps it was fitting that so controversial and paradoxical a figure as Maddox would "guide" Georgia toward the new days of black legal equality—and also of subtler white resistance. "He is a bubbling, orgasmic, petty volcano of inconsistencies, dribbling his gray lava in every direction," journalist Robert Sherrill wrote. "The source of the hot subterranean bed from whence it flows . . . is unfathomable." Maddox was a perfect symbol for the white southerner in changing times:

> This makes him one of the truest representatives of his people and a perfectly logical choice to be their leader, for in his personality is caught up all the moon phases of Dixie's personality—the love-hate response to the black man, the patriot-subversive response to the federal government, the rebel-slave response to authority, the pitying-sadistic response to the underdog, the populist-planter response to economic needs.

Maddox was a truer reflection of his Georgia constituents than the slick Bo Callaway or the 1940s reformer Ellis Arnall. In July 1964, Maddox had been at the fore of one of the great challenges to the southern way of life. That Georgia elected a man who opted to close his business instead of integrate was perhaps a step back toward Jim Crow. But Maddox often baffled liberal doubters just as surely as he surprised his Klan supporters. He showed that the white South would not quickly shake off its old habits and behaviors, but neither could it resist all efforts to change.[86]

Shadows of the man who waved pistols in 1964 trailed Maddox later in life. "I want my race preserved," Maddox said in a 2001 interview with the Associated Press, "and I hope most everybody else wants theirs preserved. I think forced segregation is illegal and wrong. I think forced racial integration is illegal and wrong. I believe both of them to be unconstitutional." To his death, Maddox kept up his membership in the Sons of Confederate Veterans and the Military Order of the Stars and Bars. He ran again for governor in 1974, and although he lost handily to the racially moderate George Busbee, Maddox still won 40 percent of the vote. He remained a powerful figure in Georgia politics, and served as lieutenant governor to Jimmy Carter, although the two often quarreled. Zell Miller, who had been Maddox's executive secretary, would later serve in the U.S. Senate. Sam Nunn picked up an important early endorsement from Maddox, and parlayed it into a long and distin-guished senatorial career. Although Maddox's views grew more and more out of step with the times, his political legacy stayed strong.[87]

Even in death, Maddox could not escape the 1960s. He died on June 25, 2003, during the same week that Ivan Allen, Jr., and Maynard Jackson passed away. Allen was the mayor of Atlanta during the 1960s who famously testified before Congress in favor of the Civil Rights Act. Jack-son was elected the first black mayor of Atlanta—and of any major southern city—in 1972. That week in June 2003, Georgians again grap-pled with the ghosts of their racial past. The three men, linked in life and death, represented different symbols of the age of civil rights: Allen the white politician who saw the light of racial moderation; Jackson the black man who completed the ascent from the vestiges of slavery to the halls of power; Maddox the lawless, loud, and bumbling segregationist who rode his defense of Jim Crow to the statehouse, then saw himself drift to the margins while his region transformed. The 1970s had little room for Lester Maddoxes. Whites who wished to remain obstacles in the path of black freedom could not do it with ax handles, guns, and bravado. Maddox's forte was not subtlety; his time was one of drama. At his Atlanta funeral, a tape recording played Lester Maddox himself singing "I'll Fly Away." It would have been more fitting had Maddox bicycled backward, "Pickrick drumstick" in hand, toward the sunset.

Two years before Lester Maddox's funeral, Ollie McClung, Jr., closed the doors of Ollie's Barbecue for good. If Maddox went out with a bang, McClung quietly faded from the Birmingham scene at the turn of the twenty-first century—but only after decades of success. Integration did not cripple business, as the McClungs had feared; indeed, their restau-rant grew more popular over time. Because of highway construction, Ollie's Barbecue moved in 1968 to a new Birmingham location. It pros-pered there for three decades, and withstood the 1989 death of Ollie Sr. After seventy-two years in Birmingham, Ollie Jr. moved his restaurant to the suburbs in 1999. On its last day of business in the city, Birmingham residents—white and black—lined up for hours to savor the same barbecue on which many of them had been raised. Ollie's Barbecue lasted only two years in the town of Hoover. Few could concentrate on their newspapers on the morning of September 11, 2001, but those who did discovered that Ollie's Barbecue had closed the previous day.[88]

The twenty-first-century South still retained ties to its racial past. In the person of Maurice Bessinger, those stories of barbecue, fried chicken, and civil rights refused to die. Bessinger presided over Maurice's Piggie Park, a chain of barbecue restaurants in the Columbia, South Carolina, area. Bessinger gained notoriety not only for his yellow, mustard-based barbecue sauce, but also for his stance on civil rights. Bessinger's flagship restaurant in West Columbia was as much a symbol of segregation as the Pickrick. During the 1950s and 1960s, Bessinger headed the National Association for the Preservation of White People. Well into the late 1960s, he denied blacks access to the main dining room. While the Supreme Court eventually barred that practice, it could do nothing about the tracts that circulated around his Piggie Park restaurant— tracts hallowing slavery and the Confederacy. Although segregationist icons like Maddox and George Wallace had softened their messages or moved to the fringes, Bessinger did neither. In 2000, South Carolina's state legislature voted to remove the Confederate flag from the dome of the capitol. Bessinger then lowered the American flag that waved over the Piggie Park headquarters and raised up a Confederate battle flag. In turn, major grocery stores removed Piggie Park sauce and frozen barbecued pork from their aisles. Bessinger claimed the boycott violated his rights, and repeated some tropes of another era. "The stores are just yielding to outside pressure from people who want to destroy the Constitution and remake America to fit their globalism strategy." Forty years after the Civil Rights Act became law, a barbecue owner invoked constitutional rights and decried outside influences. That legacy of the 1960s reared its head at the Cracker Barrel, a national chain of restaurants that traded on the tastes, recipes, and paraphernalia of an older South. In 2004, the Justice Department accused the Cracker Barrel of discrimination against African-American customers; the business settled out of court. In Arkansas, Georgia, Mississippi, and North Carolina restaurants, government investigators found that some white servers refused to wait on African-American diners, while blacks received generally worse treatment than whites. Moreover, Cracker Barrel Old Country Store managers "often directed, participated in, or condoned the discriminatory behavior." In 2004, some Cracker Barrel branches successfully recreated southern history, down to its most painful details.[89]

Many southern businessmen adapted pragmatically to the reality that the Civil Rights Act created. In 1973, Senator Sam Ervin grumbled that "we've gotten reconciled to" the new law. But no matter how much practical adjustment occurred, most whites remained in principle opposed to the federal imposition of black rights. Even if their mannerisms, behavior, and words did not always show it, that opposition was clear in their votes. In 1964, Arizona Republican Barry Goldwater opposed the Civil Rights Act; Louisiana, Alabama, Mississippi, Georgia, and South Carolina rewarded him with their votes. Nationwide, Lyndon Johnson crushed Goldwater 486–52 in the electoral college, and by a popular margin of 61 percent to 39 percent. Yet in that landslide defeat, Republicans envisioned a path to their future triumphs. The 1964 election showed that for many white southerners, race was a primary political concern. And as the decade wore on, issues of civil rights migrated from the South to the North, and changed from problems of legal equality to those of economics, urban riots (or "law and order"), and busing. White opposition to civil rights became a national issue. In the 1968 presidential election, southern states moved more fully against the Democratic Party. Few would again vote Democratic. The Civil Rights Act not only changed life in southern towns, but the resentment it spurred began to transform national politics.[90]

White southerners who voted solidly Democratic through much of the twentieth century became bedrock Republicans by the mid-1970s. As much as anything else, this was the legacy of the Civil Rights Act. But if white southerners voted in national elections against civil rights supporters, in some locales they found themselves in the minority. Less than a year after the Civil Rights Act became law, Congress passed the Voting Rights Act. It fostered a different sort of revolution. Soon, serving barbecue or fried chicken to black customers would be the least of white southerners' concerns. In some areas of the South, those African-Americans rose to political dominance. "White rights" had a new challenger; it often went by the name of Black Power.

FIVE

"Softly, the Unthinkable": The Contours of Political and Economic Change

IF THE CIVIL RIGHTS MOVEMENT sought a grail, it was the vote. For African-Americans, integrated schools, equal access to public accommo-dations, and changes in racial attitudes remained empty achievements as long as the ballot eluded them. Southern towns could fester under segre-gationist control; blacks would remain under the heel of white authority, and at the mercy of white whims. Even in the midst of the Montgomery boycott, Martin Luther King knew that seats on buses were nothing compared to the vote. "The key to the whole solution of the South's problem is the ballot," King declared in May 1956. "Until the colored man comes to this point he will have a hard struggle. When he gets the ballot, he can wield political power and come into his own. . . . The chief weapon in our fight for civil rights is the vote." The vote could help deliver to blacks the promises of equality, freedom, and power. That was precisely what many white southerners feared.[1]

For a decade after the Civil War, federal troops guarded voting places as former slaves cast their ballots; some blacks ascended into the echelons of political office. Whites charged that African-Americans abused their voting privileges, engaged in corruption, and stood generally unfit for democracy. After the Compromise of 1877 ended Reconstruction's exper-iment in black freedom, federal troops hurried out of Dixie and left southerners to their own devices. White political control returned under the specter of mob intimidation and Ku Klux Klan violence. A century afterward, many white southerners still believed tales of black incom-petence and Klan redemption. In the 1890s, some state governments removed blacks from the voting rolls. After that decade's Populist revolt threatened the Democratic Party's stranglehold on the region, every southern state adopted measures to disenfranchise blacks. Many states inaugurated literacy tests and imposed poll taxes. Others implemented what came to be known as the "grandfather clause." It established stiff educational requirements for all voters, but exempted those who had been eligible to vote before January 1, 1867. In effect, only whites were exempt. The few blacks who were not excluded by literacy tests, poll taxes, or grandfather clauses ran up against the white primary. Democrats operated their party primaries as private clubs, and barred African-Americans. With these Jim Crow measures reinforced by lynch law, white southerners—and the Democratic Party—wielded dominance through much of the twentieth century. In 1900, about 3 percent of voting-age black southerners were registered to vote. That percentage had increased little by 1940. In 1944, the Supreme Court struck at the South's political order when it outlawed the white primary. A decade later, the court's *Brown v. Board of Education* ruling and the nascent black freedom struggle exposed a powerful challenge to white supremacy. Some whites understood that threat; many others denied what they saw, or looked the other way.[2]

By the end of the 1950s, a handful of blacks attended integrated schools in Clinton, Nashville, and Little Rock; thousands more voted in Atlanta and other cities. But whites in the rural Black Belt continued to suggest that such changes could never reach them. In 1957, Hale County, Alabama, contained 22,000 people, two-thirds of whom were black. Situated in the state's western cotton country, whites in the town of Greensboro viewed the growing civil rights ferment with detachment and confusion. "There are furrowed brows in this county seat," a *Newsweek* reporter cabled on August 30, 1957. "Old timers sit on the steps of the courthouse and wonder, 'What's happening to the South?' " The world of Greensboro, Alabama, was enough divorced from urban areas for whites to persist in their delusions. "Those big cities may be giving in," a local businessman allowed, "but the day will never come in our lifetime or in the lifetime of our children that what has happened in Nashville will ever happen in Greensboro." In that town of 2,800, whites remained fused to old racial views. "If we let nigger children in the schools, we will have trouble with our workers, and we will end up with hatred on both sides," a gas station attendant declared. "Folks have got to understand that if we let the niggers have the vote, then they will put all the white men out of office." With every ounce of their muscle, whites in rural Alabama sought to deprive blacks of the vote. Failure on that score would spell a reality so horrific as to be unthinkable.[3]

Eight years later, events in nearby Dallas County helped those night-mares to materialize. The civil rights movement dramatized the plight of disenfranchised southern blacks, and few states illuminated the battle over voting rights more clearly than Alabama. While the 1964 Civil Rights Act eradicated much legal inequality, there were many types of discrimination it failed to touch. In particular, SCLC and SNCC pointed out that the law failed to authorize federal protection of black voter reg-istration. Many rural counties and Deep South towns still used literacy tests to stymie black registration. In Alabama, 19 percent of black adults were registered to vote. Only Mississippi had a lower percentage. To highlight those realities, civil rights groups moved into Selma, a town King called "a symbol of bitter-end resistance to the civil rights move-ment in the Deep South." Much as Bull Connor's violence in Birming-ham spurred the proposal of the Civil Rights Act, so SCLC hoped a display of violence in Selma would force Americans to realize the horrors of black disenfranchisement, and push Congress toward stricter voting rights legislation. In this calculus, white resistance would help blacks toward legal equality—but only if that resistance was ugly enough to arouse the nation.[4]

In Jim Clark, Selma possessed a sheriff who had proven himself capa-ble of such ferocity. Clark and his local "posse" routinely brutalized blacks and barred them from voting. Cattle prods and horse whips main-tained white supremacy in Selma. "The posse-men . . . are strangers to beauty and grace and are indeed the saddest looking people to be seen anywhere in the world," Elizabeth Hardwick wrote in *The New York Review of Books*, albeit with some exaggeration. They "have only the nothingness of racist ideas . . . and that is all." The 1964 elections had threatened to change the face of Selma. In November, Joe Smitherman had dislodged the local political machine and won the mayor's office. When SCLC and SNCC arrived, Smitherman had no interest in making Selma synonymous with segregationist violence. He understood that white aggression was essential to SCLC's goal. "They picked Selma just like a movie producer would pick a set. You had the right ingredients, I mean you would have to have seen Clark in his day, he had a helmet liner like General Patton, he had the clothes, the Eisenhower jacket . . . an example of the Old South." Smitherman appointed Wilson Baker as public safety director, and ordered Baker to peacefully enforce the law.

At first, Clark acted with restraint. No initial outbursts of violence greeted the civil rights groups. But under the sustained pressure of local blacks who dramatically demanded voting rights, "outside agitators," and the media's prolonged glare, Clark began to buckle. A group of marchers refused to move from in front of the courthouse (which housed the board of registrars) on January 19, and Clark became enraged. He roughed up a black woman, and photos of the scene reached front pages of national newspapers. The next day, Clark ushered marchers toward a side door of the courthouse. They demanded to use the front door, and although Clark refused, Baker eventually granted their request. By day's end, Clark had arrested 226 marchers. Two weeks later, that number climbed to 2,400.[5]

Sheriff Jim Clark's violent tactics would soon spur the federal government to act on black voting rights, but in the meantime, Clark galvanized a different group—Selma's African-American community. Through the 1950s and 1960s, the civil rights movement had its detractors on the black side of the racial divide as well as the white. A sizable number of blacks built thriving businesses and wielded a modicum of power within the system of segregation. Funeral directors, barbers, ministers, schoolteachers, and principals had carved slices of success out of the Jim Crow world. Sudden mass demonstrations could cause unwelcome disruptions for this minority of African-Americans. Powerful whites had picked Dallas County's black leaders, and bequeathed to them powers of their own. Any black leader who then criticized the status quo—racial, political, or otherwise—could expect to be stripped of his own strength. Reverend Claude Brown was one of the most powerful African-Americans in Selma before the civil rights struggle, and Brown found himself torn by the coming tumult. Leaders like Brown saw the obvious appeal of racial change, but they feared the civil rights movement. When SNCC workers first came to Selma in 1963, the town's leading churches kept healthy distances. Reverend D. V. Jemison had built Tabernacle Baptist Church into a temple of renown, local power, and relative conservatism. In 1963, the new pastor of Tabernacle—L. L. Anderson—supported the burgeoning protest movement. Anderson offered his church for the memorial service of Samuel Boynton, a local businessman and head of the "relatively nonmilitant" Dallas County Voters League. The deacons and congregation denied the use of Tabernacle for Boynton's memorial. They worried that their church would be bombed, and its precious stained-glass windows shattered. Few leading

blacks believed mass struggle offered much chance of success; and even
if it did result in change, their power would be undeniably diminished
in a new racial and political order. The typical southern black businessman "wanted to avoid alienating the police, the civil rights workers, his
customers, his suppliers, and everyone else," wrote J. L. Chestnut, an
African-American lawyer in Selma. All of this pointed up an irony.[6]

The most successful and best educated African-Americans—those
most capable of organization—were frequently the most skeptical of the
civil rights struggle. Their livelihoods were bound up with a social order
they loathed but on which they depended. The preachers, teachers, and
the middle class in general "would be the very persons who would lead
and staff a voter registration effort," J. L. Chestnut mused. "But the ties
they had to the white ruling hierarchy—the ties that established them as
leaders—made them the least likely group of all to become involved.
They had the most—the best jobs, the largest homes—and therefore the
most to lose." These blacks accommodated, although they rarely submit-
ted, to Jim Crow and Jim Clark. While this middle class constituted a
formidable obstacle to change, it also produced the civil rights struggle's
transcendent leader, Martin Luther King, Jr. His father, Martin Luther
King, Sr., presided over Atlanta's Ebenezer Baptist Church, and raised
the family in a comfortable home in the Sweet Auburn neighborhood.
"Daddy" King, a leading Republican, might have seemed an unlikely
man to nurture the era's icon of black protest. But when the civil rights
movement burst onto the southern scene in the mid-1950s, it swept up
the young minister of Montgomery's Dexter Avenue Baptist Church—
Martin Luther King, Jr.—and anointed him its leader. In Selma, it unified a previously balkanized African-American community in the name
of black voting rights.[7]

By the time the Selma campaign reached its apogee in the spring
of 1965, Claude Brown's Reformed Presbyterian Church, Anderson's
Tabernacle, and the other leading local churches—First Baptist Church
and Brown Chapel African Methodist Episcopal Church—had agreed to
house mass meetings. But those changes in reverends and their congregations were not the most stunning. On January 22, 110 of Selma's
African-American schoolteachers marched for civil rights. Toothbrushes
in hand and sporting their best attire, the pillars of the middle-class
African-American community marched through their neighborhoods
and to the courthouse. Clark and his police force wielded nightsticks to
force the schoolteachers down the steps. Twice more the teachers com-

posed themselves and ascended; twice more they were shoved back. When the schoolteachers returned to Sylvan Street, three hundred African-American teenagers and children gave their teachers an impassioned ovation. Dallas County Voters League leader F. D. Reese declared, according to Taylor Branch, "that if the teachers were not afraid to march for the right to vote, *nobody* should be afraid." The morticians soon organized their own march to the courthouse, and the barbers followed. As the longtime faces of black accommodation took to the streets, local whites trembled.[8]

Gusts blew from Selma across rural Alabama. Blacks in Marion, the seat of Perry County, caught the fever of protest. African-Americans boycotted stores and schools, and by February 4, six hundred high school students were jailed. On February 18, five hundred blacks attempted to march across the town square to the jail. State troopers attacked them. Hours later, a trooper shot a young black pulpwood cutter named Jimmie Lee Jackson. Jackson died of his wounds on February 26. The Selma campaign had become wracked by feuds between SCLC and SNCC, but Jackson's death lent it new life. Thousands mourned at services for Jackson, and they began to talk of a protest march to the statehouse. SCLC endorsed the idea, and urged African-Americans from rural Alabama to march on Montgomery and demand voting rights during the legislature's special session. King announced that a march from Selma to Montgomery would occur on Sunday, March 7. On Saturday, sixty whites paraded to the Selma courthouse to express solidarity with the black struggle. Again a hotbed of activity, Selma awaited March 7—a day that would come to be known as "Bloody Sunday."[9]

While the marchers' stated destination was Montgomery, it quickly became apparent that they would have trouble getting out of Selma. Five hundred twenty-five African-Americans streamed out of Brown Chapel AME Church, up Sylvan Street, and walked the six blocks to Broad Street, Selma's main thoroughfare. They continued onto the Edmund Pettus Bridge, which spanned the Alabama River. A phalanx of fifty state troopers and fifteen mounted possemen waited. Donning gas masks and brandishing nightsticks, the troopers stood shoulder to shoulder across the highway. One hundred white spectators looked on. The marchers made their way slowly across the bridge, in two lines. A voice boomed over an amplifier, informing the marchers that their actions were illegal, and ordering them to halt. SCLC's Hosea Williams asked to have a word with the troopers, but they denied his request. There was nothing to discuss. The previous day, George Wallace had ordered state troopers to stop the march. The troopers told the marchers they had two minutes to disperse, and a foreboding silence settled over the bridge. Suddenly, the line of troopers morphed into a flying wedge and bolted toward the mass of motionless blacks, who fell to the ground under the stampede. Victims screamed, horses thundered across the bridge, and white spectators "whooped and cheered." Jim Clark yelled, "Get those god-damned niggers! And get those god-damned white niggers!" Troopers lobbed tear gas canisters into the crowd of retreating and injured blacks. Flailing nightsticks were barely visible through the haze, but cries and the sounds of cracking heads were audible. Brown Chapel quickly became a makeshift emergency room. Television cameras broadcast the images across America. King vowed that on Tuesday, a march would span the entire fifty miles to Montgomery. Thousands of clergy, activists, and civil rights supporters descended upon Selma. District Judge Frank Johnson banned the Tuesday march, so King led 2,500 people across the bridge, then back to Brown Chapel. That night, local segregationists beat a Boston reverend, James Reeb, to death. A week later, Judge Johnson authorized the Selma-to-Montgomery march. It would begin on March 21.[10]

The horrors on the Edmund Pettus Bridge exposed black disenfranchisement as a violation of the national creed too flagrant for many Americans to miss. On March 15, President Johnson addressed a joint session of Congress and announced his support for a voting rights bill. Johnson described himself as "a man whose roots go deeply into southern soil," one aware of "how agonizing racial feelings are." He declared that African-Americans must have voting rights, and noted, "It is not just the Negroes, but it is really all of us, who must overcome the crippling legacy of bigotry and injustice." The proposed bill would enable federal officials to enter blacks' names on the books, and outlaw discriminatory voting qualifications. The bill would apply immediately to Alabama, Mississippi, Georgia, Louisiana, Virginia, South Carolina, and parts of North Carolina. To Tom Wicker of the *New York Times*, "Mr. Johnson's accent and emphasis imparted an unmistakable determination." It was not only that the president of the United States had become a public supporter of civil rights, but he was a white southerner. Johnson's remarkable actions made the writer Ralph Ellison recall "an old slave-born myth . . . of the flawed white Southerner who while true to his southern roots has confronted the injustices of the past and been

redeemed." Ellison called Johnson the greatest president for racial justice. "Such a man, the myth holds, will do the right thing however great
the cost, whether he likes Negroes or not. . . . The figure evoked by this
myth . . . is a man who has so identified with his task that personal considerations have become secondary." Ellison hoped and suspected that
Lyndon Johnson had become such a man, and such a leader.* In Johnson's
March 15 speech, that portrait did not seem too far off. As Senator Sam
Ervin sat in disgust and Louisiana's Allen Ellender "slumped gloomily in
his seat," Tennessee's Albert Gore enthusiastically applauded and Mike
Mansfield—the majority leader—fought off tears. "It is wrong to deny
any person full equality because of the color of his skin," Johnson
intoned. His words could not be misconstrued. In his peroration, Johnson articulated in his southern accent the mantra of the freedom struggle:
"And we . . . shall . . . overcome." To African-Americans, his words were
sweet melodies; to many white southerners, they stung like daggers.[11]

Thousands of black marchers soon nudged Johnson's bold words to
the periphery of white consciousness. The Selma-to-Montgomery march
began as planned on Sunday, March 21, with King in the lead. Some
eight thousand marchers departed from Brown Chapel, with almost two
thousand federal troops at their side. From corners in downtown Selma
to anonymous reaches of Route 80, white onlookers absorbed the scene.
Those who had howled with delight at the Bloody Sunday attack now
jeered. Along stretches of the state highway, whites alternately shouted
insults, waved Confederate flags, and snapped photographs. At one
point, a group of white children, armed with toy rifles, ran toward the
march and shouted, "Nigger Lover! White Nigger!" Georgia Roberts, a
Selma black, reflected, "I never thought I'd see the day when we'd dare to
march against the white government in the Black Belt of Alabama." But
march they did, even through Lowndes County and into the cradle of the
Confederacy.[12]

Under armed guard, the marchers encountered little violence during their four-day procession. They demanded the vote, something the

---

*Johnson showed many flaws on the racial issue. From his 1949 "We of the South" speech to
his handling of the Mississippi Freedom Democratic Party at the 1964 Democratic convention,
Johnson's life and political career were filled with conflict on the question of black civil rights.
Many Johnson scholars have explored the various arguments surrounding this issue. See Robert A.
Caro's biography for the years preceding his presidency: *The Path to Power* (New York, 1982); *The
Means to Ascent* (New York, 1990); *Master of the Senate* (New York, 2002). For a laudatory inter-
pretation of Johnson's presidency and civil rights, see Nick Kotz, *Judgment Days: Lyndon Baines
Johnson, Martin Luther King, Jr., and the Laws That Changed America* (Boston, 2005).

nation's president had already publicly endorsed. Federal and local judges were beginning to bring the black franchise to Selma and its environs. But none of that lessened the wonder the march inspired. On Thursday morning, March 25, the marchers swooped into Montgomery and through its west side residential neighborhoods. Thousands of local blacks and newly arrived supporters from out of state joined the ranks. By the time the march reached the capitol building, its numbers had swelled beyond twenty-five thousand. For a morning, a mostly black sea overtook George Wallace's Alabama.

The march made a deep impression on Montgomery's inhabitants. At the midtown Jefferson Davis Hotel, black maids peered out the windows as the white patrons stood dazed on the hotel's marquee. Black porters gazed out the Whitley on one side as white customers watched from the other. The *New York Herald Tribune*'s Jimmy Breslin recounted the epic scene. At the city's hotels and banks, drugstores and groceries, white faces pressed against windows. "At first the faces were set and the lips formed curses. Dr. Martin Luther King, the enemy, was coming by. And behind King were some rows of straggly dressed people in shoes that were caked with mud. The faces at the windows smiled." But those smirks turned to grimaces, and they altered under the realization that white supremacy was dying—not simply on the surface, but with the prospect of political change. "The people kept coming. They came in soggy clothes, with mud on their feet, and they walked in silence and with their heads up in the air, high up in the air, with the chins stuck out and the eyes straight ahead, and they came for an hour and a half and the faces at the windows changed." For more than an hour, black marchers walked by. With their gait, their posture, and their cause, they sought to bury Jim Crow for good. "The South is all gone," a man told Assistant Attorney General John Doar. "A whole way of life is going right into memory." Doar concurred, "That's right. That's just what it is." Alabama state senator Roland Cooper was one who denied that possibility. When asked the meaning of the march, Cooper commented, "Don't mean nothin' at all. Jes' take a look at them. They jes' a pack of coons." The changes would not be instantaneous, but they would be substantial. "Roland Cooper stood and watched his world change and he didn't even know it," Breslin wrote. "And he will not know it until he sees, some day, the registration figures in Wilcox County, Alabama, where niggers never have voted." When that day came, Cooper would be fighting for his job.[13]

The Voting Rights Act hastened that new day's arrival. Unlike the

Civil Rights Act, which had inspired prolonged debate, the Voting Rights Act did not invite filibusters and political warfare. Little more than a year after the ink had dried on the Civil Rights Act, Lyndon Johnson signed the Voting Rights Act into law on August 6, 1965. SNCC's John Lewis called the bill's passage "every bit as momentous and significant . . . as the Emancipation Proclamation." It had immediate effects. On August 9, Attorney General Nicholas Katzenbach designated nine counties to receive federal examiners—Dallas County, Alabama, among them. By August 14, black voter registration in Selma had doubled. A week after the federal examiners arrived, black registration quadrupled in the nine affected counties—from 1,764 to 6,998. "The whole thing's so ridiculous I haven't gotten over laughing at it yet," Jim Clark said. That November, federal registrars moved into thirty-two Deep South counties. Blacks wasted little time in amassing political might. In Alabama's western Black Belt, Greene, Macon, and Wilcox counties contained black majorities on the 1966 voting rolls. In Lowndes, where not one black was registered in the spring of 1965, a full 49.4 percent of the county's voters (2,758) had registered by 1966. More than 10,000 blacks had registered in Dallas County by that time, accounting for 45 percent of the electorate. A year after the Voting Rights Act was signed, almost half of all the adult blacks in the Deep South had registered. Segregationists like Jim Clark would not laugh for long.[14]

Clark scarcely imagined that an influx of black voters would ultimately spell his political doom. The sheriff ran for reelection in 1966, with Wilson Baker as his opposition. Before the election, Clark was asked whether he thought the newly registered blacks would vote. "If they can find their way into town," he snickered. Months before, civil rights activist James Bevel had remarked: "If we get out and work [for voter registration] Jim Clark will be picking cotton with my father in about two years." While a majority of whites voted for Clark in the May Democratic primary, Baker rode black support to victory. The civil rights movement reshaped Baker's career. Known as a hard-line racial conservative in the 1950s, Baker refashioned himself amid the epic events. During the civil rights campaign, Baker met regularly with King. He successfully projected himself as a figure of reason, compromise, law, and order. This contrasted sharply with Jim Clark's image. Clark ran as an independent in the November election, but lost again. In the final tally, Baker garnered 8,088 votes to Clark's 7,699. The removal of Sheriff Clark was the first step in Dallas County's political

transformation. In 1964, Selma contained 6,000 voters—all but 2 percent of them white. By 1968, blacks alone counted for 5,000 of the city's
registered voters. Clark had violently embodied Jim Crow. During the
1965 civil rights campaign, he sported a button on his lapel that read,
"Never." Black votes buried this kind of intransigence, even if they did
not stamp out all of segregation's political remnants. After his victory,
Wilson Baker maintained, "I am a segregationist. But I am a realist
about those social changes." In 1968, a black candidate opposed Mayor
Joe Smitherman in his bid for reelection. But by that point, Smitherman
had already built support in the black community. Sensing the mounting political tide, he began to embrace African-American voters. He
took two-thirds of the vote to win reelection, and would remain the
mayor of Selma until 2000, when he lost to an African-American, James
Perkins.[15]

Racism alone could no longer define southern politics. Before the
Voting Rights Act was passed, vows to maintain segregation were standard parts of political platforms. Even so-called moderates pledged segregation. "Prior to 1967," recalled Reuben Anderson, the first black
appointed to the Mississippi Supreme Court, "any politician who said
anything other than 'nigger' was destined for defeat." With the rise of
black voters, candidates had to appeal to both races. "Long as we didn't
have no black voters in there at all, the [one] could holler nigger the
loudest, he's the one got elected," remembered Roosevelt Williams, an
African-American worker at Birmingham's U.S. Steel. "After Selma,
Voting Rights Act passed . . . things began to change." By 1966, blacks
had won spots on the school board in several Mississippi, Georgia, and
Louisiana counties. Black ballots spelled new southern realities, for
African-Americans and whites alike.[16]

THE LIFE OF GEORGE WALLACE lends itself to many parables. Wallace
towered over Alabama politics for two decades, while he made his mark
on the nation. After all his victories and defeats, Wallace could tell many
different tales that burrowed into larger truths about the South and the
age of civil rights. Wallace hailed from the town of Clio, in the Alabama
Black Belt. During the late 1940s, the young Wallace campaigned for
local office each day in the one suit he owned. By 1962, he was Alabama's
governor. But his up-by-the-bootstraps story had only begun. In 1964,
1968, and 1972, Wallace waged campaigns for the presidency. His
strong showing in Wisconsin's 1964 Democratic primary announced

him as a national force, one whose issues eventually would become a part of Richard Nixon's successful 1968 Republican platform. Wallace became a formidable third party in his own right. A 1972 assassination attempt permanently paralyzed him, but he returned to the political scene a decade later, and won yet another gubernatorial campaign. Wallace had ascended from humble origins and achieved iconic status in American politics.

Wallace rooted his power in a fiery defense of segregation. But he first came of political age in the years after World War II as an acolyte of Big Jim Folsom, Alabama's populist—and racially moderate—governor. Wallace won a judgeship in 1952, while still linked to Folsom. As the post-*Brown* winds whipped toward "massive resistance," Wallace attempted to distance himself from Folsom's racial politics. The wildly ambitious Wallace positioned himself as a defender of Jim Crow in his 1958 campaign for the statehouse, but attorney John Patterson was able to raise doubts about Wallace's segregationist credentials. After Patterson defeated him, Wallace vowed that no politician would ever "outnigger" him again. None ever did.[17]

After Wallace won the governor's office in 1962, he delivered a historic inaugural address. With a single cutting phrase, Wallace wrote himself into one of the era's most gripping dramas. Months after Ole Miss exploded in insurrection during the university's integration, and months before Birmingham became the epicenter of the civil rights movement, George Wallace exuded defiance from the Montgomery capitol:

> Today I have stood, where once Jefferson Davis stood, and took an oath to my people. It is very appropriate then that from this Cradle of the Confederacy, this very Heart of the Great Anglo-Saxon Southland . . . we sound the drum for freedom. . . . In the name of the greatest people that have ever trod this earth, I draw the line in the dust and toss the gauntlet before the feet of tyranny . . . and I say . . . segregation now . . . segregation tomorrow . . . segregation forever.

Wallace's line, "segregation forever," etched itself into the nation's consciousness. He maintained a working relationship with Bull Connor—Birmingham's public safety director who turned fire hoses and dogs on protesters, and sent children off in paddy wagons. Wallace ordered troopers to Selma's Edmund Pettus Bridge in 1965. The fractured skulls in Selma, and the other ghastly acts of violence and murder throughout the state, all occurred on George Wallace's watch. While Wallace did not encourage all of those acts (and many of them he did), he apologized for none of them. For his uncompromising stance on civil rights as well as for his deft ability to eviscerate northern liberals, Wallace remained a hero to many white southerners. In May 1965, mere months after the violence in Selma, Wallace's approval rating among southern whites stood at 79 percent.[18]

Not even George Wallace was impervious to the coming transformations. As the 1960s ended, Wallace adapted himself to the changing political climate—one in which southern blacks came to possess clout. Encouragement of racial violence would now be punished, not rewarded. The cry of "segregation forever" would ring hollow amid the crumbling racial order. Even as Wallace derided the "black bloc vote," he knew that someday soon he might have to court it. As riots roared across northern cities and buses rolled from black neighborhoods to white schools, northern whites became more receptive to Wallace's racial appeals. In the 1970s, he employed a vocabulary that prized "law and order" and individual responsibility as it railed against "welfare queens" and the federal government. In private, Wallace's rhetoric changed little. And on the campaign trail, he still used the racial issue to win white votes. While Wallace stopped uttering the word "segregation," he defeated Albert Brewer with bald racial rhetoric. As Alabama's 1970 gubernatorial primary runoff approached, Wallace distributed leaflets that featured photographs of seven young African-American boys crowded around a white girl. "Wake Up, Alabama!" the leaflets read. They charged, "Blacks Vow to Take Over Alabama," and asked voters, "Is this the image you want?" Yet by his 1971 inaugural, Wallace seemed something of a different leader. The man who had closed Tuskegee schools in 1963 now said that Americans "ought to have non-discrimination in public schools." He claimed he had "always been a moderate," and the once bitter opponent of the Civil Rights Act now supported "public accommodations open to all." Wallace continued to exploit white racial fears for political gain, yet he seemed to have changed course. In 1972, the *Birmingham News* editorialized, "The governor is a far cry from the dedicated segregationist who . . . threw the gauntlet down to defend white supremacy." That year, Wallace again hit the presidential campaign trail. He charged through Maryland, a state he had barely lost in 1964. As Wallace waded into a crowd, a would-be assassin fired multiple shots. Confined to a wheelchair after that, Wallace never again stoked the passion and rage that earlier brought him fame and power.[19]

Driven by an intimate knowledge of human pain, a religious rebirth, and an acceptance of the South as an interracial political land, Wallace began to seek forgiveness for his segregationist sins. In 1979, he telephoned John Lewis, Georgia congressman and former head of SNCC. Years before, Lewis's skull had been cracked on the Edmund Pettus Bridge. Now Lewis and Wallace drank coffee together in Lewis's living room. Wallace then called many old civil rights leaders and nemeses, begging forgiveness of them all. Wallace hired black staffers, prayed in black churches, and held black hands. In 1982, he ran again for governor of Alabama—and won. *Time* reported, "a fairly large number of Alabama blacks have . . . joined the Wallace tribe." In the Democratic primary, 65 percent of blacks voted against Wallace. But that left a full 35 percent who supported him. As *Boston Globe* reporter Wil Haygood later asked, "How was he to know he'd meet the same folks coming down that he met coming up?" Wallace said to Haygood in 1993, "Segregation was wrong. But that was then, and I'm happy it's over with." In this new South, Wallace sought penance for his part in the old racial world—as he hoped for salvation in the next.[20]

George Wallace hashed out all of these issues when he sat down for a 1986 interview. The event was filmed as part of *Eyes on the Prize,* a film series on the civil rights movement. Callie Crossley, an African-American woman, served as Wallace's interviewer. The discussion occurred in the governor's office, where Wallace repeatedly bragged about a particular honorary degree on his wall—one from the Tuskegee Institute. The cognitive dissonance reached its peak when the old embodiment of segregationist defiance now pressed an African-American woman about whether she possessed a degree from the renowned black college. Crossley admitted that she did not. Throughout the interview, Wallace mixed boasts and smoke screens, honesty and insincerity, pretense and insight. He spoke openly of his upbringing in the Alabama Black Belt, where "I was born and raised among black people and they're my friends." He added, "Our black people are some of our finest citizens." To whites, segregation did not constitute "an antagonism toward black people, and that's what some people can't understand. . . . In fact, white southerners did not believe it was discrimination." That said, Wallace professed no nostalgia for the Jim Crow past. "It was not the kind of system we ought to have, it's gone forever, thank goodness." When asked about his famous inaugural speech declaring otherwise, Wallace admitted he had erred. "Segregation could not last and it shouldn't have lasted." The interview teemed with such contrasts. The governor who first glimpsed the hands of communists in the Birmingham church bombing now claimed he demanded that the perpetrators "ought to burn the bottom of the electric chair out." Wallace practiced a further sort of historical revisionism when he asserted that "there never was a single confrontation between blacks and whites during that time in Alabama," and that on Selma's Edmund Pettus Bridge "not a single person was harmed to the extent of having to go to the hospital." Sheriff Jim Clark made the same claim in his own 1986 interview with the *Eyes on the Prize* team. The Wallace interview possessed its awkward moments; Crossley only managed a soft "okay" after Wallace claimed that few problems existed between whites and blacks. When Wallace turned to the issue of his own legacy, the interview reached a crescendo.[21]

More than once, George Wallace displayed a sharp awareness of his own influence on American politics. "I talked about the Supreme Court usurpation of power, I talked about the big central government. Isn't that what everybody talks about now. Isn't that what Reagan got elected on?" Without using the terms "Southern Strategy" or "silent majority," Wallace alluded to their power. He glimpsed a similarity between the presidential elections of the 1960s and that of 1984. "Reagan got elected by one of the biggest votes . . . ever . . . by saying those very same things I said way back yonder when I ran for the presidency myself." Wallace saved his grandest appeals for the issues of racial reconciliation. He realized that his actions in the 1960s had jeopardized his legacy—but true to form, he alleged that the media had singled him out. He drew a parallel between his opposition to civil rights laws and that of Lyndon Johnson, Barry Goldwater, and southern senators William Fulbright, Sam Ervin, Richard Russell, and Lister Hill. Referring to Johnson's actions in the 1940s and early 1950s, Wallace asserted that the former president "has filibustered and talked more against civil rights bills than I ever did in my whole entire life." Wallace could not understand why Johnson enjoyed a reputation as a friend of civil rights while he, Wallace, remained a symbol of racism. "You rehabilitated him. You rehabilitated Fulbright. You rehabilitated all these other distinguished fine Americans. But you won't rehabilitate me." The man who once cried "segregation forever" seemed to wish he never had. In George Wallace's Alabama, a new political day had truly arrived. The governor now desired forgiveness, reconciliation, and rehabilitation.[22]

Whether George Wallace deserved any of that was an open question. Reasonable people could debate how deeply he had changed. But in a sense, that was beside the point. Former *Newsweek* bureau chief Joseph Cumming reflected: "If you've got African-Americans who've got the vote, you're not going to get demagoguery. . . . That was the beauty of it!" Black voters had changed southern politics in ways previously unimaginable. They began to influence the careers of the most racist white politicians—even George Wallace.[23]

The Voting Rights Act ushered a host of changes into southern politics. It was responsible for the fact that the "the word 'segregation' has virtually disappeared from the political vocabulary," as a *Birmingham Post-Herald* editor said in 1966. Some of the political changes were apparent in the "conversions" of leaders like George Wallace. Others were evident in the success of the Republican Party, as over decades white southerners shifted by the millions from the Democratic camp to the Republican. Still more became visible only in the faces of newly enfranchised African-Americans who voted under the guard of armed marshals, and whites who worried about their future. For some of these changes, one had to pry deep beneath the surface, into hearts and minds. For others, numbers and statistics themselves told profound tales.[24]

Black voting registration skyrocketed in the seven southern states where the Voting Rights Act assigned federal examiners. No state exhibited starker changes than Mississippi, where less than 1 percent of voting-age blacks were registered in 1947. That percentage lagged at 5 percent in 1956, and 6.7 percent in 1964. By 1967, nearly 60 percent of voting-age blacks were on the Mississippi rolls. The transformation in Alabama was almost as thorough. While 1 percent of voting-age Alabama blacks registered in 1947 and 19 percent in 1964, nearly 57 percent were registered in 1968. By 1970, 68 percent of Mississippi adult blacks and 64 percent of those in Alabama were registered. The statistics tell a story of revolution, but it took time for blacks to cement their numbers in political power. As the percentage of registered Alabama blacks grew dramatically, politicians made concerted efforts to register more whites. From 1964 to 1967, the number of registered Alabama blacks increased by 248,432; the white electorate grew by 276,622. Across the entire South, white southerners accounted for about 65 percent of new registrants. In Alabama, the percentage of whites who were registered increased from 69 percent in 1964 to a whopping 95 percent in 1969. In Mississippi, the white percentage shot up from 70 percent to 90 percent. The Voting Rights Act put thousands more southern voters on the rolls—not just blacks, but whites as well.[25]

In a further irony, the centers of white political power within the South shifted radically. Since Jim Crow's first days, Black Belt whites had held a disproportionate share of power. A white minority had dominated rural politics, and extended its grip over state affairs. Many southern states adopted political systems similar to Georgia's, with the county as the principal voting unit. Whereas hundreds of thousands made up the electorate in urban counties like Jefferson (where Birmingham was situated), a few thousand whites in Lowndes had a similar amount of influence. In Lowndes County, blacks outnumbered whites, 12,000 to 3,000, yet no black had ever attempted to register in the twentieth century. Blacks counted in population figures, but they could not vote. Therefore, each Black Belt white wielded much more power with his vote than each urban voter. The Supreme Court struck down these sorts of county-unit systems in 1962 and 1964 decisions, and the Voting Rights Act dealt Black Belt whites a final blow. With the influx of black voters, planters were outnumbered. Fortresses of conservative white rule suddenly became regional citadels of progressivism.[26]

The portrait was stunning. In 1970, a cluster of Black Belt Alabama counties had African-American majorities—Greene, Hale, Perry, Dallas, Wilcox, Lowndes, Macon, Sumter, Marengo, and Bullock. Nine of those counties qualified as Alabama's most "liberal," according to voting results: they gave the most support for the interracial National Democratic Party of Alabama, for Hubert Humphrey in his 1968 campaign for the presidency, and for George McGovern in 1972. Only twenty-three of Alabama's sixty-nine counties gave George Wallace less than 65 percent of the votes in the 1974 gubernatorial primary; those nine with black majorities were all among them. Black Belt counties were transformed from centers of planter rule to oases of increasingly liberal politics in a still conservative—and fast becoming Republican—South. Nixon strategist Kevin Phillips commented, "This new Negro voting power turned the same Black Belts which had been the Dixiecrat, Republican, or states' rights bastions of 1948–64 into the *best* national Democratic counties in the Deep South." Two worlds struggled to emerge: one featured white Republicans; in the Black Belt, democracy assumed an African-American cast. As Alabama native Virginia Durr pointed out,

" 'Black Power' . . . is only majority rule by another name." To whites in the Black Belt, the move to Republicanism was of little initial consequence; far more momentous was the living and breathing manifestation of black power.[27]

2

WHEN CIVIL RIGHTS DEMONSTRATORS trooped through the Alabama Black Belt, a sense of disbelief pervaded white communities. Many whites remained willfully indifferent, and intentionally ignorant, of the changes that threatened to engulf them. Before the 1960s, the prospect of black political rule seemed at best a cruel joke. "The niggers would take over the county if they could vote in full numbers," a white cotton ginner said in the 1950s. "They'd stick together and vote blacks into every office in the county . . . think what the black SOB's would do to you!" It was not a thought that he seriously entertained. The cotton ginner uttered those words not in the way one would issue a prediction, but as one might hallucinate a barely imaginable future. Well into the 1960s, most Black Belt whites harbored a deep paternalism. They agreed with Macon County legislator Sam Engelhardt, who said, "I do not believe the Negroes of my county are ready to take an active part in politics." State Senator Roland Cooper and Sheriff Jim Clark spoke for a large segment of white Alabamians; Cooper thought of civil rights marchers as a meaningless "pack of coons," and Clark laughingly dismissed the thousands of registered blacks as "ridiculous." For rural whites, the concept of African-Americans in power smacked of the absurd. A black official at the Tuskegee Institute termed it an "Alice-in-Wonderland climate that prevails in so much of the Alabama Black Belt." When Greene County resident Eugene Johnston peddled the idea of an all-white private school in 1965, he found little local support. It was not that whites in Greene County desired integrated schools; far from it. They would not allow themselves even to anticipate desegregation. Johnston "was considered a bit kooky or at least out of line with a tasteless joke," wrote *Newsweek*'s Joseph Cumming. And the suggestion of black government was one step further from their notions of the possible. "The idea of 'nigras' taking over the county government was simply an idea that could not be taken seriously. It was a non-idea."[28]

It was a wonder that Greene County whites seemed so far removed from this possibility, for those very "non-ideas" spelled reality in nearby

Macon County. Even in the Black Belt, Macon County stood out. Of about 26,000 residents, 84 percent were African-American—the highest percentage in the nation. The town of Tuskegee held a population of 6,500 and boasted the famed Tuskegee Institute, the black college that Booker T. Washington founded. African-American voting drives began in the years after World War II. By 1958, 1,218 Macon County blacks had registered to vote—they made up more than one-third of the electorate. In Tuskegee, blacks accounted for 40 percent of the voters. This was too much for whites to tolerate. The Alabama legislature gerrymandered Tuskegee's city boundaries to exclude all but twelve of the registered African-Americans. The U.S. Department of Justice could not miss so overt a maneuver. In one action spurred by the otherwise ineffectual 1957 Civil Rights Act, the Justice Department filed a lawsuit against Macon County. The Supreme Court struck down the gerrymander in 1961, and African-Americans in Macon County continued to register.[29]

White concerns about black power predated the gerrymander controversy. In 1951, Sam Engelhardt could glimpse African-Americans' future political clout. In an attempt to ensure eternal white control, he suggested that the legislature abolish Alabama's Black Belt counties. In 1958, a committee was created to study the potential abolition of Macon County. These proposals, along with the gerrymander, further galvanized Macon blacks. In response, they boycotted Tuskegee stores. By the spring of 1958, half of the town's white-owned retail businesses had failed. "The Negroes want complete control," charged a white Tuskegee housewife. "They will do anything to get it." In the 1960 elections, Tuskegee voters traded in their conservative local government for more pragmatic administrators. Conciliation of black demands replaced racial antagonism. White moderates grew more outspoken and attempted to ease the seemingly inevitable transition to a biracial polity. By the summer of 1963, the number of black Macon County voters approached that of whites.[30]

In the autumn general elections, Tuskegee had nine hundred black voters and one thousand whites. African-Americans combined with white moderates to elect a progressive mayor—Charles Keever—and a biracial city council. "We are aware of the break with tradition which our taking office symbolizes," read the city council's public statement of October 5. "Today may . . . mark the end of one era and the beginning of another." The political change did not accompany integration in restaurants, churches, or neighborhoods, but it nonetheless heralded a new day in Alabama. Immediately, the council paved streets in the black neighborhood. Whites "have had to face the reality of the Negro vote," said a Tuskegee Institute official. Many remnants of the "Alice-in-Wonderland" mystique vanished from this Black Belt county.[31]

The events of 1965 had a profound effect upon politics and race in Macon County. Blacks could not ignore the brutality in Selma and the dramatic march to Montgomery. SNCC made inroads at Tuskegee Institute, and students staged protests to demand integration at churches and businesses. In January 1966, a white gas station owner named Marvin Segrest shot and killed Sammy Younge, a black SNCC organizer. Outrage dissolved black support for biracial coalitions; led by student activists, blacks nominated many of their own for office. In 1966, Macon County black voters outnumbered whites 7,130 to 4,997 (59 percent to 41 percent). Against the counsel of older Tuskegee Institute leaders, many Macon blacks supported African-American Lucius Amerson for sheriff. Amerson won the Democratic primary runoff with 53 percent of the vote. While some whites began to accept the gradual "descent" into biracial politics, the thought of a black sheriff was too much for many to bear. Whites had always arbitrated the law and dispensed justice; they would now be at the mercy of such forces. Those who once countenanced coalition politics now decried what they saw as a "black takeover." "We were on the brink of total integration," said the white chief deputy sheriff, Jack Askew. "Now we've been set back." Amerson won handily in the November election. A month later, a white jury acquitted Segrest of murder charges after the trial was moved from Tuskegee to Opelika. Almost two thousand blacks swarmed City Hall to protest, where Mayor Keever was heard mumbling the words to "We Shall Overcome." Later the protest turned unruly. Students splashed black paint on a statue of a Confederate soldier that stood in Tuskegee's town square. The statue gained a yellow stripe down its back, and was adorned with the words "Black Power." That was how Tuskegee, in the winter of 1966, came to possess a Confederate statue and sheriff both of the same color—black.[32]

Amerson's election and the student upheaval further dramatized an already dramatic reality. As Gene Roberts wrote in the *New York Times Magazine,* "One chunk of Alabama soil is no longer the political province of the white man." Although some Macon County whites accommodated themselves to the new racial and political order, "a still larger group of whites tries as best it can to cling to the old ways." L. O. Hall, the white constable, plotted to undermine Amerson's authority. Hall found an old statute in state law that empowered the constable—in competition with the sheriff—to serve warrants and arrest suspects. "Most people won't have to deal with Amerson at all." If blacks won political office, some whites would simply refuse to recognize their power. Other whites disliked such an underhanded plan, and preferred to obey the law—in its intent as well as its letter. "We are dividing up over this," said a leading segregationist, "like we have divided up over most everything else since this civil-rights business started." In this respect, Tuskegee resembled New Orleans, Athens, the Mississippi Delta, and everywhere else integration traveled. Black rights wrought white division.[33]

Amerson solidified his power in the 1970 elections, and blacks won many more offices. After the 1972 elections, only one white remained on the city council. Black power in Macon County had become almost routine. In 1972, Johnny Ford challenged Mayor Keever. Ford, an African-American, had some trouble garnering support from blacks as well as from whites. In a place where race meant everything, Johnny Ford had a white wife. Ford knew what he was up against. "Oh man—a mixed marriage in the South? In the Alabama Black Belt? I got to be crazy. Maybe somewhere else, but not here, not in Macon County, not yet. A thousand years maybe—but not now." Many whites hoped it would be generations before interracial marriage came to Alabama. "For the white citizens of Tuskegee," Marshall Frady wrote in the magazine *New Times,* "being presided over by a black mayor married to a white woman would have seemed a realization of their most garish nightmares of the Sixties." More and more, Black Belt whites seemed to be living their nightmares. Amerson campaigned with Ford to help him shore up black votes. In the end, Ford defeated Keever by 124 votes. By Ford's third term in 1980, Tuskegee was almost entirely African-American. Fewer than six hundred whites remained within the city limits. Those who stayed resigned themselves to the reality of black political power. As one segregationist leader said before Amerson first took office in 1967, "The sun will still rise in the East and set in the West." That was about all Tuskegee whites could count on.[34]

FOR WHITES IN EUTAW, the Greene County seat, even such constants seemed uncertain. As some parts of Dixie looked forward to an industrialized "New South," many Greene County whites pined for the past. The story of Greene in the twentieth century was partly a tale of decline. Once a rich center of cotton production, Greene County had gradually and consistently lost people and wealth. In the days of slavery, it was the largest county in Alabama. In 1900, it counted a population of 24,182. By 1960, that number was 13,600; and by 1970, it had decreased to 10,650. Almost 40 percent of its workforce still was engaged in agriculture. Greene was the second poorest county in Alabama, and the fifth poorest in the nation. Eutaw's hilltop mansions, with their stately columns and inviting porticoes, projected an image of the county's past. Some white families still lived in the quarters that had housed them since antebellum times. It was a white population that once had reaped the profits of cotton, a people who had not yet adapted to realities— economic, social, racial, or political—of life in the second half of the twentieth century. This entire portrait led *Newsweek*'s Joseph Cumming to describe the drive from "the neon-gaudy highways around Tuscaloosa into lonely and uncluttered Greene County" as a voyage "from Technicolor into black and white." Heading into Greene felt like stepping back in time.[35]

The civil rights movement left Greene County virtually untouched until the passage of the Voting Rights Act. As blacks made up more than 75 percent of the population, they quickly surpassed whites on the voting rolls. Suddenly a political minority, few Greene whites knew exactly what had hit them. Life in Greene had been tranquil for them before blacks gained power. Although a few blacks had registered in the years following World War II, they numbered only a handful. County laws required that an already qualified voter had to vouch for any potential voter. In 1950, whites stopped vouching for blacks. Most whites believed that life could continue unchanged. "Before blacks assumed power," said William McKinley Branch, the first black probate judge, "there was never any local initiative by the white power structure to attract industry. White people were satisfied with their position, and they didn't want to upset things." Greene whites, like others in the Black Belt, embraced traditional myths about "their" African-Americans. As Sheriff Bill Lee said in 1966:

> We never . . . had a problem here with our colored people. We in
> this county feed 'em and take care of 'em, they get their groceries
> for nothing and the government gives 'em their luxuries with

their welfare checks. They know the law's not gonna bother 'em
here. . . . It's just the best place in the world for a colored person
to live.

Soon, it was one of the few places in the United States where African-
Americans wielded complete control over local government.[36]

In 1966, the same year that Lucius Amerson ran for sheriff of Macon
County, African-American Thomas Gilmore mounted a bid for the
Greene County sheriff's seat. Bill Lee was not only the incumbent, but a
sheriff by blood. From 1922 to 1954, Lee's father and brother had alternately occupied the sheriff's office. For sixteen years more, Bill Lee carried on the legacy. Gilmore embodied an obvious threat. "It would be
hard to exaggerate the harrowing implications in those days for the rural
white Southerner of a black running for sheriff of his county," Marshall
Frady wrote in Newsweek. "The sheriff was a kind of absolute totem
image of all authority and order out in the Southern countryside."
Whites in Eutaw fretted. "Goddam, nothing could be worse than this,"
one confided to Frady. "This is Armageddon." In the county, black voters
outnumbered whites by a margin of 3,927 to 2,001. It seemed that only
black fear or white trickery could prevent a Gilmore victory. Gilmore
was confident that the election would bring a new day to Greene
County—not only for blacks, but also for whites. "This election is actually gonna help the white man as much as us . . . this is gonna change
the white man in ways he ain't even thought about. . . . We gonna help
the white folks around her[e] believe in the whole race of man." Before the
May election, Martin Luther King made his way into Greene County.
"We are not Bill Lee's children. We are no white man's children," King
told a church congregation outside Eutaw. "For all these years, the white
man has been bloc-voting to keep us down. . . . Now we gonna engage in
a bloc vote to get back up on our feet." The black bloc vote was more
than a figment of white politicians' imaginations. In Greene County, it
would begin to replace white despotism with black equality.[37]

Eutaw whites nervously awaited the May 4 primary. Election night
carried the weight of ritual in that town of 2,800, and returns were
always posted on a courthouse blackboard. As the night unfolded, whites
would gather on the town square and celebrate their "democracy." But
anxiety, not revelry, accompanied the 1966 election. Although the courthouse displayed no blackboards on this night, word quickly got out that
Probate Judge Dennis Herndon was keeping a tally in his office. The

room soon teemed with a crowd that grew tenser as Gilmore's lead increased. By nine o'clock, the black candidate for sheriff led by more than twenty votes. That lasted until the absentee box arrived, and with it complimentary Pepsi from the Dairy Queen. Only one out of the 200 absentee votes went for Gilmore, and Bill Lee retained the sheriff's office by a margin of 290 votes. Frady reported that whiskey soon replaced Pepsi in the Dairy Queen cups, and jubilation displaced anguish. Greene County whites did not register a convincing victory, but they staved off black rule. Lee, though, knew his days were numbered. "You just can't expect fifteen hundred people to be able to keep beating off twenty-seven hundred. It just stands to reason they bound to win something eventually." For a time, whites enjoyed their reprieve. Few were interested in having their souls saved or their eyes opened to the "*whole* race of man," as Thomas Gilmore had said. "The white Southerner negotiated his way through such challenges" of the civil rights years not "as a moral adventure," Frady wrote, but as an "elemental tribal matter of embattlement and survival." Greene County whites had become an embattled political minority, but for the moment, they survived.[38]

The political wars had just begun. In November, four defeated black candidates—Gilmore among them—filed legal appeals. They charged that whites had illegally transferred votes into the absentee box on election night. By the time of the 1968 local elections, this suit was still pending. In that year's Democratic primary, four black candidates ran for the county commission and two for the school board. All six candidates lost. George Wallace still dominated Alabama's Democratic Party, and its primary was not fertile terrain for blacks. In response to this statewide problem, John Cashin—a black Huntsville dentist—helped to found the National Democratic Party of Alabama (NDPA). It offered an alternative to black candidates who could not puncture Alabama's Democratic Party. The six black candidates accepted Cashin's invitation to run on the NDPA ticket in Greene County's November general election. Judge Herndon dubiously disqualified them all. When the U.S. Supreme Court ordered Herndon to place their names back on the ballot, Herndon balked. The Supreme Court voided the results of the 1968 election; a new one would take place in July 1969. Greene County whites like Herndon might try to delay black rule, but they were ultimately helpless to prevent it.[39]

The summer of 1969 consistently delivered the unbelievable to Americans. Neil Armstrong walked on the moon, Woodstock pulsated, and the fledgling New York Mets won the World Series. For residents of Greene County, Alabama, in that summer local government passed from white to black hands. In the July special election, African-Americans won four of the five spots on the county commission and claimed a three-to-two majority on the school board.

One year later, Thomas Gilmore again ran for sheriff against Bill Lee. William McKinley Branch challenged Dennis Herndon for probate judge, and blacks sought complete control of the county commission. Other blacks ran, on the NDPA ticket, for most every county office—including coroner, circuit clerk, and the last two seats on the school board. The NDPA also supported Jack Drake, a twenty-five-year-old white lawyer, in his bid for circuit judge. Some whites were savvy and flexible enough to ride—rather than try to halt—the political tide. Drake attempted to unseat the incumbent, seventy-five-year-old Emmett Hildreth, perhaps the richest man in Eutaw and a polarizing embodiment of Greene's wealthy white (and segregationist) past. The 1970 election was a signal event for the whites of Greene County, for it asked them either to respond to the challenges of political and racial change or, as journalist Joseph Cumming wrote, to become "trapped forever in the backwaters." Whites like Drake adapted to the challenge; those like Lee and Herndon chose a different response. Lee, Herndon, and other white incumbents plotted their counterattack and formed a new party. "It would be damn foolishness to run for sheriff in this county on the same ticket as George Wallace," Lee said in 1970, four years after he won office on that very ticket. Whites called their party the Alabama Advancement Association (AAA), claimed that it would cater to blacks, and offered as its emblem a black-and-white spotted horse. Those facts notwithstanding, the "Spotted Horse Party" ran all white candidates and possessed no visible black support. Gilmore called the formation of the AAA "a desperate act of self-preservation by a few desperate people." If the Spotted Horse Party signified whites' attempts to preserve their political well-being, it could only be judged a failure.[40]

At two o'clock in the morning on November 4, the honking of automobile horns and the ringing of telephones awakened residents of Eutaw's black neighborhood. Euphoria spread through the neighborhood as word of the election results got around. African-American candidates swept all the major county offices. William McKinley Branch ousted Dennis Herndon as probate judge, Wadine Williams defeated Mary Yarbrough for circuit clerk, Gilmore triumphed over Lee, and the county commission and school committee both became all black. Before the election, the *Birmingham News* noted that it "marked the strongest challenge to white political supremacy Alabama has witnessed since Reconstruction Days." The next day, the *News* reported, the NDPA's victories left Greene County "in complete black power." On October 31, George Wallace had warned of "the black bloc vote," and said, "if you let them elect a governor, they'll control politics at the state capitol for the next 50 years." Wallace won, but the new political day settled ominously on Greene County whites. A local at Jimmy's Grill in Eutaw worried, "Things are going to be in a helluva mess in the county with them running it." While the blacks' victories were complete, they were far from landslides. Branch defeated Herndon by 92 votes, and Gilmore wrested the sheriff's office from Lee by a margin of 87 votes. His family's legacy thus finished, Lee griped, "It's a hell of a thing to let them . . . take over by only 90 votes." Across the Alabama Black Belt, whites' fears were coming true. H. O. Williams became the sheriff of Bullock County, and John Hulett won the office in Lowndes; Lucius Amerson also won reelection in Macon County. Many Black Belt whites could empathize with the Greene County official who said, "It isn't the end of the world, it just seems like it."[41]

Some whites refused to step into a world that seemed so transformed. Dennis Herndon and Mary Yarbrough filed lawsuits and charged that the elections were illegal. They maintained that black candidates did not meet various legal requirements for office, including stipulations involving residency and criminal records. Before the election, Judge Emmett Hildreth had Jack Drake disqualified by just such a tactic. But it did not work for Herndon and Yarbrough, who soon withdrew their suits. In January 1971, Herndon was convicted of contempt for his role in the disputed 1968 election. While whites exhausted their last efforts to stymie black political rule in the county, the city administration of Eutaw remained in white hands. Eutaw's population contained roughly equal numbers of blacks and whites. Mayor William Tuck characterized the white community as "hurt," "stunned," and "humiliated." Tuck and his brother, Edwin, ran a grocery across the street from the courthouse. The presence of African-American officeholders could not shake the Tuck brothers from their racial views. "We thought we had a lot more colored friends," Mayor Tuck grumbled. Edwin Tuck said, "The general thinking of the Negro people, the good, sturdy black citizens, is that Greene County has taken a step backward." Black power may have brought democracy to Greene, but it took longer to change some white attitudes. Still, the realities of political power in Greene County required whites to begin to respect and work with blacks. Otherwise, they would be consigned to the margins of society. "What the white people have got to realize," said newly elected Judge Branch, "is that black folks are their best friends." Here was something that Black Belt whites had been paternalistically insisting upon for decades; now it was a prospect they would honestly have to confront.[42]

The stark changes in Greene County went largely unnoticed by many in the South and across the nation. Marshall Frady's article on the 1966 election found its way into the pages of *Newsweek,* the *New York Times* ran one piece after blacks won victories in the 1970 elections, and a handful of other articles appeared in southern publications like the *Louisville Courier-Journal* and *New South.* Of course, the county received news coverage when Martin Luther King—and later Ralph Abernathy—visited. Even the *Birmingham News* ran only the occasional piece on the NDPA's success, Herndon's lawsuit, or "Alabama Bill" Lee and his family's stranglehold on the county sheriff's office. Joseph Cumming, chief of *Newsweek*'s southern bureau, more widely publicized the remarkable events in Greene County. Before the transition to black political power, Cumming had been to Greene County only once—immediately after the Voting Rights Act had been passed in 1965. Years later, Cumming remembered Greene as "rural, dark," and "out of the mainstream." The passage of the Voting Rights Act remade that world, he recalled. After the law passed, armed federal marshals stood watch over polling places—and a palpable feeling of change hung in the air. The Voting Rights Act marked "the beginning of political empowerment of Southern blacks." Then, and not before, "change began down deep." Cumming returned to Greene County eight years later, in 1973. He found that while blacks breathed with a new life, "a nameless sort of anxiety" gripped whites. It was the anxiety of a shocked people.[43]

Joseph Cumming stumbled into *Newsweek*'s southern bureau in 1957, months before President Eisenhower called the National Guard into Little Rock. William Emerson, a friend of Cumming's, had recently opened the magazine's Atlanta bureau. Cumming caught his break when Emerson needed some legwork on Eisenhower's golf trips to Augusta National. Thirty-one years old at the time and the father of four, Cumming considered himself a "moderate" on race. He soon occupied "a ringside seat at the most dramatic social revolution in the USA this century." Cumming came up in a family of New Deal Democrats, one that imbued him with a certain sensitivity toward racial issues. "There's absolutely nothing unusual about me," he reflected later. It was not that Cumming rebelled against the social customs of the South, but he did not defend them either. Cumming's moderation primed him for the great social cataclysm he would one day cover. "That was just the sensibility I was raised with, so that's why I was perfect for the civil rights movement, to be a reporter. I was sympathetic. I didn't think it was being biased to be sympathetic to black people who wanted their American rights." John Lewis once labeled as "sympathetic referees" the bevy of journalists who covered the civil rights movement. Joseph Cumming fit that description.[44]

After Cumming rose to become bureau chief, he hired Marshall Frady as a staff writer. Cumming knew Frady's article about the 1966 Greene County elections, and he followed from afar the events in Eutaw. In the early 1970s, Frady bought a small farm in Camden, South Carolina. A well-known journalist, Frady hosted a three-day house party that attracted writers and editors from up and down the eastern seaboard. Cumming met editors of *Playboy* who wished to run an article on "a county where the blacks are taking over." Cumming suggested a piece on Greene, and the *Playboy* editors agreed to read it. In 1973, Cumming spent a month in Eutaw. "I put in at a hotel and kind of spread myself . . . and let it be known I was in town to do an article on civil rights." That was the last thing many whites in Eutaw wanted to hear.[45]

Cumming developed a keen understanding of people caught up in the throes of social and political change. He came to probe the contours of the civil rights movement's impact—on white people as well as blacks. Months after Cumming left Greene County, he finished the article. It numbered some thirty-six typed pages, and unfolded the story of one county's experience with racial change. Cumming captured that transformation in the title he chose: "Softly, the Unthinkable." *Playboy* ultimately passed on the article; "it just wasn't juicy enough for them," Cumming later explained. In the spring of 1974, an organ of the Southern Regional Council published a version of the article. Parts of the original were edited, and *Southern Voices* renamed it "Greene County, Ala.: The Hope of the Future." Missing from the published version was Cumming's dramatic opening. "The 'nigras,' of course, were always there. They were part of the landscape of the county, like swamps and thunder: working in yards as gardeners, in homes as cooks, in the fields as laborers; riding in pickup trucks with sun-coarsened white men, on logging jobs or tending cattle." Greene County whites conceived of "their Negroes" as little more than objects in a landscape, but the civil rights movement—and in rural Alabama, the 1965 Voting Rights Act—transformed African-Americans into actors. Before that law was passed, such a transformation had seemed to whites unbelievable. "To have . . . suggested that one day blacks might vote themselves into dominant political power would have been to murder sleep . . . to stir the slumbering rape fantasy and the waking nightmare of social chaos and political anarchy. It was unthinkable." By 1970, the inconceivable had become stark reality.[46]

In Cumming's portrait of Greene County, noblesse oblige and the old plantation mentality characterized many more whites than did the brutality of the Ku Klux Klan. But that relative restraint took nothing away from the political achievements of Greene's African-Americans. "The black ascendancy was an outright political miracle. . . . Even now both blacks and whites seem too stunned from the historic event to quite know what to do with it." Cumming heard warnings from many Eutaw whites—warnings that the town was paranoid, that he would never know what whites were really thinking. "They tell you everybody's getting along fine but they're really suffering on the inside," an anonymous woman said. "You'll never know." Despite those doubts, Cumming glimpsed progress and undeniable transformation. In a county whose population and economy were in rapid decline, Cumming saw what he thought "few who live there can see: there is . . . possibility in the air. . . . In small, slow ways a few people are beginning to stir with life in the context of a new, enlarged reality." He argued that while black political power spurred white resentment, in an ironic way it also built hope. Whites were changing, at least on the surface. They treated blacks with a new calm and courtesy. Whites soon had no choice but to accept interracial coalition politics. "They will not have to change so much," Cumming reflected, "but they will have to grow considerably." This distinction between change and growth seemed vital. Whites might not have to mature much on questions of race, but they would have to adapt.[47]

After blacks gained power, the proverbial ball rolled into the whites' court. Whites could respond to the events with flexibility, innovation, and compromise, or they could cling to old ways and attitudes. "The first five years of this epoch of the miracle belonged to the blacks," wrote Cumming, a self-described "romantic." "From 1965 to 1970 they were in resonance with the civil rights movement as it swept across rural Alabama like a gust, like a ghost cloud filled with the sounds of battle, like an Old Testament epic." The pressing question of the 1970s was whether whites could embrace these new forms of political life. "The next years whites will have to make their own existential choice. For them it will not be a breaking out—they are too much part of their own history for that—but a matter of opening out, of dealing with the daily realities in wider terms of time and space." Cumming knew it was unrealistic to think white southerners might completely turn their backs on histories, customs, and ways of life. A revolution would never occur inside most Greene County whites. Without many other options, however, they would have to adjust. As Cumming sharply distinguished between change and growth, he also emphasized the difference between adaptation and survival. "Whites will not 'survive' if survival is the limit of their striving." Mere survival would not be enough; whites would have to take some action.[48]

One family embodied the ways Greene County's white citizens grappled with the past and future. The Banks family had wielded power for as long as most locals could remember, dating back to the establishment of Banks and Co., in 1889. When Ralph Banks, Sr., died in 1959, he left his wife and three sons—Jamie, Phil, and Ralph, Jr.—with wealth and influence. Jamie, the youngest, became head of Banks and Co., and chairman of the board at Eutaw's only bank, Merchants and Farmers. Once the civil rights movement penetrated Greene County, it sent the three brothers in different directions. In 1970, Jamie was forty years old and owned more land than any other person in the county. Phil also worked at Banks and Co.; together they strode out the front door of the business at nine o'clock each morning and into Jimmy's Restaurant. Bradly Brown, owner of the popular Cotton Patch Restaurant, dairy farmer Peter McLean, and a handful of other friends joined them there every weekday. "The main function of this nine o'clock coffee session seemed to be for the men to re-assure each other that things *are* going to the dogs," Cumming wrote. "Out of the specific topics such as land prices, beef market, government programs, sorry labor come generalizations on the decline of values, the breakdown of discipline and . . . work ethic and, in general, despair over forces seeking to disrupt the cherished way." Race, and the recent black "takeover," factored heavily into their complaints. " 'Nigras' or, sometimes 'niggers' come out to be a major cause and symbol of their woes." Whites like Jamie Banks had new worries, and their fears drifted toward one target—African-Americans, now emboldened with their rights and politically ascendant.[49]

The story of Ralph Jr. was more complex. Born in 1925, Ralph was the eldest brother. In physical description, Cumming likened him to Andrew Jackson—"Ralph has the same long jaw, high forehead, ruddy cheeks and intensity of expression with its flickering hints of storm." Banks was a man "high strung . . . hurrying, scurrying, and restless," who chain-smoked and was given as quickly to wit as he was to rage. During the late 1960s, Ralph Banks helped shape white political resistance in Greene County. While Thomas Gilmore and William Branch ran for office, Banks drew up plans to stop them. Banks realized—before many others did—that whites would have to adjust to retain political power. An attorney with a sharp political mind, Banks quickly grasped that blacks were in the majority and that they would never pull a lever for George Wallace's party. Banks helped to create the Spotted Horse Party. He tried to woo voters, black and white, in order to defeat black candidates. "Through those years of conflict," Cumming wrote, Banks "developed a genuine sense of hostility" toward blacks. "It was his high dedication to prevent William Branch and Tom Gilmore from winning power over whites." In November 1970, Banks lost when Branch and Gilmore won. But in an act that revealed an astute political sense, Branch immediately asked Banks to serve as county attorney and deputy county solicitor. "Are you out of your mind?" Banks wondered. "I have fought you tooth and nail for five years." Branch knew what county whites thought of the black "takeover." In Banks, the county government would gain an experienced attorney and more backing among local whites. Banks agreed. "It was not particularly heroic of Ralph to accept these county jobs," Cumming noted. With them came a decent salary, handsome retirement benefits, and a modicum of power. But Banks's acceptance of the positions kept alive the possibility of interracial politics in Greene County.[50]

Ralph Banks served in a government controlled by blacks, but it was not clear how that changed his racial views. After four years in the county government, "blacks in general" still "do not trust Ralph Banks," Cumming wrote in 1974. "He does not go out of his way to inspire their confidence. Neither his . . . inflection in pronouncing 'Negro' nor his sparing use of courtesy titles reflect any change in attitude toward blacks from days before the civil rights movement." Banks might have black colleagues and superiors, but he still said "nigra." Yet his dealings with blacks in the county government became too intimate and serious for them not to leave a mark. After years of working together in the courthouse, Banks and Gilmore developed a close relationship. It "approaches a man-to-man friendship, transcending the traditional structured racial friendships in the South." When Gilmore began his 1974 reelection bid, Banks volunteered to manage his campaign. As a former architect of white resistance came to spearhead a black man's campaign for sheriff, the transition seemed complete. Among the transformations the Voting Rights Act set into motion, few seemed more stunning than that one. Yet Joseph Cumming argued, "Ralph has not really had to 'change' to come to this relationship." Banks still considered himself a conservative, and the county's new politics failed to touch parts of his social life. But the fact of change was too plain to deny. Into the 1970s and even in the most rural reaches of Alabama, the civil rights movement swept up whites like Ralph Banks and started them on political trajectories they had barely contemplated.[51]

The political tempest engulfed others of Ralph Banks's ilk. While his brothers gathered at Jimmy's Restaurant each morning, Ralph shared coffee in his office with Breck Rogers. Rogers, "a certified aristocrat from one of the top county families," served as county tax assessor in the black-controlled government. Rogers, like Banks, came to his "uneasy position accidentally." Through the late 1960s, Rogers remained a Democrat. But he saw the political winds shifting. His office did not come up on the 1970 ballot, so Rogers kept his position amid the black "takeover." In 1972, the NDPA asked Rogers to run for reelection on its ticket. Rogers found himself in a morass, since he knew the NDPA would run a candidate against him if he did not accept. Rogers knew also that he risked alienating whites if he ran on the NDPA ticket. In the end, Rogers did run on the NDPA ticket—and he won. The friendship between Breck Rogers and Ralph Banks was borne aloft on the wings of a black political revolution. "That Breck and Ralph have daily coffee together, usually alone . . . has a symbolic significance neither of them would like to admit," Cumming wrote. "As fellow conservative white Southerners, they would not like the idea that they are carriers of the hope of some kind of coalition politics." As two of the Banks boys drank coffee at Jimmy's Restaurant and complained about the direction of the county under black political leadership, their older brother worked with that very political leadership, and no longer sipped his morning coffee in public.[52]

Eugene Johnston was the brains behind Warrior Academy, Greene County's all-white private school. As the years passed, however, Johnston fell into the clutches of—and ultimately embraced—the county's racial changes. A Selma native, Johnston was the product of an upper-middle-class upbringing. Born in 1932, he followed the traditional lines of paternalism and hierarchy in his relationship with blacks. After a stint in the navy and some years of engineering training, Johnston returned to the Alabama Black Belt. He became manager of a Greene County soybean and fertilizer plant, which joined a farm cooperative known as Centrala. The civil rights struggles of the 1960s brought "labor troubles" to Centrala. Black farmers demanded membership. This ferment forced Johnston to realize that if black farmers could gain co-op membership, black children could attend integrated schools, black citizens could vote, black workers could become foremen, and black candidates could gain political office. Within a matter of years, many of those possibilities spelled reality in Greene. In those same years, Johnston lost his job at Centrala. He took solace in the Episcopal Church, and sought employment from the black county government. Two conversions, religious and racial, touched his life.[53]

Still out of work into the 1970s, Johnston jumped when the position of golf course manager opened. The Greene County Golf Course had become one prominent symbol of the changes afoot. In 1968, the white-controlled county government began building a nine-hole course outside Eutaw. The black government finished the project, and locals—including Ralph Banks and Bill Lee—regularly flocked to the links. Now Eugene Johnston applied for a job there. During Johnston's unemployed years he had begun "to re-think his traditional attitude on race." The act of applying for a county job cemented that reevaluation. "All at once the roles were reversed," Johnston recalled of his job interview with Judge Branch. "All my life I had looked down on the black man. Now I had to consider him at least an equal. You can't look down on somebody you're asking for a job." Johnston got the job, and with it a black boss. As manager of the golf course, Johnston was determined to open dialogue between blacks and whites. White residents accounted for about 90 percent of the golfers, but the black government operated it. Johnston established many programs, among them an interracial greens committee. Just the fact that blacks and whites sat down at meetings and attempted to work together counted for progress in Greene County, and Johnston was responsible for some of it. The black electoral victory spelled the unthinkable in more ways than one. And Eugene Johnston, better than most Greene whites, appreciated the point of Joseph Cumming's writing. In fact, he penned Cumming a letter in June of 1973. "Eutaw should pay you $20,000 for the story," Johnston suggested. "If people here could take it to heart, we couldn't pay enough. And I'm sure . . . that some eyes will be opened. . . . I was having such a good time that the impact came on 'Softly—the Unthinkable.' "[54]

From a regional perspective, the achievement of black power in Greene County was an exceptional example. Out of 1,139 counties in the eleven southern states, 89 of them had majority-black voting-age populations in 1968. And only 35 of those accumulated an electorate that was mostly black. Out of those, just a handful—Greene County and Macon County in Alabama, Hancock County in Georgia, several areas in Mississippi, and a few other scattered locales—could boast of "black power" in the county government. By 1980, 21 of 80 counties with black majorities had yet to elect a single African-American official. But the numbers did little to alleviate white fears. Two years after the death of Martin Luther King, residents of Greene County experienced the transformation from unquestioned white rule to previously unthinkable black power. If their story is taken seriously, the civil rights movement stretched far beyond the dramatic events in Selma in 1965 or Memphis in 1968. In some black-majority towns, the civil rights movement did not really begin until African-Americans assumed political power. From the Civil Rights Act of 1964 to the advent of black political power in the late 1960s and early 1970s, white southern voters navigated a changing political terrain. Elections from 1964 to 1976 encompassed at least two different types of political transformations, and many different degrees of change in between. A few counties underwent the transformation from white power to black control. But those changes were the exceptions. The rule was inscribed in a different transformation—one in which white voters revolted from the Democratic Party.[55]

3

IN 1964, black southerners wielded little electoral might as white politicians trumpeted their opposition to the Civil Rights Act. Because Lyndon Johnson backed the bill, many white southerners worried whether the national Democratic Party was committed enough to segregation. When Sam Ervin responded to constituent mail regarding the

Civil Rights Act, he asserted that Republican congressional leaders were responsible for the "Second Reconstruction." Ervin could already sense that the Democratic Party would have to fight for its life in the South. In a June 23 letter to one constituent, Ervin noted, "We have faced dark days before. During Reconstruction, somewhat similar bills were passed." He also took pains to blame the bill's passage on Republican congressional leaders. Four southern states voted Republican in the 1952 presidential election, five did so in 1956, and three in 1960. Even before Barry Goldwater campaigned through Dixie, Katherine Foster of Yanceyville, North Carolina, had begun to question the Democratic Party. "When I read the headlines that the Civil Rights Bill had been passed I felt like I had been betrayed." By championing the bill, Lyndon Johnson "committed political suicide." Foster knew many Democrats, and "as one voice they say and mean it that they will never vote for a Johnson ticket, that they would rather vote republican first and they will. We who have been democrats all our life hate to change over but we feel we can not go along with a man who has sold us out. When November comes the people's voice will be heard."[56]

From squeaks in North Carolina to roars in the Deep South, white voters made known their disaffection with the national Democratic Party and its civil rights legislation. Lyndon Johnson won the general election by a landslide, and he won a majority South-wide. But Johnson believed that in due time his passage of the Civil Rights Act would cost the Democratic Party. After signing the bill, Johnson confided to White House aide Bill Moyers, "We just delivered the South to the Republican Party for years to come." It was already clear that Johnson did not speak for the Deep South. During the 1964 campaign, a Charleston, South Carolina, mob had chanted, "Johnson is a Communist. Johnson is a nigger lover." Just four years earlier, 58 percent of Black Belt residents had voted for John F. Kennedy. By 1964, 60 percent of them voted Republican. "I have been a Democrat all my life until now," wrote seventy-two-year-old Mrs. J. B. Segrest of East Tallassee, Alabama. "They have ruined the nation. . . . We cannot say who or what kind of people we have to associate with and live with. We cannot rule our homes. LBJ, the federal court, and the Communists have taken over." In opposing civil rights legislation, the Republican Arizona senator better represented whites in the Deep South than did the Democratic president—native Texan though he was. "Mr. Goldwater's views reflect ours," wrote Birmingham's Mary Compton. "We will continue to oppose unconstitutional thinking." Another Birmingham resident, Fred Blanton, complained, "For voting for Mr. Goldwater I was called a racist and worse." Goldwater's southern appeal rested primarily on his resistance to civil rights. *The Nation* dubbed Goldwater's GOP "counter-revolutionary." This was the GOP that former Dixiecrat Strom Thurmond joined that year. The Republicans "made it plain they didn't want the vote of Negroes," said a Georgia politician, "and they didn't get it. All they got even if it was enough to win this time, was the bitter backlash to the civil rights act." Although rural areas remained the region's least developed, Black Belt whites' early support for Republican presidential candidates suggested the South's future rather than its past.[57]

In the four years between 1964 and 1968, events in the nation and the region altered both political landscapes. If white southerners had long considered issues of race when they went to the ballot box, the upheaval of the 1960s made race a defining issue in national politics. Martin Luther King's call for nonviolence gradually gave way to more militant strategies, embodied by the proponents of Black Power and members of the Black Panther Party. After the civil rights movement won legal equality, it moved toward more divisive issues—problems of economics, residential segregation, and power. Riots stretched from the Watts neighborhood of Los Angeles in 1965 and Cleveland in 1966 to Detroit, Newark, and hundreds more cities in 1967. King's 1968 assassination punctuated the breakout of racial tension, as riots flared even in Washington, D.C. Amid this chaos, mounting racial fear led Mississippi senator James Eastland to declare, in 1966, "The sentiment of the entire country . . . now stands with the Southern people." The new political power of blacks, and the recent turns to radicalism and violence, brought about widespread white resentment.[58]

White southerners trembled and seethed at images of black rebellion. Ray Compton, a forty-seven-year-old Texas farmer, spoke for many others when he decried the smoldering urban disorders. Compton, a World War II veteran, said, "I could get 40 or 50 of my old South Pacific buddies with grease guns and stop all these damn riots." The Democratic Party not only passed epic civil rights legislation and waged a "war on poverty," but its policies appeared even worse in light of the recent riots. While liberals provided federal funds to the impoverished, poor urban dwellers seemed to be tearing down America's cities. But white southerners did not uniformly deplore black actions. Charlotte resident Joe Denmark admitted that King's 1968 death awakened within him many sympathies. A native of eastern North Carolina, Denmark noted that not all white southerners begrudged African-Americans their rights and threatened to put down riots with "grease guns." "There are many 'whites' like me, who have borne the Negro no ill will, and have followed with interest + good will his efforts to attain *honest* equality." Denmark urged Congressman Charles Raper Jonas to pass a 1968 open housing bill that would ban racial discrimination in housing sales, and demonstrated that not all white southerners were numb to the tragedy of King's death. Still, many others reacted like Martha Adcock, of Durham. "When President Johnson asked the flag to be lowered for [King]," she wrote in April 1968, "this was the greatest disgrace and dishonor that has ever been given the flag of our country." Most white southerners sided with Ray Compton and Martha Adcock. While they did not all want to personally quash riots, many sought leaders who would divert funds away from the lawless ghettoes, clamp down on black rebellion, and restore "law and order."[59]

Richard Nixon and George Wallace, in their different ways, both took advantage of that sentiment. As the 1968 presidential election approached, Ralph McGill wrote, "Race and the spin-off issue of 'law and order' and the dangerous and exaggerated rhetoric of its presentation became the big emotional 'thing.'" Following Goldwater's success in Dixie, Nixon deployed a "Southern Strategy" in his effort to outpoll the Democratic nominee, Vice President Hubert Humphrey. Nixon tailored his campaign to white concerns.* As one North Carolina woman con-

---

*Nixon took some of his cues on the "Southern Strategy" from Kevin Phillips. Phillips argues that the 1968 election results signaled the death knell of the "Democratic Party for its ambitious social programming and inability to handle the urban and Negro revolutions." Nixon claimed that he did not simply pick up where Goldwater left off. "The idea that Goldwater started the Southern Strategy is bullshit," Nixon insisted. Goldwater "ran as a racist candidate . . . and he won the wrong [southern] states." Nixon believed the key to the South lay in conservatives who constituted the emergent suburban middle class, people more receptive to subtleties like "law and order" than outright resistance to civil rights. Historian Matthew Lassiter agrees, and he marshals impressive evidence to make this case. Lassiter argues that the Republicans' success in the South hinged on the expanding middle-class corporate economy in places like Atlanta, Charlotte, and their booming suburbs, rather than on racial backlash rooted in the Black Belt. He cited the fact that the GOP won the votes of 44 percent of those whites who said they favored desegregation. And yet it was one thing to support the principle of integration, and another to back the amalgam of practices that it required. Kevin Phillips, *The Emerging Republican Majority* (New Rochelle, NY, 1969), p. 25; Matthew Lassiter, *The Silent Majority: Suburban Politics in the Sunbelt South* (Princeton, NJ, 2005), pp. 227, 239, 275, 303. Also see Dan Carter, *The Politics of Rage: George Wallace, the Origins of the New Conservatism, and the Transformation of American Politics* (Baton Rouge, 1995), pp. 326–27.

fessed, "We are really afraid with the colored right in our backyard." With promises of "law and order," Nixon would fight Wallace for the vote of every last white southerner like her. Nixon attempted to fashion the GOP as a sort of midpoint between Wallace's shameless racial rhetoric and the Democrats' racial liberalism. Attempting to capture middle-class white voters, especially in the fast-growing suburbs, he dressed up Wallace's barbed language in a more respectable vernacular. Americans still knew what he was talking about. Asked to define "law and order," one white responded: "Get the niggers. Nothing else." Nixon's strategy promised enormous dividends. There were plenty of white southern votes to be had.[60]

On November 5, Nixon eked out a victory over Humphrey. Nixon won 34.7 percent of southern votes, and Wallace picked up 34.4 percent. Humphrey garnered 31 percent of the South's popular vote, almost all of it from African-Americans. About 12 percent of white southerners, situated mainly in mountain counties, voted for Humphrey. The vice president won only in Texas. Nixon and Wallace divided the other ten states of the Old Confederacy. Nixon picked up Virginia, North Carolina, South Carolina, Tennessee, and Florida; Wallace took the rest. Mrs. M. D. Jones of Mableton, Georgia, explained, "Many who voted for Nixon would have voted for Wallace if they had not been told so often that a vote for Wallace would be a vote for Humphrey." She was likely referring to Nixon ads that advised southerners not to "divide" their vote. Polls found that 80 percent of southern Wallace voters preferred Nixon to Humphrey. As Jones continued, "We want . . . the right to sell our homes to who we please . . . and put control of schools back to the states where it belongs." Atlanta mayor Ivan Allen lamented that many white southerners cast their ballots around the issue of race. "The deep South . . . has not fully recovered from the racial problem." Many southern politicians began to follow Strom Thurmond's lead. Georgia comptroller general James Bentley was one who switched his allegiance from Democratic to Republican before the 1968 campaign. Bentley surmised, "I doubt the Wallace voters will go back to the Democratic Party." He was largely correct.[61]

A perspective that pictured white southern voters simply as racists could not fully account for their swing into the Republican fold. Among them were scores of middle-class parents who felt that the party of Lincoln—better than the party of liberalism—articulated their fears and their hopes. The Republican Party drew in some white southerners who, earlier in the decade, had stood horrified at the sight of segregationist mobs. Now they deplored riots, feared a civil rights struggle shorn of its nonviolent heart, and chafed under court-ordered school integration, busing, and the tax burden imposed by an active federal government. In a letter dated May 5, 1969, Charlotte resident Peggy Ruth made those feelings known to Nixon. "This letter will never reach your hand . . . but if there is a giant tally sheet somewhere that says 'this one for, this one against,' I want my letter to be on the tally sheet *for* reason, not necessarily *against* integration." Ruth considered herself a supporter of desegregation in principle, but the tactics of the time drew her ire. "Integration, and the methods currently being used to force it, is the reason for this letter." A self-described "southerner who disapproved when white parents stood in doorways of public schools to bar black students from entry," Ruth "would welcome blacks into the neighborhood, and thus into our neighborhood school." She stressed that she worked hard, paid her taxes, and did so "to afford a home near the school of my choice so that my elementary-age children can walk to classes." Above all else, Ruth resented "the possibility that my children, who live three blocks from the school we chose to move near, may be bused to another section of town to attend a school not of my choice." Ruth voted for Nixon because she pictured him "as a defender of law and reason." She deplored busing, a prospect that whites in Charlotte directly confronted. With the Supreme Court's decision in *Swann v. Charlotte-Mecklenburg,* Charlotte became the first southern metropolis to experience busing. "I believe integration is right, that it isn't going to happen voluntarily, that there must be some kind of force." She understood that the government had to do something, but why must it bus white children away from their neighborhoods? Ruth advised Nixon that Americans had glimpsed only the beginning of a massive political wave. "This country is headed for a middle-class rebellion the like of which has never before in history been seen." This rebellion sank its roots in the South, and carried Republicans to victory in four of the next five presidential elections.[62]

Democrats could remain competitive in local races, but only if they replaced the homilies of national liberalism with an approach better attuned to the needs and concerns of a white South in the depths of social change. With various mixes of Democratic progressivism and southern conservatism, Jimmy Carter, John West, Edwin Edwards, Dale Bumpers, and Reubin Askew won the statehouses in Georgia, South Carolina, Louisiana, Arkansas, and Florida. "The sometimes agonizing trail of history has just about overtaken the Democratic party in the Deep South," *Delta Democrat-Times* columnist Paul Pittman argued in 1969. He cited "a growing disaffection with the party on the part of the average white voter in the South." Two years later, moderate Democrat William Waller won the state house in Mississippi. As the 1970s began, still nothing seemed fated about southern politics. In 1952, three-quarters of southern whites identified themselves as Democrats. By 1964, that number had dwindled to two-thirds; by 1968, just half of southern voters still defined themselves as Democrats. Yet only 20 percent called themselves Republicans. That left a substantial number of votes up for grabs. As the 1972 election approached, the *Atlanta Constitution*'s editors warned readers against "blind allegiance to either the Republicans or Democrats." Republicans possessed considerable momentum, but many whites in the region were ready to support whoever spoke to their issues.[63]

As the 1972 presidential campaign opened, George Wallace looked to be that man. In 1968, when Wallace won the votes of 10 million Americans, his third-party candidacy possessed a fledgling nature. Wallace mounted a full-scale national campaign in 1972, and ran for the Democratic nomination. As busing became a major issue, Wallace went on the attack. Southern voters were instantly receptive to his descriptions of busing as "social scheming" that threatened the "health and safety of your child, regardless of color." His message also began to gain some popularity in the North. *Alexander v. Holmes* brought school integration to the deepest reaches of the rural South in 1969, and the Supreme Court legalized busing two years later. Those whites who had staved off racial change through the 1960s, it seemed, could not evade it in the 1970s. Wallace's pitch resonated with them. In Florida's March Democratic primary, Wallace drubbed Humphrey, 42 percent to 19 percent—mainly on the strength of the busing issue. Two months later, he won two-thirds of the vote in Tennessee, and 51 percent in North Carolina. Nixon had won these three states in 1968, and he took notice. In May, Arthur Bremer's bullets brought Wallace's campaign to an abrupt halt. Still, Wallace's initial success suggested the direction of the southern electorate.[64]

Richard Nixon did not miss the cues. On the campaign trail in 1972, he made sure that white southerners understood his message was still "law and order." While the Vietnam War consumed much of the campaign, Nixon and Democrat George McGovern also contrasted sharply on domestic issues. On busing, Nixon tried to strike a balance between "forced integration" and "segregation forever." He did not question the

Supreme Court's ruling, but tried to remain the champion of "neighbor-hood schools." Well before the election, Nixon's victory seemed certain. On November 3, Birmingham resident Frank Sieverman reflected upon Nixon's southern appeal. "The underlying reason for Mr. Nixon's strength is our racial fear, of which busing is but one obvious aspect." Despite the surge in black voter registration, white voters in the South still outnum-bered African-Americans four to one. And Nixon carried the South by a margin almost that large. He not only swept the South in the 1972 presi-dential election, but did so with 71 percent of the vote. Massachusetts was the only state McGovern won. Moreover, Nixon won 86 percent of the ballots of southern white Protestants. According to the *Birmingham News,* "The Republican Party is willing to provide an honored place for Wal-lace's followers among its 'new majority.' " In 1968, Nixon and Wallace had polled a combined 69 percent of southern votes. In 1972, Nixon's 71 percent suggested that he had won the votes of 1968 Wallace supporters. About 35 percent of white southerners pulled the Republican lever for the first time in their lives. *Atlanta Constitution* editor Reg Murphy recounted the story of one rural Georgian who had never before voted for the "silk-stocking party." The lifelong Democrat recalled, "I went on up to the courthouse . . . and stomped on in. . . . I messed around as long as I could. Then there wasn't a thing in the world to do but vote." The result clearly tickled him. "I voted for a damn Republican," he guffawed. "I just couldn't vote like all the hippies," the man explained. "I'm not saying I'll ever vote Republican again . . . I'm just not saying." As Murphy wrote, "His dilemma has occurred in hundreds of Southern households in recent weeks." In the South, McGovern shrouded the Democratic lever in disgrace, while Nixon played racial fears, division over the war, and resentment of liberalism to Republican advantage.[65]

State and congressional battles revealed different political metamor-phoses. In Georgia, African-American Andrew Young ran for a congres-sional seat on the Democratic ticket. A respected former member of King's inner circle, Young picked up the *Atlanta Constitution*'s endorse-ment on November 1. The *Constitution* noted, approvingly, that Young was "on record" in opposition to "massive busing in Atlanta." Young gained the support of white moderates, while his campaign sent bro-chures to blacks that proclaimed the 1972 election the "opportunity of a century." (Georgia's only previous black representative, Jefferson Long, won election in 1870.) Young's opponent, Republican Rodney Cook, mostly avoided race during the campaign. But finally and desperately, Cook ran an ad that showed a photo of him next to a haggard-looking Young. It asked, "What's the Difference?," and tried to highlight Young's blackness. Young defeated Cook, 53 percent to 47 percent. In a district that was 62 percent white, Young picked up the votes of about one-fifth of the district's whites. "I don't know if a black man could be elected in a 62 per cent white district in any of our Northern cities right now," Young said, and called it "a tribute to Atlanta to be able to rise above its racial heritage." Young became one of more than one thousand black elected officials in the South.[66]

While Young rolled to victory in Georgia, so did Richard Nixon. After Richard Russell passed away, Sam Nunn won his vacated Senate seat. Nunn ran as an anti-busing and "law and order" candidate on the Democratic ticket. In North Carolina and Mississippi, Republicans Jesse Helms and Trent Lott won seats in the Senate and the House, respectively. The lessons of the 1972 elections were decidedly mixed. It was unclear whose victory would be the more enduring symbol—Nixon's landslide presidential win, Andrew Young's historic achievement, the triumph of a young centrist Democrat (Sam Nunn) in Georgia, or the Republican wave that Lott and Helms rode. In no southern state were the lessons more muddled than Florida. Republican legislators forced a referendum onto the ballot that asked voters whether they supported a constitutional amendment against "forced busing," and to "guarantee the right of each student to attend the appropriate public school near his home." Reubin Askew, the liberal Democratic governor, countered with another referendum: "Do you favor providing an equal opportunity for quality education for all children regardless of race, creed, color or place of residence and oppose a return to a dual system of public schools?" Seventy-four percent of Floridians favored the amendment against "forced busing," while 79 percent of them favored the referendum on equal education. White Floridians were ready to support school integration in theory, but the reality was far messier.[67]

A series of evolutions and revolutions characterized southern politics in the age of civil rights. Which change one emphasized, and how forcefully, often depended upon perspective. When *New York Times* correspondent Roy Reed gave an interview in 1974, he stressed neither the southern drift toward the Republican Party nor the advent of black political power. Instead, Reed saw the most striking changes in the defeats of once powerful segregationists. When Dale Bumpers beat Orval Faubus in the 1970 Democratic gubernatorial runoff, "Arkansas had come more than just ten years forward, but a full generation." Glancing around the new political land in 1974, "there are no . . . Faubuses . . . left," Reed reflected. "Not even George Wallace is an Orval Faubus any more, giving him his full due. The politics of race has changed and therefore these people have changed." To Reed, the essential point was that "white politicians don't ignore black votes any longer." Many politicians themselves affirmed this suggestion. In the 1970s, "the white politician tends to become much more sensitive to the black community," attested Louisiana's Edgar Mouton. "That was my experience." That was also the experience of Greene County whites. For many in heavily black areas, the signal political transformation of the era involved the move from white dominance to biracial rule. But if one considers national politics as the frame of reference, and looks at the South with forty years of hindsight, the drift to the Republicans assumes a paramount vitality. In one of the civil rights movement's more enduring legacies, it pushed white southerners and the Republican Party toward a lasting, and powerful, alliance. Of the six men elected president since Lyndon Johnson, four were Republicans; the other two were southern Democrats. White southerners increasingly held the key to the presidency.[68]

The party turnaround could not be denied. In 1975, the Voting Rights Act came up for renewal. Two-thirds of southern Democrats in the House voted to extend the act; two-thirds of southern Republicans voted against the extension. As the Republican Party began to morph into a sanctuary for southern whites, it was often hard to gauge how much political change had pulsed through the South. By 1976, fully 1,847 African-Americans held elected offices in the South. That was a staggering number, but it amounted to less than 5 percent of the region's total number of officeholders. It came nowhere close to representing southern blacks as a whole, who made up more than 20 percent of the South's population. John Lewis called those African-Americans elected to office "products of a revolution" and noted, "these officials now have an unparalleled opportunity to usher in another era of revolutionary change." In 1976, Jimmy Carter gained the presidency on a platform that partly pledged support for civil rights. Black southern voters were instrumental in his victory. As Lewis put it, "The hands that picked cotton had now picked a president." Some saw Carter's election as the culmination of the civil rights era, but they had only four years to wait for the backlash of the "Reagan Democrats." Still, black political power brought some of what it promised. For example, biracial government changed the face of towns like Selma, as the *New York Times* reported in 1978. "The dark, dirt streets trod by the marchers are now paved and lighted." While the civil rights movement changed many facets of life, whites continually devised plans to blunt its effects.[69]

Even where African-Americans voted in sizable numbers, white southerners employed various devices to curb blacks' electoral power. Memphis was one city that ingeniously manipulated voting statutes to preserve white political control. African-Americans in Memphis voted through the 1940s and 1950s. Indeed, they were important cogs in Mayor Ed Crump's machine. By 1959, blacks accounted for 30 percent of Memphis's registered voters. After Crump's rule ended and his machine ceased to dominate political offices, blacks sought election to many local positions. Memphis whites responded with three basic ploys to weaken black voting strength: the primary runoff, the majority-vote requirement, and the at-large designations of some city council positions. The runoff and majority-vote requirement ensured that even if black candidates fared well, they would in the end have to run one-on-one against whites. As two-thirds of Memphis voters were white, they could defeat any black candidate. The designation of some city councilors as at-large ensured that even if blacks were voted in from majority-black districts, whites could always elect the at-large candidates—and keep a disproportionate amount of power over local government. Whites in other cities and states replicated these types of measures, and even where African-Americans began to constitute 30 and 40 percent of the registered voters, their political power remained less than their number. In 1963, the Georgia legislature adopted the majority-vote law to curb black power. Lester Maddox owed his 1966 gubernatorial victory to that system. In North Carolina, a black state legislator named Mickey Michaux co-sponsored a bill to eliminate runoffs in 1973. The bill failed, and nine years later Michaux became a victim of that very device. In 1982, Michaux ran for Congress. With 44 percent of the vote, he won the first Democratic primary election; Tim Valentine placed second, with 33 percent. In the runoff, Valentine bested Michaux, 54 percent to 46 percent. Yet Michaux's defeat was due to more than just the runoff system. In 1981, North Carolina redrew its congressional districts. Even in Michaux's Second Congressional District, where the percentage of African-Americans was highest, a black candidate could not command a majority. For years after the Voting Rights Act became law, white southerners wielded redistricting, along with many other tools, to ward off the threat of black political power.[70]

White southerners did not yield political power easily, and they were even less interested in black demands for economic equality. Greene County blacks ran the county government by 1970, but they could not effect all the change they wished. Shortly after the black "takeover," Warrior Academy—the all-white private school—began to thrive. In the mid-1970s, a majority of the county's white students attended Warrior. Most Greene County whites still sent their children there in 1983. The same man, William Tuck, remained Eutaw's mayor until 1980. Into that decade, black unemployment in the county hovered around 22 percent; barely 2 percent of whites were without jobs. The Voting Rights Act may have transformed the county's politics, but it did little to change the stark economic realities in Greene. While Greene County whites had to adjust to the new political day, they continued to control other levers of power. In 1973, Joseph Cumming reported in *Newsweek* that "change thus far has been largely cosmetic; whites still control the bulk of land and wealth." Even where the most unthinkable sorts of changes occurred, parts of white society remained untouched. Many blacks may have believed that political power promised economic equality, but whites made sure that no redistribution of wealth ensued.[71]

4

ANY ATTEMPT TO ASSESS the impact of the civil rights movement must encompass other forces that gripped the South. Not all the changes southerners experienced were attributable to the civil rights movement—nor were its limitations responsible for what stayed the same. The civil rights movement was the primary motor of change in Dixie, but not the only one. Automation swept over farms, and the agrarian South rapidly industrialized. Towns strained to lure industries southward. Mechanization softened the nature of fieldwork, while sharecropping and tenant farming died silent deaths. As much as the civil rights protester or the black officeholder thrust white southerners toward a new world, so did the combine, the skyscraper, and the air conditioner. In the three decades after World War II, economic and demographic revolutions altered the face of the South. A mainly rural area became increasingly urban and suburban. The economy's center shifted from plantations and cotton fields to factories and office buildings. Yet wealth rarely changed hands. Those who held economic power before cities sprouted and blacks gained their rights still possessed it afterward. Landowners still lorded over vast acreage, while white workers filled a disproportionate share of the region's job openings. Businesses often moved southward to capitalize on cheap labor, but workers did not always cooperate. Race cleaved southerners, and so did class. Poor whites experienced the civil rights years in ways different than the newly emergent suburban middle class or their wealthier employers. For all of them, structural changes brought new rhythms to everyday life. From expanding business centers to contracting farms and abandoned sharecropper shacks, economic transformation revealed the contours of a new society—as the old vestiges resided nearby.

Before World War II, the South was a rural place. More than 40 percent of its people resided on farms, and two-thirds of southerners lived in hamlets of less than 2,500. Out of a total population of 35 million, only one in five lived in a metropolitan area. The region was by far the country's most impoverished, and few Deep South residents enjoyed the amenities of the twentieth century. Less than one-third of Georgians, for instance, possessed indoor plumbing or owned their homes. After the war, industry pulled people off the farms and into the factories, from rural areas into cities. "The mechanical cotton picker and the flame-thrower are forcing an agricultural revolution on the South," the Southern Regional Council's Guy Johnson declared. By 1950, the vast majority of southern workers were not involved in agriculture. The number of agricultural workers exceeded nonagricultural workers only in Mississippi; Arkansas was the only other state where farmworkers comprised more than 45 percent of the workforce. During the 1950s, thousands of nonagricultural jobs opened across the region.[72]

Even before the first sit-ins occurred in 1960, the South was a changed land. That year, only 15 percent of southerners lived on farms. Almost half of the population congregated in metropolitan districts, and by the mid-1960s, a clear majority of southerners lived in or around cities. In 1964 alone, automation ended forty thousand unskilled and semiskilled jobs per week as black unemployment grew to twice that for whites. "What about the . . . Bulldozer Revolution?" C. Vann Woodward asked. "It has come on the South with a swiftness that is without precedent and with an irresistible momentum." A majority of Georgians owned their homes, six in ten had indoor plumbing, and 80 percent had televisions. "Not since that autumn of 1792 when young Eli Whitney came to Georgia," Ralph McGill wrote in 1968, "have so many forces sifted and sorted out the South." Within that nascent environment, white southerners molded new lives for themselves.[73]

Attention focused on the flight from the farm. Yet life was transformed not only for those who fled farms, but for those who stayed on them. Racial and economic realities on the farm changed as they did throughout the South, but not always in similar ways. Large tenant plantations ballooned into fully automated "neo-plantations"—where power became increasingly concentrated in a smaller number of white owners. In 1940, tenants and owners operated roughly the same number of farms. Over the next three decades, control of farms shifted steadily into the hands of owners. By 1969, as tenant farming fell by the wayside and as workers streamed from the countryside to the cities, 88 percent of farms were owner-operated. In three decades, the total number of southern farms dropped from three million to barely more than one million. Slowly, white southerners came to operate a higher percentage of farms than blacks. Although the civil rights movement helped some blacks ascend into the urban middle class, it aided few of those in the field. Of the one million farms that were owner-operated in 1969, 93 percent of those owners were white. African-Americans still tilled white-owned land, even if they no longer did so as tenants. Rural landowners burned and destroyed sharecropper shacks by the thousands. After World War II, Guy Johnson predicted, "The social . . . effects of mechanization will soon begin to make themselves felt." But if demographic and economic shifts brought any changes in the social order on large farms and plantations, they were not immediately clear. "We used to own our slaves," a landowner in Belle Glade, Florida, said in 1960. "Now we just rent them." Beyond and beneath the statistics of change, rural whites combined old attitudes with new conditions.[74]

In the same Alabama Black Belt counties that hosted stunning political shifts, economic realities reflected more of the old than the new. Although African-Americans gained control of the government in Greene County, land remained largely in white hands. Through the 1960s, whites (who comprised about 20 percent of the population) owned 76 percent of the county's nearly 300,000 acres of farmland. Their economic power remained unchallenged through the "black take-over." Greene County whites' median family income continued to be almost five times that of blacks. In Lowndes County, the economic chasm stretched even wider.

Lowndes "is dirt-poor as it always was," journalist Andrew Kopkind wrote in 1975. "Its population of black farmers and their families who live on the margins of the cotton fields and the grazing pastures is still economically subservient to the small white minority in the sprawling farmhouses and . . . columned stately homes." Although the African-American majority elected some black officeholders in Lowndes, economic change did not follow. "We can vote now and we got a few colored people in office," Hayneville farmer Bill Grant explained, "but we still got real problems getting food and buying clothes and shoes and things." In 1975, whites owned about 90 percent of the land. Whites in Lowndes "still know that the state legislature and the governor will protect them," said black sheriff John Hulett, "if it comes down to a question of property." Across the rural South, the color of economic power remained white—even in those places that experienced the transition to black political strength.[75]

To African-Americans, that was a hard and blunt truth. Unita Blackwell, a Mississippi farmer, became the first black mayor of Mayersville in 1977. "They is the power," Blackwell said of local whites. "They got the money." Writing in 1981, black journalist Chet Fuller described the paycheck as "a more powerful controller than a hundred vicious dogs." The civil rights movement rid the South of its Bull Connors, Jim Clarks, and other flagrant manifestations of segregation. But to many blacks, Fuller wrote, the bottom line remained unchanged:

> The niggers are still working in the fields, or in the stomachs of these mills and factories. Still working in the dust, dirt, and filth, just like always. People have been too quick to speak of the New South. They have been influenced by the sight of a few black faces in elective office. But that is not power, only the illusion of power. . . . Economics is still the great controller. . . . Whites, through their economic might, still have the power to strangle us or let us breathe.

Although the same process of social change enveloped both African-Americans and whites, their filters of experience sharply differed. Where blacks groped toward equality under new national laws, whites glimpsed the "oppression" of the federal government. As blacks gained the franchise and voted Democratic, whites began to vote Republican. And when blacks looked at the continued economic power of whites, they began to wonder how much had really changed. Yet in light of the jarring social, political, and racial transformations, whites believed the era had been tumultuous enough. They had already ceded plenty.[76]

Industrialization left the wealthy with their money and power intact, but at the same time it altered the lives of many white southern workers. When "the word automation exploded onto the American scene," the *Birmingham News* reported in 1969, it brought "both terror and dreams of glory." For workers in Scott, Mississippi, mechanization penetrated into the far reaches of life. A tiny town in the Delta, Scott contained little more than a post office, a main street with a handful of stores, and a cotton gin. "The world's largest cotton plantation," operated by Delta & Pine Land Company, surrounded the town. Gradually, machines replaced Delta & Pine workers. Eighty hand laborers once did the work of one "hoe machine." While many workers left farms, those who stayed reaped the benefits of progress. New houses sprouted in Scott; they all boasted central heating, modern bathrooms, and kitchen appliances. Workers spilled out of the 38,000-acre plantation and into town. This was part of the company's plan. "We'd like to move everybody off the farm into Scott," said Early Ewing, Jr., vice president of Delta & Pine. By 1969, that vision neared fruition. The town's population was a little more than 1,000, spread across 323 families. Only two Scott residents were not employed by Delta & Pine, and they worked at the post office. Industrialization dragged even the most insulated and isolated of southern towns into the twentieth century. In addition to the new housing, Scott built a recreation center, a baseball field, and a hospital. "The machine may have sent people away from the farm," the *Delta-Democrat Times's* Pat Roberts wrote in 1969, "but for the ones who've stayed, it has meant a new way of life." While many still worked on the plantations, they now lived in a quickly modernizing town. Workers who once harvested the fields by hand now manned machines. Even in dark corners of the rural South, industry upended old patterns of life. But not all patterns. Workers still lived in a company town, directly under Delta & Pine's control. And by 1969, Scott had finished construction of two new swimming pools—one for whites and the other for blacks.[77]

From company towns to plantations, industrial advance deposited twin legacies in the Mississippi Delta. Machines ended thousands of jobs even as they created more comfortable lifestyles for those who remained employed. The march of new economic forces changed relationships between owners and workers. Company managers and plantation masters remained lords of all they surveyed. But their business style lost much of its paternalism. As black deference died with the civil rights movement, so did the "compassion" of wealthy whites. If the 1960s brought changes in economics, politics, and race relations, it also exposed some of southern society's rougher edges. Around Scott, company heads burned down tenant shacks and lured their workers into town. On the farms of nearby Louise, landowners severed all their ties to that old tradition—real or imagined—of noblesse oblige.

Plantations defined much of the land in Louise, and in Humphreys County. The smallest plantations contained a hundred acres, and the largest stretched for many miles. As late as 1960, plantations housed anywhere from ten to forty families. Tenants inhabited shacks strewn across dirt roads, and remained dependent upon owners. It was an "authoritarian world," Anthony Dunbar wrote for the Southern Regional Council, "ruled by a planter, where families earn with their sweat . . . the privilege of staying alive." Dunbar later reflected that "the real life on the plantations in the 1960s was . . . reminiscent of the lovely and glorified heritage of old Dixie." On one particular Louise plantation, thirty tenant families worked the land through the 1950s. By 1969, just six men worked those same fields. Only those skilled enough to operate machines stayed on; the others boarded trains or thumbed rides to New Orleans, Chicago, and destinations in between.[78]

Efficient machines and growing cities did not by themselves account for all this upheaval on the land. The Minimum Wage Law of 1966 complicated planters' efforts to employ bevies of unskilled laborers. Before the law took effect, tenant farmers in Louise earned about $3 each day. The new Minimum Wage Law, first implemented in 1967, mandated a salary of $1 per hour. By 1969, that wage ascended to $1.30. While some planters in Louise skirted the law, most complied—and they fired unskilled laborers. "At first, the machines started throwin' people off the plantation," a black worker recalled. "After the wage law came along that made plantation owners buy more machines and put more people off." Laborers streamed away from the farms.[79]

In the Deep South, as across America, racial lines were also class lines. In 1966, Humphreys County held nearly 16,000 residents. Of 2,493 African-American families, 2,324 lived below the poverty line. Out of 1,418 white families, by contrast, 484 were poor. Those class divisions shaped the social worlds of Louise whites. Planters controlled poor whites as they did poor blacks, while agents on the plantation composed a thin middle class. As both cause and effect of their economic power, planters dominated local politics. All but one of Louise's city councilmen were planters. Few blacks even realized they could vote if they wished. African-Americans called the city council the "White Citizens' Council," and it may as well have been. The city council focused on two aims: to retain planters' economic power, and to keep the races separate. Problems with that latter objective were apparent well before the days of civil rights. For almost twenty years, the owner of a large plantation just outside Louise was married to a black woman. With firearms, he fended off disapproving neighbors. This exception to racial conformity also proved the general rule. Through the early 1970s, planters maintained political and economic supremacy. Up until 1975 Humphreys County registrar G. H. Wood tried to resist the Voting Rights Act. "The planter governs the community," Dunbar wrote. "Almost everyone works for him. In Louise, and . . . in the Delta, the interests of the plantation are the interests of the community." Even if the civil rights movement did not bring rapid political change to Louise, it altered historic relationships between the races.[80]

More than landowners and businessmen, many planters perceived themselves as heads of large families. In the days of slavery, masters might care for their chattel when sick, lavish gifts and feasts on their slaves during Christmas, or allow their workers a small modicum of autonomy within the larger reality of bondage. Even after the "peculiar institution" of slavery was abolished, it was not clear how much had changed between plantation masters and black workers. Sharecropping became a halfway point between slavery and freedom, and well into the twentieth century, tenants and sharecroppers depended upon landowners for their survival. "A point perhaps not yet overstated," Dunbar wrote of Louise planters in 1969, "is that when people spend their lives depending upon others, the 'others' do not feel like oppressors; they feel paternalistic." Into the late 1960s, planters continued to think of black workers as dependent children. The civil rights movement presented that mind-set with an inescapable challenge. In Louise, "most planters viewed the loan that they extended to get a family through the winter more as a kind act, the sort that men must perform occasionally, rather than as one link in a chain of bondage." To the workers, the chains were all too real—even if they were no longer literal. As the civil rights movement assaulted Jim Crow and its concomitant attitudes, the planter perceived "a massive rejection of the decency with which he had tried to live his life." Soon, the compassionate planter of old (and perhaps also of myth) became the merciless manager.[81]

The plantation's communal character succumbed to mechanization, the civil rights movement, and the charge toward agricultural efficiency. If white landowners ever felt bonds of affection for their workers, by the 1960s they saw laborers mainly as drains on capital. "The kindness that might once have played a part in the relationship between planter and tenant is disappearing," Dunbar wrote. "Callousness between management and labor" replaced it. Until the 1960s, Louise landowners often permitted tenants to maintain "truck gardens." Tenants grew vegetables and raised hogs on small patches of land. With industrialization, planters began to maximize profit and land. Outhouses pocked the tenant's front lawn, while cotton and soybean crops crowded his doorstep. Those workers who became old or injured could expect to soon depart. "No tenants not working regularly can believe the boss who says, 'You can live here as long as you need to.' They have seen too many families, believing the same promise, who were told one afternoon to leave . . . so that the house into which they were born could be burned and planted over in cotton." More than ever, the goal of profit overwhelmed all others.[82]

Planters had always been businessmen. But if landowners once protected their workers as they would valuable investments, mechanization and wage laws made those laborers expendable. At the same time, economic advances and civil rights struggles lent workers a new dignity and humanity. The events of the post–World War II period stripped the protective layering that shielded black workers from white landowners. "The power of the planter is not guarding over them; it is seemingly aimed directly at them," Dunbar wrote. Planters "do not care whether the black man in the Delta starves or not." For those whites who had prided themselves on paternalism, the age of civil rights was a profoundly perplexing and deeply revealing time.[83]

For almost every white southerner, it was a time of uncertainty and insecurity. In that respect, the plantation was not unique. Through the 1960s and into the 1970s, events altered white lives and turned communities upside down—in models of the New South like Atlanta, as well as in rural areas everywhere from the Delta to the Piedmont. In Rocky Mount, North Carolina, a white woman who grew up on a plantation gave the tumult on the farm a different spin. Identified as A.W., she returned to her Nash County home during the 1970s, when she was in her twenties. A.W. detailed how her father and brothers burned tenant houses, deducted taxes from the workers' pay, fired those who failed to show up on holidays, and considered installing a rent-free trailer park to further tie the workers to the land. This was the "new paternalism":

> I was born in 1948 into an essentially feudal system on a farm in Nash County in which everybody knew his "place" and stayed in it. My place was to be a good little southern girl and behave myself at all times, principally by staying out of the way. . . .
>
> Now the circle has come around to the beginning again. I am at home with my four brothers on the farm—we see ourselves as "saving our way of life." . . . Why? We love it—we are tied to it and see it as threatened.
>
> What place do the blacks have in our plan or scheme? We are burning down the tenant houses have abolished the take-out-30 c an hour from their pay envelope—give them their "bonus" (their hard-earned money) at Christmas time after you've taken out taxes—We want to put in a trailer park (no rent) on our land so we can keep them tied to us—some of them are learning because they don't like the new rules—you're fired if you don't come in to work on Easter Monday or if you come to work drunk—This is the new paternalism and my father has almost had cardiac arrest—I think we see these people as adults, whereas to him they're still children—but he has failed and the struggle, the clash of the 2 generations is going to have no winner—he'll go down with us or rise up with us or "be ground into the dust" (my brother's expression). . . .
>
> We recognize our dependence on them and feel that they have been cheated of the rewards for their sweat—or they can leave—I think that's when they'll really be free—we want the feudalism to be dead—but can you do it by only burning tenant houses?

The new generation was not so naive as to think that burning tenant houses could erase decades of paternalism. Indeed, a "new paternalism" was waiting to take its place. The civil rights movement achieved many goals, yet it did not bury "racism" and "paternalism" altogether. They reappeared in different incarnations.[84]

WHITE SOUTHERNERS WERE NOT only lords of the economy. Many of them were its serfs. Although southern workers saw improvements in their lifestyle in the decades after World War II, their wages remained lower than those of workers in any other region. Southern industry was in its infancy during the 1960s, but that alone did not account for the workers' low salaries. Anti-unionism sank deep roots in the South. It fit with the regional aversion to political change. Black protesters, "outside agitators," communists, Yankees, and union organizers often blended together to threaten the southern way of life. The South witnessed few union successes. The Southern Tenant Farmers' Union posted impressive achievements in the 1930s, and Winston-Salem tobacco workers waged a powerful labor movement during the 1940s. In both cases, African-Americans played large roles in the union efforts. White workers needed nothing more to encourage skepticism. To them, unionism reeked of subversion. While many white laborers scorned unionism, it was all the more loathsome to Dixie's captains of industry.[85]

Southern businessmen glimpsed their future prosperity in the stuff of cheap labor. In a land whose agricultural flavor had only recently faded, local power brokers realized that the region's affordable and plentiful supply of workers gave it economic appeal. With that selling point, boosters lured businesses southward. Chambers of Commerce boasted that their towns had no "labor problems." A Selma Chamber of Commerce brochure from 1953 read: "LABOR: There is in Selma . . . a large reservoir of colored labor which is rapidly being released from agricultural work. . . . It is 100% native born, untainted and willing and eager to work. We also have white labor." Southern workers—black and white—became commodities to be sold and traded. It was vital that these workers were recently "released from agricultural work." On the farm, there was little talk of unions. The new workers would presumably harbor little interest in any such schemes. Amid the civil rights tumult of the 1960s, boosters had an extra responsibility: they not only sought to convince prospective businesses that unions were feeble, but also that their towns had been unaffected by the civil rights movement. Monroe, Louisiana's, boosters reminded industrialists that their city had endured "no riots . . . no marches . . . no demonstrations . . . no teacher strikes." In this light, one might think back to the protestations of Albany, Georgia's, leaders and realize that politicians and editors were not simply naive. They had a large stake in claiming that Martin Luther King, Jr., would never turn their community "upside down." If he did, it might become less attractive to northern businesses.[86]

As a group, white workers feared integration in general—and their black counterparts in particular. A 1957 survey of southern trade unions found that in two-thirds of locals, "most" white members opposed school integration. "Most" also held "antagonistic feelings" toward African-Americans. "Most" was the questionnaire's strongest category of response. As the national labor movement began to support black demands for civil rights, "most" of the white members in more than one-third of southern locals began to oppose national unions like the AFL-CIO. In the aftermath of the *Brown v. Board of Education* decision, leaders of southern locals attested to "strained relations between white and Negro workers, even to the point of breaking off all conversation and contact." After AFL-CIO head George Meany pledged support for civil rights, workers in a Rome, Georgia, papermakers' union sent him a letter of disapproval. The members wrote in February 1956 to express "our protest and profound disappointment in your stand in the segregation issue in the South." They spoke for many other white laborers across the region.[87]

The very design of some workplaces prevented interracial contact. At Mylcraft Manufacturing in North Carolina's Northampton County, a high wall down the middle of the plant separated white workers from blacks. It remained that way until 1965. Soon thereafter, southern workplaces like Mylcraft buckled to the mandates of the Civil Rights Act. Among white workers, that law caused an uproar. The eventual mixing of races in the workplace "really created a furor among the white members," remembered Thomas Knight, a worker at Reliance Manufacturing in Hattiesburg, Mississippi, and later an organizer for the Amalgamated Clothing Workers. In the late 1960s, the affiliated membership of the state union dropped by twelve thousand. "This was the toll that racial prejudice has taken on our state body." A preoccupation with cheap labor combined with the racial prejudices of white workers to cripple many efforts toward southern unionization.[88]

Like white proprietors and small businessmen, many workers opposed the Civil Rights Act. The law affected workplaces as directly as it did rib shacks, motels, or restaurants. Selina Burch, president of the Communications Workers of America (CWA), remembered that in the South, blacks worked only as janitors and elevator operators. The Civil Rights Act changed all that, and such changes sat poorly with white workers. "When Southern Bell started hiring blacks as switchboard operators, the phones in the CWA office were ringing off the wall. Members of the union were demanding that we stop it, hollering that if niggers came to work, they were going to walk off their jobs." Although CWA workers did not in fact walk out, they were not the only workers who despised the new law. As senators filibustered during the spring of 1964, a 165-member Atlanta union voiced its support for Senator Richard Russell and the southern cause. Local 65 of the American Stereotypers and Electrotypers Union wrote, "The law would impair (or destroy) our rights as Americans in the following way: As rights as seniority as members of Organized Labor. Seniority is the base upon which Unionism is founded. . . . Our right to seek employment according to our qualification. . . . Our rights as Labor Unions to choose our own members." While the civil rights movement challenged white workers' domination over unions and workplace practices, the cry of "white rights" resonated with the laboring class.[89]

As the American Stereotypers and Electrotypers Union conveyed to Richard Russell, workers' cherished seniority system was the nub of the matter. When the civil rights movement struck at the racialized system of job promotions, it caused white laborers untold distress. In the Jim Crow years, nearly every southern factory operated with two lines of progression—one for white workers, the other for blacks. Individuals accumulated seniority rights, but they could bid only on jobs allotted for their own race. White jobs were invariably better, and commanded higher salaries. The black freedom struggle threatened this system, and the Civil Rights Act shattered it. Many white laborers considered integration the most wrenching experience of their working lives; it merged two working worlds into one, and endangered the advantages that their whiteness had granted. As Mobile paper worker Plez Watson reflected, "1964 brought a new era for all of us." While he accepted the changes in time, they were at first almost impossible to abide. "No man should be denied having the same paid job that he's working on . . . but it took me a lot of years to actually see how wrong it was . . . it took a long, long time." The 1964 law began a tortuous process. Watson's mill had been segregated since 1941, and initially he found the changes "devastating." All of a sudden, two lines of progression became one. Blacks could bid on white jobs, and at those companies that later adopted affirmative action policies, African-American workers even gained "superseniority" rights that enabled several of them to vault past older white workers. "The rules give them their rights and you couldn't stop it," Watson recalled. "That was a devastating thing . . . for the white workers it turned our world upside down." If some white southerners shrugged

off integrated water fountains or quickly accepted desegregated train
cars, many others had trouble absorbing the changes in their workplaces.[90]

In the 1960s and 1970s, the issues of race and civil rights overwhelmed other concerns at southern workplaces. Joe McCullough was
secretary of the local at Savannah's Union Camp paper factory from 1960
to 1994. He remembered the meeting in which white workers learned
the details of the company's affirmative action program. "They thought
it was the end of the world." One laborer estimated that 90 percent of
union meetings dealt with civil rights. The new laws, and the new realities they forced, dominated the working world. McCullough recalled the
first black worker placed on a white job at Union Camp. "It was an odd-
ity, everybody was out there looking at him. . . . It was . . . something
unusual . . . it was something you could see, you could see that the faces
was changing. . . . I'd never seen civil rights movements, I'd never seen
this before in my life." Even in those southern towns that witnessed few
public protests or demonstrations, the effects of the civil rights movement were hard to miss. Racial change did not always pierce white
minds or homes, but it often reached ballot boxes and schools—and
finally penetrated thousands of workplaces.[91]

AS THOUGH INTEGRATION ITSELF were not a trying enough ordeal
for southern workers, those who wished to unionize had to confront
prospects just as daunting. Where workers displayed interest in unions,
southern communities often united to crush their desires. The town of
Hamburg, Arkansas, lured Bernstein & Son Shirt Corporation to its
environs in 1961. Soon 93 of 123 employees signed up with the Amalgamated Garment Workers. Businessmen, ministers, and newspaper editors joined forces with Bernstein's management to break the union.
The union ultimately lost the election, 67–43. Similar fights erupted
throughout the region, as in Moore County, North Carolina, during
1966. The National Labor Relations Board (NLRB) intervened to ensure
fairness for the union at the Southern Pines Proctor-Silex plant. But the
union never stood much of a chance. Repeated episodes of anti-union
intimidation marred the vote, and the NLRB then voided the election.
As the county readied for another vote, Carthage's *Moore County News*
titled its lead editorial on September 29, 1966, "Vote Against the
Union." Citing as evidence the nullification of the election, the *News*
railed, "The federal government is determined to collectivize us all."

School integration was bad enough, the *News* noted, and now the NLRB was meddling in the affairs of Proctor-Silex. "Another tentacle reaches out to pull us under. IT MUST BE CUT OFF. If you know any worker at the plant, let him kno[w] the danger that he and the community is facing, and urge him to vote AGAINST union representation. By so doing he will be voting FOR his own individual freedom, and a full paycheck." Carthage's newspaper could not have summed up the union's fate any more clearly. "There is no place for a union in this county."[92]

Through the 1970s, southern states remained opposed to unions. By 1976, all eleven members of the Old Confederacy possessed right-to-work laws. Only nine other states in America had passed laws that enabled workers to stay out of the union in organized plants. Organizers in the South knew the odds they were up against. Milford Allen, a native of Anderson, South Carolina, worked more than fifteen years for the Textile Workers Union of America before he began to organize with the International Ladies Garment Workers Union. When Allen held a meeting for workers at one of William Carter Co.'s knitting mills in Barnesville, Georgia, only twenty-four of them attended; four were white. "This is a tough business," Allen told the prospectives. "Some of you gonna get fired." To the bitter end, southern companies resisted unions and fought their advances. Corporate heads preferred the vernacular of paternalism to the language of war. It was a paternalism many had plied on the farm, and they adapted it easily to the factory. "I frankly don't feel our folks see the need for a third party to represent them," said Joe Lanier, Jr., president of the Georgia textile company West Point-Pepperell. "We have no adversary relationship." For the old construction "our Negroes," employers readily substituted "our folks." The subject changed from black civil rights protesters to organizing workers of any stripe. But similar myths prevailed.[93]

Black workers bore the brunt of both sorts of paternalism, which a 1968 sanitation workers' strike in Memphis brought to the fore. In February, 1,300 garbage workers (virtually all of them African-Americans) went on strike to protest meager wages, unsafe working conditions that led to the deaths of two workers, and a "rainy day" policy that often deprived them of pay. The strike lured a national labor union—the American Federation of State, County, and Municipal Employees—and attracted Martin Luther King and SCLC. Yet Memphis whites did not see this struggle as an episode in the black quest for freedom; to them, it was a devious plot. The strike transformed the accommodating southern black of yore into a political actor who demonstrated with signs that averred, "I Am a Man." Whites believed there had to be more to this cataclysm than simple human dignity. They thought "outsiders"—most likely of the communist and Yankee variety—had concocted this confrontation. The presence of the union, and the fact of labor strife, played even more forcefully into white myths.

Mayor Henry Loeb claimed that he had a close relationship with the garbagemen in the Public Works Department, of which he was a former commissioner. According to U.S. Undersecretary of Labor James Reynolds, dispatched to Memphis after King's assassination there, Loeb was "a captive of attitudes and a captive of generations of attitudes which were awfully difficult to remove from one's thinking." These views made it nearly impossible for whites like Loeb to understand the strikers' demands for union recognition. The local newspapers lambasted the strike. "The bluster, swagger and insolence of the men purporting to represent city garbage workers cannot be construed as 'bargaining,' " the *Commercial Appeal* editorialized. It drew explicit analogies to communism and war. "They 'negotiate' with Mayor Henry Loeb and the City of Memphis somewhat like the Viet Cong and Hanoi do with South Vietnam and the United States." From the strike's first day, Loeb claimed that the workers' actions were illegal. Loeb's conviction was rooted not only in a certain reading of law, but also in a belief about African-Americans' proper "place." Memphis blacks saw that paternalism for what it was. A garbage worker's wife recalled, "He was telling them like you tell a little child, 'Go on back to work, I'll give you some candy,' or 'Stop that!' " Whites could not believe that the strike spun out of any legitimate demands. "Memphis had been designated a target for the hard focus of big-time union power," the *Commercial Appeal* opined. White Memphis's response to the garbage strike was a function not only of traditional racial attitudes, but also of a powerful streak of anti-unionism. Loeb could not give up the thought that some outside force had manipulated him. He felt he could protect the workers better than the union could, and he sincerely believed he understood and spoke for the garbagemen. In turn, most whites in Memphis—with the exception of a handful of college students and ministers—strongly backed Loeb. Supporters of the workers hid their garbage, and let it fester out of sight. Whites who opposed the strike allowed their garbage to pile up high. Blocks and blocks of waste in Memphis testified not only to white attitudes toward the civil rights movement, but also to their views of labor unions.[94]

Two months before the Memphis strike began, and about a five-hour drive away, a different kind of strike was broken in Laurel, Mississippi. While an all-black union prevailed in Memphis, racial divisions wracked Laurel workers and sealed their defeat. In the spring of 1967, pulpwood workers at Laurel's Masonite plant waged a strike. Until the 1964 passage of the Civil Rights Act, blacks and whites had organized two different locals. By the time of the 1967 strike, Local 5-443 of the International Woodworkers of America represented them both. Jones County was a Klan hotbed for most of the civil rights years, and race continued to cleave workers. Although the Civil Rights Act had abolished segregated locals, the Masonite workers remained separated. In effect, two locals comprised 5-443: whites made up three-quarters of the membership, and blacks the remaining quarter. Its leadership was entirely white. Although the leaders did not stir up racial division, some of the rank and file were members of the Klan. When the local decided to organize a strike, Masonite management knew that race concerns could still trump class. The company "Klan-baited" Local 5-443 and spread rumors that the KKK controlled the union. Masonite executives exploited tensions aroused by the civil rights movement to isolate striking white workers.[95]

Union organizers suggested that Masonite had deviously orchestrated the strike. Because the union was gaining strength, the company acted to destroy it. "That strike was set up," said Granville Sellers, vice president of the local. "Jesus Christ himself couldn't have prevented it." Posing as the ally of black workers, the company integrated showers and washrooms—moves that were compelled by law, but that Masonite executives knew would cause friction between whites and blacks. In a final effort to stoke the fires of white workers, Masonite promoted a number of blacks. Sure enough, this action further fanned the flames of an already dissatisfied white workforce. Led by its all-white leadership, the union decided to strike. Many black workers saw the strike as racially motivated. While two hundred African-Americans supported the strike, three hundred went back to work and helped to break it. A casualty of racial tensions, the Laurel strike ended in December 1967. Some progressives had long hoped that segregation's downfall would free black and white workers to unify along class lines, but the situation in Laurel indicated precisely the opposite. It seemed that integration only further embittered workers.[96]

When the strike failed, the Southern Conference Educational Fund entered town—in hopes of forging that fanciful alliance between the downtrodden of both races. After careful organizing and extended discussion, African-American workers began to see Masonite's "Klan-baiting" for what it was. And white workers ceded partial control of the union to blacks. In 1971, Masonite changed its system for measuring quantities of wood. Workers who hauled wood—and who were paid by the amount they hauled—made less money. The union helped to establish a picket line, and Masonite quickly found its wood supply depleted. No longer able to "Klan-bait," the Masonite corporation revived another anti-union tool: the red brush. "They call us Communist," said W. H. Pulliam, a thirty-year-old white pulpwood worker. "They're the Communists. Masonite, that's who's the Communist. . . . We're just a bunch of poor people trying to make a living." The outlines of a class consciousness began to emerge. And Charles Evers noticed it. While campaigning for governor of Mississippi, Evers stopped in Laurel to make a speech in September 1971. White workers made up half of the audience. "I've always known that the poor black and the poor white would some day get together," said Evers, awed by the interracial crowd. "Thank God, it's beginning to happen here in Jones County." Of course, many of the white workers drove to the Evers rally in pickup trucks adorned with "WALLACE" stickers.[97]

The South's largest industry was textiles, and whites dominated its workforce.* In 1960, only 3 percent of textile workers were black. The South, and particularly the Carolinas, comprised the heart of the nation's textile industry; about 90 percent of American mills were in the South. Textile workers received wages far below those of many other industries. Historically, the textile industry served as a "route to economic freedom," Roy Reed wrote in the New York Times, "for those other slaves to the plantation system, the white hill people." For many whites, textiles was the first rung on a large economic ladder. Mills pulled workers off the fields and eventually vaulted them into wage-paying positions. With the South's growth in the years after World War II, higher-

---

*While textiles were the South's largest "traditional" industry, a host of defense-related industries—when taken together—were far bigger. The military grounded southern growth from 1952 to 1962, and by 1973, more southerners worked in defense-related industries than in textiles, synthetics, and apparel combined.

paying businesses—chemical and electronic industries, for example—lured whites away from the textile mills. In response, the textile industry began to look elsewhere for cheap labor—specifically, in the black community. To stay competitive, textile firms hired more blacks, paid more money, and moved slowly from the Piedmont areas toward the Black Belt. Yet the need to stay competitive only partially explained the integration of the textile industry. The Civil Rights Act and subsequent federal lawsuits forced textile companies to integrate. Following the 1964 legislation, virtually every major textile company—Burlington Industries, Dan River Mills, and J. P. Stevens among them—faced lawsuits to desegregate their workforces.[98]

By 1966, African-Americans accounted for almost 10 percent of the South's textile workforce. In the Carolinas, whites made up 91 percent of textile workers. Yet they comprised only 65 percent of the industry's service workers and manual laborers; in contrast, more than 99 percent of officials, managers, and technicians were white. The fact that whites ran the textile industry did not make it unique. But in a region that powerfully resisted unions, the textile industry's resistance seemed particularly savage. Despite gradual wage increases, textile workers were still paid so little that, in 1967, North Carolina workers made less than those in any other state.[99]

In the late 1960s, Carolina textile workers moved into action. In 1966, workers at Elkin's Chatham Manufacturing Co., just west of Winston-Salem, demanded better contracts. Employees at the National Spinning Co. in Whiteville, a town near coastal Wilmington, were fired for union activity. The company's hardball tactics backfired, and fueled further worker unrest. National Spinning eventually reinstated the group. Through 1966 and 1967, workers at Greensboro's Cone Mills struggled to secure better contracts. The NLRB cited Cone Mills for "unfair labor practices, including the threatening, coercing, and firing of employees for union activity and refusal by the company to bargain in good faith." In February 1967, employees at seven Cone Mills plants waged three-day strikes. They gathered support from various local ministers, professors, and students. The Textile Workers Union of America planned a state-wide meeting for April 23. Editors of the University of North Carolina at Chapel Hill's *Daily Tarheel* backed the workers. "It will probably be a long and bitter fight. But it will be worth it, for what's involved is the bringing of some members of North Carolina's textile industry—kicking and screaming if necessary—across the threshold of the 20th Century."

Strike talk swirled around some textile plants as the workers' old deference receded. And the changes of the 1960s eventually dragged textile bosses—and also white workers—into the twentieth century.[100]

Erwin Mills dominated a small North Carolina town of the same name, situated between Fayetteville and Raleigh. Erwin straddled the Piedmont and the Black Belt. As late as 1969, a conspicuous billboard shrouded the nearby interstate. It featured a white-cloaked man on horseback, clutching a burning cross. The sign read, "You are in the heart of Klan Country. Welcome to North Carolina . . . Help Fight Integration & Communism!" For African-Americans who began to work at Erwin Mills, the setting did not seem inviting. But this was in some ways a new South, and workers at Erwin accepted the mill's integration without violent opposition.[101]

If interracial friendships were not the rule, neither was outright hostility. Rufus Cross was one worker who embodied the "cracker" stereotype. In 1949, he hitched a ride from Bainbridge, Georgia, up to Erwin. Cross worked at Erwin Mills for twenty years before the company hired black laborers. When Cross said, "The ones they hired, they act like niggers," he was actually issuing a perverse sort of compliment. "They're real nice. Act like [they're] friends. We try to get along. As fir as I know, they ain't had a bit of trouble, all through the mill." While a white weaver named Paul Carroll alleged that some blacks were "lazy," he admitted, "I get along with 'em just fine. . . . They're just another working man." Bradley Caudle, a weaver for twenty-two years, said, "It won't bother me. If they tend to their business, I will, too." Betty Long had worked as a spinner for twenty-six years. "The good Lord made us all alike. We'll get along and it's better than the farm." While such reactions did not herald racial unity, they seemed at least to promise a future of peace. Occurrences like these led the *New York Times* to report, "The bugaboo about the unwillingness of white employees to work side by side with Negroes has been virtually laid to rest." Compared with white workers' uproar about the Civil Rights Act, this seemed like rapid progress. In an industry with a reputation for racism, an industry that had been 97 percent white until 1960, and in a town that still bore the KKK's mark, one might not have expected tolerance from white workers. Yet there was a vital distinction between tolerating working alongside a black worker and tolerating his seniority rights. The *New York Times* article did not broach the topics of black promotion or affirmative action, subjects much more distressing to whites. Perhaps Erwin workers' actions signaled less a tolerance or an embrace of blacks than what journalist Roy Reed termed "a kind of shocked innocence in many white Carolinians these days."[102]

There was little innocence in Kannapolis, North Carolina. Charles Cannon, the chairman of Cannon Mills, owned everything in town, right down to the water supply. In 1969, Kannapolis would have been North Carolina's tenth-biggest city if it was incorporated; since it was not, residents—black and white—were deprived of the right to vote on local matters. The downtown area was pristine, the police were on Cannon's payroll, and all housing was segregated. "Kannapolis whites don't call 'Negroes' blacks—or, for that matter, 'Negroes,' " the *Wall Street Journal* explained. "From Mr. Cannon on down, the term is 'nigger.' But in speaking of a Kannapolis resident, it usually is 'good nigger'; that's what whites feel most of the local blacks are." Charlie Cannon's fiefdom remained firmly tethered to the mores and practices of a different era. When the federal government moved to end segregated housing in April 1969, a Kannapolis resident asked, "What do you want—a race riot?" Yet the 1960s brought racial change even to Kannapolis, as it did to most southern communities. Shortly before the Civil Rights Act passed in 1964, Cannon Mills took down the "colored" signs. And Cannon hired its first African-American millworker that year. By the early 1980s, one-quarter of the company's twenty-two thousand workers were black. In Kannapolis, anti-unionism proved more dogged than racial discrimination. It was not until 1999 that workers at Pillowtex Fieldcrest Cannon mills finally voted to unionize.[103]

If change could ripple into Kannapolis, it could penetrate any town, company, or workforce. In 1973, there were almost 700,000 textile workers in the South; apparel was the next largest industry, with 422,000 workers. In eight southern states (everywhere except Louisiana, Arkansas, and Texas), more than 20 percent of all manufacturing workers labored in textile mills. Textiles remained a high-volume, low-profit-margin industry. This assured mill hands that they would remain the lowest-paid industrial workers both in the South and throughout the nation. In 1973, their average hourly wage of $2.79 stood 35 cents lower than the southern average for industrial laborers, and a full $1.22 below the national average. For all these reasons, southern textile workers would have seemed natural allies of unions. But by 1973, only 70,000 of 700,000 belonged to the Textile Workers Union of America.[104]

Through the 1960s and 1970s, the TWUA campaigned among

workers at the "Big Three" textile firms—Burlington Industries, J. P. Stevens, and Deering-Milliken. Quickly, Stevens moved to the forefront of that fight. Between 1965 and 1976, the NLRB convicted Stevens of fifteen separate labor law violations. Stevens fired pro-union workers, harassed them, and denied them overtime. When employees in States-boro, Georgia, voted for a union, Stevens simply closed down the plant. Stevens's anti-unionism possessed little subtlety. "This company was fir-ing people the same day they signed the union card," said Reed Johnston, the NLRB's regional director at Winston-Salem. "Doing it blatantly." Stevens insisted that issues between workers and management would be "settled amicably," and that the union could only bring "friction, terror-ism, and fear." Administrative law judge Bernard Ries observed that Stevens conducted labor negotiations "with all the tractability and open-mindedness of Sherman at the outskirts of Atlanta."[105]

With good reason, the TWUA intensified its focus on J. P. Stevens. In 1973, workers at Stevens plants in Roanoke Rapids, North Carolina, began to consider the TWUA's appeal. In that town of fourteen thou-sand, more than one-quarter worked in one of Stevens's seven mills. The company had aggressively recruited black workers in its effort to keep wages at a minimum. In eighty-one Stevens mills South-wide, almost 13 percent of its workers were African-Americans in 1969. By 1973, that figure had risen to 20 percent. Given this reality, Stevens executives—like Masonite executives before them—glimpsed a way to cripple the union drive. Although whites outnumbered blacks by a ratio of more than three to one in the Roanoke Rapids mills, Stevens executives believed they could stoke white fears of a black takeover. On April 25, 1973, J. P. Stevens sent letters to its workers. Presented as a message to black workers, the letter was in fact intended to scare whites:

> A special word to our black employees. It has come repeatedly to our attention that it is among you that the union supporters are making their most intensive drive—that you are being insistently told that the union is the wave of the future for you especially—and that by going into the union in mass, you can dominate it and control it in this plant.

In the end, the company's racial appeals fell on deaf ears.[106]

While white laborers experienced integration of the workplace as a great trauma, the decade that elapsed between the mid-1960s and the mid-1970s seemed to have worn away some of the initial shock and resentment. For instance, black and white workers at J. P. Stevens now played together on the company's intramural softball team. Although racial hostilities had not completely subsided, they no longer seemed omnipresent. In August 1974, workers voted for TWUA representation. Crystal Lee Jordan dramatized the majority's sentiment. A lifelong mill worker, Jordan was also the daughter of mill workers. She hoped the family line would stop there. "If they became mill workers, she said to [her three] children, then she wanted life to be better for them than it had been for her. So, she said, she had joined the union." Jordan took a generational view. She started to see her own troubles in light of those her parents had endured—and those that she wanted her own children to avoid. When the TWUA came to Roanoke Rapids in April 1973, "It got me thinking about my parents, about me. . . . Cotton-mill workers are known as trash by some, and I knew this union was the only way we could have our own voice, make ourselves better." While workers in Roanoke Rapids met with success, thousands more textile laborers remained unorganized.[107]

A 1976 advertisement in *Forbes* symbolized the Tar Heel State's priorities. "North Carolina has a commitment to provide the most favorable climate to industry that is possible." By that year, previously agricultural North Carolina had become America's eighth-most-industrialized state. Unions languished while industry thrived. Only 6.8 percent of North Carolina's nonagricultural workers belonged to unions; South Carolina was the only state with a lower ratio, at 6.6 percent. No other southern state approached those low levels of unionization. Texas and Mississippi both counted 12 percent of their workforce in unions, and even that was less than half of the 1976 American average—25 percent. A writer for *The Progressive* believed a great showdown between two historic forces was in the offing. "In North Carolina . . . the battle between labor and capital is still in its infancy. It is a replay of the struggles witnessed elsewhere in America from the 1880s through the 1930s." Those epic confrontations never came to the South. While the civil rights movement placed the old racism on its last legs, anti-unionism still enjoyed its heyday. By 1988, less than 5 percent of workers in the Carolinas belonged to unions.[108]

Unions' continued futility in Dixie highlighted the general frustrations of poor white southerners. For them, the years after World War II were marked by a mix of confusion, upheaval, resentment, and progress. The South's rapid industrialization and urbanization contributed to economic improvements for poor whites. In North Carolina, for example, working families' incomes were half the national average in 1950; by 1970, they were 80 percent of the U.S. average. But North Carolina workers were still poor. And while every extra bit helped, money was not the only concern—especially during a period as dynamic as the age of civil rights. For the most part, laboring whites lived their day-to-day lives well beneath the media's radar. Attention focused on protesting African-Americans, Klansmen who fought them, or politicians whom the rest of the nation considered proxies for poor whites—George Wallace, Bull Connor, or even Jimmy Carter. As journalist Ron Duncan wrote, "common" whites' actual responses to the civil rights movement were still unknown:

> Since the successes of the civil rights movement, little notice has been given to the poor white people and how they are reacting and adjusting to the changed role of Negroes. Bull Connor's dogs and George Wallace's school door defiance were perhaps instructive, but basically they were political and mass media histrionics. What was the common white person feeling, and how was he handling this new world that was culturally quaking under him?

The civil rights movement overturned integral parts of the South's social hierarchy. However difficult life might have been for poor whites, their skin color had once conferred upon them rights and privileges denied to blacks. "These white peons never believed they were poor in the way that Negroes were poor," Harry Golden wrote in *The Nation*. "White men had hope." Southern whites had long lived on the empowering side of segregation; many now found themselves on the "wrong side" of the civil rights revolution.[109]

For decades, demagogic politicians fueled racial fears—and then convinced poor whites to vote those concerns. In the civil rights years, anxieties of generations met with unsettling realities. From the integration of schools and neighborhoods to the struggle for employment, poor whites felt the first effects of the civil rights movement. To be a poor white is "to be taught all your life that the bogeyman is a Negro," Duncan wrote, "and then have him move next door." The experience was deeply unnerving. Duncan wrote about Claude Workman, one poor white in Durham, North Carolina. "His is not the world of the private white school and club. He feels first hand the law that can desegregate the public housing projects in the middle of a city but rarely touch the white neighborhoods located out past a sort of economic dew line." As in New Orleans during 1960, poor whites felt the hard impact of desegregation. The integration of New Orleans schools not only threatened a racial order, but also carried with it a crisis of class. Poor whites felt picked on by the powerful men who ran the city, and class divisions helped turn an episode of desegregation into a battle of whites against whites. When integration traveled to other southern communities—in the form of African-American students, customers at burger joints, or mill workers—poor whites knew that their lives would be more deeply affected than those of their upper-class counterparts. The affluent often lived in a world of safety valves, one that included all-white private schools, country clubs, and exclusive suburbs. That world was closed off to working-class southerners. To wealthier whites, the civil rights movement could often remain a montage of popular images—episodes they had heard about or seen on television, protests that worried them, changes that upset their businesses or threatened their political might, but rarely realities that they had to confront daily. To poor whites, however, integration often brought a new way of life.[110]

That new order stared poor whites in the face. Raymond Wheeler of the Southern Regional Council said as much in 1968. "Where desegregation has taken place, the poorer, uneducated white, least able to cope with the change, has become the most involved. Upper-class neighborhoods stay lily white, while public housing is desegregated. Restaurants, movies, public pools . . . are desegregated. Country clubs, private schools, and dining clubs remain all-white." Wheeler's assessment was mostly on the mark. But it betrayed a bias endemic to well-educated whites of most every political bent, liberal and conservative alike. They tended to blame the vagaries of racism upon poor whites. Wheeler considered the poor and uneducated "least able to cope with the change." Some events—like the episodes in New Orleans's Ninth Ward— highlighted that point. But Wheeler's generalization was questionable at best. His belief rested on a stereotype that stretched back in time. It suggested the manner in which Black Belt planters and urban moderates had long sneered at less fortunate "rednecks" and upcountry whites. The Mississippi Delta scion William Alexander Percy summed up that mind-set in his 1941 classic, *Lanterns on the Levee.* Percy termed poor whites "intellectually and spiritually . . . inferior to the Negro." That bias cut deep in southern society. Clara Lee Sharrard, who grew up in Lexington, Virginia, in the 1950s, recalled the importance of class.

There were "real class divisions, all the way through school. My father would say, 'Well, you can't associate with this person because their great-grandfather was a bootlegger.' . . . Everybody knew everybody's pedigree and it was very definitely a class society." Into the twenty-first century, "poor whites are looked down upon at least as much as blacks." And although the civil rights movement won legal equality for African-Americans, it left poor whites with little to boast about.[111]

While many poor whites harbored various degrees of racism, their habitual prejudices often helped to mask racism's systemic nature. Those who wielded power also possessed a deep investment in white supremacy. Wealthy industrialists often doubled as leading "country-club Klanners." Affluent whites might not employ the word "nigger" at the dinner table, but they did plenty to hamstring blacks' quest for equality. Deep prejudices animated both sides of the white South's class divide. It was not until he reached high school that Atlanta doctor Richard Franco discovered how southern racism cut across class lines. "It took a good while for me to realize that there were many examples of people who I regarded as educated and enlightened on many issues . . . intelligent, articulate, successful professionals," and yet in their "attitudes on blacks there was a real blind spot there." Higher education or social status could confer many things, but racial tolerance was not necessarily one of them. Of course, some polls showed a correlation between level of education and tendency to support integration. In 1956, 28 percent of white southerners with a college education supported token school integration; 15 percent of high school graduates favored it; and only 5 percent of white southerners with less education showed support for desegregation. By 1964, 20 percent of the least educated supported school integration; 32 percent of high school graduates did, and almost half of college-educated white southerners affirmed their support. Still, more than half of white southern college graduates opposed token integration. This hardly displayed an enlightenment on race. Moreover, those in the upper class had the means, ability, and power to do much more to preserve segregation than the working class could. And they often wielded that power.[112]

From the murder of Emmett Till in 1955 to the beatings on Selma's Edmund Pettus Bridge a decade later, the civil rights years burned a certain image of racism into the American consciousness. The sheriff, filling station attendant, or other working-class white man—often drawling and poorly educated—became a symbol of American prejudice. The mind's eye latched on to the photos of southern brutality, and equated racism with its most visible agents. Doubtless, that picture conveyed more than a few grains of truth. Just as certain, it cloaked the fact that a cadre of powerful men stood behind every brutal southern sheriff and every vicious purveyor of prejudice. Politicians, businessmen, lawyers, professors, and otherwise "respectable" leaders of southern communities gave the requisite winks and nods to the enforcers of segregation—and quite often they gave much more. Bigotry knew no class lines; what found expression at the bottom of white southern society often began at the top. For every Jim Clark or Bull Connor, there were many more discreet—and far more powerful—men. In Selma, Judge James Hare dictated the vicious response to segregation. "The orders came directly from Hare," J. L. Chestnut remembered. "Though big, burly Jim Clark became the symbol of white resistance in Selma . . . James A. Hare was the commander in chief of the forces of white resistance." Hare sought injunctions in courtrooms, prosecuted blacks, and fumed against the freedom struggle. He invested these maneuvers and rhetoric with a confected aura of order, peace, and reason. "James Hare was a sort of 1960s version of an 1860s plantation owner," Chestnut asserted. "Jim Clark was his overseer, the lower-class white man who ran the fields and controlled the slaves." Many others agreed with Chestnut's analysis. Across the scattered sites of the civil rights movement, *Newsweek* reporter and native North Carolinian Karl Fleming found that to be the case. Through his many dealings with southern sheriffs, Fleming came to believe that the "police were only as good—or bad—as their bosses—the white power structure." As Fleming recounted in his 2005 memoir, "It was only when they had the tacit or real approval—and sometimes active encouragement—from political and business leaders that cops, or even ordinary racists and Klansmen, behaved brutally toward Negroes."[113]

In Birmingham, Klansmen bombed black churches and homes in a reign of terror. According to native daughter Diane McWhorter, that violence possessed "respectable underpinnings." The city's elite establishment fostered the KKK "and created the brutal conditions that incited a magnificent nonviolent revolution." In that city whose wealth depended upon the steel industry, the modern civil rights movement grew from the "rib of organized labor." Leading industrialists responded with "a 'grassroots' counteroffensive of hooded vigilantes and the queerest Tory politician in history, a loudmouthed hick named Bull Connor." In this story, the redneck sheriff rose to power as a tool of the elite. James Simpson stood foremost among them, the biggest of Birmingham's "Big

Mules." Simpson—a corporation lawyer and founder of a bank—molded Connor into the "czar of Birmingham City Hall." When Bull Connor turned loose his attack dogs on unarmed black protesters, he was unleashing the fury of country club power brokers. Crass working-class racial sentiment worked hand in hand with the machinations and justifications of the powerful. As dissident Mississippi newspaperman Ira Harkey put it in 1967, "On the question of race there is no measurable difference in mentality between an educated, obviously polished white southerner in his immaculate garb and the grubbiest, most morally illiterate white lout plastered with mud and manure. They are twins." Together, southern whites of all social and economic classes fueled a system of segregation and a way of life that in the face of the civil rights challenge alternated among shock, devastation, vigilance, and violence. Neither poor whites nor wealthy ones were equipped to handle the changes that the civil rights movement set in motion.[114]

Some hoped that the civil rights movement might finally free southern whites, rich and poor, from their heritage of racial degradation. There were two ways to view it. From one perspective, the poor white's dreaded bogeyman had moved next door, assumed a spot alongside him on the assembly line, and now sent his children to the same school. Whites who thought this way recoiled from nightmares made real. But from another perspective, some believed poor whites would not have to view blacks as bogeymen. No longer impelled to detest blacks and discriminate against them, whites were finally liberated. John Jennings, a Wilmington, North Carolina, resident and regional director of the United Transport Service Employees Union, believed in that promise. "Some day the poor white man will realize that [the] only hope . . . is for him to join hands with the black-man in one common goal of making a great society in this land in which I love but can not enjoy." Whether that hope would come to possess any basis in reality was a question only time could answer.[115]

SIX

The Price of Liberation

THE CIVIL RIGHTS MOVEMENT advanced through the South with the force of a revolution. The "Second Reconstruction," like its historical namesake, produced staggering change even as it met with sobering continuity. When the struggles subsided and Americans began to measure the impact of the civil rights movement, black southerners, quite naturally, became the subjects of their assessment. Observers couched the extent of progress—or stagnation—in terms of black freedom, black voting rights, black education, and black poverty. But as long as the spotlight remained solely on blacks, Americans underestimated the full power of the civil rights movement. For the black freedom struggle also reshaped the lives of white southerners, and worked its way into whites' practices and habits—even into some minds and hearts. Whites did not have to be Klansmen or SNCC workers, politicians or Citizens' Councilors, to feel the seismic shifts. The civil rights movement changed all sorts of white southerners, in all sorts of ways. Some accommodated to new social, racial, and political orders. Many others attempted to fend off those changes, or to postpone their effects. Through the civil rights years, still others perceived something different: the outlines of their own liberation.

Even before the civil rights movement reached its apogee, the region's most celebrated intellectuals articulated that notion. Amid the rise of the Citizens' Councils and in the aftermath of Emmett Till's murder, William Faulkner could see the beginnings of the conflict that would envelop his beloved Mississippi. Writing in the winter of 1955, Faulkner hoped that white southerners could avoid violent confrontations over the issue of race. As the Supreme Court had recently done, Faulkner called "inevitable" the coming "changes in social relations." He hoped whites would accept them with grace. The preservation of their own freedom depended on whites' abilities to accept change, before it was thrust upon them—either by newly empowered blacks or federal intervention. "The question is no longer of white against black," but "whether or not white people shall remain free." To other writers, the premise that whites already had their freedom—and that they needed to *remain* free—was itself debatable. For Robert Penn Warren, the question was whether integration could *make them* free. Warren believed that if whites greeted desegregation with peace, they could put to rest their most violent fears and bewitching demons. Once whites realized that "desegregation is just one small episode in the long effort for justice," Warren wrote in 1956, they might unload the burdens of generations. "That perspective . . . is a liberating one. It liberates you from yourself." To Warren, the peaceful advent of integration could bring with it white liberation. Few expressed that sentiment better than Virginia Durr, who wrote from her Montgomery home in the midst of the bus boycott. "I do so long for a breath of freedom from this ever present . . . feeling of being . . . suffocated by the crowding walls of racial prejudice," Durr wrote on May 23, 1956. "But the Negroes have had it much worse and they are struggling to free us all." Early on in the black struggle, Durr glimpsed whites' freedom.[1]

Many African-Americans understood Durr's meaning. Martin Luther King, Jr.'s, "Letter from Birmingham City Jail" originally contained a lengthy section on how the civil rights movement would liberate whites. Somewhere in the transition from King's scribblings on smuggled scraps of newspaper to the typed treatise the world now knows, the section on white freedom was cut. But that idea persisted, from civil rights leaders on down to fieldhands. At a 1961 mass meeting in Albany, Georgia, Ralph Abernathy cried out to the crowd, "I want the white man to be free." The audience chorused back, "I do, too." Robert Pleas, a sharecropper who lived near Athens, Mississippi, could easily distinguish the "right decent" whites from the "bad ones." In a state dominated by segregationists, Pleas realized that the "all-right ones" were "gagged up. But we're going to set them good ones free—ourselves and them." Liberation could travel across the color line. Fannie Lou Hamer, the Sunflower County sharecropper who joined the Mississippi Freedom Democratic Party and vaulted to national prominence, sensed that white liberation was bound with black freedom. "There ain't no telling how many . . .

nights [the white man] slept not wanting things to be like they had been all the time. So that's the price for freedom, too. He is not free until I am free." While scholars have argued that white liberty depended—for its conceptual definition as well as its actual existence—upon the subjugation of blacks, this idea was turned on its head. In this dynamic vision, blacks who struggled for their rights might also liberate whites from a past guided by a system of oppression.[2]

From Delta plantations to the pages of *The New Yorker,* that notion of interdependence resonated. James Baldwin's *The Fire Next Time,* published in 1963, became an instant classic. In Baldwin's formulation, "*Whoever debases others is debasing himself.* This is not a mystical statement but a most realistic one, which is proved by the eyes of any Alabama Sheriff." In Birmingham's Bull Connor or Selma's Jim Clark, one might see Baldwin's point. Few men better epitomized the degradation of the Jim Crow South, or stooped lower to maintain segregation. Whites grew up in a world where the "order of nature" spelled white supremacy and black inferiority. That world distorted reality, and prevented whites from realizing the democracy and freedom of which their rhetoric so grandly spoke. The only way for any Americans to attain freedom, Baldwin wrote, was to embrace the nation and all its people, not just parts of it or some of them. "We, the black and the white, deeply need each other here if we are really to become a nation—if we are really, that is, to achieve our identity, our maturity, as men and women." The problem was that whites worshipped a false history of liberty—when in fact that past smacked more accurately of oppression. They clung to racial myths and fancied them worldly truths. "The white man is himself in sore need of new standards, which will release him from his confusion and place him once again in fruitful communion with the depths of his own being." For Baldwin, this was not mystical. It had everything to do with American history, inequality, and racial stereotypes—all of which debased white and black alike by prizing falsehoods over realities and blinding whites to the work that still remained.[3]

The brilliance of Baldwin's vision was in its insistence that whites would play only passive roles in that process. Instead, blacks became the agents of American freedom. "The price of the liberation of the white people is the liberation of the blacks." Whites were too trapped in their histories and their inventions to take an active role in change. Blacks, in freeing themselves, could also free whites. Baldwin's "Letter to My Nephew," penned on the centennial of the Emancipation Proclamation, composed one part of *The Fire Next Time.* He noted that racism stemmed not from black inferiority, but from white inhumanity and fear. Whites constructed visions of blacks that suited those fears. Prior to the civil rights years, "the black man . . . functioned in the white man's world as a fixed star, as an immovable pillar." But the civil rights movement changed all that. As the African-American "moves out of his place, heaven and earth are shaken to their foundations." In this world of upheaval, whites did not know precisely how to react. "They are, in effect, still trapped in a history which they do not understand; and until they understand it, they cannot be released from it." Baldwin counseled his nephew that he, and other African-Americans, would liberate whites. "The really terrible thing is that *you* must accept *them.* . . . We, with love, shall force our brothers to see themselves as they are, to cease fleeing from reality and begin to change it." One hundred years after slaves gained a kind of freedom, blacks—and not whites—would fulfill America's promises. "The country is celebrating one hundred years of freedom one hundred years too soon. We cannot be free until they are free." Baldwin's vision spelled out how blacks could bring about white liberation. Here was an idea that African-American author James Weldon Johnson articulated decades before. "The race question involves the saving of black America's body and white America's soul."[4]

The roots of that notion stretched deep into the past, far beyond James Weldon Johnson and his writings in the early twentieth century. Since the inception of the "peculiar institution," slaves and slaveholders alike speculated that the system of bondage brutalized white masters as well as black chattel. Guilt and degradation stained whites, even as they wielded the whip and brandished the lash. Of course, whites were not beaten, lynched, whipped, or shackled. If they were indeed oppressed by slavery and segregation, it must be acknowledged that their burdens were of a wholly different order than black sufferings. Still, from Thomas Jefferson to Frederick Douglass, various writers articulated the idea that racism degraded whites—and that African-Americans could free them. After Douglass witnessed a slave auction, he vouched for "the brutalizing effects of slavery upon both slave and slaveholder." In his master's wife, Douglass observed this process at close range. The woman was pious, warm, and tenderhearted when Douglass met her. But her participation in slavery "soon proved its ability to divest her of those heavenly qualities." The experience of degradation and oppression changed this woman. "Slavery proved as injurious to her as it did to me." The idea was that bondage deprived the oppressor of his humanity as much as the victim. It was a notion as old as the existence of human slavery—and it did not apply solely to that condition. George Orwell perceived a similar dynamic in the experience of colonization. He wrote in 1936, "When the white man turns tyrant it is his own freedom that he destroys." Released from the grip of tyranny in the age of civil rights, many white southerners began to reach toward their own freedom.[5]

SOME WHITES UNDERSTOOD the historic stakes of the civil rights years, and framed them in the vernacular of white freedom and oppression. When Atlanta's Sibley Commission held its 1960 public forums on closed schools and token integration, one Methodist minister was among those who spoke up for desegregation. Lester Rumble had served as a minister in Monroe, Georgia, during the infamous lynchings of 1946. "The terrible crime of Monroe is a guilt of us all," Rumble had told his congregation. By 1960, he had moved to Atlanta. Rumble still felt the burden of living as a white man in an oppressive society, and suggested that the liberation of whites hung in the balance of the fight over school integration. "How long, Sir, will we white people of the South continue to be discounted . . . before the rest of our country and the world because we insist on perpetuating a Master-Servant Society, that enslaves the so-called Master as well as the so-called Servant?" In 1961, *Atlanta Journal* columnist Margaret Long conceived of the civil rights movement in similar terms. She reached that sentiment after attending a theatrical performance of *Finian's Rainbow* at Atlanta University. The African-American students dramatized a scene in which an Irish spell turned a southern demagogue black, and the students erupted in laughter. That display gave Long insight into the black freedom struggle. "They suffer, forgive, insist and love—for our liberations as well as their own. We oppress, resist, fear and deny them—for our own privilege. So we have scarcely earned the larger freedom of their laughter." The civil rights years opened Long's eyes, as they did those of many other whites. New ways of seeing were evident in white citizens who had their attitudes transformed by the scenes of black protest, white cheerleaders who began to shuffle and sway alongside black girls, white proprietors who saw that the onset of integration did not cripple their businesses, and white politicians who discovered a language above and beyond racism. Of course, there were many stories to the contrary—of white politicians who simply packaged racial appeals in different wrappings, white students who fled public schools, and citizens who clung even more defensively to their traditional racial views. For those like Margaret Long, however, the civil rights movement promised a laughter that could liberate.[6]

If Long, Faulkner, Warren, Rumble, and Durr hoped for white liberation, and Baldwin asserted that blacks could deliver it, the views of other white southerners lent those ideas further credence. In 1962, a white lawyer issued a prediction to Robert Coles. "By the time we are in the 1970's . . . we will have a much better South, which means the white man will at last be liberated from the role of oppressor of his Negro neighbor." Although words like "liberation" and "oppression" carried echoes of profundity, the whole business of freeing oneself could in fact be much more pedestrian. By 1961, the Southern Regional Council's Leslie Dunbar was confident that blacks would gain their rights, and that white resisters would go down to defeat. But "the typical white southerner will shrug his shoulders, resume his stride and go on." Dunbar agreed that the civil rights movement possessed a freeing effect, but the substance of that freedom was more prosaic than lofty. "He can manage well enough, even if the patterns change. There is now one fewer fight which history requires of him. He has done his ancestral duty. He is free of part of his load, he can relax a bit more." Perhaps the civil rights movement allowed white southerners finally to rest.[7]

That rest would not come easily. Dunbar noted that for white southerners to truly free themselves from an oppressive past, they would have to face up to wrongs, and experience conflict. The process would not be gentle or simple. True rest could occur only after a battle, not in place of one. "Neither can the typical white man give up without a fight." Whites would have to be beaten—in Dunbar's language, they would have to be subjected to high heat and annealed—before they could be freed. Moreover, the civil rights years left marks on people that they might not even recognize until later. As Tuskegee mayor Johnny Ford said, "There's just a lot of folks here who, I gotta admit, still hadn't realized yet they were freed the same time the Negroes were." SCLC's Wyatt Tee Walker commented, "At the time . . . white people didn't understand. . . . This was as much for them as it was for black folks." Without even comprehending what was happening, white southerners gained opportunities for freedom and release.[8]

Some journalists became powerful advocates for the concept of white liberation. Hodding Carter, editor of Greenville, Mississippi's, *Delta*

Democrat-Times, believed the civil rights movement freed the white southerner more than the black. Before the civil rights years, Carter reflected, "any white who didn't agree with the white majority . . . was to be treated as a traitor . . . there were . . . one hell of a lot of people who were just scared." The civil rights struggle opened up the Magnolia State and the South to dissenters and moderates. "I'll tell you who's really free in Mississippi for the first time," he said in 1974. "It's not the black man, who still is economically . . . as much in bondage as he ever was. By God, the white Mississippian is free. . . . You can't write Mississippi the closed society anymore. And an awful lot of whites are never going to go back willingly." Few southern newsmen gained more acclaim than Hodding Carter, but none ascended higher than Howell Raines. An Alabama native, Raines became editor-in-chief of the *New York Times* in 2001. He articulated, with heightened optimism, the idea of white freedom. "Of all the lessons Martin Luther King, Jr., tried to teach us," Raines wrote in 1977, "the hardest for white Southerners to understand was that the Civil Rights Movement would free us, too." Raines himself learned those truths as a young boy in Birmingham, and his source was the family's black maid. Through eye-opening discussions about race in the 1950s, Grady Williams "had given me the most precious gift that could be received by a pampered white boy growing up in that time and place. It was the gift of a free and unhateful heart." Before the days of civil rights protest in Birmingham, Howell Raines had already been "freed."[9]

The observation that the civil rights struggle would free white southerners came in many forms. Some of the more eloquent expressions belonged to Pat Watters, a journalist from South Carolina. Blacks who struggled for civil rights "made possible the most important, and most necessary change of all, the freeing of whites as well as blacks from the curse of racism." In so many different ways, Watters wrote in 1969, "Southerners were free at last. . . . The good little white child need no longer be racist; the dutiful white citizen need no longer discriminate; 'good' Negroes need no longer demean themselves." Silence might not paralyze "nice" people, and blacks would be finally free of degradation. This was a hopeful vision—perhaps a naive one—but it captured the minds, and corresponded to the experiences, of many white southerners.[10]

Some whites forged that sense of liberation through the fervor of specific events. For others, liberation remained a powerful idea, a notion, a creature of the mind. Florence Mars lived in Philadelphia, Mississippi, during the infamous 1964 murders of civil rights workers. While some

Neshoba County whites understood the perpetrators' motives, others wallowed in shame and guilt over the actions of their neighbors. When seven men were finally prosecuted and convicted, Mars and her friends felt a deep sense of release. "We felt like we had been liberated, that those people on that jury had really saved us." Other whites attested to similar feelings, stemming from different circumstances. For Warren Ashby, a Greensboro resident, freedom came in the mid-1960s—and it was a freedom of the mind. Several years after the Greensboro sit-ins, and amid civil rights victories like the Civil Rights Act and the Voting Rights Act, Ashby began to feel a genuine liberty. Most important, he felt free to think as he liked. "It was mid '60[s] before I felt psychologically free in the South." Margaret Anderson, a teacher in Clinton, Tennessee, emphasized that mental dimension of liberation. She remembered a poor white boy who, during the first months of integration in Clinton schools, had visceral reactions to contact with African-Americans. When he returned to the school years later and chatted with Anderson, the civil rights movement had worked a remarkable transformation. "Sam was now free of mental slavery. His children would not be shackled as he had been." In that moment, Anderson glimpsed the liberation of minds for generations to come.[11]

Pat Watters spoke of salvation, and Marshall Frady called it a release. Whatever term was used, many white southerners felt that the civil rights years had removed a great burden from their shoulders. The weight of a long and bloody past seemed to be lifting. The civil rights movement began a wide-ranging process, Watters wrote, that penetrated white southerners to their very core. It announced a new force afoot in the South, one that produced "a snapping loose suddenly of bonds in a process that, once begun, could not be stopped until all were gone . . . so that those of us who had been by history and conditioning completely tied down were to be completely free—whether we wanted to be, could without fear be, or not." Watters covered passionate mass meetings in Albany, witnessed numerous beatings in Deep South towns, and encountered thousands of people touched by the changes that coursed through the land. When he thumbed through his old notebooks decades later, he tried to "find salvation." Watters believed the civil rights movement extended that promise to all whites, whether they knew it at the time or not.[12]

During his tenure in the White House, Lyndon Johnson attempted to seize on this promise. Native Texan that he was, Johnson tried to achieve not only the legal freedom of African-Americans—but also the liberation of southern whites. In a 1965 radio and television address devoted to the Voting Rights Act, Johnson tackled both the cause of civil rights crusaders and the plight of white southerners. "I also know how difficult it can be to bend long years of habit and custom to grant" blacks their freedom. While Johnson deplored injustice "anywhere in the American mansion," he suggested that space always existed "for understanding toward those who see the old ways crumbling." For white southerners caught in a dying social order and afraid of the impending one, Johnson had these words: "It must come. It is right that it should come. And when it has, you will find that a burden has been lifted from your shoulders too." Johnson continued to explain that segregation was a sort of lie. Although it may have seemed natural to many, Jim Crow was founded on the presumption of black inferiority. That falsity wreaked havoc in whites. "It is not just a question of guilt. . . . It is that men cannot live with a lie and not be stained by it." The president from the Texas Hill Country was saying that when white southerners honestly confronted the unjust past, and began to accept the interracial future, they would relieve themselves of a crushing weight.[13]

TO GROW UP WHITE in the twentieth-century South was in part to become a master of mental tricks. Whites convinced themselves of black inferiority, even in the face of black struggle. "White Southerners necessarily had to learn how to transform other humans into objects having no real connections to themselves," Marshall Frady wrote. From Montgomery to Memphis and beyond, African-Americans made plain their humanity and gave the lie to whites' objectifications. In places like Americus, Georgia, it took time for whites to realize that. After schools integrated in 1970, Frady tracked a "meeting of strangers" in that Southwest Georgia town. Soon Americus High's football team was half white and half black. It acted as a force to bring blacks and whites— players, parents, and fans—together. While sports and other youth activities began to pierce the divisive facades of racial myth, they could also drive the races far apart. When white students organized a festive homecoming dance, their parents included on the invitations: "No blacks admitted. . . . Make sure no blacks see this." The invitations also carried the signature of white student body leader Charles Warren. Racial chaos soon threatened the school. African-Americans led chants in the halls, and promised to quit the football team. Warren made an

impassioned apology in front of the entire school. The ordeal opened
Warren's eyes, and those of many white students. "People just weren't
used to thinking very carefully about something we might do or say
would hurt a black man." The experience of integration changed that.
Some whites started to see the humanity in blacks, and that enabled
them to better embrace the humanity in themselves.[14]

Whites emerged from a metaphorical darkness. Frady wrote, "The
aftermath of the homecoming crisis suggests that this generation of
Southern white is finally and fully encountering in open daylight, even if
under constraint and impressments, the black Southerner." The experience "might at last work a release from the elusive curse of those old
myriad devious reflexes of mind, dullings of spirit and inward brutaliza-
tions which have endured from that primeval slave-system mentality."
Six months after Frady's article appeared in *Life,* in February 1971,
Joseph Cumming came to a similar conclusion in his writings about
school integration in the Deep South. White southerners had come a
long way, Cumming wrote. "There was . . . a certain pride that something had been accomplished, that the South, so long belabored for its
benighted racial attitudes had . . . been liberated of a great burden." As
black students entered white schools, the stains of prejudice began to
leave some white minds and bodies.[15]

Martin Luther King, Jr.'s, unique leadership was instrumental in that
process. Few whites had to examine the missing section of King's "Letter
from Birmingham City Jail" to understand what he offered. Four years
after King's death, *Atlanta Constitution* columnist Hal Gulliver argued
that "King's principal effect on this nation was not as a leader of black
people but as a leader of white people . . . he spoke to the conscience of
white Americans and confronted them with themselves and with the
manifest injustices of racial segregation." African-Americans discovered
many leaders during the civil rights years. While none loomed larger
than King, various eminent figures emerged, all with different styles—
from Thurgood Marshall's leadership in the courtroom to Malcolm X's
evolving vision, Stokely Carmichael's "Black Power," and the Black Panthers' agenda for revolution. In each town and city in the South, and in
many others across the country, black leaders asserted themselves. But
few of them engendered in whites anything other than fear and anger.
King offered whites comfort, even redemption. "Hate is always tragic. It
is as injurious to the hater as it is to the hated. It distorts the personality
and scars the soul." And King offered a way for white southerners to heal

those age-old wounds. Of course, millions of white southerners rejected King's message and plotted against him. But many others found themselves drawn in by King's righteous words, glued to his image on the television set, and beguiled by a prophetic message that crossed the color line and appealed to their better selves.[16]

Atlanta doctor Richard Franco was one of them. Franco found himself deeply moved—and more than a little changed—by King's appeals. "When Martin Luther King came along, that was really dramatic because he spoke to the moral liberation not only of blacks, but the moral liberation of whites," Franco recalled in 2003. White southerners had created "a system in which you denied the value of humans. That put such a burden on you of living in a false world. In a sense, whites were going to be liberated from their own mischief, from their own demons." In King, Franco saw an African-American who spoke directly and eloquently to the white experience—even as he marshaled armies of black protesters. All told, Franco noted that the process of white liberation was messy and difficult. "That burden was relieved," but not willfully ceded. "It wasn't enlightened self-interest" that led whites to see through falsities and free themselves. As Leslie Dunbar had written, white southerners had to lose a battle in order to achieve their own freedom. Franco reflected, "It was . . . the second defeat of the Civil War." Many white southerners believed they had lost their freedom during the days of the first Reconstruction. During the second Reconstruction, they attained freedom of another sort.[17]

After enduring such an experience, one came out on the other end a different person. In a deeply religious region, some southerners began to feel secular rebirths. "Reconstructed southerners are the most attractive people there are," Virginia Durr boasted in 1967. "They know from experience the ease of evil ways, and the difficulty breaking away from them. . . . We emancipated southerners are really prizes!" Durr revisited a thought that Ralph Ellison fixed upon in "The Myth of the Flawed White Southerner." Once a white racist saw the light, Ellison believed, he would take up the side of equality with more passion than any moderate ever could. "The white Southern man who gets converted to the cause," National Urban League head Vernon Jordan said in 1976, "why, he would die for you." The strength behind the conviction remained, but the conviction itself changed—from a belief in segregation to that of equal rights. Joel Williamson, a historian who grew up in South Carolina, administered a slight turn of the screw. To Williamson, all remnants of that previous person—the one who defended segregation—would cease to exist. "In order for an individual white person to let black people go," he wrote in 1984, "the white person, in a sense, had to die, had to cease to be in an important way what he or she had been." One of Williamson's students at the University of North Carolina attested to that very experience. P.M.P. split time in his childhood between Beaulaville, North Carolina, and Alexandria, Virginia. He served in the navy during the 1960s, and came to Chapel Hill for his education in the 1970s. By 1972, P.M.P. realized he had undergone a thorough racial change. He was soon "rejecting the Southern aristocrat type of life." As proof, he had lost both "desire and need" for a black servant. "I feel as a result that I am dying and being reborn into a New type [of] Southerner. I want to be my best self, not just myself, for I know that I have my fears and prejudices of Black people still to some degree." P.M.P. knew that for as long as he lived, he would retain some degree of prejudice. Yet he still felt reborn. A racial transformation did not always have to be self-immolating to be true.[18]

Joseph Cumming agreed that southerners were on the verge of something completely new. They were both excited and weary, Cumming wrote in *Georgia* magazine in 1972, for they could at last begin to shape their minds and hearts and lives as they wished—without prime reference to the issue of race. "I know that now we . . . are free to start a new history." Still, Cumming confessed, "I don't know which way we are likely to go." For an extended moment, white southerners possessed the opportunity to embrace a new world rooted in racial equality. Perhaps it was not likely, but it was possible. Cumming expanded on those ideas in a 1975 column for the *Athens Observer.* "When the South lost the Civil War and then, a hundred years later, lost the civil rights battles in Congress, it meant the lifting of a great burden from our heart." There was something new in the land:

> There was a spiritual and psychic dilation; we were free. All possibilities were enlarged, we were ready for an expanded idea of love. We faced—and do face—new problems and larger challenges; but no more do we have to be vexed with the ritual of never calling a black man Mr., never allowing a black woman her choice of seats on the bus, never permitting a black family to stroll through a public park.

The civil rights movement was about breaking down physical and legal barriers, but it also allowed white southerners to reimagine their lives and worlds.[19]

Claims about white liberation possessed an ethereal quality. They were more often tied to lofty speculation about the "psyche" or the "soul" than to practice and reality. Perhaps for this reason, the ideas behind white liberation could compel and enchant. When white southerners said they had been freed, they were talking about an experience that was intensely personal and subjective. It seemed more the stuff of poetry than history. Quite a few white southerners claimed they had been liberated, and it was not difficult to see why. But those who attested to emancipation seemed to be a small minority, and the power of their claims stemmed in part from the grandeur of their language. In the end, the concept of liberation commanded the most strength as a metaphor. It was almost impossible to generalize or to verify. Whether a white southerner experienced freedom was partly up to him—a matter that concerned his own individual past, his mind, and his heart. For these reasons, it became easy for writers to get carried away with the idea of "white liberation." Yet that idea had some undeniable basis in reality, even as its exalted vernacular often spun far away from that root. At bottom it was a claim about how deeply lives and attitudes had changed—or, at the very least, how the post–civil rights South carried the potential for those changes. None could deny that white children who grew up in the 1970s were raised in a freer region than the land of their parents. These white children were not required by law to discriminate. If some chose to call that "liberation," it was difficult to argue with them. And if their claims about "liberation" sometimes seemed too divorced from the world of actions and practices, those lofty ideas could also come back down to earth.

Richardson Preyer, a North Carolina member of the House of Representatives, entered that case for white liberation into the *Congressional Record.* Concerned about the racial strife and tension that hampered American cities—North and South—in the late 1960s and early 1970s, Preyer gained insight into such problems when he read a report by the Greensboro Chamber of Commerce. With candor and sensitivity, the chamber confronted the issue of race relations. Its report, entitled "Something's Got to Give," examined "twelve attitudes which affect the community's ability to solve its human relations problems," Preyer explained to the House on May 27, 1970. It delved into the rise and fall of Jim Crow, and rigorously analyzed the relationship between custom and law, ways of life and southern institutions. It showed how Jim Crow laws touched every aspect of life for both whites and blacks—from jobs, education, and housing to religious practices, voting rights, and even nutrition. The legal system of Jim Crow "confined both black and white within the geographic, psychological, social and economic walls of racial ghettos," the report argued. "Once confined behind such walls it was possible to conceal the black man's problems, to desensitize whites to his presence and his needs, to permit the larger community to shape the dimensions of his destiny, to say 'we have no racial problems—our niggers are happy.' " Institutional walls between the races buttressed prejudices and stereotypes as they trapped whites and blacks in their own worlds. "Through a successful program to confine, conceal and control the black, the larger community also created a life style, a pattern of living, a system of relationships which structured a social pattern controlling the personal lives of blacks and whites." Racial oppression not only permeated voting booths and classrooms, but based an entire southern way of life upon a stifling of blacks' livelihood. This truth formed the backbone of the white social fabric as much as the black. Although whites possessed more everyday freedom than their African-American counterparts, that freedom was nonetheless rooted in a basic confinement and isolation.[20]

Any change in this social structure, the Greensboro Chamber of Commerce argued, meant a change in day-to-day life for whites. "If the community is to deal with cultural racism, each and every person, white and black, must accept fundamental changes in the ways his life is organized. This will produce change in his private clubs, his churches, his schools, his neighborhood and his home." Here were the changes that seeped into the lives of many white southerners during the age of civil rights. And the report contended that these changes had the capacity to free whites.[21]

This argument made particular sense in reference to the long sweep of southern history. Whites may have been miffed when they had to accept seats near the back of the bus—they might have called that a sort of oppression, rather than an emancipation. But the Greensboro Chamber of Commerce maintained that those acts comprised the true marks of a free society:

> The framers of the Jim Crow system . . . failed to anticipate one
> fatal flaw in the system. While it succeeded in limiting the freedom of the black man, it also succeeded in limiting the freedom of

the white man. As the black man was forced to the back of the bus, the white man was forced to the front. As the black man was forced to the back door of the restaurant, the white man was forced to the front door. As the black man was forced to create and support his "freedom churches," the white man was forced to maintain his closed church.

Through the civil rights years, the southern bus persisted as a powerful symbol of freedom and oppression. The lines that demarcated white and black also separated front from back. The racial pecking order was literal and physical, and seats on the bus defined its details. After Jim Crow fell, whites sometimes found themselves at the back of the bus, in the spaces that had for years constituted degradation. Like front seats on buses, all of the facilities into which Jim Crow "forced" whites were normally cleaner, better kept, and of a higher quality. But just because white accommodations were better than black ones, they did not necessarily make whites any "freer." In their own way, these first-class white facilities were also destructive. "The black ghetto, when subtracted from the total community, leaves an afflicted remainder—the white ghetto." The white "ghetto" may have in fact been a suburb or a beautiful tree-lined street. Jim Crow made it possible for white life to be simultaneously comfortable and oppressive. The Greensboro Chamber of Commerce came to hope for the "liberation of white and black together from this heritage of bondage." As Jim Crow fell, whites moved to the back of the bus and gained a modicum of freedom.[22]

2

WHILE THE CIVIL RIGHTS REVOLUTION did not bring a full-fledged military battle, it created new social and political orders that one might expect only a military conflict to produce. Southerners struggled to emerge from their past, to put aside the years of conflict and the history of violence. The remnants of the tattered old order exposed a civil society and a way of life plunged into flux. If the South did not look precisely like other war-torn nations, or like Dixie after the Civil War, it faced similar questions. When the struggles subsided, white southerners wondered how to live with African-Americans. Whites finally had to face the people against whom their ancestors had discriminated, at times had even enslaved or lynched. Now these people had risen up; their demands and achievements thoroughly affected the texture of white life. "After the revolution came the difficult part," New Orleans attorney Anthony Dunbar wrote. "It is the reconciliation of people who in the past have disliked even the way the other smelled." The question of what to do next—of how to amble toward a tolerable future while the violent past still festered—lurked beneath southern life.[23]

Some whites suggested that the nonviolent thrust of the civil rights movement allowed them a historic chance at reconciliation. If white liberation followed black struggle, then reconciliation was something the races would have to achieve together. Individuals in many other lands ravaged by strife, conflict, and war often held out this hope—a hope for closure, perhaps, for the end of guilt and hate and shame, and the beginning of something new. Historian and native southerner David Goldfield observed, "The manner in which blacks conducted the movement—as a moral, religious crusade rather than as a war of retribution and vindication—offered the promise of reconciliation." Because the civil rights movement often emphasized the healing power of love, it left open the prospect of an interracial communion in the years to come.[24]

That hope for reconciliation, while grounded in substance, conflicted with various realities. During the 1970s, Reverend Will Campbell found such clashing evidence in an Alabama tavern. The manager admitted that his business had no choice except to serve African-Americans. "But we break every glass they drink out of. There ain't no law against that." Campbell noted that legal equality meant little if it was practiced as such. "It's sure not reconciliation." Campbell began to sour on liberal visions, those that said all southerners were free to become their best selves. Dreams of racial reconciliation failed to jibe with the South that Campbell knew.[25]

The irony was that Campbell himself had felt liberated by the civil rights movement. Yet he knew that his individual experience could not ground a region-wide transformation. This fact highlighted the subjective nature of the "liberation" experience. Some believed the onset of the 1970s signaled the terminus of the civil rights movement, but Campbell suggested that the struggle was still beginning. Whites were just starting to grapple, and were finally free to wrestle, with all that had occurred. "You gave me my freedom," Campbell told a black minister and friend. "I'm sorry I couldn't do more to give you yours. . . . I know I am more free than when it began. . . . The civil rights movement may be over for black people. It is far from over for whites." Because many changes in southern life were lasting, the civil rights movement endured. Yet Campbell had less hopeful reasons for believing that the struggle persisted. By the 1970s and 1980s, many white southerners had not yet confronted, and had hardly accepted, those racial changes. The struggle for racial change would continue, for many were still not free.[26]

In this vein, some observers wondered whether reconciliation was a reasonable goal to expect of a society or a people, in any circumstance—especially when it came to race in America. In 1965, Mississippi author Walker Percy wrote, "Mississippi is even now beginning to feel its way toward what might be called the American settlement of the racial issue." That settlement had little to do with reconciliation or liberation. It was better represented by an "ambiguous state of affairs which is less a solution than a more or less tolerable impasse." Impasses, rather than reconciliation, defined the limits of some whites' hopes. "Southerners of goodwill have persisted in the illusion that racial animus is a remnant of the era of white supremacy," wrote southern historian J. Mills Thornton, "that will slowly give way to harmony if the various sources of tension can be removed." Yet by the late twentieth century, racial frictions seemed a constitutive part of the society. Joseph Cumming harbored a similar skepticism about southerners' abilities to effect meaningful racial reconciliation. "I would like to believe this version of the vision but I cannot," he wrote in 1971. "The South I know just isn't equipped for existential voyages." For some whites who observed the South of the 1970s, racial tension hovered as a fact of life and harmony remained a naive goal.[27]

Other southern thinkers shared a specific hope about race relations. Blacks and whites had always forged close relationships in the South, they claimed. The problem was that friendship and intimacy came without equality, and fondness was distorted when wrapped in discrimination. Many whites hoped that once black equality removed that layer of discrimination, only the familiarity would be left. On those twin pillars of friendship and equality, southerners could build an interracial world.

James McBride Dabbs, the "squire" of Rip Raps plantation in South Carolina, best articulated that hope. In an interview during the late 1960s, Dabbs insisted that white southerners loved African-Americans; he asserted with equal force that love remained empty without justice. The civil rights movement could supply the missing piece of the equation, he believed. Racial equality could make love meaningful again, and peel away the discrimination from every interaction. Dabbs added that this could never occur until white southerners came to grips with their past. He argued that whites needed to confront the legacy of slavery, the Civil War, and Jim Crow before they could meet blacks on genuine terms of equality. "Let us admit it; the South has done great wrong. More has happened to the South than to any other region in the nation. We've had more history. . . . It's been too rich for many of us, we couldn't take it." Dabbs termed this a perpetual state of "historical indigestion," an inability among southerners to honestly tackle the vicissitudes of their past. Dabbs argued that southerners had witnessed more trauma, and more history, than other Americans. Black southerners, who experienced "two centuries of slavery, one century of second class citizenship, and now the beginning of true citizenship," qualified as the nation's most mature people. African-Americans suffered and persisted, reflected and struggled. Through it all, they gained a "tragic sense of life." If whites wanted to grow as people, and southern states as societies, they would also have to face their history. Future growth, Dabbs believed, depended upon southerners' capacities to reckon with a rich past. As the years unfolded into the 1970s, it was questionable whether any of Dabbs's hopes would be realized. The South did not look like a land of racial harmony, nor a testing ground for reconciliation. Neither did any other part of America. One explanation for that inability to reconcile pulsed through the words of James McBride Dabbs. While some white southerners confronted and accepted the pain of their region's racial past, many more preferred to forget.[28]

White southerners tried their best to ignore the civil rights movement while it occurred, and just as many attempted to disregard it afterward. During the civil rights years, local leaders—from newspaper editors in Albany, Georgia, to the mayor of New Orleans—counseled white citizens to proceed as though nothing unusual had happened. The *Albany Herald* mocked Martin Luther King, Jr.'s, claim that he would turn the city "upside down," while Chep Morrison boasted about "just how little is going on." Both statements were made amid pitched battles over black civil rights. Although city leaders tried to ignore efforts for racial equality, newspapers in New Orleans and Albany carried front-page stories about those events. Yet other southern newspapers did not dignify the civil rights movement with press coverage. John Carroll was an editor of the Lexington, Kentucky, *Herald-Leader* from the late 1970s until 1991. A running joke in the newsroom had it that the *Herald-Leader* ought to print a "clarification": "It has come to our attention that *The Herald* neglected to cover the civil rights movement. We regret the omission." That the newspaper failed to cover the civil rights movement did not make it unique. Like many other southern newspapers at the time, it effectively belittled—and missed the chance to chronicle—the unfolding revolution. As Hodding Carter III reflected, "A revolution was going on, and ignoring it was pretending it was a few flecks of foam on top of the waves." For whites, ignorance was a far easier thing than openness.[29]

In the civil rights years, certain southern towns became infamous for the racial violence perpetrated on their soil—Philadelphia and Money, Mississippi; Birmingham, Alabama; and many more. Such locales, where civil rights ferment had disappeared from the surface of life like so many bad dreams, awakened from their racial slumbers at the turn of the twenty-first century. A new generation of southern prosecutors, wielding new evidence, launched a host of investigations into some of the civil rights era's crimes. These prosecutors and their explorations would inaugurate a sort of regional redemption. "Evidence of a 'New South'—a term I never liked—was everywhere," wrote *Boston Globe* reporter and Mississippi native Curtis Wilkie, "but the old, conflicted South still existed." In this land caught between continuity and change, "I found a characteristic that had been missing in my days at the *Clarksdale Press Register:* a desire for reconciliation." At long last, some white southerners sought a rendezvous with justice. "The effort to track down and convict the men responsible for the civil rights murders had become a ritual of atonement and redemption, an exercise almost religious in its nature. The sins of a segregated society could not be swept away in a single swoop, but it seemed clear to me that the people of my home state were committed to justice." The white South could revisit and extirpate its collective sins and move toward reconciliation.[30]

In 1967, eighteen Mississippi men were tried in the notorious slayings of James Chaney, Mickey Schwerner, and Andrew Goodman. Seven of them were convicted—on federal civil rights violations rather than murder charges. By 1973, all seven men had been released. In Neshoba County and the town of Philadelphia, the murders remained an open wound. Florence Mars and her friends felt freed when the men were convicted, but for many other local residents, no sense of liberation ensued. Mars described the community's initial reaction as a "mass nervous breakdown." Into the 1980s and 1990s, blacks pressed for a reexamination of the case—or at least a historical monument to recognize the deaths. Few local whites supported either of those ideas. During the

1995 campaign for governor, the legacy of the crime reared its head. In 1989, Democrat Dick Molpus, former Mississippi secretary of state, had offered an apology to the families of Goodman, Chaney, and Schwerner. In the governor's race six years later, that remark cost Molpus precious political capital among Mississippi whites. When the Neshoba County Fair hosted a gubernatorial debate, Republican incumbent Kirk Fordice raised the specter of the 1964 murders and Molpus's 1989 statement. "I don't think we need to keep running this state by 'Mississippi Burning,' apologizing for what happened 30 years ago." Fordice won the election, and even carried Neshoba County—Molpus's backyard.[31]

James Prince, the publisher of the *Neshoba Democrat*, likened how locals viewed the 1964 incident to the way they might regard a terrible car crash. "I think that people are still in shock, and bringing up the details is too painful." Prince pointed out that such shock produced a dissonance between words and actions. "Everyone says they want to move on, but we can't move on until we acknowledge what happened." In the spring of 2004, white southerners still seemed bedeviled by the problem of "historical indigestion." Seventy-one-year-old Stanley Dearman, the former editor of the *Neshoba Democrat*, noted that the murders left indelible marks. Try as Philadelphia residents might to forget about the incident, those exercises were destined to fail. "I can say without exaggeration that in 40 years, not a single day has gone by that I don't think about those boys. . . . It's just something you can't wash off. People may not want to talk about it but it will never go away. The thing won't let us forget." As fifty-year-old Linda Jenkins, owner of Carousel Gifts, Pools, and Spa, remarked, "It's part of history and we can't sweep it under the rug. . . . But we have to move on. . . . The less said about it the better." Myra Johnson, a seventy-nine-year-old drugstore clerk, believed that an emphasis on that awful episode would only invite more pain. "I'm sorry it happened but I can't do anything about it . . . we should be more forgiving instead of bringing it up every year." For Jenkins and Johnson, forgiveness and acknowledgment of the past also meant "moving on" and not "bringing it up every year." Many years after the civil rights movement, white southerners made a concerted effort to forget the very past that continued to define them.[32]

During the 1960s, Jackson's *Clarion-Ledger* led the opposition to Freedom Summer volunteers and other "outside agitators." The newspaper helped inflame local sentiment against civil rights workers like Chaney, Schwerner, and Goodman. Decades later, the same paper agitated for justice in that case. *Clarion-Ledger* reporters and editors would not let the story die, and in the 1990s, the paper published a series of articles about the crime and its perpetrators. Mississippi attorney general Mike Moore began reinvestigating the case in 1999, and his successor—Jim Hood—formally reopened it in December 2004. On January 7, 2005, Neshoba County district attorney Mark Duncan charged a local man in the murders. A lifelong Neshoba resident, Duncan was only four years old when the crime bathed his county in infamy. After the arraignment, Duncan insisted that he did not take action just to heal Philadelphia's wounds. "But . . . if that's what it does, I'm all for it."[33]

Edgar Ray Killen stood accused of the 1964 murders. The seventy-nine-year-old was a preacher at a small local church; he owned a sawmill business and a twenty-acre farm in the neighboring town of Union. Killen lived in a ranch house, and exhibited a tablet of the Ten Commandments in his front yard. He also served as a Kleagle in the Ku Klux Klan during the 1960s. Prosecutors alleged that Killen rounded up a gang to kill the three civil rights workers. When seven others were convicted of civil rights violations in 1967, Killen escaped punishment because the all-white jury could not reach an agreement. The only hold-out said she could never convict a preacher. Killen never displayed any sorrow for the murdered men. In a 1999 interview, he referred to Chaney, Schwerner, and Goodman as communists. "I'm sorry they got themselves killed. But I can't show remorse for something I didn't do." In a separate interview with the *Clarion-Ledger* that same year, Killen cited the Bible's support for racial separation—while he also mentioned his close black friends. "I have some very good black friends. . . . I regret to say that there are not too many of them that I trust." In that interview, Killen denied any affiliation with the Klan and lauded the shooting of Martin Luther King.[34]

This rekindling of past horrors dredged up different emotions in local whites. After the arraignment, a bomb threat forced the courthouse to evacuate. Killen's brother knocked down a cameraman. "Get all of your shots now," J. D. Killen said. "We're going to make sure you're not around for the funeral. My brother's innocent." Scenes like these recalled the charged energy of the 1960s—an age that smacked of distant memories at some times, and at others seemed like current events. Billy Wayne Posey, one of the men convicted in 1967, was now subpoenaed to testify before the grand jury. "After 40 years to come back and do something like this is ridiculous, like a nightmare." Posey wished the past could disappear. A thirty-year-old barber (who trimmed Killen's hair before the trial) worried that the revival of the case would exert a negative influence. "The South already has a bad reputation. This isn't going to help us live it down." Others were not so sure. Joe Mulholland, a sixty-eight-year-old lawyer, hoped that a resolution in this case would complete the white South's racial transformation. "We've changed since then . . . I just hope there's some closure and that we can move on." Justice would have to occur before white Mississippians could overcome their "historical indigestion," and truly move forward. "You've got to open the wound and clean it before it can heal," James Prince reflected. "It's as if we've had this open gash on the arm for 40 years and have done nothing but put a bandage on it." Billy Wayne Posey's nightmare was James Prince's elixir. The two contrasting reactions epitomized the conflict that "atonement cases" produced across the region, when they reopened the wounds of the southern past.[35]

The decade from the mid-1990s to 2005 witnessed several such trials. Since 1989, southern states have reexamined twenty-three civil rights murders. Among the more notorious cases, in 1994 a Mississippi jury convicted Byron de la Beckwith of Medgar Evers's murder; four years later, former KKK imperial wizard Sam Bowers was convicted of murdering Vernon Dahmer; a Birmingham jury convicted Thomas E. Blanton, Jr., and Bobby Frank Cherry, in 2001 and 2002, of the 16th Street Church bombing that killed four girls; in 2003, Ernest Avants was convicted of Ben Chester White's 1966 murder near Natchez. Numerous other cases have been reopened, from Mississippi to South Carolina and Florida. In 2000, Georgia governor Roy Barnes ordered a full reexamination of the 1946 lynchings in Monroe. The original FBI report named fifty-five suspects, and at least two survive. District Attorney Ken Wynne promised no action without new evidence. In search of that same type of evidence, federal authorities exhumed Emmett Till's body on June 1, 2005. Fifty years after Till's death, events began to create a full circle. The mangled corpse of a young Chicago boy had once ignited the struggles of an era. Decades later, that same corpse symbolized a nation's effort to grapple with the conflicted legacy of an age.[36]

Yet the perpetrators of the most infamous civil rights crime roamed free in 2005. Ironically, the words of Sam Bowers helped to fuel the prosecution's case. In a 1999 interview with the *Clarion-Ledger*, Bowers boasted that the ringleader of the Neshoba murders had escaped punishment. Six years later, the state of Mississippi and Neshoba County presented new evidence against the remaining defendants from the 1967 case. The grand jury indicted one man for murder—Killen. Suddenly, white Mississippians who had fought for years to bury the pain of the past would have to relive it. As Philadelphia residents alternately anticipated and dreaded Killen's trial, the old crime slowly began to dominate conversation.

The *Clarion-Ledger* immediately applauded Killen's indictment as "a reckoning of blood and justice that is long overdue." Some Philadelphia residents, like the newspaper editors, entertained hopes that the trial would cleanse the hurt of a generation. "I think it's about time," sixty-one-year-old Harmon O'Neal, a former worker for the state Department of Transportation, said in January 2005. "We were all ready for this to happen. I think it will be a cleansing, a healing for all of us." Other locals agreed. Steve Wilkerson, the fifty-two-year-old owner of Steve's on the Square, remarked, "We've all had to carry that around for a long, long time, and it's time to deal with it." Such sentiments were not unanimous, but they did seem to reflect the majority view. While other residents counseled their neighbors to "let it go," or "stop living in the past," the *Clarion-Ledger* argued that even this rhetoric cloaked a deep and unacknowledged pain. "That response has only masked a feeling of collective guilt so grave that righting it seemed an impossible task," the newspaper editorialized on January 23. "The result has been a stalemated mix of doubt, shame, guilt, not fading from memory, but digging deeper, still rending race relations—an old wrong, growing older, that would not go away, with no clear way to right it." So many sentiments dwelled together inside white Mississippians. For those who had lived through the violent rule of white supremacy in the Magnolia State, the doubt and resentment had gnawed for decades. Now the 2005 trial brought a host of feelings that community residents confronted—or evaded—in various ways.[37]

When Killen sustained a work-related injury, it delayed the trial, and gave Mississippians time to reflect. *Clarion-Ledger* columnist Orley Hood stepped back and took stock. "Where does that leave us, you and me, Mississippians in 2005, inheritors of this unwelcome legacy of moral cowardice and government depravity?" Hood posed the question of the civil rights murders' relevance in the twenty-first century. "What sort of baggage do we carry from Emmett Till, Vernon Dahmer, Medgar Evers,

Chaney-Schwerner-Goodman and countless other innocents targeted by our elected officials and their minions in—God forbid—our name?" As the trial loomed, white Mississippians debated those questions. Some glimpsed opportunities to address the past; others feared its ghosts. "The thing that bothers me most," Steve Wilkerson confessed, "is when people say, 'Why do y'all want to bring that up?' " Many locals must have caused Wilkerson considerable discomfort. Hugh Thomasson, a businessman, termed the victims "outside troublemakers" in a letter to the *Neshoba Democrat*. "The media has profited for four decades by smearing Neshoba County and Mississippi. I ask, 'When is enough enough?' " In interviews conducted by that same vilified media, many Philadelphia residents—like hairdresser Cindy Young—echoed the plea to "stop living in the past." And Thomasson was not the only one who revived the contentious controversy about "outsiders." At one point during the trial, Mark Duncan beseeched the jurors, "Tell me you'll treat them like they were from here and were our neighbors." When the trial finally began, it represented many things to many people. For some, it brought unwelcome reminders of a trying time—the national press, "outsiders," an exacting revisiting of the county's most traumatic event. For others, it carried the hope of resolution, catharsis, and even justice. So much was riding on Killen's trial; it finally commenced on June 15, 2005—almost forty-one years behind schedule.[38]

Reminders of the past loomed too large for anyone to miss. Journalists descended on Philadelphia, a few stray Klansmen protested near the courthouse, and mothers and widows of the deceased—Carolyn Goodman, Fannie Lee Chaney, and Rita Schwerner Bender—appeared in the town where their relatives' lives had been taken. The prosecution employed as evidence testimony delivered in the 1967 federal trial. Because many former witnesses had long since passed away, stand-ins peered at scripts and read their words into the record. The courtroom drama enveloped the town of 7,300, in which only a few degrees separated most residents. Edgar Ray Killen had himself previously presided at the funerals of Judge Marcus Gordon's parents. After the prosecution rested its case on June 18, rumors began to circulate that the jury was split. Many citizens worried about the fallout that would ensue if Killen were somehow acquitted. But the racially mixed jury (nine whites and three African-Americans) soon returned with a verdict. Their decision came on June 21, the exact date on which Schwerner, Chaney, and Goodman had met their deaths. The jury found Killen guilty of three counts of manslaughter, but not murder. Each offense carried a maximum of twenty years in prison.

Many Mississippians breathed a sigh of relief. Justice seemed to have prevailed, and the demons of their past were on their way to being exorcised. Still, debate coursed through the town and the local newspapers. Some openly wondered whether it would serve any purpose to lock up an infirm elderly man. "There are no benefits to putting him in jail," volunteered sixty-four-year-old Jackson resident Henry Rosenthal. "They should let the man alone," agreed thirty-nine-year-old Ben Smith, of Forest, Mississippi. "It happened 41 years ago," said Pearl resident Sheila Shaw, who was three years old in 1964. "He's 80 years old. Let dead dogs lie." In some pockets of the state, a few unreconstructed white southerners still harbored racial resentments they had acquired in the days of Jim Crow. The Killen case offered them a chance to vent. Brandon, Mississippi, resident Constance McDowell wrote a letter to the *Clarion-Ledger* in which she excoriated all the old villains: "The 'Philadelphia three' and Emmett Till were long past and forgotten until *The Clarion-Ledger* and other left-wing media . . . decided to go digging around in ancient histories in the hopes of committing more 'legal lynching' against old, helpless and probably innocent victims of vicious persecution like Byron de la Beckwith, Ernest Avants and others." In at least one mind, the bogeymen of southern history still lived. McDowell averred that she believed racial separation was ordained by God. Most outrageously, she referred to the cases against Beckwith, Avants, and now Killen as "legal lynchings." Equal justice, McDowell protested, did not apply to "defenders of the Southern way of life"—those who "fought outside revolutionaries 'fire with fire' in the 1950s and 1960s." She railed against the "War of Northern Aggression" and bemoaned the destruction of Western civilization. "You believe in 'collective guilt,'" she chided the *Clarion-Ledger*, "and want every loyal white in Mississippi to publicly recant and apologize for believing in racial segregation and white rule." McDowell offered no such apologies. By 2005, however, the vehemence of McDowell's views placed her in a minority—albeit a still highly visible one. C. J. Vance of Greenville lamented, "After reading some of the comments in . . . *The Clarion Ledger,* I see many Mississippians haven't changed much."[39]

Yet the verdict gratified many in the Magnolia State, and scores of residents applauded the dispensing of justice. "I think he should pay for what he did," suggested twenty-one-year-old Rankin County resident

Abby Philley. "I think [any others connected with the killings] should be brought to trial." Angela London of Jackson agreed. "He got what he deserved. You're never too old for justice to be served." In the ensuing dialogue, many argued that Killen should have received a murder conviction. For them, Judge Gordon's sentencing was a tonic. Gordon meted out the law's harshest sentence, handing Killen a total of sixty years in prison, twenty years for each crime. This ensured that Killen would join Sam Bowers in state prison. The state that civil rights advocates once termed the "Closed Society," and "the middle of the iceberg" that was white supremacy, finally sanctioned an official thaw.[40]

Although Americans had traded the overt discrimination of the Jim Crow years for a more ambiguous future, the past had a knack of reappearing. Sometimes the remnants of history caught southerners unawares; at other times, the past was thrust purposefully to the surface. Ronald Reagan chose to launch his 1980 presidential campaign in Philadelphia, Mississippi, with full knowledge of Neshoba County's historical symbolism. Reagan reached out to white southerners, as Richard Nixon had in 1968 and 1972. While Nixon appealed to "law and order," Reagan gave a speech in Philadelphia about states' rights. By the twenty-first century, the South was again "solid" in presidential elections—for the Republicans. Republican power in Dixie originated during the upheaval of the civil rights era. Yet in the thirty-six years between Nixon's "Southern Strategy" and George W. Bush's back-to-back sweeps of the South, a national consensus came to regard Jim Crow as an unseemly blight. Martin Luther King became a celebrated, if sanitized, American hero, and "diversity" a widely sought goal. In such a climate, those who came of age in the segregated South—or those who courted its voters—began to tiptoe around history. The southern past admitted of an increasing fragility. And not everyone handled it with delicacy.

Trent Lott, a native of Carroll County, Mississippi, who later rose to the top spot in the U.S. Senate, discovered firsthand the power and persistence of that past. Lott's father was a sharecropper who moved the family to the Gulf Coast town of Pascagoula when he accepted a job at Ingalls shipyard. Trent Lott's political ambitions were apparent by high school. He attended college at Ole Miss, where he became president of Sigma Nu fraternity. As a cheerleader, Lott developed a reputation for waving the Confederate battle flag (the school's emblem) on the football field during games. In the autumn of Lott's senior year, James Meredith integrated the university. A day after Governor Ross Barnett delivered a defiant speech on the football field, a bloody riot ensued. Lott tried to foster peace, and ordered all of the Sigma Nu brothers away from the riot. While Lott distanced himself from violence, he had done his part to uphold segregation. A year before, he had helped lead a region-wide effort to keep blacks out of Sigma Nu. Tom Johnson, who would go on to become president of Cable News Network, was a Sigma Nu member at the University of Georgia. While Johnson also voted to ban blacks from Sigma Nu, he soon underwent a "huge awakening" when violence followed on the heels of integration in Georgia. Lott experienced no such racial awakening.[41]

Lott finished law school at Ole Miss, then departed for Washington in 1968. He became a top aide to William Colmer, the powerful Democratic congressman from Pascagoula. When Colmer retired in 1972, he supported Lott in his bid for the seat. In a surprising and shrewd move, Lott ran as a Republican. Lott understood the political tide sweeping the South, and he swam with it. As Nixon carried the South in a landslide, Lott won election easily. Some of Lott's actions in the House bore the stamp of his past. In 1978, he led an attempt to posthumously restore Jefferson Davis's American citizenship. Five years later, he voted against a holiday for Martin Luther King, explaining his action by saying, "We have not done it for a lot of other people that were more deserving." Lott averred that in the 1984 Republican platform, "the spirit of Jefferson Davis lives." While he became an intelligent and increasingly powerful politician, Lott never addressed issues about his region's racial past. Nobody who knew Lott accused him of racism or prejudice; he possessed something much more subtle, and somehow nearly as insidious. While Lott had nothing against African-Americans personally, he never grappled with an important fact: the southern past that he celebrated and often invoked was rooted in racial discrimination. If some white southerners attested to liberation or racial conversions, and others buried the past or attempted to evade it, Lott did neither. He made his way in the new racial order and ascended in national politics, but displayed an uncritical attitude toward the conflict and inequality that shaped his own history.[42]

Lott won election to the Senate, and later became its majority leader. He earned a reputation as a disciplined politician and successful party leader. But Lott's past brought him down. In December 2002, speaking at Strom Thurmond's one hundredth birthday party, Lott remarked that if Thurmond had won the presidency in 1948 (on the Dixiecrat platform of segregation), "we wouldn't have had all of these problems." Lott added that he was "proud" Thurmond won Mississippi. Days passed before journalists pounced on the remark, but they eventually did. It came to light that Lott had made similar statements before; this one did not seem to be a mere slip of the tongue. Under fire, Lott issued a public apology on December 13. "Segregation is a stain on our nation's soul," he began. Lott recalled that Mississippians grew up with segregation, but "we worked hard to overcome that and to bring about reconciliation and to work together. I grew up in an environment that condoned policies and views that we now know were wrong and immoral, and I repudiate them. Let me be clear. Segregation and racism are immoral." As his political livelihood hung in the balance, Lott finally confronted the wrongs of segregation. With mention of reconciliation and repudiation, Lott hoped for redemption. He admitted surprise that his remarks produced such a furor. "I mean obviously I had a blind spot." As leading Republicans discussed whether to oust Lott from the Senate leadership, he attempted to make up for lost time and came out for affirmative action. But it was not enough to save his post. With the backing of President George W. Bush, another white southerner—Bill Frist of Tennessee— assumed the Senate's top position.[43]

Trent Lott's ordeal fueled a media frenzy, and suddenly the nation's periodicals were rife with insight about the way Americans—and specifically southerners—dealt with their racial past. The editors of the *New York Times* observed, "Southern white politicians who lived under segregation and the civil rights movement either repress the thought that anything terrible went on in their region or remember it all the time." The editors made a significant distinction. Trent Lott certainly fell into the former category—even if he did not completely repress thoughts about the racial past, he did not give it any public notice either. Senator Robert Byrd, a West Virginia Democrat, was a southern politician of the latter type. Byrd helped to lead the resistance against the 1964 Civil Rights Act, and also had been a member of the Klan. Byrd repeatedly confessed those sins. "This is an albatross around my neck that I will always wear. You will read it in my obituary that I was a member of the K.K.K." Because of the racial origins of southern Republicans' power, the party wore a similar albatross. Yet Byrd fessed up to a past that Republicans preferred to hide. What made Lott "toxic to the Republican fraternity," columnist Frank Rich wrote, "was his careless revelation of its darkest predilections." The Republicans had skeletons in their closet, and Trent Lott rattled them.[44]

Lott's predicament was a classic case of a man unable to outrun his past. Edward Ball, a South Carolina native and the author of *Slaves in the Family,* described Lott as a man who "lost a wrestling match with his Southern past." In the end, the lurking ghosts of slavery, sharecropping, Jim Crow, and civil rights pinned Lott to the mat. "In the South, the past is like a bothersome pest that we try to keep hidden," Ball wrote. "From time to time it likes to crawl out of the muck and into the full sun. Our region's remarkable story—which includes the prolific beasts of slavery and Jim Crow—forms the backdrop of everyday Southern life, from politics to schools, churches to gardening clubs." Ball, like James McBride Dabbs, glimpsed in the southern past a unique resilience. The scars of southern history ran so deep that individuals had to confront their experiences if they ever wished to control them. If one did not face his past, he would remain subject to its sway. And there was no telling when history would decide to bubble to the surface. Trent Lott learned that the hard way. "There are several ways to deal with the vexed legacy of slavery and exploitation that have left America with a caste system, and not just in the South," Ball continued. "One can deny its ubiquitous aftermath and pretend that the easy social command held by white people grows out of a natural authority." Apart from denial, the only other alternative was to deal directly with the discomfort aroused by history. "One can come to grips with it, which is much harder—and which Senator Lott avoided until his deathbed conversion." Lott had been unable to take that step.[45]

The whole process was never as easy, or as natural, as some commentators seem to suggest. The very act of "confronting" one's past is itself fraught with ambiguity. Perhaps this would entail a psychological or spiritual journey. Maybe it would compel inner reflection; it might also require actions and deeds. But the Republican Party, and popular American opinion in the twenty-first century, expected of their politicians much less than that. They only wanted Lott to realize that for one who represented the state of Mississippi and the nation, it was important to acknowledge the injustice of Jim Crow. By 2002, American politics would tolerate no more Dixiecrat apologists. Public figures would not have to become advocates for racial equality in the here and now—only to admit the most obvious wrongs of the past. One could say, with Edward Ball, that "the tragic past keeps coming back." One could also say that some white southerners, Trent Lott apparently among them, never quite absorbed the lessons of the civil rights movement.[46]

In this episode, some observers glimpsed hope for the Republican Party. Trent Lott exposed an ignoble aspect of the party's recent rise to power, and in effect opened that subject for discussion.* "It could be a hangover for them, or it could be cathartic," said Don Fowler, a South Carolina native and former Democratic National Committee chairman. Along with reconciliation, liberation, and salvation, Fowler raised another notion—catharsis—that assumes a prominent place in the dialogue about the post–civil rights South. As the protracted struggles of the civil rights years came to a close, many southerners found themselves in need of a cleansing or release.[47]

In theory and in history, the idea of catharsis was associated with the stage. Tragic dramas could effect emotional purges in their audiences. These notions found some parallels in the history of the American South. The specters of bondage and Jim Crow invested life in the South with a tragic quality. Even defenders of those systems realized they were lamentable. The long lives of slavery and segregation damaged their African-American victims, but also dehumanized white perpetrators. Suffering would persist until all were released from history's burdens. In Aristotle's classic insights, tragic drama contained many components. It involved a gripping plot, depicted scenes of suffering, and inspired pity and fear in its audience. "He who hears the tale told will thrill with horror and melt to pity at what takes place." Few who honestly confronted the arc of southern history could hide their horror at its inhumanity and oppression, nor could they help harboring sympathy and pity for its many victims. In the end, a proper dramatic tragedy effected in its audience a release, a purging of pain, a catharsis.[48]

If southern history contained such tragedy, the civil rights movement was the agent that would bring about a collective catharsis. Some white southerners invoked analogies to ancient Greece to explain their land. "If the Civil War was our 'Iliad,' " Joseph Cumming proposed in 1997, "the Civil Rights struggle was our 'Odyssey,' our epic narrative of how the South, in a struggle with itself, shed the leaden burden of official segre-

---

*In 2005, the Republican National Committee chairman offered an apology for the "Southern Strategy." Ken Mehlman said at the Indiana Black Expo: "Some Republicans gave up on winning the African-American vote, looking the other way or trying to benefit politically from racial polarization. . . . I am here today as the Republican chairman to tell you we were wrong." *New York Times,* July 15, 2005.

gation . . . of how we, black and white, could finally shout 'free at last!' "
Cumming likened the South's journey to a classical epic, in which freedom awaited at the end of the trek. Will Campbell possessed a vision
that drew similar parallels with Greek epics, but his was far less optimistic. While Cumming's play ended in liberation for white southerners, Campbell's vision, true to the tragic story line, ended in darkness.
Campbell believed everyone—black and white alike—was a victim, and
remained such. "What we were dealing with here was a human tragedy.
Everybody is involved in this and at the end of the drama . . . they all
may be lying dead on the stage, but they're all innocent and they're all
guilty." To Campbell, the southern story did not culminate in freedom
for all, but in something more ominous.[49]

While both Campbell and Cumming referenced the dramatic analogy,
neither used the idea of catharsis in its technical sense. In a 1965 article
about Martin Luther King, Jr., historian August Meier made a more
direct connection. Meier showed how King, and the movement he came
to embody, effectively penetrated the conscience of whites. But King
not only unearthed emotion and guilt; he also provided an answer, a
way out, a path toward release. King played upon and exploited whites'
guilt, Meier argued, but also declared his belief in their salvation. King
promised that direct action would win black freedom, just as "it will
purify, cleanse, and heal the sickness in white society. . . . King first
arouses the guilt feelings of whites and then relieves them . . . like a
Greek tragedy, King's performance provides an extraordinary catharsis
for the white listener." This was part of King's genius; he held out hope
for whites. Because of that hope, more whites listened to him—and
were moved by him—than were affected by other civil rights leaders.
King left whites "feeling purified and comfortable." His oratory emboldened white hopes, encouraged whites to accept the black struggle for
equality, and eventually to free themselves. He achieved a "verbal catharsis." With the help of King's words, whites began to purge themselves of
racial sins.[50]

The metaphor of the stage wielded a commanding power. During the
civil rights years, most whites in the South felt themselves trapped
between the extremes of segregationist defiance and black equality.
While few of them welcomed the black freedom struggle, fewer violently resisted. The vast majority only hoped that upheaval would die
down, and that it would not overwhelm their lives. They could do little
to prevent the massive demonstrations and protests, the legal and politi-

cal changes—they could only watch. The drama unfolded not only on television sets, but before their very eyes. That drama occurred in white homes, schools, businesses, at ballot boxes and workplaces, even in minds and hearts. All their world was a stage.

The featured actors were not powerful whites, but the descendants of slaves and the progeny of sharecroppers. Whites comprised the audience. With alternating degrees of shock and confusion, awe and despair, chagrin and elation, whites remained spectators through much of the ordeal. But at various times and in certain places, they were drawn into the middle of the drama. When the struggles died down, as at the end of a dramatic performance, some felt a cathartic release.

Kentucky native Elizabeth Hardwick articulated this kind of vision. She portrayed Selma segregationists as adrift in darkness, scarcely aware that they were awaiting illumination. "So many of these white people are lost to history, waiting for the light to shine on them, waiting for some release from darkness." The civil rights movement offered that release. Hardwick detected this not only in the social changes that the movement produced, but in its very spirit. She thought the civil rights movement could replace stale oppression with vibrant righteousness. Hardwick believed even the staunchest segregationists had no choice but to acknowledge this promise. "The racists . . . see before them something more than voting rights. They sense the elation, the unexpected release." The developing black drama could purify white souls.[51]

Pat Watters confirmed that this actually occurred. Through the civil rights years, Watters himself felt cleansed and healed. Few experiences in Watters's life gripped him with such power and emotion as did the Albany Movement. As a reporter, Watters covered mass meetings, marches, demonstrations, and boycotts. He sat in churches, walked dirt roads, and huddled in crowds. Watters felt transformed by the new energy in his native land. This was particularly poignant on the 1961 day that Watters first heard the song "We Shall Overcome":

> I had not heard the song before, did not catch all the words, but did feel all through me the spirit of it, its force and its meaning. . . . I stood on the shoulder of the road, listening, and out of a lifetime of the way it used to be . . . out of all my life of acquiescence in the evil and *their* acquiescence. . . . Out of all my southern experience, I listened and heard them saying in the song that the way things used to be was no more, was forever ended.

Then came the release for Watters. It had nothing to do with a stage or a performance, and everything to do with his land's racial past. "Knowing all that that meant for them, and for me, I cried. I cried for the first time in many years, cried unabashedly, cried for joy—and hope." For a moment, the South's ugly history dissolved in Pat Watters's tears.[52]

3

WHEN WHITES CLAIMED they had been liberated, they were often discussing something tangible. They were wondering how deeply the South had changed, and how profoundly their lives, attitudes, and institutions had been affected. They asked whether this was a fundamentally new land, with transformed individuals and social structures, or not. Where change occurred, the process was often complex. It crept up unannounced and seeped in through back channels. Throughout the civil rights years, and even after the famous struggles became memory and history, the forces of change and continuity fought each other. Their battleground was everyday southern life, white as well as black.

Differing degrees of change and continuity came to light in the stark contrasts among individual experiences. While a few whites had supported integration all along, many others arrived accidentally at pro-integration positions—positions forged in the heat of momentous events. Though Margaret Conner's role in the 1960 New Orleans school crisis was unique, her reactive embrace of integration was not. Jerry Clower, the renowned humorist, traveled a similar path. Clower grew up on Route 4 in Liberty, Mississippi, and imbibed the traditional views of his southern upbringing. "Racial prejudices just run deeper than any other sin in the world. I know this, because I've experienced this." During the high tide of the civil rights years, Clower's prejudices began to recede. It was not that black protesters awakened inside him some sense of justice or morality, but the vehemence of segregationists repulsed him. "I was a segregationist; the integrationists didn't change me! It was the Ross Barnetts that changed me." Clower recalled James Meredith's attempt to integrate Ole Miss. When Governor Barnett helped rouse white Mississippians to defiance of integration, he moved Clower to acceptance. "The Governor of the state of Mississippi clenching his fists screaming, 'Never, Never!!' . . . This is what changed me. You needn't say the do gooders . . . changed me; it was folks who were so . . . full of racial hatred that changed me." Although Clower began to oppose segregationists, his lifestyle did not undergo a complete overhaul. In 1973, Clower admitted he would be "hurt" if his daughter had married a black man; he also warned her against marrying a Catholic. It showed that an acceptance of integration could not always compel an erosion of one's entire worldview. White southerners like Clower did not embrace racial equality so much as they began to loathe the worst expressions of racial prejudice.[53]

The process of change could move surprisingly fast. Both Clower and Conner altered their positions quickly in response to events. Peter Klopfer witnessed some of this in North Carolina. In 1958, Klopfer moved near Durham, to teach at Duke; it was the first time he had been south of Washington, D.C. The locals possessed attitudes so ingrained that Klopfer deemed them immutable. "While we came to see them as not being vindictive individuals, still we also saw that they had been so thoroughly conditioned that we could not imagine any change occurring in their lifetime. . . . I thought it would take . . . a full generation to change a single individual's attitude, and that would mean several generations before social attitudes altogether would be changed." But Klopfer witnessed an overhaul in a matter of months and years. Soon, he would hear—and come to tell—tales of "the tenant farmers and the boss farmers . . . literally sitting at the table together." By the 1970s, Klopfer saw that many racial attitudes had undergone rapid shifts.[54]

Virginia Durr observed that upheaval from her Montgomery home. A native Alabamian who came to embrace civil rights during the New Deal period, Durr established herself, through her voluminous letters, as one of the white South's keenest social critics. As blood spilled on Selma's bridge, Durr lamented that such horrors made little difference in whites' racial views. On April 19, 1965, she perceived "absolutely no signs in the white community of any change of heart or mind." The Voting Rights Act passed in August of that year, but did little to chip away at white prejudice. "Rather than seeing any lightening of the prejudice," Durr wrote on September 21, "it seems to me it is being strengthened." Alabama blacks registered to vote at a higher rate, but so did whites. The following spring, voters propelled Lurleen Wallace (George's first wife and his political proxy) to victory in the gubernatorial primary. In 1966, the Deep South still seemed frozen in the attitudes of the Jim Crow era. But in the age of civil rights, tumultuous days and months could rapidly melt away customs that had stood for centuries. Less than a year later, Durr pinpointed a profound change that few southern whites could deny.

"I think a big change has come," she wrote on January 17, 1967. "You find it everywhere, which is evident in listening to any private conversation of any white southerner . . . who may be integrationist or most of course, segregationists, but they realize the Negro is not what he used to be." That fact alone, that "the Negro is not what he used to be," forced unavoidable changes to the surface of southern whites' lives.[55]

Change knew no ideological lines. It touched progressives like Virginia Durr and Klansmen like Calvin Craig. Craig joined the Atlanta-area Klan in 1960, citing emotions about "the Negro question, or you might say threat, which we all seen back then." By 1963, Craig had ascended to the position of grand dragon. He launched a drive to register white voters, and tried to involve the Klan in more respectable—or at least more mainstream—activities. This caused an internal rift, and Craig later resigned. His break with the Klan started him on a trajectory that led to a racial conversion. In 1968, Craig ran for sheriff of Fulton County, vowing that if he won the election, he would hire black deputies. Moderates and liberals viewed the newly enlightened Calvin Craig with suspicion, while he also attracted segregationists' scorn. "I feel like a drunk who converted himself and joined the church and hasn't drunk in years—and yet people still say he's a drunk," said Craig. By 1969, his conversion was complete. "I spent a lot of time resisting those changes. I think I was wrong." Craig came to see the error of his ways.[56]

Hastings Wyman chronicled a change neither as thorough as Craig's nor as speedy as those that Klopfer observed. Wyman worked for Strom Thurmond during the 1970s, and shared the senator's historic contempt for civil rights. As Wyman came to know some African-Americans, his beliefs about black inferiority started to fade. "By degrees, the old segregationist became a believer in a free and fair society, though not necessarily a bleeding-heart liberal. My experience is not a rarity for white Southerners." Crucially, Wyman's change came in gradations. Cataclysmic events like the "battle of Ole Miss" did not shake Wyman from his racial views; the process was much slower. "It didn't happen all at once, like being saved at a revival." Almost every white southerner changed in some way as a result of the civil rights movement. The question was how, to what extent, and in what sense. Each individual had a different answer. James McBride Dabbs wrote, in 1969, "There's been a tremendous change . . . from the South that said 'Never!' . . . But much of it has been pragmatic change, an admission that open resistance is hopeless. Change of heart, what religious people call conversion, comes much slower." To say one "changed" did not, by itself, reveal anything profound, for change admitted of many meanings.[57]

Joseph Cumming found racial change both undeniable and hard to detect. "The black man moved suddenly out of the category of being understood and loved with a household-pet kindness and closer to being a human and a citizen, difficult and demanding." Still, it was easy for some whites to ignore and avoid that shift. "On the golf courses, in church, at board meetings and on the . . . motorcycles interweaving themselves in the Shrine parade," Cumming wrote in 1969, "the change of a segregated pattern of life is almost invisible." Although some signs and symbols announced a new South, many facets of life looked the same as before. Whites, in general, "have not suffered any real inconvenience to their daily lives or their inner visions." Twin legacies dwelled side by side. Some whites experienced serious changes of heart and mind. Others devoted themselves to resistance for as long as possible. In 1978, former Hattiesburg segregationist leader M. W. Hamilton averred that white southerners' minds had not undergone much transformation. "The Citizen's Council was basically set up to prevent integration of the schools and the general society. The people of the South didn't want it, and of course still don't want it." Evidence abounded to support Hamilton's view.[58]

Attitudes changed overnight only rarely, and sometimes they never did. Southerners who wrote letters to *Time* in 1976 had their doubts about the extent of change. "The only change I can see in the past 50 years," observed Helen Doyle of Fort Myers, Florida, "is that the Dixiecrats have finally registered as Republicans." At the level of national politics, many channeled the same old beliefs into a different party allegiance. Mary Caperton Bowles Dale, a ninety-two-year-old from Columbia, Tennessee, shared that core skepticism. "The South is changing, but the 'upper crust' has resisted so far. There is more flexibility in its thinking and actions, but down deep little real change." Thirty years after the race riot in Columbia, Dale saw evidence of acquiescence, but not full-fledged transformation.[59]

For anyone who observed white southerners in the aftermath of the civil rights struggle, it was impossible not to see both truths: enormous change and evident continuity. *Newsweek*'s Karl Fleming detected both when he returned to his native South in 1970. Because the landscape looked the same, because whites still held power, because blacks often lived in the same shotgun houses and struggled through the same poverty, "the temptation, coming home, is to say that nothing has changed." But Fleming refused to give himself wholly to that temptation. "Except for the encroachment of a few more factory buildings and a lot more plastic franchise eateries, the South looks just about the way it always has. Yet it has changed and changed profoundly in the decade since the sit-ins and the Freedom Rides." Fleming noted the transformations conferred by courtesy titles, the integration of public accommodations, and voting rights. Through their struggles, African-Americans "have forced white people to recognize their common humanity, if not their claim to real equality. The Deep South used to say *never;* the extent to which it has changed since I left—and the extent to which it has acquiesced in the change—was stunning." As Fleming visited the towns made famous by the civil rights movement, he discovered a white South marked alternately by acceptance, resistance, resignation, and fear of integration.[60]

Cecil Wallace, George's cousin, ran a barbershop in Montgomery. While Wallace resigned himself to the existence of integration, he had a clear idea of where to draw the line. "Us ole Alabama boys don't care about niggers eating in hotels and cafés and such. But they aren't setting down to dinner in our homes yet." Clarence Mitchell, an insurance salesman in Philadelphia, Mississippi, felt similarly—but saw few available options. "If the niggers want to come to white schools, let 'em come. We don't care. We resent this forcing but there's no way to resist. It's like looking down the barrel of a cannon—you can't fight back with a pea shooter." Whites like Cecil Wallace and Clarence Mitchell seemed only slightly concerned with integration of public facilities, although they were not enamored of the idea. Their grudging acceptance was a sign of how little, materially, whites had given up. "The price of peace . . . was pathetically small," Fleming noted. "The ballot, some jobs, desegregation in various public places." While the concessions were sometimes difficult to see, they still left whites feeling embittered. This irony struck Karl Fleming hard. "The white people I saw believe they have given up a lot. One can in fact see the changes in the day-to-day conditions of Negro life as trivial. . . . But to do so would be to forget that even the simplest recognition of human dignity of black people has been a painful concession for whites." Those differing perspectives underscored the divided legacy of the civil rights movement. Depending upon one's point of view, the degree of change could seem either monumental or minuscule.[61]

For years afterward, some white southerners remained unrepentant.

Ross Barnett was a symbol of segregationist intransigence in the civil rights years, and he remained one for decades. Calvin Craig, the former grand dragon of the Ku Klux Klan, admitted he was wrong. Ross Barnett did not. "I didn't make any mistakes," Barnett said in an interview during the 1980s. "I don't think of a thing I'd have done differently. I used the best judgment in everything I did and everything I said." Some of those who joined the mob to "defend" Ole Miss against James Meredith and the federal government agreed. "I didn't want the black guy in there," said one Greenwood native who joined the mob as a freshman. "I would have been happy if they'd have killed every fucking marshal there," he reflected in 2000. "Plus that nigger. I still feel that way." His brother, one year older, concurred. "If I had to go do it over again, I probably would have fought a little harder." For these white Mississippians, there was little promise of conversion, redemption, liberation, reconciliation, or catharsis—only the contested terrain of the past, and embitterment over its legacy. Brodie Crump was a columnist for Hodding Carter's *Delta Democrat-Times*. In 1974, at the age of seventy-six, Crump continued to pine for the Jim Crow past. "Fifty years ago it sort of went back to the old antebellum times. . . . Those were the good old days." They were the days of black oppression and unquestioned white dominance. Crump admitted, "I'm not crazy about these days."[62]

From the Mississippi Delta to the Upper South, tales of continuity were as common as stories of transformation. Clara Lee Sharrard returned to her hometown of Lexington, Virginia, in 1969, when she got married. At that point, blacks and whites still did not patronize the same restaurants or eat at the same tables. When Sharrard's father passed away in 1974, she insisted that one of his African-American co-workers serve as a pallbearer. "The roof is still standing over the funeral home . . . the whole world didn't end with that. . . . So, by '74, things were starting to change. But still, not a lot." Change was coming in fits and starts, although it did not promise any revolution. In the 1980s and 1990s, Sharrard visited her elder relatives in eastern North Carolina. For that generation, old racial attitudes persisted. "As I listened to the older folks, people in their seventies and eighties, attitudes really have not changed," she said in 2003. "They tolerate each other, but no acceptance of African-Americans at all. . . . Even up to this day." Across the South, whites looked back and observed a curious mix of progress and retreat.[63]

Joseph Cumming perceived that same commingling of resistance and change. "Here we are in the South today, 40 years later," he wrote in

1997, "moving along nicely without Jim Crow; whites automatically use courtesy titles. Otherwise, we're not that different from then." Whites and blacks addressed one another differently, with less overt discrimination. Aside from that, Cumming wondered how much had been transformed. Yet he still insisted that a revolution had occurred. It could be seen in whites' experiences during the civil rights years. "Did something happen? Did anybody see it? Who remembers? . . . Yes, something happened. A revolution." That revolution infiltrated many white homes. "As a white Southerner, I experienced the schisms this change wrought among whites, the friendships cleaved in bitter words, generations scowling across their gap of years, family Sunday dinners ruined with chairs slammed back from the table, napkins hurled at the centerpiece." Not even the dinner table was immune from social upheaval.[64]

Scholars argue over the extent of change that the civil rights movement wrought. They debate whether it was lasting or fleeting, whether it stretched to the depths of society or merely scratched its surface, whether it shattered a social structure or only frayed its edges. For many whites, and in many different ways, change was both undeniable and inescapable. Much of it came with a force more powerful than a napkin hurled at the centerpiece. Ralph Ellison famously wrote, "Southern whites cannot walk, talk, sing, conceive of laws or justice, think of sex, love, the family or freedom without responding to the presence of Negroes." During the civil rights years, many whites began to understand exactly what he meant. For parents in New Orleans, restaurateurs in Birmingham, residents of Albany, and local politicians in Eutaw, Ellison's words morphed into reality. African-Americans forced those whites to respond to their presence, confront their demands, choose sides, and recognize uncomfortable truths. In the face of school integration in New Orleans's Ninth Ward, Margaret Conner metamorphosed into an accidental radical. As Albany blacks gathered at churches and raised their voices in song, whites began to see (even when they insisted otherwise) that these were not the deferential African-Americans of myth. In Greene County, Alabama, the changes were stunningly palpable. Ralph Banks, the architect of an effort to maintain white political power, came—in just a few years—to assist the black sheriff's reelection campaign. In 1965, Eugene Johnston garnered support for an all-white private school. A decade later, he brokered interracial compromises and worked under a black boss. In Birmingham, Ollie McClung, Sr., battled integration of his barbecue restaurant all the way to the Supreme Court. After McClung lost the case, he desegregated with remarkable ease. These stories, and many others, testify to the civil rights movement's transformative power.[65]

Participants and observers both introduced a spate of terms that attempted to summarize and package those changes. They hailed white "liberation," "catharsis," or "reconciliation," and touted the unfolding events as the "Second Reconstruction" or the "civil rights movement." All these terms failed to capture the entirety of what occurred in the South during the decades after World War II. Of course, any single phrase must falter under the weight of diverse and complex experiences. It was a time when such experiences overwhelmed words, events swallowed ideas, and a whole society—a way of life previously invested with an aura of immutability—struggled to catch up with the civil rights movement's rapid march. That society contained within it untold differences, and millions of people who encountered the emerging world through the prism of their own past. So much was written about the spell of history and the power of a southern past that would not die. And yet the question finally became, as it will always become, about the future—about what this revolution would yield. The civil rights movement braved enormous resistance and attracted widespread rejection, but it nonetheless built the outlines of a new society. Its impact endured far from the sites of the marches, the tense courthouses, the venerable churches with their spirited mass meetings. Arguments at the dinner table, lessons in interracial classrooms, or interactions between employers and laborers often revealed the depths—and defined the limits—of those changes. Some white southerners embraced the novel aspects of this world; others refused to accept the nascent social order; still more walked gingerly across its threshold.

On his farm outside Chapel Hill, North Carolina, Hugh Wilson described a great transition in racial attitudes. During the 1960s, Wilson helped to drag black protesters out of businesses. By 1974, he had started to see past the distorting mirror of race. Wilson reflected that some of his friends and neighbors "think about themselves as a white person rather than as a person, who happens to be white." Wilson came to see the error of this outlook, and began to envision a world that drew no color lines. In the end, he issued a prophecy that was at once simple and complex: "There will be people again some day."[66]

4

AT SOME POINT, most studies of American race relations in the twentieth century meander ineluctably toward the hefty treatise of a Swedish sociologist. For its encyclopedic range, Gunnar Myrdal's *An American Dilemma,* published in 1944, possesses no rival. Time has not diminished the importance of Myrdal's work. But the written word can lose relevance in the face of the next day's events. Myrdal published his book one year before the end of World War II—a decade prior to the *Brown v. Board of Education* decision, and twenty years before the passage of the Civil Rights Act. "The Negro, as a minority, and a poor and suppressed minority at that, in the final analysis, has had little other strategy open to him than to play on the conflicting values in the white majority group," Myrdal wrote. "That is the situation even today and will remain so in the foreseeable future. In that sense, 'this is a white man's country.' " When the civil rights revolution coalesced, African-Americans asserted their autonomy on the national stage. Yet blacks remained, and still remain, a relatively powerless minority—one that bears a disproportionate burden of the nation's poverty. While America is less a "white man's country" today than ever before, Myrdal's stark formulation carries more truth than many would feel comfortable admitting.[67]

Myrdal grounded his approach in a realism that still resonates. White Americans held the power, Myrdal argued. Any existing "race problem" was something whites would have to resolve. It was a white problem. "Although the Negro problem is a moral issue both to Negroes and to whites in America, we shall in this book have to give *primary* attention to what goes on in the minds of white Americans. . . . Practically all the economic, social, and political power is held by whites. . . . It is thus the white majority group that naturally determines the Negro's 'place.' " While Myrdal subtitled his book "The Negro Problem and Modern Democracy," he frankly stated that the problem resided in the laps of whites. "The Negro's entire life, and, consequently, also his opinions on the Negro problem, are, in the main, to be considered as secondary reactions to more primary pressures from the side of the dominant white majority." Yet as Myrdal wrote the book's conclusion, he sensed that America's recent entry into World War II—and African-Americans' mounting efforts for equality—signaled something important. "There is bound to be a redefinition of the Negro's status in America as a result of this War. . . . The exact nature of this structural change in American society cannot yet be foreseen." While Myrdal continued to insist that "the Negro problem has its existence in the [white] American's mind," he also realized that African-Americans would soon have something to say about their plight.[68]

Although Myrdal could not foresee the precise outlines of the civil rights movement, his work carried its share of prophecy. As the war mounted against foreign fascism, race riots flared at home. "*America can never more regard its Negroes as a patient, submissive minority.* Negroes will continually become less well 'accommodated.' They will organize for defense and offense. They will be more and more vociferous." While Myrdal continued to believe that the "race problem" was rooted in white minds, he began to see that a newly emboldened African-American populace possessed the potential to shake the racial order. In more than sixty years since *An American Dilemma* was published, a bevy of books have focused on the perspective of African-Americans—through their experiences, voices, and points of view. The civil rights movement bears primary responsibility for that correction of the historical record. When African-Americans won rights, they also regained control of their own histories. And they did even more: blacks affected the lives and attitudes of that "dominant white majority" in ways that Myrdal could not have imagined.[69]

Shortly after the Voting Rights Act was passed in the summer of 1965, a group of journalists revived the concept of the "white man's problem." But this time it was African-Americans who did so. In August, *Ebony* devoted a special issue to "The White Problem in America." As Lerone Bennett, Jr., introduced the idea, "The problem of race in America, insofar as that problem is related to packets of melanin in men's skins, is a white problem." Through the American centuries, and across much of the Western world, whites made invidious racial distinctions, and constructed societies based on those notions of difference. As whites clung to discriminatory ideas and practices, their "problem" gained depth and intensity. Whites *invented* the "race problem," Bennett asserted; white fears and frailties continued to fuel its divisive power. And the civil rights movement deepened the "American dilemma." Whites could no longer navigate the "race problem" in their own way, or on their own timetable. African-Americans who demanded equality also forced whites to either accept or resist their pleas. Blacks decided to risk all for freedom, and whites had to respond.[70]

While race was a white problem, John Killens argued, it also became the black man's burden. When whites built "fences" between the races, they in fact trapped themselves. "The hope of America, indeed its sole salvation, is that the Freedom Movement will tear the fences down and bring this country into the family of mankind. This is a part of the black man's burden." If whites produced and intensified the problem, blacks— in their struggle for freedom—could bring about its resolution. Era Bell Thompson reached a similar conclusion in an article entitled "Some of My Best Friends Are White." Thompson's piece was primarily aimed at fellow African-Americans. It counseled them on how to help whites through a period of profound adjustment. "We must stand by while they emerge from the shock of finding that, shorn of his stereotypes, the Negro is a normal, living and breathing American." For some white southerners, this was an eye-opening—even a liberating—realization. For others, it contained a threat.[71]

Ebony concluded with an article by James Baldwin. In the two years since *The Fire Next Time,* Baldwin's views remained consistent. Yet plenty of jarring events occurred in America, and the civil rights movement was beginning to change shape. Watts exploded, the Mississippi Freedom Democratic Party was denied full representation at the 1964 Democratic convention in Atlantic City, John F. Kennedy had been assassinated and Malcolm X after him, and black rights gained the full majesty of the law. "Black Power" was then more a whisper than a cry, and fissures between civil rights leaders and organizations were only starting to appear.

Baldwin participated in the Selma-to-Montgomery march, and what he saw reinforced many of his beliefs. Baldwin witnessed jeering southern whites, that very group about whom his writing had been so prescient. "The great, unadmitted crime is what he has done to himself." As he had in *The Fire Next Time,* in his 1965 article Baldwin emphasized whites' inability to deal honestly with their racial past. "The fact that . . . white Americans, have not yet been able to . . . face their history, to change their lives—hideously menaces this country." Whites' difficulties in overcoming realities of discrimination made the "race problem" in fact a "white problem," Baldwin felt. Most white Americans "are dimly, or vividly, aware that the history they have fed themselves is mainly a lie, but they do not know how to release themselves from it, and they suffer enormously from the resulting personal incoherence." As victims of past evils, blacks grappled with history's pain. But most whites attempted to forget or evade a past in which they—or their leaders or ancestors—were perpetrators.[72]

Baldwin had a lesson for Americans, one he had culled from Henry James's *The Ambassadors:* "Trust life, and it will teach you, in joy and sorrow, all you need to know." Baldwin thought that many whites lacked the capacity, or the depth of feeling, that this trust required. Because many southern whites lived in worlds guided by racial discrimination, fear—and not trust—became their governing concept. But it would have to be otherwise if whites wished to free themselves. "Jazz musicians know this. Those old men and women who waved and sang and wept as we marched in Montgomery know this. White Americans, in the main, do not know this. They are still trapped." White Americans created myths, stereotypes, tropes, and lies to explain and justify the racial status quo. Until whites ceased producing such deceptions, Baldwin argued, they would continue to shape—and to deepen and worsen—America's "race problem."[73]

To emphasize the "white problem" in America, one did not have to downplay the recent achievements or the historic struggles of African-Americans. The August 1965 issue of *Ebony* was a welcome corrective to much of the writing on civil rights. It illuminated neither black protesters nor white violence, but highlighted what had long lurked at the heart of America's racial troubles. From slavery times to the last days of the civil rights movement, the problem was that whites did not respect black freedoms, and refused to elevate African-Americans to the plane of human dignity. Whites kept blacks down, and they justified that oppression by pointing to the disparities it generated. As James Baldwin, Lerone Bennett, Jr., and others wrote, to call race a "white problem" was not to suggest that whites alone could solve it. On the contrary, the civil rights struggle showed that blacks themselves would lead the push toward equality. Yet after African-Americans had done this, after they had risen up, destroyed segregation, gained voting rights, elected black officials, and much more, they still had not conquered the "white problem." That problem manifested itself in every southern town that the civil rights movement gripped—from Albany and Atlanta to Eutaw and Birmingham.

By the middle of the 1970s, epic events no longer hogged headlines. The media introduced the "Sunbelt," the "New South," and the "Americanization of Dixie" as it bade the old South "farewell." The shopping mall and the condominium replaced the mass meeting and the billy club as emblems of the region. "It was as if, since those summers of danger and outrage in the sixties," Marshall Frady wrote in 1974, "a whole century had quietly passed in the deeps of Dixie." Seeking to convey a similar sense, *Time* devoted an entire 1976 issue to "The South Today," and allowed that "integration has a way to go in the South," but the "ugly confrontations of the '50s and '60s, the bombings and Klan revivals, the school riots and statehouse harangues seem as remote as the Dred Scott decision." The nation's attention drifted northward—toward urban riots and busing crises. But some southern communities still had not witnessed widespread school integration or black officeholders. In those areas, the civil rights movement had not yet arrived. By the 1970s, in coastal McIntosh County, Georgia, residents had yet to elect an African-American, place one on a jury, or hire a black person as anything but an unskilled laborer or domestic worker. As Melissa Fay Greene wrote, "In 1971 the epic of the civil rights movement was still a fabulous tale about distant places to the black people of McIntosh." When Americans think back on the 1960s, many refer less to a specific period of time than to a certain feeling—they conjure images of flux, tumult, the spirit of political protest, and either the wonder or the horror of a changing world. In this sense, the 1960s came to different places at different times. In McIntosh County, Georgia, as in Tupelo, Mississippi, that tumultuous time arrived a decade late. In the middle of the 1970s, Tupelo African-Americans took to the streets to protest the shooting of black citizens by two police officers. Thinking they had already made it through the 1960s unscathed, Tupelo whites responded to the demonstrations with shock. "I just don't understand it all," a middle-aged white woman confessed to journalist Chet Fuller. "We've always had good relations with our blacks here in Tupelo. We didn't have all that nasty business they had other places in the sixties." Fuller replied, "You've got it now. . . . You've got the sixties ten years after everybody else." Depending upon time and place, different southern locales experienced the civil rights years in a variety of ways. The "civil rights movement" did not so much as arrive in some places until ten years after the passage of the Voting Rights Act.[74]

THROUGH THE 1970s, many whites were still experiencing their first moments of integration—in schools, in businesses, or on buses. As they reacted and adjusted, whites helped define the contours of this new racial order. They could no longer subjugate blacks by law, but neither did they have to live near them, send their children to schools with them, or shop in stores owned by them. If a new way of life had arrived, it brought manifold dilemmas. Today, the center of Eutaw, Alabama, exhibits the civil rights movement's mixed legacy. The Banks & Co. building still stands sentinel over the town. Just a block away, the refurbished courthouse glitters. That old den of white power now bears a new name: Judge William McKinley Branch Courthouse. Further down the road, the extent of racial change seems more ambiguous. A caricature of a growling tiger announces Eutaw High School, where most black students attend. Warrior Academy, for which an exiting interstate traveler will immediately see signs even in 2005, is tucked further away. Its rolling hills and leafy trees still shelter many white children of Greene County from the harsh truth of a world transformed.

Some signs and symbols heralded a changing South, just as other markers suggested a land still stuck in the racial mores of the past. But the South experienced a radical change in racial demographics. By the 1990s, nothing about race was binary. The old dualities of black and white could no longer withstand an influx of Latinos into southern towns, factories, and fields. Latinos joined many blacks and poor whites at the bottom of the economic ladder; they worked in the most menial jobs. Latinos' arrival on the scene did not soften tensions between blacks and whites. It only made race relations that much more complex.

In Bladen County, North Carolina, the substantial number of Native Americans had always defined race as something beyond black and white. The rapid influx of Mexicans further muddled that picture. Many Mexicans moved into North Carolina shortly after the meatpacking industry relocated there. Before the 1980s, packing plants dotted the Midwest. But they soon came south, attracted by the lack of unions and the promise of cheap labor. The Smithfield Packing Company made Tar Heel, North Carolina, the home of the world's largest pork production plant. In the factory, as in the surrounding towns, four distinct worlds developed—white, black, Latino, and Native American. Whites, and often Native Americans, were employed as supervisors, foremen, or boxers. Mexicans, blacks, and prisoners on work release toiled on the conveyer belts, slaughtered hogs, and sliced them into pieces. While workers on the conveyer belt made about $8 per hour in 2001, jobs on the "killing floor" could pay as much as $12. Those jobs were held mostly by African-Americans. "We built this country and we ain't going to hand them everything," one black man said of the Mexicans. The locker rooms and cafeterias were both self-segregated. Four bars hugged the nearby interstate, one for members of each race. Hostility and confusion characterized interactions between the races. If whites and blacks both disdained the Mexicans in their midst, the feeling was mutual. Mercedes Fernández, a Mexican immigrant, quickly picked up on the dominant racial stereotypes. "Blacks don't want to work. . . . They're lazy. . . . They live in the past. They are angry about slavery, so instead of working, they steal from us." Among blacks, Mexicans, and whites, new racial tensions—and in many ways, more complicated ones—began to brew. "There's a day coming soon where the Mexicans are going to catch hell from the blacks," said African-American Wade Baker, "the way the blacks caught it from the whites." Class tension festered beneath it all, just as it had during the age of civil rights.[75]

A white man named Billy Harwood, who was imprisoned in 1994, started work at Smithfield after his release in 2001. Aghast at the number of Mexicans, Harwood wondered aloud, "What the hell's going on?" By that year, fully one-third of the babies born at the health clinic in neighboring Robeson County were Latino. As Charlie LeDuff reported in the *New York Times,* Harwood "was Rip Van Winkle standing there." He had been locked up for seven years, and missed the birth of a new kind of southern racial order. Suddenly, he found himself thrust into the middle of it. Harwood still believed his skin color conferred on him a certain kind of advantage. While Harwood found the work terrible, he could take solace. "At least I ain't a nigger. I'll find other work soon. I'm a white man." By 2001, the influx of Mexican laborers came to have an ironic effect on African-Americans. As Mexicans squeezed some blacks out of their jobs and generally drove down the price of labor, they seemed to elevate African-Americans within the social order. Frustrated by incessant conversations in Spanish at the factory, one old white man commented, "The tacos are worse than the niggers." This new racial order contained some unmistakable stamps of the old.[76]

The ghosts of the past that haunted the South still came in only two colors. Into the 1980s, 1990s, and the twenty-first century, there were more than enough of those apparitions to go around. In some of the most obvious ways, the racial landscape looked the same as it ever did. Whites were still much wealthier than blacks, still far better educated on the whole, and most of them still lived in heavily white neighborhoods or towns. At some moments, the decades since *Brown v. Board of Education* seemed to have brought few lasting changes. There were always different

Souths, depending on where the beholder fixed his eye. One could witness a changed land, replete with legal equality for all, the dissipation of racial fears, the termination of racial violence, and healthy and integrated polities, economies, businesses, and schools. Just as easily, one might hear a stray epithet slipped into a sentence. More likely, one could glimpse a row of dilapidated all-black houses in the shadows of mansions inhabited by whites, or observe crumbling public schools that teemed with blacks while burgeoning private schools catered to privileged whites. Most business executives still were white; many of the household workers, busboys, and bellhops still were black. White southerners knew that these were not history's accidents, but its cold results.

De facto segregation marked the South; as such, Dixie resembled much of America. If many parts of the nation were beginning to look similar in the post–civil rights era, the region's stark historical distinctions still preserved shreds—and sometimes multitudes—of differences. Dixie's unique dialects persisted, the South had its own brand of weather, its particular cuisine, and southerners still prided themselves on a slower rhythm to life. But that was not all. Many southerners in the 1980s, 1990s, and beyond had lived through the most important social changes in twentieth-century America. It was now undeniable that African-Americans desired continued progress toward economic equality, political power, and social and cultural freedom. But questions still lingered about the nature of white southerners' desires. Some embraced the advances of blacks; most preferred to forget a past that still dogged them. It was easier not to remember the violence, the marches, the dislocations. Life was more comfortable if one did not always recall the time he started addressing blacks with courtesy titles, the autumn his daughter attended school with a black girl, or the November day he saw a black name printed on the ballot. Most white southerners preferred to ignore the reality of this everyday revolution. The atmosphere that reigned in Natchitoches, Louisiana, was one that pervaded many southern towns. As Ginger Thompson of the *New York Times* reported in 2001, "Not talking about race is at the heart of a social contract, rooted in the slave-owning past, that governs all sorts of black-white relationships—or nonrelationships." And so the trek toward a racially just society remains agonizingly slow—not because blacks wanted it that way, but often out of deference to the rhythms and preferences of whites' lives. As Curtis Tate, a Natchitoches African-American, observed, "They are the ones who can't handle the truth. . . . Isn't it the same for all black people, that we have to be careful to make white people comfortable?" In that respect, if a racial problem persisted, it could be accurately termed a "white problem."[77]

Carl Rowan, an African-American journalist, contributed an article to the 1965 *Ebony* issue. In it he neatly summarized the expansive character—and the enduring impact—of the civil rights movement. "The civil rights 'revolution' in America can never be merely a *Negro* revolution. Whether white Americans will it so or not, their futures, their hopes, their children's well being, are caught up in the racial turmoil that engulfs our land." As the civil rights struggles upended and recast everyday life in thousands of towns, white southerners variously accepted, rejected, and absorbed the untold effects of that interracial revolution.[78]

Notes

Introduction: Change Seeps In

1. Interview with Hugh Wilson, by Wendy Watriss and Reginald Kearney (June 5, 1974), Duke University Oral History Program, Duke University Special Collections.
2. Ibid.
3. *Albany Herald* (Albany, GA), July 17, 1962.
4. *Newsweek* Collection, Box 11, Folder: Segregation, Emory University Special Collections; Robert Coles, *Children of Crisis: A Study of Courage and Fear* (Boston, 1967), p. 288.
5. Robert Coles, *Farewell to the South* (Boston, 1972), p. 377; Coles, *Children of Crisis*, p. 239.
6. As Mississippi native Robert Canzoneri wrote, "Reconstruction was the name of a nightmare nobody dared tell before breakfast for fear it would come true." Robert Canzoneri, *"I Do So Politely": A Voice from the South* (Boston, 1965), p. 89; interview with Joe Smitherman, by Blackside Inc. (December 5, 1985), Washington University Libraries, Film and Media Archive, Henry Hampton Collection; Margaret Jones Bolsterli, *Born in the Delta: Reflections on the Making of a Southern White Sensibility* (Knoxville, 1991), p. 126; Marshall Frady, *Southerners: A Journalist's Odyssey* (New York, 1980), p. xiv; James McBride Dabbs, *Who Speaks for the South?* (New York, 1964), p. 336; James McBride Dabbs, "Civil Rights in Recent Southern Fiction" (1969), p. 41, Southern Regional Council Papers, 1944–1968, Reel 220. Wyatt Tee Walker also expressed a version of this idea in a 1965 interview: "I think the white man may [now] feel that he is, in a sense, at the mercy of history, whereas, the Negro, in a sense, is guiding or directing." Robert Penn Warren, *Who Speaks for the Negro?* (New York, 1965), p. 230.
7. Jimmy Breslin, "Changing the South," *New York Herald Tribune,* March 26, 1965; Coles, *Children of Crisis,* p. 8; William Chafe, notes from interview with Ed Hudgins, William Henry Chafe Oral History Collection, Duke University Special Collections.
8. Interview with Clay Lee, by Orley Caudill (July 8, 1980), Civil Rights in Mississippi Digital Archive, The Center for Oral History and Cultural Heritage, The University of Southern Mississippi.
9. The literature on the civil rights movement is vast. Books that tell some of the stories of white southerners include, but are not limited to, J. Mills Thornton, *Dividing*

Lines: Municipal Politics and the Struggle for Civil Rights in Montgomery, Birmingham, and Selma (Tuscaloosa, 2002); Diane McWhorter, *Carry Me Home: Birmingham, Alabama—The Climactic Battle of the Civil Rights Revolution* (New York, 2001); Charles Eagles, *Outside Agitator: Jon Daniels and the Civil Rights Movement in Alabama* (Chapel Hill, 1993); Robert Norrell, *Reaping the Whirlwind: The Civil Rights Movement in Tuskegee* (New York, 1985); William Chafe, *Civilities and Civil Rights: Greensboro, North Carolina, and The Black Struggle for Freedom* (New York, 1980); David Goldfield, *Black, White and Southern: Race Relations and Southern Culture, 1940 to the Present* (Baton Rouge, 1990); John Dittmer, *Local People: The Civil Rights Struggle in Mississippi* (Urbana, 1994); Matthew Lassiter, *The Silent Majority: Suburban Politics in the Sunbelt South* (Princeton, 2005); Dan Carter, *The Politics of Rage: George Wallace, the Origins of the New Conservatism, and The Transformation of American Politics* (Baton Rouge, 2000); David Chappell, *Inside Agitators: White Southerners in the Civil Rights Movement* (Baltimore, 1994); David Chappell, *A Stone of Hope: Prophetic Religion and the Death of Jim Crow* (Chapel Hill, 2004); Kevin Kruse, *White Flight: Atlanta and the Making of Modern Conservatism* (Princeton, 2005). For a seminal review essay in the field, see Steven Lawson, "Freedom Then, Freedom Now: The Historiography of the Civil Rights Movement," *American Historical Review,* Vol. 96, No. 2 (April 1991), pp. 456–71.

10. Charles Eagles, "Toward New Histories of the Civil Rights Era," *Journal of Southern History,* Vol. 66, No. 4 (November 2000), pp. 816, 843; Kevin Mattson, "Civil Rights Made Harder," *Reviews in American History,* Vol. 30 (December 2002); Jacquelyn Dowd Hall, "The Long Civil Rights Movement and the Political Uses of the Past," *Journal of American History,* Vol. 91, No. 4 (March 2005), p. 1235; Peter Ling, "Tales of White Birmingham," *Reviews in American History,* Vol. 30 (December 2002), p. 308.

11. Roy Blount, Jr., "Being from Georgia," in Hugh Ruppersburg, ed., *Georgia Voices,* Vol. 2: *Nonfiction* (Athens, GA, 1994), p. 502; Charles Payne, *I've Got the Light of Freedom: The Organizing Tradition and the Mississippi Freedom Struggle* (Berkeley, CA, 1995), pp. 418–19; Adam Fairclough, *Race and Democracy: The Civil Rights Struggle in Louisiana, 1915–1972* (Athens, GA, 1995), p. 167.

12. Thornton, *Dividing Lines,* p. 2; Harold Fleming, "The State of Public Opinion in the South" (October 22, 1956), Southern Regional Council Papers, 1944–1968, Reel 45.

13. Interview with Hugh Wilson, by Wendy Watriss and Reginald Kearney (June 5, 1974), Duke University Oral History Program.

14. H.S. (June 24, 1975), Joel Williamson Exams, University of North Carolina at Chapel Hill.

15. Ben Smith to Sam Ervin (December 2, 1963), Sam J. Ervin Papers, Southern Historical Collection, Wilson Library, University of North Carolina at Chapel Hill.

16. Toni Morrison, *Playing in the Dark: Whiteness and the Literary Imagination* (Cambridge, MA, 1992), p. 64; Nathan Irvin Huggins, *Revelations: American History, American Myths* (New York, 1995), p. 275; David R. Roediger, *The Wages of Whiteness: Race and the Making of the American Working Class* (New York, 1991); Edmund Morgan, *American Slavery, American Freedom: The Ordeal of Colonial Virginia* (New York, 1975); Leon Litwack, *Trouble in Mind: Black Southerners in the Age of Jim Crow* (New York, 1998).

17. Interview with Hugh Wilson, by Wendy Watriss and Reginald Kearney (June 5, 1974), Duke University Oral History Program.

ONE

Prelude: In the Wake of the War, 1945–1955

1. *Fort Worth Star-Telegram,* August 14, 1945, and *Robesonian* (Lumberton, NC), December 4, 1945, both cited in Guy B. Johnson, "Race Relations in the South—A Challenge to Christian Agencies," address to Conference of Southern YMCA Secretaries, Atlanta, GA (December 8, 1945), Papers of the North Carolina Council on Human Relations, Southern Historical Collection, University of North Carolina at Chapel Hill.

2. Samuel Stouffer, Edward Suchman, Leland DeVinney, Shirley Star, and Robin Williams, eds., *The American Soldier: Adjustment During Army Life* (Princeton, 1949), Vol. 1, pp. 519–20, 558, 570, and Vol. 2, pp. 637–38, 643; Pete Daniel, "Going Among Strangers: Southern Reactions to World War II," *Journal of American History,* Vol. 77, No. 3 (December 1990), pp. 886–911.

3. Johnson, "Race Relations in the South—A Challenge to Christian Agencies."

4. Frank Smith, *Congressman from Mississippi* (New York, 1964), p. 59; interview with Claude Ramsay, by Orley Caudill (April 28, 1981), Civil Rights in Mississippi Digital Archive. For another essential story of the war's transformative power, see Ira Harkey, *The Smell of Burning Crosses: An Autobiography of a Mississippi Newspaperman* (Jacksonville, IL, 1967), pp. 205–7.

5. John Egerton, *Speak Now Against the Day: The Generation Before the Civil Rights Movement in the South* (New York, 1994), p. 210; Fred Powledge, *Free at Last?: The Civil Rights Movement and the People Who Made It* (Boston, 1991), pp. 48–49, 177.

6. Stouffer et al., *The American Soldier,* Vol. 1, pp. 591–93; interview with Wilson Evans II, by Orley Caudill (June 11, 1981), Civil Rights in Mississippi Digital Archive.

7. Harris Wofford, "A Preliminary Report on the Status of the Negro in Dallas County, Alabama," in David Garrow, ed., *We Shall Overcome: The Civil Rights Movement in the United States in the 1950's and 1960's* (Brooklyn, 1989), Vol. 3, pp. 65–68.

8. Ibid.; Stouffer et al., *The American Soldier,* Vol. 2, pp. 637, 643. Neil McMillen writes: "Without exception, these returning veterans found more continuity than change in their Mississippi hometowns." McMillen, "Fighting for What We Didn't Have: How Mississippi Black Veterans Remember World War II," in Neil McMillen, ed., *Remaking Dixie: The Impact of World War II on the American South* (Jackson, 1997), p. 106. On white veterans and the war's racial meaning, also see Jennifer Brooks, "Winning the Peace," in Glenn Feldman, ed., *Before* Brown: *Civil Rights and White Backlash in the Modern South* (Tuscaloosa, 2004).

9. Studs Terkel, *"The Good War": An Oral History of World War II* (New York, 1984), pp. 152–53, 156–57.

10. Ibid., pp. 370–71.

11. McMillen, "Fighting for What We Didn't Have," pp. 100, 105.

12. Bruce Schulman, *From Cotton Belt to Sunbelt: Federal Policy, Economic Development, and the Transformation of the South, 1938–1980* (New York, 1991), p. 101; Numan V. Bartley, *The New South, 1945–1980* (Baton Rouge, 1995); James Cobb, *The Most Southern Place on Earth: The Mississippi Delta and the Roots of Regional Identity* (New York, 1992), p. 204; *Newsweek* Collection, Box 11, Folder: Segregation Story (1959); Daniel,

"Going Among Strangers," pp. 886, 895; Morton Sosna, "Introduction," in McMillen, ed., *Remaking Dixie*, p. xiv; "Distribution of Agricultural and Nonagricultural Workers in the South, 1950," Southern Regional Council Papers, 1944–1968, Reel 21; interview with Arthur Lemann, by Bernard Lemann (January 3, 1991), Friends of the Cabildo Oral History Program, City Archives, New Orleans Public Library; Schulman, *From Cotton Belt to Sunbelt,* p. 102. Schulman also documents the point that industrialization of the South began during the New Deal, even if it did not reach full force until after World War II.

13. Gail Williams O'Brien, *The Color of the Law: Race, Violence, and Justice in the Post-World War II South* (Chapel Hill, 1999), p. 127.

14. Wofford, "A Preliminary Report on the Status of the Negro in Dallas County, Alabama," p. 4; Goldfield, *Black, White, and Southern,* pp. 48–49; V. O. Key, *Southern Politics in State and Nation* (New York, 1949), p. 7.

15. Patricia Sullivan, *Days of Hope: Race and Democracy in the New Deal Era* (Chapel Hill, 1996). Sullivan also shows that blacks and whites attempted, and at times succeeded, in building black and white class-based alliances in the South before World War II—in the 1930s.

16. Guy Johnson, address to the Southern Regional Council, Atlanta, GA (November 13, 1946), Papers of the North Carolina Council on Human Relations; Egerton, *Speak Now Against the Day,* pp. 365–66; Richard Dalfiume, *Desegregation of the U.S. Armed Forces: Fighting on Two Fronts, 1939–1953* (Columbia, MO, 1969), p. 133.

17. Egerton, *Speak Now Against the Day,* pp. 365–67; Mary L. Dudziak, *Cold War Civil Rights: Race and the Image of American Democracy* (Princeton, 2000), pp. 18–19; *Atlanta Constitution,* July 19, 1946.

18. *Atlanta Constitution,* July 21–23, 26, 1946. See Brooks, "Winning the Peace," for more on the election and the war's legacy.

19. Stephen Tuck, *Beyond Atlanta: The Struggle for Racial Equality in Georgia, 1940–1980* (Athens, GA, 2001), p. 28; *Atlanta Constitution,* July 21–24, 1946.

20. *Atlanta Constitution,* July 23, 1946. For a more detailed portrait of the sordid affair, see Robert Sherrill, *Gothic Politics in the Deep South: Stars of the New Confederacy* (New York, 1968), pp. 42–44; Jack Bass and Walter DeVries, *The Transformation of Southern Politics: Social Change and Political Consequences Since 1945* (New York, 1976), p. 137.

21. *Atlanta Constitution,* July 28, 30, 1946.

22. Ibid., July 29, 1946.

23. Ibid., July 18, 30, 1946; Egerton, *Speak Now Against the Day,* p. 369; Tuck, *Beyond Atlanta,* p. 80.

24. O'Brien, *The Color of the Law,* pp. 1–28.

25. Ibid., p. 188.

26. Historian Gail Williams O'Brien quoted Campbell to make the case about poor white southerners and their lack of status anxiety (ibid., p. 244); Stouffer et al., *The American Soldier,* Vol. 2, p. 618. Historian Pete Daniel has argued that working-class southerners became much more interested in farming, stock-car racing, and rock and roll than they were in defending Jim Crow. "Preserving segregation became the cause of middle-class and elite whites." Pete Daniel, *Lost Revolutions: The South in the 1950s* (Chapel Hill, 2000), p. 179.

27. *Washington Post,* May 20, 1946.

28. O'Brien wrote, "World War II veterans comprised the most volatile element in the crowd." Sociologist Samuel Stouffer and his colleagues conducted a poll that showed only 15 percent of American soldiers defined the war in moral terms. Furthermore, they sharply distinguished what came before and after from the war itself. Historian Harvard Sitkoff has argued that the war years were not a watershed in black militancy, much less white tolerance. And Neil McMillen has asserted that black soldiers, like whites, "declined to invest wartime experience with postwar meaning." O'Brien, *The Color of the Law*, p. 11; Stouffer et al., *The American Soldier*, Vol. 2, pp. 432–40. For the essays by Sitkoff, McMillen, and others, see McMillen, ed., *Remaking Dixie*. Also see Brooks, "Winning the Peace."

29. Interview with Wilson Evans II, by Orley Caudill (June 11, 1981), Civil Rights in Mississippi Digital Archive; Egerton, *Speak Now Against the Day*, pp. 365, 375, 369.

30. Wofford, "A Preliminary Report on the Status of the Negro in Dallas County, Alabama," p. 44.

31. Southern Regional Council Papers, 1944–1968, Reel 18; George Gallup, ed., *The Gallup Poll: Public Opinion, 1935–1971* (New York, 1972), Vol. 3, pp. 797, 810.

32. Smith, *Congressman from Mississippi*, p. 101; letter from Mrs. W. C. Todd to Ralph McGill (September 30, 1957), Ralph McGill Papers, Emory University Special Collections.

33. Floyd Goodman to Charles Raper Jonas (March 1965), Charles Raper Jonas Papers, Southern Historical Collection, University of North Carolina at Chapel Hill; Wofford, "A Preliminary Report on the Status of the Negro in Dallas County, Alabama," p. 68.

34. *Atlanta Constitution*, July 26, 1946; Robert Caro, *Master of the Senate* (New York, 2003), p. 708.

35. Smith, *Congressman from Mississippi*, pp. 100–102.

36. Goldfield, *Black, White, and Southern*, pp. 67–69; Egerton, *Speak Now Against the Day*, pp. 531–32; William Chafe, *Never Stop Running: Allard Lowenstein and the Struggle to Save American Liberalism* (New York, 1993), pp. 88–91.

37. Jeff Woods, *Black Struggle, Red Scare: Segregation and Anti-Communism in the South, 1948–1968* (Baton Rouge, 2004), pp. 30–31, 46–47; Patricia Sullivan, ed., *Freedom Writer: Virginia Foster Durr, Letters from the Civil Rights Years* (New York, 2003), p. 30.

38. *Atlanta Constitution*, May 28, 1954; letter from Mrs. Jewell Lamm to Charles Raper Jonas (July 17, 1956), Charles Raper Jonas Papers; *American Experience: The Murder of Emmett Till*, PBS, 2003 (http://www.pbs.org/wbgh/amex/till/filmmore/pt.html).

39. Mrs. Jewell Lamm to Charles Raper Jonas (July 17, 1956); L. G. Blodgett to Charles Raper Jonas (June 11, 1957); Milton Clapp, Jr., to Charles Raper Jonas (September 25, 1957), Charles Raper Jonas Papers. On North Carolina's "progressive mystique," see Chafe's *Civilities and Civil Rights*.

40. Louis Schulz to the Southern Regional Council (November 20, 1956), Southern Regional Council Papers, 1944–1968, Reel 44.

41. Interview with Richard Franco, by author, Atlanta, GA (June 24, 2003).

42. Southern Regional Council Papers, 1944–1968, Reel 44; "South Cover—pegged to 1961 school opening," *Newsweek* Collection, Box 12, Folder: Segregation—School Opener 1961.

43. Wofford, "A Preliminary Report on the Status of the Negro in Dallas County, Alabama," pp. 25, 72–73.

44. Ibid., pp. 63, 8.

45. Ibid., p. 58.

46. Ibid., pp. 72, 25.

47. Ibid., pp. 31, 34.

48. Daniel, "Going Among Strangers," p. 886; Bartley, *The New South,* pp. 23, 123, 134; William Emerson dispatch from Birmingham, Alabama (August 27, 1953), *Newsweek* Collection, Box 11.

49. *Atlanta Constitution,* May 18, 25, 1954. "By the time of the *Brown* decision in 1954," historian David Goldfield writes, "southern white leaders had already drawn the battlelines." Goldfield, *Black, White, and Southern,* pp. 63, 77.

50. J. L. Chestnut and Julia Cass, *Black in Selma: The Uncommon Life of J. L. Chestnut, Jr.* (New York, 1990), p. 81; *Atlanta Constitution,* May 18–19, 1954 (editorial from *Birmingham News* also excerpted in *Atlanta Constitution*).

51. Sullivan, ed., *Freedom Writer,* p. 72; Egerton, *Speak Now Against The Day,* p. 613; interview with Phyllis Franco, by author, Atlanta, GA (June 25, 2003).

52. *Atlanta Constitution,* May 18, June 4, 1954.

53. Interview with Richard Franco, by author.

54. "Southern Baptist Convention," Southern Regional Council Papers, 1944–1968, Reel 220; Chappell, *A Stone of Hope,* p. 5.

55. Ralph McGill, "The Agony of the Southern Minister," *New York Times Magazine* (September 27, 1959); "Ministers Losing Pastorates," Southern Regional Council Papers, 1944–1968, Reel 21; Mark Newman, *Getting Right with God: Southern Baptists and Desegregation* (Tuscaloosa, 2001), p. 43.

56. "Ministers Losing Pastorates," Southern Regional Council Papers, 1944–1968, Reel 21; "Presbytery Upholds Eviction of Minister by Durant's Church," from the *Clarion-Ledger* (November 30, 1955), Southern Regional Council Papers, 1944–1968, Reel 45.

57. Michael Friedland, *Lift Up Your Voice Like a Trumpet: White Clergy and the Civil Rights and Antiwar Movements 1954–1973* (Chapel Hill, 1998), pp. 19–20, 32; Newman, *Getting Right with God,* pp. 25–26; Reese Griffin to George Mitchell (June 16, 1956), Southern Regional Council Papers, 1944–1968, Reel 45.

58. *Albany Herald,* July 17, 1962; Sullivan, ed., *Freedom Writer,* p. 80.

59. John Hope Franklin, "The Great Confrontation: The South and the Problem of Change," *Journal of Southern History,* Vol. 38 (February 1972), reprinted in Patrick Gerster and Nicholas Cords, eds., *Myth and Southern History* (Chicago, 1974), pp. 305–6. A century before *Brown,* prior to the Civil War, "slaveholding families acknowledged by their conversations and daily conduct a relationship with their blacks that was riddled with ambiguity," historian Leon Litwack wrote. Similar dynamics prevailed before the civil rights movement. Leon Litwack, *Been in the Storm So Long: The Aftermath of Slavery* (New York, 1979), p. 4.

TWO

"Our Negroes" No More

1. David Cohn, *Where I Was Born and Raised,* 2nd rev. ed. (South Bend, IN, 1967), pp. 161–62; Sarah Patton Boyle, *The Desegregated Heart: A Virginian's Stand in Time of*

Transition (New York, 1962), p. 35. Boyle became a well-known writer, with articles published in national journals and magazines.

2. Interview with James McBride Dabbs, by Dallas Blanchard (1965–1968), Fellowship of Southern Churchmen Interviews, Southern Oral History Program Collection, Southern Historical Collection, University of North Carolina at Chapel Hill.

3. Letter to Charles Raper Jonas (name withheld, August 24, 1957); Clarence Morison to Charles Raper Jonas (September 25, 1957), Charles Raper Jonas Papers.

4. "Opinions and Attitudes in the Community," Clinton, Tennessee, *Newsweek* Collection, Box 13, Folder: Segregation—Clinton Schools; Roscoe Griffin, "A Tentative Description and Analysis of the School Desegregation Crisis in Sturgis, Kentucky" (August 31–September 19, 1956), Southern Regional Council Papers, 1944–1968, Reel 21.

5. Griffin, "A Tentative Description and Analysis of the School Desegregation Crisis in Sturgis Kentucky"; Chafe, *Civilities and Civil Rights,* pp. 9, 28–29.

6. Howard Zinn, "Albany," January 8, 1962, pp. 3–6, Southern Regional Council Papers, 1944–1968, Reel 220; William Styron, "The Quiet Dust," in Willie Morris, ed., *The South Today: 100 Years After Appomattox* (New York, 1965), p. 20.

7. Interview with John Carswell, by Lois Gilman and Wendy Watriss (June 1974), Duke University Oral History Program.

8. David Vann, a lawyer, was elected mayor of Birmingham in 1975. Interview with David Vann, by Blackside Inc. (November 1, 1985), Washington University Libraries; Powledge, *Free at Last?,* pp. 10–11, xix–xx.

9. Interview with Jan Robertson, by Blackside Inc. (May 8, 1986), Washington University Libraries; interview with Joe Smitherman, by Blackside Inc. (December 5, 1985), Washington University Libraries; interview with John Carswell, by Lois Gilman and Wendy Watriss (June 1974), Duke University Oral History Program; Warren, *Who Speaks for the Negro?,* p. 12.

10. David Halberstam, "A Good City Gone Ugly," *The Reporter* (March 31, 1960), in *Reporting Civil Rights: American Journalism,* Vol. 1: *1941–1963* (New York, 2003), p. 442; Chafe, *Civilities and Civil Rights,* p. 71; *Atlanta Constitution,* January 26, 1961; Dan Wakefield, "Eye of the Storm," *The Nation* (May 7, 1960).

11. Boyle, *The Desegregated Heart,* pp. 84–85, 299; Jack Davis, *Race Against Time: Culture and Separation in Natchez Since 1930* (Baton Rouge, 2001), p. 195.

12. Wakefield, "Eye of the Storm."

13. Milton Elliott to Ralph McGill (May 26, 1961), Ralph McGill Papers.

14. W. E. B. Du Bois, *The Souls of Black Folk* (1903; New York, 1989), pp. 92–105.

15. *New York Times,* August 16, 1962; Du Bois, *The Souls of Black Folk,* p. 102.

16. *Albany Herald,* July 31, 1962.

17. Ibid., August 7, 1962.

18. John Ricks, " 'De Lawd' Descends and Is Crucified: Martin Luther King, Jr. in Albany, Georgia," *Journal of Southwest Georgia History,* Vol. 2 (Fall 1984), pp. 3–14, reprinted in Garrow, ed., *We Shall Overcome; Albany Herald,* June 24, 1962; Pat Watters, *Down to Now: Reflections on the Southern Civil Rights Movement* (Athens, GA, 1971), p. 151. The identity of the quoted preacher is unclear in Watters's book.

19. Watters, *Down to Now,* p. 166.

20. *Albany Herald,* May 31, June 29, July 13, 1962.

21. *New York Times,* July 16, 1962; *Albany Herald,* July 21, 22, 24, 1962; Taylor Branch, *Parting the Waters: America in the King Years, 1954–63* (New York, 1988), p. 606.

22. *Albany Herald,* July 22, 24, 1962.

23. Ibid., July 21, 25, 27, August 9, 1962. Hundreds more whites chimed in with statements that elucidated the general mind-set. Albany's Mrs. R. J. Williams wrote, "The 'way of life' in the deep South was calm and happy and good will prevailed between the races until outside influences moved in." A "citizen and mother" agreed: "We had harmony and understanding until these radicals came here." An anonymous Albanian added, "We've never had any race problem here until this mess." Yet another writer contended, "Here in Albany the white and colored have gotten along quite well." "I am of that group of white citizens of the South, generally referred to as the best friend the Negro race has, or has ever had," maintained E. S. Winn of Fitzgerald.

24. Ibid., July 18, 26, 1962.

25. Ibid., August 4, 1962; *New York Times,* August 16, 1962.

26. *Albany Herald,* July 18, 25, 1962; *New York Times,* August 18, 1962; *Albany Herald,* August 12, 1962.

27. *New York Times,* July 25, 1962.

28. Ibid., February 14, 1965.

29. Michael Chalfen, " 'The Way Out May Lead In': The Albany Movement Beyond Martin Luther King, Jr.," *Georgia Historical Quarterly,* Vol. 79, No. 3 (Fall 1995), p. 561.

30. Watters, *Down to Now,* pp. 206–7.

31. *New York Times,* July 27, 1962.

32. Frances Pauley to Albany citizens (July 30, 1962), Frances Pauley Papers, Box 10, Folder 1, Emory University Special Collections. The figure 400 combines the number who responded directly to Pauley with those who published responses to her in the *Albany Herald.* One can assume that the *Herald* did not publish all of the letters that it received concerning Pauley.

33. Arthur Johnston to Frances Pauley (undated), Frances Pauley Papers, Box 10, Folder 1.

34. Rudolph Greer to Frances Pauley (August 6, 1962), Box 10, Folder 2; W. H. Swinney to Frances Pauley (August 6, 1962), Box 10, Folder 1; J. W. Scruggs to Frances Pauley (undated), Box 10, Folder 1; Milton Merts to Frances Pauley (August 10, 1962), Box 10, Folder 2; Paul Dauier to Frances Pauley (August 6, 1962), Frances Pauley Papers, Box 10, Folder 2; *Albany Herald,* August 27, 1962.

35. Eagles, *Outside Agitator,* p. ii; Milton Merts to Frances Pauley (August 10, 1962), Frances Pauley Papers, Box 10, Folder 2; *Albany Herald,* August 11, 15, 1962.

36. *New York Times,* August 13, 1962; anonymous to Frances Pauley, Box 10, Folder 1; Florence Barbee to Frances Pauley, Frances Pauley Papers, Box 10, Folder 2.

37. Milton Merts to Frances Pauley (August 10, 1962), Box 10, Folder 2; Mrs. R. W. Schultz to Frances Pauley (August 16, 1962), Box 9; W. H. Swinney to Frances Pauley (August 6, 1962), Frances Pauley Papers, Box 10, Folder 1, *Albany Herald,* August 18, July 14, August 13, 1962.

38. Watters, *Down to Now,* p. 197; *Albany Herald,* August 18, July 14, August 13, 1962.

39. *Albany Herald,* August 9, 18, 1962; J. W. Scruggs to Frances Pauley (undated), Frances Pauley Papers, Box 10, Folder 1; interview with James McBride Dabbs, by Dallas Blanchard, Southern Oral History Program.

40. *Albany Herald,* August 3, 25, 27, 1962; Tuck, *Beyond Atlanta,* 147; Reese Cleghorn, "Epilogue in Albany: Were the Mass Marches Worthwhile?," *The New Republic* (July 20, 1963), p. 18.

41. *Albany Herald,* August 21, 1962.

42. Ibid., August 28, 29, 1962.

43. Ibid., August 7, 16, 22, 23, 1962.

44. Ibid., August 31, 1962.

45. Anonymous to Frances Pauley, Box 10, Folder 1; "True Albanian" to Frances Pauley, Frances Pauley Papers, Box 10, Folder 1; *Albany Herald,* August 12, 1962.

46. The John Birch Society funded many of the billboards, and the Citizens' Councils many others. Woods, *Black Struggle, Red Scare,* p. 131.

47. Rosalind Frame to Richard Russell (June 9, 1964), Richard B. Russell, Jr., Collection, Box 39, Correspondence: June 9–11, 1964, Civil Rights series, Georgia subseries, Richard B. Russell Library for Political Research and Studies, University of Georgia Libraries, Athens.

48. *Jackson Daily News,* January 9, 1961, September 19, 1962; McWhorter, *Carry Me Home,* p. 518.

49. Reese Cleghorn, "Radicalism: Southern Style: A Commentary on Regional Extremism of the Right" (Atlanta, 1968), Southern Regional Council Papers, 1944–1968, Reel 171; letter from Council of Federated Organizations to congressmen (December 1964), Mississippi State Sovereignty Commission Records, SCR ID# 6-44-0-2-1-1-1, Mississippi Department of Archives and History, http://www.mdah .state.ms.us; Anne Braden, "The House Un-American Activities Committee: Bulwark of Segregation" (1964), Mississippi State Sovereignty Commission Records, SCR ID# 6-44-0-11-1-1-1.

50. Dittmer, *Local People,* pp. 58, 60; Woods, *Black Struggle, Red Scare,* pp. 93–98; Albert Jones to Mrs. Hugh Rodman, Jr. (January 26, 1961), Mississippi State Sovereignty Commission Records, SCR ID# 2-63-1-42-1-1-1.

51. *Mississippi Handbook for Political Programs,* Council of Federated Organizations, 1964, Student Non-Violent Coordinating Committee Papers, 1959–1972 (Sanford, NC: Microfilm Corporation of America, 1982), Reel 41; Tom Scarbrough report (April 22, 1963), Mississippi State Sovereignty Commission Records, SCR ID# 1-71-0-3-2-1-1.

52. Interview with Clay Lee, by Orley Caudill (July 8, July 23, 1980), Civil Rights in Mississippi Digital Archive.

53. *House Un-American Activities Committee Guide to Subversive Organizations,* Mississippi State Sovereignty Commission Records; *New York Herald Tribune,* September 3, 1964; David Harris, *Dreams Die Hard* (New York, 1982), p. 53.

54. Woods, *Black Struggle, Red Scare,* p. 148; "Red Warning by a Dixie Moderate," *San Francisco Chronicle,* April 13, 1965; Gallup, ed., *The Gallup Poll,* p. 1971.

55. Fairclough, *Race and Democracy,* p. 324; "Americanism v. Communism," Mississippi State Sovereignty Commission Records, SCR ID# 99-49-0-6-1-1-1, SCR ID# 99-49-0-2-1-1-1, SCR ID# 99-49-0-4-1-1; Smith, *Congressman from Mississippi,* pp. 276–77.

56. Smith, *Congressman from Mississippi*, pp. 100–101; letter from Phillip Bryan to Charles Raper Jonas (July 24, 1962), Charles Raper Jonas Papers; *Jackson Daily News*, December 2, 1961; Woods, *Black Struggle, Red Scare*, p. 53.

57. A. L. Hopkins Report (June 2, 1967), Mississippi State Sovereignty Commission Records, SCR ID# 1-92-0-61-1-1-1.

58. Martha Adcock to Charles Raper Jonas (April 1968), Charles Raper Jonas Papers; Cleghorn, "Radicalism: Southern Style," p. 9. For examples of anti-communism's continued appeal in 1968 and 1972, see Curtis Wilkie, *Dixie: A Personal Odyssey Through Events That Shaped the Modern South* (New York, 2001), p. 170; Carter, *The Politics of Rage*, p. 452.

59. *New York Times*, August 18, September 5, 1962, July 5, 1963; Cleghorn, "Epilogue in Albany," p. 16.

60. *New York Times*, July 5, 1963; Cleghorn, "Epilogue in Albany," pp. 17–18.

61. *New York Times*, July 10, 11, 1964; *Albany Herald*, July 30, 1964; *New York Times*, March 21, 1971.

62. *New York Times*, October 8, 1967; *Albany Herald*, June 4, 1970.

63. *Albany Herald*, June 8, 1970.

64. Ibid., June 12, 1970.

65. *New York Times*, March 21, 1971; *Greensboro News & Record*, November 15, 2000.

66. *Albany Herald*, June 16, 1970, July 10, 24, 1964.

67. Ibid., November 27, 1968; Howard Zinn, "Albany: A Study in National Responsibility" (Atlanta, 1962), Southern Regional Council Papers, 1944–1968, Reel 219.

68. Lillian Smith, "No Easy Way, Now," *The New Republic* (December 16, 1957), pp. 13–14.

69. *Atlanta Constitution*, May 18, 1963; Susan Bresler, "Impressions—Louisville, Ga.—July to August 3, 1966," Southern Regional Council Papers, 1944–1968, Reel 171.

70. Mississippi State Sovereignty Commission Records, SCR ID# 1-115-0-5-1-1-1; North Carolina Fund Poll, Papers of the North Carolina Council on Human Relations.

71. Garry Wills, "Martin Luther King Is *Still on the Case*," *Esquire* (August 1968).

72. Willie Morris, *Yazoo: Integration in a Deep-Southern Town* (New York, 1971), pp. 30–31; Melissa Fay Greene, *Praying for Sheetrock* (Reading, MA, 1991), p. 188.

73. St. Marc (1975), Joel Williamson Exams.

74. Leslie Dunbar, "The Changing Mind of the South: The Exposed Nerve" (1964), in Leslie Dunbar, *The Shame of Southern Politics: Essays and Speeches* (Lexington, KY, 2002), pp. 25–42.

75. Newman, *Getting Right with God*, pp. 20, 48; Melany Neilson, *Even Mississippi* (Tuscaloosa, 1989), p. 99; interview with Clara Lee Sharrard, by author, Springfield, MA (August 2003).

76. On the question of southern ministers' defense of segregation, historians remain divided. David Chappell, in *A Stone of Hope* (2004), takes pains to argue that southern white ministers "did not contribute much, and showed little enthusiasm for, the defense of legal segregation." Moreover, Chappell maintains that white supremacists' primary error was their failure to unify churches in an active campaign against black civil rights. His argument challenges much of the previous scholarship. Mark New-

man's *Getting Right with God* contains a well-documented chapter on the Southern Baptists' religious support for segregation. J. Wayne Flynt found no precise link between "fundamentalist theology and resistance to integration"; in his *Alabama Baptists,* he writes that "southern racism fed off biblical literalism." Chappell, *A Stone of Hope,* pp. 112–13, 318; J. Wayne Flynt, *Alabama Baptists: Southern Baptists in the Heart of Dixie* (Tuscaloosa, 1998), p. 458.

77. Newman, *Getting Right with God,* p. 20; Will Campbell, "A Man Had Two Sons," Nashville, TN (May 6, 1959), Southern Regional Council Papers, 1944–1968, Reel 44. On the subject of the civil rights movement and religion, see also Charles Marsh's *God's Long Summer: Stories of Faith and Civil Rights* (Princeton, 1997), which explores the connection between religion and white supremacy (often through Klan leader Sam Bowers), and also the strength that civil rights supporters derived from their faith.

78. R. L. Herrington to Ralph McGill (October 5, 1962), Ralph McGill Papers, Box 24, Folder 5; *Newsweek* Collection, Box 14, Folder: Segregation—Religion. For the story of one St. Augustine minister who did take a stand, see Taylor Branch, *Pillar of Fire: America in the King Years, 1963–65* (New York, 1998), pp. 383, 266. Reporter Karl Fleming commented in his 2005 memoir, "The dominant white Methodist and Baptist churches, and their numerous Southern off-shoots, stayed all but silent." Karl Fleming, *Son of the Rough South: An Uncivil Memoir* (New York, 2005), p. 258.

79. Chappell, *A Stone of Hope,* p. 133; *Newsweek* Collection, Box 14, Folder: Segregation—Religion; McGill, "The Agony of the Southern Minister."

80. Branch, *Pillar of Fire,* pp. 121, 263–64; Friedland, *Lift Up Your Voice Like a Trumpet,* p. 102; W. J. Cunningham, *Agony at Galloway: One Church's Struggle with Social Change* (Jackson, 1980), pp. 3, 12, 18, 29, 37, 121; interview with W. J. Cunningham, by Orley Caudill (August 6, 1981), Civil Rights in Mississippi Digital Archive.

81. James Washington, ed., *A Testament of Hope: The Essential Writings and Speeches of Martin Luther King, Jr.* (San Francisco, 1991), pp. 344–46; Friedland, *Lift Up Your Voice Like a Trumpet,* pp. 78–79, 131; S. Jonathan Bass, *Blessed Are the Peacemakers: Martin Luther King, Jr., Eight White Religious Leaders, and the "Letter from Birmingham Jail"* (Baton Rouge, 2001), pp. 235–36; Branch, *Parting the Waters,* pp. 741–42, 745.

82. Newman, *Getting Right with God,* pp. 83, 63, 32; Cunningham, *Agony at Galloway,* p. 145; interview with W. J. Cunningham, by Orley Caudill (August 6, 1981), Civil Rights in Mississippi Digital Archive; Bolsterli, *Born in the Delta,* p. 131.

83. Interview with Robert Humphreys, by Matisha Wiggs (March 6, 2001), Southern Oral History Program.

84. *Delta-Democrat Times,* July 1, 1969.

85. Cohn, *Where I Was Born and Raised,* p. 38; Smith, *Congressman from Mississippi,* p. 104; interview with Joe Smitherman, by Blackside Inc. (December 5, 1985), Washington University Libraries; Wofford, "A Preliminary Report on the Status of the Negro in Dallas County," p. 60; interview with Imogene Wilson, *Behind the Veil: Documenting African-American Life in the Jim Crow South, 1940–1997,* Duke University Special Collections; Wilkie, *Dixie,* p. 55; Hodding Carter, *Where Main Street Meets the River* (New York, 1953), excerpt reprinted in *Reporting Civil Rights,* Vol. 1, pp. 136–37.

86. Interviews with Alice Giles and Cora Flemming, *Behind the Veil;* interview with Ms. Vernon Keys, by Homer Hill (March 19, 1994), Civil Rights in Mississippi Digi-

tal Archive; Branch, *Pillar of Fire,* p. 283; McWhorter, *Carry Me Home,* pp. 196–202; interview with Edgar Mouton, by Jack Bass (January 13, 1974), Southern Oral History Program.

87. *Atlanta Constitution,* May 20, 1963.

88. Mississippi (July 1, 1964), *Newsweek* Collection, Box 14, Folder: Segregation—Mississippi, School Opens.

89. Fairclough, *Race and Democracy,* pp. 342–61; clipping, Mississippi State Sovereignty Commission, SCR ID# 11-11-0-4-3-1-1; James Baldwin, *Collected Essays* (New York, 1998), p. 637.

90. Powledge, *Free at Last?,* p. 98; Warren, *Who Speaks for the Negro?,* pp. 423–24, 52.

91. St. Marc (1975), Joel Williamson Exams; interview with James McBride Dabbs, by Dallas Blanchard (1965–1968), Southern Oral History Program.

92. Interview with James McBride Dabbs, by Dallas Blanchard, Southern Oral History Program.

THREE

Daughters of Dixie, Sons of the South

1. Joseph Cumming, "Integration Situationer" (August 20, 1958), *Newsweek* Collection; William Emerson, "Regarding Segregation" (1957), *Newsweek* Collection, Box 11, Folder: Segregation—Story.

2. "What We Have Learned About School Desegregation from the Experience of 500 Schools" (March 1956), Papers of the North Carolina Council on Human Relations.

3. Margaret Anderson, *The Children of the South* (New York, 1966), pp. 81, 105.

4. Harvard Sitkoff, *The Struggle for Black Equality, 1954–1992* (New York, 1993), pp. 29–31; anonymous letter to Ralph McGill (September 29, 1957), Jack King to Ralph McGill (September 30, 1957), Ralph McGill Papers.

5. Interview with Craig Rains, by Blackside Inc. (October 29, 1985), Washington University Libraries.

6. William Emerson, "Shift in the South" (1959), *Newsweek* Collection, Box 9, Folder: Moderation—Signs of; Lassiter, *The Silent Majority,* pp. 24–25.

7. James Ely, *The Crisis of Conservative Virginia: The Byrd Organization and the Politics of Massive Resistance* (Knoxville, 1976), p. 34; "Background Summary on Virginia" (August 11, 1958), Southern Regional Council Papers, 1944–1968, Reel 220; "Virginia's Public Schools," *The New Republic* (May 26, 1958).

8. Helen Fuller, "The Defiant Ones in Virginia," *New Republic* (January 12, 1959); Emerson, "Shift in the South"; Matthew Lassiter and Andrew Lewis, eds., *The Moderates' Dilemma: Massive Resistance to School Desegregation in Virginia* (Charlottesville, 1998), pp. 7, 78–79.

9. Lassiter and Lewis, eds., *The Moderates' Dilemma,* pp. 10, 72, 117–18, 123.

10. Ely, *The Crisis of Conservative Virginia,* pp. 79–80, 88–89, 122.

11. "A Background Report on School Desegregation for 1959–60," Southern Regional Council Papers, 1944–1968, Reel 220.

12. Emerson, "Shift in the South."

13. Helen Fuller, "Atlanta Is Different," *The New Republic* (February 2, 1959);

M. M. Smith, "Spring Street School—For Sale" (November 18, 1958), *Newsweek* Collection, Box 13, Folder: Segregation—Atlanta, 1958–59.

14. Lassiter, *The Silent Majority,* pp. 44–93.

15. *Atlanta Journal,* January 15, 1959; Lassiter, *The Silent Majority,* pp. 51–52, 64.

16. Lassiter, *The Silent Majority,* pp. 60, 76–77; *Atlanta Constitution,* January 4, 12, 14, 18, 1960.

17. Lassiter, *The Silent Majority,* pp. 80–84; Gary Pomerantz, *Where Peachtree Meets Sweet Auburn: A Saga of Race and Family* (New York, 1996), pp. 256–57; Sibley Commission, John Sibley Papers, Box 146, Witness Testimony Folder, Emory University Special Collections; Kruse, *White Flight,* p. 144. Neither Atlantans nor rural Georgians spoke with a single voice. Even in the Black Belt, some educational associations and ministers backed open schools. HOPE made inroads in other Georgia cities, including Columbus, Rome, and Savannah.

18. William Emerson from New Orleans (February 1954), William Emerson (1959), *Newsweek* Collection, Box 10, Folder: New Orleans Continuing; Fairclough, *Race and Democracy,* pp. 219–35.

19. "How Does Chep Morrison Stand on Segregation?," de Lesseps Morrison Papers, Folder: Integration— 1960, City Archives, New Orleans Public Library; Helen Fuller, "New Orleans Knows Better," *The New Republic* (February 16, 1959).

20. *The New Orleans School Crisis: Report of the Louisiana State Advisory Committee of the United States Commission on Civil Rights* (Washington, DC, 1961), pp. 5–6; letter from R. G. Graves to de Lesseps Morrison (April 22, 1960), de Lesseps Morrison Papers.

21. *The New Orleans School Crisis,* pp. 13, 25; *New Orleans Times-Picayune,* November 2, 1960; "New Orleans Mood" (December 12, 1960), *Newsweek* Collection, Box 14, Folder: Segregation—New Orleans School Crisis.

22. "New Orleans Mood" (December 12, 1960), *Newsweek* Collection; Urban League of Greater New Orleans, "A Summary Statement on Inter-Group Racial Problems in New Orleans (A Plan for Dealing with Them)," Victor Schiro Papers, City Archives, New Orleans Public Library; Bass and DeVries, *The Transformation of Southern Politics,* p. 179; Gerald Jaynes and Robin Williams, Jr., eds., *A Common Destiny: Blacks and American Society* (Washington, DC, 1989), p. 62; *Greenville News,* December 11, 1960; *In Motion: The African American Migration Experience,* The Schomburg Center for Research in Black Culture (http://www.inmotionaame.org); U.S. Bureau of the Census.

23. *New Orleans Times-Picayune,* November 9, 1960.

24. Ibid., November 7, 1960; Alan Wieder, *Race and Education: Narrative Essays, Oral Histories, and Documentary Photographs* (New York, 1997), p. 78; interview with Rosa Freeman Keller, by Dorothy Schlesinger (July 7, 1977), Friends of the Cabildo Oral History Program, transcription at Tulane University Special Collections; interview with Marion Bourdette, by Dorothy Mahan (May 20, 1981), Friends of the Cabildo Oral History Program; "Nation—New Orleans School," *Newsweek* Collection, Box 14, Folder: Segregation—New Orleans School Crisis.

25. "Nation—New Orleans School," *Newsweek* Collection; *New Orleans Times-Picayune,* November 15, 1960. While some scholars have written about the "New Orleans School Crisis," the subject remains under-studied in proportion to its importance. See Morton Inger, *Politics and Reality in an American City: The New Orleans School Crisis of 1960* (New York, 1960); Fairclough, *Race and Democracy;* Coles, *Children of Crisis;* Wieder, *Race and Education;* Edward Haas, *DeLesseps Morrison and the Image of Reform:*

New Orleans Politics, 1946–1961 (Baton Rouge, 1974); Liva Baker, *The Second Battle of New Orleans: The Hundred-Year Struggle to Integrate the Schools* (New York, 1996).

26. "Integration: Louisiana Nightmare," *Newsweek* (November 28, 1960); *New Orleans Times-Picayune,* November 15–17, 1960.

27. John Weintraub to de Lesseps Morrison (November 16, 1960); Paula Fussell to de Lesseps Morrison (November 16, 1960); A. L. Chapman to de Lesseps Morrison (November 15, 1960), de Lesseps Morrison Papers.

28. *New Orleans Times-Picayune,* November 18–19, 24, 1960.

29. John Steinbeck, *Travels with Charley* (New York, 1962), pp. 247, 253–55.

30. Reporter's notes (beginning "11:19 a.m. william frantz"), *Newsweek* Collection, Box 14, Folder: Segregation New Orleans II; *New Orleans Times-Picayune,* November 30, 1960.

31. "Mother, Pupil Outwait Crowd," November 29, 1960, *Newsweek* Collection, Box 14, Folder: Segregation New Orleans II; *Look* (March 14, 1961), p. 55; *Commercial Appeal* (Memphis, TN), November 29, 1960; reporter's notes (beginning "11:19 a.m. william frantz"), *Newsweek* Collection.

32. *New Orleans Times-Picayune,* December 3, 8, 1960; *Los Angeles Times,* December 3, 1960.

33. "Mother, Pupil Outwait Crowd," *Newsweek* Collection; Leo Bergman to de Lesseps Morrison (December 7, 1960), de Lesseps Morrison Papers; *New Orleans Times-Picayune,* December 7, 1960; *Los Angeles Times,* December 7, 1960.

34. Notes, Rosalie Grad (December 6, 1960), de Lesseps Morrison Papers; Edwanda and Charles Macmurdo to de Lesseps Morrison (November 16, 1960), de Lesseps Morrison Papers; *New Orleans Times-Picayune,* December 5, 7, 8, 1960; *Greenville News,* December 11, 1960.

35. *New Orleans Times-Picayune,* December 9, November 30, 1960; *Washington Post,* December 9, 1960.

36. Coles, *Children of Crisis,* pp. 13, 275–76; Alan Wieder, "One Who Stayed: Margaret Conner and the New Orleans School Crisis," *Louisiana History,* Vol. 26, No. 2 (Spring 1985), reprinted in Wieder, *Race and Education,* pp. 84–85.

37. Coles, *Children of Crisis,* pp. 276–77; clippings, *Newsweek* Collection, Box 10, Folder: New Orleans Continuing.

38. Coles, *Children of Crisis,* pp. 277–78; clippings, *Newsweek* Collection.

39. Coles, *Children of Crisis,* p. 278; clippings, *Newsweek* Collection.

40. Coles, *Children of Crisis,* pp. 14, 275; Wieder, *Race and Education,* p. 89; "Orleans Mother Stands Firm," *Atlanta Journal and Constitution,* December 11, 1960.

41. "Orleans Mother Stands Firm"; Coles, *Children of Crisis,* pp. 13, 278.

42. Coles, *Children of Crisis,* pp. 278, 14; "Orleans Mother Stands Firm."

43. "White Pupil, 9, Revives Fears in New Orleans," *Atlanta Constitution,* January 30, 1961; "School Boycott Foe Is Picketed," *Philadelphia Inquirer,* February 1, 1961; *The New Orleans School Crisis,* p. 14.

44. James Sweeney to de Lesseps Morrison (February 8, 1961); de Lesseps Morrison to James Sweeney (February 16, 1961); Laurence Daspit to Victor Wogan, Jr. (November 18, 1960), de Lesseps Morrison Papers.

45. Leo Bergman to Albert Vorspan (carbon copy to de Lesseps Morrison, December 6, 1960), de Lesseps Morrison Papers; Wieder, *Race and Education,* p. 90; *Greenville News,* December 11, 1960; Haas, *DeLesseps S. Morrison and the Image of Reform,* p. 272.

46. *New Orleans Times-Picayune,* November 26, December 14, 1960,

47. Ibid., November 29, 1960; Wieder, *Race and Education,* pp. 100, 107; *New Orleans Times-Picayune,* December 8, 22–23, 1960; Robert Coles, "How Do the Teachers Feel?," *Saturday Review* (May 16, 1964), p. 72.

48. Coles, "How Do the Teachers Feel?," pp. 72–73.

49. Coles, *Children of Crisis,* pp. 83–84.

50. Robert Coles, Report to the Southern Regional Council (1962), Southern Regional Council Papers, 1944–1968, Reel 18; Ruby Bridges, *Through My Eyes* (New York, 1999), pp. 8, 12.

51. De Lesseps Morrison to Betty Lowry (December 15, 1960); de Lesseps Morrison to David Cole (January 26, 1961); de Lesseps Morrison to Jackie Boudreaux (January 14, 1961); de Lesseps Morrison to Ed Connell (December 14, 1960), de Lesseps Morrison Papers.

52. Nancy Jones to de Lesseps Morrison (November 16, 1960); de Lesseps Morrison to Henry Meisel (January 24, 1961), de Lesseps Morrison Papers.

53. Joan Blalock to Victor Schiro (August 14, 1961); Nelda Clements to Victor Schiro (August 18, 1961); Ann Huey to Victor Schiro (August 21, 1961); Victor Schiro Papers, City Archives, New Orleans Public Library.

54. Joseph Calo to Victor Schiro (undated); H. M. Tailor to Victor Schiro (September 2, 1961), Victor Schiro Papers; "Dispossessed!," Ninth Ward Private School Association, Segregation File, City Archives, New Orleans Public Library.

55. Anne Dlugos to Victor Schiro (undated); Lysle Aschaffenburg to Victor Schiro (August 31, 1961), Victor Schiro Papers; *Times-Picayune,* August 16, 1961.

56. Interview with Marion Bourdette, by Dorothy Mahan (May 20, 1981), Friends of the Cabildo Oral History Program; Robert Coles, "Civil Rights Is Also a State of Mind," *New York Times Magazine* (May 7, 1967).

57. Interview with Marion Bourdette, Friends of the Cabildo Oral History Program; interview with Claire Chauviere, by Dorothy Mahan (October 14, 1992), Friends of the Cabildo Oral History Program.

58. Coles, Report to the Southern Regional Council (1962), Southern Regional Council Papers, 1944–1968, Reel 18; Fairclough, *Race and Democracy,* pp. 263, 453; *New York Times,* September 5, 1962; Gary Orfield, *Must We Bus?: Segregated Schools and National Policy* (Washington, DC, 1978), pp. 68, 72; Mary Lee Muller, "New Orleans Public School Desegregation," *Louisiana History,* Vol. 18 (1976), p. 76.

59. Interview with Marion Bourdette, Friends of the Cabildo Oral History Program; Coles, *Farewell to the South,* p. 310.

60. *Atlanta Constitution,* January 7, 1961.

61. Ibid., January 7, 9, 10, 1961; Robert Pratt, *We Shall Not Be Moved: The Desegregation of the University of Georgia* (Athens, GA, 2002).

62. *Atlanta Constitution,* January 11, 1961.

63. Ibid., January 11, 10, 1961; Terry Hazelwood, "Your Responsibility," *Red and Black* (January 9, 1961), Vol. 68, *Newsweek* Collection, Box 14, Folder: Segregation—University of Georgia Integration.

64. See Pratt, *We Shall Not Be Moved;* Calvin Trillin, *An Education in Georgia: The Integration of Charlayne Hunter and Hamilton Holmes* (New York, 1964); and Robert Cohen's "G-Men in Georgia: The FBI and the Segregationist Riot at the University of

Georgia, 1961," *Georgia Historical Quarterly,* Vol. 83, No. 3 (Fall 1999), pp. 508–38. Cohen establishes conclusively that the riot was a planned affair.

65. Background Report, *Newsweek* Collection, Box 14, Folder: Segregation— University of Georgia Integration.

66. *Atlanta Constitution,* January 14, 1961; Robert Cohen, "Two, Four, Six, Eight, We Don't Want to Integrate: White Student Attitudes Toward the University of Georgia's Desegregation," *Georgia Historical Quarterly,* Vol. 80, No. 3 (Fall 1996), pp. 620–21.

67. TT, JA, Math 254 Essays, Walter Danner Papers, University Archives, Hargrett Rare Book and Manuscript Library, University of Georgia Libraries.

68. 9, 23, DW, 13, HS, Math 254 Essays, Walter Danner Papers.

69. 13, JB, JG, Math 254 Essays, Walter Danner Papers.

70. JA II, JB, 2, Math 254 Essays, Walter Danner Papers.

71. MHC, RC, 17, HS, GLC, Math 254 Essays, Walter Danner Papers.

72. PC, 6, AS, Math 254 Essays, Walter Danner Papers.

73. 5, GB, JA II, Math 254 Essays, Walter Danner Papers.

74. DC, 7, Math 254 Essays, Walter Danner Papers.

75. 19, TT, 13, Math 254 Essays, Walter Danner Papers.

76. JG, CC, 17, JB, DC, GLC, Math 254 Essays, Walter Danner Papers.

77. *Atlanta Constitution,* January 18, 1961; W. C. Henson to William Tate (January 12, 1961), William Tate, Integration at University of Georgia Files, 1961–1963, University Archives, Hargrett Library, University of Georgia; Dorothy Westafu to O. C. Aderhold (January 13, 1961), O. C. Aberhold Papers, University Archives, Hargrett Library, University of Georgia.

78. Mrs. Edward Downs to William Tate (January 1961); Richard Trimble to William Tate (January 20, 1961); Arthur Murphey, Jr., to William Tate (January 20, 1961), William Tate, Integration at University of Georgia Files; *Atlanta Constitution,* January 18, 1961.

79. Pratt, *We Shall Not Be Moved,* p. 86; *Atlanta Constitution,* January 13, 24, 1961; JM, 30, Math 254 Essays, Walter Danner Papers.

80. *Atlanta Constitution,* January 13, 1961.

81. Ibid., January 20, 21, 25, 1961.

82. Pratt, *We Shall Not Be Moved,* pp. 155–58.

83. Mary Ellen Goodman, "Sanctuaries for Tradition: Virginia's New Private Schools" (February 8, 1961), p. 20, Southern Regional Council Papers, 1944–1968, Reel 220; *New York Times,* April 17, 1961; Ely, *The Crisis of Conservative Virginia,* pp. 136–38; Lassiter and Lewis, *The Moderates' Dilemma,* pp. 161, 166.

84. Joseph Cumming, "School Desegregation, Take II" (September 5, 1961), *Newsweek* Collection, Box 12, Folder: Segregation—School Opener 1961. On Atlanta's leaders, see Pomerantz, *Where Peachtree Meets Sweet Auburn,* and Kruse, *White Flight.*

85. Robert Coles, "The Desegregation of Southern Schools: A Psychiatric Study" (July 1963), Southern Regional Council Papers, 1944–1968, Reel 18; Robert Coles, "Southern Children Under Desegregation," report presented at American Psychiatric Association (May 6, 1963), Southern Regional Council Papers, 1944–1968, Reel 18.

86. Anderson, *The Children of the South,* pp. 86–87, 89, 142, 208, 107.

87. *New York Times,* September 12–13, 16, 1963; Norrell, *Reaping the Whirlwind,* p. 153.

88. Robert Coles, "How Do the Teachers Feel?," *Saturday Review* (May 16, 1964); "Little Rock Revisited—Tokenism Plus," *New York Times Magazine* (June 2, 1963); *The New South* (Winter 1968); *New York Times,* March 23, 1985.

89. Davis, *Race Against Time,* p. 237; interview with Samuel Holton, by Jenny Matthews (March 28, 2001), Southern Oral History Program; *Atlanta Constitution,* July 14, 1964; Jerry Virden to Charles Raper Jonas (July 29, 1966), Charles Raper Jonas Papers.

90. *New Orleans Times-Picayune,* September 1, 5, 1966.

91. Ibid., September 2, 9, 13–14, 20, 1966.

92. Ibid., September 15, 1966; Neilson, *Even Mississippi,* pp. 28, 34–35.

93. *Atlanta Journal and Constitution,* September 14, 1969; *The New South* (Fall 1969), p. 75; George Metcalf, *From Little Rock to Boston: The History of School Desegregation* (Westport, CT, 1983), p. 49; Lassiter, *The Silent Majority,* p. 171.

94. *Delta Democrat-Times,* May 19, June 8, 1969; Frederick Wirt, *"We Ain't What We Was": Civil Rights in the New South* (Durham, NC, 1997), p. 119.

95. *Atlanta Constitution,* September 9, 1969.

96. *Delta Democrat-Times,* July 24, August 24, 1969.

97. Ibid., August 24, October 22, 1969.

98. *The New South* (Winter 1970); interview with Charles Allen Johnson, Jr., by Mike Garvey (August 26, 1975), Civil Rights in Mississippi Digital Archive; Neil McMillen, *The Citizens' Council: Organized Resistance to the Second Reconstruction, 1954–64* (Urbana, IL, 1971); *Delta Democrat-Times,* October 27, 1969; *New York Times,* November 24, 1969; Wirt, *"We Ain't What We Was,"* p. 86.

99. *New York Times,* January 6, 1970; *Newsweek* (January 26, 1970); *The New South* (Winter 1970).

100. *Delta Democrat-Times,* October 30, November 2, 3, 1969; Metcalf, *From Little Rock to Boston,* p. 268.

101. *New York Times,* November 24, 1969; Morris, *Yazoo,* p. 29.

102. Morris, *Yazoo,* pp. 42, 89, 103–4.

103. Ibid., pp. 91–93.

104. Ibid., p. 133.

105. Jaynes and Williams, eds., *A Common Destiny,* p. 75; *The New South* (Fall 1969), p. 108; *New York Times,* May 18, 1982, March 23, 1985.

106. Lassiter, *The Silent Majority,* pp. 119–221.

107. *Atlanta Constitution,* January 15, 1970.

108. Orfield, *Must We Bus?,* p. 400; *New York Times,* January 14, 1970; *Atlanta Constitution,* January 10, 1970; Kruse, *White Flight,* pp. 5, 238.

109. *Atlanta Constitution,* January 12–15, 1970; *New York Times,* January 14, 1970.

110. *Atlanta Constitution,* May 10, 1971; *New York Times,* April 18, 1971; *Atlanta Constitution,* May 11–15, 1971.

111. Paul Gaston, "The Region in Perspective," in *The South and Her Children: School Desegregation, 1970–1971,* p. 18, Southern Regional Council Papers, 1944–1968, Reel 220.

112. Marshall Frady, "A Meeting of Strangers in Americus," *Life* (February 12, 1971); *Atlanta Constitution,* May 14, 1971.

113. Frady, "A Meeting of Strangers in Americus"; Morris, *Yazoo*, p. 21.

114. "Decatur High School," *Newsweek* Collection, Box 11, Folder: School Desegregation Situationer (November 1970); Gaston, "The Region in Perspective," p. 19.

FOUR

Barbecue, Fried Chicken, and Civil Rights: The 1964 Civil Rights Act

1. *Atlanta Journal and Constitution*, July 4, 1964; Sherrill, *Gothic Politics in the Deep South*, p. 277; Frady, *Southerners*, p. 56; *Time* (July 17, 1964), p. 26.

2. "Lester Maddox Backgrounder," *Newsweek* Collection, Box 9, Folder: Lester Maddox (August 1964); *New York Times*, September 30, 1966, June 26, 2003; Sherrill, *Gothic Politics in the Deep South*, p. 283; "Obituary: Lester Garfield Maddox, 1915–2003" (Marietta, GA, 2003).

3. Sherrill, *Gothic Politics in the Deep South*, p. 284; "Lester Maddox Backgrounder," *Newsweek* Collection, Box 9, Folder: Lester Maddox (August 1964); "P.A.S.S.," *Newsweek* Collection, Box 2, Folder: Atlanta Racial Current.

4. *Atlanta Constitution*, July 4, 7, 1964; "Lester Maddox Backgrounder," *Newsweek* Collection; Richard Cortner, *Civil Rights and Public Accommodations: The Heart of Atlanta Motel and McClung Cases* (Lawrence, KS, 2001), p. 39; *New York Times*, July 10, 18, 1964; *Albany Herald*, July 11, 1964.

5. Cortner, *Civil Rights and Public Accommodations*, p. 56; *New York Times*, August 11, 1964.

6. *New York Times*, August 12, 14, 1964.

7. Ibid., August 14, 1964.

8. Ibid., February 2, 8, 23, 1965.

9. Michael Durham, "Ollie McClung's Big Decision," *Life* (October 9, 1964), p. 31; Ollie's Barbecue (December 17, 1964), *Newsweek* Collection, Box 4, Folder: Civil Rights Cases; Cortner, *Civil Rights and Public Accommodations*, pp. 78–79.

10. Durham, "Ollie McClung's Big Decision," p. 31; Ollie's Barbecue, *Newsweek* Collection; Cortner, *Civil Rights and Public Accommodations*, p. 79.

11. Durham, "Ollie McClung's Big Decision," p. 31; Cortner, *Civil Rights and Public Accommodations*, p. 64; *Time* (July 17, 1964), p. 25.

12. *New York Times*, September 3, 18, 1964; *Montgomery Advertiser*, September 18, 1964.

13. Cortner, *Civil Rights and Public Accommodations*, p. 77; Durham, "Ollie McClung's Big Decision," p. 31.

14. Durham, "Ollie McClung's Big Decision," pp. 31–32; *Birmingham News*, December 16, 1964.

15. *Birmingham News*, December 14, 15, 16, 17, 1964; *New York Times*, December 17, 1964; Ollie's Barbecue, *Newsweek* Collection.

16. Frances Pauley to members of Georgia Council on Human Relations (July 1, 1963), Frances Pauley Papers, Box 10; Gallup, *Gallup Poll*, vol. 3, p. 1829; *Albany Herald*, July 1, 1964.

17. Iredell Hutton to Charles Raper Jonas (July 3, 1963), Charles Raper Jonas Papers.

18. Nathan Blanchard to Sam Ervin (January 10, 1964); George Colclough to Sam Ervin (June 25, 1964), Sam J. Ervin Papers.

19. L. J. Moore to Sam Ervin (June 13, 1964), Sam J. Ervin Papers; Tommy Moore, interview with author, by telephone (April 29, 2005).

20. Raymond Ingold to Sam Ervin (July 8, 1964), Sam J. Ervin Papers.

21. Benjamin Muse, "Memphis" (July 1964), pp. 33–36, Southern Regional Council Papers, 1944–1968, Reel 220.

22. Interview with Jesse Boyce Holleman, by Orley Caudill (August 9–10, September 17, 1976), Civil Rights in Mississippi Digital Archive.

23. *Albany Herald,* July 3, 1964; Peter de Lissovoy, "Mixin' in South Georgia," *The Nation* (December 21, 1964), p. 486.

24. *Albany Herald,* July 3, 1964; *Atlanta Journal and Constitution,* July 4, 1964.

25. *New York Times,* July 6, 13, 19, 1964.

26. *Time* (July 17, 1964), 25; *New York Times,* July 7, 9, 1964; *Albany Herald,* July 7, 1964.

27. David Garrow, *Bearing the Cross: Martin Luther King, Jr., and the Southern Christian Leadership Conference* (New York, 1986), p. 326; John Herbers, "Critical Test for the Nonviolent Way," *New York Times Magazine,* July 5, 1964, p. 30; Branch, *Pillar of Fire,* pp. 36–37, 111; David Colburn, *Racial Change and Community Crisis: St. Augustine, Florida, 1877–1980* (New York, 1985), pp. 46–47, 63.

28. Colburn, *Racial Change and Community Crisis,* pp. 44–71.

29. Garrow, *Bearing the Cross,* pp. 330–33; *New York Times,* June 12, 1964; Branch, *Pillar of Fire,* pp. 354–55.

30. Colburn, *Racial Change and Community Crisis,* p. 101; Garrow, *Bearing the Cross,* p. 336; Bass and DeVries, *The Transformation of Southern Politics,* p. 10.

31. Garrow, *Bearing the Cross,* p. 341; *New York Times,* July 24, 1964; Colburn, *Racial Change and Community Crisis,* p. 9.

32. "St. Augustine, July 29, 1964," *Newsweek* Collection, Box 14, Folder: Segregation—St. Augustine.

33. Ibid.; Colburn, *Racial Change and Community Crisis,* p. 128.

34. "St. Augustine, July 29, 1964," *Newsweek* Collection; Garrow, *Bearing the Cross,* p. 344; Colburn, *Racial Change and Community Crisis,* p. 112; Branch, *Pillar of Fire* p. 327.

35. Colburn, *Racial Change and Community Crisis,* pp. 114–15, 182, 203; Tom Dent, *Southern Journey: A Return to the Civil Rights Movement* (New York, 1997), pp. 201–7.

36. *New York Times,* July 12, 15, 26, 1964; *St. Petersburg Times,* November 9, 1964; Paul Good, *New South* (Summer 1966), reprinted in *Reporting Civil Rights,* Vol. 2, p. 497. For incidents at the Watts Grill near Chapel Hill, see interview with Rev. Charles Jones, Duke University Oral History Program, Duke University Special Collections. Adam Fairclough argues that segregation remained the norm in rural Louisiana following the Civil Rights Act, while many cities integrated. Fairclough, *Race and Democracy,* pp. 339–40.

37. Kruse, *White Flight,* pp. 105–30, 205–33.

38. "The Civil Rights Act: Compliance as Reported to the Georgia Council on Human Relations" (July 15, 20, 1964), Frances Pauley Papers, Box 10, Folder 6; *New York Times,* July 14, 1964; Tuck, *Beyond Atlanta,* pp. 127–53; Pat Watters, "Brunswick at the Time of the Civil Rights Act," Southern Regional Council Papers, 1944–1968, Reel 220.

39. "The Civil Rights Act: Compliance as Reported to the Georgia Council on

Human Relations" (July 15, 20, 1964), Frances Pauley Papers. For examples of that press reaction, see *New York Times,* July 12 (see map), July 26, 1964; *U.S. News & World Report* (July 20, 1964); *Birmingham News,* November 29, 1964; "5 Years Ago," *Delta Democrat-Times,* July 4, 1969.

40. "The Civil Rights Act: Compliance as Reported to the Georgia Council on Human Relations" (July 15, 20, 1964), Frances Pauley Papers.

41. Tuck, *Beyond Atlanta,* pp. 158, 176; "The Civil Rights Act: Compliance as Reported to the Georgia Council on Human Relations" (July 15, 20, 1964), Frances Pauley Papers; *New York Times,* July 9, 1964.

42. Ralph Lowe to Richard Russell (May 30, 1964), Richard B. Russell, Jr., Collection, Box 39, Correspondence: June 5–6, 1964; *New York Times,* July 16, 1964.

43. Peter de Lissovoy, "Mixin' in South Georgia," *The Nation* (December 21, 1964), pp. 487–88.

44. Ibid., p. 488.

45. Ibid., p. 489.

46. Ibid., pp. 489–90.

47. *Birmingham News,* November 29, 1964, January 30, 1965; *New York Times,* December 20, 1965; *St. Petersburg Times,* November 9, 1964.

48. Samuel Adams, "Highways of Hope Opening to Negroes in the South," *St. Petersburg Times,* November 8, 1964.

49. Ibid.; Samuel Adams, "Road of Hope Dotted by Ruts in Carolinas," *St. Petersburg Times,* November 9, 1964.

50. Samuel Adams, "Scenic Trip Yields Warmth, but Color Barrier Cumbersome," *St. Petersburg Times,* November 10, 1964.

51. Thornton, *Dividing Lines,* p. 469; *Birmingham News,* January 31, 1965; *Raleigh News and Observer* editorial, quoted in *New York Times,* December 20, 1964.

52. *Birmingham News,* December 6, 1964.

53. Frances Pauley, "Compliance with the 1964 Civil Rights Act" (October 6, 1965), Frances Pauley Papers, Box 10, Folder 6.

54. *New York Times,* December 20, 1964; Pauley, "Compliance with the 1964 Civil Rights Act," Frances Pauley Papers; *U.S. News & World Report* (July 20, 1964).

55. Mrs. Alton Bland to Charles Raper Jonas (May 28, 1963), Charles Raper Jonas Papers.

56. Mrs. Alton Bland to Charles Raper Jonas (June 4, 1963), Charles Raper Jonas Papers.

57. Mrs. Alton Bland to Charles Raper Jonas (June 8, 1963), Charles Raper Jonas Papers; Booker T. Washington, *Up from Slavery,* in *Three Negro Classics* (New York, 1999), p. 159.

58. Mrs. Alton Bland to Charles Raper Jonas (June 8, 1963), Charles Raper Jonas Papers.

59. Mr. and Mrs. J. E. Redmon to Richard Russell (June 12, 1964), Richard B. Russell, Jr., Collection, Box 39.

60. June Melvin to Charles Raper Jonas (June 19, 1963), Charles Raper Jonas Papers; F. M. Bain, Sr., and F. M. Bain, Jr., to Sam Ervin (May 1, 1964), Sam J. Ervin Papers; David McDougal to Richard Russell (May 1964), Richard B. Russell, Jr., Collection, Box 40, Correspondence: May 27, 1964; Preston Wilkes, Jr., to Charles Raper Jonas (July 9, 1963), Charles Raper Jonas Papers. As Jack Davis writes in his study of Natchez,

Mississippi, "Whites were convinced that the 'civil wrongs' legislation granted blacks not only equal rights but special rights that 'seriously impaired' the liberties of others." Davis, *Race Against Time,* p. 169.

61. June Melvin to Charles Raper Jonas (June 19, 1963), Charles Raper Jonas Papers; F. M. Bain, Sr., and F. M. Bain, Jr., to Sam Ervin (May 1, 1964), Sam J. Ervin Papers; Mrs. Romeo Powell to Sam Ervin (January 9, 1964), Sam J. Ervin Papers.

62. Mrs. Alton Bland to Charles Raper Jonas (June 8, 1963), Charles Raper Jonas Papers; F. V. Taylor to Sam Ervin (April 30, 1964), Sam J. Ervin Papers; Florence Wood to Richard Russell (May 20, 1964), Richard B. Russell, Jr., Collection, Box 40, Correspondence: May 20, 1964; *New York Times,* June 28, 2003.

63. Mary Idol Breeze to Charles Raper Jonas (June 12, 1963), Charles Raper Jonas Papers.

64. Nancy Anderson to Richard Russell (December 8, 1963), Correspondence: December 1963; Mary Ann Clarke to Richard Russell (October 24, 1963), Correspondence: October 1963; Richard B. Russell, Jr., Collection; Melvin Rockleff to Sam Ervin (May 3, 1964), Sam J. Ervin Papers.

65. Nancy Collinson to Richard Russell (March 23, 1964), Correspondence: March 1964; James O'Hear Sanders to Richard Russell (December 2, 1963), Correspondence: December 1963; Richard B. Russell, Jr., Collection.

66. Harriet Southwell to Richard Russell (December 8, 1963), Correspondence: December 1963; Richard B. Russell, Jr., Collection.

67. Audrey Wagner to Charles Raper Jonas (June 27, 1963), Charles Raper Jonas Papers; Hugh Lefler to Sam Ervin (January 21, 1964), Sam J. Ervin Papers. The textbook mentioned was co-authored by Hugh Lefler and Albert Newsome, *North Carolina: The History of a Southern State* (Chapel Hill, NC, 1954).

68. B. F. Wardlow to Richard Russell (May 22, 1964), Richard B. Russell, Jr. Collection, Box 40, Correspondence: May 1964; O. W. Hines to Sam Ervin (January 9, 1964), Sam J. Ervin Papers.

69. Mildred and Gene Carr to Richard Russell (May 14, 1964), Richard B. Russell, Jr., Collection, Box 40, Correspondence: May 20, 1964.

70. *Albany Herald,* July 3, 1964. Among the books on the construction of "whiteness" in American history, surprisingly few of them focus on the South. The one that does most closely is Grace Elizabeth Hale's *Making Whiteness: The Culture of Segregation in the South, 1890–1940* (New York, 1998). See also Roediger's *The Wages of Whiteness,* Michael Rogin's *Blackface, White Noise: Jewish Immigrants in the Hollywood Melting Pot* (Berkeley, CA, 1966), Alexander Saxton's *The Rise and Fall of the White Republic: Class Politics and Mass Culture in Nineteenth-Century America* (New York, 1990), Noel Ignatiev's *How the Irish Became White* (New York, 1995), and Morrison's *Playing in the Dark.*

71. Interview with Joe Smitherman, by Blackside Inc. (December 5, 1985), Washington University Libraries; *Albany Herald,* July 13, 1964.

72. *Albany Herald,* July 22, 1964; *Birmingham News,* December 15, 20, 1964.

73. *Atlanta Constitution,* July 18, 1964.

74. Ibid.

75. Interview with Clara Lee Sharrard, by author. For different takes on the success of the Civil Rights Act, see Tuck, *Beyond Atlanta,* pp. 193–94; Fairclough, *Race and Democracy,* p. 376; Dittmer, *Local People,* p. 402.

76. Howard Glenn to Sam Ervin (May 15, 1969), Sam J. Ervin Papers.

77. Robert Coles, "Civil Rights Is Also a State of Mind," *New York Times Magazine* (May 7, 1967); Joseph Cumming, "Birmingham Revisited" (November 30, 1964), *Newsweek* Collection, Box 2, Folder: Birmingham, AL (December 1964); Martin Luther King, Jr., "Letter from Birmingham City Jail," in Washington, ed., *A Testament of Hope,* p. 295.

78. Interview with Richard Franco, by author.

79. *New York Times,* April 27, 1985; interview with Margaret Rogers, *Behind the Veil: Documenting African-American Life in the Jim Crow South, 1940–1997,* Duke University Special Collections; *New York Times,* April 6, 1985.

80. Frady, *Southerners,* p. 71; *Atlanta Journal and Constitution,* June 26, 2003.

81. Frady, *Southerners,* pp. 55, 71; Bass and DeVries, *The Transformation of Southern Politics,* p. 142; Sherrill, *Gothic Politics in the Deep South,* pp. 285–88.

82. Frady, *Southerners,* p. 56.

83. Sherrill, *Gothic Politics in the Deep South,* p. 288.

84. Frady, *Southerners,* p. 57; Bass and DeVries, *The Transformation of Southern Politics,* p. 143; *New York Times,* June 26, 2003.

85. Frady, *Southerners,* pp. 60, 74; Sherrill, *Gothic Politics in the Deep South,* p. 280; *New York Times,* June 26, 2003.

86. Pomerantz, *Where Peachtree Meets Sweet Auburn,* p. 359; Sherrill, *Gothic Politics in the Deep South,* p. 280.

87. *New York Times,* June 26, 2003; "Obituary: Lester Garfield Maddox, 1915–2003" (Marietta, GA, 2003).

88. *Birmingham News,* June 3, 1997, December 31, 1998, September 11, 2001; *Birmingham Business Journal,* June 25, 1999, September 21, 2001.

89. *New York Times,* September 29, 2000, May 4, 2004.

90. Frady, *Southerners,* p. 107. For the complete story of the South's Republican transformation, see Earl Black and Merle Black, *The Rise of Southern Republicans* (Cambridge, MA, 2002); also see Bass and DeVries, *The Transformation of Southern Politics.*

FIVE

"Softly, the Unthinkable": The Contours of Political and Economic Change

1. Garrow, *Bearing the Cross,* p. 77.

2. Steven Lawson, *Black Ballots: Voting Rights in the South, 1944–1969* (New York, 1976), pp. 12–13; Chandler Davidson and Bernard Grofman, eds., *Quiet Revolution in the South: The Impact of the Voting Rights Act, 1965–1990* (Princeton, 1994), pp. 29–30. See also C. Vann Woodward's *The Strange Career of Jim Crow* (New York, 1955).

3. Jimmy Couey to William Emerson (August 30, 1957), *Newsweek* Collection, Box 11, Folder: Segregation—Story.

4. Davidson and Grofman, eds., *Quiet Revolution in the South,* p. 38; Garrow, *Bearing the Cross,* p. 372; *Birmingham News,* January 24, 1965.

5. Elizabeth Hardwick, "Selma, Alabama: The Charms of Goodness," *New York Review of Books* (April 22, 1965); interview with Joe Smitherman, by Blackside Inc. (December 5, 1985), Washington University Libraries; Garrow, *Bearing the Cross,* p. 391; Thornton, *Dividing Lines,* p. 481.

6. Chestnut and Cass, *Black in Selma,* p. 172; Powledge, *Free at Last?,* p. 616.

7. Chestnut and Cass, *Black in Selma,* p. 154.

8. Branch, *Pillar of Fire,* pp. 82, 554, 564.

9. Thornton, *Dividing Lines,* pp. 486–87; Carter, *The Politics of Rage,* pp. 246–47; Branch, *Pillar of Fire,* pp. 593–606.

10. *New York Times,* March 8, 1965; Thornton, *Dividing Lines,* p. 487; Carter, *The Politics of Rage,* p. 249. For the compelling story of Judge Frank Johnson, a white Alabamian who often ruled in favor of black civil rights and suffered terrible ostracism, see Jack Bass, *Taming the Storm: The Life and Times of Judge Frank M. Johnson and the South's Fight over Civil Rights* (New York, 1993).

11. *New York Times,* March 16, 1965; Ralph Ellison, "The Myth of the Flawed White Southerner," in *Going to the Territory* (New York, 1986), pp. 86–87; Garrow, *Bearing the Cross,* p. 407; Lawson, *Black Ballots,* p. 312; Renata Adler, "Letter from Selma," *New Yorker* (April 10, 1965); Carter, *The Politics of Rage,* p. 255.

12. Adler, "Letter from Selma"; Thornton, *Dividing Lines,* p. 489.

13. Garrow, *Bearing the Cross,* p. 412; Adler, "Letter from Selma"; Jimmy Breslin, "Changing the South," *New York Herald Tribune,* March 26, 1965.

14. Lawson, *Black Ballots,* pp. 321–31; *Birmingham News,* November 6, 1966.

15. Lawson, *Black Ballots,* pp. 337, 308; Thornton, *Dividing Lines,* pp. 498–99, 559–60; *Birmingham News,* November 9–12, 1966.

16. *New York Times,* April 2, 1985; interview with Roosevelt Williams, *Behind the Veil,* Duke University Special Collections.

17. There is some debate about whether Wallace actually made this comment. See Carter, *The Politics of Rage,* pp. 95–96.

18. Carter, *The Politics of Rage,* pp. 11, 262; *New York Times,* May 23, 1965.

19. Carter, *The Politics of Rage,* p. 417, also see the photo insert to view Wallace's "Wake Up Alabama" leaflet; *Birmingham News,* November 25, 1972.

20. Carter, *The Politics of Rage,* p. 460; "George Wallace Overcomes," *Time* (October 11, 1982), pp. 15–16; *New York Times,* April 4, 1986; "George Wallace Faces His Demons," *Boston Globe,* December 2, 1993.

21. Interview with George Wallace, by Callie Crossley, Blackside, Inc. (March 10, 1986), Washington University Special Collections.

22. Ibid.

23. *Interview* with Joseph Cumming, by author, May 20, 2004.

24. *New York Times,* April 17, 1966.

25. Bass and DeVries, *The Transformation of Southern Politics,* pp. 38, 206; Davidson and Grofman, eds., *Quiet Revolution in the South,* pp. 39, 374; "Voter Registration in the South, Spring–Summer, 1970," Southern Regional Council Papers, 1944–1968, Reel 170; Lawson, *Black Ballots,* pp. 233, 331.

26. Carter, *The Politics of Rage,* p. 247; Gavin Wright, *Old South, New South: Revolutions in the Southern Economy Since the Civil War* (New York, 1986), p. 259. For an exploration of Black Belt whites' traditional dominance over southern politics, see V. O. Key's *Southern Politics in State and Nation.* Key described black-majority plantation counties as the "hard core of the political South," and they "managed to subordinate the entire South to the service of their peculiar local needs." Key continued, "The politics of the South revolves around the position of the Negro." In the Black Belt, his position was most prominent. C. Vann Woodward put it another way when he argued that New

South politics were not about white supremacy, but *which whites* would rule supreme. Key, *Southern Politics in State and Nation,* p. 5; C. Vann Woodward, *Origins of the New South, 1877–1913* (Baton Rouge, 1951).

27. Bass and DeVries, *The Transformation of Southern Politics,* pp. 412–13; Sullivan, ed., *Freedom Writer,* p. 360; Kevin Phillips, *The Emerging Republican Majority* (New Rochelle, NY, 1969), p. 212.

28. Lawson, *Black Ballots,* pp. 130, 330; Norrell, *Reaping the Whirlwind,* p. 87; Breslin, "Changing the South"; *New York Times,* November 27, 1964; Joseph Cumming, "Greene County, Alabama—Softly, the Unthinkable," *Newsweek* Collection, Box 6, Folder: Greene County (October, 1973).

29. *Birmingham News,* December 1, 1966; *New York Times,* November 27, 1964; Lawson, *Black Ballots,* p. 209; Norrell, *Reaping the Whirlwind,* pp. 89, 92.

30. Norrell, *Reaping the Whirlwind,* pp. 96–97, 101, 104.

31. Ibid., p. 165; *New York Times,* November 27, 1964.

32. *New York Times,* June 2, 1966; *Birmingham News,* November 6–9, December 1, 9–10, 1966.

33. Gene Roberts, "A Kind of Black Power in Macon County, Ala.," *New York Times Magazine* (February 26, 1967). For developments in Wilcox County, see Gene Roberts, "A Remarkable Thing Is Happening in Wilcox County, Ala.," *New York Times Magazine* (April 17, 1966).

34. Norrell, *Reaping the Whirlwind,* pp. 200–204; Marshall Frady, "An Alabama Marriage," *New Times* (March 8, 1974), reprinted in Frady, *Southerners,* pp. 261–78; Roberts, "A Kind of Black Power in Macon County, Ala."

35. "Greene County, Alabama—Statistical Profile," Student Nonviolent Coordinating Committee Papers, Reel 37; "Black Power at Work," *Newsweek* (February 19, 1973); Cumming, "Greene County, Alabama—Softly, the Unthinkable," p. 11, *Newsweek* Collection; *The New Republic* (January 16, 1971), p. 11.

36. *New York Times,* August 3, 1969, September 3, 1983; Marshall Frady, "Nightwatch in Greene County," *Newsweek* (May 16, 1966). Throughout the Alabama Black Belt, it was not difficult to find evidence of traditional white racial views. In Lowndes County, during jury selection for the 1965 Viola Liuzzo trial (Liuzzo was a white Detroit woman murdered when she traveled south to assist the cause of civil rights), a prosecutor asked C. E. Bender, a worker at an auto agency near Fort Deposit, "Do you believe that a white person is superior to a Negro?" Bender responded, "Every white man believes that." As Charles Eagles writes in his history of Lowndes County, "White residents intuitively understood that the civil rights movement threatened their way of life. An end to segregation would, they believed, inevitably threaten not just their economic and political power but every aspect of their lives. . . . It had to be stopped." *New York Times,* February 14, October 19, 1965, October 31, 1966; Eagles, *Outside Agitator,* p. 144.

37. Frady, "Nightwatch in Greene County"; *Birmingham News,* November 6, 1966; Frye Gaillard, *Cradle of Freedom: Alabama and the Movement That Changed America* (Tuscaloosa, 2004), p. 319; Pat Watters and Reese Cleghorn, *Climbing Jacob's Ladder: The Arrival of Negroes in Southern Politics* (New York, 1967), p. 302.

38. Frady, "Nightwatch in Greene County."

39. *Birmingham News,* November 30, 1966; *New York Times,* August 3, 1969.

40. John Egerton, "White Incumbents, Black Challengers," *Newsweek* Collection,

Box 6, Folder: Greene County (January 2, 1973); Cumming, "Greene County—Softly, the Unthinkable," *Newsweek* Collection.

41. "Blacks' Sweep of County Alarms Alabama Whites," *New York Times,* November 5, 1970; *Birmingham News,* November 1, 3, 4, 24, 25, 1970; *Louisville Courier-Journal,* January 10, 1971.

42. *Louisville Courier-Journal,* January 10, 1971.

43. Interview with Joseph Cumming, by author; Joseph Cumming, "Lessons Learned in Black and White: An Irresistible Force," *Times-Georgian* (Carrollton, GA), February 23, 1997; Cumming, "Greene County—Softly, the Unthinkable," *Newsweek* Collection.

44. Cumming, "Lessons Learned in Black and White," *Times-Georgian,* February 16, 1997; interview with Joseph Cumming, by author; "Covering the South: A National Symposium on the Media and the Civil Rights Movement," University of Mississippi, April 3–5, 1987.

45. Interview with Joseph Cumming, by author.

46. Ibid.; Cumming, "Greene County—Softly, the Unthinkable," *Newsweek* Collection; Joseph Cumming, "Greene County, Ala.: The Hope of the Future," *Southern Voices,* Vol. 1, No. 1 (March/April 1974), pp. 22–29.

47. Cumming, "Greene County—Softly, the Unthinkable," *Newsweek* Collection; Cumming, "Greene County, Ala.: The Hope of the Future," pp. 22–29.

48. Cumming, "Greene County—Softly, the Unthinkable," *Newsweek* Collection; Cumming, "Greene County, Ala.: The Hope of the Future," pp. 22–29.

49. Cumming, "Greene County—Softly, the Unthinkable," p. 14, *Newsweek* Collection; Cumming, "Greene County, Ala.: The Hope of the Future," p. 26.

50. Cumming, "Greene County—Softly, the Unthinkable," pp. 16, 18–19, *Newsweek* Collection; Cumming, "Greene County, Ala.: The Hope of the Future," pp. 26–27.

51. Cumming, "Greene County—Softly, the Unthinkable," pp. 17, 19–20, *Newsweek* Collection; Cumming, "Greene County, Ala.: The Hope of the Future," pp. 26–27.

52. Cumming, "Greene County—Softly, the Unthinkable," pp. 15–16, *Newsweek* Collection; Cumming, "Greene County, Ala.: The Hope of the Future," p. 26. The *Birmingham News* reported that Rogers was "one of the few whites in the state to successfully seek and gain the backing of the party at the county level." In this instance, Cumming's report—that the NDPA approached Rogers—is probably more reliable, given his extensive interviewing of Rogers, Banks, Branch, and other main participants in Greene County politics. *Birmingham News,* November 8, 1972.

53. Cumming, "Greene County—Softly, the Unthinkable," pp. 23–25, *Newsweek* Collection; Cumming, "Greene County, Ala.: The Hope of the Future," p. 28.

54. Cumming, "Greene County—Softly, the Unthinkable," pp. 8–10, 25–29, *Newsweek* Collection; Cumming, "Greene County, Ala.: The Hope of the Future," pp. 24, 28–29; Eugene Johnston to Joseph Cumming (June 17, 1973), *Newsweek* Collection, Box 6, Folder: Greene County (October 1973).

55. Davidson and Grofman, eds., *Quiet Revolution in the South,* p. 376; Steven Lawson, *In Pursuit of Power: Southern Blacks and Electoral Politics, 1965–1982* (New York, 1985), p. 265. For the story of the switch to black power in Fayette, Mississippi, see *Delta Democrat-Times,* May 11, July 6, 7, 8, 1969; Watters and Cleghorn, *Climbing*

Jacob's Ladder, p. 32. For other episodes of the "unthinkable" becoming political reality, see Bass and DeVries, *The Transformation of Southern Politics,* pp. 191, 273–74. Also see Watters and Cleghorn, *Climbing Jacob's Ladder,* pp. 336–39.

56. Sam Ervin to Mittie Pickard (June 23, 1964); Katherine Foster to Sam Ervin (June 20, 1964), Sam J. Ervin Papers.

57. Nick Kotz, *Judgment Days: Lyndon Baines Johnson, Martin Luther King, Jr., and the Laws That Changed America* (Boston, 2005), pp. 154, 223, 228; *Birmingham News,* November 8, 25, 1964; "The Morning After," *The Nation* (November 16, 1964), p. 346; *Birmingham News,* November 8, 1964.

58. *New York Times,* September 30, 1966.

59. *Newsweek* (October 9, 1969), p. 52; Joe Denmark to Charles Raper Jonas (April 5, 1968); Martha Adcock to Charles Raper Jonas (April 1968), Charles Raper Jonas Papers.

60. *Atlanta Constitution,* November 2, 3, 1968; *Newsweek* (October 9, 1969), p. 45; Bartley, *The New South, 1945–1980,* p. 378; Lassiter, *The Silent Majority,* p. 237.

61. *Atlanta Constitution,* November 6, 7, 11, 12, 1968; Phillips, *The Emerging Republican Majority,* p. 286.

62. Peggy Ruth to Richard Nixon (May 5, 1969), Charles Raper Jonas Papers.

63. *Delta Democrat-Times,* October 2, 1969; *Atlanta Constitution,* November 6, 1972; Bartley, *The New South,* p. 389; *New York Times,* July 25, 2004. Hundreds of local races that occurred between 1968 and 1972 either confounded or confirmed this pattern. For more information on those elections, see Numan V. Bartley and Hugh D. Graham, *Southern Politics and the Second Reconstruction* (Baltimore, 1975); Bass and DeVries, *The Transformation of Southern Politics;* and Lassiter, *The Silent Majority,* pp. 251–74.

64. Bartley, *The New South,* p. 411; Bartley and Graham, *Southern Politics and the Second Reconstruction,* pp. 166–68; Carter, *The Politics of Rage,* p. 426.

65. *Birmingham News,* November 3, 12, 19, 1972; Bartley, *The New South,* p. 412; *Atlanta Constitution,* November 8, 10, 1972.

66. *Atlanta Constitution,* November 1, 2, 3, 6, 9, 1972.

67. Bass and DeVries, *The Transformation of Southern Politics,* pp. 127–28.

68. Roy Reed, interview with Jack Bass, Southern Oral History Program; Edgar Mouton, interview with Jack Bass, Southern Oral History Program.

69. John Lewis, "From Rosa Parks to Northern Busing," *New York Times,* December 26, 1975; Howell Raines, "Revolution in the South," *New York Times,* April 3, 1978; *Time* (September 27, 1976); John Lewis, *Walking with the Wind: A Memoir of the Movement* (New York, 1998), p. 417.

70. J. Morgan Kousser, *Colorblind Injustice: Minority Voting Rights and the Undoing of the Second Reconstruction* (Chapel Hill, NC, 1999), pp. 47, 145, 152, 171, 181, 256–57. Overall, Kousser argues, "Redistricting, not racial attitudes, primarily determined congressional policies on race in both the late nineteenth and the late twentieth centuries."

71. *New York Times,* September 3, 1983; Joseph Cumming, "Black Power at Work," *Newsweek* (February 19, 1973).

72. Bartley, *The New South,* pp. 2, 123, 134, 269; "Distribution of Agricultural and Nonagricultural Workers in the South, 1950," Southern Regional Council Papers, 1944–1968, Reel 21; Wright, *Old South, New South,* p. 257.

73. Bartley, *The New South,* pp. 23, 262; C. Vann Woodward, "The South Tomorrow," *Time* (September 27, 1976), p. 99; Woodward, *The Strange Career of Jim Crow,*

p. 192; Ralph McGill, "The South's Glowing Horizon," *Saturday Review* (March 9, 1968), p. 21.

74. Figures are based on author's calculations of data gleaned from Wright's *Old South, New South*, pp. 245–46; Southern Regional Council Papers, 1944–1968, Reel 39; Very Rony, "Sorrow Song in Black and White," *New South* (Summer 1967).

75. Memo from Stokely Carmichael, Bob Marts, Tina Harris, Alabama Staff to Staff, "Who Owns the Land in the Black Belt Counties of Alabama," Student Nonviolent Coordinating Committee Papers, Reel 37; Andrew Kopkind, "Lowndes County, Alabama: The Great Fear Is Gone," *Ramparts* (April 1975), reprinted in Andrew Kopkind, *The Thirty Years' War: Dispatches of a Radical Journalist* (New York, 1995), pp. 259, 261–62; *New York Times*, December 30, 1975; *Christian Science Monitor*, January 15, 1986.

76. Interview with Unita Blackwell, by Mike Garvey (April 21, May 12, 1977), Civil Rights in Mississippi Digital Archive; Chet Fuller, *I Hear Them Calling My Name: A Journey Through the New South* (Boston, 1981), pp. 94, 97.

77. *Birmingham News*, November 2, 1969; Anthony Dunbar, *Delta Time: A Journey Through Mississippi* (New York, 1990), pp. 169–70; "Mechanization of Scott: Times They Are a Changin'," *Delta Democrat-Times*, June 12, 1969.

78. Anthony Dunbar, *The Will to Survive: A Study of a Mississippi Plantation Community Based on the Words of Its Citizens*, p. 3, Southern Regional Council Papers, 1944–1968, Reel 220; Dunbar, *Delta Time*, p. xviii.

79. Dunbar, *The Will to Survive*, pp. 5–6.

80. Ibid., pp. 7, 11–12; Lawson, *In Pursuit of Power*, p. 231.

81. Dunbar, *The Will to Survive*, p. 13. Whether slavery was defined by brutal capitalism, negotiated reciprocity, or communal bonds has been a matter of much debate. While the literature on the subject has advanced since their seminal works, Kenneth Stampp's *The Peculiar Institution: Slavery in the Ante-bellum South* (New York, 1956) and Eugene Genovese's *Roll, Jordan, Roll: The World the Slaves Made* (New York, 1974) still frame the terms of that debate. To understand how relations between black workers and their bosses changed—or did not—after the abolition of slavery, see Leon Litwack's *Been in the Storm So Long* and *Trouble in Mind*. For an illuminating look at slaveholders, not only on large plantations but also on small farms, see James Oakes's *The Ruling Race: A History of American Slaveholders* (New York, 1982).

82. Dunbar, *The Will to Survive*, pp. 13–14. For a thorough study of these themes—and many others—in the Mississippi Delta, see Wirt, *"We Ain't What We Was."*

83. Dunbar, *The Will to Survive*, p. 14. In *The Political Economy of Slavery: Studies in the Economy and Society of the Slave South* (New York, 1965), Eugene Genovese argues, in effect, that slaveholders were not businessmen—or at the least, they were not capitalists.

84. A. W., Joel Williamson Exams.

85. See Robert Korstad's *Civil Rights Unionism: Tobacco Workers and the Struggle for Democracy in the Mid-Twentieth-Century South* (Chapel Hill, NC, 2003) for the story of Winston-Salem; Robin Kelley's *Hammer and Hoe: Alabama Communists During the Great Depression* (Chapel Hill, NC, 1990) narrates a story of African-Americans, unionism, and political struggles during the 1930s.

86. Wofford, "A Preliminary Report on the Status of the Negro in Dallas County, Alabama," p. 44; James Cobb, *The Selling of the South: The Southern Crusade for Industrial*

Development (Urbana, IL, 1993), p. 94. Cobb argues that, in fact, southern businessmen often misjudged the priorities of northern companies. Cheap and unorganized labor was not always the latter's primary need.

87. "Interim Report on Survey of Southern Trade Unions and the Race Problem" (May 10, 1957), Southern Regional Council Papers, 1944–1968, Reel 171; Timothy Minchin, *Hiring the Black Worker: The Racial Integration of the Southern Textile Industry, 1945–1980* (Chapel Hill, NC, 1999), p. 237; Timothy Minchin, *The Color of Work: The Struggle for Civil Rights in the Southern Paper Industry, 1945–1980* (Chapel Hill, NC, 1991), p. 170.

88. Letter from Ginny and Buddy Tieger (August 12, 1965), Student Nonviolent Coordinating Committee Papers, Reel 40; interview with Thomas Knight, by Charles Bolton (February 7, 1992), Civil Rights in Mississippi Digital Archive.

89. Marc Miller, ed., *Working Lives: The* Southern Exposure *History of Labor in the South* (New York, 1980), p. 283; Local 65, Electrotypers and Stereotypers Union to Richard Russell (June 1964), Richard B. Russell, Jr., Collection.

90. Minchin, *The Color of Work,* pp. 178, 174.

91. Ibid., pp. 172, 184.

92. "How a Southern Community Helped to Break a Union," *Steel Labor* (March 1966), Southern Regional Council Papers, 1944–1968, Reel 170; "Vote Against the Union," *Moore County News,* September 29, 1966, Southern Regional Council Papers, 1944–1968, Reel 170.

93. *Time* (September 27, 1976), pp. 75–76.

94. Interview with James Reynolds, by David and Carol Lynn Yellin, Washington, DC (February 4, 1972), p. 25, Sanitation Strike Archival Project, University of Memphis; *Commercial Appeal,* February 16, 1968; interview with Mr. and Mrs. L. C. Reed, by Bill Thomas, Memphis, TN (July 15, 1968), p. 8, Sanitation Strike Archival Project, University of Memphis.

95. "Labor in the South," *Southern Patriot* (January 1968); Robert Analavage, "A New Movement in the White South," Southern Regional Council Papers, 1944–1968, Reel 219; Robert Analavage, "Workers Strike Back," Southern Regional Council Papers, 1944–1968, Reel 219.

96. "Labor in the South"; Analavage, "Workers Strike Back."

97. *New York Times,* September 24, 1971; Analavage, "A New Movement in the White South"; Analavage, "Workers Strike Back."

98. *New York Times,* May 19, 1969; Cobb, *The Selling of the South,* p. 118; Schulman, *From Cotton Belt to Sunbelt,* p. 140. Minchin, *Hiring the Black Worker,* p. 4.

99. "Occupational Employment by Race in the Textile Industry in the Carolinas, 1966," Papers of the North Carolina Council on Human Relations; letter from Will Allred, Jr., to members and friends of Human Relations Councils (March 28, 1967), Papers of the North Carolina Council on Human Relations. See Minchin's *Hiring the Black Worker* for an illuminating discussion and tabulation of racial hiring practices, disparities in position, and wage rates.

100. Letter from Will Allred, Jr., to members and friends of Human Relations Councils (March 28, 1967), Papers of the North Carolina Council on Human Relations; *Union Voice,* Vol. 2, No. 9 (April 19, 1967), Papers of the North Carolina Council on Human Relations.

101. Reese Cleghorn, "The Mill: A Giant Step for the Southern Negro," *New York Times Magazine* (November 9, 1969).

102. Ibid.; *New York Times,* June 12, 1969, May 19, 1969.

103. *Wall Street Journal,* April 29, 1969; Minchin, *Hiring the Black Worker,* pp. 16, 3; *Carolina Journal,* September 22, 2003.

104. Henry Leifermann, "The Unions Are Coming," *New York Times Magazine* (August 5, 1973).

105. James Hodges, "J. P. Stevens and Union: Struggle for the South," in Gary Fink and Merl Reed, eds., *Race, Class, and Community in Southern Labor History* (Tuscaloosa, 1994), pp. 57–59.

106. Leifermann, "The Unions Are Coming"; Cobb, *The Selling of the South,* pp. 256–58.

107. Leifermann, "The Unions Are Coming."

108. Barbara Koeppel, "Something Could Be Finer than to Be in Carolina," *The Progressive* (June 1976), pp. 20, 23. Historian James Cobb argues that by the end of the 1970s, "antiunionism had supplanted racism as the South's most respectable prejudice." Cobb, *The Selling of the South,* pp. 259, 270.

109. Koeppel, "Something Could be Finer than to Be in Carolina," p. 21; Ron Duncan, "One Poor White," *New South* (1969), p. 49; *The Nation* (May 20, 1968), p. 668; McWhorter, *Carry Me Home,* p. 15. A white native of Birmingham, McWhorter wrote that she grew up on "the wrong side of a revolution."

110. Duncan, "One Poor White," p. 50.

111. Raymond Wheeler, "The Challenge to Black and White," *New South,* Vol. 24, No. 1 (Winter 1969), p. 4; William Alexander Percy, *Lanterns on the Levee,* quoted in Dunbar, *Delta Time,* p. 17; interview with Clara Lee Sharrard, by author.

112. Diane McWhorter often writes about the "country-club Klanner" in *Carry Me Home* (pp. 15–30); interview with Richard Franco, by author.

113. Chestnut and Cass, *Black in Selma,* pp. 176, 185; Fleming, *Son of the Rough South,* p. 244.

114. McWhorter, *Carry Me Home,* pp. 15, 17, 21. In an interview with *Eyes on the Prize,* lawyer and former mayor David Vann argued that Birmingham businessmen never encouraged Connor's tactics. Interview with David Vann, Washington University Libraries. Harkey, *The Smell of Burning Crosses,* p. 65.

115. John Jennings to Emory Via (August 9, 1966), Southern Regional Council Papers, 1944–1968, Reel 70.

SIX

The Price of Liberation

1. William Faulkner, quoted in James Silver, "Mississippi Must Choose," *New York Times Magazine* (July 19, 1964); Robert Penn Warren, *Segregation: The Inner Conflict in the South* (New York, 1956), p. 113; Sullivan, ed., *Freedom Writer,* p. 121.

2. On King's "Letter from Birmingham City Jail," see McWhorter, *Carry Me Home,* p. 355; Watters, *Down to Now,* p. 13; John Hersey, "A Life for a Vote," in *Reporting Civil Rights,* Vol. 2, pp. 223–24; interview with Fannie Lou Hamer, by Neil McMillen (April 14, 1972), Civil Rights in Mississippi Digital Archive.

3. James Baldwin, *The Fire Next Time* (1963), reprinted in Baldwin, *Collected Essays,* pp. 334, 293, 342.

4. Ibid., pp. 294–95; James Weldon Johnson, *Along This Way: The Autobiography of James Weldon Johnson* (New York, 1933), p. 318.

5. David Blight, ed., *Narrative of the Life of Frederick Douglass, An American Slave, Written by Himself* (Boston, 1993), pp. 59–60, 64; George Orwell, "Shooting an Elephant," in Orwell, *A Collection of Essays* (New York, 1946), p. 152.

6. *Atlanta Constitution,* July 29, 1946; Sibley Commission, Fifth Congressional District, Atlanta, GA (March 24, 1960), John Sibley Papers, Box 146, Witness Testimony Folder, Emory University Special Collections; Margaret Long, "A Southern White Views the Sit-in Movement," USNSA Civil Rights Newsletter (May 3, 1961), Southern Historical Collection.

7. Coles, *Farewell to the South,* p. 10; Leslie Dunbar, "The Annealing of the South" (1961), reprinted in Dunbar, *The Shame of Southern Politics,* p. 6.

8. Dunbar, "The Annealing of the South," p. 6; Frady, *Southerners,* p. 265; Powledge, *Free at Last?,* p. 641.

9. Interview with Hodding Carter, by Jack Bass (April 1, 1974), Southern Oral History Program; Howell Raines, *My Soul Is Rested: The Story of the Civil Rights Movement in the Deep South* (New York, 1977), pp. 23–24; Howell Raines, "Grady's Gift," *New York Times Magazine* (December 1, 1991).

10. Pat Watters, *The South and the Nation* (New York, 1969), pp. 4, 374; Pat Watters, "The South and the Nation," *New South* (Fall 1969), p. 20.

11. Interview with Florence Mars, by Thomas Healy (January 5, 1978), Civil Rights in Mississippi Digital Archive; interview with Warren Ashby, by William Chafe (September 25, 1974, and October 3, 1974), William Henry Chafe Oral History Collection, Duke University Special Collections; Anderson, *The Children of the South,* p. 116.

12. Watters, *Down to Now,* pp. 161, 11.

13. Kotz, *Judgment Days,* pp. 336–37.

14. Marshall Frady, "A Meeting of Strangers in Americus," *Life* (February 12, 1971).

15. Ibid.; Joseph Cumming, "Been Down Home So Long It Looks like Up to Me," *Esquire* (August 1971), p. 114.

16. *Atlanta Constitution,* November 13, 1972; *Delta Democrat-Times,* April 4, 1969.

17. Interview with Richard Franco, by author.

18. Sullivan, ed., *Freedom Writer,* p. 388; *Time* (September 27, 1976), p. 48; Joel Williamson, *The Crucible of Race: Black-White Relations in the American South Since Emancipation* (New York, 1984), p. 499; P.M.P. (December 19, 1972), Joel Williamson Exams.

19. Joseph Cumming, "A Final Farewell," *Georgia* (June 1972), p. 52; draft of article, Joseph Cumming to *Athens Observer* (November 18, 1975).

20. *Congressional Record* (Vol. 116, No. 87), May 28, 1970.

21. Ibid.

22. Ibid.

23. Dunbar, *Delta Time,* p. xx.

24. Goldfield, *Black, White, and Southern.* Goldfield has a section entitled "Civil Rights and White Southerners: The Fruits of Liberation," pp. 169–73.

25. Will Campbell, *Forty Acres and a Goat,* quoted in Frady, *Southerners,* p. 373.

26. Will Campbell, *Forty Acres and a Goat,* quoted in Fred Hobson, *But Now I See: The White Southern Racial Conversion Narrative* (Baton Rouge, 1999), p. 277.

27. Walker Percy, "Mississippi: The Fallen Paradise," in Morris, ed., *The South Today,* p. 78; Thornton, *Dividing Lines,* p. 582; Cumming, "Been Down Home So Long It Looks like Up to Me," p. 114.

28. Interview with James McBride Dabbs (1965–1968), by Dallas Blanchard, Southern Oral History Program; Jack Bass, "The Squire of Rip Raps," *The South Today* (December 1969).

29. *Albany Herald,* July 17, 1962; de Lesseps Morrison to Betty Lowry (December 15, 1960), de Lesseps Morrison Papers; *New York Times,* July 13, 2004.

30. Wilkie, *Dixie,* pp. 299, 323–24.

31. Interview with Florence Mars, by Thomas Healy (January 5, 1978), Civil Rights in Mississippi Digital Archive; *Clarion-Ledger* (Jackson, MS), January 7, June 15, 2005; *New York Times,* June 12, 2005.

32. "Southern Town Struggles with a Violent Legacy," *New York Times,* May 29, 2004.

33. *New York Times,* January 7–8, 2005.

34. Ibid.; *Clarion-Ledger,* June 12, 2005.

35. *New York Times,* January 7–8, 2005.

36. Gary Younge, "Racism Rebooted," *The Nation* (July 11, 2005); *Clarion-Ledger,* June 12, 2005; *New York Times,* April 3, June 2, 12, 2005.

37. *Clarion-Ledger,* January 8, 23, 2005.

38. Ibid., June 15, 12, 2005; *New York Times,* June 12, 21, 2005.

39. *Clarion-Ledger,* June 22, 2005.

40. Ibid. See James Silver, *Mississippi: The Closed Society* (New York, 1964); Robert Moses wrote from the McComb jail that he was in "the middle of the iceberg." Branch, *Parting the Waters,* p. 523.

41. *New York Times,* December 15, 2002; William Doyle, *An American Insurrection: The Battle of Oxford, Mississippi, 1962* (New York, 2001); Ellis Cose, "Lessons of the Trent Lott Mess," *Newsweek* (December 23, 2002), p. 37.

42. *New York Times,* December 15, 2002; *Newsweek* (December 23, 2002), p. 23.

43. *New York Times,* December 14, 12, 2002.

44. Ibid., December 21, 22, 2002. Southerners would doubtless point out that "terrible" racial episodes occurred everywhere in America, in New York City as well as in Pascagoula. *The Nation* opined: "In the end, as Martin Luther King, Jr., prophesied, they liberated white Americans too, including white Mississippians, by removing this historic stain from our society. Senator Lott was not saved, however." *The Nation* (December 30, 2002), p. 3.

45. Edward Ball, "Ghosts of Carolina," *New York Times,* December 22, 2002.

46. Ibid.

47. *New York Times,* December 21, 2002.

48. Aristotle, *Poetics,* translated by S. H. Butcher (New York, 1961), p. 78.

49. Joseph Cumming, "Lessons Learned in Black and White: Unforgettable Characters," *Times-Georgian,* March 2, 1997; interview with Will Campbell, by Orley Caudill (June 8, 1976), Civil Rights in Mississippi Digital Archive.

50. August Meier, "On the Role of Martin Luther King," *New Politics* (Winter 1965), in *Reporting Civil Rights,* Vol. 2, pp. 456–57.

51. Elizabeth Hardwick, "Selma, Alabama: The Charms of Goodness," *New York Review of Books* (April 22, 1965).

52. Watters, *Down to Now,* p. 54.

53. Interview with Jerry Clower, by Orley Caudill (July 12, 1973), Civil Rights in Mississippi Digital Archive.

54. Interview with Peter Klopfer (June 5, 1974), Duke University Oral History Program.

55. Sullivan, ed., *Freedom Writer,* pp. 318–19, 327, 342, 375.

56. Charles Longstreet Weltner, "My Friend Calvin," *Atlanta Magazine* (November 1969).

57. Hastings Wyman, *Chattanooga Times/Chattanooga Free Press,* February 16, 2003; John Egerton, "A Visit with James McBride Dabbs," *New South,* Vol. 24, No. 1 (Winter 1969), p. 47. For an in-depth exploration of the "white southern racial conversion narrative," probed mostly through a study of autobiographies, see Hobson, *But Now I See.*

58. Joseph Cumming, "The American Idea in the South," *Atlanta Magazine* (September 1969), p. 17; interview with M. W. Hamilton, by Orley Caudill (February 13, 1978), Civil Rights in Mississippi Digital Archive.

59. *Time* (September 27, 1976), pp. 4–6.

60. Karl Fleming, "The South Revisited After a Momentous Decade," *Newsweek* (August 10, 1970).

61. Ibid.

62. Doyle, *An American Insurrection,* pp. 173–74, 316; interview with Brodie Crump, by Orley Caudill (February 26, 1974), Civil Rights in Mississippi Digital Archive.

63. Interview with Clara Lee Sharrard, by author (Springfield, MA, 2003).

64. Cumming, "Lessons Learned in Black and White: An Irresistible Force," *Times-Georgian,* February 23, 1997.

65. Ralph Ellison, quoted in George Tindall, *The Ethnic Southerners* (Baton Rouge, 1976), p. 19.

66. Interview with Hugh Wilson, by Wendy Watriss and Reginald Kearney (June 5, 1974), Duke University Oral History Program.

67. Gunnar Myrdal, *An American Dilemma: The Negro Problem and Modern Democracy* (New York, 1944), p. lxxvi. The phrase "this is a white man's country" comes from *American Negro Slavery* (1918), by Ulrich Phillips, an early-twentieth-century historian and apologist for slavery.

68. Myrdal, *An American Dilemma,* pp. 997–98.

69. Ibid., pp. 1004, lxxv.

70. Editors of *Ebony, The White Problem in America* (Chicago, 1966), pp. 1–2, 4, 6.

71. Ibid., pp. 171, 154.

72. Ibid., pp. 174–75.

73. Ibid., pp. 180–81.

74. *Time* (September 27, 1976). See Schulman, *From Cotton Belt to Sunbelt;* Peter Applebome, *Dixie Rising: How the South Is Shaping American Values, Politics, and Culture* (New York, 1996); Coles, *Farewell to the South;* Marshall Frady, "An Alabama Marriage," *New Times* (March 8, 1974), reprinted in Frady, *Southerners,* p. 263; *Time* (Septem-

ber 27, 1976), p. 29; Greene, *Praying for Sheetrock,* p. 21; Fuller, *I Hear Them Calling My Name,* p. 200.

75. Charlie LeDuff, "At a Slaughterhouse, Some Things Never Die," in Correspondents of *The New York Times, How Race Is Lived in America* (New York, 2001), pp. 97–113.

76. Ibid.

77. Ginger Thompson, "Reaping What Was Sown on the Old Plantation," in Correspondents of *The New York Times, How Race Is Lived in America,* pp. 141, 147.

78. Editors of *Ebony, The White Problem in America,* p. 32.

Selected Bibliography

Books

Abbott, Dorothy, ed. *Mississippi Writers—Reflections of Childhood and Youth.* Volume 2: *Nonfiction.* Jackson: University Press of Mississippi, 1986.

Anderson, Margaret. *The Children of the South.* New York: Farrar, Straus & Giroux, 1966.

Applebome, Peter. *Dixie Rising: How the South Is Shaping American Values, Politics, and Culture.* New York: Times Books, 1996.

Ashmore, Harry. *Hearts and Minds: The Anatomy of Racism from Roosevelt to Reagan.* New York: McGraw Hill, 1982.

Baker, Liva. *The Second Battle of New Orleans: The Hundred-Year Struggle to Integrate the Schools.* New York: HarperCollins, 1996.

Baldwin, James. *Collected Essays.* New York: Library of America, 1998.

Bartley, Numan V. *The New South, 1945–1980.* Baton Rouge: Louisiana State University Press, 1995.

Bartley, Numan V., and Hugh D. Graham. *Southern Politics and the Second Reconstruction.* Baltimore: Johns Hopkins University Press, 1975.

Bass, Jack. *Taming the Storm: The Life and Times of Judge Frank M. Johnson, and the South's Fight over Civil Rights.* New York: Doubleday, 1993.

Bass, Jack, and Walter DeVries. *The Transformation of Southern Politics: Social Change and Political Consequence Since 1945.* New York: Basic Books, 1976.

Bass, S. Jonathan. *Blessed Are the Peacemakers: Martin Luther King, Jr., Eight White Religious Leaders, and the "Letter from Birmingham Jail."* Baton Rouge: Louisiana State University Press, 2001.

Beardslee, William. *The Way Out Must Lead In: Life Histories in the Civil Rights Movement.* Atlanta: Center for Research in Social Change, Emory University, 1977.

Bergreen, Laurence. *Louis Armstrong: An Extravagant Life.* New York: Broadway Books, 1997.

Black, Earl, and Merle Black. *The Rise of Southern Republicans.* Cambridge: Harvard University Press, 2002.

Blight, David, ed. *Narrative of the Life of Frederick Douglass, An American Slave, Written by Himself.* Boston: Bedford, 1993.

Bolsterli, Margaret Jones. *Born in the Delta: Reflections on the Making of a Southern White Sensibility.* Knoxville: University of Tennessee Press, 1991.

Boyle, Sarah Patton. *The Desegregated Heart: A Virginian's Stand in Time of Transition.* New York: Morrow, 1962.

Bragg, Rick. *All Over but the Shoutin'.* New York: Pantheon, 1997.

Branch, Taylor. *Parting the Waters: America in the King Years, 1954–63.* New York: Simon & Schuster, 1988.

———. *Pillar of Fire: America in the King Years, 1963–65.* New York: Simon & Schuster, 1998.

Bridges, Ruby. *Through My Eyes.* New York: Scholastic, 1999.

Brinkley, Alan. *Liberalism and Its Discontents.* Cambridge: Harvard University Press, 1998.

Canzoneri, Robert. *"I Do So Politely": A Voice from the South.* Boston: Houghton Mifflin, 1965.

Caro, Robert A. *Master of the Senate.* New York: Knopf, 2002.

———. *Means of Ascent.* New York: Knopf, 1990.

———. *The Path to Power.* New York: Knopf, 1982.

Carson, Clayborne, et al. *The Eyes on the Prize Civil Rights Reader: Documents, Speeches, and Firsthand Accounts from the Black Freedom Struggle, 1954–1990.* New York: Penguin, 1991.

Carter, Dan. *The Politics of Rage: George Wallace, the Origins of the New Conservatism, and the Transformation of American Politics.* Baton Rouge: Louisiana State University Press, 1995.

Carter, Hodding. *So the Heffners Left McComb.* Garden City, NY: Doubleday, 1965.

———. *Where Main Street Meets the River.* New York: Rinehart, 1953.

Cash, W. J. *The Mind of the South.* New York: Knopf, 1941.

Chafe, William. *Civilities and Civil Rights: Greensboro, North Carolina, and the Black Struggle for Freedom.* New York: Oxford University Press, 1980.

———. *Never Stop Running: Allard Lowenstein and the Struggle to Save American Liberalism.* New York: Basic Books, 1993.

Chappell, David L. *Inside Agitators: White Southerners in the Civil Rights Movement.* Baltimore: Johns Hopkins University Press, 1994.

———. *A Stone of Hope: Prophetic Religion and the Death of Jim Crow.* Chapel Hill: University of North Carolina Press, 2004.

Chestnut, J. L., and Julia Cass. *Black in Selma: The Uncommon Life of J. L. Chestnut, Jr.* New York: Farrar, Straus & Giroux, 1990.

Cobb, James. *The Most Southern Place on Earth: The Mississippi Delta and the Roots of Regional Identity.* New York: Oxford University Press, 1992.

———. *The Selling of the South: The Southern Crusade for Industrial Development, 1936–1990.* Urbana: University of Illinois Press, 1993.

Cohn, David. *Where I Was Born and Raised.* 2nd rev. ed. South Bend, IN: University of Notre Dame Press, 1967.

Colburn, David. *Racial Change and Community Crisis: St. Augustine, Florida, 1877–1980.* New York: Columbia University Press, 1985.

Coles, Robert. *Children of Crisis: A Study of Courage and Fear.* Boston: Little, Brown, 1967.

———. *Farewell to the South.* Boston: Little, Brown, 1972.

———. *Migrants, Sharecroppers, Mountaineers.* Boston: Little, Brown, 1971.

Cortner, Richard. *Civil Rights and Public Accommodations: The Heart of Atlanta Motel and McClung Cases.* Lawrence: University Press of Kansas, 2001.

Cunningham, W. J. *Agony at Galloway: One Church's Struggle with Social Change*. Jackson: University Press of Mississippi, 1980.

Curry, Constance. *Silver Rights*. Chapel Hill, NC: Algonquin, 1995.

Dabbs, James McBride. *Who Speaks for the South?* New York: Funk & Wagnalls, 1964.

Dalfiume, Richard. *Desegregation of the U.S. Armed Forces: Fighting on Two Fronts, 1939–1953*. Columbia: University of Missouri Press, 1969.

Daniel, Pete. *Lost Revolutions: The South in the 1950s*. Chapel Hill: University of North Carolina Press, 2000.

Davidson, Chandler, and Bernard Grofman, eds. *Quiet Revolution in the South: The Impact of the Voting Rights Act, 1965–1990*. Princeton: Princeton University Press, 1994.

Davis, Jack. *Race Against Time: Culture and Separation in Natchez Since 1930*. Baton Rouge: Louisiana State University Press, 2001.

Dent, Tom. *Southern Journey: A Return to the Civil Rights Movement*. New York: Morrow, 1997.

Dittmer, John. *Local People: The Civil Rights Struggle in Mississippi*. Urbana: University of Illinois Press, 1994.

Doyle, William. *An American Insurrection: The Battle of Oxford, Mississippi, 1962*. New York: Doubleday, 2001.

Du Bois, W. E. B. *Dusk of Dawn: An Essay Toward an Autobiography of a Race Concept*. New York: Harcourt, Brace, 1940.

———. *The Souls of Black Folk*. Chicago: A. C. McClurg & Co., 1903; New York: Penguin, 1989.

Dudziak, Mary L. *Cold War Civil Rights: Race and the Image of American Democracy*. Princeton: Princeton University Press, 2000.

Dunbar, Anthony. *Delta Time: A Journey Through Mississippi*. New York: Pantheon, 1990.

———. *Our Land Too*. New York: Pantheon, 1971.

Dunbar, Leslie. *The Shame of Southern Politics: Essays and Speeches*. Lexington: University Press of Kentucky, 2002.

Durr, Virginia. *Outside the Magic Circle: The Autobiography of Virginia Foster Durr*. Tuscaloosa: University of Alabama Press, 1985.

Eagles, Charles. *Outside Agitator: Jon Daniels and the Civil Rights Movement in Alabama*. Chapel Hill: University of North Carolina Press, 1993.

Ebony, Editors of. *The White Problem in America*. Chicago: Johnson, 1966.

Egerton, John. *Shades of Gray: Dispatches from the Modern South*. Baton Rouge: Louisiana State University Press, 1991.

———. *Speak Now Against the Day: The Generation Before the Civil Rights Movement in the South*. New York: Knopf, 1994.

Ellison, Ralph. *Going to the Territory*. New York: Random House, 1986.

Ely, James. *The Crisis of Conservative Virginia: The Byrd Organization and the Politics of Massive Resistance*. Knoxville: University of Tennessee Press, 1976.

Eskew, Glenn. *But for Birmingham: The Local and National Movements in the Civil Rights Struggle*. Chapel Hill: University of North Carolina Press, 1997.

Estes, Steve. *I Am a Man!: Race, Manhood, and the Civil Rights Movement*. Chapel Hill: University of North Carolina Press, 2004.

Fager, Charles. *White Reflections on Black Power*. Grand Rapids, MI: William Eerdmans, 1967.

Fairclough, Adam. *Race and Democracy: The Civil Rights Struggle in Louisiana, 1915–1972.* Athens: University of Georgia Press, 1995.

Feldman, Glenn, ed. *Before Brown: Civil Rights and White Backlash in the Modern South.* Tuscaloosa: University of Alabama Press, 2004.

Ferris, William. *Blues from the Delta.* New York: Anchor/Doubleday, 1978.

Fink, Gary, and Merl Reed, eds. *Race, Class, and Community in Southern Labor History.* Tuscaloosa: University of Alabama Press, 1994.

Fleming, Karl. *Son of the Rough South: An Uncivil Memoir.* New York: Public Affairs, 2005.

Flynt, J. Wayne. *Alabama Baptists: Southern Baptists in the Heart of Dixie.* Tuscaloosa: University of Alabama Press, 1998.

———. *Dixie's Forgotten People: The South's Poor Whites.* Bloomington: Indiana University Press, 1979.

Flynt, J. Wayne, and Dorothy Flynt. *Southern Poor Whites: An Annotated Bibliography.* New York: Garland, 1981.

Frady, Marshall. *Southerners: A Journalist's Odyssey.* New York: New American Library, 1980.

Fredrickson, George. *Racism: A Short History.* Princeton: Princeton University Press, 2002.

Friedland, Michael. *Lift Up Your Voice like a Trumpet: White Clergy and the Civil Rights and Antiwar Movements, 1954–1973.* Chapel Hill: University of North Carolina Press, 1998.

Fuller, Chet. *I Hear Them Calling My Name: A Journey Through the New South.* Boston: Houghton Mifflin, 1981.

Gaillard, Frye. *Cradle of Freedom: Alabama and the Movement That Changed America.* Tuscaloosa: University of Alabama Press, 2004.

Gallup, George H., ed. *The Gallup Poll: Public Opinion, 1935–1971,* Vol. 3. New York: Random House, 1972.

Garrow, David. *Bearing the Cross: Martin Luther King, Jr., and the Southern Christian Leadership Conference.* New York: Morrow, 1986.

Garrow, David, ed. *We Shall Overcome: The Civil Rights Movement in the United States in the 1950's and 1960's.* 3 vols. Brooklyn: Carlson, 1989.

Genovese, Eugene. *The Political Economy of Slavery: Studies in the Economy and Society of the Slave South.* New York: Pantheon, 1965.

———. *Roll, Jordan, Roll: The World the Slaves Made.* New York: Pantheon, 1974.

Gerster, Patrick, and Nicholas Cords, eds. *Myth and Southern History.* Chicago: Rand McNally, 1974.

Gerstle, Gary. *American Crucible: Race and Nation in the Twentieth Century.* Princeton: Princeton University Press, 2001.

Goldfield, David R. *Black, White, and Southern: Race Relations and Southern Culture, 1940 to the Present.* Baton Rouge: Louisiana State University Press, 1990.

———. *Still Fighting the Civil War: The American South and Southern History.* Baton Rouge: Louisiana State University Press, 2002.

Greene, Melissa Fay. *Praying for Sheetrock.* Reading, MA: Addison-Wesley, 1991.

Guralnick, Peter. *Lost Highway: Journeys and Arrivals of American Musicians.* Boston: David Godine, 1979.

Haas, Edward. *DeLesseps S. Morrison and the Image of Reform: New Orleans Politics, 1946–1961.* Baton Rouge: Louisiana State University Press, 1974.

Hale, Grace Elizabeth. *Making Whiteness: The Culture of Segregation in the South, 1890–1940.* New York: Pantheon, 1998.

Halpern, Rick, and Jonathan Morris, eds. *American Exceptionalism?: U.S. Working-Class Formation in an International Context.* New York: St. Martin's, 1997.

Hampton, Henry, and Steve Fayer. *Voices of Freedom: An Oral History of the Civil Rights Movement from the 1950s Through the 1980s.* New York: Bantam, 1990.

Harkey, Ira. *The Smell of Burning Crosses: An Autobiography of a Mississippi Newspaperman.* Jacksonville, IL: Harris-Wolfe, 1967.

Harris, David. *Dreams Die Hard.* New York: St. Martin's/Marek, 1982.

Hendrickson, Paul. *Sons of Mississippi: A Story of Race and Its Legacy.* New York: Knopf, 2003.

Hirsch, Arnold, and Joseph Logsdon, eds. *Creole New Orleans: Race and Americanization.* Baton Rouge: Louisiana State University Press, 1992.

Hobson, Fred. *But Now I See: The White Southern Racial Conversion Narrative.* Baton Rouge: Louisiana State University Press, 1999.

Huggins, Nathan Irvin. *Revelations: American History, American Myths.* New York: Oxford University Press, 1995.

Hunter-Gault, Charlayne. *In My Place.* New York: Farrar, Straus & Giroux, 1992.

Ignatiev, Noel. *How the Irish Became White.* New York: Routledge, 1995.

Inger, Morton. *Politics and Reality in an American City: The New Orleans School Crisis of 1960.* New York: Center for Urban Education, 1969.

Jacoway, Elizabeth, and David R. Colburn, eds. *Southern Businessmen and Desegregation.* Baton Rouge: Louisiana State University Press, 1982.

James, Hunter. *They Didn't Put That on the Huntley-Brinkley!: A Vagabond Reporter Encounters the New South.* Athens: University of Georgia Press, 1993.

Jaynes, Gerald, and Robin Williams, Jr., eds. *A Common Destiny: Blacks and American Society.* Washington, DC: National Academy Press, 1989.

Johnson, James Weldon. *Along This Way: The Autobiography of James Weldon Johnson.* New York: Viking Press, 1933.

Kelley, Robin. *Hammer and Hoe: Alabama Communists During the Great Depression.* Chapel Hill: University of North Carolina Press, 1990.

———. *Race Rebels: Culture, Politics, and the Black Working Class.* New York: Free Press, 1994.

Key, V. O., Jr. *Southern Politics in State and Nation.* New York: Knopf, 1949.

Killian, Lewis. *Black and White: Reflections of a White Southern Sociologist.* Dix Hills, NY: General Hall, 1994.

———. *White Southerners.* Amherst: University of Massachusetts Press, 1985.

King, Larry L. *Confessions of a White Racist.* New York: Viking, 1971.

King, Martin Luther, Jr. *Stride Toward Freedom: The Montgomery Story.* New York: Harper & Row, 1958.

———. *Why We Can't Wait.* New York: Harper & Row, 1964.

Kluger, Richard. *Simple Justice: The History of* Brown v. Board of Education *and Black America's Struggle for Equality.* New York: Knopf, 1976.

Kopkind, Andrew. *The Thirty Years' Wars: Dispatches of a Radical Journalist.* New York: Verso, 1995.

Korstad, Robert Rodgers. *Civil Rights Unionism: Tobacco Workers and the Struggle for Democracy in the Mid-Twentieth-Century South.* Chapel Hill: University of North Carolina Press, 2003.

Kotz, Nick. *Judgment Days: Lyndon Baines Johnson, Martin Luther King, Jr., and the Laws That Changed America.* Boston: Houghton Mifflin, 2005.

Kousser, J. Morgan. *Colorblind Injustice: Minority Voting Rights and the Undoing of the Second Reconstruction.* Chapel Hill: University of North Carolina Press, 1999.

Kruse, Kevin. *White Flight: America and the Making of Modern Conservatism.* Princeton: Princeton University Press, 2005.

Lassiter, Matthew. *The Silent Majority: Suburban Politics in the Sunbelt South.* Princeton: Princeton University Press, 2005.

Lassiter, Matthew, and Andrew Lewis, eds. *The Moderates' Dilemma: Massive Resistance to School Desegregation in Virginia.* Charlottesville: University of Virginia Press, 1998.

Lawson, Steven. *Black Ballots: Voting Rights in the South, 1944–1969.* New York: Columbia University Press, 1976.

———. *In Pursuit of Power: Southern Blacks and Electoral Politics, 1965–1982.* New York: Columbia University Press, 1985.

Lefler, Hugh Talmage, and Albert Ray Newsome. *North Carolina: The History of a Southern State.* Chapel Hill: University of North Carolina Press, 1954.

Lewis, John. *Walking with the Wind: A Memoir of the Movement.* New York: Simon & Schuster, 1998.

Lightle, Bill. *Made or Broken: Football and Survival in the Georgia Woods.* Austin, TX: Turn Key Press, 2004.

Litwack, Leon. *Been in the Storm So Long: The Aftermath of Slavery.* New York: Knopf, 1979.

———. *Trouble in Mind: Black Southerners in the Age of Jim Crow.* New York: Knopf, 1998.

Marsh, Charles. *God's Long Summer: Stories of Faith and Civil Rights.* Princeton: Princeton University Press, 1997.

Mayfield, Chris, ed. *Growing Up Southern: Southern Exposure Looks at Childhood, Then and Now.* New York: Pantheon, 1981.

McKnight, Gerald. *The Last Crusade: Martin Luther King, Jr., the FBI, and the Poor People's Campaign.* Boulder, CO: Westview, 1998.

McLaurin, Tim. *Keeper of the Moon.* New York: Norton, 1991.

McMillen, Neil. *The Citizens' Council: Organized Resistance to the Second Reconstruction, 1954–64.* Urbana: University of Illinois Press, 1971.

McMillen, Neil, ed. *Remaking Dixie: The Impact of World War II on the American South.* Jackson: University Press of Mississippi, 1997.

McWhorter, Diane. *Carry Me Home: Birmingham, Alabama—The Climactic Battle of the Civil Rights Revolution.* New York: Simon & Schuster, 2001.

Meacham, Jon, ed. *Voices in Our Blood: America's Best on the Civil Rights Movement.* New York: Random House, 2001.

Metcalf, George. *From Little Rock to Boston: The History of School Desegregation.* Westport, CT: Greenwood, 1983.

Miller, Marc, ed. *Working Lives: The Southern Exposure History of Labor in the South.* New York: Pantheon, 1980.

Minchin, Timothy. *The Color of Work: The Struggle for Civil Rights in the Southern Paper Industry, 1945–1980.* Chapel Hill: University of North Carolina Press, 1991.

———. *Hiring the Black Worker: The Racial Integration of the Southern Textile Industry, 1960–1980.* Chapel Hill: University of North Carolina Press, 1999.

Moody, Anne. *Coming of Age in Mississippi.* New York: Doubleday, 1968.

Morgan, Edmund. *American Slavery, American Freedom: The Ordeal of Colonial Virginia.* New York: Norton, 1975.

Morris, Willie. *Yazoo: Integration in a Deep-Southern Town.* New York: Harper's Magazine Press, 1971.

Morris, Willie, ed. *The South Today: 100 Years After Appomattox.* New York: Harper & Row, 1965.

Morrison, Toni. *Playing in the Dark: Whiteness and the Literary Imagination.* New York: Vintage, 1992.

Myrdal, Gunnar. *An American Dilemma: The Negro Problem and Modern Democracy.* New York: Harper & Row, 1944.

Neilson, Melany. *Even Mississippi.* Tuscaloosa: University of Alabama Press, 1989.

Newman, Mark. *Divine Agitators: The Delta Ministry and Civil Rights in Mississippi.* Athens: University of Georgia Press, 2004.

———. *Getting Right with God: Southern Baptists and Desegregation, 1945–1995.* Tuscaloosa: University of Alabama Press, 2001.

The New Orleans School Crisis: Report of the Louisiana State Advisory Committee of the United States Commission on Civil Rights. Washington, DC: U.S. Government Printing Office, 1961.

Correspondents of *The New York Times. How Race Is Lived in America.* New York: Times Books, 2001.

Norrell, Robert. *Reaping the Whirlwind: The Civil Rights Movement in Tuskegee.* New York: Knopf, 1985.

Oakes, James. *The Ruling Race: A History of American Slaveholders.* New York: Knopf, 1982.

O'Brien, Gail Williams. *The Color of the Law: Race, Violence, and Justice in the Post–World War II South.* Chapel Hill: University of North Carolina Press, 1999.

Orfield, Gary. *Must We Bus?: Segregated Schools and National Policy.* Washington, DC: Brookings Institution, 1978.

Orwell, George. *A Collection of Essays.* New York: Harcourt Brace Jovanovich, 1946.

Ownby, Ted, ed. *The Role of Ideas in the Civil Rights South.* Jackson: University Press of Mississippi, 2002.

Parsons, Sarah Mitchell. *From Southern Wrongs to Civil Rights: The Memoir of a White Civil Rights Activist.* Tuscaloosa: University of Alabama Press, 2000.

Payne, Charles M. *I've Got the Light of Freedom: The Organizing Tradition and the Mississippi Freedom Struggle.* Berkeley: University of California Press, 1995.

Phillips, Kevin. *The Emerging Republican Majority.* New Rochelle, NY: Arlington House, 1969.

Pomerantz, Gary. *Where Peachtree Meets Sweet Auburn: A Saga of Race and Family.* New York: Simon & Schuster, 1996.

Powledge, Fred. *Free at Last?: The Civil Rights Movement and the People Who Made It.* Boston: Little, Brown, 1991.

Pratt, Robert. *We Shall Not Be Moved: The Desegregation of the University of Georgia.* Athens: University of Georgia Press, 2002.

Raines, Howell. *My Soul Is Rested: The Story of the Civil Rights Movement in the Deep South.* New York: Penguin, 1977.

Ransby, Barbara, ed. *Deep in Our Hearts: Nine White Women in the Freedom Movement.* Athens: University of Georgia Press, 2000.

Reporting Civil Rights: American Journalism, 1941–1973. 2 vols. New York: Library of America, 2003.

Robinson, Armstead, and Patricia Sullivan, eds. *New Directions in Civil Rights Studies.* Charlottesville: University Press of Virginia, 1991.

Roediger, David R. *The Wages of Whiteness: Race and the Making of the American Working Class.* New York: Verso, 1991.

Roediger, David R., ed. *Black on White: Black Writers on What It Means to Be White.* New York: Schocken, 1998.

Rogers, Kim Lacy. *Righteous Lives: Narratives of the New Orleans Civil Rights Movement.* New York: New York University Press, 1993.

Rogin, Michael. *Blackface, White Noise: Jewish Immigrants in the Hollywood Melting Pot.* Berkeley: University of California Press, 1996.

Ruppersburg, Hugh, ed., *Georgia Voices.* Vol. 2: *Nonfiction.* Athens: University of Georgia Press, 1994.

Saxton, Alexander. *The Rise and Fall of the White Republic: Class Politics and Mass Culture in Nineteenth-Century America.* New York: Verso, 1990.

Schulman, Bruce. *From Cotton Belt to Sunbelt: Federal Policy, Economic Development, and the Transformation of the South, 1938–1980.* New York: Oxford University Press, 1991.

———. *The Seventies: The Great Shift in American Culture, Society, and Politics.* New York: Free Press, 2006.

Segrest, Mab. *Memoir of a Race Traitor.* Boston: South End, 1994.

Sherrill, Robert. *Gothic Politics in the Deep South: Stars of the New Confederacy.* New York: Ballantine, 1968.

Silver, James. *Mississippi: The Closed Society.* New York: Harcourt, Brace & World, 1964.

Sitkoff, Harvard. *The Struggle for Black Equality, 1954–1992.* New York: Hill & Wang, 1993.

Smith, Frank. *Congressman from Mississippi.* New York: Pantheon, 1964.

———. *Look Away from Dixie.* Baton Rouge: Louisiana State University Press, 1965.

Smith, Lillian. *Killers of the Dream.* New York: Norton, 1949.

Stampp, Kenneth. *The Peculiar Institution: Slavery in the Ante-bellum South.* New York: Knopf, 1956.

Steinbeck, John. *Travels with Charley: In Search of America.* New York: Viking, 1962.

Stouffer, Samuel, Edward Suchman, Leland DeVinney, Shirley Star, and Robin Williams, eds. *The American Soldier: Adjustment During Army Life.* 2 vols. Princeton: Princeton University Press, 1949.

Sullivan, Patricia. *Days of Hope: Race and Democracy in the New Deal Era.* Chapel Hill: University of North Carolina Press, 1996.

Sullivan, Patricia, ed. *Freedom Writer: Virginia Foster Durr, Letters from the Civil Rights Years.* New York: Routledge, 2003.

Terkel, Studs. *"The Good War": An Oral History of World War II.* New York: New Press, 1984.

Thornton, J. Mills. *Dividing Lines: Municipal Politics and the Struggle for Civil Rights in Montgomery, Birmingham, and Selma.* Tuscaloosa: University of Alabama Press, 2002.

Three Negro Classics. New York: Bard/Avon Books, 1999.

Tindall, George. *The Ethnic Southerners.* Baton Rouge: Louisiana State University Press, 1976.

Trillin, Calvin. *An Education in Georgia: The Integration of Charlayne Hunter and Hamilton Holmes.* New York: Viking, 1964.

———. *U.S. Journal.* New York: Dutton, 1971.

Tuck, Stephen. *Beyond Atlanta: The Struggle for Racial Equality in Georgia, 1940–1980.* Athens: University of Georgia Press, 2001.

Warren, Robert Penn. *Segregation: The Inner Conflict in the South.* New York: Knopf, 1956.

———. *Who Speaks for the Negro?* New York: Knopf, 1965.

Washington, James, ed. *A Testament of Hope: The Essential Writings and Speeches of Martin Luther King, Jr.* San Francisco: Harper San Francisco, 1991.

Watters, Pat. *Down to Now: Reflections on the Southern Civil Rights Movement.* Athens: University of Georgia Press, 1971.

———. *The South and the Nation.* New York: Pantheon, 1969.

Watters, Pat, and Reese Cleghorn. *Climbing Jacob's Ladder: The Arrival of Negroes in Southern Politics.* New York: Harcourt Brace, 1967.

Wieder, Alan. *Race and Education: Narrative Essays, Oral Histories, and Documentary Photography.* New York: Peter Lang, 1997.

Wilkie, Curtis. *Dixie: A Personal Odyssey Through Events That Shaped the Modern South.* New York: Simon & Schuster, 2001.

Williamson, Joel. *The Crucible of Race: Black-White Relations in the American South Since Emancipation.* New York: Oxford University Press, 1984.

Wirt, Frederick. *"We Ain't What We Was": Civil Rights in the New South.* Durham, NC: Duke University Press, 1997.

Woods, Jeff. *Black Struggle, Red Scare: Segregation and Anti-Communism in the South, 1948–1968.* Baton Rouge: Louisiana State University Press, 2004.

Woodward, C. Vann. *The Burden of Southern History.* Baton Rouge: Louisiana State University Press, 1968.

———. *Origins of the New South, 1877–1913.* Baton Rouge: Louisiana State University Press, 1951.

———. *The Strange Career of Jim Crow.* New York: Oxford University Press, 1955.

Wright, Gavin. *Old South, New South: Revolutions in the Southern Economy Since the Civil War.* New York: Basic Books, 1986.

Zinn, Howard. *The Southern Mystique.* New York: Knopf, 1964.

Manuscript Sources

The Center for Oral History and Cultural Heritage, University of Southern Mississippi, Hattiesburg, Mississippi

Oral Histories, Civil Rights in Mississippi

Film and Media Archive, Washington University Special Collections, St. Louis, Missouri

Eyes on the Prize Interviews, Henry Hampton Collection

Louisiana Division, New Orleans Public Library, New Orleans, Louisiana

Mayor de Lesseps S. Morrison Records, City Archives

Mayor Victor H. Schiro Records, City Archives

`   Save Our Schools File
        Segregation File
        Friends of the Cabildo Oral History Program (audiotapes)

McWhorter Library, University of Memphis, Memphis, Tennessee
        Sanitation Strike Archival Project

Richard B. Russell Library for Political Research and Studies, University of Georgia
Libraries, Athens, Georgia
        Richard B. Russell Papers

Southern Historical Collection, Wilson Library, University of North Carolina at Chapel
Hill, Chapel Hill, North Carolina
        Charles Raper Jonas Papers
        Sam J. Ervin Papers
        Papers of the North Carolina Council on Human Relations
        Southern Oral History Program
        New Bern Oral History Project
        Fellowship of Southern Churchmen Interviews
        Listening for a Change
        Jack Bass and Walter DeVries Collection

Special Collections, Duke University, Durham, North Carolina
        Duke University Oral History Program
        William Henry Chafe Oral History Collection
        Behind the Veil: Documenting African-American Life in the Jim Crow South, 1940–1997

Special Collections, Tulane University, New Orleans, Louisiana
        Friends of the Cabildo Oral History Program (transcriptions)

Special Collections and Archives Division, Robert W. Woodruff Library, Emory University, Atlanta, Georgia
        Newsweek Collection
        Frances Freeborn Pauley Papers
        John Sibley Papers
        Ralph McGill Papers

University Archives, Hargrett Rare Book and Manuscript Library, University of Georgia Libraries, Athens, Georgia
        Walter Danner Papers
        William Tate Papers
        O. C. Aderhold Papers

Microfilm Collections

Southern Regional Council Papers, 1944–1968 (Ann Arbor, MI: University Microfilms
        International), 1984.

Student Nonviolent Coordinating Committee Papers, 1959–1972 (Sanford, NC: Microfilm Corporation of America), 1982.

Digital Sources

Civil Rights in Mississippi Digital Archive, University of Southern Mississippi http://www.lib.usm.edu/~spcol/crda/

Eyes on the Prize interviews, Washington University Special Collections http://library.wustl.edu/units/spec/filmandmedia/hampton/eyes1interviews.html

In Motion: The African American Migration Experience, The Schomburg Center for Research in Black Culture, http://www.inmotionaame.org

Mississippi State Sovereignty Commission Records, Mississippi Department of Archives and History, http://www.mdah.state.ms.us

Sources in Author's Possession (audiotapes and/or transcripts)

Interview with Joseph Cumming
Interview with Phyllis Franco
Interview with Richard Franco
Interview with Tommy Moore
Interview with Clara Lee Sharrard
Joel Williamson Exams, courtesy of Joel Williamson
"Obituary: Lester Garfield Maddox, 1915–2003" (Marietta, GA, 2003)

Newspapers

Albany Herald (Albany, GA)
Atlanta Constitution (Atlanta, GA)
Atlanta Journal (Atlanta, GA)
Birmingham News (Birmingham, AL)
Boston Globe (Boston, MA)
Chattanooga Times/Free Press (Chattanooga, TN)
The Christian Science Monitor (Boston, MA)
Clarion-Ledger (Jackson, MS)
Commercial Appeal (Memphis, TN)
Delta Democrat-Times (Greenville, MS)
Greensboro News & Record (Greensboro, NC)
Greenville News (Greenville, SC)
Jackson Daily News (Jackson, MS)
Los Angeles Times (Los Angeles, CA)
Louisville Courier-Journal (Louisville, KY)
Montgomery Advertiser (Montgomery, AL)
New Orleans Times-Picayune (New Orleans, LA)
New York Herald Tribune (New York, NY)
New York Times (New York, NY)
Philadelphia Inquirer (Philadelphia, PA)
San Francisco Chronicle (San Francisco, CA)

St. Petersburg Times (St. Petersburg, FL)
Times-Georgian (Carrollton, GA)
The Wall Street Journal (New York, NY)
Washington Post (Washington, DC)

Periodicals

Atlanta Magazine
Birmingham Business Journal
Carolina Journal
Esquire
Georgia
Life
Look
The Nation
The New Republic
New South
Newsweek
The New Yorker
The New York Review of Books
New York Times Magazine
The Progressive
The Reporter
The Saturday Evening Post
The Saturday Review
Southern Voices
The South Today
Time
U.S. News & World Report

Acknowledgments

When I first conceived of this project, almost four years ago, I never could have imagined the journey that ensued. As the seed of an idea developed into the book that I feel fortunate to have produced, quite a few people lent me their hands, exercised their minds, and opened their homes. This book belongs to all of them.

Leon Litwack, my adviser at the University of California, Berkeley, guided me through every step. He helped with the initial conception of the project, directed me through research treks to the South, cast a critical eye on each paragraph and chapter, and offered tremendous help with the book contract. Waldo Martin also read much of the manuscript in its early stages. Along with others in the UC-Berkeley History Department—among them Robin Einhorn, Margaret Chowning, Reggie Zelnik, and Jim Kettner—he shepherded me through the graduate program. Patricia Sullivan's thorough comments on the manuscript, and her general help launching me into the academic world, have proved invaluable. Tom Leonard read over every chapter, and was always generous with his time.

Joe Cumming never tired. He sat down for an interview; sent me articles, clippings, and photographs; e-mailed his recollections, and gave me feedback on the chapter whose title bears his mark: "Softly, the Unthinkable." Lee Formwalt offered incisive comments on my chapter about Albany. Robby Cohen was a great help with my section on the integration of the University of Georgia, and I thank him for the opportunity to present my work in his NYU classroom. Joel Williamson gave me helpful comments while I was formulating my topic, and he provided me with a gold mine of primary documents.

I am ever grateful to Phyllis and Richard Franco. They shared many stories from their past, and welcomed me like family into their beautiful Atlanta home. Tommy Moore was also friendly and forthcoming, and regaled me with photos and mementos from Moore's Barbecue in New Bern. Clara Lee Sharrard not only took the time to revisit her Virginia childhood with me, but put up with Jeremy Sharrard, Daniel Oppenheimer, and me throughout our excellent years in Springfield, Massachusetts.

I cannot possibly mention every individual who was gracious enough to respond to my various entreaties by phone or mail. Some who met with me, offered crucial advice, or provided a good meal or shelter during my various research sojourns to the South include William Chafe, James Cobb, Robert Coles, Paul Duval, Steve Estes, William

Ferris, Raymond Gavins, Jacquelyn Dowd Hall, Tom Hallock, John Inscoe, Matt Lassiter, Betsy Lerner, Jim and Joan Martin, Gary Pomerantz, and Harry Watson.

Any young historian quickly learns that his staunchest allies work in the archives. Their prodigious knowledge, labor, and skill became indispensable. In particular, I would like to thank John White and the rest of the staff at the Southern Historical Collection in Chapel Hill; Randy Gue, Teresa Burk, and the staff at Emory University's Special Collections; Wayne Everard and his staff at the New Orleans Public Library; Linda McCurdy and others at Duke University's Rare Book, Manuscripts, and Special Collections Library; the staffs at the Hargrett Library and the Richard Russell Library at the University of Georgia; and Chris Pepus at Washington University's Special Collections.

Generous grants from the Jacob K. Javits Fellowship, under the auspices of the U.S. Department of Education, and the UC-Berkeley History Department made these research trips—and this project—possible. Two of my colleagues in the History Department, Joyce Mao and Jen Burns, gave me helpful advice on several chapters. Camilo Trumper, Celso Castilho, Tim Rose, and many more dear friends made my graduate school years unforgettable—from the Bay Area's assorted basketball courts to its extraordinary cafés.

My undergraduate advisers at Oberlin College have been instrumental in my intellectual growth. Gary Kornblith helped to guide me through my first major historical research project, and Norman Care taught me countless lessons about the world of learning.

As for the title of this book, I must acknowledge Dallas Frazier, the man who penned the song "There Goes My Everything." My two close collaborators, Nina Morrison and Scott Sokol, helped me to arrive at that title—one I think captures my subject. Which brings me to white southerners in general, and specifically to the many hundreds of people I have quoted. As a Springfield, Massachusetts, native with a Berkeley tag and a suspicious hankering for barbecue, I could not help feeling at times like an unwelcome outsider. But almost every southerner I met, or with whom I corresponded, welcomed me to their towns and into their past.

My editors at Alfred A. Knopf have been helpful and gracious through this process. I would like to thank Ashbel Green for taking on my project and offering varied suggestions, and Luba Ostashevsky and Sara Sherbill for their help on various facets of the book. Others I would like to thank: production manager Tracy Cabanis, text designer Wesley Gott, cover designer Carol Devine Carson, production editor Ellen Feldman, copyeditor Fred Chase, and proofreaders Susan VanOmmeren and Laura Starrett.

Finally, I want to thank my family. Their achievements are mine, as mine are theirs. They have provided all the love, compassion, thought, respect, and space that I could wish for. This book is dedicated to my parents, Fred and Betsy Sokol. I would also like to recognize and thank my grandparents, all of whom remain models of resilience: Saul Sokol, Mazie Sokol, Jim Pirtle, and Lucy Pirtle. My brother, Scott Sokol, deserves the highest praise for his ability to commiserate with me in the bad times and always revel in the good. Nina Morrison has bestowed upon me untold gifts. Her love has seen me through each day in Berkeley, San Francisco, and now Brooklyn; together, we will celebrate many more.

Index

Permissions Acknowledgments

Grateful acknowledgment is made to the following for permission to reprint previously published material:

Little, Brown and Co., Inc.: Excerpts from *Children of Crisis: A Study of Courage and Fear, Volume 1*, by Robert Coles, copyright © 1964, 1965, 1966, 1967 by Robert Coles. Reprinted by permission of Little, Brown and Co., Inc.

Routledge: Excerpts from *Freedom Writer: Virginia Foster Durr, Letters from the Civil Rights Years,* edited by Patricia Sullivan, copyright © 2003 by Taylor & Francis Books, Inc. Reprinted by permission of Routledge/Taylor & Francis Group, LLC.

Photo Credits

The author and publisher would like to thank the following individuals and institutions for permission to reprint images in the art insert:

Page 1: Corbis

Page 2: *Look* Magazine Collection, Library of Congress, Prints & Photographs Division, photographer: G. Thoma Kersh

Page 3: Tommy Moore

Page 4: Copyright by *The Birmingham News,* 2005, photographer: Jones. All rights reserved. Reprinted with permission.

Page 5: *(top)* Joseph Cumming; *(bottom)* Portrait of Frances Pauley, Frances Pauley Papers, Manuscript, Archives, and Rare Book Library, Emory University

Page 6: *(top)* Joseph Cumming; *(bottom)* Al Clayton & Southern Historical Collection, University of North Carolina at Chapel Hill

Page 7: Al Clayton & Southern Historical Collection, University of North Carolina at Chapel Hill

Page 8: author

AN AMERICAN INSURRECTION
James Meredith and the Battle of Oxford, Mississippi, 1962
by William Doyle

In 1961, a black veteran named James Meredith applied for admission to the University of Mississippi—and launched a legal revolt against white supremacy in the most segregated state in America. Meredith's challenge ultimately triggered what *Time* magazine called "the gravest conflict between federal and state authority since the Civil War," a crisis that exploded into a chaotic battle between thousands of white civilians and a small corps of federal marshals. The defeat of the uprising was a turning point in the civil rights struggle, and *An American Insurrection* brings this event to life.

History/978-0-385-49970-5

COLORED PEOPLE
A Memoir
by Henry Louis Gates, Jr.

In a coming-of-age story as enchantingly vivid and ribald as anything by Mark Twain or Zora Neale Hurston, Gates recounts his childhood in the mill town of Piedmont, West Virginia, in the 1950s and 1960s, and ushers readers into a now-vanished "colored" world. *Colored People* is a pungent and poignant masterpiece of recollection that extends and deepens our sense of African American history even as it entrances us with its bravura storytelling.

Autobiography/978-0-679-73919-7

THE PECULIAR INSTITUTION
by Kenneth M. Stampp

"In ten sparkling chapters the book details and illuminates every aspect of slavery. . . . Slavery is viewed not as a method of regulating race relations, not as an arrangement that was in its essence paternalistic, but as a practical system of controlling and exploiting labor. How the slaves worked, how they resisted bondage, how they were disciplined, how they lived their lives in the quarters, and how they behaved toward each other and toward their masters are themes which receive full exploration. . . . The materials are handled with imagination and verve, the style is polished, the factual evidence is precise and accurate. Some scholars will disagree with the conclusions. No one can afford disregarding them."
—Frank W. Klingberg, *American Historical Review*
History/978-0-679-72307-3

PLAYING IN THE DARK
Whiteness and the Literary Imagination
by Toni Morrison

Toni Morrison's brilliant discussions of the "Africanist" presence in the fiction of Poe, Melville, Cather, and Hemingway leads to a dramatic reappraisal of the essential characteristics of our literary tradition. She shows how much the themes of freedom, individualism, manhood, and innocence depended on the existence of a black population that was manifestly unfree—and that came to serve white authors as embodiments of their own fears and desires. Written with the artistic vision that has earned Toni Morrison a pre-eminent place in modern letters, *Playing in the Dark* is a persuasive work of literary criticism that promises to change the way we read American literature.

Literary Criticism/978-0-679-74542-6

BEEN IN THE STORM SO LONG
The Aftermath of Slavery
by Leon F. Litwack

Based on hitherto unexamined sources: interviews with ex-slaves, diaries and accounts by former slaveholders, this "rich and admirably written book" (Eugene D. Genovese, *The New York Times Book Review*) aims to show how, during the Civil War and after Emancipation, blacks and whites interacted in ways that dramatized not only their mutual dependency, but the ambiguities and tensions that had always been latent in "the peculiar institution." Winner of the Pulitzer Prize and the National Book Award.

History/978-0-394-74398-1

ALL OVER BUT THE SHOUTIN'
by Rick Bragg

Rick Bragg grew up dirt-poor in northeastern Alabama, seemingly destined for either the cotton mills or the penitentiary, and instead became a Pulitzer Prize–winning reporter. This is the story of Bragg's father, a hard-drinking man with a murderous temper and the habit of running out on the people who needed him most. But at the center is Bragg's mother, who went eighteen years without a new dress so that her sons could have school clothes. Evoking these lives—and the country that shaped and nourished them—with compassion, Rick Bragg brings home the love and suffering that lie at the heart of every family. The result is unforgettable.

Memoir/978-0-679-77402-0

ROLL, JORDAN, ROLL
The World the Slaves Made
by Eugene D. Genovese

"The most profound, learned and detailed analysis of Negro slavery to appear since World War II. It covers an incredible range of topics and offers fresh insights on nearly every page. . . . Genovese's great gift is his ability to penetrate the minds of both slaves and masters, revealing not only how they viewed themselves and each other, but also how their contradictory perceptions interacted."

—David B. Davis, *The New York Times Book Review*

History/978-0-394-71652-7

SIMPLE JUSTICE
The History of Brown v. Board of Education *and Black America's Struggle for Equality*
by Richard Kluger

Simple Justice is the definitive history of the landmark case *Brown v. Board of Education* and the epic struggle for racial equality in this country. Combining intensive research and original interviews with surviving participants, Richard Kluger provides the fullest possible view of the human and legal drama in the years before 1954, the cumulative assaults on the white power structure that defended segregation, and the step-by-step establishment of a team of inspired black lawyers who could successfully challenge the law. Kluger has updated his work with a new final chapter covering events and issues that have arisen since the book was first published, including developments in civil rights and recent cases involving affirmative action.

History/978-1-4000-3061-3

THE MIND OF THE SOUTH
by W. J. Cash

Ever since its publication in 1941, *The Mind of the South* has been recognized as a path-breaking work of scholarship and as a literary achievement of enormous eloquence and insight in its own right. From its investigation of the Southern class system to its pioneering assessments of the region's legacies of racism, religiosity, and romanticism, W. J. Cash's book defined the way in which millions of readers—on both sides of the Mason-Dixon line—would see the South for decades to come. This fiftieth-anniversary edition of *The Mind of the South* includes an incisive analysis of Cash himself and of his crucial place in the history of modern Southern letters.

History/978-0-679-73647-9

SONS OF MISSISSIPPI
A Story of Race and Its Legacy
by Paul Hendrickson

They stand as if the photograph were being taken at a church picnic and not during one of the pitched battles of the civil rights struggle. None of them knows that the image will appear in *Life* magazine or that it will become an icon of its era. The year is 1962, and these seven white Mississippi lawmen have gathered to stop James Meredith from integrating the University of Mississippi. One of them is swinging a billy club. More than thirty years later, Paul Hendrickson sets out to discover who these men were, what happened to them after the photograph was taken, and how racist attitudes shaped the way they lived their lives. But his ultimate focus is on their children and grandchildren, and how the prejudice bequeathed by the fathers was transformed, or remained untouched, in the sons.

History/978-0-375-70425-3

CONFEDERATES IN THE ATTIC
Dispatches from the Unfinished Civil War
by Tony Horwitz

Propelled by his boyhood passion for the Civil War, Tony Horwitz embarks on a search for places and people still held in thrall by America's greatest conflict. The result is an adventure into the soul of the unvanquished South, where the ghosts of the Lost Cause are resurrected through ritual and remembrance. Written with Horwitz's signature blend of humor, history, and hard-nosed journalism, *Confederates in the Attic* brings alive old battlefields and new ones: "classrooms, courts, country bars" where the past and the present collide in explosive ways. Poignant and hilarious, it speaks to anyone who has ever felt drawn to the dark romance of the Civil War.

Civil War/Travel/978-0-679-75833-4

VINTAGE AND ANCHOR BOOKS
Available at your local bookstore, or visit www.randomhouse.com.